# The Home Brew

Third edition

## Reviews and comments on previous editions

"As the author states in his introduction, the recipes are primarily intended for Full Mash brewers but many could be adapted for partial mashing or extract brewing. The book assumes the reader is already versed in the basic techniques of brewing, this is not a "how to brew" manual. That said, you don't need to have years of experience - pick a recipe and just give it a go.

Les Howarth has assembled beer recipes from almost 350 breweries, some of them long gone but many brewing today. He has collated the data from numerous sources, and it is a wonder that existing brewers divulge this information. The recipes do vary in detail: some specify the percentages of each type of malt that make up the grist, some even specify the ratio of hops to use. Others only list the malt and hop ingredients with no guidance to ratios. The book provides the original gravity figure and the bitterness in IBUs, and the home brewer must call upon his/her knowledge of brewing theory to calculate a suitable amount of malt and hops to achieve the desired result; there are some examples in the book to help. If you know the desired colour of the beer this can guide you in malt selection. Hop ratios can be chosen based upon the brewer's experience of their flavour characteristics. Specific yeast strains are not specified since these are unlikely to be available to a home brewer; use your judgement to choose a suitable yeast strain from those readily available, e.g. a fruity ester yeast for an Old ale, a neutral one for a golden ale. Given the vast amount of variable factors involved in creating a beer, one should expect to repeat a recipe more than once with minor tweaking before getting it just how you like it.

For me the major appeal of this book is trying to recreate beers I know and like. I tried brewing an old favourite for a good friend of mine, a strong bitter he used to drink often but sadly no longer available since the brewery was closed in the year 2000. The first attempt was slightly too dark (I guesstimated too much chocolate malt) but otherwise a very good flavour match. After quaffing several pints each we both agreed it was a superb brew!

I have made two attempts to replicate my personal all-time favourite bitter (also no longer available) and the second brew is a pretty close match; I am confident number 3 will be nearing perfection.

This book has enough brewing recipes to keep you going for life, and it is very satisfying to recreate the beers of one's youth and indeed those of today. If you are an enthusiastic brewer I'd say this book is money well spent, and highly recommend it. For those of you who have not tried full mash brewing at home, how does top quality real ale for 35 pence a pint sound? Cheers!"

Nicholas Mayes on Amazon.co.uk

"This amazing monster-size book gives home brewers detailed ingredient information for more than 2000 commercial European beers. Many of these beers are no longer commercially brewed, so the only way to taste them now is to brew them at home. The Home Brewer's Recipe Database also offers an interesting historical insight into the way some British brewers have adjusted their recipes and provides justification for breaking some brewing "rules" with your own creations."

BeerBooks.com

"Homebrewers will be amazed at how simple some beers are, and also to find out about some "secret" ingredient that otherwise might go undetected-knowledge that might just take your beer over the top."

K. Florian Kemp, All About Beer

"Have been brewing lots recently and have used the formula from your book to calculate the malt bill and the alpha acid content to good effect."

John McGarva, owner of Tryst Brewery, Scotland

"This is a vast collection of recipes for European beers, mostly from the UK and Belgium. The depth of each recipes varies, but usually includes the type of malts and hops and the general specs, like gravity and bittering units. To clone a beer you will have to do some calculations to figure out how much malt and hops to use for your particular system and volume. There isn't any information on yeast or water treatment, though. Overall, a good resource for trying to clone English and Belgian ales."

Benjy Edwards on Amazon.com

"I love British beer. Unfortunately you can not get much of a variety here. So I am forced to brew my own. This book, while covering beers from all over the world) is, to me, invaluable in trying to recreate a beer I had in Britain or create a similar beer. It is also very helpful in that it lists (mostly) malts and hops used in the various beers. This helps you understand what makes a beer you like (or dislike) taste the way it does. I love this book and am grateful that I stumbled across it as it is not in your normal brewing references."

Sleepy Fox on Amazon.com

# The Home Brewer's Recipe Database

## Third edition

## Les Howarth

To Larry
thanks for setting me
brewing in the USA!

Les Howarth

First edition published 2002 by iUniverse

Republished 2004 by iUniverse Star

Second edition published 2009 by Lulu

This edition published by Lulu™

www.lulu.com

ISBN: 978-1-326-45098-4

To my darling Mara

# Table of Contents

# Foreword to First Edition

Craft Brewing has become a marginalised branch of a discredited hobby called homebrewing. Nevertheless, brewing good beer at home is the second oldest profession and has always been the main weapon with which beer lovers have protected the quality of their beverage. It is no different today. The Craft Brewing Association has done as much to pull homebrew from its slough of despond called "kits" as CAMRA has done to protect the microbrewery and the cask ale.

Against this background we have a few brave and incredibly knowledgeable writers who are prepared to continue to publish i.e. protect our historical heritage. Les Howarth's contribution will make a major input to this genre.

A craft brewer's greatest thrill is to brew a beer they remember but can no longer buy. Now Les has given us the most comprehensive hard copy database of all time.

It won't be easy to recreate beers we know and love; ingredients and techniques evolve all the time. Les has given us a record of what we are aiming for, which will never be lost again. It is now up to us to do the rest.

Clive La Pensée, December 2001

Author of *The Historical Companion to House-Brewing*

and *The Craft of House-Brewing.*

# Acknowledgements

I'd like to thank everyone who has assisted or encouraged me on my brewing journey and exploration of good beer. Rather than attempting and failing to name everyone individually I will list the main groups of people I have been involved with. When I wrote the first edition of this book I was living in Scotland which is why I thanked the members of Scottish Craft Brewers[1] for their encouragement and assistance in my home brewing activities. When I completed the second edition I had moved down to England so thanked Cambridge Craft Brewers. I'd now like to add the North West Essex branch of the Campaign for Real Ale[2] and the Oxford Brewers Group[3] to this list. Now, as I am writing this I am living in Illinois near Chicago, it is the turn of the Midnight Carboys[4] to join me on my ongoing home brewing journey.

I'd also like to belatedly thank my uncle and namesake, Les Howarth, who started me on this journey by buying me a home winemaking book for Christmas some time back in the 1970s.

Les Howarth

---

[1] www.scottishcraftbrewers.org
[2] www.northwestessex.camra.org.uk
[3] www.oxfordbrewers.com
[4] www.midnightcarboys.com

# List of Abbreviations

AAU:   Alpha-acid units ($\alpha$-acid units).

ABV:   Alcohol by volume.

ABW:   Alcohol by weight.

b-c:   Bottle-conditioned.

EBC:   European Brewing Convention.

EBU:   European Bittering Units.

IBU:   International Bittering Units.

°L:    Degrees Lovibond.

OG:    Original Gravity.

°P:    Degrees Plato.

SG:    Specific Gravity.

SRM:   Standard Reference Method.

WGV:   Whitbread Goldings Variety.

# Introduction

This is not a recipe book, it is an ingredient information book. There are a number of reasons for this. Firstly, often I have been unable to obtain sufficient information from which to be able to formulate a recipe. In order to formulate a recipe I might have to make assumptions about proportions and quantities which, without a lot of taste testing to compare with the commercial product, would amount to little more than guesses. This leaves you, the brewer, to make your own assumptions if you wish to attempt to clone a commercial beer. You'll need to brew the beer, taste it, compare with the commercial beer, make adjustments and brew again etc. I wouldn't want to take all that fun away from you! Of course, such experimentation is not possible if the commercial beer is no longer in production, but we can certainly have some fun attempting to reproduce extinct beers. Secondly, I have rarely used a recipe as published since I'll either want to brew a different volume of beer and/or the author of the recipe will have designed it using some assumptions about my abilities as a brewer which may not be correct. Also, what units would I use? Each brewer has his own preferences and I'm a bit anachronistic in that I brew using Imperial measurements, so I have to convert recipes given in either Metric or U.S. units. Finally, I have no desire to infringe copyright nor adversely affect the royalties of authors of recipe books who have gone to some effort on our behalf to test recipes and provide us with the results of their research. I have therefore deliberately not included complete details for data obtained from recipe books. I have hopefully pointed the way for you to find the information for yourself.

This book is the result of my collecting of a database over the years for my own use in designing craft brew recipes. I have used the database in two ways. Firstly, I have found it useful for attempting to replicate favourite brews at home, especially for beers that were sadly no longer in commercial production. When attempting to "clone" a beer like this, it is likely that the first attempt will not fully achieve the intended result, but careful tasting should allow one to tweak the recipe and/or process to get closer to the target. In that sense, this book doesn't claim to provide clone recipes but a starting point for you to try to develop your own clone recipes.

The second way I have used the recipe information in this book is as a basis for experimenting with a new (to me) ingredient. For example, if I want to try out a particular variety of hop then I might search the database for a beer that has used that hop and formulate a recipe on that basis. In this instance I am not making any serious attempt to brew a clone but simply using the ingredient information as a framework for brewing a beer with the given hop variety. My logic is that if a commercial brewery has decided that the hop variety works well with certain other ingredients in a certain style of beer then that is as good a place for me to start myself. I'd also hope that this prevents me from settling into a standard trial recipe and becoming "stale" as a brewer.

Finally, this book may be of interest to beer lovers who are curious about what ingredients are used in the concoctions that they drink.

I have given information (next chapter) on how to convert the ingredient information supplied in this book into a recipe that you can use. This conversion can usually be performed with just two equations, which the craft brewer can customise depending upon their preferred units and experience with their own equipment and procedures.

No two breweries or brewers are the same. Equipment and procedures differ with consequent effects on beer flavour. Also, ingredients change from season to season and this is especially true of hop α-acid (alpha-acid) contents. There will also be inevitable changes in water, water treatment, yeast and yeast handling. Given all of this, exact replication of a commercial beer will be impossible, but I have discovered that it is possible to get remarkably close to the "real thing" on many occasions without going to a huge amount of extra effort.

I have not included any tasting notes, but have added occasional notes and photographs relating to my experiences of these beers. For tasting notes, I refer you to either my original source references, the annual editions of the CAMRA (Campaign for Real Ale) Good Beer Guide[5] or other beer guide books. Of course, the best suggestion is that you search out a good pub and/or beer festival to taste them for yourself. Sadly this is not possible in many cases due to the demise of breweries.

Brewing of these recipes can be performed using "full mash" techniques, as used by the commercial breweries, and this is what I have assumed in providing my conversion procedures. However, there is no reason why this database could not be used as inspiration for craft brewers that use either "extract" or "partial mash" techniques. I have not given any information on the brewing process since several excellent books already describe the brewing process in detail. Some of these are listed in a bibliography towards the end of this book.

In many cases I have made the distinction between bottled beers. This is because bottled beers are frequently different from their draught versions. In the case of bottle-conditioned beers there is often a slight increase in alcoholic strength due to the use of priming sugars. Also, the practice of dry hopping is not

---

[5] *Good Beer Guide*, published annually by CAMRA, St. Albans. www.camra.org.uk

possible with bottled beer. However, in some cases, where the bottled and draught beer data is essentially identical, I have not made this distinction.

I have found that this database has been a great help to my brewing over the years. I hope that it will also be of assistance to you. Happy brewing!

## *Index*

The index should assist the reader in not only finding references to particular types of hops or malt but also the broader range of ingredients used in beer recipes from allspice to white pepper. I encourage you to explore the index but, of course, whether you decide to experiment with some of the more bizarre ingredients is entirely up to you.

## *Historical beers*

A new feature that I have included in this edition is recipe details and an index category for "Historical beers", indexed generally by the year of the recipe. While the term "historical" could be applied to any beer no longer brewed, I have used it for ingredient data for recipes for beers either brewed before the middle of the 20th century or modern beers based on research on historical recipes. Since brewing prior to the Industrial Revolution tended to be a relatively small-scale process it has not always been possible to categorise this data under the heading of a brewing company. In such cases, the ingredient information has been included under a "Historical recipes" heading.

I strongly recommend that anyone interested in brewing history should search out the work of the Durden Park Beer Circle[6], Clive La Pensée[7] and Ron Pattinson in his many books and/or his *Shut Up About Barclay Perkins* blog[8].

In a sense it may be argued that brewing has come full circle and the modern home brewer has a lot in common with the earliest brewers. The information in this book should assist the brewer who wishes to attempt to brew modern versions of these old beers and/or find further reading on the subject. One of the many things I enjoy about home brewing is researching old recipes and techniques and attempting to use these as a (frequently tenuous) basis for some sort of story that I can tell about my beers.

## Organic beers

Another new index category that I have included in this edition is for "Organic beers". I have decided to do this rather than index ingredients as being organic. This category is for beers that the brewers claim to include at least some organic ingredients.

The original versions of many historical beers should also be organic, even if their modern recreations are not.

---

[6] John Harrison et al, *Old British Beers and How To Make Them*, 3rd edition, Durden Park Beer Circle (2003).; Www.DurdenParkBeer.org.uk.

[7] Clive La Pensée, *The Historical Companion to House-Brewing*, Montag Publications, Beverley (1990); Clive La Pensée, *The Craft of House-Brewing*, Montag Publications, Beverley (1996); Clive La Pensée and Roger Protz, *Homebrew Classics: India Pale Ale*, CAMRA, St. Albans (2001); Clive La Pensée and Roger Protz, *Homebrew Classics: Stout and Porter*, CAMRA, St. Albans (2003).

[8] http://barclayperkins.blogspot.com/ ; http://www.lulu.com/shop/search.ep?contributorId=474752.

# Recipe Design

If a home or craft brewer is supplied with information on original gravity, bitterness units, proportions of each type of grain, sugar and hops used for a commercial beer, then it is possible to create a recipe that comes close to that beer. In cases where not all of this information is available it is possible to make educated guesses to fill in the gaps in knowledge. In this chapter I shall describe how to take the information supplied in the main body of this book and create a recipe for use in your own craft brewery. In my own brewing I tend to use Imperial units so I shall describe my recipe design process using these units and then I shall also give the relevant equations for both Metric and USA units.

I shall describe the process for one of my own beer recipes. These would be the recipe details for my "B2K Millennium Ale" which I brewed as a variation of an old favourite (Dave Line's recipe for Gibbs Mew Bishop's Tipple[DL], also see under Gibbs Mew, Salisbury, England in the main section of this book) tweaked in the general direction of a Belgian Tripel. The raw details (as might be supplied in this database) for this beer would be:

**B2K Millennium Ale**: OG: 1075. Malt: 70% Pale malt, 7.5% Crystal malt, 2.5% Roast Caramalt, 20% Golden syrup. Hops: 33% Fuggles, 33% Hallertau, 33% Tettnang. Late hops: Saaz. Others: Coriander seeds. IBU: 50. Source: Les Howarth.

The first piece of information required in designing a recipe is the original gravity (OG) of the beer. This is the specific gravity (SG) of the wort prior to fermentation and is a measure of the density of the wort relative to the density of water. The OG is useful information for us because it allows us to

---

[DL] Dave Line, *Brewing Beers Like Those You Buy*, Amateur Winemaker Publications, Andover (1978); Revised by Roy Ekins, Nexus Special Interests, Swanley (1995).

calculate the total amount of grains and sugars we require to obtain the target strength of beer.

Where possible I have supplied the OG, but if this has not been available I have either given the alcohol by volume (ABV) or degrees Plato (°P). The ABV can be accurately calculated from the difference between the OG and the specific gravity of the finished beer. However, as a very rough guide:

$$OG = 1000 + (10 \times ABV)$$

So, for example, an ABV of 3.5%, 4% or 5.2% will approximately correspond to an OG of 1035, 1040 or 1052 respectively.

To a good approximation °P can be coverted to OG by the following equation:

$$OG = 1000 + 4 \times °P$$

So, for example, a °P of 8°P, 10.5% or 16% will approximately correspond to an OG of 1032, 1042 or 1064 respectively.

Having obtained a target OG, we need to know what the potential extract of each ingredient in the malt bill is as well as the extraction efficiency of our mashing and sparging process. The potential extract differs for each ingredient and tables giving these are given in most good craft brewing books. While it is perfectly possible to do a detailed calculation on the basis of these figures, I have found that taking an average value for the entire malt bill works very well. I use a value for pale malt since this is usually the main component and the other ingredients usually have similar potential extracts. I use a potential extract of 30 degrees of extract per pound gallon. This means that the potential extract of 1lb of grain would result in an SG of 1030 in 1 gallon of extract. So could we say that to obtain 3 gallons of beer at OG1075 we would need 75 × 3 ÷

30=7.5lb of malt? No, because we will never achieve 100% extract efficiency. In fact, it would be undesirable to attempt to achieve this because over-sparging tends to extract tannins from the grain that result in unpleasant harshness in the final beer. We therefore need to factor in our extract efficiency when designing the recipe. The calculation therefore becomes:

$$\text{Total weight of malt} = \frac{100 \times (\text{Target OG} - 1000) \times \text{Target volume/gal}}{30 \times \text{efficiency/\%}} \text{ lb}$$

You will be able to get a good indication of your likely extract efficiency from your own brewing experience. I have found that my extract efficiency reduces as the total weight of my malt bill increases, which means that I can end up in a diminishing returns scenario such that any potential increase in OG by adding extra grain is offset by the reduction of extract efficiency. Also, the extract efficiency calculation only strictly applies to the grain part of the malt bill that is mashed and sparged and not the sugars, which are added at the boiling stage. Nevertheless, I have found that including the entire malt and sugar bill in the above calculation works well enough for my purposes.

From my experience with my brewing procedure the best method of achieving OG1075 would be to aim for a final brew length (volume) of 3 gallons and expect an extract efficiency of around 75%. Inserting these values into the above equation results in:

$$\text{Total weight of malt required} = \frac{100 \times (1075 - 1000) \times 3}{30 \times 75} \text{ lb}$$

$$\text{Total weight of malt required} = \frac{100 \times 75 \times 3}{30 \times 75} \text{ lb}$$

$$\text{Total weight of malt required} = 10 \text{ lb}$$

So we now know the total amount of grain and sugar required to achieve our target OG and volume. Since, in this case, we have information about the proportions of ingredients in our malt bill, it is a simple matter to calculate the quantities of each ingredient required. This means that in our recipe we will need 7lb (70%) Pale malt, 12 oz (7.5%) Crystal malt and 4 oz (2.5%) Roast Caramalt in our mash tun. We will also need 2lb (20%) of Golden syrup added during the boil.

Normally most of the hops are added at the start of the boil and provide bitterness as well as some hop flavours and aromas. Where possible, I have supplied the IBU (International Bittering Units) values for the beers. The IBU gives the target bitterness level of the beer. Where IBUs are not available it is possible to make an educated guess based on the beer style. A useful, but not universally agreed on, set of style guidelines is available from the Beer Judge Certification Program (BJCP)[9]. Tables giving such information are also available in most good homebrew books (see the Bibliography chapter at the end of this book for some recommendations). The final IBU will depend upon the quantity and bitterness value of the hops added during the boil and the efficiency of bitterness extraction (or "utilisation"), which will depend on your boiling time and conditions. The bittering power of hops is determined by their $\alpha$-acid content, which depends on the variety, weather conditions during the year of harvesting and the age and storage conditions of the hops. The $\alpha$-acid content of hops is usually printed on their packaging these days, but if not most good homebrew books give tables of such information which can act as a guide. A good discussion of this subject is given in Ray Daniels' *Designing Great Beers*[10].

[9] www.bjcp.org/stylecenter.php
[10] Ray Daniels, *Designing Great Beers*, Brewers Publications, Boulder (1996).

When more than one hop is used for bittering, it is a matter of choice whether the proportions used are based simply on weight or the proportion of bittering power that each hop variety supplies. Since the latter approach should give the most consistent results, this is what I shall describe here.

The bitterness of a beer in IBUs is given by:

$$IBU = \frac{\text{Weight of hops/oz} \times \alpha\text{-acid/\%} \times \text{Utilisation/\%}}{1.6 \times \text{Volume brewed/gal}}$$

This can be rearranged to:

$$\text{Weight of hops} = \frac{1.6 \times \text{Volume brewed/gal} \times IBU}{\alpha\text{-acid/\%} \times \text{Utilisation/\%}} \quad oz$$

In this example we have a target IBU of 50 and we are using 3 types of bittering hop. We are therefore aiming for a bittering contribution from each type of hop of around 16.7. We have no way of knowing what the utilisation will be unless we have been able to analyse the IBU values of previous brews. Considering this and the uncertainties due to the unknown changes of α-acid in our hops during storage[11], we can only make an educated guess at our utilisation. Graham Wheeler[12] suggests a value of 20% but Daniels and Papazian[13] suggest higher utilisation values. The best way of deciding an appropriate utilisation for your procedure is by taste. If your beers seem to be too bitter try increasing your utilisation value for future brews. For my system, I have found that Wheeler's 20% seems to produce beers having similar bitterness to the target commercial beers so that is the figure I shall use in this example.

---

[11] BeerSmith, and probably other brewing software, includes a calculator for the effects of hop age and storage conditions upon α-acid.

[12] Graham Wheeler, *Home Brewing-The CAMRA Guide*, CAMRA, St. Albans (1993).

[13] Charlie Papazian, *The Home Brewer's Companion*, Avon Books, New York (1994).

If our available Fuggles hops have an α-acid content of 4.0%, then we can calculate how much we need to use to achieve our target IBU. Using the above equation we obtain:

$$\text{Weight of hops} = \frac{1.6 \times 3 \times 16.7}{4.0 \times 20} \text{ oz}$$

$$\text{Weight of Fuggles hops} = 1 \text{ oz}$$

If the Tettnang and Hallertau hops have α-acid contents of 3.0 and 3.4% respectively, then a similar calculation shows that we would require 1.33 and 1.18 oz respectively to achieve our target IBU contribution for each of 16.7. So for equal IBU contributions from each of the hop varieties we require different amounts of each variety because of their different α-acid contents.

In principle there would be no reason not to use 1, 1.33 and 1.18 ounces of each of the Fuggles, Tettnang and Hallertau hops respectively. However, my scales effectively only read to a precision of ¼ oz so I would probably choose to slightly change the hop quantities accordingly. I might choose to use 1, 1.25 and 1.25 ounces respectively of each hop variety. I could then back-calculate using the equation for IBU above to double check that such an adjustment isn't likely to throw me significantly off target. Doing this results in the IBU contributions from the hops being 16.7, 15.6 and 17.7 respectively.

We now need to decide how much late hops to add. Fortunately this isn't massively critical. In my experience adding a generous measure of late hops at the end of the boil works well. As a very rough guide to quantity I would use around 50% of the total weight of bittering hops. In this case the bittering hops total 3.5 oz so I would probably add around 2 oz of the Saaz hops at the end of the boil. Adding at the end of the boil ensures that the late hops will have zero contribution to the bitterness of the beer. So, in this case, the α-acid content of the Saaz hops would be irrelevant.

The recipe also calls for an addition of crushed coriander seed. I would add these at the same time as the late hops and again the quantity is a matter of taste. In this case I would probably add 1 ounce.

So, to summarise, my homebrew recipe for my "B2K" would be:

| | |
|---|---|
| Mash tun: | 7lb Pale malt, 12oz Crystal malt, 4oz Roast Caramalt. |
| Start of boil: | 2lb Golden syrup, 1oz Fuggles, 1.25oz Tettnang and 1.25oz Hallertau hops. |
| End of boil: | 2oz Saaz hops, 1oz crushed coriander seed. |

Having prepared the wort according to the desired recipe, the next stage is fermentation which requires yeast as an essential ingredient. Not all yeast strains are the same and the yeast used by a brewer can have a significant effect on the flavour of the resulting beer.

## US Units

The only important difference for us between Imperial and US units is the difference between the US and Imperial gallon. 1 Imperial gallon = 1.2 US gallons. The calculations therefore become:

$$\text{Total weight of malt} = \frac{100 - (\text{Target OG} - 1000) \times \text{Target volume} / \text{US gal}}{36 \times \text{Efficiency} / \%} \text{ lb}$$

$$IBU = \frac{\text{Weight of hops}/\text{oz} \times \alpha\text{-acid}/\% \times \text{Utilisation}/\%}{1.34 \times \text{Volume brewed}/\text{US gal}}$$

$$\text{Weight of hops} = \frac{1.34 \times \text{Volume brewed}/\text{US gal} \times IBU}{\alpha\text{-acid}/\% \times \text{Utilisation}/\%} \text{ oz}$$

## *Metric Units*

In Metric units, the calculations become:

$$\text{Total weight of malt} = \frac{100 - (\text{Target OG} - 1000) \times \text{Target volume}/\text{litres}}{300 \times \text{Efficiency}/\%} \text{ kg}$$

$$IBU = \frac{\text{Weight of hops}/\text{g} \times \alpha\text{-acid}/\% \times \text{Utilisation}/\%}{10 \times \text{Volume brewed}/\text{litres}}$$

$$\text{Weight of hops} = \frac{10 \times \text{Volume brewed}/\text{litres} \times IBU}{\alpha\text{-acid}/\% \times \text{Utilisation}/\%} \text{ g}$$

## *Brewing Software*

I have found that the above calculations have worked well for me, but mention must also be made of the wide availability of brewing software that can also assist in recipe formulation. Examples of such software include Beersmith[14], StrangeBrew[15], Beer Alchemy[16], BrewMath[16], Beertools Pro[17], Promash[18] and many others.

---

[14] BeerSmith.com
[15] StrangeBrew.ca
[16] KentPlaceSoftware.com
[17] BeerTools.com
[18] Promash.com

# Ingredient Information

## Malt

The malt bill lists the grains and sugars used in the recipes. Where possible, proportions are given. In some cases this totals more than 100%, but usually it will be found that the grains added during the mash should add up to 100% whilst the sugar added during the boil comprises the extra. However, in some cases the total is not 100% for any apparent reason! Even though sugars are usually added during the boil, I have included such additions in this section purely for convenience.

As will be apparent, the brewers have sometimes been somewhat vague about what ingredients they use. This is particularly the case when they have used a range of euphemisms for added sugar. I have used the brewers' own terminology and I leave it up to you to decide which ingredient to use based on this. Some brewers use caramel as a colouring agent and this has been listed under the Malt heading even though it might normally be added during the boil. There are a range of names given for crystal or caramel malt/caramalt. I have attempted to standardise naming where possible, but the wide range of terminology used for these malts has meant that I've had to accept what the various sources have named these malts to a large extent. I leave the brewer to interpret the information supplied as they wish.

In cases where we do not have information on proportions of malts it is possible to make educated guesses based on the beer style. Most good craft brewing books give guides to the limits on proportions of each type of malt. As a general rule, as a grain becomes darker and more strongly flavoured it would be used in smaller proportions in the malt bill.

Some recipes have included rice and/or oat hulls, but I have omitted these from the ingredient information since I consider that these additives are processing aids rather than ingredients that directly contribute a characteristic to the finished beer.

## *Hops*

Normally most of the hops are added at the start of the boil and provide bitterness as well as some hop flavours and aromas. When hop varieties have been described as being added for aroma it has been assumed here that they have been added as late hops. Late hops are hops added towards the end of the boil and/or at the end of the boil. In some cases dry hopping has been specified, which is the addition of hops to the finished beer in the cask. In some cases, dry hopping is performed by adding hops to the fermentation vessel. If dry hopping has been specified but without naming the variety of hop used, then I have simply put "Yes" next to the Dry hops sub-heading. It is reasonable to assume that the dry hops would be one or more of the varieties already listed in the recipe and is more likely to be an "aroma hop" than a "bittering hop". This is based on conventional brewing practice, but in recent years a number of unusual hopping procedures such as "first wort hopping" and "mash hopping" have been proposed by some craft brewers. Where such practices have been used by commercial breweries I have captured these in the Index. It is up to the craft brewer to experiment with their hopping procedures.

The sources of ingredient are not consistent in their naming of hop varieties so I have generally not given any indication of the country of origin of the hops nor have I made any distinction between Goldings and East Kent Goldings. I have given either "Hersbrücker" or "Hallertau Hersbrücker" as "Hersbrücker". Some of the alternative names for hops are given in the Index.

## Yeast

Because of the difficulties involved in obtaining samples of the correct yeast strains for commercial beers (especially from breweries that are no longer in business) I have generally made no attempt to suggest yeast strains to be used when formulating recipes. I leave you to experiment with the yeast strains available to you.

## Others

Some brews have fruit, herbs, spices and/or other ingredients in their recipe. Some of these ingredients are difficult to classify under any particular category so I have included them all under "Others". It would be normal procedure to add spices at the same stage as the late hops. Fruit may be added later in process, either in the primary fermenting vessel or along with dry hops.

## IBU

International Bittering Units are identical to European Bittering Units (EBU). I have omitted this information when it has been supplied as part of a published recipe.

## Beer Colour

The colour of the beer may be a clue to estimating the proportions of darker malts in the malt bill. Where possible, beer colours have been given as EBC (European Brewing Convention) units of colour. Other authors have given detailed discussions of the use of colour[19]. However, the addition of caramel and/or coloured sugars and many other factors can upset such calculations. Therefore colour can be a rather unreliable indication of the recipe but for those willing to attempt the use of such calculations, the equation to calculate beer colour from the recipe composition is of the form:

$$\text{Beer colour} = \frac{\text{Factor} \times \text{Grain weight} \times \text{Grain colour}}{\text{Beer volume}}$$

Or, for more than one type of grain:

$$\text{Beer colour} = \frac{\text{Factor} \times \sum (\text{Grain weight} \times \text{Grain colour})}{\text{Beer volume}}$$

where $\Sigma$ (Grain weight x Grain colour) represents the sum of the products of the weights and colours of each grain in the malt bill. This equation can be expanded to include as many grains or sugars as you wish in your recipe. The factor in the above equations will obviously depend on the units for weight and volume. Approximations for this are given in Table 1.

**Table 1: Colour calculation factors**

| Units | Factor |
|---|---|
| Imperial | 0.83 |
| USA | 1.0 |
| Metric | 8.36 |

A selection of grain colours are given in Table 2.

---

[19] Charlie Papazian, *The Home Brewer's Companion*, Avon Books, New York (1994); Ray Daniels, *Designing Great Beers*, Brewers Publications, Boulder (1996).

## Table 2: Grain Colours[20]

| Grain | Colour / EBC |
|---|---|
| Pale malt | 5 - 6 |
| Pilsner / Lager malt | 2.5 - 3 |
| Mild ale malt | 6 - 7 |
| Wheat malt | 3 - 4 |
| Vienna malt | 6 - 8 |
| CaraPils malt | 3 - 15 |
| Light Munich malt | 13 - 15 |
| Dark Munich malt | 20 - 25 |
| Carahell malt | 20 - 30 |
| Caramalt | 23 - 28 |
| CaraMunich / CaraMünch malt | 80 - 100 |
| Crystal malt | 80 – 300 (usually ~120) |
| Amber malt | 90 - 110 |
| Brown malt | 120 - 150 |
| Special B malt | 500 |
| Roast Caramalt | 800 |
| Chocolate malt | 800 - 1200 |
| Roast Barley | 1000 - 1550 |
| Black malt | 1250 - 1500 |

The brewing software mentioned in the previous chapter can perform these calculations automatically.

Given that beer colour also depends on the proportion of colour extracted from the malt, which depends on mash time, mash pH, sparge conditions, degree of grain crushing etc. as well as other factors such as degree of aeration, hop rates, boil time or boil conditions, then it is perhaps not surprising that colour calculations are an approximation. However, in my experience, brewing to achieve a given colour using the above equations and data can produce results that are very close to the target colour so colour calculations can assist your recipe design.

---

[20] Charlie Papazian, *The Home Brewer's Companion*, Avon Books, New York (1994); Graham Wheeler, *Home Brewing-The CAMRA Guide*, CAMRA, St. Albans (1993); and various other sources.

## Source

This gives my source of the ingredient information either directly (e.g. Web site or other reference) or according to the key below.

150 = *150 Classic Clone Recipes*[150]. This is a special clone recipe issue of *Brew Your Own* magazine.

A,G&B − Martyn Cornell, *Amber, Gold & Black*, The History Press, Stroud (2010).

BA = Joshua M. Bernstein, *Brewed Awakening*, Sterling Epicure, New York (2011).

BBB = Roger Putman, *Beers and Breweries of Britain*, Shire Publications, Princes Risborough (2004).

BC = Tess and Mark Szamatulski, *Beer Captured: Homebrew Recipes for 150 World Class Beers*, Maltose Press, Trumbull (2001). I've noticed that this book often gives higher OGs than other sources. The recipes also tend to give extra ingredients over and above other sources. I leave the brewer to draw their own conclusions.

BLAM = Stan Heironymus, *Brew Like a Monk: Trappist, Abbey, and Strong Belgian Ales and How to Brew Them*, Brewers Publications, Boulder (2005).

BSC = BeerSmith Cloud. This is the official BeerSmith beer recipe sharing site that includes some recipes provided by commercial breweries. Www.beersmithrecipes.com

---

[150] *150 Classic Clone Recipes: The best of Brew Your Own* [http://brewyourownstore.com/clone.html].

BY = Bill Yenne, *Guinness® - The 250-year quest for the perfect pint*, Wiley, Hoboken (2007).

BYO = *Brew Your Own* magazine, Manchester Center, VT. Www.byo.com. This magazine publishes many clone recipes, including some developed from data in this book. Some of these can be found on their web site, see byo.com/recipes-tag.

CB = Tess and Mark Szamatulski, *Clone Brews: Homebrew Recipes for 150 Commercial Beers*, Storey Books, North Adams (1998). This book does not appear to feature increased OGs or more complex recipes to the same extent as the later Szamatulskis' book, *Beer Captured* (above).

CYBI = Can You Brew It - The Jamil Show podcasts[21]. Jamil Zainasheff's series of *Can You Brew It* shows are aimed at brewers wishing to clone commercial beers. These shows involve designing a recipe from the available data, brewing a beer, tasting it and then adjusting the recipe (if necessary) to bring it closer to target and repeating the process. These shows are a very useful resource for educating brewers (including myself) on how to develop a clone recipe from the starting ingredient information, such as that available in this book. For these entries, I have attempted to capture the main features of the interviews with the brewers. For many extra details and discussion of the results of trial clone brews I strongly suggest that you listen to the relevent podcasts.

DAW = David Alan Woolsey, *Libations of the Eighteenth Century*, Universal Publishers, USA (1997).

DL = Ingredient information from Dave Line[DL]. I believe that the ingredient information in Dave Line recipes are quite accurate but he gives no indication of

---

[21] www.thebrewingnetwork.com/shows/The-Jamil-Show
[DL] Dave Line, *Brewing Beers Like Those You Buy*, Amateur Winemaker Publications, Andover (1978); Revised by Roy Ekins, Nexus Special Interests, Swanley (1995).

IBUs since home brewers in the late 1970s were generally ignorant of IBUs and hops were not supplied with α-acid information. If you want to assume some sort of average α-acid for the various hop varieties, then you will have to take into account that these may have changed since then due to new farming techniques, improved storage etc. You may want to reduce the amount of hops in the boil to allow for this but I have found that you can get very good results from Dave Line recipes by not worrying about IBUs and using the hop quantities given. Indeed, this is what I did for most of my first 10 years of craft brewing. Some of the Dave Line recipes are for use with malt extract only. In these cases I have ignored the malt extract part of the recipe.

DP = The Durden Park Beer Circle[22] has done much work researching and brewing historical beer recipes. They have collected their interpretations of historical recipes in *Old British Beers and How To Make Them*[DP].

EBA = Roger Protz, *The European Beer Almanac*, Lochar Publishing, Moffat (1991).

GAM = The Great America Microbrewery Beer Book[GAM]. The ingredient information in this book is somewhat difficult to interpret and there are some obvious errors. I have therefore adapted the data making the assumptions that 2-row barley is pale malt and 6-row barley is lager malt rather than unmalted barley. I have also attempted to correct the data as best I can, although if in any doubt I have omitted the suspect data.

---

[22] Www.durdenparkbeer.org.uk.
[DP] John Harrison et al, *Old British Beers and How To Make Them*, 3rd edition, Durden Park Beer Circle (2003).
[GAM] Jennifer Trainer Thompson, *The Great American Microbrewery Beer Book*, Ten Speed Press, Berkeley (1997).

GW = Graham Wheeler[GW] has published several beer recipe books. Graham tends to add black malt to his recipes for colour adjustment. Where he appears to have done this I have ignored these additions.

HB = Roger Protz, *Heavenly Beer*, Carroll & Brown, London (2002).

HF/MHF = *Homebrew Favorites*[HF] and *More Homebrew Favorites*[MHF] are collections of many recipes including some clones. Acknowledgement is given to the brewers who developed these recipes. There are also some recipes that include ingredients given in the Further Ingredients chapter which may be a useful starting point for brewers wishing to experiment with something unusual.

JE1, 2, 3, 4, 5 and 6 are the 1st (1998)[JE1], 2nd (1999)[JE2], 3rd (2001)[JE3], 4th (2003)[JE4], 5th (2004)[JE5] and 6th (2006)[JE6] editions of the *Good Bottled Beer Guide* by Jeff Evans respectively.

JHF = Recipes based on interpretations of *Real Ale Almamac* data using *BeerSmith* software by Norman are published on Jim's Homebrew Forum[JHF].

MHF = See under HF.

MO = Marc Ollosson, *Real Ales for the home brewer*, Nexus Special Interests, Hemel Hempstead (1997).

---

[GW] Graham Wheeler and Roger Protz, *Brew Your Own Real Ale at Home*, CAMRA, St. Albans (1993). Graham Wheeler and Roger Protz, *Brew Classic European Beers at Home*, CAMRA, St. Albans (1995). Graham Wheeler and Roger Protz, *Brew Your Own British Real Ale at Home*, CAMRA, St. Albans (1998). Graham Wheeler, *Brew Your Own British Real Ale*, 3rd edition, CAMRA, St. Albans (2009).
[HF] Karl F. Lutzen and Mark Stevens, *Homebrew Favorites*, Storey, North Adams (1994).
[MHF] Karl F. Lutzen and Mark Stevens, *More Homebrew Favorites*, Storey, North Adams (1997).
[JE1] Jeff Evans, *Good Bottled Beer Guide*, CAMRA Books, St. Albans (1998).
[JE2] Jeff Evans, *Good Bottled Beer Guide*, CAMRA Books, St. Albans (1999).
[JE3] Jeff Evans, *Good Bottled Beer Guide*, CAMRA Books, St. Albans (2001).
[JE4] Jeff Evans, *Good Bottled Beer Guide*, CAMRA Books, St. Albans (2003).
[JE5] Jeff Evans, *Good Bottled Beer Guide*, CAMRA Books, St. Albans (2004).
[JE6] Jeff Evans, *Good Bottled Beer Guide*, CAMRA Books, St. Albans (2006).
[JHF] Jim's Homebrew Forum, www.jimsbeerkit.co.uk/forum/viewtopic.php?t=8174.

NACB = Scott R. Russell, *North American Clone Brews*, Storey Books, Pownal (2000). I've noticed that many of the recipes in this book bear little relationship to ingredient information published by the brewers themselves on their web sites.

PP = Www.PintPicker.co.uk. An independent database of UK real ales.

RP1, 2, 3, 4 and 5 are the 1st (1989)[RP1], 2nd (1991)[RP2], 3rd (1993)[RP3], 4th (1995)[RP4] and 5th (1997)[RP5] editions of the *Real Ale Almanac* by Roger Protz respectively. RP means that I have provided edited, condensed information based on several editions of the *Real Ale Almanac*.

SHB = Stephen Harrod Buhner, *Sacred and Herbal Healing Beers*, Siris Books, Boulder (1998). This book includes recipes for ancient meads, beers and other drinks. I have not included reference to any of these recipes in this book but have provided brief details of some of the unusual ingredients used in the Further Ingredients chapter.

SMB = Patrick Higgins, Maura Kate Kilgore and Paul Hertlein, *Secrets fron the Master Brewers*, Fireside, NewYork (1998).

SUABP = *Shut Up About Barclay Perkins*, blog by Ron Pattinson at http://barclayperkins.blogspot.com. A very useful resource on the history of brewing.

TBBK = Jeff Evans, *The Book of Beer Knowledge*, CAMRA Books, St. Albans (2007).

[RP1] Roger Protz, *The Real Ale Drinker's Almanac*, Lochar Publishing, Moffat (1989).
[RP2] Roger Protz, *The Real Ale Drinker's Almanac*, 2nd edition, Lochar Publishing, Moffat (1991).
[RP3] Roger Protz, *The Real Ale Drinker's Almanac*, 3rd edition, Neil Wilson Publishing, Glasgow (1993).
[RP4] Roger Protz, *The Real Ale Drinker's Almanac*, 4th edition, Neil Wilson Publishing, Glasgow (1995).
[RP5] Roger Protz, *The Real Ale Drinker's Almanac*, 5th edition, Neil Wilson Publishing, Glasgow (1997).

VB = Ron Pattinson, *The Home Brewer's Guide to Vintage Beer*, Quarry Books, Beverly, MA (2014). This is highly recommended for brewers wishing to replicate historical beers.

W = J.D.Wetherspoon is a large pub company in the UK who sell a range of guest ales (information about which is provided in their *Wetherspoonnews* newsletter and website www.jdwetherspoon.co.uk) and also have regular beer festivals. These sources of information have provided some details of beer ingredients.

WB = *What's Brewing*, the monthly newspaper of the Campaign for Real Ale (CAMRA). This code is also used for ingredient information published in the companion *Beer* magazine.

Web = Data obtained from brewer's own web site as given in the brewery heading.

# Recipe Information

## *Argentina*

### .   *Antares, Mar del Plata. Www.antaresbeer.com*

**Kolsch**: ABV: 5%. Malt: Pilsner malt. Hops: Cascade. Late hops: Saaz. Source: Web.

**Porter**: ABV: 5.5%. Malt: Pilsner malt, Chocolate malt, Caramel malt. Hops: Cascade. Late hops: Fuggles. Source: Web.

**Scotch Ale**: ABV: 6%. Malt: Pilsner malt, Chocolate malt. Hops: Cascade. Late hops: Fuggles. Source: Web.

**Imperial Stout**: ABV: 8.5%. Malt: Pilsner malt, Chocolate malt, Caramel malt. Hops: Cascade. Late hops: Fuggles. Source:Web.

**Barley Wine**: ABV: 10%. Malt: Pilsner malt, Munich malt, Caramel malt. Hops: Cascade. Late hops: Fuggles. Source: Web.

### .   *Buller, Buenos Aires. Www.bullerpub.com*

**Oktoberfest**: Malt: Munich malt, Vienna malt. Source: Web.

### .   *Cerveceros Caseros (Home Brewers in Argentina)*

**Web:** www.cerveceroscaseros.com.ar

## *Australia*

### .   *Carlton & United Breweries, Melbourne*

**Fosters Lager**: OG: 1046. Malt: Lager malt, Flaked rice, Sugar. Hops: Hallertau. Source: DL. OG: 1047-48. Malt: Pilsner malt, Crystal malt, Sugar. Hops: Hersbrücker. Late hops: Hersbrücker, Styrian Goldings. Source: CB.

**Guinness Foreign Extra Stout**: Others: Guinness flavour extract. Source: BY.

### .   *Castlemaine Perkins, Brisbane*

**XXXX Bitter**: OG: 1044. Malt: Pale malt, Flaked maize, Sugar. Hops: Hallertau. Source: DL.

### .   *Coopers, Adelaide*

**Sparkling Ale**: OG: 1055-58. Malt: Pale malt, Crystal malt, Sugar, optional Aromatic malt. Hops: Pride of Ringwood. Late hops: Pride of Ringwood. Source: 150/CB. OG: 1058. Yeast: Yeast Lab A01 Australian ale. Source: Craig D. Amundsen, MHF.

**Cooper's Best Extra Stout**: OG: 1064-67. Malt: Pale malt, Crystal malt, Roast barley, Chocolate malt, Sugar. Hops: Pride of Ringwood. Late hops: Styrian Goldings. Source: CB.

**Vintage Ale**: ABV: Around 7.5% but varies from year to year. Malt: Pale malt, Crystal malt, Sugar. Hops: Pride of Ringwood, optional Saaz, optional Hallertau. Source: WB.

### . *Esk Brewing, Launceston, Tasmania*

**Razor Edge Lager**: OG: 1050-51. Malt: Pilsner malt, Crystal malt, Sugar. Hops: Pride of Ringwood. Late hops: Hersbrücker, Styrian Goldings. Source: CB.

### . *South Australian Brewing Company, Adelaide*

**Southwark Bitter**: OG: 1041. Malt: Pale malt, Flaked maize, Sugar. Hops: Goldings. Source: DL.

**West End Export Lager**: OG: 1058-60. Malt: Pilsner malt, Crystal malt, Chocolate malt. Hops: Pride of Ringwood. Late hops: Hersbrücker, Saaz. Source: CB.

### . *Tooth & Co., Sydney*

**Reschs Pilsner**: OG: 1043. Malt: Lager malt, Flaked maize, Sugar. Hops: Hallertau. Source: DL.

# Austria

### . *Stiftsbrauerei Schlägl, Schlägl*

**Doppelbock**: ABV: 7%. Malt: Pale malt, Vienna malt. Hops: Local hops. Source: HB.

### . *Schloßbrauerei Eggenberg, Vorchdorf*

**MacQueens Nessie Whisky Malt Red Beer**: ABV: 7.5%. Malt: Scotch whisky malt. Hops: Hallertau. IBU: 27. Source: EBA. OG: 1075-80. Malt: Pale malt, Crystal malt, Vienna malt, Belgian Aromatic malt, Whiskey or Peat-smoked malt. Hops: Hersbrücker. Late hops: Styrian Goldings. Source: CB.

**Urbock 23°**: ABV: 9.3%. Malt: 40% Light Munich malt, 60% Pilsner malt. Hops: 59% Hallertau, 41% Saaz. Source: EBA/GW.

**Samichlaus**: OG: 1139. Malt: Pilsner malt, Vienna malt, CaraHell® malt, Sugar. Hops: Northern Brewer. Late hops: Tettnang, Hallertau Mittelfrüh. Source: 150. ABV: 14%. Malt: Pale malts, Dark malts. Hops: Hersbrücker, Styrian Goldings. Source: HB.

### . *Hofbrau Kaltenhausen, Salzburg*

**Edelweiss Dunkel Weissbier**: OG: 1051-53. Malt: Pale malt, Wheat malt, Crystal malt, CaraVienne malt, Honey malt. Hops: Hersbrücker. Source: CB.

### Josef Sigl Brauerei, Obertrum

**Weizen Gold**: ABV: 5.2%. Malt: 65% Pale malt, 35% Wheat malt. Hops: Hallertau. Late hops: Hallertau. IBU: 29. Source: EBA/GW.

### Steirische Bräuindustrie, Graz

**Gösser Export**: ABV: 5%. Malt: Pale malt, Crystal malt/Caramalt, Flaked maize, Flaked rice. Hops: Hallertau, Spalt, Styrian Aurora, Goldings, Super Styrian Goldings. IBU: 20. Source: EBA.

## Belgium

### Brouwerij van de Achelse Kluis, Hamont-Achel

**Achelse Blond**: ABV: 4%. Malt: Pilsner malt. Hops: Goldings, Hersbrücker, Saaz. Source: HB.

**Achelse Bruine**: ABV: 5%. Malt: Pilsner malt, Caramalt. Hops: Goldings, Hersbrücker, Saaz. Source: HB.

**Achel Bruin Extra**: OG: 1090. Malt: Pilsner malt, Chocolate malt, Sucrose, Caramel syrup. Hops: Saaz. IBU: 28. Source: BLAM.

### Brasserie d'Achouffe, Achouffe

**La Chouffe**: OG: 1080. Malt: 87% Pilsner malt, 5% Crystal malt, 8% White Sucrose. Hops: 39% Goldings, 24% Styrian Goldings, 37% Saaz. Others: Coriander seeds, Cumin seeds, Caraway seeds. Source: EBA/GW.

**Mc Chouffe**: ABV: 9.2%. Malt: Pilsner malt, Brown candi sugar, Honey. Hops: Styrian Goldings, Goldings. Others: Spices. Source: EBA.

**N'Ice Chouffe**: OG: 1099-1102. Malt: Pilsner malt, Special B malt, CaraMunich malt, Crystal malt, Aromatic malt, Candi sugar. Hops: Styrian Goldings. Late hops: Styrian Goldings, Saaz. Others: Thyme, Vanilla bean, Bitter orange peel. Source: BC.

### Angerik, Brussels

**Boerke**: OG: 1055-57. Malt: Pilsner malt, Munich malt, CaraMunich malt, Biscuit malt, Aromatic malt, Candi sugar, Golden syrup. Hops: Styrian Goldings. Late hops: Styrian Goldings, Challenger, Saaz. Source: BC.

### Bavik de Brabandere, Bavikhove

**Petrus Tripel**: OG: 1073-75. Malt: Maris Otter pale malt, CaraVienne malt, Aromatic malt, Candi sugar. Hops: Styrian Goldings. Late hops: Styrian Goldings, Willamette. Others: Sweet Orange peel. Source: CB.

## Huisbrouwerij Boelens, Belsele

**Bieken**: OG: 1084-86. Malt: Pilsner malt, Honey malt, Aromatic malt, Biscuit malt, Candi sugar, Honey. Hops: Styrian Goldings. Late hops: Styrian Goldings, Goldings. Source: BC.

## Bosteels, Buggenhout

**Karmeliet Tripel**: OG: 1081. Malt: Pilsner malt, Wheat malt, Oat malt, Barley, Wheat, Oats, Sucrose. Hops: Styrian Goldings, Saaz. Others: Coriander and other Spices. IBU: 20. Source: BLAM. OG: 1082-83. Malt: Pilsner malt, Wheat malt, Aromatic malt, Flaked oats, Candi sugar. Hops: Challenger. Late hops: Styrian Goldings, Saaz. Others: Sweet Orange peel, Coriander seeds. Source: BC.

**Kwak Pauwel Belgian Ale**: OG: 1081-86. Malt: Pilsner malt, Munich malt, Special B malt, Candi sugar. Hops: Challenger. Late hops: Styrian Goldings, Saaz. Source: CB.

**DeuS**: OG: 1102. Malt: Pale malt, Acid malt, Dextrose/Candi sugar. Hops: Tettnang. Others: Coriander. Source: 150.

## Brasserie Cantillon, Brussels

**Geuze**: OG: 1052. Malt: 65% Pale malt, 35% Wheat. Hops: Fuggles, Belgian Star. EBC: 9. Source: EBA/GW.

**Framboise**: ABV: 5%. Malt: 65% Pale malt, 35% Wheat. Hops: Fuggles, Belgian Star. Others: Raspberries. Source: EBA.

**Kriek**: ABV: 5%. Malt: 65% Pale malt, 35% Wheat. Hops: Fuggles, Belgian Star. Others: Cherries. Source: EBA.

**Rosé de Gambrinus**: Note: Blend of **Framboise** and **Kriek**. Source: Roger Protz, *The Ultimate Encyclopedia of Beer*, Prion, London (1995).

## Brasserie Caracole, Falmignoul

**Saxo**: OG: 1065. Malt: Pilsner malt, Wheat, Sugar. Hops: Saaz. Others: Coriander. IBU: 21. Source: BLAM.

**Nostradamus**: OG: 1083. Malt: Pilsner malt, Munich malt, 2 Caramel malts, Aromatic malt, Wheat malt, Sucrose. Hops: Hallertau, Saaz. IBU: 20. Source: BLAM.

## Chimay, Abbaye Notre-Dame de Scourmont, Forges

**Chimay Red / Rouge**: OG: 1063. Malt: Pilsner malt, Caramel malt. Hops: Hallertau, Yakima or Galena. IBU: 28. EBC: 45. Source: EBA/HB. OG: 1075. Malt: Pale malt, Black malt, Sugar, Honey. Hops: Hallertau, Goldings. Source: DL. OG: 1061. Malt: Pilsner malt, Caramel malt, Wheat starch, Sugar. Hops: American. Late hops: Hallertau. IBU: 19. Source: BLAM. OG: 1068-71. Malt: Maris Otter pale malt, Aromatic malt, CaraMunich malt, Chocolate malt, Candi sugar. Hops: Tettnang. Late hops: Styrian Goldings, Hersbrücker. Source: CB.

**Chimay White / Blanc**: OG: 1071. Malt: Pilsner malt, Caramel malt, Wheat. Hops: Hallertau, Yakima. IBU: 30. EBC: 25. Source: EBA. Malt: Pilsner malt, Caramalt. Hops: Hallertau, Galena. Source: HB.

**Chimay Blue / Bleu / Grande Réserve:** OG: 1081. Malt: Pilsner malt, Caramel malt. Hops: Hallertau, Yakima. Source: EBA. OG: 1086-88. Malt: Pilsner malt, Special B malt, CaraMunich malt, Chocolate malt, Aromatic malt, Dark candi sugar. Hops: Yakima Magnum. Late hops: Hersbrücker. Others: Grains of Paradise. Source: BC. Malt: Pilsner malt. Hops: Hallertau, Galena. Source: HB.

### .   *Brewery Clarysee NV, Krekelput-Oudenaarde*

**St. Hermes Ale**: OG: 1072-78. Malt: Pilsner malt, Aromatic malt, Biscuit malt, Vienna malt, Rauchmalz, Candi sugar. Hops: Styrian Goldings. Late hops: Styrian Goldings. Source: CB.

### .   *De Brabandere, Bavikhove*

**Petrus Oud Bruin**: OG: 1055-56. Malt: Pilsner malt, Acid malt, CaraVienne malt, Chocolate malt, Dark candi sugar. Hops: Styrian Goldings. Others: Steamed Oak chips. Yeast: Lactobacillus delbrueckii. Source: BC.

### .   *Corsendonk*

Note: See Du Bocq and Van Steenberge.

### .   *De Dolle Brouwers, Esen*

**Arabier**: OG: 1075. Malt: Munich malt, Amber malt, Torrefied malt, Candi sugar. Hops: Spalt, Saaz, Goldings. Source: EBA.

**Stille Nacht**: OG: 1077-80. Malt: Pilsner malt, Aromatic malt, Crystal malt, Biscuit malt, Honey malt, Candi sugar, Golden syrup, Wild honey. Hops: Nugget. Late hops: Styrian Goldings. Yeast: Lactobacillus delbrueckii. Source: BC.

**Boskeun**: OG: 1078-81. Malt: Pale malt, Crystal malt, Aromatic malt, Corn sugar, Candi sugar. Hops: Goldings. Late hops: Saaz. Others: Sweet Orange peel, Grains of Paradise. Source: CB.

**Oerbier**: OG: 1090. ABV: 7.5%. Malt: Munich malt, Amber malt, Torrefied malt, Candi sugar. Hops: Spalt, Saaz, Goldings. IBU: 26. EBC: 76. Source: EBA.

### .   *De Koninck, Antwerp*

**De Koninck Pale**: OG: 1048. Malt: Pale malt, Vienna malt. Hops: Saaz. IBU: 24. Source: BLAM.

**De Koninck Blond**: OG: 1057. Malt: Pilsner malt, Sucrose. Hops: Saaz. IBU: 28. Source: BLAM.

### De Smedt, Opwijk

**Affligem Blond**: OG: 1065. Malt: Pilsner malt, Munich malt. Hops: Hallertau, Spalt, Styrian Goldings. IBU: 24. Source: BLAM.

**Affligem Abbey Tripel**: OG: 1083-86. Malt: Pilsner malt, Aromatic malt, Candi sugar. Hops: Challenger, Styrian Goldings. Late hops: Styrian Goldings. Others: Sweet Orange peel. Source: CB.

**Affligem Noël Christmas Ale**: OG: 1093-95. Malt: Pilsner malt, Aromatic malt, CaraMunich malt, Biscuit malt, Chocolate malt, Honey malt, Candi sugar. Hops: Challenger, Styrian Goldings. Late hops: Styrian Goldings. Others: Cinnamon. Source: BC.

### Du Bocq, Oud-Turnhout

**Corsendonk Abbey Pale Ale**: OG: 1076-78. Malt: Pilsner malt, Munich malt, Aromatic malt, Biscuit malt, Candi sugar, Sugar. Hops: Styrian Goldings. Late hops: Saaz. Others: Sweet Orange peel, Bitter orange peel, Coriander seeds. Source: BC.

### Brasserie Dubuisson, Pipaux, Hainauet

**Scaldis Belgian Special Ale**: OG: 1115-1116. Malt: Pilsner malt, Maris Otter pale malt, Aromatic malt, CaraMunich malt, Candi sugar. Hops: Styrian Goldings. Late hops: Styrian Goldings, Goldings. Source: BC.

**Scaldis Noel**: OG: 1116-1120. Malt: Maris Otter pale malt, Pale malt, Crystal malt, Toasted pale malt, Candi sugar. Hops: Goldings. Late hops: Styrian Goldings, Goldings. Dry hops: Goldings. Source: CB.

### Brasserie Dupont, Tourpes

**Saison Dupont**: OG: 1064-67. Malt: Pilsner malt, Wheat malt, Vienna malt, Candi sugar. Hops: Styrian Goldings. Late hops: Goldings. Others: Curaçao Orange peel. Source: CB.

**La Moinette Blonde**: OG: 1086-87. Malt: Pilsner malt, Acid malt, Crystal malt, Aromatic malt, Biscuit malt, Candi sugar. Hops: Goldings. Late hops: Goldings. Others: Sweet Orange peel. Source: BC.

### Duvel Moortgat, Breendonk-Puurs

**Duvel**: OG: 1070. Malt: Pale or Pilsner malt(s). Hops: Saaz, Styrian Goldings. IBU: 30. Source: EBA/BLAM. OG: 1072. Malt: Pilsner malt, CaraPils malt, Sugar. Hops: Styrian Goldings. Late hops: Saaz. Source: 150. OG: 1079-82. Malt: Pilsner malt, Crystal malt, Aromatic malt, Candi sugar, Corn sugar. Hops: Styrian Goldings. Late hops: Styrian Goldings, Saaz. Source: CB. Notes: I remember being very pleasantly surprised by this classic beer the first time I tasted it. It is lovely and should be served in its own special glass in order to contain the large fluffy head and fruity aroma.

**Maredsous 8**: OG: 1069. Malt: Pilsner malt, Caramalt, Roast malt, Dextrose. Hops: Saaz, Styrian Goldings. IBU: 29. Source: BLAM.

### Brasserie Ellezelloise, Ellezelles

**Hercule**: OG: 1087-89. Malt: Pilsner malt, Torrefied wheat, Chocolate malt, Roast barley, Candi sugar, Sugar. Hops: Goldings. Late hops: Goldings. Others: Steamed light toast Oak chips. Source: BC.

### Brasserie Fantôme, Soy

**Fantôme Saison Style Ale**: OG: 1078-79. Malt: Pilsner malt, Wheat malt, Aromatic malt. Hops: Hersbrücker, Goldings. Late hops: Goldings. Others: Curaçao Bitter orange peel, Coriander seeds, Grains of Paradise, Strawberry juice, Raspberry juice. Source: BC.

### Brasserie Friart, Le Roeulx

**St. Feuillien Abbey Ale**: OG: 1068-71. Malt: Pilsner malt, Aromatic malt, Crystal malt, Candi sugar. Hops: Styrian Goldings. Late hops: Styrian Goldings. Others: Curaçao Orange peel, Sweet Orange peel, Coriander seeds, Crushed Juniper berries. Source: CB.

**St. Feuillien Tripel**: OG: 1080-81. Malt: Pilsner malt, Aromatic malt, Biscuit malt, Candi sugar. Hops: Styrian Goldings. Late hops: Styrian Goldings. Others: Coriander seeds, Grains of Paradise, Sweet Orange peel, Juniper berries. Source: BC.

### Brasserie de Gouden Boom, Bruges

**Blanche de Bruges**: OG: 1048-49. Malt: Pilsner malt, Flaked wheat, Flaked oats, Biscuit malt, Candi sugar. Hops: Styrian Goldings. Late hops: Saaz. Others: Curaçao Orange peel, Coriander seeds, Crushed Cumin seeds, Crushed Grains of Paradise. Source: CB.

**Brugse Tripel**: OG: 1091-92. Malt: Pilsner malt, Aromatic malt, Biscuit malt, Candi sugar. Hops: Styrian Goldings. Late hops: Styrian Goldings. Source: BC.

### Gruut, Ghent. Www.gruut.be

**White**: ABV: 5%. Malt: Wheat malt. Hops: None. Others: Secret herb and spice mix. Source: WB.

**Blonde**: ABV: 5.5%. Hops: None. Others: Secret herb and spice mix. Source: WB.

**Amber**: ABV: 6.6%. Hops: None. Others: Secret herb and spice mix. Source: WB.

**Brown**: ABV: 8%. Hops: None. Others: Mixed nuts, Secret herb and spice mix. Source: WB/Web.

Notes: The use of a herb and spice mix called a gruit is an ancient practice that predates the use of hops. It is possible that this mix comprises Sweet Gale (Bog Myrtle), Mugwort, Yarrow, Heather, Juniper berries, Ginger, Caraway seeds, Sage, Rosemary, Aniseed and/or Cinnamon. Source: WB.

### Gueuzestekerij Hanssens, Dworp

**Hanssens Kriek**: OG: 1062-63. Malt: Pilsner malt, Wheat malt, Acid malt. Hops: Saaz. Others: Cherry concentrate. Source: BC.

. *Het Anker, Mechelen*

**Emperor of the Grand Cru / Cuvée van de Keizer**: OG: 1101. Malt: Pilsner malt, Caramel malt, Maize. Hops: Challenger. Others: Secret Spices. IBU: 24. Source: BLAM.

. *De Kluis Brouwerij van Hoegaarden, Hoegaarden*

**Hoegaarden White / Witte van Hoegaarden**: OG: 1048. Malt: 45% Wheat, 5% Oats, 50% Malted barley. Hops: 60% Goldings, 40% Saaz. Late hops: Saaz. Others: Coriander seed, Curaçao Orange peel. EBC: 8. Source: EBA/GW. OG: 1048-50. Malt: Pilsner malt, Wheat malt, Aromatic malt, Flaked wheat, Flaked oats. Hops: Goldings. Late hops: Goldings, Saaz. Others: Bitter orange peel, Coriander seeds, Cumin seeds. Source: BC.

**Verboden Vrucht (Forbidden Fruit)**: OG: 1087-91. Malt: Pilsner malt, Special B malt, CaraMunich malt, Biscuit malt, Sugar. Hops: Challenger. Late hops: Styrian Goldings. Others: Coriander seeds, Bitter orange peel. Source: BC.

. *Van Honsebrouck Brewery Chateau d'Inglemunster, Inglemunster*

**Kasteel Bier**: OG: 1102-1103. Malt: Pilsner malt, Munich malt, Aromatic malt, Biscuit malt, Candi sugar, Golden syrup. Hops: Styrian Goldings. Late hops: Styrian Goldings. Others: Bitter orange peel. Source: BC.

. *Huyghe, Melle*

**Duinen Dubbel Belgian Abbey Ale**: OG: 1078-80. Malt: Pilsner malt, CaraMunich malt, Special B malt, Aromatic malt, Biscuit malt, Chocolate malt, Amber candi sugar. Hops: Northern Brewer. Late hops: Brewers Gold. Source: BC.

**Delerium Tremens**: OG: 1084-85. Malt: Pilsner malt, Munich malt, Biscuit malt, Aromatic malt, Candi sugar, Golden syrup. Hops: Styrian Goldings. Late hops: Styrian Goldings, Saaz. Others: Grains of Paradise. Source: BC.

. *Interbrew, Leuven*

**Stella Artois**: OG: 1050. Malt: Lager malt, Wheat malt. Hops: Hallertau, Saaz. Late hops: Saaz. Source: DL.

**Leffe Blond**: OG: 1064. Malt: Pilsner malt, Pale malt, Maize. Hops: Hallertau, Saaz. IBU: 25. Source: BLAM. OG: 1067-68. Malt: Pilsner malt, Munich malt, Biscuit malt, Aromatic malt, Honey malt, Candi sugar. Hops: Pride of Ringwood. Late hops: Styrian Goldings. Source: BC.

. *Kerkom, Sint-Truiden*

**Bink Tripel**: OG: 1083. Malt: Pilsner malt (two varieties), Sucrose. Hops: Goldings, Challenger. Late hops: Saaz. IBU: 38. Source: BLAM.

. *Lefebvre Brewery, Quenast. Www.brasserielefebvre.be*

**Newton**: ABV: 3.5%. Others: Blend of apple juice and **Blanche**. Source: Web.

**Blanche de Bruxelles**: ABV: 4.5%. Malt: 40% Wheat malt. Others: Bitter orange peel, Coriander. Source: Web.

**Barbar Belgian Honey Ale**: OG: 1079-83. Malt: Pilsner malt, Wheat malt, CaraVienne malt, Gambrinus Honey malt, Clover honey, Candi sugar. Hops: Hersbrücker. Late hops: Styrian Goldings. Others: Curaçao Orange peel, Coriander. Source: CB.

**Floreffe Prima Melior**: ABV: 8%. Malt: Brewing sugar. Others: Anise, Coriander. Source: Web.

### . Liefmans, Oudenaarde

**Fruitesse**: ABV: 4.2%. Others: Strawberry juice, Raspberry juice, Elderberry juice, Bilberry juice. Source: W.

**Goudenband**: OG: 1052. Malt: 69% Pale malt, 5% Crystal malt, 2% Chocolate malt, 12% Torrefied barley, 12% Flaked maize. Hops: Saaz, WGV. EBC: 60. Source: EBA/GW.

**Kriekbier**: OG: 1052. Malt: Pale malt, Crystal malt, Chocolate malt, Torrefied barley, Flaked maize, Caramel. Hops: Saaz, WGV. Others: Cherries. IBU: 20. Source: EBA.

**Frambozenbier**: OG: 1053. Malt: Pale malt, Crystal malt, Chocolate malt, Torrefied barley, Flaked maize, Caramel sugar. Hops: Saaz, WGV. IBU: 19. Source: EBA.

### . Lindemans, Vlezenbeek

**Lindeman's Framboise**: OG: 1061-63. Malt: Pilsner malt, Wheat malt, Flaked wheat, Gambrinus Honey malt. Hops: Saaz. Others: Elderberries, Raspberry concentrate. Source: CB.

### . Maes, Kontich-Waarloos

**Maes Pils**: Malt: Mainly Czech malt. Hops: Saaz. Source: Roger Protz, *The Ultimate Encyclopedia of Beer*, Prion, London (1995).

### . Brasserie d'Orval, Villers-devant-Orval

**Orval**: OG: 1055. Malt: 86.5% Beauce, Gratinais, Unterfranken and Prisma pale malts, 13.5% CaraVienne malt, White candi sugar. Hops: Hallertau, Styrian Goldings. Dry hops: optional Goldings. IBU: 38-40. Source: EBA/BLAM. OG: 1059. Malt: Pale malt, Vienna malt, Crystal malt, Cane sugar. Hops: Hersbrücker. Late hops: Styrian Goldings. Dry hops: optional Styrian Goldings. Yeast: Wyeast #3522/White Labs WLP530 and Wyeast #3526/White Labs WLP650. IBU: 33. SRM: 12. Source: 150/BYO. OG: 1059-62. Malt: Pale malt, Crystal malt, CaraVienne malt, Candi sugar. Hops: Styrian Goldings, Hersbrücker. Late hops: Styrian Goldings. Dry hops: Styrian Goldings. Others: Curaçao Orange peel, Coriander seeds. Source: CB. ABV: 6.2%. Malt: Four or five varieties of spring barley malts, small amount of Crystal malt. Hops: Hallertau, Styrian Goldings: Dry hops: Goldings. Source: HB. Malt: Pale malt, Caramalt, Candi sugar. Hops: Hallertau, Goldings. Source: Roger Protz, *The Ultimate Encyclopedia of Beer*, Prion, London (1995). Malt: Pale malt, "small proportion of" Caramel malt, Liquid candi sugar. Hops: Hallertau, Styrian Goldings, Strisselspalt. Dry hops: Yes. Source: orval.be.

## . *Brasserie Piedboeuf, Jupille sur Meuse*

**Jupiler**: OG: 1047. Malt: Pale malt, Rice. IBU: 24.5. Source: EBA.

## . *Brasserie des Pères Trappistes de Rochefort, Rochefort*

**Rochefort 6**: ABV: 7.5%. Malt: Pilsner malt, Munich malt. Hops: Styrian Goldings, Hallertau. Source: HB.

**Rochefort 8**: ABV: 9.2%. Malt: Pilsner malt, Munich malt. Hops: Styrian Goldings, Hallertau. Source: HB.

**Rochefort 10**: OG: 1096. Malt: Pilsner malt, Caramel malt, Wheat starch, White sugar, Dark sugar. Hops: Styrian Goldings, Hallertau. Others: Coriander. IBU: 27. Source: BLAM. OG: 1109-1110. Malt: Pilsner malt, Biscuit malt, CaraMunich malt, Munich malt, Chocolate malt, Amber candi sugar. Hops: Styrian Goldings, Hersbrücker. Late hops: Hersbrücker, Styrian Goldings. Source: BC. ABV: 11.3%. Malt: Pilsner malt, Munich malt. Hops: Styrian Goldings, Hallertau. Source: HB.

## . *Abbaye des Rocs, Montignes-sur-Roc. Www.abbaye-des-rocs.com*

**Abbaye des Rocs**: ABV: 9%. Malt: Seven malts, No sugar. Hops: Belgian, German and Czech hops. Source: Web.

**Spéciale Noël**: ABV: 9%. Malt: Seven malts. Hops: Belgian, German and Czech hops. Source: WB.

## . *Rodenbach, Roeselare*

**Rodenbach**: OG: 1048. Malt: Pale malt, CaraMunich malt (Vienna malt), Flaked maize. Hops: Brewers Gold. IBU: 14. Source: EBA.

**Grand Cru**: OG: 1064. Malt: Pale malt, CaraMunich malt (Vienna malt), Flaked maize. Hops: Brewers Gold. IBU: 14. Source: EBA. OG: 1053-55. Malt: Pale malt, Flaked maize, Vienna malt, CaraVienne malt, Acid malt, Chocolate malt, Lactose, Corn sugar. Hops: Styrian Goldings. Late hops: Brewers Gold, Goldings. Others: Steamed Oak chips. Source: CB.

## . *Sint-Bernadus, Watou*

**St. Bernardus 12**: OG: 1090. Malt: Pilsner malt, Black malt / Dark malt, Sugar, Caramel syrup. Hops: Target, Saaz. IBU: 22. Source: BLAM.

## . *Brasserie St-Feuillien, Le Roeulx*

**St. Feuillien Tripel**: OG: 1074. Malt: Pilsner malt, CaraPils malt, Sugar. Hops: Saaz, Styrian Goldings, Spalt. IBU: 28. Source: BLAM.

### Brouwerij de Silly, Silly

**Double Enghien Blonde Ale**: OG: 1073-78. Malt: Pilsner malt, Aromatic malt, Biscuit malt, Vienna malt, Candi sugar. Hops: Styrian Goldings. Late hops: Styrian Goldings. Source: CB.

**Scotch Silly**: OG: 1078-82. Malt: Pale malt, Crystal malt, Aromatic malt, Whiskey or Peat-smoked malt, Candi sugar, Glucose syrup. Hops: Goldings. Late hops: Goldings. Source: CB.

**Piraat Ale IPA**: OG: 1103-1106. Malt: Pilsner malt, Crystal malt, CaraVienne malt, Aromatic malt, Candi sugar. Hops: Brewers Gold. Late hops: Styrian Goldings. Others: Coriander seeds. Source: CB.

### Slaghmuylder, Ninove

**Witkap-Pater Abbey Single Ale**: OG: 1059-62. Malt: Pilsner malt, Crystal malt. Hops: Styrian Goldings. Late hops: Saaz. Others: Sweet Orange peel, Coriander seeds, Lemon peel. Source: CB.

### Van Steenberge, Ertvelde

**Corsendonk Monk's Brown Ale**: OG: 1070-72. Malt: Pilsner malt, CaraMunich malt, Aromatic malt, Biscuit malt, Chocolate malt, Candi sugar. Hops: Styrian Goldings. Late hops: Styrian Goldings. Others: Bitter orange peel. Source: BC.

**Gulden Draak**: OG: 1104-1109. Malt: Pilsner malt, Pale malt, Wheat malt, Crystal malt, Aromatic malt, CaraMunich malt, Biscuit malt, Candi sugar. Hops: Brewers Gold. Late hops: Styrian Goldings. Source: CB.

### Sterkens, Meer

**St. Paul Double Ale**: OG: 1059-61. Malt: Pilsner malt, CaraMunich malt, Aromatic malt, Biscuit malt, Chocolate malt, Dark candi sugar. Hops: Styrian Goldings. Late hops: Saaz. Source: BC.

**St. Sebastiaan Golden Belgian Ale**: OG: 1076-78. Malt: Pilsner malt, Munich malt, Aromatic malt, Biscuit malt, Candi sugar, Sugar. Hops: Brewers Gold. Late hops: Hersbrücker, Styrian Goldings. Source: BC.

### Strubbe, Ichtegem

**Vlaskop**: OG: 1056. Malt: Pilsner malt, Aromatic malt. Hops: Styrian Goldings. Late hops: Styrian Goldings. Others: Dried Lemon peel, Dried Orange peel, Coriander seeds. Source: BC.

### Brouwerij der Trappisten van Westmalle, Westmalle

**Westmalle Dubbel**: OG: 1063. Malt: Pilsner malt, Caramel malt, Dark malt, Dark sugar. Hops: Tettnang, Saaz, Styrian Goldings. IBU: 24. Source: BLAM/HB. OG: 1070-71. Malt: Pilsner malt, CaraMunich malt, Chocolate malt, Biscuit malt, Dark candi sugar. Hops: Styrian Goldings. Source: BC.

**Westmalle Tripel**: OG: 1081. Malt: Pilsner malt, Sugar. Hops: Tettnang, Saaz, Styrian Goldings, sometimes others. IBU: 39. Source: BLAM/150/HB. OG: 1088-90. Malt: Pilsner malt, Aromatic malt, Candi sugar. Hops: Styrian Goldings. Late hops: Tettnang, Hersbrücker, Saaz. Source: CB. Hops: Saaz. Source: HB. ABV: 9%. Malt: Pale malt, Candi sugar. Hops: Styrian Goldings. Source: Roger Protz, *The Ultimate Encyclopedia of Beer*, Prion, London (1995).

. *Brouwerij Westvleteren, Westvleteren*

**Blond / Green Cap**: ABV: 5.6%. Malt: Pale malt, Candi sugar. Hops: Northern Brewer. Source: HB.

**Westvleteren 8**: OG: 1072. Malt: Pilsner malt, Pale malt, Sucrose, Caramel. Hops: Northern Brewer, Hallertau, Styrian Goldings. IBU: 35. Source: BLAM.

**Westvleteren Abt 12°**: OG: 1105-1106. Malt: Pilsner malt, Special B malt, CaraMunich malt, Biscuit malt, Aromatic malt, Chocolate malt, Candi sugar. Hops: Styrian Goldings. Late hops: Hersbrücker, Styrian Goldings. Source: BC.

# Bermuda

. *Bermuda Triangle Brewing, Southampton*

**Wilde Hogge Amber Ale**: OG: 1056-60. Malt: Pale malt, Dextrin malt, Crystal malt, Vienna malt, Chocolate malt, Maltodextrin. Hops: Northern Brewer. Late hops: Tettnang, Styrian Goldings. Source: CB.

# Brazil

. *Cervejaria Sul Brasileira, Toledo*

**Xingu Black Beer**: OG: 1062-63. Malt: Lager malt, Dextrin malt, Crystal malt, Vienna malt, Chocolate malt, Black malt. Hops: Yakima Magnum. Late hops: Hersbrücker. Source: CB.

# Cameroon

. *Guinness, Douala*

**Foreign Extra Stout**: Others: Guinness flavour extract. Source: BY.

# Canada

. *Bières de la Nouvelle France, Saint-Paulin, Québec*

**Ambrée de Sarrasin**: OG: 1055. Malt: Pale malt, Crystal malt, Flaked oats, Wheat malt, Buckwheat. Hops: Saaz. Late hops: Hallertau. Source: NACB.

## Big Rock, Calgary, Alberta

**Warthog Cream Ale**: OG: 1045. Malt: Pale malt, Crystal malt. Hops: Willamette. Late hops: Centennial. Source: 150.

## Brasserie Brasal, La Salle, Québec

**Brasal Bock**: OG: 1082-83. Malt: Pale malt, Dextrin malt, Crystal malt, Vienna malt, Chocolate malt. Hops: Tettnang. Late hops: Hersbrücker. Source: CB.

## Brasserie Seigneuriale, Boucherville, Québec

**Seigneuriale Réserve**: OG: 1075. Malt: Belgian pale malt, Crystal malt, Special B malt, CaraMunich malt, Wheat malt. Hops: Brewers Gold. Late hops: Saaz. Source: NACB.

## Les Brasseurs du Nord, Blainville, Québec

**Boréale Noire**: OG: 1055. Malt: Pale malt, Crystal malt, Flaked oats, Roast barley, Black malt. Hops: Goldings. Late hops: Northern Brewer, Goldings. Source: NACB.

## Creemore Springs Brewery, Creemore, Ontario

**Creemore Springs Premium Lager**: OG: 1050. Malt: Lager malt, CaraPils malt, Munich malt, Vienna malt. Hops: Hallertau. Late hops: Saaz. Source: NACB. OG: 1048. Malt: Pale malt, Pilsner malt, Crystal malt. Hops: Saaz. Late hops: Saaz. Source: 150.

## Labbatt, Ontario / Toronto / Vancouver

**Labbatt Blue**: OG: 1045. Malt: Pilsner malt, Flaked maize, Pale malt, Corn sugar. Hops: Hallertau. Late hops: Hallertau, Saaz. Source: 150.

**Guinness Foreign Extra Stout**: Others: Guinness flavour extract. Source: BY.

## McAuslan Brewery, Montréal, Québec

**Griffon Brown Ale**: OG: 1040. Malt: Mild ale malt, CaraPils malt, Chocolate malt, Sugar. Hops: Willamette. Late hops: Willamette. Source: NACB.

**St. Ambroise Stout**: OG: 1058. Malt: Pale malt, Munich malt, Flaked oats, Special B malt, Roast barley. Hops: Bullion. Late hops: Willamette. Source: NACB.

## Molson, Vancouver, Toronto and Montréal

**Molson Ice**: OG: 1055-59. Malt: Pale malt, Flaked maize, Crystal malt. Hops: Tettnang. Late hops: Hersbrücker, Tettnang. Source: CB.

## Moosehead, St. John, New Brunswick and Dartmouth, Nova Scotia

**Moosehead Lager**: OG: 1045. Malt: Lager malt, CaraPils malt, Flaked maize. Hops: Tettnang. Late hops: Tettnang, Hallertau. Source: NACB.

**Ten Penny Ale**: OG: 1052. Malt: Pale malt, Wheat malt, Crystal malt, CaraPils malt, Cornstarch, Maltodextrin. Hops: Cluster, Goldings. Late hops: Goldings. Source: Neil C. Gudmestad, HF.

. *Niagara Falls Brewing Company, Niagara Falls, Ontario*

**Maple Wheat Ale**: OG: 1084. Malt: Pale malt, Wheat malt, Maple syrup. Hops: Willamette. Source: CB.

. *Sleeman Brewing & Malting Company, Guelph, Ontario*

**Sleeman Steam Beer**: OG: 1048. Malt: Lager malt, CaraPils malt, Flaked rice. Hops: Mount Hood. Late hops: Hallertau. Source: NACB.

. *Unibroue, Chambly, Québec*

**Blanche de Chambly**: OG: 1051. Malt: Lager malt, Wheat malt, Candi sugar. Hops: Hersbrücker. Others: Curaçao Bitter orange peel, Coriander. Source: CB.

**Quelquechose**: OG: 1085. Malt: Pale malt, Crystal malt, Wheat malt. Hops: Brewers Gold. Others: Cherries. Source: NACB.

**Trois Pistoles**: OG: 1085-86. Malt: Pilsner malt, Crystal malt, CaraMunich malt, Biscuit malt, Chocolate malt, Candi sugar, Golden syrup. Hops: Styrian Goldings. Late hops: Styrian Goldings, Saaz. Others: Anise, Bitter orange peel. Source: BC.

**La Fin du Monde**: OG: 1086. Malt: Belgian Pilsner malt, Crystal malt, Wheat malt, CaraVienne malt, Candi sugar. Hops: Perle. Late hops: Styrian Goldings. Source: NACB.

. *Upper Canada Brewing Company, Toronto, Ontario*

**Maple Brown Ale**: OG: 1056. Malt: Mild ale malt, Crystal malt, Chocolate malt, Munich malt, Maple syrup. Hops: Fuggles. Late hops: Goldings. Source: NACB.

. *Wellington County Brewery, Guelph, Ontario*

**County Ale**: OG: 1052. Malt: Pale malt, Crystal malt, Chocolate malt, Wheat malt. Hops: Willamette. Late hops: Goldings. Source: NACB.

. *Yukon Brewing Company, Whitehorse, Yukon*

**Arctic Red**: OG: 1054. Malt: Pale malt, Crystal malt, Patent black malt, Munich malt. Hops: Goldings. Late hops: Cascade. Source: 150.

# China

. *Cheerday, Qiandaohu*

**Luckys**: Malt: Rice. Hops: Qingdao. Source: W.

. *Tsing-Tao, Quingdao*

**Tsing-Tao**: OG: 1047-48. Malt: Rice, Pale malt, Crystal malt, Rice syrup. Hops: Tettnang, Saaz. Late hops: Saaz. Source: CB.

## Costa Rica

. *Cerveceria Costa Rica, Heredia*

**Cerveza Imperial**: OG: 1051-52. Malt: Lager malt, Flaked maize, Crystal malt, Sugar. Hops: Tettnang. Late hops: Saaz. Source: CB.

## Cuba

. *Cerveceria Bucanero, Hoguin*

**Cristal**: OG: 1047-50. Malt: Pilsner malt, Flaked maize, Crystal malt. Hops: Tettnang. Late hops: Saaz, Tettnang. Source: BC.

## Cyprus

. *Keo, Limassol*

**Keo Beer**: OG: 1046-48. Malt: Pilsner malt, Crystal malt. Hops: Saaz. Late hops: Saaz. Source: CB.

## Czech Republic

. *Budweiser Budvar, Budejovice*

**Budweiser Budvar**: OG: 1049. Malt: Pilsner malt, Hops: Saaz. EBC: 4. Source: EBA/GW. OG: 1051-53. Malt: Pilsner malt, Crystal malt, Munich malt, Aromatic malt. Hops: Saaz. Late hops: Saaz. Source: BC.

. *Gambrinus, Plzen*

**Gambrinus**: OG: 1048. Malt: 90% Pilsner malt, 10% Sucrose. Hops: Saaz. Late hops: Saaz. EBC: 3. Source: EBA/GW.

. *Herold, Breznice*

**Black Chalice**: ABV: 4.8%. Hops: Saaz. Source: W.

. *Klásterni Pivovar, Prague*

**Svaty Norbert Pale**: ABV: 5.2%. Malt: Pale malt. Hops: Saaz. Source: HB.

**Svaty Norbert Dark**: ABV: 6.2%. Malt: Four malts. Hops: Saaz. Source: HB.

*   *Nova Paka Brewery, Nova Paka*

**Kumburak Bohemian Pilsner**: OG: 1051-53. Malt: Pilsner malt, Dextrin malt, Crystal malt, Vienna malt, Maltodextrin. Hops: Saaz. Late hops: Saaz. Source: CB.

*   *Plzensky Prazdroj Urquell, Plzen*

**Pilsner Urquell**: OG: 1048. Malt: Pilsner malt. Hops: Saaz. Late hops: Saaz. IBU: 40. Source: EBA/DL. Malt: Pilsner malt, Vienna malt, Munich malt, CaraPils malt. Hops: Cluster. Late hops: Saaz. Source: 150. OG: 1050-53. Malt: Pilsner malt, Crystal malt, Munich malt. Hops: Saaz. Late hops: Saaz. Source: CB.

# Denmark

*   *Carlsberg Brewery, Copenhagen*

**Elephant**: OG: 1065. Malt: 88% Pilsner malt, 12% Sugar. Hops: Hallertau. EBC: 5. Source: EBA/GW. OG: 1069-70. Malt: Lager malt, Crystal malt, Corn sugar. Hops: Hersbrücker. Late hops: Hersbrücker, Saaz. Source: CB.

# El Salvador

*   *Cerveceria La Constacia, San Salvador*

**Pilsener of El Salvador**: OG: 1047-48. Malt: Rice, Lager malt, Crystal malt, Vienna malt, Aromatic malt, Rice syrup. Hops: Saaz, Hersbrücker. Late hops: Styrian Goldings. Source: CB.

# England

*   *Acorn, Barnsley. Www.acorn-brewery.co.uk*

**Lightness**: ABV: 3.6%. Hops: Fuggles. Source: Web.

**Yorkshire Pride**: ABV: 3.7%. Hops: Styrian Savinjski Goldings, Challenger. Source: Web.

**Barnsley Bitter**: ABV: 3.8%. Malt: Maris Otter pale malt. Hops: English. Source: Web.

**Darkness**: ABV: 4.2%. Malt: Roast malts. Hops: Fuggles. Source: Web.

**Quantum**: ABV: 4.5%. Malt: Lager malt. Hops: Fuggles, Goldings. Source: WB.

**England's Dreaming**: ABV: 4.5%. Malt: Roast Crystal malts. Source: Web.

**God Save The Queen**: ABV: 4.5. Hops: Sovereign, English. Source: Web.

**Mild**: OG: 1034/5. Malt: Maris Otter pale malt, Crystal malt (optional Invert sugar, Laevuline), Caramel. Hops: Fuggles, Goldings. IBU: 20. EBC: 120. Source: RP

**Bitter (BB)**: OG: 1036. Malt: Maris Otter pale malt (optional Invert sugar), Caramel. Hops: Fuggles, Goldings (optional Challenger). Dry hopping: Fuggles. IBU: 33. Source: RP/EBA.

**Southwold Bitter**: OG:1037. Malt: Pale malt, Roast barley, Crystal malt. Hops: Fuggles, Goldings. Late hops: Goldings. Dry hops: Goldings. Source: DL.

**Old**: OG: 1042. Malt: Maris Otter pale malt, Crystal malt (optional Invert sugar, Laevuline), Caramel. Hops: Fuggles, Goldings. IBU: 23. EBC: 100. Source: RP.

**Extra**: OG: 1043. Malt: Maris Otter pale malt, Crystal malt, Invert sugar, Caramel. Hops: Fuggles, Goldings, Challenger. Late hops: Fuggles. IBU: 36. EBC: 30. Source: RP.

**Regatta**: OG: 1045. Malt: 100% Pipkin pale malt. Hops: Goldings. Dry hops: Goldings. IBU: 28. EBC: 8-10. Source: RP5/JHF.

**Suffolk Strong Ale**: OG: 1046-47. Malt: Pale malt, Crystal malt, Chocolate malt, Invert sugar. Hops: Fuggles. Late hops: Fuggles, Goldings, Challenger. Source: BC.

**Barley Mow**: OG: 1047. Malt: Maris Otter pale malt, Crystal malt, Amber malt. Hops: Fuggles, Goldings. Late hops: Fuggles. IBU: 33. EBC: 40. Source: RP4/5.

**May Day Ale**: OG: 1047. Malt: Maris Otter pale malt, Amber malt. Hops: Goldings. Late hops: Fuggles, Goldings. Dry hops: Fuggles, Goldings. IBU: 40. EBC: 16-20,. Source: RP.

**American-style IPA**: ABV: 4.8%. Malt: Pale malt, Crystal malt, Munich malt, Wheat malt. Hops: Columbus, Chinook, Cascade, Centennial, Willamette. Source: Web.

**Oyster Stout**: OG: 1048. Malt: Maris Otter pale malt, Crystal malt, Chocolate malt, Roast barley. Hops: Fuggles. IBU: 33. EBC: 200. Source: RP5.

**Broadside**: OG: 1049. Malt: Maris Otter pale malt, Crystal malt, Invert sugar, Caramel. Hops: Fuggles, Goldings, Challenger. Late hops: Fuggles. IBU: 33. EBC: 38. Source: RP. Hops: First Gold. Source: Web.

**Tally Ho**: OG: 1075. Malt: Maris Otter pale malt, Crystal malt, (optional Brown malt, Invert sugar, Laevuline), Caramel. Hops: Fuggles, Goldings. IBU: 28. EBC: 120. Source: RP/Web. OG: 1088. Malt: Pale malt, White sugar. Hops: Fuggles. Notes: Recipe from 1878. Source: DP.

**Innovation**: Hops: Boadicea, Columbus, Styrian Goldings. Source: Web.

**Sole Bay Celebratory Ale**: Malt: Pilsner malt, Muscovado sugar, Demerara sugar. Hops: Nelson Sauvin. Source: Web.

### . Alcazar, Nottingham

**Mocha Stout** (b-c): ABV: 5%. Malt: Maris Otter pale malt, Crystal malt, Roast barley, Chocolate malt. Hops: Target, Goldings. Others: Chocolate essence, Coffee essence. Source: JE6.

**Maple Magic** (b-c): ABV: 5.5%. Malt: Maris Otter pale malt, Crystal malt, Amber malt, Roast barley, Chocolate malt, Maple syrup. Hops: Goldings, Fuggles, Challenger, Northdown. Others: Nutmeg, Cinnamon, Cloves. Source: JE6.

**Bombay Castle IPA** (b-c): ABV: 6.5%. Malt: Maris Otter pale malt. Hops: Progress, Goldings. Source: JE6.

### . Ales of Kent, Maidstone

**Defiance** (b-c): ABV: 4.1%. Malt: Maris Otter pale malt, Crystal malt, Flaked maize. Hops: Fuggles, Goldings. Source: JE3.

**Stiltman** (b-c): ABV: 4.3%. Malt: Maris Otter pale malt, Crystal malt, Roast malt, Wheat malt. Hops: First Gold, Goldings. Source: JE3.

**Smugglers Glory** (b-c): ABV: 4.8%. Malt: Maris Otter pale malt, Crystal malt, Roast malt, Chocolate malt. Hops: Fuggles, Goldings. Source: JE3.

**Farmers Harvest** (b-c): ABV: 5%. Malt: Maris Otter pale malt. Hops: Hallertau Hersbrücker, Saaz. Source: JE3.

### . Alewife, Harleston

**Harvest Ale** (b-c): ABV: 4.5%. Malt: Pale malt, Crystal malt. Hops: Challenger. Source: JE4/5.

**Dark Skies Stout** (b-c): ABV: 4.6%. Malt: Pale malt, Chocolate malt. Hops: Styrian Goldings. Source: JE4/5.

**Festival Ale** (b-c): ABV: 6.5%. Malt: Pale malt, Chocolate malt, Roast barley. Hops: Goldings. Source: JE4/5.

**Hunter's Moon** (b-c): ABV: 6.8%. Malt: Pale malt, Crystal malt. Hops: Mixed English. Source: JE4/5.

### . Ampleforth Abbey, Ampleforth

**Double** (b-c): ABV: 7%. Malt: Pale malt, Wheat malt, Crystal malt, Chocolate malt, Munich malt, Soft brown sugar. Hops: German Northern Brewer, Styrian Savinjski Goldings. Yeast: Trappist, probably Rochefort. Source: www.guardian.co.uk/lifeandstyle/2012/jun/19/ ampleforth-abbey-monastic-beer-secrets.

### . Anglo Dutch Brewery, Dewsbury

**Kletswater** (b-c): ABV: 4%. Malt: Maris Otter pale malt, Crystal malt, Wheat malt. Hops: Pilgrim, First Gold. Source: JE5.

**Tabatha** (b-c): ABV: 6%. Malt: Lager malt. Hops: Pilgrim, First Gold, Fuggles. Others: Coriander. Source: JE5.

### . *Archers Ales, Swindon*

**Village Bitter**: OG: 1035. Malt: 95% Halcyon pale malt, 5% Crystal malt. Hops: Progress, WGV. Late hops: Styrian Goldings. Source: RP4/5.

**Best Bitter**: OG: 1040. Malt: 95% Pale malt, 5% Crystal malt. Hops: WGV, Fuggles. Late hops: WGV or Goldings. Source: RP.

**IPA**: ABV: 4.2%. Hops: Cascade, Willamette. Source: W.

**Blackjack Porter**: OG: 1046. Malt: 88% Pale malt, 10% Black and other Dark malts, 2% Wheat malt. Hops: WGV, Fuggles. Late hops: WGV or Goldings. Source: RP.

**Golden Bitter**: OG: 1046. Malt: 100% Blended Pale malt. Hops: Progress, WGV. Late hops: WGV or Goldings. IBU: 36. Source: RP. Note: **Archers Golden** is a superb ale.

**Golden Bitter** (b-c): ABV: 4.7%. Malt: Maris Otter and Halcyon pale malt. Hops: Progress, WGV, Styrian Goldings, Goldings. Source: JE1. Malt: Maris Otter pale malt, Lager malt, CaraPils malt. Hops: Progress, WGV, Styrian Goldings, Goldings. Source: JE2/3.

**ASB**: OG: 1048. Malt: 95% Pale malt, 5% Crystal malt. Hops: Sunshine, Fuggles. Late hops: Goldings. Source: RP1.

**Headbanger / Old Cobleigh's**: OG: 1065. Malt: 95% Halcyon pale malt, 5% Crystal malt. Hops: Sunshine, Fuggles or Progress, WGV. Late Hops: Goldings or WGV. Source: RP. Notes: I once had a soporific experience with this beer in an Oxford pub. This beer deserves more respect than I gave it on that occasion.

### . *Arkells Brewery, Swindon*

**John Arkell Bitter (BB) / 2B**: OG: 1032. Malt: 90-92% Pipkin pale malt, 6% Crystal malt, 2-4% Sugar. Hops: Goldings, Fuggles/Progress. Late hops: Goldings or Fuggles. IBU: 28. EBC: 25. Source: RP.

**Brown Jack Best Brown Ale** (bottled): ABV: 3.5%. Malt: Roast barley, Sugar. Hops: Fuggles. Source: DL.

**Arkell Best Bitter (3Bs) / 3B**: OG: 1039-1040. Malt: 88% Pipkin pale malt, 10% Roast barley or Crystal malt, 2% Sugar. Hops: Goldings, Progress or Fuggles. Late hops: Fuggles or Goldings. IBU: 30. EBC: 35. Source: RP. Malt: Pale malt, Flaked maize, Roast barley, Sugar. Hops: Bramling Cross, Fuggles. Late hops: Goldings. Dry hops: Goldings. Source: DL.

**Mash Tun Mild**: OG: 1040. Malt: 66% Pipkin pale malt, 30% Crystal malt and Chocolate malt, 4% Sugar. Hops: Fuggles. IBU: 24. EBC: 100. Source: RP2/3/4/5/JHF/GW.

**Kingsdown Ale**: OG: 1052. Malt: 86% Pipkin pale malt, 12% Roast barley or Crystal malt, 2% Sugar. Hops: Progress, Goldings. Late hops: Fuggles or Goldings. IBU: 32. EBC: 43. Source: RP. OG: 1060. Malt: Pale malt, Black malt, Sugar. Hops: Fuggles, Goldings. Source: DL.

**Noel**: OG: 1055. Malt: 92% Pipkin pale malt, 6% Crystal malt, 2% Sugar. Hops: Goldings, Fuggles. Late hops: Goldings. IBU: 36. EBC: 30. Source: RP3/4/5.

### . *Arundel Brewery, Arundel*

**Best Bitter**: OG: 1040. Malt: 88% Pale malt, 12% Crystal malt. Hops: Fuggles, Goldings. Source: RP3/4/5.

**Sussex Gold**: OG: 1042. Malt: 100% Pale malt. Hops: Goldings. Source: RP4/5. Hops: Cascade, Goldings. Source: W.

**Stronghold**: OG: 1050. Malt: 90% Pale malt, 10% Crystal malt. Hops: Fuggles, Goldings. Source: RP3/4/5.

**Old Knucker**: OG: 1055. Malt: 82% Pale malt, 12% Crystal malt, 6% Chocolate malt. Hops: Fuggles, Goldings. Source: RP3/4/5.

### . *Ash Vine Brewery, Frome*

**Trudoxhill Bitter**: OG: 1034.5. Malt: Triumph pale malt, Crystal malt, Wheat malt. Hops: Goldings, Fuggles. Source: RP3.

**Bitter**: OG: 1037.5 – 1039.8. Malt: Triumph or Maris Otter pale malt, 1% Crystal malt, optional Wheat malt. Hops: Challenger and/or WGV. Late hops: Goldings. Source: RP.

**Penguin Porter** (b-c): ABV: 4.2%. Malt: Maris Otter pale malt, Crystal malt, Black malt. Hops: Fuggles, Challenger, Goldings. Source: JE1/2.

**Challenger**: OG: 1042.8 – 1044.5. Malt: Triumph or Maris Otter pale malt, 8.5% Crystal malt, optional Wheat malt. Hops: Challenger. Late hops: Goldings, Fuggles. Source: RP.

**Black Bess Porter**: OG: 1044.5 – 1046. Malt: 90% Triumph or Maris Otter pale malt, 6% Crystal malt, optional Wheat malt, 0.2% Black malt, 3.6% Chocolate malt, optional Roast barley. Hops: Challenger and/or WGV. Late hops: Goldings, Fuggles. Source: RP.

**Munro's Mickey Finn**: OG: 1047.5. Malt: Maris Otter pale malt. Hops: Challenger. Late hops: Challenger, Goldings. Source: RP5.

**Tanker**: OG: 1049. Malt: Triumph pale malt, Crystal malt, Black malt, Wheat malt. Hops: Fuggles, WGV. Late hops: Goldings. Source: RP2/3.

**Longleat** (b-c): ABV: 5%. Malt: Maris Otter pale malt, Crystal malt. Hops: Fuggles, Challenger, Goldings. Others: Raisins, Brandy essence. Source: JE2.

**Hop & Glory** (b-c): ABV: 5%. Malt: Maris Otter pale malt. Hops: Challenger, Goldings. Source: JE1/2.

**Hop & Glory**: OG: 1058. Malt: Triumph pale malt, Crystal malt, Wheat malt, Black malt. Hops: Goldings, Challenger, Fuggles. Source: RP3. OG: 1052-1053.5. Malt: 100% Maris Otter pale malt. Hops: Challenger and optional WGV. Late hops: Goldings. Source: RP4/5.

### . Aston Manor Brewery Company, Birmingham

**Mild / Chandlers Mild**: OG: 1032. Malt: Golden Promise pale malt, Chocolate malt, Brewer's Invert sugar. Hops: Fuggles, Northdown. IBU: 22. Source: RP2/3.

**Bitter / Chandlers Bitter**: OG: 1036. Malt: Golden Promise pale malt, Brewer's Invert sugar. Hops: Fuggles, Northdown. Source: RP2.

### . Atlantic Brewery, Treisaac

**Gold** (b-c): ABV: 4.6%. Malt: Pale malt, Wheat malt. Hops: Fuggles, First Gold. Others: Root ginger. Source: JE6.

**Blue** (b-c): ABV: 4.8%. Malt: Pale malt, Crystal malt, Chocolate malt, Black malt, Wheat malt. Hops: Fuggles, First Gold. Source: JE6.

**Red** (b-c): ABV: 5%. Malt: Pale malt, Crystal malt, Wheat malt. Hops: Fuggles, First Gold. Source: JE6.

**Discovery** (b-c): ABV: 5.5%. Others: Limes, Chillies, Ginger. Source: WB.

### . Ballard's Brewery, Petersfield

**Midhurst Mild**: OG: 1034. Malt: 74% Pipkin pale malt, 8.5% Crystal malt, 6% Chocolate malt, 11.5% Torrefied wheat. Hops: Fuggles. Source: RP3/4/5.

**Trotton Bitter**: OG: 1036. Malt: 90% Pipkin and Triumph pale malt, 10% Crystal malt. Hops: Fuggles. Late hops: Goldings. Source: RP1/2/3/4/5.

**Best Bitter**: OG: 1042. Malt: 90% Pipkin and Triumph pale malt, 10% Crystal malt. Hops: Fuggles. Late hops: Goldings. Source: RP1/2/3/4/5/JE3.

**Best Bitter** (b-c): ABV: 4.2%. Malt: Pearl pale malt, Crystal malt. Hops: Goldings, Fuggles. Source: JE4/5/6.

**Golden Bine**: OG: 1042. Malt: 97% Pipkin pale malt, 3% Torrefied wheat. Hops: Fuggles. Late hops: Goldings. Source: RP4/5.

**King's Table** (b-c): ABV: 4.2%. Malt: Pearl pale malt, Torrefied wheat. Hops: Fuggles, Goldings. Source: JE5.

**Nyewood Gold** (b-c): ABV: 5%. Malt: Pipkin or Pearl pale malt, optional Torrefied wheat. Hops: Phoenix. Source: JE3/4/5/6.

**Volcano**: OG: 1060. Malt: Triumph pale malt, Crystal malt. Hops: Fuggles. Late hops: Goldings. Source: RP2.

**Wassail**: OG: 1060. Malt: 85% Pipkin and Triumph pale malt, 15% Crystal malt. Hops: Fuggles. Late hops: Goldings. Source: RP1/2/3/4/5. OG: 1062. Malt: Pale malt, Crystal malt, Patent black malt. Hops: Fuggles. Late hops: Goldings. Source: BC.

**Wassail** (b-c): ABV: 6%. Malt: Pipkin or Pearl pale malt, Crystal malt. Hops: Fuggles, Goldings. Source: JE1/2/3/4/5/6.

**Early Daze** (b-c): ABV: 8.7%. Malt: Pipkin pale malt, Crystal malt. Hops: Goldings, Fuggles. Source: JE3.

**Old Episcopal**: OG: 1092. Malt: 90% Pipkin pale malt, 9.8% Crystal malt, 0.2% Chocolate malt. Hops: Fuggles, Goldings. Source: RP3.

**Foxy** (b-c): ABV: 9.3%. Malt: Pearl pale malt, Crystal malt. Hops: Goldings. Source: JE4.

**WMD** (b-c): ABV: 9.4%. Malt: Pearl pale malt, Crystal malt. Hops: Fuggles, Goldings. Source: JE5.

**Off the Wall**: OG: 1094. Malt: 87.95% Pipkin pale malt, 11.8% Crystal malt, 0.25% Chocolate malt. Hops: Fuggles. Late hops: Goldings. Source: RP4/5.

**Pom's Delight** (b-c): ABV: 9.6%. Malt: Pearl pale malt, Crystal malt. Hops: Fuggles, Goldings. Source: JE6.

**Blizzard** (b-c): ABV: 9.8%. Malt: Pipkin pale malt, Crystal malt, Chocolate malt. Hops: Fuggles, Phoenix. Source: JE1.

**Wild**: ABV: 4.7%. Note: Blend of 52% **Mild** and 48% **Wassail**. Source: RP5.

**Trout Tickler**: OG: 1102-106. Malt: Pale malt, Crystal malts, Chocolate malt. Hops: Fuggles. Late hops: Goldings, Styrian Goldings. Source: BC.

**Trout Tickler** (b-c): ABV: 9.9%. Malt: Pipkin pale malt, Chocolate malt, Crystal malt. Hops: Fuggles, Phoenix. Source: JE2.

### .  Banks's & Hanson's, Wolverhampton

**Hanson's Bitter**: OG: 1035. Malt: Mainly Maris Otter pale malt with some Halcyon and Pipkin pale malt. Hops: Fuggles, Goldings. Dry hops: Yes. IBU: 27. EBC: 25. Source: RP3.

**Hanson's Mild Ale**: OG: 1036. Malt: Maris Otter pale malt, Halcyon pale malt, Pipkin pale malt, Crystal malt, Caramalt. Hops: Fuggles, Goldings. IBU: 25. EBC: 50. Source: RP3/4/5/GW.

**Banks's Mild Ale / Banks's Ale**: OG: 1036. Malt: Maris Otter pale malt, Halcyon pale malt, Pipkin pale malt, Caramel. Hops: Fuggles, Goldings. IBU: 25. EBC: 40. Source: RP3/4/5. OG: 1035. Malt: Mild ale malt, Crystal malt, Flaked barley, Sugar. Hops: Fuggles, Goldings. Source: 150.

**Banks's Bitter**: OG: 1038. Malt: Maris Otter pale malt, Halcyon pale malt, Pipkin pale malt. Hops: Fuggles, Goldings. IBU: 33. EBC: 23. Source: RP3/4/5.

## Banks & Taylor Brewery, Shefford

**Shefford Mild**: OG: 1035. Malt: 95% Pale malt, 5% Crystal malt, Caramel. Hops: Challenger. Late hops: Fuggles, Goldings. IBU: 30. Source: RP2/3/4/5.

**Shefford Bitter**: OG: 1038. Malt: 95% Pale malt, 5% Crystal malt. Hops: Challenger, Fuggles, Goldings. Late hops: Fuggles, Goldings. IBU: 40. Source: RP1/2/3/4/5/W/JE6.

**Shefford Pale Ale (SPA)**: OG: 1041. Malt: 87% Pale malt, 7% Crystal malt, 6% Wheat malt. Hops: Fuggles, Goldings. IBU: 36. Source: RP1/2/3/4/5.

**Millennium Gold / Golden Fox** (b-c): ABV: 4.1%. Malt: Pearl pale malt, Wheat malt. Hops: Styrian Goldings. Source: JE6.

**Black Dragon Mild** (b-c): ABV: 4.3%. Malt: Mild ale malt, Crystal malt, Black malt, Roast barley, Wheat malt. Hops: Goldings. Source: JE4/5/6.

**Edwin Taylor's Extra Stout**: OG: 1042. Malt: 84% Pale malt, 16% Roast barley. Hops: Challenger, Hallertau. Source: RP2/3/4/5/GW.

**Edwin Taylor's Extra Stout** (b-c): ABV: 4.5%. Malt: Halcyon or Pearl pale malt, Brown malt, Roast barley. Hops: Challenger. Source: JE2/3/4/5/6.

**Dragonslayer**: OG: 1045. Malt: 95% Pale malt, 5% Wheat malt. Hops: Fuggles, Goldings, Challenger. Source: RP4/5.

**Dragonslayer** (b-c): ABV: 4.5%. Malt: Halcyon or Pearl pale malt, Wheat malt. Hops: Goldings, Challenger. Source: JE2/3/4/5/6.

**Old Bat**: OG: 1045. Malt: 100% Halcyon pale malt. Hops: Hallertau, Fuggles, Goldings. Source: RP3/4/5.

**Old Bat** (b-c): ABV: 6%. Malt: Halcyon or Pearl pale malt, Crystal malt, Brown malt. Hops: Fuggles. Source: JE2/3/4.

**Shefford Old Strong (SOS)**: OG: 1050. Malt: 95% Pearl pale malt, 5% Crystal malt. Hops: Fuggles, Goldings. Source: RP1/2/3/4/5/JE5/6.

**Shefford Old Dark (SOD)**: OG: 1050. Malt: 95% Pearl pale malt, 5% Crystal malt, Caramel. Hops: Fuggles, Goldings. Source: RP1/2/3/4/5/JE5.

**SOD** (b-c): ABV: 5%. Malt: Pearl pale malt, Crystal malt, Black malt. Hops: Challenger, Goldings. Source: JE6.

**Juliet's Revenge**: OG: 1050. Malt: 98% Halcyon pale malt, 2% Crystal malt. Hops: Challenger. Late hops: Fuggles. Dry hops: Fuggles. Source: RP5.

**Shefford Wheat Beer**: OG: 1050. Malt: 50% Halcyon pale malt, 50% Wheat malt. Hops: Fuggles. Source: RP5/JHF.

**2XS**: OG: 1059. Malt: 92% Pale malt, 8% Crystal malt. Hops: Challenger, Fuggles, Goldings. IBU: 40. Source: RP2/3/4/5.

**Black Bat**: OG: 1064. Malt: 90% Pale malt, 10% Crystal malt. Hops: Challenger, Fuggles, Goldings. IBU: 42. Source: RP2/3/4/5.

**Black Old Bat** (b-c): ABV: 6.5%. Malt: Halcyon or Pearl pale malt, Crystal malt, Black malt. Hops: Fuggles. Source: JE2/3/4/5.

### . *Barclay Perkins, London*

**Table Beer**: OG: 1030. Malt: Pale malt, Brown malt, Amber malt. Hops: Goldings. Yeast: Wyeast #1098/Wyeast #1099. Notes: Recipe from 1804. IBU: 17. SRM: 22. Source: VB.

**IPA**: OG: 1044. Malt: Pale malt, Lager malt, Flaked maize, No.3 invert sugar. Hops: Goldings, Fuggles. Dry hops: Styrian Goldings. Yeast: Wyeast #1098/Wyeast #1099. Notes: Recipe from 1939. IBU: 41. SRM: 12. Source: VB.

**DBA**: OG: 1046. Malt: Pale malt, Lager malt, Crystal 60L malt, Flaked maize, No.3 invert sugar, Caramel. Hops: Fuggles, Northern Brewer. Yeast: Wyeast #1098/Wyeast #1099. Notes: Recipe from 1936. IBU: 48. SRM: 20. Source: VB.

**XLK**: OG: 1052. Malt: Pale malt, Flaked rice, No.1 invert sugar. Hops: Fuggles. Yeast: Wyeast #1098/Wyeast #1099. Notes: Recipe from 1899. IBU: 60. SRM: 5. Source: VB.

**Hhd**: OG: 1054. Malt: Pale malt, Brown malt, Amber malt, Black malt, Crystal malt, No.3 invert sugar. Hops: Fuggles. Yeast: Wyeast #1098/Wyeast #1099. Notes: Porter recipe from 1886. IBU: 56. SRM: 45. Source: VB.

**TT**: OG: 1055. Malt: Pale malt, Brown malt, Amber malt. Hops: Goldings. Yeast: Wyeast #1098/Wyeast #1099. IBU: 67. SRM: 27. Notes: Recipe from 1804. OG: 1060. Malt: Pale malt, Brown malt, Amber malt. Hops: Goldings. Yeast: Wyeast #1098/Wyeast #1099. Notes: Recipe from 1821. IBU: 72. SRM: 22. OG: 1060. Malt: Pale malt, Brown malt, Black malt. Hops: Goldings, Cluster. Yeast: Wyeast #1098/Wyeast #1099. Notes: Recipe from 1848. IBU: 73. SRM: 24. OG: 1033. Malt: Mild malt, Amber malt, Brown malt, Roast barley, Crystal malt, Flaked oats, Caramel, No.3 invert sugar. Hops: Goldings, Fuggles. Yeast: Wyeast #1098. Notes: Recipe from 1936. IBU: 25. SRM: 38. Source: VB.

**EI**: OG: 1055. Malt: Pale malt, Brown malt, Black malt, Crystal 60L malt. Hops: Goldings. Yeast: Wyeast #1098/Wyeast #1099. Notes: Recipe from 1867. IBU: 68. SRM: 30. Source: VB.

**Export India Porter**: OG: 1060. Malt: Pale malt, Roast barley, Brown malt. Hops: Fuggles. Notes: Recipe from 1855. Source: DP.

**Brown Stout**: OG: 1066. Malt: Pale malt, Amber malt, Brown malt. Hops: Fuggles. Notes: Recipe from 1804. Source: DP.

**BSt**: OG: 1070. Malt: Pale malt, Brown malt. Hops: Goldings. Yeast: Wyeast #1098/Wyeast #1099. Notes: Recipe from 1805. IBU: 92. SRM: 28. OG: 1083. Malt: Pale malt, Brown malt, Amber malt, Black malt. Hops: Goldings. Yeast: Wyeast #1098/Wyeast #1099. Notes: Recipe from 1832. IBU: 120. SRM: 28. Source: VB.

**BS**: OG: 1071. Malt: Pale malt, Brown malt, Amber malt, Black malt, Crystal 60L malt, No.3 invert sugar. Hops: Goldings, Fuggles. Yeast: Wyeast #1098/Wyeast #1099. Notes: Recipe from 1887. IBU: 60. SRM: 42. Source: VB.

**KK**: OG: 1073. Malt: 57% Mild malt, 15.5% American Pale malt, 9.8% Flaked maize, 2.7% Crystal 120L malt, 15% No.1 invert sugar. Hops: 56.7% Goldings, 31.3% Hallertau, Dry hops: 11.9% Goldings. Yeast: Wyeast #1968/White Labs WLP002/Nottingham. IBU: 107. SRM: 25. Notes: Burton ale recipe from 1909. Source: SUABP. OG: 1056. Malt: Pale malt, Lager malt, Mild malt, Crystal 40L malt, Flaked maize, Caramel. Hops: Fuggles, Bramling Cross, Northern Brewer. Yeast: Wyeast #1098/Wyeast #1099. Notes: Recipe from 1936. IBU: 52. SRM: 20. Source: VB.

**BS Ex**: OG: 1076. Malt: Pale malt, Brown malt, Amber malt, Black malt, Crystal 60L malt, No.3 invert sugar. Hops: Goldings, Fuggles. Yeast: Wyeast #1098/Wyeast #1099. Notes: Recipe from 1899. IBU: 122. SRM: 36. OG: 1103. Malt: Mild malt, Amber malt, Brown malt, Black malt, No.2 invert sugar. Hops: Goldings. Yeast: Wyeast #1098/Wyeast #1099. Notes: Recipe from 1924. IBU: 159. SRM: 48. Source: VB.

**PA**: OG: 1079. Malt: Pale malt. Hops: Goldings. Yeast: Wyeast #1098/Wyeast #1099. Notes: Recipe from 1805. IBU: 87. SRM: 6. Source: VB.

**IBSt (Imperial Brown Stout)**: OG: 1101. Malt: Pale malt, Brown malt, Amber malt, Black malt. Hops: Goldings. Yeast: Wyeast #1098/Wyeast #1099. Notes: Recipe from 1848. IBU: 200. SRM: 41. Source: VB. OG: 1085. Malt: Pale malt, Amber malt, Roast barley, Brown malt. Hops: Fuggles. Notes: Recipe from 1832. OG: 1107. Malt: Pale malt, Amber malt, Roast barley, Brown malt. Hops: Goldings. Notes: Recipe from 1856. Source: DP.

**KKKK (October Ale)**: OG: 1106. Malt: Mild malt. Hops: Goldings. Notes: Recipe from 1870. Source: DP.

**XXXX**: OG: 1120. Malt: Pale malt. Hops: Fuggles. Notes: Recipe from 1836. Source: DP.

### .   Barron's Brewery, Silverton

**Exe Valley Bitter**: OG: 1041.5. Malt: 95%. Pale malt, 5% Roast barley. Hops: Fuggles. Source: RP1.

**Devon Glory**: OG: 1049. Malt: 95% Pale malt, 5% Roast barley. Hops: Fuggles. Source: RP1.

Note: Barron's brewery expanded and became the *Exe Valley Brewery* (qv) in 1991.

### .   Bartrams, Bury St. Edmunds

**Marld** (b-c): ABV: 3.4%. Malt: Mild ale malt, Amber malt, Roast barley, Flaked barley. Hops: Galena, Goldings. Source: JE4/5/6.

**Rougham Ready** (b-c): ABV: 3.6%. Malt: Pale malt, Crystal malt. Hops: Variable. Notes: Organic. Source: JE5/6.

**Premier Bitter** (b-c): ABV: 3.7%. Malt: Maris Otter pale malt, Crystal malt, Chocolate malt. Hops: Challenger, Fuggles, Goldings. Source: JE4/5/6.

**Little Green Man** (b-c): ABV: 3.8%. Malt: Pale malt. Hops: Pacific Gem, Hallertau or First Gold. Others: Coriander. Source: JE4/5/6.

**Red Queen** (b-c): ABV: 3.9%. Malt: Maris Otter pale malt, Crystal malt, Chocolate malt. Hops: Challenger, Fuggles, Goldings. Source: JE4/5/6.

**Green Man** (b-c): ABV: 4%. Malt: Pale malt. Hops: Hallertau, Perle, Pacific Gem. Others: Coriander. Source: JE4. Hops: First Gold. Source: JE5/6.

**Headway** (b-c): ABV: 4%. Malt: Pale malt, Crystal malt. Hops: Variable. Notes: Organic. Source: JE5.

**Pierrot** (b-c): ABV: 4%. Malt: Maris Otter pale malt, Caramalt. Hops: Tettnang, Saaz, Fuggles, Goldings. Source: JE4/5/6.

**The Bee's Knees** (b-c): ABV: 4.2%. Malt: Maris Otter pale malt, CaraPils malt, Wildflower honey. Hops: Challenger, Ahtanum, Fuggles. Others: Coriander. Source: JE4/5/6.

**Catherine Bartram's IPA** (b-c): ABV: 4.3%. Malt: Pale malt. Hops: Fuggles, First Gold. Source: JE4/5/6.

**Jester Quick One** (b-c): ABV: 4.4%. Malt: Maris Otter pale malt, Crystal malt, Chocolate malt. Hops: Ahtanum. Source: JE4/5/6.

**Coal Porter** (b-c): ABV: 4.5%. Malt: Pale malt, Crystal malt, Barley extract. Hops: Variable. Notes: Organic. Source: JE5/6.

**Stingo!** (b-c): ABV: 4.5%. Malt: Pale malt, Honey. Hops: Hallertau, Perle. Others: Coriander. Notes: Organic. Source: JE4/5/6.

**Captain Bill Bartram's Best Bitter** (b-c): ABV: 4.8%. Malt: Maris Otter pale malt, Crystal malt. Hops: Fuggles, Goldings. Source: JE4/5/6.

**The Captain's Cherry Stout** (b-c): ABV: 4.8%. Malt: Mild ale malt, Crystal malt, Black malt, Chocolate malt, Smoked malt. Hops: Galena, Fuggles, Goldings. Others: Cherries. Source: JE4/5/6.

**Captain's Stout** (b-c): ABV: 4.8%. Malt: Mild ale malt, Crystal malt, Chocolate malt, Black malt, Smoked malt. Hops: Galena, Fuggles, Goldings. Source: JE4/5/6.

**Damson Stout** (b-c): ABV: 4.8%. Malt: Mild ale malt, Crystal malt, Chocolate malt, Black malt, Smoked malt. Hops: Galena, Fuggles, Goldings. Others: Damsons. Source: JE4/5/6.

**Beer Elsie Bub** (b-c): ABV: 4.8%. Malt: Maris Otter and Halcyon pale malt, Amber malt, Torrefied wheat, Wildflower honey. Hops: Challenger, Fuggles, Goldings. Others: Coriander. Source: JE4/5/6.

**Suffolk 'n' Strong** (b-c): ABV: 5%. Malt: Pale malt, Crystal malt. Hops: Variable. Notes: Organic. Source: JE5/6.

**Xmas Holly Daze** (b-c): ABV: 5%. Malt: Maris Otter pale malt, Crystal malt. Hops: Fuggles, Goldings. Source: JE4/5/6.

**New Year Daze** (b-c): ABV: 5.2%. Malt: Maris Otter pale malt, Crystal malt, Roast barley/Roast malt. Hops: Fuggles, Goldings. Source: JE4/5/6.

**Mother in Law's Tongue Tied** (b-c): ABV: 9%. Malt: Maris Otter pale malt. Hops: Galena, Tettnang, Hallertau. Source: JE5/6.

## . *Barum, Barnstaple*

**Original** (b-c): ABV: 4.4%. Malt: Pipkin pale malt, Roast malt, Crystal malt. Hops: Goldings, Fuggles, Challenger. Source: JE3/4/5.

**Breakfast** (b-c): ABV: 5%. Malt: Pipkin pale malt, Roast malt, Wheat malt. Hops: Goldings, Challenger. Source: JE3/4/5.

**Challenger** (b-c): ABV: 5.6%. Malt: Pipkin pale malt, Roast malt, Wheat malt. Hops: Challenger. Source: JE3/4/5.

**Barnstablasta** (b-c): ABV: 6.6%. Malt: Pipkin pale malt, Chocolate malt, Crystal malt, Wheat malt. Hops: Goldings, Challenger. Source: JE3/4/5.

## . *Bass*

**Tuborg Pilsner Lager** (bottled): OG: 1031. Malt: Lager malt, Flaked maize, Wheat malt. Hops: Hallertau. Source: DL.

**Bass / Toby Light Ale** (bottled): OG: 1035. Malt: Pale malt, Sugar. Hops: Fuggles, Bramling Cross. Source: DL.

**Worthington E** (keg): ABV: 4%. Malt: Crystal malt, Sugar. Hops: Fuggles. Dry hops: Hop extract. Source: DL.

**Red Triangle** (b-c): Note: See **Masterpiece IPA**, Museum Brewing Company.

**Porter No.4**: OG: 1076. Malt: Pale malt, Brown malt, Black malt. Hops: Fuggles. Notes: Recipe from 1874. Source: DP.

## . *Bass, Burton-on-Trent*

**Draught Bass**: OG: 1043. Malt: 100% Halcyon pale malt, 10% Maltose syrup. Hops: Challenger, Northdown. Dry hops: Northdown. IBU: 26. EBC: 19. Source: RP3/4/5. OG: 1045. Malt: Pale malt, Crystal malt, Sugar. Hops: Goldings, Fuggles. Late hops: Goldings. Dry hops: Goldings. Source: DL.

**Bass Export Pale Ale**: OG: 1048. Malt: 95% Halcyon pale malt, 5% Crystal malt. Hops: Challenger, Goldings, Northdown. EBC: 18. Source: EBA/GW. Malt: Pale malt, Flaked maize, Crystal malt, Roast barley. Hops: Northern Brewer. Late hops: Northern Brewer. Source: 150.

**Bass Ale**: OG: 1051-53. Malt: Pale malt, Crystal malt. Hops: Northdown. Late hops: Northdown, Challenger. Source: CB.

**Bass Continental**: ABV: 6.5%. Malt: Pale malt, Crystal malt, Sugar. Hops: Northdown. Late hops: Northdown. Notes: Last brewed around 1950. It was brewed for Belgium and based on Bass recipes from the 1850s. Source: Pete Brown, *Hops and Glory*, Macmillan, London (2009).

**Bass 1874 IPA**: ABV: 7%. Dry hops: 1lb per barrel. IBU: 60-92. Source: Pete Brown, *Hops and Glory*, Macmillan, London (2009).

**Bass 1840-1939 IPA**: Hops: Goldings, up to 25% US hops, German hops, Belgian hops. Source: Pete Brown, *Hops and Glory*, Macmillan, London (2009).

**No. 2**: OG: 1097. Malt: Pale malt. Hops: Fuggles. Notes: Recipe from 1874. Source: DP.

Note: See Museum Brewing Company.

### . *Bass Mitchells & Butlers, Birmingham*

**M & B Mild**: OG: 1033.5-1034.9. Malt: 94.1% Halcyon pale malt, 3.5% Crystal malt, 2.4% Black malt, 17.9% Maltose syrup, 0.3% Caramel. Hops: Challenger, Northdown. IBU: 24. EBC: 48-53. Source: RP3/4/5.

**M & B Brew XI**: OG: 1038 – 1040. Malt: Pipkin pale malt, 0 - 2.4% Black malt, 8.25% Maltose syrup, 0.06% Caramel. Hops: Challenger, Northdown. IBU: 27. EBC: 18-20. Source: RP.

**Worthington White Shield** (b-c): OG: 1051. Malt: 96.2% Pale malt, 3.8% Crystal malt, 18.4% Maltose syrup. Hops: Challenger, Northdown or Fuggles, Goldings. Late hops: Goldings. Dry hops: Goldings. IBU: 40. EBC: 20.5. Source: RP4/5/DL. Notes: This is a classic bottle-conditioned pale ale that has unfortunately suffered from repeatedly being brewed in different locations. It was originally brewed in Burton-on-Trent before being moved to Sheffield, Birmingham, King & Barnes in Horsham before returning to Burton-on-Trent where it is currently brewed in the Bass Museum. Also see **Worthington White Shield**, Bass, Sheffield, **Worthington White Shield**, King & Barnes, **Worthington White Shield**, Museum Brewing Company and **Worthington White Shield**, Coors, Burton-on-Trent.

### . *Bass, Sheffield*

**Mild XXXX**: OG: 1032. Malt: 89% Pale malt, 4% Crystal malt, 7% Maltose syrup. Hops: Challenger, optional Northdown. Late hops: Goldings, optional Target. IBU: 22. EBC: 66 – 74. Source: RP.

**Special Bitter**: OG: 1034. Malt: 83% Pale malt, 1.3% Crystal malt, 6.1% Wheat malt. Hops: Challenger, Goldings, Northdown, Progress. Dry hops: Yes. IBU: 26. EBC: 21. Source: RP3/4/5.

**Light 5 Star**: OG: 1030 – 1032. Malt: 83% Pale malt, 1.3% Crystal malt, 6% Wheat flour. Hops: Challenger, optional Northdown. IBU: 23. EBC: 18. Source: RP.

**Stones Best Bitter**: OG: 1038. Malt: 80% Pipkin or Halcyon pale malt, 20% Glucose syrup, optional Crystal malt. Hops: Challenger, optional Northdown. Late hops: Goldings, Progress. Dry hops: Bramling Cross or Goldings. IBU: 28. EBC: 13. Source: RP. Note: When I lived in Sheffield I drank more of this beer than any other.

**Worthington White Shield**: OG: 1051. Malt: Halcyon pale malt, Pipkin pale malt, Black malt, optional Crystal malt. Hops: Challenger, Northdown. IBU: 40. EBC: 20.5. Source: RP. Notes: See **Worthington White Shield**, Bass Mitchells & Butlers, **Worthington White Shield**, King & Barnes, **Worthington White Shield**, Museum Brewing Company and **Worthington White Shield**, Coors, Burton-on-Trent.

## George Bateman & Son, Wainfleet

**Dark Mild**: OG: 1033. Malt: 60-89% Pipkin or Maris Otter pale malt, 9-12% Crystal malt, 2-4% Wheat malt, 0-19% Invert sugar, 4-5% Caramel. Hops: Goldings, optional Challenger. IBU: 22. EBC: 106. Source: RP. Malt: 83% Pale malt, 12% Crystal malt, 5% Chocolate malt. Hops: 60% Goldings. Late hops: 40% Challenger. IBU: 24. EBC: 92. Source: Martin Cullimore via Cambridge Craft Brewers. Malt: Maris Otter pale malt, Crystal malt, Flaked wheat. Hops: Challenger. Late hops: Goldings. Source: GW.

**XB Bitter**: OG: 1036-7. Malt: 73.5-89% Pipkin or Maris Otter pale malt, 6-8% Crystal malt, 2.5-4% Wheat flour, 0-18% Invert sugar. Hops: Challenger, Goldings. IBU: 28. EBC: 26-7. Source: RP.

**Valiant Bitter**: OG: 1043. Malt: 90% Pipkin or Maris Otter pale malt, 10% Invert sugar. Hops: Goldings. IBU: 29. EBC: 22. Source: RP4/5.

**Pour With Care** (b-c): ABV: 4.5%. Malt: Maris Otter pale malt, Wheat malt, Crystal malt. Hops: Goldings, Challenger. Source: JE3/4/5.

**Hooker**: Hops: Liberty, Challenger, Styrian Goldings. Source: W.

**XXXB Bitter**: OG: 1048-1049. Malt: 72-87% Pipkin or Maris Otter pale malt, 7.5-12% Crystal malt, 0-3% Wheat flour, 15-18% Invert sugar. Hops: Challenger, Goldings. IBU: 37. EBC: 40-42. Source: RP/W.

**Salem Porter**: OG: 1049-50. Malt: 72-75% Pipkin or Maris Otter pale malt, 8-11% Crystal malt, 3-5% Roast barley, 0-2% Wheat flour, 12% Invert sugar. Hops: Challenger, Goldings. IBU: 36. EBC: 95-120. Source: RP.

**Victory Ale**: OG: 1056-1059. Malt: 66-90% Pipkin or Maris Otter pale malt, 3-5% Crystal malt, 0-5% Wheat flour, 15-25% Invert sugar. Hops: Goldings. IBU: 32. EBC: 32. Source: RP.

**Winter Warmer**: OG: 1058. Malt: 66% Pipkin pale malt, 6.5% Roast barley, 4.5% Wheat, 23% Invert sugar. Hops: Goldings. Source: RP2/GW.

### Bath Ales, Warmley. Www.bathales.com

**S.P.A.**: OG: 1038. Malt: 88% Maris Otter pale malt / Lager malt, 10% Amber malt, 2% Wheat malt. Hops: First Gold. Late hops: First Gold. Dry hops: First Gold. Source: RP5/JHF/Web.

**Summer's Hare**: ABV: 3.9%. Malt: Wheat malt. Hops: Bramling Cross, Chinook. Source: Web.

**Ginger Hare**: ABV: 3.9%. Malt: Maris Otter pale malt, Wheat malt. Hops: Goldings. Others: Root ginger. Source: Web.

**Dark Side**: ABV: 4%. Malt: Dark roast malts, Wheat malt. Hops: Fuggles. Source: Web.

**Gem Bitter**: OG: 1041. Malt: 90% Maris Otter pale malt, 8% Crystal malt, 1% Wheat malt, 1% Chocolate malt. Hops: Challenger. Late hops: Goldings. Dry hops: Goldings. Source: RP5/Web.

**Gem** (b-c): ABV: 4.8%. Malt: Maris Otter pale malt. Hops: Goldings, Challenger. Source: JE3/4/5.

**Golden Hare**: ABV: 4.4%. Malt: Maris Otter pale malt, Wheat malt. Hops: Goldings. Source: Web.

**Barnsey**: ABV: 4.5%. Malt: Maris Otter pale malt, Crystal malt, Wheat malt, Chocolate malt. Hops: Bramling Cross. Source: Web.

**Barnstormer**: OG: 1047. Malt: 88% Maris Otter pale malt, 10% Crystal malt, 2% Wheat malt. Hops: Bramling Cross. Late hops: Goldings. Dry hops: Goldings. Source: RP5.

**Festivity**: ABV: 5%. Malt: Maris Otter pale malt, Crystal malt, Chocolate malt, Roast barley, Wheat malt. Hops: Challenger, Bramling Cross. Source: JE4/5/W/Web.

**Wild Hare**: ABV: 5%. Malt: Wheat malt, Pale malt. Hops: English hops. Notes: Organic. Source: Web.

### Daniel Batham & Son, Brierley Hill

**Mild Ale**: OG: 1036. Malt: 100% Golden Promise pale malt or 100% Maris Otter pale malt, Caramel. Hops: Fuggles, Northdown. Dry hops: Goldings. Source: RP1/2/3/4/5.

**Best Bitter**: OG: 1043.5. Malt: 100% Golden Promise pale malt or 100% Maris Otter pale malt. Hops: Fuggles, Northdown. Dry hops: Goldings. Source: RP1/2/3/4/5.

### Bazens', Salford

**Flatbac** (b-c): ABV: 4.2%. Malt: 100% Maris Otter pale malt. Hops: Cascade, Styrian Goldings, Hallertau. Source: JE6.

**Knoll St. Porter** (b-c): ABV: 5.2%. Malt: Maris Otter pale malt, Chocolate malt, Smoked malt, Chocolate wheat malt, Crystal wheat malt, Rye malt, Oat malt. Hops: Green Bullet. Source: JE6.

## Beartown Brewery, Congleton

**Ambeardextrous**: OG: 1036. Malt: 85% Maris Otter pale malt, 10% Wheat malt, 4% Amber malt, 1% Black malt. Hops: Challenger. Late hops: Northdown. Source: RP5.

**Hoppy Rambler**: OG: 1038. Malt: 90% Maris Otter pale malt, 10% Wheat malt. Hops: Challenger. Late hops: Styrian Goldings. Source: RP5.

**Kodiak Gold** (b-c): ABV: 4%. Malt: Maris Otter pale malt, Wheat malt. Hops: Northdown, Challenger. Source: JE5.

**Bitter**: OG: 1040. Malt: 85% Maris Otter pale malt, 10% Wheat malt, 5% Crystal malt. Hops: Challenger. IBU: 35. Source: RP4.

**Bearskinful**: OG: 1040. Malt: 85% Maris Otter pale malt, 10% Wheat malt, 5% Crystal malt. Hops: Challenger. Late hops: Styrian Goldings. IBU: 35. Source: RP5/JHF.

**Bearskinful** (b-c): ABV: 4.2%. Malt: Maris Otter pale malt, Crystal malt, Wheat malt. Hops: Challenger. Source: JE5.

**Babymaker**: OG: 1040. Malt: 80% Maris Otter pale malt, 10% Crystal malt, 2% Chocolate malt, 8% Wheat malt. Hops: First Gold. Late hops: Cascade. Source: RP5.

**Polar Eclipse Oatmeal Stout**: OG: 1046. Malt: 73% Maris Otter pale malt, 3% Wheat malt, 7% Oat malt, 9% Chocolate malt, 8% Crystal malt. Hops: Northdown, Challenger. Late hops: Styrian Goldings. Source: RP5/JHF.

**Polar Eclipse** (b-c): ABV: 4.8%. Malt: Maris Otter pale malt, Crystal malt, Chocolate malt, Oat malt, Wheat malt. Hops: Northdown, Challenger. Source: JE5.

**Bruins Ruin**: OG: 1048. Malt: 85% Maris Otter pale malt, 10% Wheat malt, 5% Crystal malt. Hops: Challenger, Goldings. Late hops: Goldings. Source: RP5.

**Black Bear** (b-c): ABV: 5%. Malt: Maris Otter pale malt, Crystal malt, Chocolate malt, Wheat malt. Hops: Northdown, Challenger. Source: JE5.

**Spirityule**: OG: 1055. Malt: 72% Maris Otter pale malt, 3% Wheat malt, 14% Oat malt, 8% Chocolate malt, 3% Crystal malt. Hops: Northdown. Late hops: Challenger, Styrian Goldings. Source: RP5.

**Bear Ass Bitter**: OG: 1038. Malt: 80% Maris Otter pale malt, 10% Wheat malt, 2% Chocolate malt, 2% Oat malt, 6% Crystal malt. Hops: Challenger, Northdown. Late hops: Styrian Goldings. Source: RP5.

## Beavertown, London, www.BeavertownBrewery.com

**Neck Oil**: ABV: 4.3%. Malt: Low colour pale malt. Hops: Simcoe, Magnum, Columbus, Mosaic, Centennial, Galaxy, Amarillo, Vic Secret. IBU: 35. Source: Web.

**Pig Swill**: ABV: 5.2%. Malt: Pale malt, Cara Gold malt, Wheat malt, Munich malt. Hops: Magnum, Cascade. IBU: 35. Source: Web.

**Gamma Ray**: ABV: 5.4%. Malt: Pale malt, Cara Gold malt, Caramalt, optional Wheat malt. Hops: Columbus, optional Citra, optional Calypso, Amarillo, Bravo, optional Magnum. IBU: 44-55. Source: Web.

**Smog Rocket**: ABV: 5.4%. Malt: Pale malt, Smoked malt, Crystal malt, Munich malt, Oats, Caramalt, Brown malt, Chocolate malt, Black malt. Hops: Magnum, Chinook. IBU: 29. Source: Web.

**Bravo**: ABV: 5.6%. Malt: Pale malt, Caramalt, Wheat malt, Cara Gold malt. Hops: Magnum, Columbus, Bravo. IBU: 40. Source: Web.

**Black Yeti**: ABV: 5.6%. Malt: Pale malt, Pale chocolate malt, Carafa® II malt, Crystal malt, Oats. Hops: Summit, Magnum, Mount Hood. IBU: 55. Source: Web.

**O-Mega**: ABV: 5.8%. Malt: Pale malt, Caramalt, Wheat malt, Cara Gold malt. Hops: Summit, Magnum, Apollo. IBU: 45. Source: Web.

**Saison 34**: ABV: 6%. Malt: Pale malt, Pilsner malt, Munich malt, Wheat malt. Hops: Goldings, Magnum, Saaz. IBU: 23. Source: Web.

**8 Ball**: ABV: 6.2%. Malt: Pale malt, Caramalt, Rye malt, Crystal rye malt, Cara Gold malt, Pale crystal malt. Hops: Columbus, Citra, Galaxy, Vic Secret, Pacific Jade. IBU: 65. Source: Web.

**Spiced Pumpkin**: ABV: 7.2%. Malt: Pale malt, Munich malt, Crystal malt, CaraPils malt, Amber malt, Brown sugar. Hops: Magnum, Saaz. Others: Maple syrup roasted pumpkin, Nutmeg, Cloves, Cardamom, Cinnamon, Ginger. IBU: 25. Source: Web.

**Black Betty**: ABV: 7.4%. Malt: Pale malt, Cara Gold malt, Carafa® II malt, Carafa® III malt, Caramalt. Hops: Chinook, Columbus, Citra, optional Magnum. IBU: 60-75. Source: Web.

**Imperial Lord Smog Almighty**: ABV: 9%. Malt: Pale malt, Wheat malt, Chocolate malt, Munich malt, Smoked malt, Crystal malt, Black malt, Oats, Brown malt, 5 sugars. Hops: Magnum, Chinook. IBU: 110. Source: Web.

### . *The Beer Engine, Newton St. Cyres*

**Rail Ale**: OG: 1037. Malt: 96% Pale malt, 4% Crystal malt. Hops: Challenger, Goldings. Source: RP1/2/3/4/5.

**Piston Bitter**: OG: 1044. Malt: 96.6% Pale malt, 2% Crystal malt, 1.4% Chocolate malt. Hops: Challenger, Goldings. Source: RP1/2/3/4/5/JHF.

**Sleeper Heavy**: OG: 1055. Malt: 96.6% Pale malt, 2.4% Crystal malt, 1% Chocolate malt. Hops: Challenger, Goldings. Source: RP1/2/3/4/5.

### . *Bells Brewery & Merchants, Ullesthorpe*

**Rainmaker** (b-c): ABV: 4.1%. Malt: Maris Otter pale malt, Crystal malt, Wheat malt. Hops: Fuggles, Bramling Cross. Source: JE6.

**Victor** (b-c): ABV: 4.1%. Malt: Maris Otter pale malt, Crystal malt, Wheat malt. Hops: Cascade, Columbus. Source: JE6.

**Vulcan** (b-c): ABV: 4.1%. Malt: Maris Otter pale malt, Crystal malt. Hops: Cascade, Bramling Cross. Source: JE6.

**Smalley's Stout** (b-c): ABV: 4.2%. Malt: Maris Otter pale malt, Roast barley. Hops: Goldings. Source: JE6.

**TP Buck** (b-c): ABV: 4.3%. Malt: Maris Otter pale malt, Crystal malt, Torrefied wheat. Hops: Cascade. Source: JE6.

**Dreamcatcher** (b-c): ABV: 4.6%. Malt: Maris Otter pale malt, Chocolate malt. Hops: Fuggles, Saaz. Source: JE6.

**India Pale Ale** (b-c): ABV: 4.8%. Malt: Maris Otter pale malt, Crystal malt. Hops: Columbus, Challenger. Source: JE6.

**What the Duck** (b-c): ABV: 5.5%. Malt: Maris Otter pale malt, Crystal malt, Wheat malt. Hops: Bramling Cross. Source: JE6.

**Mucky Duck** (b-c): ABV: 6%. Malt: Maris Otter pale malt, Crystal malt. Hops: Fuggles, Cascade. Source: JE6.

### Belvoir, Old Dalby

**Star Bitter** (b-c): ABV: 3.9%. Malt: Maris Otter pale malt, Crystal malt, Chocolate malt, Torrefied wheat. Hops: Target, Goldings, Progress. Source: JE5/6.

**Beaver Bitter** (b-c): ABV: 4.3%. Malt: Maris Otter pale malt, Crystal malt, Chocolate malt. Hops: Challenger, Progress, Bramling Cross, Goldings. Source: JE4/5/6.

**Peacock's Glory** (b-c): ABV: 4.7%. Malt: Maris Otter pale malt, Crystal malt. Hops: Target, Progress, Goldings. Source: JE4/5.

**Old Dalby** (b-c): ABV: 5.1%. Malt: Maris Otter pale malt, Crystal malt, Chocolate malt. Hops: Challenger, Progress, Bramling Cross, Goldings. Source: JE4/5/6.

**Super Star** (b-c): ABV: 5.6%. Malt: Maris Otter pale malt, Crystal malt, Chocolate malt, Torrefied wheat. Hops: Target, Goldings, Progress. Source: JE6.

### Bentley's Yorkshire Brewery, Leeds

**No. 3**: OG: 1080. Malt: Pale malt, Demerara sugar. Hops: Fuggles. Notes: Recipe from 1896. Source: DP.

### Beowulf, Brownhills

**Dragon Smoke Stout** (b-c): ABV: 5.3%. Malt: Pearl pale malt, Black malt, Roast barley, Flaked barley. Hops: Goldings, Northern Brewer. Source: JE6.

### . Berrow Brewery, Burnham-on-Sea

**BBBB or 4Bs**: OG: 1038. Malt: Pale malt, Crystal malt. Hops: Fuggles, Goldings. Source: RP1/2/3/4/5.

**Topsy Turvey**: OG: 1055. Malt: 100% Pale malt. Hops: Fuggles, Goldings. Dry hops: Yes. Source: RP1/2/3/4/5.

### . Best's, Chatham

**John Wells Pale Ale**: OG: 1092. Malt: Pale malt. Hops: Fuggles. Notes: Recipe from 1775. Source: DP.

**Mr. Faunes Amber Ale**: OG: 1110. Malt: Pale amber malt. Hops: Fuggles. Notes: Recipe from 1775. Source: DP.

**Yorkshire Keeping Beer**: OG: 1134. **Small Beer**: OG: 1040-5. Malt: Pale malt. Hops: Fuggles. Notes: Parti-gyle recipes from 1763. Source: DP.

### . Betwixt, New Ferry

**Sunlight** (b-c): ABV: 4.3%. Malt: Maris Otter pale malt. Hops: Goldings. Source: JE6.

### . Big Lamp Brewers, Newcastle-upon-Tyne

**Big Lamp Bitter**: OG: 1038. Malt: 95% Pale malt, 5% Crystal malt, 20% Invert sugar. Hops: Fuggles, Styrian Goldings. Late hops: Goldings. IBU: 30. Source: RP1/2/3/4/5/GW.

**Big Lamp Special**: OG: 1050. Malt: 88% Pale malt, 12% Crystal malt, 15% Invert sugar. Hops: Goldings, Styrian Goldings. Source: RP1.

**Prince Bishop Ale**: OG: 1044. Malt: 100% Pale malt, optional 16% Invert sugar. Hops: Goldings, Styrian Goldings or Fuggles. Late hops: Goldings. Source: RP.

**Old Genie**: OG: 1070. Malt: 90-3% Pale malt, 5-10% Crystal malt, 0-11% Invert sugar, 0-2% Chocolate malt. Hops: Fuggles. Late hops: Goldings. IBU: 44. Source: RP.

**The Big 21** (b-c): ABV: 11%. Malt: Pale malt, Crystal malt, Chocolate malt, Invert sugar. Hops: Fuggles, Goldings. Source: JE1.

### . Bird In Hand, Hayle

**Speckled Parrot** (b-c): ABV: 5.5%. Malt: Maris Otter pale malt, Crystal malt. Hops: Goldings, Fuggles. Source: JE3/4.

### . Bishops Brewery, London

**Thirsty Willies Bitter**: ABV: 3.7%. Malt: 98% Pale malt, 2% Crystal malt. Hops: Bramling Cross. Late hops: Styrian Goldings. Source: RP5.

**Cathedral Bitter**: ABV: 3.7%. Malt: 94% Pale malt, 6% Crystal malt. Hops: Bramling Cross. Source: RP5.

**Mitre Best Bitter**: ABV: 4.2%. Malt: 94% Pale malt, 6% Crystal malt. Hops: Styrian Goldings. Late Hops: Mount Hood. Dry hops: Bramling Cross. Source: RP5.

**Cardinal Winter Ale**: ABV: 4.7%. Malt: 80% Pale malt, 20% Crystal malt. Hops: Bramling Cross. Late hops: Styrian Goldings. Source: RP5.

**Willies Revenge**: ABV: 4.7%. Malt: 98% Pale malt, 2% Crystal malt Hops: Bramling Cross. Late hops: Styrian Goldings. Source: RP5.

### . *Black Bull Brewery, Fenny Bentley*

**Dovedale Bitter**: OG: 1036. Malt: Halcyon pale malt, small % Wheat malt, smaller % Crystal malt. Hops: Fuggles, Liberty. Source: RP4/5.

**Best Bitter**: OG: 1040. Malt: Halcyon pale malt, Wheat malt, Crystal malt, Chocolate malt, Black malt. Hops: Fuggles, small % Liberty. Source: RP4/5.

**Raging Bull**: OG: 1048. Malt: Halcyon pale malt, Wheat malt, Crystal malt, Chocolate malt, Black malt. Hops: Fuggles, small % Liberty, Source: RP4/5.

### . *Black Sheep Brewery, Masham. Www.BlackSheepBrewery.com*

**Best Bitter**: OG: 1039. Malt: 85% Maris Otter pale malt, 5% Crystal malt, 10% Torrefied wheat, 0.005% Roast malt extract. Hops: Fuggles, Goldings, Progress and optional Challenger. Late Hops:. Fuggles. IBU: 19. EBC: 19. Source: RP.

**Special Strong Bitter**: OG: 1044. Malt: 83% Maris Otter pale malt, 7% Crystal malt, 10% Torrefied wheat, 0.005% Roast malt extract. Hops: Fuggles, Goldings, Progress and optional Challenger. Late hops: Goldings. IBU: 36. EBC: 26. Source: RP. OG: 1047-48. Malt: Maris Otter pale malt, Crystal malt, Torrefied wheat, Roast barley. Hops: Progress. Late hops: Fuggles, Challenger, Goldings. Source: BC.

**Riggwelter**: OG: 1056. Malt: 70% Maris Otter pale malt, 6% Crystal malt, 10% Chocolate malt, 9% Torrefied wheat, 0.005% Roast malt extract. Hops: Fuggles, Challenger, Goldings, Progress. Late hops: Goldings. IBU: 39. EBC: 60. Source: RP5/JHF.

### . *Blackawton Brewery, Totnes/Saltash*

**Dart Mild**: OG: 1036.5. Malt: 84% Pale malt, 11% Crystal malt, 5% Chocolate malt. Hops: Progress. Source: RP5.

**Bitter**: OG: 1037.5. Malt: Pale malt, Crystal malt. Hops: Challenger, Goldings, Northern Brewer. Source: RP1. Malt: Pale malt, Crystal malt. Hops: Goldings or Styrian Goldings. Dry hops: Yes. IBU: 26. Source: RP.

**Devon Gold**: OG: 1040.5. Malt: Pale malt. Hops: Goldings or Styrian Goldings. Dry hops: Yes. IBU: 21. Source: RP4/5.

**Shepherds Delight**: OG: 1042. Malt: 60% Pale malt, 40% Wheat malt. Hops: Styrian Goldings. Others: Fresh Coriander. Dry hops: Styrian Goldings. Source: RP5.

**Forty Four / 44 Special**: OG: 1044.5. Malt: Pale malt, Crystal malt. Hops: Challenger and/or Goldings. Dry hops: Goldings. IBU: 25. Source: RP.

**Headstrong**: OG: 1051.5. Malt: Pale malt, Crystal malt. Hops: Challenger and/or Goldings. Dry hops: Goldings. IBU: 25. Source: RP.

**Winter Fuel**: ABV: 4.6-5%. Malt: 75% Pale malt, 25% Crystal malt. Others: Christmas Spices. Source: RP4/5.

**Winter Fuel** (b-c): ABV: 5%. Malt: Pale malt, Crystal malt, Chocolate malt, Torrefied wheat. Hops: Progress, Goldings. Others: Mace, Ginger, Lemons. Source: JE4/5/6.

**Devon Gold Export** (b-c): ABV: 5%. Malt: Pipkin pale malt, Crystal malt. Hops: Styrian Goldings. Source: JE1/2.

**Head Strong** (b-c): ABV: 5.2%. Malt: Pale malt, Crystal malt, Wheat malt. Hops: Styrian Goldings, Progress, Challenger. Source: JE4/5. Malt: Pale malt, Crystal malt, Torrefied wheat. Hops: Styrian Goldings, Progress, Challenger. Source: JE6.

### . *Blatch's Brewery, Theale*

**Porter**: OG: 1070. Malt: Pale malt, Amber malt, Brown malt. Hops: Fuggles. Notes: Recipe from 1848. Source: DP.

### . *Blencowe, Barrowden*

**Beach Boys** (b-c): ABV: 3.8%. Malt: Maris Otter pale malt, Caramalt, Wheat malt. Hops: Challenger, Fuggles, Styrian Goldings. Source: JE5.

**Bevin Boys** (b-c): ABV: 4.5%. Malt: Maris Otter pale malt, Crystal malt, Caramalt, Wheat malt. Hops: Bramling Cross, Cascade. Source: JE5.

**Danny Boys** (b-c): ABV: 4.6%. Malt: Maris Otter pale malt, Crystal malt, Chocolate malt, Munich malt, Caramalt, Roast barley, Black Treacle. Hops: Bramling Cross, Cascade. Others: Liquorice. Source: JE5.

**Boys with Attitude** (b-c): ABV: 6%. Malt: Maris Otter pale malt, Crystal malt, Caramalt, Wheat malt. Hops: Bramling Cross, Cascade. Source: JE5.

### . *Blue Anchor, Helston*

**Jubilee Ale** (b-c): ABV: 4.5%. Malt: Pipkin pale malt. Hops: Goldings. Source: JE4/5/6.

**Spingo Middle**: ABV: 5%. Malt: Pipkin pale malt. Hops: Goldings. Source: HB/JE3/4/5/6.

**Spingo Bragget** (b-c): ABV: 6%. Malt: Pipkin pale malt, Honey. Hops: None. Others: Apple juice. Source: JE5/6.

**Spingo 800**: ABV: 6%. Malt: Pipkin pale malt, Honey. Hops: None. Others: Apple juice. Source: HB/JE3.

**Spingo Special**: ABV: 6.6%. Malt: Pipkin pale malt. Hops: Goldings. Source: HB/JE3/4/5/6.

**Christmas Special / Easter Special** (b-c): ABV: 7.6%. Malt: Pipkin pale malt, Crystal malt. Hops: Goldings. Source: JE4/5/6.

**Easter Special** (b-c): ABV: 7.8%. Malt: Pipkin pale malt. Hops: Goldings. Source: JE4.

### . *Blythe, Hamstall Ridware*

**Blythe Bitter** (b-c): ABV: 4%. Malt: Pale malt. Hops: Goldings, Fuggles, Cascade. Source: JE6.

**Chase Bitter** (b-c): ABV: 4.4%. Malt: Pale malt, Crystal malt. Hops: Goldings, Challenger. Source: JE6.

**Staffie** (b-c): ABV: 4.4%. Malt: Pale malt, Torrefied wheat. Hops: Chinook, Cluster. Source: JE6.

**Palmer's Poison** (b-c): ABV: 4.5%. Malt: Pale malt, Crystal malt, Flaked maize, Black malt. Hops: Goldings, Challenger. Source: JE6.

**Old Horny** (b-c): ABV: 4.6%. Malt: Pale malt, Crystal malt, Black malt, Torrefied wheat. Hops: Goldings, Styrian Goldings, Challenger. Source: JE6.

### . *Boddingtons Brewery, Manchester*

**Mild / OB Mild / Oldham Mild**: OG: 1032. Malt: 83-5% Pale malt, 9-10% Crystal malt, 2-3% Chocolate malt, 4% Cane sugar, Caramel. Hops: Fuggles, Goldings and optional Bramling Cross, WGV. IBU: 22-24. EBC: 80. Source: RP./GW

**Bitter**: OG: 1035. Malt: 95.5% Pale malt, 1.5% Patent black malt, 3% Cane sugar. Hops: 8% Bramling Cross, 35% Fuggles, 30% Goldings, 5% Northern Brewer, 22% WGV. Source: RP1/2. Malt: 95% Pale malt, 2% Patent black malt, 3% Cane sugar. Hops: Fuggles, Goldings, WGV. IBU: 30. Source: RP3/4/5/GW. OG: 1037-38. Malt: Maris Otter pale malt, Crystal malt, Patent black malt, Invert sugar. Hops: Fuggles, Goldings. Late hops: Fuggles, Goldings, WGV. Source: BC.

**OB Bitter / Oldham Best Bitter**: OG: 1038. Malt: 86-7% Pale malt, 5-6% Crystal malt, 8% Cane sugar, optional Caramel. Hops: Fuggles, Goldings, Styrian Goldings. Late Hops: optional Goldings. IBU: 32. EBC: 23. Source: RP.

### . *Boggart, Manchester*

**Steaming** (b-c): ABV: 9%. Malt: Pale malt, Wheat malt. Hops: Challenger, Galena. Source: JE4/5.

**Rocket Fuel** (b-c): ABV: 14%. Malt: Pale malt, Amber malt, Wheat malt. Hops: Nugget, Liberty. Source: JE4/5.

### . *Border Brewery Company, Tweedmouth*

**Old Kiln Bitter**: OG: 1036. Malt: 94% Halcyon pale malt, 6% Crystal malt. Hops: 50% Fuggles, 50% Goldings. Source: RP4.

**Special Bitter**: OG: 1037. Malt: 98% Halcyon or Maris Otter pale malt, 2% Crystal malt. Hops: Fuggles, Goldings or Challenger. Late hops: Optional Goldings, Styrian Goldings. Dry hops: Goldings, Styrian Goldings. IBU: 30. EBC: 12. Source: RP.

**Old Kiln Ale**: OG: 1038-40. Malt: 87% Camargue or Halcyon pale malt, 13% Crystal malt. Hops: 50% Fuggles, 50% Goldings. IBU: 30. EBC: 25. Source: RP3/4. Malt: Maris Otter pale malt, Crystal malt, Amber malt, Chocolate malt. Hops: Challenger, Fuggles, Goldings. Late hops: Goldings, Styrian Goldings. IBU: 30. EBC: 25. Source: RP5.

**Noggins Nog**: OG: 1042. Malt: 89% Halcyonor Maris Otter pale malt, 8% Crystal malt, 3% Chocolate malt. Hops: Fuggles, Goldings. Late hops: Fuggles, Goldings. IBU: 20. EBC: 100. Source: RP.

**Rampart Bitter**: OG: 1047. Malt: Maris Otter pale malt, Crystal malt, Amber malt. Hops: Challenger. Late hops: Fuggles, Goldings. IBU: 30. EBC: 15. Source: RP5.

**S.O.B.**: OG: 1049. Malt: 92% Halcyon pale malt, 7% Crystal malt, 1% Chocolate malt. Hops: Fuggles, Goldings. IBU: 30. EBC: 15. Source: RP4. Malt: Maris Otter pale malt, Crystal malt, Amber malt. Hops: Challenger. Late hops: Fuggles, Goldings. IBU: 30. EBC: 15. Source: RP5.

### . *Bradfield Brewery, High Bradfield*

**Farmers Stout** (b-c): ABV: 4.5%. Malt: Fanfare pale malt, Chocolate malt, Crystal malt, Roast barley. Hops: Goldings, Fuggles. Source: JE6.

**Farmers Pale Ale** (b-c): ABV: 5%. Malt: Fanfare pale malt. Hops: Goldings, Fuggles. Source: JE6.

### . *W. H. Brakspear & Sons, Henley-on-Thames*

**Mild / XXX / Henley Dark Mild**: OG: 1030. Malt: 96% Maris Otter pale malt, 3% Crystal malt, 1% Black malt, 10% No.2 invert sugar, Optional less than 1% Roast malt extract. Hops: 95% Fuggles, Goldings optional Styrian Goldings. Dry Hops: Yes, optional 5% Challenger oil. IBU: 33. EBC: 33-45. Source: RP.

**Bitter / PA**: OG: 1035. Malt: 96% Maris Otter pale malt, 3% Crystal malt, 1% Black malt, 10% No.2 invert sugar. Hops: 95% Goldings, Fuggles and optional Styrian Goldings. Dry hops: Yes, optional 5% Challenger oil. IBU: 38. EBC: 23. Source: RP/HB.

**Special Bitter / SBA**: OG: 1043-4. Malt: 96% Maris Otter pale malt, 3% Crystal malt, 1% Black malt, 10% No.2 invert sugar. Hops: 95% Goldings, Fuggles and optional Styrian Goldings. Dry hops: Yes, optional 5% Challenger oil. IBU: 46. EBC: 27. Source: RP/HB/JHF. Malt: Pale malt, Crystal malt, Flaked maize, Sugar. Hops: Goldings, Fuggles. Late hops: Goldings. Dry hops: Goldings. Source: DL.

**Old / XXXX**: OG: 1043. Note: **SBA** with added colour. Source: RP1/2/3/4/5.

**Ted & Ben's Organic Beer** (b-c): ABV: 4.6%. Malt: Scarlet pale malt, Crystal malt. Hops: Goldings, Hallertau. Source: JE3.

**Live Organic / Organic Beer** (b-c): ABV: 4.6%. Malt: Pale malt, Crystal malt. Hops: Goldings, Target, Hallertau. Source: JE3/6.

**OBJ**: OG: 1050. Malt: 96% Maris Otter pale malt, 3% Crystal malt, 1% Black malt, 10% No.2 invert sugar, Less than 1% Roast malt extract. Hops: 95% Goldings, Fuggles, Styrian Goldings and WGV, 5% Challenger oil. Dry hops: Yes. IBU: 48. EBC: 40. Source: RP4/5.

**Vintage Ale** (b-c): ABV: 5.5%. Malt: Maris Otter pale malt, Crystal malt, Pale amber malt, Rye crystal malt. Hops: Fuggles. Source: JE1. Note: The recipe and strength of this beer changes each year.

**Vintage Henley** (b-c): ABV: 5.5%. Malt: Maris Otter pale malt, Amber malt, Rye crystal malt. Hops: Fuggles. Source: JE3.

**Millennium** (b-c): ABV: 6.3%. Malt: Pale malt. Hops: Fuggles, Goldings. Source: JE2. Note: This was brewed instead of the **Vintage Ale** in 2000.

**50/- Pale Ale**: OG: 1063. Malt: Pale malt, Lager malt. Hops: Fuggles, Goldings. Notes: Recipe from 1865. Source: DP.

**Amber Strong**: OG: 1070. Malt: Pale amber malt. Hops: Fuggles. Notes: Recipe from 1795. Source: DP.

**26° Porter Extra**: OG: 1071. Malt: Pale malt, Amber malt, Brown malt. Hops: Fuggles. Notes: Recipe from 1810. Source: DP.

**Porter**: OG: 1071. Malt: Pale malt, Brown malt, Black malt. Hops: Fuggles. Notes: Recipe from 1835. Source: DP.

**Triple** (b-c): ABV: 7.2%. Malt: Maris Otter pale malt, Crystal malt, Black malt. Hops: Northdown. Late hops: Cascade. Dry hops: Cascade (in secondary fermenter). Source: JE6.

**March Strong Ale**: OG: 1082. Malt: Pale malt. Hops: Fuggles. Notes: Recipe from 1798. Source: DP.

**140/-**: OG: 1100. Malt: Pale malt, Amber malt. Hops: Fuggles. Notes: Recipe from 1810. Source: DP.

## . *Bramcote Brewing Company, Nottingham*

**Hemlock Bitter**: OG: 1040. Malt: 85% Maris Otter pale malt, 10% Crystal malt, 5% Wheat malt. Hops: Fuggles. Late hops: Goldings. Source: RP5. Note: Became the *Castle Rock Brewery* in 1998.

### . Brancaster, King's Lynn

**IPA** (b-c): ABV: 3.7%. Malt: Maris Otter pale malt, Caramalt, optional Roast barley. Hops: Fuggles, Brewers Gold. Source: JE5/6.

**Old Les** (b-c): ABV: 5%. Malt: Maris Otter pale malt, Caramalt, Roast barley. Hops: Challenger, Fuggles. Source: JE5/6.

### . Brandy Cask Pub & Brewery, Pershore

**Whistling Joe**: OG: 1037. Malt: 90% Maris Otter pale malt, 10% Crystal malt. Hops: Cascade. Late hops: Cascade, Goldings. IBU: 30. Source: RP5.

**Brandysnapper**: OG: 1040. Malt: 100% Maris Otter pale malt. Hops: Challenger. Late hops: Challenger, Goldings. IBU: 34. Source: RP5.

**John Baker's Original**: OG: 1048. Malt: 96% Maris Otter pale malt, 2% Crystal malt, 2% Chocolate malt. Hops: Challenger. Late hops: Challenger, Goldings. IBU: 22. Source: RP5.

### . Branscombe Vale Brewery, Seaton

**Branoc**: OG: 1037. Malt: 45% Triumph pale malt, 45% Maris Otter pale malt, 0.7% Chocolate malt, 5% Wheat flour, 4% Flaked maize or 60% Pipkin pale malt, 38% Maris Otter pale malt, 0.5% Chocolate malt, 0.5% Wheat flour, 1% Flaked maize. Hops: Challenger. Late hops: Goldings. Source: RP.

**Drayman's Best Bitter** (b-c): ABV: 4.2%. Malt: Pipkin pale malt, Crystal malt. Hops: Phoenix. Source: JE4. Malt: Pipkin pale malt, Chocolate malt. Hops: Bramling Cross, Phoenix. Source: JE5/6.

**Own Label**: OG: 1044. Malt: 65% Pipkin pale malt, 30% Maris Otter pale malt, 3% Crystal malt, 1% Chocolate malt, 1% Flaked maize. Hops: Willamette. Late hops: Goldings. Source: RP5.

**Summa That**: OG: 1049. Malt: 40% Pipkin pale malt, 56% Maris Otter pale malt, 4% Flaked maize. Hops: Challenger. Late hops: Goldings. Source: RP5.

**Olde Stoker**: OG: 1052. Malt: 46% Triumph or Pipkin pale malt, 46% Maris Otter pale malt, 3% Chocolate malt, 5% Wheat flour. Hops: Challenger. Late hops: Goldings. Source: RP.

**Yo Ho Ho!**: OG: 1062. Malt: 40% Pipkin pale malt, 54% Maris Otter pale malt, 1% Black malt, 4% Crystal malt, 1% Roast barley. Hops: Challenger. Late hops: Goldings. Source: RP5.

### . Brentwood Brewing Company, Brentwood

**Summer Virgin**: Malt: Pale malt, Lager malt, Torrefied wheat. Hops: Challenger. Late hops: Chinook, US First Gold. Source: WB.

### Brewster's, Stathern

**Jezebel** (b-c): ABV: 4.8%. Malt: Maris Otter pale malt, Caramalt. Hops: Bramling Cross. Source: JE6.

**Mata Hari** (b-c): ABV: 4.8%. Malt: Maris Otter pale malt, Crystal malt. Hops: Fuggles, Progress, Northdown. Source: JE6.

**Vale Pale Ale** (b-c): ABV: 4.5%. Malt: Maris Otter pale malt, Caramalt. Hops: Cascade, Northdown, Goldings. Source: JE4/5.

### Bridgewater Ales, Salford

**Amber Ale**: OG: 1040. Malt: 94% Pale malt, 6% Crystal malt. Hops: Styrian Goldings, Goldings. Source: RP3/4/5.

**Coppernob**: OG: 1045. Malt: 90% Pale malt, 10% Crystal malt. Hops: Styrian Goldings, Fuggles. Source: RP3/4/5.

**Sunbeam**: OG: 1052. Malt: 100% Pale malt. Hops: Styrian Goldings, Goldings. Source: RP3/4/5.

### Bristol Beer Factory, Bristol. Www.bristolbeerfactory.com

**Red**: ABV: 3.8%. Malt: Maris Otter pale malt, Crystal malt, Roast barley, optional Rye crystal malt. Hops: Challenger. Late hops: Bramling Cross. Source: Web.

**Bristol Stout**: ABV: 4%. Malt: 7 malts including Flaked oats. Source: Web.

**No. 7**: ABV: 4.2%. Malt: Maris Otter pale malt, Crystal malt, optional Wheat malt. Hops: Challenger. Late hops: Fuggles. Source: Web.

**Sunrise**: ABV: 4.4%. Malt: Maris Otter pale malt, CaraPils malt, optional Crystal malt, optional Wheat malt. Hops: Pioneer. Late hops: Pioneer or Goldings. Source: Web.

**Milk Stout**: ABV: 4.5%. Malt: Maris Otter pale malt, Crystal malt, Chocolate malt, Black malt. Hops: Challenger. Source: Web.

**Gold**: ABV: 5%. Malt: Maris Otter pale malt, CaraPils malt. Hops: Pioneer. Late hops: Pioneer. Source: Web.

**Smiles Exhibition/Bristol Exhibition**: Malt: Maris Otter pale malt, Crystal malt, Chocolate malt, optional Wheat malt. Hops: Challenger or Pilgrim. Late hops: Fuggles. Source: Simon Bartlett/web. See **Exhibition**, Smiles Brewing Company, Bristol.

### British Oak Brewery, Dudley

**Castle Ruin**: OG: 1038. Malt: Triumph pale malt, 10% Wheat malt. Hops: Challenger, Fuggles. Late hops: Goldings. Source: RP2/3.

**Eve'll Bitter**: OG: 1042. Malt: 89% Triumph pale malt and Crystal malt, 10% Wheat malt, 1% Black malt. Hops: Challenger, Fuggles. Late hops: Goldings. Source: RP2/3.

**Colonel Pickering's Porter**: OG: 1046. Malt: 85% Triumph pale malt and Crystal malt, 5% Black malt, 10% Wheat malt. Hops: Challenger, Fuggles. Late hops: Goldings. Source: RP2/3.

**Dungeon Draught**: OG: 1050. Malt: 85% Triumph pale malt and Crystal malt, 5% Black malt, 10% Wheat malt. Hops: Challenger, Fuggles. Late hops: Goldings. Source: RP2/3.

**Old Jones**: OG: 1060. Malt: 85% Triumph and Crystal malt, 5% Black malt, 10% Wheat malt. Hops: Challenger, Fuggles. Late hops: Goldings. Source: RP2/3.

## . Broadstone, Retford

**Two Water Grog** (b-c): ABV: 4%. Malt: Pearl pale malt, Crystal malt, Rye crystal malt, Roast barley. Hops: Northdown, Bramling Cross. Source: JE4/5.

**Black Abbot** (b-c): ABV: 5%. Malt: Pearl pale malt, Crystal malt, Rye crystal malt, Roast barley. Hops: Northdown. Source: JE4/5.

**Broadstone Gold** (b-c): ABV: 5%. Malt: Pearl pale malt. Hops: Northdown. Source: JE4/5.

## . Matthew Brown, Blackburn

**Mild**: OG: 1032. Malt: Pale malt, Crystal malt, Wheat, Flaked maize, Cane sugar, Caramel. Hops: Goldings, Fuggles. Source: RP1.

**Bitter**: OG: 1035. Malt: Pale malt, Wheat, Flaked maize, Cane sugar. Hops: Goldings, Fuggles. Source: RP1.

## . Brunswick Brewing Company, Derby

**Brunswick Recession Ale**: OG: 1033. Malt: Maris Otter pale malt, Crystal malt. Hops: Northdown. Source: RP3.

**Celebration Mild**: OG: 1033. Malt: Maris Otter pale malt, Crystal malt, Roast barley, No.3 invert sugar. Hops: Challenger. Source: RP3.

**Fat Boy Stout**: OG: 1040. Malt: Maris Otter pale malt, Crystal malt, Roast barley. Hops: Challenger, Northdown. Source: RP3.

**Brunswick First Brew**: OG: 1042. Malt: Maris Otter pale malt, Flaked maize, Torrefied wheat. Hops: Challenger, Goldings. Source: RP3.

**Brunswick Second Brew**: OG: 1042. Malt: Maris Otter pale malt, Crystal malt. Hops: Challenger, Goldings. Source: RP3.

**Railway Porter**: OG: 1045. Malt: Maris Otter pale malt, Roast barley, No.3 invert sugar. Hops: Goldings. Source: RP3.

**Brunswick Festival Ale**: OG: 1046. Malt: Maris Otter pale malt, Flaked maize, Torrefied wheat. Hops: Challenger, Goldings. Source: RP3.

**Old Accidental**: OG: 1050. Malt: Maris Otter pale malt, Crystal malt. Hops: Challenger, Goldings. Source: RP3.

**Owd Abusive**: OG: 1066. Malt: Maris Otter pale malt, Crystal malt, No.3 invert sugar. Hops: Challenger, Goldings. Source: RP3.

### . Buffy's Brewery, Tivetshall St. Mary

**Bitter**: OG: 1038.5. Malt: 90% Pipkin pale malt, 6% Crystal malt, 3% Wheat malt, 1% Roast barley. Hops: Fuggles, Goldings. Source: RP4/5.

**Polly's Folly**: OG: 1040. Malt: 98% Halcyon pale malt, 2% Crystal malt. Hops: Fuggles. Late hops: Goldings, Mount Hood. Source: RP4/5.

**Best**: OG: 1046. Malt: 96% Pipkin pale malt, 3.5% Crystal malt, 0.5% Roast barley. Hops: 40% Fuggles, Goldings. Source: RP4/5.

**Buffy's Ale**: OG: 1049. Malt: 97% Halcyon pale malt, 1.56% Crystal malt, 0.7% Wheat malt, 0.7% Roast barley. Hops: 50% Fuggles, 50% Goldings. Source: RP4/5.

**Buffy's Strong Ale**: OG: 1060. Malt: 97% Halcyon pale malt, 1.5% Crystal malt, 0.75% Wheat malt, 0.75% Roast barley. Hops: Fuggles, Goldings. Source: RP4/5.

### . Bunce's Brewery, Salisbury

**Benchmark**: OG: 1033-5. Malt: 84% Maris Otter pale malt, 7.5% Crystal malt, 8.5% Wheat flour or Torrefied wheat. Hops: Goldings and Challenger or Omega. Late hops: Optional Goldings. Source: RP/GW.

**Vice Beer**: OG: 1035. Malt: 50% Maris Otter pale malt, 50% Wheat malt. Hops: Goldings. Source: RP3/4/5.

**Pigswill**: OG: 1040. Malt: Maris Otter pale malt, Crystal malt, Torrefied wheat. Hops: Goldings. Source: RP3/4/5.

**Best Bitter**: OG: 1042. Malt: 84% Maris Otter pale malt, 7.5% Crystal malt, 8.5% Wheat flour or Torrefied wheat. Hops: Goldings and Challenger or Omega. Source: RP.

**Sign of Spring**: OG: 1044. Malt: Maris Otter pale malt, Torrefied wheat. Hops: Goldings, Challenger. Source: RP4/5. Notes: This beer is a light green colour so a green food dye is obviously an extra ingredient. I drank a few pints of this brew in an Edinburgh pub and had several people coming up and asking me what I was drinking. I started telling them that it was a pint of Crème de Menthe…

**Danish Dynamite**: OG: 1050. Malt: 91% Maris Otter pale malt, 9% Torrefied wheat. Hops: Cascade, Challenger. Source: RP4/5.

**Stig-Swig**: OG: 1050. Malt: Maris Otter pale malt, Torrefied wheat. Hops: Challenger, Sweet Gale leaves. Source: RP5.

**Rudolph**: OG: 1050. Malt: Maris Otter pale malt, Crystal malt, Wheat malt, Black malt, Torrefied wheat. Hops: Goldings. Source: RP4/5.

**Old Smokey**: OG: 1050. Malt: 88% Maris Otter pale malt, 3.5% Brown malt, 8.5% Wheat flour or Torrefied wheat. Hops: Goldings and Challenger or Omega. Source: RP1/2/3/4. Malt: Maris Otter pale malt, Crystal malt, Wheat malt, Black malt, Torrefied wheat. Hops: Challenger, Goldings. Source: RP5.

### . *Burrington Brewery, Burrington*

**DNA (Dark Newt Ale)**: ABV: 4.4%. Malt: Maris Otter pale malt, Crystal malt, Dark crystal malt, Wheat malt, Crystal wheat malt, Torrefied wheat. Hops: First Gold, Willamette. Source: JE6.

### . *Burton Bridge Brewery, Burton upon Trent*

**Midsummer Ale**: OG: 1038. Malt: 100% Pipkin pale malt. Hops: Challenger. Source: RP2/3.

**Summer Ale**: OG: 1038. Malt: 95% Pipkin pale malt, 5% Invert sugar. Hops: Challenger. Dry hops: Styrian Goldings. Source: RP4/5.

**XL**: OG: 1039. Malt: 95% Maris Otter or Pipkin pale malt, 5% Crystal malt, optional 5% Invert sugar. Hops: 50% Target, 50% Challenger. Late hops: optional Challenger. Dry hops: Target. Source: RP/MO.

**Sovereign Gold**: ABV: 4%. Hops: Northdown. Late hops: Hops: Cascade. Source: W.

**Bridge Bitter**: OG: 1042. Malt: 95% Maris Otter or Pipkin pale malt, 5% Crystal malt, optional 5% Invert sugar. Hops: 33% Target, 67% Challenger. Late hops: optional Challenger. Dry hops: Styrian Goldings. Source: RP/MO.

**Burton Porter**: OG: 1044. Malt: 92% Maris Otter or Pipkin pale malt, 5% Crystal malt, 3% Chocolate malt. Hops: 50% Target, 50% Challenger. Source: RP.

**Burton Porter** (b-c): ABV: 4.5%. Malt: Pipkin pale malt, Crystal malt, Chocolate malt. Hops: Target, Challenger. Source: JE1/2/3/4/5/6.

**Spring Ale**: OG: 1045. Malt: 90% Pipkin pale malt, 3% Crystal malt, 5% Invert sugar. Hops: Northdown, Challenger. Dry hops: Challenger. Source: RP4/5.

**Staffordshire Knot Brown Ale**: OG: 1047. Malt: 83% Pipkin pale malt, 4% Crystal malt, 1% Chocolate malt, 12% Invert sugar. Hops: Northdown. Source: RP4/5.

**Battle Brew**: OG: 1049. Malt: 90% Pipkin pale malt, 5% Crystal malt, 5% Invert sugar. Hops: 67% Challenger, 33% Target. Dry hops: Styrian Goldings. Source: RP4/5.

**Bramble Stout** (b-c): ABV: 5%. Malt: Pale malt, Chocolate malt. Hops: Challenger. Others: Blackberry juice. Source: JE2/3/4/5/6/TBBK.

**Derbyshire Estate Ale** (b-c): ABV: 5%. Malt: Maris Otter pale malt. Hops: Northdown, Fuggles, Goldings. Source: JE4/5.

**Top Dog Stout**: OG: 1050. Malt: 69% Maris Otter pale malt or Pipkin pale malt, 21% Roast barley, 10% Chocolate malt. Hops: Challenger. Source: RP2. Malt: 72% Pipkin pale malt, 21% Wheat, 7% Chocolate malt. Hops: Challenger. Source: RP3/4/5.

**Burton Festival Ale**: OG: 1055. Malt: 94% Maris Otter or Pipkin pale malt, 5% Crystal malt, 1% Chocolate malt. Hops: 50% Target, 50% Challenger. Source: RP1.

**OX (Old Expensive)**: OG: 1065. Malt: 88-94% Maris Otter or Pipkin pale malt, 5% Crystal malt, 1% Chocolate malt, 0-6% Sugar. Hops: 50% Target, 50% Challenger. Source: RP.

**Empire Pale Ale** (b-c): ABV: 7.5%. Malt: Pipkin pale malt, Invert sugar. Hops: Challenger. Dry hops: Styrian Goldings. Source: RP5/JE2/3/4/5/6. Malt: Pipkin pale malt. Hops: Challenger. Source: JE1.

**Tickle Brain** (b-c): ABV: 8%. Malt: Pipkin pale malt, Crystal malt, optional Chocolate malt, Invert sugar. Hops: Northdown. Source: JE1/2/3/4/5/6.

## . *Burtonwood Brewery, Warrington*

**Dark Mild / Mild**: OG: 1032. Malt: 69-77% Pipkin and Maris Otter Pale malt, 7-8% Crystal malt, 2-9% Black malt, 7-9% Torrefied wheat, 6-12% Invert sugar, 0-2% Caramel. Hops: Challenger, Fuggles and Progress, Goldings, WGV, Northern Brewer and/or Brewers Gold. IBU: 22. EBC: 135. Source: RP.

**Bitter**: OG: 1036-7. Malt: 65-80% Pipkin and/or Maris OtterPale malt, 6-7% Crystal malt, 7-10% Torrefied wheat, 6-19% Invert Cane sugar. Hops: Challenger, Fuggles and Progress, Goldings, Styrian Goldings, Brewers Gold, WGV and/or Northern Brewer. Dry hops: Yes. IBU: 22-8. EBC: 24. Source: RP.

**James Forshaw's Bitter**: OG: 1038-9. Malt: 74% Maris Otter or Pipkin + Maris Otter pale malt, 11% Crystal malt, 8% Torrefied wheat, 7% Liquid sugar. Hops: Brewers Gold, Challenger, Fuggles, WGV and Northern Brewer, Progress, Goldings and/or Styrian Goldings. Dry hops: Yes. IBU: 35. EBC: 36. Source: RP.

**Top Hat**: OG: 1046. Malt: 78-80% Maris Otter pale malt, 7% Crystal malt,7% Torrefied wheat, 6-8% Liquid sugar. Hops: Brewers Gold, Challenger, Fuggles, Goldings, Progress, WGV and optional Styrian Goldings. Dry hops: Yes. IBU: 35. EBC: 30. Source: RP.

**Buccaneer**: OG: 1052. Malt: 71-5% Pipkin pale malt, 0.5-4% Crystal malt, 9-9.5% Torrefied wheat, 15-6% Liquid sugar. Hops: Brewers Gold, Challenger, Fuggles, Goldings, Progress, WGV and optional Styrian Goldings. Dry hops: Yes. IBU: 35. EBC: 15. Source: RP.

## . *Burts Brewery, Newport, Isle of Wight*

**Bitter**: OG: 1030. Malt: Pale malt. Hops: Fuggles, Goldings, Northern Brewer. Source: RP1.

**Parkhurst Porter**: OG: 1037. Malt: 74% Pipkin pale malt, 13.2% Crystal malt, 6.2% Chocolate malt. Hops: Challenger. Source: RP4.

**Nipper Bitter**: OG: 1035. Malt: 95.4% Pipkin pale malt, 3.6% Crystal malt, 1% Chocolate malt. Hops: Goldings, Target. Late hops: Goldings. Source: RP5.

**Ventnor Pale Ale (VPA)**: OG: 1040. Malt: Pale malt. Hops: Fuggles, Goldings, Northern Brewer. Source: RP1.

**Ventnor Premium Ale (VPA)**: OG: 1041. Malt: 94% Pipkin pale malt, 4.4% Crystal malt, 1.6% Chocolate malt. Hops: Challenger, Goldings, Target. Source: RP4.

**Vectis Premium Ale (VPA)**: OG: 1041. Malt: 94.2% Pipkin pale malt, 4.5% Crystal malt, 1.3% Chocolate malt. Hops: Goldings, Target. Late hops: Goldings. Source: RP5.

**Newport Nobbler**: OG: 1043. Malt: 91-92.6% Pipkin pale malt, 7.4-9% Torrefied wheat or Wheat malt. Hops: Goldings, Challenger. Late hops: Goldings. Source: RP.

**Tanner Bitter**: OG: 1046. Malt: 94% Pipkin pale malt, 4.5% Crystal malt, 1.5% Chocolate malt. Hops: Challenger, Goldings, Target. Source: RP4.

**Old Vectis Venom**: OG: 1050. Malt: 89.5-91% Pipkin pale malt, 3.5-3.8% Crystal malt, 0.2-5% Chocolate malt, 4.7-6.8% Wheat malt. Hops: Goldings and Challenger or Target. Late hops: Goldings, Cascade. Source: RP.

Notes: See Island Brewery and Ventnor Brewery.

### . Bushy's Brewery, Braddan, Isle of Man

**Bushy's Dark Mild**: OG: 1035. Malt: 82.6% Pipkin pale malt, 13.2% Crystal malt, 4.2% Chocolate malt. Hops: Fuggles, Challenger. Late hops: Yes. Source: RP3/4/5.

**Best Bitter/Bitter**: OG: 1038. Malt: 94.75% Pipkin pale malt, 5% Crystal malt, 0.25% Chocolate malt. Hops: Challenger, Fuggles and Goldings or Northern Brewer. Dry hops: Fuggles or Challenger. Source: RP.

**Celtibration Ale**: OG: 1040. Malt: 100% Pipkin pale malt. Hops: Fuggles. Dry hops: Fuggles. Source: RP5.

**Old Bushy Tail**: OG: 1045. Malt: 94% Pipkin pale malt, 4.5% Crystal malt, 1.5% Chocolate malt. Hops: Fuggles, Goldings and optional Challenger. Late hops: Challenger. Dry hops: Fuggles. Source: RP/JHF.

**Bushy's** (b-c): ABV: 4.5%. Malt: Maris Otter pale malt, Chocolate malt, Crystal malt. Hops: Goldings, Fuggles. Source: JE3.

**Celebration Ale**: OG: 1060. Malt: Pale malt, Crystal malt, Chocolate malt. Hops: Challenger, Fuggles, Goldings. Dry hops: Fuggles. Source: RP2/3.

### . Butcombe Brewery, Butcombe

**Bitter**: OG: 1039. Malt: 95% Maris Otter pale malt, 5% Crystal malt. Hops: Northdown, Yeoman, Northern Brewer. IBU: 31-5. EBC: 20. Source: RP2/3/4/5/JHF.

**Wilmots Premium Ale**: OG: 1048. Malt: 95% Maris Otter pale malt, 5% Crystal malt, 2% Wheat malt, 0.5% Chocolate malt. Hops: Fuggles. Late hops: Fuggles. IBU: 28. EBC: 30. Source: RP5.

**Brunel IPA**: ABV: 5%. Hops: Goldings, Fuggles. Source: W.

### . *Butterknowle Brewery, Bishop Aukland*

**Bitter**: OG: 1036. Malt: Halcyon or Maris Otter pale malt, Crystal malt. Hops: Challenger. IBU: 40. EBC: 18-28. Source: RP.

**Festival Stout**: OG: 1038. Malt: Pale malt, Crystal malt, Chocolate malt, Roast barley. Hops: Challenger. Source: RP2.

**Banner Bitter**: OG: 1040. Malt: 95% Maris Otter pale malt, 5% Crystal malt. Hops: Styrian Goldings. IBU: 38. EBC: 17. Source: RP4/5.

**Conciliation Ale**: OG: 1042. Malt: Halcyon or Maris Otter pale malt, Crystal malt, Chocolate malt. Hops: Challenger. IBU: 38. EBC: 34. Source: RP2/3/4/5.

**Conciliation Ale** (b-c): ABV: 4.3%. Malt: Maris Otter pale malt, Crystal malt, Pale chocolate malt. Hops: Challenger. Source: JE1.

**Black Diamond**: OG: 1050. Malt: Halcyon or Maris Otter pale malt, Crystal malt, Roast barley. Hops: Challenger. IBU: 41. EBC: 72. Source: RP3/4/5.

**High Force**: OG: 1060. Malt: Halcyon or Maris Otter pale malt, Crystal malt, 10% Sugar. Hops: Challenger. IBU: 36. EBC: 31. Source: RP3/4/5.

**High Force** (b-c): ABV: 6.2%. Malt: Maris Otter pale malt, Crystal malt. Hops: Challenger. Source: JE1.

**Old Ebenezer**: OG: 1080. Malt: Halcyon or Maris Otter pale malt, Crystal malt, Roast barley, 10% Sugar. Hops: Challenger. IBU: 30-6. EBC: 82. Source: RP.

### . *Butts, Hungerford*

**Le Butts** (b-c): ABV: 5%. Malt: Pale malt, Wheat malt. Source: JE4/5/6.

**Coper** (b-c): ABV: 6%. Hops: Goldings, Fuggles. Source: JE6.

### . *Robert Cain & Company, Liverpool*

**Cain's Dark Mild**: OG: 1033.5. Malt: Spring and Winter Pale malts, Chocolate malt, Roast barley, Wheat. Hops: Target. Late hops: Goldings. Dry hops: Goldings. EBC: 130-150. Source: RP4/5.

**Cain's Brewery Bitter**: OG: 1035.5. Malt: Maris Otter pale malt/Halcyon pale malt, Chocolate malt. Hops: Target. Late hops: Goldings. Dry hops: Northdown. IBU: 30. EBC: 18. Source: RP5.

**Cain's Traditional Bitter**: OG: 1038.5. Malt: Maris Otter pale malt/Halcyon pale malt, Chocolate malt, Wheat, Dark cane sugar. Hops: Target. Late hops: Goldings. Dry hops: Goldings. IBU: 28. EBC: 30. Source: RP5.

**Cain's Finest Bitter**: ABV: 4%. Hops: Styrian Goldings. Source: W.

**Cain's Formidable Ale**: OG: 1048. Malt: Maris Otter pale malt, small % Sugar, Wheat. Hops: Target. Late hops: Goldings. Dry hops: Northdown. IBU: 30. EBC: 14-16. Source: RP5.

## . *Camden Brewery Company, London*

**S**: OG: 1048. Malt: Pale malt, Lager malt, Black malt, Crystal 60L malt, No.3 invert sugar, Caramel. Hops: Spalt, Fuggles. Yeast: Wyeast #1098/Wyeast #1099. Notes: Recipe from 1922. IBU: 35. SRM: 30. Source: VB.

**PA**: OG: 1055. Malt: Pale malt, Lager malt, Glucose. Hops: Fuggles, Goldings. Yeast: Wyeast #1098/Wyeast #1099. Notes: Recipe from 1922. IBU: 73. SRM: 4. Source: VB.

**WA**: OG: 1066. Malt: Pale malt, Crystal 40L malt, Flaked maize, No.3 invert sugar, Caramel. Hops: Fuggles, Brewers Gold. Yeast: Wyeast #1098/Wyeast #1099. Notes: Recipe from 1924. IBU: 89. SRM: 22. Source: VB.

## . *Camden Town Brewery, London. Www.CamdenTownBrewery.com*

**Pale Ale**: ABV: 4%. Malt: Pilsner malt, Munich malt, Pale crystal malt, Wheat malt. Hops: Citra, Cascade, Amarillo, Columbus. IBU: 38. Source: Web.

**Gentleman's Wit**: ABV: 4.3%. Malt: Wheat malt, Pilsner malt. Hops: Perle. Others: Bergamot. IBU: 15. Source: Web.

**Ink**: ABV: 4.4%. Malt: Pale malt, Roast barley, Chocolate malt, Caramalt. Hops: Northdown, Pacific Gem. IBU: 51. Source: Web.

**Hells**: ABV: 4.6%. Malt: Pilsner malt. Hops: Hallertau Tradition, Perle. IBU: 20-24. Source: Web.

**Pils**: ABV: 4.6%. Malt: Pilsner malt. Hops: Zeus, Simcoe, Centennial. IBU: 36. Source: Web.

**Alsace Alt**: ABV: 4.6%. Malt: Pilsner malt, Munich malt, Pale crystal malt, Black malt. Hops: Aramis, Bouclier. IBU: 38. Source: Web.

**Apricot & Rosemary Wit**: ABV: 4.8%. Others: Apricots, Rosemary. Notes: Collaboration with The Kernel and Partizan breweries (both London). Source: Web.

**God Save the Elk**: ABV: 4.8%. Malt: Pilsner malt, Munich malt. Hops: Magnum, Chinook, Galaxy. Notes: Collaboration with The Flying Elk pub, Sweden. Source: Web.

**Black Friday**: ABV: 5.2%. Malt: Pilsner malt, Roast malt. Hops: Magnum, Saaz, Motueka. IBU: 40. Source: Web.

**Pumkin Spiced Lager**: ABV: 5.2%. Malt: Maris Otter pale malt, Dark crystal malt, Special B malt, Aromatic malt, Vienna malt. Hops: Hallertau Tradition. Others: Baked pumpkin. IBU: 16. Source: Web.

**One Hells of a Beaver**: ABV: 5.2%. Malt: Pilsner malt, Munich malt, Caramalt, Cara Gold malt. Hops: Magnum, Columbus, Citra, Amarillo, Bravo, Calypso. IBU: 55. Notes: Collaboration with Beavertown Brewery, London. Source: Web.

**Emperor Nero**: ABV: 5.8%. Malt: Pilsner malt, Munich malt, Light crystal malt, Chocolate malt, Roast malt. Hops: Simcoe, Chinook, Citra, Perle. IBU: 58. Source: Web.

**Flue Faker**: ABV: 5.8%. Malt: Beechwood smoked Pilsner malt, CaraPils malt, Special B malt. Hops: Saaz. IBU: 26. Source: Web.

**Versus Mohawk**: ABV: 5.8%. Malt: Pilsner malt, Munich malt, Pale crystal malt, Carafa® Special malt. Hops: Simcoe, Mosaic, Columbus, Galaxy. IBU: 65. Notes: Collaboration with Mohawk Brewing Company, Sweden. Source: Web.

**Versus Italy**: ABV: 5.8%. Malt: Pilsner malt, Munich malt, Pale crystal malt, Black malt. Hops: Hallertau Mittelfrüh, Hallertau Tradition, Hersbrücker, Pacifica, Motueka. IBU: 45. Notes: Collaboration with Birrificio Italiano, Birra del Borgo and Brewfist, Italy. Source: Web.

**Versus Petrus**: ABV: 6%. Malt: Belgian Pale malt, Pilsner malt, Special B malt, Aromatic malts, Roast malt. Hops: Saaz, First Gold. IBU: 45. Notes: Collaboration with Brouwerij de Brabandere, Belgium. Source: Web.

**IHL (India Hells Lager)**: ABV: 6.2%. Malt: Pilsner malt, Munich malt, CaraPils malt. Hops: Magnum, Simcoe, Chinook, Mosaic. IBU: 55. Source: Web.

**Indian Summer**: ABV: 6.2%. Malt: Pilsner malt, Munich malt, CaraPils malt. Hops: Simcoe, Magnum, Chinook, Mosaic. IBU: 52. Source: Web.

**Barrel Aged IHL (India Hells Lager)**: ABV: 7.2%. Malt: Pilsner malt, Munich malt, CaraPils malt. Hops: Simcoe, Magnum, Chinook, Mosaic. IBU: 54. Notes: Aged for 6 months in Bourbon and Tequila casks. Source: Web.

**Beer 2013**: ABV: 8.8%. Malt: Pilsner malt. Hops: Saaz, Styrian Goldings. IBU: 28. Source: Web.

**Beer 2014**: ABV: 9.5%. Malt: Pilsner malt, Carafa® malt, CaraRed® malt, Munich malt, Pale crystal malt, CaraPils malt, Chocolate malt, Caramalt. Hops: Magnum, Chinook, Perle, Galaxy. IBU: 28. Notes: Lagered for 5 months in Bourbon casks. Source: Web.

### . *Camerons Brewery Company, Hartlepool*

**Traditional Bitter**: OG: 1036. Malt: 72% Pale malt, 7% Crystal malt, 9% Flaked maize, 12% Sugar. Hops: Fuggles. Late hops: Goldings. Source: GW/RP1/2.

**Bitter**: OG: 1036. Malt: 86% Pipkin and/or Maris Otter pale malt, 6% Crystal malt, 6% Brewing sugar. Hops: Challenger. Late hops: Goldings, Fuggles. IBU: 30-32. EBC: 27. Source: RP.

**Strongarm**: OG: 1040. Malt: 62-79% Maris Otter pale malt, 13-16% Crystal malt, 0-8% Flaked maize, 8-14% Sugar. Hops: Fuggles or Challenger. Late hops: Goldings and/or Fuggles. IBU: 32. EBC: 52. Source: GW/RP/JHF.

**Strongarm Premium**: OG: 1045. Malt: Pale malt, Crystal malt, Flaked maize, Sugar. Hops: Fuggles, Goldings. Source: RP1.

### . *Cannon Brewery, Wellingborough*

**Light Brigade**: OG: 1036. Malt: 90% Maris Otter pale malt, 5% Crystal malt, 5% Wheat malt. Hops: Challenger, Goldings. Source: RP4/5.

**Cannon Pride**: OG: 1042. Malt: 90% Maris Otter pale malt, 5% Crystal malt, 5% Wheat malt. Hops: Challenger, Goldings. Source: RP4/5.

**Florrie Night-in-ale**: OG: 1048. Malt: 90% Maris Otter pale malt, 5% Crystal malt, 5% Wheat malt. Hops: Challenger, Goldings. Source: RP4/5.

**Cannon Fodder**: OG: 1055. Malt: 87% Maris Otter pale malt, 7% Crystal malt, 6% Wheat malt. Hops: Challenger, Goldings. Source: RP4/5.

### . *Cannon Royal Brewery, Ombersley*

**KPA**: OG: 1034. Malt: 100% Maris Otter pale malt. Hops: Challenger, Goldings, Bramling Cross, Fuggles, Northdown. Source: RP4/5.

**Mild**: OG: 1037. Malt: Maris Otter pale malt, Crystal malt, Torrefied wheat. Hops: Challenger, Goldings, Bramling Cross, Fuggles, Northdown. Source: RP4/5.

**Arrowhead**: OG: 1039. Malt: 100% Maris Otter pale malt 0-5% Torrefied wheat. Hops: Bramling Cross, Challenger, Northdown. Late hops: Challenger, Goldings, Bramling Cross, Fuggles. Dry hops: Yes. Source: RP.

**Buckshot**: OG: 1045. Malt: Maris Otter pale malt, Amber malt, Torrefied wheat. Hops: Challenger, Goldings, Bramling Cross, Fuggles, Northdown. Source: RP4/5.

**Heart of Oak**: OG: 1054. Malt: Maris Otter pale malt, Amber malt, Crystal malt, Torrefied wheat. Hops: Challenger, Goldings, Bramling Cross, Fuggles, Northdown. Late hops: Styrian Goldings. Source: RP4/5.

### . *Canuk, Rowley Regis*

**Mick's Mix** (b-c): ABV: 5%. Malt: Maris Otter pale malt, Caramalt, Amber malt, Wheat malt. Hops: Challenger, Northdown, Styrian Goldings. Source: JE2.

### . *Carlsberg, Northampton*

**Special Brew** (bottled): OG: 1080. Malt: Lager malt, Flaked maize, Golden syrup. Hops: Hallertau. Late hops: Hallertau. Source: DL.

### Cartmel Brewery, Kendal

**Pride**: OG: 1035. Malt: Halcyon pale malt, Roast barley, Crystal malt. Hops: Challenger. Late Hops: Styrian Goldings. Source: RP5.

**Lakeland Gold**: OG: 1038.5. Malt: Halcyon pale malt, Crystal malt. Hops: Challenger. Late hops: Styrian Goldings. Source: RP5.

**Thoroughbred**: OG: 1044. Malt: Halcyon pale malt, Crystal malt, Amber malt, Roast barley. Hops: Challenger. Late hops: Styrian Goldings. Source: RP5.

### Castle Eden Brewery, Hartlepool

**Higsons Mild**: OG: 1032. Malt: 75% Pale malt, 5% Crystal malt, 10% Torrefied wheat, 6% Brewing sugar, 4% Caramel. Hops: Galena, Target. Late hops: Styrian Goldings. IBU: 22. EBC: 85. Source: RP4. Notes: See **Mild**, Higsons and **Higson's Best Mild**, Whitbread, Sheffield.

**Eden Bitter**: OG: 1037. Malt: 88% Pale malt, 5% Crystal malt, 7% Torrefied wheat. Hops: Galena, Target. Late hops: Styrian Goldings. IBU: 27. EBC: 18. Source: RP4.

**Higsons Bitter**: OG: 1038. Malt: 75% Pale malt, 5% Crystal malt, 10% Torrefied wheat, 10% Brewing sugar. Hops: Target and optional Galena. Late hops: Styrian Goldings. IBU: 32. EBC: 23. Source: RP. Notes: See **Bitter**, Higsons and **Higson's Best Bitter**, Whitbread, Sheffield.

**Castle Eden Ale**: OG: 1040. Malt: 70% Pale malt, 10% Torrefied wheat, 20% Sugar. Hops: Target. Late hops: Styrian Goldings. Dry hops: Styrian Goldings. IBU: 23. Source: RP/MO. Notes: I once had an absolutely superb pint of Castle Eden Ale served to me in a pub in Sheffield. The pint slipped down very quickly indeed so I returned to the bar for a refill…and they had run out!

**Old Dambusters**: OG: 1043. Malt: 87% Pale malt, 3% Crystal malt, 10% Torrefied wheat. Hops: Galena, Target. Late hops: Styrian Goldings. IBU: 37. EBC: 18. Source: RP4/5.

**Whitbread Porter**: OG: 1052. Malt: 76% Pale malt, 20% Brown malt, 2% Chocolate malt, 2% Black malt. Hops: Goldings. Late hops: Goldings. Dry hops: Styrian Goldings. IBU: 36-40. EBC: 290. Source: RP3/4/MO.

**Winter Royal**: OG: 1054. Malt: 95% Pale malt, 5% Crystal malt. Hops: 100% Target. Late hops: optional Styrian Goldings. IBU: 36. EBC: 36. Source: RP3/4/MO.

**Fuggles Imperial IPA**: OG: 1055. Malt: 90% Pale malt, 10% Torrefied wheat. Hops: Fuggles. Late hops: Fuggles. Dry hops: Fuggles. IBU: 42. EBC: 14. Source: RP4/5.

### Castle Rock Brewery, Nottingham

**Hemlock Bitter** (b-c): ABV: 4.1%. Malt: Maris Otter pale malt, Crystal malt, Torrefied wheat. Hops: Goldings, Fuggles. Source: JE6.

**Elsie Mo** (b-c): ABV: 4.7%. Malt: Low colour Maris Otter pale malt, Torrefied wheat. Hops: Goldings, Styrian Goldings, Challenger. Source: JE6.

### *. Chelmsford Brewery, Chelmsford*

**Porter**: OG: 1070. Malt: Pale malt, Amber malt, Brown malt, Black malt. Hops: Fuggles. Notes: Recipe from 1853. Source: DP.

**Samson Ale**: OG: 1081. Malt: Pale malt. Hops: Fuggles. Notes: Recipe from 1853. Source: DP.

**Old Tom**: OG: 1088. Malt: Pale malt. Hops: Fuggles. Notes: Recipe from 1854. Source: DP.

**Old Ale**: OG: 1090. Malt: Pale malt. Hops: Fuggles. Notes: Recipe from 1855. Source: DP.

### *. Cheriton Brewhouse, Alresford*

**Pots Ale**: OG: 1037. Malt: 97% Halcyon pale malt, 3% Crystal malt. Hops: Challenger. Source: RP3/4/5.

**Cheriton Best**: OG: 1040.8. Malt: Halcyon pale malt, Crystal malt, Chocolate malt. Hops: Challenger. Source: RP4/5.

**Diggers Gold**: OG: 1044.5. Malt: 97% Halcyon pale malt, 3% Crystal malt. Hops: Challenger. Source: RP4/5.

### *. Chiltern Brewery, Aylesbury*

**Chiltern Ale**: OG: 1036. Malt: 90-93% Maris Otter pale malt, 3-10% Crystal malt, Invert sugar. Hops: Challenger. Late hops: Fuggles, Goldings. Source: RP.

**Beechwood Bitter**: OG: 1041-3. Malt: 90-93% Maris Otter pale malt, 7-10% Crystal malt, Invert sugar. Hops: Challenger. Late hops: Fuggles, Goldings. Source: RP.

**Copper Beech**: ABV: 4.4%. Malt: Maris Otter pale malt. Hops: Challenger. Source: WB.

**Glad Tidings** (b-c): ABV: 4.6%. Malt: Maris Otter pale malt, Chocolate malt, Roast barley. Hops: Bramling Cross. Others: Nutmeg, Coriander, Orange peel. Source: JE5/6.

**John Hampden's**: OG: 1048. Malt: 97% Maris Otter pale malt, 3% Crystal malt, Sugar. Hops: Fuggles. Late hops: Fuggles. Source: RP5.

**Three Hundreds Old Ale**: OG: 1050. Malt: 85-87% Halcyon or Maris Otter pale malt, 13-15% Crystal malt, Roast barley, Invert sugar. Hops: Challenger. Late hops: Fuggles, Goldings. Source: RP.

**Bodgers Barley Wine** (b-c): OG: 1080. Malt: Halcyon or Maris Otter pale malt, optional Invert sugar, optional Malt extract. Hops: Challenger. Late hops: Fuggles, Goldings. Source: RP/JE1/2/3/4/6. ABV: 8.5%. Malt: Maris Otter pale malt. Hops: Fuggles, Goldings. Source: JE5.

## . Chiltern Valley, Henley-on-Thames

Note: See Old Luxters Farm Brewery.

## . Church End, Shustoke

**Nuns Ale** (b-c): ABV: 4.5%. Malt: Pale malt, Crystal malt. Hops: Green Bullet, Cascade, Amarillo. Source: JE4/5/6.

**Rugby Ale** (b-c): ABV: 5%. Malt: Maris Otter pale malt, Crystal malt, Amber malt, Chocolate malt. Hops: Hersbrücker or Northdown. Source: JE1/2/3/4/5.

**Arthur's Wit** (b-c): ABV: 6%. Malt: Pale malt, Torrefied wheat. Hops: Cascade, Mount Hood. Source: JE4/5/6.

## . City of Cambridge, Cambridge

**Jet Black** (b-c): ABV: 3.7%. Malt: Maris Otter pale malt, Crystal malt, Caramalt, Roast malt. Hops: First Gold. Source: JE4/5/6.

**Boathouse Bitter / Easter Bunny** (b-c): ABV: 3.8%. Malt: Maris Otter pale malt, Crystal malt. Hops: First Gold, Cascade. Source: JE3/4/5.

**Hobson's Choice** (b-c): ABV: 4.1%. Malt: Maris Otter pale malt, Caramalt. Hops: First Gold. Source: JE2/3/4/5/6.

**Trinity** (b-c): ABV: 4.3%. Malt: Maris Otter pale malt, Crystal malt, Caramalt, Roast barley. Hops: First Gold, Cascade. Source: JE6.

**Blend '42'** (b-c): ABV: 4.4%. Malt: Maris Otter pale malt, Crystal malt, Caramalt, Roast malt. Hops: First Gold. Source: JE3/4.

**Sunset Square** (b-c): ABV: 4.4%. Malt: Maris Otter pale malt, Crystal malt, Caramalt, Roast barley. Hops: First Gold. Source: JE4/5/6.

**Drummer Street Stout** (b-c): ABV: 4.5%. Malt: Maris Otter pale malt, Crystal malt, Roast malt, Torrefied wheat. Hops: Challenger, Goldings. Other: Sea salt. Source: JE4/5.

**Mich'aelmas** (b-c): ABV: 4.6%. Malt: Maris Otter pale malt, Crystal malt, Caramalt, Roast barley. Hops: First Gold, Cascade. Source: JE3/4/6.

**New Model Ale** (b-c): ABV: 4.6%. Malt: Maris Otter pale malt, Crystal malt, Caramalt, Roast barley. Hops: First Gold, Bramling Cross. Source: JE6.

**Atomsplitter / Atomic Ale / Patron Saint** (b-c): ABV: 4.7%. Malt: Maris Otter pale malt, Crystal malt, Caramalt, optional Roast barley. Hops: First Gold. Source: JE1/2/3/4/5/6.

**Darwin's Downfall** (b-c): ABV: 5%. Malt: Maris Otter pale malt, Crystal malt, Caramalt, Roast barley. Hops: First Gold. Source: JE3/4/5/6.

**Holly Heaven** (b-c): ABV: 5.1%. Malt: Maris Otter pale malt, Crystal malt, Caramalt, Roast barley. Hops: First Gold. Source: JE6.

**Parkers Porter** (b-c): ABV: 5.3%. Malt: Maris Otter pale malt, Crystal malt, Caramalt, Roast barley. Hops: First Gold. Source: JE3/4/5/6.

**Bramling Traditional** (b-c): ABV: 5.5%. Malt: Maris Otter pale malt, Crystal malt, Caramalt, Roast barley. Hops: First Gold, Bramling Cross. Source: JE3/4/5/6.

### . *H.B.Clark & Company, Wakefield*

**Clark's HB**: OG: 1033. Malt: Pale malt, 4% Crystal malt, 1% Chocolate malt. Hops: Challenger. Source: RP1.

**Garthwaite Special**: OG: 1035. Malt: Pale malt, 4% Crystal malt, 1% Chocolate malt. Hops: Challenger. Source: RP1.

**Traditional Bitter**: OG: 1037. Malt: Pale malt, 4% Crystal malt, 1% Chocolate malt. Hops: Challenger. Source: RP1/2/3. OG: 1038. Malt: Halcyon pale malt, Crystal malt, Torrefied wheat, Roast barley. Hops: Challenger or Omega or Target. Late hops: Styrian Goldings. Source: RP4/5.

**Mild**: OG: 1038. Malt: Pale malt, Crystal malt, Chocolate malt. Hops: Challenger. Source: RP2.

**Festival Ale**: OG: 1042. Malt: Halcyon pale malt, Crystal malt, Torrefied wheat. Hops: Styrian Goldings. Late hops: Styrian Goldings. Source: RP4/5.

**Burglar Bill**: OG: 1044. Malt: Pale malt, 4% Crystal malt, 1% Chocolate malt. Hops: Challenger. Dry hops: Challenger. Source: RP1/2/3. Malt: Halcyon pale malt, Crystal malt, Torrefied wheat, Roast barley. Hops: Styrian Goldings. Late hops: Styrian Goldings. Source: RP4/5.

**Winter Warmer**: OG: 1060. Malt: Halcyon pale malt, Crystal malt, Torrefied wheat, Roast barley. Hops: Challenger or Omega or Target. Source: RP4/5.

**Hammerhead**: OG: 1055. Malt: Pale malt, 4% Crystal malt, 1% Chocolate malt. Hops: Challenger. Source: RP1/2/3. Malt: Halcyon pale malt, Crystal malt, Torrefied wheat, Roast barley. Hops: Challenger or Omega or Target. Source: RP4/5.

**T'owd Dreadnought**: OG 1080. Malt: Halcyon pale malt, Torrefied wheat. Hops: Challenger or Omega or Target. Source: RP4/5.

**Ram's Revenge**: OG: 1046. Malt: Halcyon pale malt, Crystal malt, Torrefied wheat, Roast barley. Hops: Challenger or Omega or Target. Late hops: Styrian Goldings. Source: RP4/5.

### . *Clarke's Organic, Dewsbury*

**COB No.1** (b-c): ABV: 4.2%. Hops: Cascade. Source: JE5.

**Bright Bay** (b-c): ABV: 5%. Hops: Pacific Gem. Source: JE5.

### . Clearwater, Great Torrington

**Cavalier Ale** (b-c): ABV: 4%. Malt: Pipkin pale malt, Crystal malt, Chocolate malt. Hops: Challenger, Goldings. Source: JE4/5.

**1646** (b-c): ABV: 4.8%. Malt: Pipkin pale malt, Crystal malt. Hops: Goldings. Source: JE4/5.

**Oliver's Nectar** (b-c): ABV: 5.2%. Malt: Pipkin pale malt, Crystal malt, Roast barley. Hops: Challenger, Goldings. Source: JE4/5.

### . Coach House Brewing Company, Warrington

**Coachman's Best Bitter**: OG: 1037. Malt: 86% Maris Otter pale malt, 14% Crystal malt. Hops: Fuggles, Goldings. Dry hops: Yes. IBU: 28. EBC: 30. Source: RP3/4/5.

**Ostlers Summer Pale Ale**: OG: 1037. Malt: 94.8% Maris Otter pale malt, 5.2% Pale crystal malt. Hops: Hersbrücker. IBU: 28. EBC: 18. Source: RP5.

**Honey Pot Bitter**: ABV: 3.8%. Hops: Target. Source: W.

**Gunpowder Strong Mild**: OG: 1039. Malt: 94% Maris Otter pale malt, 3% Crystal malt, 3% Chocolate malt. Hops: Fuggles, Goldings. IBU: 28. EBC: 200. Source: RP3/4/5/JHF.

**Squires Gold**: OG: 1042. Malt: 87.5% Maris Otter pale malt, 12.5% Amber malt. Hops: Hallertau, Hersbrücker, Pacific Gem. Dry hops: Yes. IBU: 38. EBC: 21. Source: RP3/4/5.

**Innkeeper's Special Reserve**: OG: 1045. Malt: 84% Maris Otter pale malt, 16% Crystal malt. Hops: Fuggles, Goldings. Dry hops: Yes. IBU: 32. EBC: 42. Source: RP3/4/5/JHF.

**Post Horn Premium Ale**: OG: 1050. Malt: 94.5% Maris Otter pale malt, 5.5% Pale crystal malt. Hops: Fuggles, Target. Dry hops: Yes. IBU: 38. EBC: 18. Source: RP4/5.

**Taverners Autumn Ale**: OG: 1050. Malt: 97% Maris Otter pale malt, 3% Pale crystal malt. Hops: Target. Late hops: Cascade. Source: RP5.

**Blunderbus**: OG: 1055. Malt: 90.25% Maris Otter pale malt, 6.5% Chocolate malt, 3.25% Black malt. Hops: Fuggles, Goldings. IBU: 40. EBC: 240. Source: RP3/4/5.

**Anniversary Ale**: OG: 1060. Malt: 91% Maris Otter pale malt, 9% Crystal malt. Hops: Fuggles, Goldings. Late hops: Yes. IBU: 35. EBC: 38. Source: RP3/4/5.

### . Cobb & Co., Margate

**Amber Small Beer**: OG: 1042. Malt: Pale malt, Amber malt. Hops: Fuggles. Notes: Recipe from 1823. Source: DP.

**Porter**: OG: 1068. Malt: Pale malt, Brown malt. Hops: Fuggles. Notes: Recipe from 1783. Source: DP.

**Amber Ale**: OG: 1072 or 1081. Malt: Pale malt, Amber malt. Hops: Fuggles. Notes: Recipe from 1823. Source: DP.

**Dark Amber Ale**: OG: 1076. Malt: Pale amber malt, Brown malt. Hops: Fuggles. Notes: Recipe from 1812. Source: DP.

**Sixpenny Ale**: OG: 1085. Malt: Pale malt, Amber malt. Hops: Fuggles. Notes: Recipe from 1785. Source: DP.

### . *Cobra Beer, London*

**King Cobra** (b-c): See Cobra Beer, Kielce, Poland.

### . *Combe Martin Brewery, Combe Martin*

**Past-Times** (b-c): ABV: 3.9%. Malt: Pale malt, Crystal malt, Demerara sugar. Hops: Jeanette, Admiral. Source: JE6.

### . *Christopher Columbus, Woking*

**The Millennium Celebration Ale** (b-c): ABV: 8%. Malt: Maris Otter pale malt. Hops: Goldings, Early Bird. Source: JE2.

### . *Commercial Brewing Company, Keighley*

**Keighlian Mild**: OG: 1034. Malt: Two pale malts, Crystal malt. Hop: Goldings, Styrian Goldings. EBC: 20-24. Source: RP3.

**Becksider**: OG: 1034. Malt: 85% Pale malt, 8% Crystal malt, 7% Chocolate malt. Hops: Goldings. EBC: 100. Source: RP3/4/5.

**Wayfarer Mild**: OG: 1034. Malt: Pale malt, Crystal malt, Chocolate malt. Hops: WGV. EBC: 50. Source: RP4/5.

**Keighlian Bitter**: OG: 1036. Malt: 97% Pale malt, 3% Crystal malt. Hops: 100% Goldings. EBC: 24-26. Source: RP3.

**Alesman Bitter**: OG: 1036. Malt: 97% Pale malt, 3% Crystal malt. Hops: Goldings. EBC: 24-26. Source: RP4/5.

**Neary's Stout**: OG: 1040. Malt: Pale malt, Roast barley, Crystal malt, Chocolate malt. Hops: WGV. EBC: More than 100. Source: RP4/5.

**Wild Boar**: OG: 1040. Malt: Pale malt, Chocolate malt. Hops: Northdown, WGV. EBC: 22-26. Source: RP4/5.

**Worth Bitter**: OG: 1045. Malt: 100% Pale malt. Hops: Goldings, Styrian Goldings. EBC: 12-14. Source: RP3/4/5.

**Porter**: OG: 1045. Malt: 85% Pale malt, 5% Chocolate malt, 10% Crystal malt. Hops: Goldings, Styrian Goldings. EBC: 100. Source: RP3/4/5.

**Old Toss**: OG: 1065. Malt: 80% Pale malt, 10% Crystal malt, 10% Chocolate malt. Hops: Goldings. EBC: 100. Source: RP3/4/5.

### Coniston Brewing Company, Coniston

**Bluebird Bitter**: OG: 1036. Malt: 95% Maris Otter pale malt, 5% Crystal malt. Hops: Challenger. Late hops: Challenger. IBU: 36-38. EBC: 21-22. Source: RP5/JE2/3/4/5/6/JHF. OG: 1043-44. Malt: Maris Otter pale malt, Crystal malt, Torrefied wheat, Roast barley. Hops: Challenger. Late hops: Challenger, Styrian Goldings. Source: BC.

**Bluebird XB** (b-c): ABV: 4.4%. Malt: Maris Otter pale malt, Crystal malt, Torrefied wheat. Hops: Challenger, Mount Hood. Source: JE6.

**Old Man Ale** (b-c): ABV: 5%. Malt: Maris Otter pale malt, Crystal malt, Roast barley. Hops: Challenger. Source: JE3/4/5/6.

### Cook Brewery Company, Bockhampton

**Yardarm Special Bitter**: OG: 1052. Malt: 90% Pale malt, 10% Crystal malt, Black malt. Hops: Target. Late hops: Fuggles. Source: RP3.

### Coors, Burton-on-Trent. Www.carling.com

**Carling Black Label** (bottled): OG: 1039. Malt: Lager malt. Hops: Hallertau or variety of English hops. Source: DL/Web.

**Worthington White Shield** (b-c): ABV: 5.6%. Malt: Pearl pale malt, Crystal malt. Hops: Fuggles, Northdown, Goldings/Challenger. Source: JE4/5/6. Notes: See **Worthington White Shield**, Bass, Sheffield, **Worthington White Shield**, Bass Mitchells & Butlers, **Worthington White Shield**, King & Barnes and **Worthington White Shield**, Museum Brewing Company.

**Bullion** (b-c): ABV: 6.5%. Malt: Pearl pale malt. Hops: Fuggles, Goldings, Northdown. Source: JE4.

**P2** (b-c): ABV: 8%. Malt: Halcyon pale malt, Crystal malt, Black malt. Hops: Fuggles, Goldings. Source: JE4/5/6. Note: See Museum Brewing Company.

**No. 1 Barley Wine** (b-c): ABV: 10.5%. Malt: Halcyon pale malt. Hops: Fuggles, Goldings. Source: JE4/5/6. Note: See **No. 1 Barley Wine**, Museum Brewing Company.

### Coors, Tadcaster

**Bass Mild**: OG: 1032. Malt: Mild ale malt, Black malt, Sugar. Hops: Challenger. Late hops: Goldings. IBU: 22. EBC: 74. Source: GW. Note: See **Mild XXXX**, Bass, Sheffield.

### Cornish Brewery Company, Redruth

**Draught Steam Bitter**: OG: 1038. Malt: 100% Pale malt. Hops: Fuggles, Goldings, Progress. IBU: 30. Source: RP1/2.

**Royal Wessex Bitter**: OG: 1042. Malt: 85% Pale malt and Crystal malt, Invert sugar. Hops: Fuggles, Goldings, Progress. IBU: 32. Source: RP1/2.

**Churchill Amber**: OG: 1050-2. Malt: 71.3% Pale malt, 8.9% Crystal malt, 9.6% Amber malt, 10.2% Invert sugar. Hops: Fuggles, Goldings, Progress. IBU: 32. EBC: 35. Source: EBA/GW.

**JD Dry Hop Bitter**: OG: 1032. Malt: 85% Pale malt and Crystal malt, Invert sugar. Hops: Fuggles, Goldings, Progress. Dry hops: Yes. IBU: 24. Source: RP1/2.

**Original**: OG: 1037-8. Malt: 85% Pale malt and Crystal malt, Invert sugar. Hops: Fuggles, Goldings, Progress. Dry hops: Yes. IBU: 24. Source: RP1/2/3.

### .   Corvedale, Craven Arms

**Teresa's Birthday Party** (b-c): ABV: 4%. Malt: Maris Otter pale malt, Crystal malt, Wheat malt. Hops: Northdown, 93/50 trial hops. Source: JE3.

**Teresa's Birthday** (b-c): ABV: 4.2%. Malt: Maris Otter pale malt, Crystal malt, Wheat malt. Hops: Northdown, Susan. Source: JE4/5. ABV: 4.5%. Hops: Northdown, Pilgrim. Source: JE6. Notes: The strength of this beer is increased by 0.1% every January.

**Katie's Pride** (b-c): ABV: 4.3%. Malt: Maris Otter pale malt, Crystal malt, Chocolate malt, Wheat malt. Hops: Jenny. Source: JE6.

**Norman's Pride** (b-c): ABV: 4.3%. Malt: Maris Otter pale malt, Crystal malt, Wheat malt. Hops: Northdown. Source: JE3/4/5/6.

**Secret Hop** (b-c): ABV: 4.5%. Malt: Maris Otter pale malt, Crystal malt, Wheat malt. Hops: 93/50 trial hops/Susan. Source: JE3/4/5/6.

**Dark and Delicious** (b-c): ABV: 4.6%. Malt: Maris Otter pale malt, Crystal malt, Chocolate malt, Wheat malt. Hops: Northdown, 93/50 trial hops/Susan. Source: JE3/4/5/6.

Notes: The 93/50 trial hops were Wye College (now sadly closed) experimental hops that were subsequently named Susan. Scottish Craft Brewer Bill Cooper has also brewed using Wye College trial hops and he was once also kind enough to pass on to me some of their Target control variety. Given the high α-acid content (12.2%) and quantity he supplied me as well as its reputation (it is not generally considered to have good flavour or aroma), I decided that its best use would be as a late hop rather than as a bittering hop. Accordingly, I did a search of this database to find suitable beers that used Target as a late or dry hop, and designed recipes accordingly. The two beers I based my recipes on were **Wye Valley Brew 69** and **Burton Bridge XL**. Both brews were successful and apparently when James "Dougall" McCrorie tasted the former he said it was the best beer he'd ever tasted that used Target hops! I'm not sure how much of a compliment this was. This is just one way in which this database has aided me in "breaking the rules" and making best use of a particular ingredient.

### .   Cotleigh Brewery, Wiveliscombe

**Harrier SPA**: OG: 1036. Malt: Pale malt, Crystal malt, optional Chocolate malt. Hops: Fuggles, Goldings, Northdown. Source: RP.

**Tawny Bitter**: OG: 1040. Malt: Pale malt, Crystal malt. Hops: Fuggles, Goldings and Northdown or Challenger. Source: RP.

**Barn Owl Bitter**: OG: 1045. Malt: Pale malt, Crystal malt. Hops: Fuggles, Goldings, Northdown. Source: RP4/5/W.

**Old Buzzard / Buzzard**: OG: 1048. Malt: Pale malt, Crystal malt, Chocolate malt. Hops: Fuggles, Goldings, Northdown. Source: RP1/2/3/4/5/JE6.

**Red Nose Reinbeer** (b-c): ABV: 5%. Malt: Optic pale malt, Crystal malt, Chocolate malt. Hops: Goldings, Fuggles, Northdown. Source: JE5.

**Peregrine Porter** (b-c): ABV: 5%. Malt: Pale malt, Crystal malt, Chocolate malt, Brown malt, Black malt. Hops: Fuggles, Goldings, Challenger. Source: JE6.

**Monmouth Rebellion**: OG: 1050. Malt: Pale malt, Chocolate malt. Hops: Goldings. Source: RP2/3.

## .   *Cottage Brewing Company, Lovington*

**Southern Bitter**: OG: 1037. Malt: Pale malt, Crystal malt. Hops: Challenger. Late hops: Styrian Goldings. Source: RP5.

**Wheeltappers**: OG: 1040. Malt: Pale malt, Crystal malt, Chocolate malt. Hops: Challenger. Late hops: Styrian Goldings. Source: RP5.

**Somerset & Dorset (S & D)**: OG: 1043. Malt: Paie malt, Crystal malt, Chocolate malt. Hops: Challenger. Source: RP5.

**Golden Arrow**: OG: 1043. Malt: Pale malt. Hops: Challenger. Late hops: Styrian Goldings. Source: RP5.

**Old Freckled Ken / Our Ken**: OG: 1044. Malt: Pale malt, Crystal malt, Chocolate malt. Hops: Challenger. Late hops: Styrian Goldings. Source: RP5.

**Goldrush**: OG: 1048. Malt: Pale malt. Hops: Challenger. Late hops: Cascade. Source: RP5.

**Great Western Real Ale (GWR)**: OG: 1054. Malt: Pale malt, Crystal malt, Chocolate malt. Hops: Challenger. Source: RP5.

**Norman's Conquest**: OG: 1066. Malt: Pale malt, Crystal malt, Chocolate malt. Hops: Challenger. Source: RP5.

**Norman's Conquest** (b-c): ABV: 7%. Malt: Maris Otter pale malt, Crystal malt, Chocolate malt. Hops: Challenger. Source: JE1/5.

## .   *Cottage Economy by William Cobbett*

**1850 Ale**: Malt: 2 bushels (68lb) of malted barley. From what is written my guess is the nearest modern equivalent would be pale malt. Hops: 1.5lb good hops. There is no indication but some good advice about selecting good quality hops. Water: Soft water. Notes: There is a single infusion mash that lasts about 2.5 hours and the the first runnings should provide 18 UK gallons of ale wort. There is apparently no sparging. The hops are added and the wort is boiled for 1 hour and the hops strained out (and reserved for use in the Small beer recipe below) and allowed to cool to 70°F before about half a pint of yeast is pitched. The yeast is optionally mixed with some wheat or rye flour before pitching, but I'd suggest that you omit this step. Fermentation is conducted at 55°F. The wort is skimmed during fermentation.

**1850 Small beer**: After running off the ale wort from the above recipe, 36 gallons of boiling water is added to the mash tun, the mash stirred and left for one hour before drawing off the wort. Hops: The strained hops from the ale recipe above are added to the wort along with a further half a pound of fresh hops and boiled for an hour. The hops are strained out, discarded and the wort is allowed to cool. In this case 3 pints of yeast are added. The rest of the process is as for the ale recipe above

Notes: *Cottage Economy* by William Cobbett was originally published as a series of pamphlets in 1821-22 and then 15 editions of a book through to 1850. It has been republished by Verey & Von Kanitz, Abbeydore (2000) and this version is the source of the ingredient information given here. Cobbett's views on the relative merits of drinking beer or tea make amusing reading and I can only agree with his comments!

> "...nothing is more common than for country gentlemen, who have a dislike to die by poison, bring their home-brewed beer to London.", William Cobbett

## .  *Country Life, Abbotsham*

**Old Appledore** (b-c): ABV: 4.2%. Malt: Maris Otter pale malt, Crystal malt, Roast malt, Wheat malt. Hops: Fuggles, Goldings. Source: JE4/5. ABV: 3.7%. Malt: Maris Otter pale malt, Roast barley. Hops: Fuggles, Goldings. Source: JE6.

**Baa Tenders Best** (b-c): ABV: 4.2%. Malt: Maris Otter pale malt, Roast malt. Hops: Challenger. Source: JE6.

**Wallop / Pot Wallop** (b-c): ABV: 4.4%. Malt: Maris Otter pale malt, optional Wheat malt. Hops: Fuggles, Goldings. Source: JE4/5/6.

**Golden Pig** (b-c): ABV: 4.7%. Malt: Maris Otter pale malt. Hops: Challenger, Goldings. Source: JE3/4/5. Malt: Maris Otter pale malt, Crystal malt. Hops: Challenger. Source: JE6.

**Lacey's Real Lager** (b-c): ABV: 5.2-5.4%. Malt: Lager malt. Hops: Mount Hood, Hersbrücker. Source: JE5.

**Country Bumpkin** (b-c): ABV: 6%. Malt: Maris Otter pale malt, Chocolate malt. Hops: Challenger, Goldings. Source: JE3/4/5/6.

## .  *Courage, Barnsley*

**Barnsley Bitter**: OG: 1037. Malt: Pale malt, Crystal malt, Flaked maize, Sugar. Hops: Fuggles, Goldings. Late hops: Goldings. Source: DL.

### . Courage, Bristol

**Bitter Ale**: OG: 1030-1. Malt: Halcyon pale malt, Pipkin pale malt, Crystal malt, Black malt, Brewing sugar. Hops: Target and/or Omega, Zenith, Hallertau, Styrian Goldings. Dry hops: Hop oil. IBU: 24. EBC: 23. Source: RP.

**George's Bitter Ale**: OG: 1032. Malt: 84% Halcyon and Puffin pale malt, 6% Crystal malt, 10% Black malt, Brewing sugar. Hops: Target. Late hops: Hallertau, Styrian Goldings. Dry hops: Hop oil. IBU: 22. EBC: 23. Source: RP4/5.

**Best Bitter**: OG: 1039. Malt: 84% Halcyon and Puffin pale malt, 6% Crystal malt, 10% Black malt, Brewing sugar. Hops: Target and/or Omega, Zenith, Hallertau, Hersbrücker, Styrian Goldings. Late hops: Hallertau, Styrian Goldings. Dry hops: Hop oil. IBU: 27-30. EBC: 25. Source: RP. OG: 1040. Malt: Pale malt, Crystal malt, Flaked barley, Demerara sugar. Hops: Goldings, Northern Brewer. Late hops: Goldings. Source: DL.

**Directors**: OG: 1046. Malt: 84% Halcyon and Puffin pale malt, 6% Crystal malt, 10% Black malt, Brewing sugar. Hops: Target and/or Omega, Zenith, Hallertau, Styrian Goldings. Late hops: Hallertau, Styrian Goldings. Dry hops: Hop oil. IBU: 33-35. EBC: 28. Source: RP. OG: 1047-51. Malt: Pale malt, Crystal malt, Sugar. Hops: Target. Late hops: Hersbrücker, Styrian Goldings. Source: CB.

### . Courage, Staines

**Light Ale**: OG: 1032. Malt: Pale malt, Mild malt, Crystal 40L malt, Flaked maize, No.3 invert sugar. Hops: Fuggles, Bramling Cross, Northern Brewer. Yeast: Wyeast #1098/Wyeast #1099. Notes: Recipe from 1965. IBU: 31. SRM: 12. Source: VB.

**Tavern Keg** (keg): OG: 1039. Malt: Crystal malt, Flaked barley, Sugar. Hops: Fuggles, Hop extract. Source: DL.

**Draught John Courage** (keg): OG: 1045. Malt: Pale malt, Crystal malt, Torrefied barley, Sugar. Hops: Goldings, Northern Brewer. Source: DL.

**Directors Bitter**: OG: 1046. Malt: Pale malt, Crystal malt, Barley syrup, Sugar. Hops: Goldings, Fuggles. Late hops: Goldings. Dry hops: Goldings. Source: DL.

**London Ale**: OG: 1062. Malt: Pale malt. Hops: Fuggles. Notes: Recipe from 1820. Source: DP.

**Double Stout**: OG: 1064. Malt: Pale malt, Brown malt, Black malt, No.3 invert sugar, No.4 invert sugar. Hops: Strisselspalt, Fuggles. Yeast: Wyeast #1098/Wyeast #1099. Notes: Recipe from 1918. IBU: 33. SRM: 44. Source: VB.

**KKK**: OG: 1072. Malt: 44.1% English Pale malt, 22.9% American Pale malt, 10.1% Crystal 55L malt, 9% Flaked maize, 12.4% No.3 invert sugar. Hops: 45.5% Goldings. Late hops: 22.7% Goldings. Dry hops: 31.8% Goldings. Yeast: White Labs WLP002, Wyeast #1968 or Nottingham. IBU: 41. SRM: 50. Notes: Burton ale recipe from 1937. Source: SUABP.

**Imperial Double Stout Porter**: OG: 1095. Malt: Pale malt, Brown malt, Black malt, Sugar. Hops: Fuggles. Notes: Recipe from 1914. Source: DP.

**Imperial Russian Stout** (bottled): OG: 1103. Malt: Pale malt, Crystal malt, Chocolate malt, Black malt, Sugar. Hops: Fuggles. Source: DL. Malt: Pale malt, Crystal malt, Chocolate malt, Roast barley, Black malt, Black Treacle. Hops: Target. Late hops: Target. Others: Steamed Oak chips. Source: CB. Notes: See **Imperial Russian Stout**, Scottish & Newcastle Beer Production, Scotland and **Imperial Russian Stout**, John Smith's Brewery, Tadcaster.

### . *Thomas Cox, Ware*

**XXX Fine Ale**: OG: 1075. Malt: Pale malt. Hops: Goldings. Notes: Recipe from 1858. Source: DP.

### . *Cox & Holbrook, Buxhall*

**Goodcock's Winner** (b-c): ABV: 5%. Malt: Maris Otter pale malt, Chocolate malt, Caramalt. Hops: Fuggles. Source: JE3/4.

**Iron Oak Single Stout** (b-c): ABV: 5%. Malt: Maris Otter pale malt, Crystal malt, Roast barley, Flaked barley. Hops: Northdown. Others: Toasted Oak chips. Source: JE3/4.

**Remus** (b-c): ABV: 5%. Malt: Maris Otter pale malt, Crystal malt, Caramalt. Hops: Cascade. Source: JE3/4.

**Stormwatch** (b-c): ABV: 5%. Malt: Maris Otter pale malt, Chocolate malt, Wheat malt, Roast barley. Hops: Fuggles, Goldings. Source: JE3/4.

**Stowmarket Porter** (b-c): ABV: 5%. Malt: Maris Otter pale malt, Chocolate malt, Wheat malt, Roast barley, Flaked barley. Hops: Fuggles. Source: JE3/4.

**Uncle Stan** (b-c): ABV: 5%. Malt: Maris Otter pale malt, Chocolate malt, Crystal malt. Hops: Fuggles. Source: JE3/4.

### . *Cropton Brewery Company, Pickering*

**King Billy Bitter**: OG: 1037. Malt: Pale malt. Hops: Challenger. Late hops: Goldings. Source: RP4/5.

**King Billy Bitter** (b-c): ABV: 3.6%. Malt: Pale malt. Hops: Challenger, Goldings. Source: JE1/2/3/4/5/6.

**Endeavour** (b-c): ABV: 3.8%. Malt: Pale malt. Hops: Challenger, Goldings. Source: JE4/5/6.

**Two Pints Best Bitter**: OG: 1040-2. Malt: 85% Pale malt, 15% Crystal malt. Hops: Goldings, Challenger. Source: RP1/2/3/4/5/JE1/2/3/4/5/6.

**Honey Farm Bitter / Honey Gold** (b-c): ABV: 4.2%. Malt: Pale malt, Honey. Hops: First Gold. Source: JE1/2/3/4/5/6.

**Scoresby Stout**: OG: 1042. Malt: 75% Halcyon pale malt, 15% Crystal malt, 10% Roast barley. Hops: Challenger. Late hops: Goldings. Source: RP3/4/5/JE1/2/3/4/5/6.

**Uncle Sams Bitter** (b-c): ABV: 4.4%. Malt: Pale malt, Crystal malt. Hops: Cascade. Source: JE1/3/4/5/6.

**Uncle Sams**: OG: 1048. Malt: 100% Pale malt, 5% Torrefied wheat. Hops: Cascade. Source: RP5.

**Rudolph's Revenge** (b-c): ABV: 4.6%. Malt: Pale malt, Crystal malt, Roast barley. Hops: Styrian Goldings, Challenger, optional Cascade. Source: JE1/2/3/4/5. Hops: Styrian Goldings, Cascade. Source: JE6.

**Yorkshire Moors** (b-c): ABV: 4.6%. Malt: Pale malt, Crystal malt, Roast malt. Hops: Challenger, Styrian Goldings. Source: JE4/5. Hops: Fuggles, Progress. JE6.

**Backwoods Bitter** (b-c): ABV: 5.1%. Malt: Pale malt, Crystal malt, Roast malt. Hops: Styrian Goldings, Challenger. Source: JE1/2/3.

**Backwoods**: OG: 1053. Malt: 91% Pale malt, 8% Crystal malt, 1% Roast malt, 5% Torrefied wheat. Hops: Challenger. Late hops: Styrian Goldings. Source: RP5.

**Monkman's Slaughter** (b-c): ABV: 6%. Malt: Pale malt, Crystal malt, Roast malt. Hops: Goldings, Challenger. Source: JE1/2/3/4/5/6.

**Special Strong Bitter**: OG: 1060-2. Malt: Pale malt, Crystal malt. Hops: Goldings, Challenger. Source: RP1/2/3/4.

## .  *Crouch Vale Brewery, South Woodham Ferrers*

**Woodham Bitter / IPA**: OG: 1035-6. Malt: 88% Pale malt, 7% Wheat malt, 5% Crystal malt. Hops: Challenger, Northdown, Progress, WGV. Late hops: Goldings. Malt: 47.5% Halcyon pale malt, 47.5% Maris Otter pale malt, 5% Crystal malt. Hops: Challenger or Omega. Late hops: Goldings or Challenger. Dry Hops: Goldings or Challenger. IBU: 32. EBC: 25. Source: RP/MO.

**Best Mild / Best Dark Ale**: OG: 1036. Malt: 95% Pale malt (Halcyon pale malt, Pipkin pale malt, Maris Otter pale malt or Triumph pale malt), 5% Roast barley. Hops: Challenger, Goldings. IBU: 30. EBC: 50. Source: RP. Malt: Mild ale malt, Roast barley. Hops: Challenger. Late hops: Goldings. Source: MO.

**Best Bitter**: OG: 1038-9. Malt: 93-94.5% Pale malt, 6.5-7% Crystal malt. Hops: Challenger, Northdown, Progress and/or WGV. Late hops: Goldings. Dry hops: Goldings. Source: RP/MO. OG: 1040. Malt: 48% Halcyon pale malt, 46% Maris Otter pale malt, 2% Roast barley. Hops: Omega. Late hops: Challenger. Dry hops: Challenger. IBU: 35. EBC: 31. Source: RP5/JHF.

**Millennium Gold**: OG: 1042. Malt: 50% Maris Otter pale malt, 50% Halcyon pale malt. Hops: Challenger, optional Omega. Late hops: Goldings or Challenger. Dry hops: Goldings or Challenger. IBU: 35. EBC: 22. Source: RP/MO.

**Kursaal Flyer**: OG: 1045. Malt: 97-98.5% Halcyon or Maris Otter pale malt, 0-3% Crystal malt, 0-1.5% Roast barley. Hops: Omega. Late hops: Challenger. Dry hops: Challenger. IBU: 35. EBC: 24. Source: RP.

**Strong Anglian Ale / SAS**: OG: 1048. Malt: 88% Pale malt, 7% Wheat, 5% Crystal malt or 47% Halcyon pale malt, 47% Maris Otter pale malt, 6% Crystal malt. Hops: Challenger, Northdown, Goldings, Progress, WGV and/or Omega. Late hops: Goldings or Challenger. Dry hops: Goldings or Challenger. IBU: 37. EBC: 29. Source: RP/MO.

**Essex Porter**: OG: 1050. Malt: 88% Pale malt, 7% Wheat, 5% Crystal malt, Roast barley or 45% Halcyon pale malt, 45% Maris Otter pale malt, 6% Crystal malt, 4% Roast barley. Hops: Omega or Challenger and optional Northdown, Goldings. Late hops: Goldings or Challenger. Dry hops: Challenger. IBU: 37. EBC: 98. Source: RP.

**Santa's Revenge**: OG: 1058. Malt: 37.5% Halcyon pale malt, 37.5% Maris Otter pale malt, 5% Crystal malt, 20% Sugar. Hops: Challenger, optional Omega. Late hops: Goldings or Challenger. Dry hops: Goldings or Challenger. IBU: 37. EBC: 23. Source: RP/MO.

**Willie Warmer**: OG: 1060. Malt: 35% Halcyon pale malt, 35% Maris Otter pale malt, 5% Roast barley, 25% Sugar. Hops: Challenger, optional Omega. Late hops: Goldings or Challenger, Omega. IBU: 40. EBC: 100. Source: RP/MO.

## . *Cuckmere Haven Brewery, Cuckmere Haven*

**Cuckmere Best**: OG: 1041-2. Malt: 96% Halcyon or Maris Otter pale malt, 4% Crystal malt, 15% Invert sugar. Hops: Bramling Cross. Late hops: Fuggles, Goldings. Dry hops: Goldings. Source: RP.

**Saxon King Stout**: OG: 1042-4. Malt: 87.5% Halcyon pale malt, 12.5% Roast barley or 75% Halcyon or Maris Otter pale malt, 12.5% Roast barley, 12% Amber malt, Invert sugar. Hops: Challenger. Late hops: Fuggles. Source: RP.

**Gentleman's Gold**: OG: 1044-6. Malt: 90% Halcyon pale malt, 10% Amber malt or Caramalt. Hops: Fuggles, Goldings. Dry hops: Yes. Source: RP4/5.

**Guv'nor**: OG: 1046-8. Malt: 85% Halcyon or Maris Otter pale malt, 3.5% Crystal malt, 11.5% Amber malt or Caramalt. Hops: Fuggles, Goldings. Dry hops: Goldings. Source: RP4/5.

**Golden Peace**: OG: 1056. Malt: Halcyon or Maris Otter pale malt, Amber malt, Crystal malt, Wheat malt, Invert sugar. Hops: Bramling Cross, Challenger. Late hops: Goldings. Dry hops: Goldings. Source: RP5.

**Fuggl'olmullable**: OG: 1067. Malt: 87.5% Halcyon and Maris Otter pale malt, 12.5% Amber malt, 2.5% Crystal malt, 3.5% Chocolate malt, Invert sugar. Hops: Fuggles. Others: Cinnamon, Cloves. Source: RP4/5.

**Velvet Dark Mild / Dark Secret Mild**: OG: 1048. Malt: 75% Halcyon or Maris Otter pale malt, 25% Crystal malt, Invert sugar. Hops: Fuggles, Goldings. Source: RP4/5.

### . Daleside Brewery, Harrogate

**Monkman's Slaughter**: OG: 1060. Malt: Pale malt, Crystal malt. Hops: Challenger, Goldings. Source: RP5.

### . Dark Star, Haywards Heath

**Hophead**: ABV: 3.8%. Hops: Cascade. Source: W.

**Espresso**: ABV: 4.2%. Other: Coffee beans. Source: WB.

**Porter** (b-c): ABV: 5.5%. Malt: Maris Otter pale malt, Crystal malt, Brown malt, Black malt, Caramalt. Hops: Target, Styrian Goldings. Source: JE5.

**Critical Mass** (b-c): ABV: 7.4%. Malt: Maris Otter pale malt, Munich malt, Crystal malt, Black malt, Chocolate malt, Roast barley. Hops: Hallertau, Perle. Source: JE5.

### . Darwin, Crook

**Richmond Ale** (b-c): ABV: 4.5-4.8%. Malt: Pale malt, Crystal malt, Brown malt, Black malt. Hops: Fuggles, Goldings. Source: JE1/2/3/4/5/6.

**Hammond's Porter** (b-c): ABV: 4.7%. Malt: Pale malt, Crystal malt, Black malt, Maize, Sugar. Hops: Fuggles. Source: JE4/5.

**Saint's Sinner** (b-c): ABV: 5%. Malt: Pale malt, Black malt, Roast barley. Hops: Fuggles, Challenger. Source: JE1

**Extinction Ale** (b-c): ABV: 8.2-8.3%. Malt: Pale malt, Crystal malt. Hops: Fuggles, Goldings. Source: JE2/3/5.

**Hammond's Stingo** (b-c): ABV: 10%. Malt: Pale malt, Maize, Black malt, Sugar. Hops: Fuggles. Source: JE4/5.

### . Davenports Brewery, Birmingham

**Best Mild Ale**: OG: 1035. Malt: 79% Maris Otter pale malt, Crystal malt, Chocolate malt, Caramel. Hops: Goldings, Northdown, Challenger, Target. Source: RP1.

**Wem Best Bitter**: OG: 1037.5. Malt: 77% Maris Otter pale malt, Crystal malt, Barley syrup, Cane sugar. Hops: Fuggles, Goldings. Source: RP1.

**Traditional Bitter**: OG: 1038.5. Malt: 72% Maris Otter pale malt, Crystal malt, Barley syrup, Cane sugar. Hops: Goldings, Northdown, Challenger, Target. Dry hops: Styrian Goldings. Source: RP1. Malt: Pale malt, Crystal malt, Wheat malt, Sugar. Hops: Goldings, Fuggles. Late hops: Goldings. Dry hops: Goldings. Source: DL. Note: See **Davenports Original**, Highgate Brewery.

**Wem Special Bitter**: OG: 1042.5. Malt: 80% Maris Otter pale malt, Crystal malt, Barley syrup, Cane sugar. Hops: Fuggles, Goldings, others. Source: RP1.

### Dent Brewery, Dent

**Bitter**: OG: 1036. Malt: 95% Halcyon pale malt, 4.5% Crystal malt, 0.5% Roast barley. Hops: Northdown optional Fuggles. Source: RP.

**Ramsbottom**: OG: 1044. Malt: 90% Halcyon pale malt, 9% Crystal malt, 1% Roast barley. Hops: Northdown optional Fuggles. Source: RP/JHF.

**T'Owd Tup**: OG: 1055-8. Malt: 86% Halcyon pale malt, 9.5% Crystal malt, 4.5% Roast barley. Hops: Northdown. Source: RP3/4/5.

### Doghouse, Redruth

**Biter** (b-c): ABV: 4%. Malt: Optic pale malt, Crystal malt. Hops: Northdown, Styrian Goldings. Source: JE5/6.

**Dozey Dawg** (b-c): ABV: 4.4%. Malt: Optic pale malt, Crystal malt. Hops: Pilot, Cascade. Source: JE5/6.

**Cornish Corgi** (b-c): ABV: 4.5%. Malt: Optic pale malt, Crystal malt. Hops: Pilot, Styrian Goldings. Source: JE5/6.

**Dogfight** (b-c): ABV: 4.7%. Malt: Optic pale malt, Crystal malt, Chocolate malt, Roast barley. Hops: Pilot, Cascade. Source: JE5/6.

**Staffi Stout** (b-c): ABV: 4.8%. Malt: Optic pale malt, Black malt, Roast barley, optional Crystal malt. Hops: Fuggles, Goldings. Source: JE4/5/6.

**Bow Wow** (b-c): ABV: 5%. Malt: Optic pale malt, Crystal malt, Chocolate malt, Roast barley, optional Torrefied wheat. Hops: Challenger. Source: JE4/5/6.

**Dingo Lager** (b-c): ABV: 5%. Malt: Lager malt. Hops: Hallertau. Source: JE4/5/6.

**Colliewobbles / Christmas Tail** (b-c): ABV: 5.8%. Malt: Optic pale malt, Crystal malt, Chocolate malt, Roast barley, Torrefied wheat. Hops: Fuggles, Goldings. Source: JE5/6.

### Donnington Brewery, Stow-on-the-Wold

**BB**: OG: 1036. Malt: 90% Maris Otter pale malt, 10% Invert sugar. Hops: Goldings or Fuggles. Source: RP.

**XXX**: OG: 1035-6. Malt: 85-90% Maris Otter pale malt, 10% Invert sugar, 0-5% Caramel. Hops: Goldings or Fuggles. Source: RP.

**SBA**: OG: 1042. Malt: 90% Maris Otter pale malt, 10% Invert sugar. Hops: Fuggles. IBU: 30-2. EBC: 18. Source: RP2/3/4/5. OG: 1040. Malt: Pale malt, Flaked barley, Roast barley, Sugar. Hops: Goldings, Fuggles. Late hops: Goldings. Dry hops: Goldings. Source: DL.

### Dorset Brewing Company, Weymouth. Www.dbcales.com

**Harbour Master**: ABV: 3.6%. Malt: Malt: Maris Otter pale malt. Hops: Bramling Cross, First Gold. Source: Web.

**Best**: ABV: 4.0%. Malt: Maris Otter pale malt. Hops: Styrian Goldings, Cascade. Source: Web.

**Chesil**: ABV: 4.1%. Malt: Optic lager malt, Cara Gold malt. Hops: Sovereign, Lubelski. Source: Web.

**Coastguard**: ABV: 4.1%. Malt: Maris Otter pale malt, Wheat malt. Hops: First Gold, Ammonite. Source: Web.

**Weymouth JD 1742** (b-c): ABV: 4.2%. Malt: Maris Otter pale malt. Hops: Challenger, Mount Hood. Source: JE5/Web.

**Steam Beer** (b-c): ABV: 4.5%. Malt: Lager malt, Black malt, Wheat malt. Hops: Cascade. Source: JE5.

**Steam**: ABV: 4.5%. Malt: Maris Otter pale malt, Chocolate malt. Hops: Centennial, Chinook. Source: Web.

**Ammonite**: ABV: 4.5%. Malt: Maris Otter pale malt. Hops: Magnum, Perle, First Gold. Source: Web.

**Portland Porter**: ABV: 4.7%. Malt: Maris Otter pale malt, Crystal malt, Chocolate malt, Black malt. Hops: Magnum, Goldings. Source: Web.

**Jurassic** (b-c): ABV: 4.7%. Malt: Pale malt, Crystal malt. Hops: Hallertau, Saaz. Source: JE5. Hops: Hallertau. Source: W.

**Durdle Moor**: ABV: 5%. Malt: Maris Otter pale malt, Wheat malt. Hops: Cascade, Brewers Gold, Fuggles. Source: JE5/Web.

**Silent Knight** (b-c): ABV: 5.9%. Malt: Maris Otter pale malt, Wheat malt, Chocolate malt. Hops: Bramling Cross. Source: JE5.

**Silent Knight**: ABV: 5.9%. Malt: Maris Otter pale malt, Wheat malt. Hops: Bramling Cross. Source: Web.

Note: Formerly Quay Brewery.

## . *Dorsetshire Brewery Co., Sherbourne*

**Dorset Ale**: OG: 1065. Malt: Pale malt. Hops: Fuggles. Notes: Recipe from 1891. Source: DP.

## . *Dow Bridge, Lutterworth*

**Bonum Mild** (b-c): 3.6%. Malt: Maris Otter pale malt, Crystal malt, Chocolate malt, Black malt. Hops: Goldings, Fuggles. Source: JE6.

**Ratae'd** (b-c): 4.3%. Malt: Maris Otter pale malt, Crystal malt. Hops: Goldings, Fuggles. Source: JE6.

**Fosse** (b-c): 4.8%. Malt: Maris Otter pale malt, Crystal malt, Chocolate malt. Hops: Goldings, Fuggles. Source: JE6.

### . *Downton Brewery Company, Downton*

**Chimera India Pale Ale** (b-c): 7%. Malt: Pale malt, Maize. Hops: Goldings, Pioneer. Source: JE6.

### . *Dunn Plowman, Kington*

**Old Jake** (b-c): ABV: 4.8%. Malt: Maris Otter pale malt, Wheat malt, Flaked barley, Roast barley. Hops: Fuggles, Goldings. Source: JE3/4/5.

**Golden Haze** (b-c): ABV: 5%. Malt: Maris Otter pale malt, Wheat malt. Hops: First Gold. Others: Coriander, Orange peel. Source: JE5.

**Kyneton Ale** (b-c): ABV: 5%. Malt: Maris Otter pale malt, Crystal malt, Black malt/Wheat malt. Hops: Fuggles, Goldings. Source: JE3/5.

**Crooked Furrow** (b-c): ABV: 6.5%. Malt: Maris Otter pale malt, Crystal malt, Black malt. Hops: Fuggles, Goldings. Source: JE2/3/4/5.

### . *Durham Brewery, Bowburn*

**Magus**: OG: 1039.5. Malt: 86.5% Halcyon pale malt, 11.2% Wheat malt, 2.3% Crystal malt. Hops: Challenger, Goldings, optional Target, Saaz, Styrian Goldings. Source: RP.

**Celtic**: OG: 1042.5. Malt: 88% Halcyon pale malt, 11% Wheat malt, 1% Roast barley. Hops:. Fuggles, Northdown. Source: RP4/5.

**Cloister** (b-c): ABV: 4.5%. Malt: Maris Otter pale malt, Crystal malt. Hops: Challenger, Target, Columbus, Saaz. Source: JE3/4/5. Malt: Maris Otter pale malt, Lager malt, Wheat malt, Crystal malt. Hops: Cascade, Target, Columbus, Saaz. Source: JE6.

**Graduation** (b-c): ABV: 4.5%. Malt: Pale malt, Lager malt, Wheat malt. Hops: Target, Saaz, Cascade, Styrian Goldings, Goldings. Source: JE4.

**Black Bishop**: OG: 1045. Malt: Pale malt, Oat malt, Roast barley, Black malt, Crystal malt. Hops: Challenger, Target. Source: RP5.

**Bede's Chalice** (b-c): ABV: 4.8%. Malt: Pale malt, Crystal malt. Hops: Target, Goldings. Source: JE3.

**Pagan**: OG: 1049. Malt: 86.5% Halcyon pale malt, 9.3% Wheat malt, 3% Crystal malt, 1.2% Amber malt. Hops: Challenger, Goldings, Fuggles. Source: RP4/5.

**Evensong** (b-c): ABV: 5%. Malt: Maris Otter pale malt, Crystal malt. Hops: Goldings. Source: JE3/4/5. Malt: Maris Otter pale malt, Crystal malt, Amber malt, Munich malt, Wheat malt. Hops: Challenger, Goldings, Fuggles. Source: JE6.

**Black Bishop** (b-c): ABV: 5.5%. Malt: Pale malt, Amber malt, Black malt, Roast barley. Hops: Northdown, Fuggles. Source: JE3.

**Black Abbot** (b-c): ABV: 5.6%. Malt: Maris Otter pale malt, Lager malt, Munich malt, Pale chocolate malt, Black malt, Rye crystal malt, Wheat malt. Hops: Saaz, Northdown. Source: JE4/5.

**Sanctuary**: OG: 1058.5. Malt: 87.9% Halcyon pale malt, 7.3% Wheat malt, 3.3% Crystal malt, 1.5% Roast barley, optional Amber malt. Hops: Challenger/Fuggles, Goldings, Northdown, Target. Source: RP.

**Sanctuary** (b-c): ABV: 6%. Malt: Pale malt, Crystal malt, Caramel. Hops: Challenger, Fuggles, Goldings. Source: JE3.

**St. Cuthbert** (b-c): ABV: 6.5%. Malt: Maris Otter pale malt, Crystal malt. Hops: Challenger, Target, Columbus, Goldings, Saaz. Source: JE3/4/5. Malt: Maris Otter pale malt, Crystal malt, Wheat malt. Hops: Challenger, Target, Columbus, Goldings, Saaz. Source: JE6.

**White Magic** (b-c): ABV: 7%. Malt: Maris Otter pale malt. Hops: Goldings. Source: JE5.

**Benedictus** (b-c): ABV: 8%. Malt: Maris Otter pale malt, Crystal malt, optional Wheat malt. Hops: Goldings, Target, Saaz, Styrian Goldings, optional Columbus. Source: JE3/4/5/6.

**Temptation** (b-c): ABV: 10%. Malt: Maris Otter pale malt, Lager malt, Black malt, Roast barley, Wheat malt. Hops: Target, Goldings. Source: JE4/5. Malt: Maris Otter pale malt, Brown malt, Amber malt, Roast barley, Wheat malt. Hops: Target, Goldings. Source: JE6.

## . *Earl Soham Brewery, Earl Soham*

**Gannet Mild** (b-c): ABV: 3.3%. Malt: Maris Otter pale malt, Crystal malt, Black malt. Hops: Fuggles, Goldings. Source: JE5/6.

**Victoria Bitter** (b-c): ABV: 3.6%. Malt: Maris Otter pale malt. Hops: Fuggles, Goldings, Styrian Goldings. Source: JE4. Malt: Maris Otter pale malt, Crystal malt. Hops: Fuggles, Goldings, WGV. Source: JE5/6.

**Sir Roger's Porter** (b-c): ABV: 4%. Malt: Maris Otter pale malt, Crystal malt, Black malt, Roast barley. Hops: Fuggles, Styrian Goldings, Goldings. Source: JE5/6.

**Gold** (b-c): ABV: 4%. Malt: Maris Otter pale malt, Crystal malt. Hops: Brewers Gold. Source: JE5/6.

**Albert Ale** (b-c): ABV: 4.4%. Malt: Maris Otter pale malt, Crystal malt, Black malt, Roast barley. Hops: WGV, Goldings. Source: JE5/6.

**Empress India Premium Pale Ale** (b-c): ABV: 4.7%. Malt: Maris Otter pale malt, Crystal malt. Hops: WGV, Fuggles, Goldings. Source: JE5.

## . *E&S Elland (Eastwood & Sanders), Elland*

**Beyond the Pale** (b-c): ABV: 4-4.2%. Malt: Maris Otter pale malt, Amber malt, Wheat malt. Hops: Challenger, Centennial, Cascade, First Gold. Source: JE5.

**1872 Porter** (b-c): ABV: 6.5%. Malt: Maris Otter pale malt, Amber malt, Chocolate malt, Brown malt, Muscovado sugar, Molasses. Hops: Goldings, Challenger, First Gold. Source: JE5.

### . *Eldridge Pope & Co., Dorchester*

**Dorchester Bitter**: OG: 1032-3. Malt: Maris Otter pale malt, Pipkin pale malt, Crystal malt, Sugar. Hops: Fuggles, Goldings or Challenger, Northdown. Dry hops: Goldings. IBU: 21. Source: RP.

**Konig Pilsner** (bottled): OG: 1035. Malt: Lager malt, Flaked rice, Sugar. Hops: Hallertau, Goldings. Source: DL.

**Best Bitter**: OG: 1036. Malt: Maris Otter pale malt, Pipkin pale malt, Crystal malt, Sugar. Hops: Fuggles, Goldings or Challenger, Northdown. Dry hops: Goldings. IBU: 25. Source: RP.

**Blackdown Porter**: OG: 1040. Malt: Pipkin pale malt, Roast malt. Hops: Challenger, Northdown. Late hops: Goldings. IBU: 30. EBC: 150. Source: RP.

**Thomas Hardy Country Bitter**: OG: 1041. Malt: Maris Otter pale malt, Pipkin pale malt, Crystal malt, Sugar. Hops: Fuggles, Goldings or Challenger, Northdown. Dry hops: Goldings. IBU: 27. Source: RP.

**Royal Oak**: OG: 1048. Malt: Maris Otter and/or Pipkin pale malt, Crystal malt, Sugar. Hops: Fuggles, Goldings or Challenger, Northdown or Fuggles, Styrian Goldings. Dry hops: Goldings. IBU: 30-35. Source: RP/EBA. Malt: Pale malt, Crystal malt, Flaked barley, Soft dark brown sugar. Hops: Fuggles. Late hops: Goldings. Dry hops: Goldings. Source: DL.

**Goldie Barley Wine**: OG: 1090. Malt: 65% Maris Otter pale malt, 35% Pilsner malt. Hops: 41% Fuggles, 23% Styrian Goldings, 36% Goldings. IBU: 40-50. EBC: 13. Source: EBA/GW.

**Thomas Hardy's Ale** (bottled) OG: 1125. Malt: 100% Pipkin or Maris Otter pale malt, optional Lager malt. Hops: Goldings, Fuggles, Challenger and/or Northdown. Late hops: Styrian Goldings. Dry hops: Styrian Goldings. IBU: 60-75. Source: RP/DL. OG: 1123-1125. Malt: Maris Otter pale malt, Amber malt, Crystal malt, Peat-smoked malt. Hops: Goldings, Northern Brewer. Late hops: Fuggles, Goldings. Dry hops: Fuggles, Goldings. Source: CB.

Notes: After a management buy out, the Eldridge Pope brewery became the Thomas Hardy Brewery in 1997 and then the Thomas Hardy Burtonwood Brewery in 1998. Unfortunately, the brewing of the classic Thomas Hardy's Ale ceased during these changes, but Phoenix Imports bought the brand and it is now brewed by O'Hanlon's. Also see Thomas Hardy Brewery and O'Hanlon's.

## Elgood & Sons, Wisbech

**Cambridge Bitter**: OG: 1035-1037.5. Malt: 88-91% Pipkin or Triumph pale malt, Wheat flour/Torrefied wheat, Flaked maize, Roast barley, Invert sugar. Hops: Fuggles, optional Challenger. IBU: 27-32. EBC: 28-30. Source: RP.

**EB / Bitter**: OG: 1036. Malt: Mild ale malt, Wheat, Flaked maize, Invert sugar, optional Roast barley, Caramel. Hops: Fuggles. Source: RP.

**Black Dog Mild**: OG: 1036.5. Malt: 77-80% Pipkin pale malt, Flaked maize, Torrefied wheat, Roast barley, Invert sugar. Hops: Fuggles. IBU: 25. EBC: 100. Source: RP4/5. Malt: 77% Pale malt, 20% Wheat malt, 4-6% Roast barley, 4-6% Crystal malt, 6% Invert sugar. Source: Cambridge Craft Brewers.

**Feelgood Fresh**: ABV: 3.7%. Hops: Bramling Cross. Source: WB.

**Bicentenary Pageant Ale**: OG: 1043.8. Malt: 85-88% Pipkin pale malt, Crystal malt, Flaked maize, Invert sugar. Hops: Challenger. EBC: 35. Source: RP4/5.

**Golden Newt**: OG: 1044.5. Malt: 80% Pipkin pale malt, Amber malt, Oat malt, Wheat malt, Rye malt. Hops: Fuggles, Challenger. Dry hops: Yes. IBU: 30. EBC: 15-20. Source: RP5.

**GSB / Greyhound Strong Bitter**: OG: 1045-1050.8. Malt: 88-91% Mild ale malt or Triumph pale malt or Pipkin pale malt, Wheat, Flaked maize, Invert sugar, optional Roast barley, optional Caramel. Hops: Fuggles. IBU: 35. EBC: 32-40. Source: RP.

**Barleymead**: OG: 1048.5. Malt: Pipkin pale malt, Crystal malt, 10% Invert sugar. Hops: Challenger. EBC: 20. Source: RP4/5.

**Flag Porter**: OG: 1051-53. Malt: Pale malt, Crystal malt, Brown malt, Chocolate malt. Hops: Goldings. Late hops: Fuggles. Source: CB.

**North Brink Porter**: OG: 1055.8. Malt: 82-88% Pipkin pale malt, Amber malt, Crystal malt, Chocolate malt. Hops: Fuggles. EBC: 100. Source: RP4/5.

**Wenceslas Winter Warmer**: OG: 1075.5. Malt: 88-91% Pipkin pale malt, Torrefied wheat, Flaked maize, Roast barley, Invert sugar. Hops: Fuggles, Challenger. EBC: 50-60. Source: RP4/5.

**Winter Warmer**: OG: 1080. Malt: Mild ale malt, Wheat, Flaked maize, Roast barley, Invert sugar. Hops: Fuggles. Source: RP2/3.

## Elveden, Thetford

**Stout** (b-c): ABV: 5%. Malt: Maris Otter pale malt, Roast barley, Wheat, Molasses. Hops: Boadicea. Source: JE5/6.

**Elveden Ale** (b-c): ABV: 5.2%. Malt: Maris Otter pale malt, Wheat. Hops: Boadicea. Source: JE5/6.

. *English Wines, Tenterden*

**Curious Brew Admiral Porter** (b-c): ABV: 5%. Malt: Pale malt, Crystal malt, Amber malt, Black malt, Chocolate malt. Hops: Admiral, Goldings. Source: JE6.

. *Enville Ales, Stourbridge*

**Bitter**: OG: 1039. Malt: 94% Maris Otter pale malt, 6% Crystal malt, 10% No.1 invert sugar. Hops: Challenger, Goldings. Late hops: Fuggles. Dry hops: Fuggles. IBU: 22. EBC: 22. Source: RP5.

**Mild**: OG: 1044. Malt: 92.5% Maris Otter pale malt, 7.5% Crystal malt, No.1 invert sugar, Dark brown sugar, Caramel. Hops: Challenger, Goldings. Late hops: Challenger, Goldings. Dry hops: Yes. IBU: 24. EBC: 52. Source: RP5.

**Simpkiss Bitter**: OG: 1039. Malt: 81-94% Maris Otter pale malt, 3-6% Crystal malt, 4-5% Wheat malt, 10-12% No.1 invert sugar. Hops: Challenger, Goldings, optional Northdown. Late hops: Fuggles. Dry hops: Fuggles. IBU: 38. EBC: 22. Source: RP.

**Enville Ale**: OG: 1045. Malt: 83-88% Maris Otter or Pipkin pale malt, 0-2% Crystal malt, 0-5% Wheat malt, 10% No.1 invert sugar, optional Honey. Hops: Challenger, Goldings, optional Northdown. Late hops: Saaz or Challenger, Goldings. Dry hops: Saaz. IBU: 21-30. EBC: 15-25. Source: RP.

**Enville Ale** (b-c): ABV: 4.5%. Malt: Maris Otter pale malt, Honey. Hops: Challenger, Goldings. Source: JE3/4.

**IPA**: OG: 1048. Malt: 100% Maris Otter pale malt, 10% Wheat malt, Hops: Challenger, Goldings. Late hops: Challenger, Goldings. Dry hops: Yes. IBU: 25. EBC: 25. Source: RP5.

**Gothic Ale**: OG: 1052. Malt: 77% Pipkin pale malt, 13% Dark malt, 10% Roast barley or 79-90% Maris Otter pale malt, 8-10% Black malt, 3-5% Wheat malt, 10% Sugar. Hops: Challenger, optional Goldings. IBU: 30-35. Source: RP.

**Gothic Ale** (b-c): ABV: 5.2%. Malt: Maris Otter pale malt, Crystal malt, Black malt, Wheat malt, Honey. Hops: Challenger, Fuggles. Source: JE3/4.

. *Everards Brewery, Leicester*

**Burton Mild/Mild**: OG: 1033. Malt: 92% Maris Otter pale malt, Flaked maize, Caramel. Hops: Fuggles, Challenger, Goldings. Dry hops: Yes. IBU: 15. EBC: 75. Source: RP1/2.

**Mild**: OG: 1036. Malt: 92% Maris Otter pale malt and Crystal malt, Torrefied wheat. Hops: Fuggles, Challenger. Late hops: Goldings. IBU: 15. EBC: 75. Source: RP3/4.

**Beacon Bitter**: OG: 1036. Malt: 87-91% Maris Otter pale malt and Crystal malt, Torrefied wheat, Cane sugar or Wheat syrup. Hops: Fuggles, Challenger. Late hops: Goldings. Dry hops: Goldings. IBU: 25. EBC: 20. Source: RP.

**Tiger Best Bitter**: OG: 1041. Malt: 88% Maris Otter pale malt and Crystal malt, Wheat syrup, Flaked maize or Torrefied wheat. Hops: Fuggles, Challenger. Late hops: Goldings. Dry hops: Goldings. IBU: 26. EBC: 25. Source: RP.

**Old Original**: OG: 1050. Malt: 95% Maris Otter pale malt and Crystal malt, Flaked maize or Torrefied wheat, Cane sugar or Wheat syrup. Hops: Fuggles, Challenger. Late hops: Goldings. Dry hops: Goldings. IBU: 28. EBC: 31. Source: RP.

**Daredevil**: OG: 1068. Malt: 72% Maris Otter pale malt and Crystal malt, Wheat syrup. Hops: Fuggles, Challenger. Late hops: Goldings. IBU: 40. EBC: 44. Source: RP4/5.

**Old Bill**: OG: 1070. Malt: 71% Maris Otter pale malt and Crystal malt, Cane sugar or Wheat syrup. Hops: Challenger, Fuggles. Late hops: Goldings. IBU: 33. EBC: 44. Source: RP.

### . *Sydney Evershed, Burton-upon-Trent*

**2**: OG: 1080. Malt: Pale malt, No.2 invert sugar. Hops: Goldings, Cluster. Yeast: White Labs WLP026. Notes: Burton ale recipe from 1892. IBU: 92. SRM: 9. Source: VB.

### . *Evesham Brewery, Evesham*

**Asum Ale**: OG: 1038. Malt: 95% Maris Otter pale malt, Crystal malt, Chocolate malt, small % Wheat malt. Hops: Challenger, Fuggles. Dry hops: Yes. Source: RP4/5.

**Asum Gold**: OG: 1050. Malt: Maris Otter pale malt, Crystal malt, Chocolate malt, small % Wheat malt. Hops: Challenger, Fuggles. Source: RP4/5.

### . *Exe Valley Brewery, Exeter*

**Exe Valley Bitter**: OG: 1038-9. Malt: 95% Pale malt, 5% Crystal malt. Hops: Goldings, Fuggles / Willamette. Source: RP/GW.

**Devon Summer**: OG: 1039. Malt: 100% Pipkin pale malt. Hops: Fuggles, Target. Source: RP5.

**Hope** (b-c): ABV: 4.3%. Malt: Optic pale malt. Hops: Challenger, Goldings. Source: JE4.

**Spring Beer**: OG: 1044. Malt: 100% Pipkin pale malt. Hops: Willamette, Goldings or Fuggles, Target. Late hops: Yes. Source: RP.

**Autumn Glory**: OG: 1045. Malt: 93% Pipkin pale malt, 7% Crystal malt. Hops: Fuggles, Goldings. Source: RP5.

**Devon Glory**: OG: 1047. Malt: 95% Pale malt, 5% Roast barley. Hops: Fuggles. Source: RP2. Malt: 95% Pipkin pale malt, 5% Crystal malt. Hops: Goldings, Fuggles / Willamette. Source: RP3/5.

**Devon Glory** (b-c): ABV: 4.7%. Malt: Optic pale malt, Crystal malt, Chocolate malt. Hops: Fuggles, Goldings, Challenger. Source: JE4/5. Malt: Optic pale malt, Crystal malt, Wheat malt, Chocolate malt. Hops: Challenger. Source: JE6.

**Exeter Old Bitter**: OG: 1047. Malt: 95% Pipkin pale malt, 5% Crystal malt. Hops: Fuggles, Goldings. Dry hops: Yes. Source: RP5.

**Dob's Best Bitter**: OG: 1049. Malt: 95% Pipkin pale malt, 5% Crystal malt. Hops: Goldings, Willamette/Fuggles. Source: RP.

**Winter Glow**: OG: 1058. Malt: 94% Pipkin pale malt, 5% Crystal malt, 1% Chocolate malt. Hops: Fuggles, Goldings. Source: RP5.

Note: This was previously the Barron's Brewery (qv).

### . *Exmoor Ales, Wiveliscombe*

**Exmoor Ale**: OG: 1039. Malt: Pale malt, Crystal malt. Hops: Challenger, Fuggles, Goldings. IBU: 40. EBC: 30. Source: RP1/2/3/4/5.

**Exmoor Dark**: OG: 1042. Malt: Pale malt, Crystal malt. Hops: Challenger, Fuggles, Goldings. Dry hops: Yes. Source: RP1.

**Exmoor Gold**: OG: 1045. Malt: 100% Pale malt. Hops: Challenger, Fuggles, Goldings. Source: RP1/2/3/4/5/GW. Hops: Goldings, Fuggles. Source: W.

**Exmoor Hart**: OG: 1049. Malt: Pale malt, Crystal malt, Chocolate malt. Hops: Challenger, Fuggles. Late hops: Goldings. IBU: 35. EBC: 40. Source: RP5.

**Exmoor Stag**: OG: 1050. Malt: Pale malt, Crystal malt. Hops: Challenger, Fuggles, Goldings. IBU: 35. EBC: 35. Source: RP2/3/4/5.

**Exmoor Beast**: OG: 1066. Malt: Pale malt, Crystal malt, Chocolate malt. Hops: Challenger, Fuggles, Goldings. IBU: 40. EBC: 120. Source: RP3/4/5. Hops: Challenger, Goldings. Source: W.

### . *Fallen Angel, Battle*

**St. Patrick's Irish Stout** (b-c): ABV: 3.1%. Malt: Pale malt, Roast barley, Chocolate malt. Source: JE6.

### . *Farmer's Ales, Maldon Brewing Company, Maldon*

**A Drop of Nelson's Blood** (b-c): ABV: 3.8%. Malt: Maris Otter pale malt, Crystal malt, Black malt. Hops: Cascade, First Gold. Other: Brandy. Source: JE6.

**Sweet Farmer's Ale** (b-c): ABV: 4%. Malt: Maris Otter pale malt, Crystal malt, Chocolate malt, Honey. Hops: Fuggles. Source: JE6.

**The Hotel Porter** (b-c): ABV: 4.1%. Malt: Maris Otter pale malt, Roast barley, Rolled oats. Hops: Challenger, Goldings. Source: JE6.

**Puck's Folly** (b-c): ABV: 4.2%. Malt: Lager malt. Hops: Goldings. Source: JE6.

**Edward Bright Stout** (b-c): ABV: 4.8%. Malt: Maris Otter pale malt, Chocolate malt. Hops: Goldings. Source: JE6.

### Featherstone Brewery, Leicester

**Hows Howler**: OG: 1036. Malt: Maris Otter pale malt, Crystal malt, Wheat malt. Hops: Challenger, Willamette. Source: RP4/5.

**Stout**: OG: 1037. Malt: 50% Pale malt, 50% Wheat malt, Black malt. Hops: Challenger. Source: RP4/5.

**Best Bitter**: OG: 1042. Malt: Maris Otter pale malt, Crystal malt, Wheat malt. Hops: Willamette. Source: RP4/5.

**Stage Ale**: OG: 1045. Malt: Maris Otter pale malt, 20% Crystal malt, Wheat malt. Hops: 50% Challenger, 50% Willamette. Source: RP4/5.

**Vulcan Bitter**: OG: 1049. Malt: Maris Otter pale malt, Wheat malt. Hops: Willamette. Source: RP4/5.

**Kingstone Strong**: OG: 1058. Malt: Maris Otter pale malt, Crystal malt, Wheat malt, Chocolate malt. Hops: Challenger, Willamette. Source: RP4/5.

### Felstar, Felsted

**Crix Gold** (b-c): ABV: 4%. Malt: Lager malt, Caramalt, Wheat malt. Hops: First Gold, Jenny, Brewers Gold. Source: JE4/5/6.

**Hops & Glory** (b-c): ABV: 4%. Malt: Maris Otter pale malt, Crystal malt, Chocolate malt, Wheat malt. Hops: Fuggles, Brewers Gold. Source: JE4/5/6.

**Chick Chat** (b-c): ABV: 4.1%. Malt: Maris Otter and Pearl pale malt, Chocolate malt, Torrefied wheat. Hops: Fuggles, Bramling Cross. Source: JE5/6.

**Grand Crix** (b-c): ABV: 4.1%. Malt: Maris Otter pale malt, Crystal malt, Caramalt, Barley. Hops: Bramling Cross, Ruth. Other: Root ginger, Coriander. Source: JE4/5/6.

**Lord Kulmbach** (b-c): ABV: 4.4%. Malt: Maris Otter pale malt, Lager malt, Crystal malt, Black malt, Wheat malt. Hops: Fuggles, Brewers Gold. Source: JE4/5/6.

**Hoppin' Hen** (b-c): ABV: 4.5%. Malt: Maris Otter and Pearl pale malt, Crystal malt, Roast barley, Wheat malt. Hops: First Gold, Jenny, Hersbrücker. Source: JE4/5/6.

**Old Crix** (b-c): ABV: 4.5%. Malt: Maris Otter pale malt, Crystal malt, Chocolate malt, Wheat malt. Hops: First Gold, Perle. Dry hops: Perle. Source: JE4/5/6.

**Wheat** (b-c): ABV: 4.8%. Malt: Pearl pale malt, Crystal malt, Wheat malt, Roast barley. Hops: Mount Hood. Source: JE5/6.

**Good Knight** (b-c): ABV: 5%. Malt: Maris Otter pale malt, Crystal malt, Caramalt, Roast barley, Chocolate malt. Hops: Bramling Cross, First Gold, Perle. Source: JE4/5/6.

**Peckin' Order** (b-c): ABV: 5%. Malt: Lager malt, Crystal malt, Wheat malt. Hops: Perle, Brewers Gold. Source: JE4/5/6.

**Peckin' Python** (b-c): ABV: 5%. Malt: Lager malt, Crystal malt, Wheat malt. Hops: Perle, Brewers Gold. Other: Nettles. Source: JE6.

**Red Wheat Lager** (b-c): ABV: 5%. Malt: 60% Lager malt, 40% Wheat malt, Maple syrup. Hops: Horizon. Late hops: Hersbrücker. Source: JE6.

**Roosters Rest** (b-c): ABV: 5%. Malt: Maris Otter pale malt, Caramalt, Torrefied wheat, Torrefied barley. Hops: Bramling Cross, Jenny, Hersbrücker. Source: JE4/5.

**Jet-Lager** (b-c): ABV: 5.2%. Malt: Lager malt, Chocolate malt, Crystal malt, Invert sugar. Hops: Brewers Gold. Dry hops: Mount Hood. Source: JE6.

**Dark Wheat** (b-c): ABV: 5.4%. Malt: Pearl pale malt, Wheat malt, Black malt, Chocolate wheat malt. Hops: Mount Hood. Source: JE5/6.

**Lord Essex** (b-c): ABV: 5.4%. Malt: Maris Otter pale malt, Caramalt, Wheat chocolate malt, Roast barley. Hops: Mount Hood, Phoenix. Source: JE5/6.

**Haunted Hen** (b-c): ABV: 6%. Malt: Maris Otter pale malt, Caramalt, Chocolate malt, Wheat chocolate malt, Torrefied wheat. Hops: Goldings, Jenny, Hersbrücker. Source: JE4/5/6.

**Howlin' Hen** (b-c): ABV: 6.5%. Malt: Maris Otter and Pearl pale malt, Wheat malt, Roast barley. Hops: Goldings, Jenny, Hersbrücker. Source: JE5/6.

## . *Fenland, Chatteris/Little Downham*

**St. Audrey's Ale** (b-c): ABV: 3.9%. Malt: Maris Otter pale malt, Crystal malt. Hops: Fuggles, First Gold. Source: JE6.

**Babylon Banks** (b-c): ABV: 4.1%. Malt: Maris Otter pale malt, Munich malt, Chocolate malt, Black malt. Hops: Pilot, Goldings. Source: JE6.

**Osier Cutter** (b-c): ABV: 4.2%. Malt: Maris Otter pale malt, Lager malt. Hops: Challenger, Styrian Goldings. Source: JE6.

**Smokestack Lightning** (b-c): ABV: 4.2%. Malt: Maris Otter pale malt, Crystal malt, Caramalt, Black malt, Chocolate malt. Hops: First Gold, Goldings, Fuggles. Source: JE6.

**Sparkling Wit** (b-c): ABV: 4.5%. Malt: Maris Otter pale malt, Wheat malt, Oat malt, Honey. Hops: First Gold. Others: Grains of Paradise, Coriander. Source: JE1/2. Malt: Maris Otter pale malt, Wheat malt, Honey. Hops: First Gold. Others: Coriander. Source: JE6.

**Doctor's Orders** (b-c): ABV: 5%. Malt: Maris Otter pale malt, Crystal malt, Caramalt. Hops: First Gold, optional Challenger. Source: JE1/2/6.

## Flagship Brewery, Chatham

**Capstan**: OG: 1038. Malt: 87% Maris Otter pale malt, 7.5% Crystal malt, 5% Wheat malt, Chocolate malt, Roast barley. Hops: Fuggles, WGV. Source: RP5.

**Ensign Ale**: OG: 1042. Malt: 89% Maris Otter pale malt, 4% Crystal malt, 6.5% Wheat malt, Chocolate malt, Roast barley. Hops: Fuggles, WGV. Source: RP5.

**Spring Pride**: OG: 1042. Malt: 82% Maris Otter pale malt, 10.4% Crystal malt, 7% Wheat malt, Chocolate malt, Roast barley. Hops: Fuggles. Source: RP5.

**Friggin in the Riggin**: OG: 1045. Malt: 83% Maris Otter pale malt, 9.5% Crystal malt, 6.5% Wheat malt, Chocolate malt, Roast barley. Hops: Fuggles, WGV, Progress. Source: RP5.

**Nelson's Blood**: OG: 1045. Malt: 81% Maris Otter pale malt, 13.5% Crystal malt, 5.4% Wheat malt, Chocolate malt. Hops: Fuggles, WGV, Progress. Source: RP5.

**Crow's Nest Ale**: OG: 1048. Malt: 83% Maris Otter pale malt, 9.5% Crystal malt, 6.5% Wheat malt, Chocolate malt, Roast barley. Hops: Fuggles, WGV, Progress. Source: RP4.

**Futtock**: OG: 1050. Malt: 77% Maris Otter pale malt, 14% Crystal malt, 8.5% Wheat malt, Chocolate malt, Roast barley. Hops: Fuggles, WGV, Progress. Source: RP5.

**Gangplank Ale**: OG: 1055. Malt: 81% Maris Otter pale malt, 2.5% Chocolate malt, 13.5% Crystal malt, 2.5% Wheat malt, Roast barley. Hops: Fuggles, WGV, Progress. Source: RP5.

## Flower and Sons, Stratford-on-Avon

**XXX**: OG: 1032. Malt: 82.14% Pale malt, 7.14% No.3 invert sugar, 7.14% Lactose, 3.57% Malt extract. Hops: 100% Fuggles. Yeast: White Labs WLP007. IBU: 22. SRM: 24. Notes: Mild recipe from 1955. Source: SUABP.

**BX (Brownex)**: OG: 1034. Malt: 79.25% Pale malt, 3.77% Crystal 60L malt, 7.55% No.3 invert sugar, 7.55% Lactose, 1.89% Malt extract. Hops: 80% Fuggles, 20% Goldings. Yeast: White Labs WLP007. IBU: 19. SRM: 23. Notes: Brown ale recipe from 1955. Source: SUABP.

**IPA**: OG: 1034. Malt: 93.32% Pale malt, 5.01% No.1 invert sugar, 1.67% Malt extract. Hops: 100% Goldings. Yeast: White Labs WLP007. IBU: 36. SRM: 6. Notes: Recipe from 1955. Source: SUABP.

**Stout**: OG: 1040. Malt: 59.39% Pale malt, 3.73% Crystal 60L malt, 7.58% Wheat malt, 7.58% Black malt, 7.58% No.3 invert sugar, 11.31% Lactose, 2.83% Malt extract. Hops: 100% Fuggles. Yeast: White Labs WLP007. IBU: 35. SRM: 75. Notes: Recipe from 1955. Source: SUABP.

**OB (Original Bitter)**: OG: 1043. Malt: 92.11% Pale malt, 5,26% No.1 invert sugar, 2.63% Malt extract. Hops: 100% Goldings. Yeast: White Labs WLP007. IBU: 41. SRM: 7. Notes: Bitter recipe from 1955. Source: SUABP.

**Christmas Porter**: OG: 1066. Malt: Pale malt, Brown malt, Black malt, White sugar. Hops: Fuggles. Notes: Recipe from 1872. Source: DP.

**SA (Shakespeare Ale)**: OG: 1075. Malt: 77.64% Pale malt, 4.79% Crystal 60L malt, 4.79% No.3 invert sugar, 12.78% Malt extract. Hops: 33.3% Fuggles, 66.7% Goldings. Yeast: White Labs WLP007. IBU: 68. SRM: 21. Notes: Strong Ale recipe from 1955. Source: SUABP.

**XXX March Ale**: OG: 1123. Malt: Pale malt, White sugar. Hops: Fuggles. Notes: Recipe from 1872. Source: DP.

### . *Flying Firkin (Dent Brewery)*

**Aviator**: OG: 1038. Malt: 85% Halcyon pale malt, 10% Crystal malt, 5% Wheat malt. Hops: Northdown. Late hops: Styrian Goldings. Source: RP5.

**Kamikaze**: OG: 1048. Malt: 80% Halcyon pale malt, 10% Caramalt, 10% Wheat malt. Hops: Northdown, Fuggles. Late hops: Styrian Goldings. Source: RP5/JHF.

### . *Fox, Heacham*

**Perfick** (b-c): ABV: 3.7%. Malt: Maris Otter pale malt, Pale chocolate malt. Hops: First Gold, Bramling Cross, Goldings. Others: Vanilla extract. Source: JE5.

**Branthill Best** (b-c): ABV: 3.8%. Malt: Maris Otter pale malt, Amber malt, Pale chocolate malt, Torrefied wheat. Hops: Phoenix, Cascade, First Gold. Source: JE5/6.

**Drop of Real Norfolk** (b-c): ABV: 3.8%. Malt: Maris Otter pale malt, Torrefied wheat. Hops: Styrian Goldings, Fuggles. Source: JE6.

**Heacham Gold** (b-c): ABV: 3.9%. Malt: Lager malt, Wheat malt. Hops: Cascade, Phoenix, First Gold. Source: JE5/6.

**Nina's Mild** (b-c): ABV: 3.9%. Malt: Maris Otter pale malt, Crystal malt, Black malt, Chocolate malt, Torrefied wheat. Hops: Challenger, Fuggles. Source: JE6.

**LJB** (b-c): ABV: 4%. Malt: Maris Otter pale malt, Crystal malt, Chocolate malt. Hops: Challenger, Fuggles, Target. Source: JE5/6.

**Red Knocker** (b-c): ABV: 4.2%. Malt: Maris Otter pale malt, Crystal malt. Hops: First Gold, Cascade, Fuggles. Source: JE5/6.

**Branthill Norfolk Stout** (b-c): ABV: 4.3%. Malt: Maris Otter pale malt, Torrefied wheat. Hops: Bramling Cross, Fuggles. Source: JE6.

**Branthill Light** (b-c): ABV: 4.3%. Malt: Maris Otter pale malt, Torrefied wheat. Hops: Challenger, Bramling Cross, Cascade. Source: JE5.

**Cerberus Norfolk Stout** (b-c): ABV: 4.5%. Malt: Maris Otter pale malt, Crystal malt, Torrefied wheat, Wheat, Roast barley. Hops: Fuggles. Source: JE5/6.

**Peddars Sway** (b-c): ABV: 5%. Malt: Maris Otter pale malt, Crystal malt, Pale chocolate malt. Hops: Challenger, Fuggles, Target. Source: JE5.

**Heacham Kriek** (b-c): ABV: 5.1%. Malt: Maris Otter pale malt, Crystal malt, Chocolate malt, Black malt. Hops: Target, Bramling Cross, Fuggles, Cascade. Others: Cherries. Source: JE6.

**Nelson's Blood** (b-c): ABV: 5.1%. Malt: Maris Otter pale malt, Crystal malt, Black malt, Chocolate malt. Hops: Target, Bramling Cross, Fuggles, Cascade. Others: Cloves, Nelson's Blood rum. Source: JE6.

**IPA** (b-c): ABV: 5.2%. Malt: Maris Otter pale malt, Crystal malt. Hops: Target, First Gold. Source: JE5/6.

**Punt Gun** (b-c): ABV: 5.9%. Malt: Maris Otter pale malt, Crystal malt, Black malt, Torrefied wheat. Hops: Fuggles, Bramling Cross. Source: JE5/6.

### *Freeminer Brewery, Coleford / Cinderford*

**Bitter**: OG: 1038. Malt: Maris Otter pale malt, Crystal malt, Wheat malt. Hops: Fuggles, Goldings. IBU: 30. Source: RP3/4/5.

**Bitter** (b-c): ABV: 4%. Malt: Maris Otter or Optic pale malt, Crystal malt. Hops: Goldings, Fuggles. Source: JE1/2/3/4.

**Waterloo** (b-c): ABV: 4%. Malt: Maris Otter or Optic pale malt, Crystal malt. Hops: Cascade, First Gold, Goldings. Source: JE3/5/6.

**Swift & Bold**: ABV: 4.5%. Hops: Fuggles, Goldings. Late hops: First Gold. Source: WB.

**Speculation Ale**: OG: 1047. Malt: Maris Otter pale malt, Crystal malt, Chocolate malt, Roast barley. Hops: Fuggles, Goldings. Dry hops: Yes. IBU: 40. Source: RP4/5.

**Speculation Ale** (b-c): ABV: 4.7%. Malt: Maris Otter or Optic pale malt, Crystal malt, Chocolate malt. Hops: Fuggles, Goldings. Source: JE1/2/3/4/5/6.

**Gold Miner** (b-c): ABV: 5%. Malt: Optic pale malt, Pale crystal malt. Hops: First Gold. Source: JE4/5/6.

**Shakemantle Ginger Ale** (b-c): ABV: 5%. Malt: Maris Otter or Optic pale malt, optional Wheat malt. Hops: Goldings. Others: Ginger. Source: JE1/2/3/4. OG: 1050-51. Malt: Maris Otter Pale malt, Wheat malt. Hops: Fuggles. Late hops: Goldings. Others. Ginger. Source: BC.

**Morrisons The Best** (b-c): ABV: 6%. Malt: Optic pale malt, other malts. Hops: First Gold, Fuggles, Goldings. Source: JE6.

**Trafalgar IPA** (b-c): ABV: 6%. Malt: Maris Otter or Optic pale malt, Crystal malt. Hops: Goldings. Source: JE1/2/3/4/5/6.

**Deep Shaft Stout**: OG: 1060. Malt: Maris Otter pale malt, Oat malt, Roast barley. Hops: Fuggles, Goldings. Dry hops: Yes. IBU: 45-50. Source: RP4/5. OG: 1062-64. Malt: Maris Otter pale malt, Wheat malt, Roast barley, Flaked oats. Hops: Fuggles. Late hops: Goldings. Source: BC.

**Deep Shaft Stout** (b-c): ABV: 6.2%. Malt: Maris Otter or Optic pale malt, Wheat malt, Roast barley, Oat malt. Hops: Fuggles. Source: JE1/2/3/4.

### . *Fremlins, Faversham*

**Bitter**: OG: 1035. Malt: 70% Pale malt, 4% Crystal malt, 12% Torrefied wheat, 14% Sugar. Hops: Hop extract. Dry hops: Styrian Goldings. Source: RP1.

**Pompey Royal**: OG: 1043. Malt: 67.5% Pale malt, 7.5% Crystal malt, 12.5% Torrefied wheat, 12.5% Sugar. Hops: Hop extract, Styrian Goldings. Dry hops: Styrian Goldings. Source: RP1.

**ISPA**: OG: 1075. Malt: Pale malt, White sugar, Demerara sugar. Hops: Fuggles. Late hops: Yes. Notes: Recipe from 1876. Source: DP.

### . *Frog & Parrot, Sheffield*

**Roger & Out** (b-c): ABV: 12.5%. Malt: Malt extract. Hops: Challenger, Goldings, Styrian Goldings. Source: JE1/2/3/4/5. Notes: When I lived in Sheffield I visited the Frog & Parrot on several occasions. The draft version of this beer was available in one-third pints and you received a certificate for each glass you had until you'd had a full pint. I collected several sets of such certificates and always remember noticing the effects of this powerful brew after the third glass, but then upon switching to more normal beer I would actually apparently sober up. I can only assume that this rather odd effect was because I was getting more water into my system.

### . *Frog Island Brewery, Northampton*

**Best Bitter**: OG: 1040. Malt: 91% Maris Otter pale malt, 6% Crystal malt, 3% Wheat malt. Hops: Target. Late hops: Fuggles. Dry hops: Fuggles. Source: RP4/5.

**Shoemaker**: OG: 1044. Malt: 88% Maris Otter pale malt, 10% Crystal malt, 2% Wheat malt. Hops: Target. Late hops: Cascade. Dry hops: Cascade. Source: RP5/JHF.

**Natterjack** (b-c): ABV: 4.8%. Malt: Maris Otter pale malt, Wheat malt. Hops: Target, Goldings. Source: JE3/4/5/6.

**Natterjack**: OG: 1049. Malt: 93-4% Maris Otter pale malt, 6-7% Wheat malt. Hops: Target. Late hops: Styrian Goldings. Dry hops: Styrian Goldings. Source: RP4/5/JHF.

**Fire-bellied Toad** (b-c): ABV: 5%. Malt: Maris Otter pale malt, Crystal malt, Wheat malt. Hops: Phoenix. Source: JE1/2/3/4/5/6.

**Croak & Stagger** (b-c): OG: 1053. Malt: 88% Maris Otter pale malt, 5% Crystal malt, 5% Chocolate malt, 2% Wheat malt. Hops: Target, Cascade. Late hops: Cascade. Source: RP5/JE1/2/3/4/5/6.

### Fromes Hill Brewery, Ledbury

**Buckswood Dingle**: OG: 1038. Malt: 94% Maris Otter pale malt, 6% Crystal malt. Hops: Goldings, Challenger. Source: RP5.

**Overture**: OG: 1043. Malt: 92% Maris Otter pale malt, 8% Crystal malt. Hops: Goldings, Challenger, Fuggles. Source: RP5.

### Fuller, Smith & Turner, London

**P**: OG: 1031. Malt: 62.96% Pale malt, 11.11% Black malt, 7.41% Flaked barley, 3.7% No.2 invert sugar, 11.11% No.3 invert sugar, 3.7% No.4 invert sugar. Hops: 100% Fuggles. Yeast: White Labs WLP002. IBU: 28. SRM: 29. Notes: Porter recipe from 1946. Source: SUABP.

**Hock**: OG: 1033. Malt: Alexis pale malt, Amber malt, Crystal malt, Caramel. Hops: Target. IBU: 20. EBC: 90. Source: RP4.

**PA**: OG: 1035. Malt: 77.42 % Pale malt, 16.13% Flaked barley, 3.23% No.2 invert sugar, 3.23% Glucose. Hops: 100% Fuggles. Yeast: White Labs WLP002. IBU: 32. SRM: 12. Notes: Pale ale recipe from 1946. Source: SUABP.

**Chiswick Bitter**: OG: 1034. Malt: 90% Alexis and Chariot pale malt, 3% Crystal malt, 7% Flaked maize, Caramel. Hops: Target, Northdown, Challenger. Late hops: Goldings, Challenger, Northdown. Dry hops: Yes. IBU: 28. EBC: 21. Source: RP.

**Summer Ale**: OG: 1037. Malt: 85% Alexis and Chariot pale malt, 15% Wheat malt. Hops: Target. Late hops: Saaz. IBU: 22. EBC: 13. Source: RP.

**London Pride**: OG: 1040. Malt: 90% Alexis and/or Chariot pale malt, 3% Crystal malt, 7% Flaked maize, Caramel. Hops: Target, Northdown, Challenger. Late hops: Challenger, Northdown. IBU: 30. EBC: 24. Source: RP/JHF. Malt: Pale malt, Crystal malt, Demerara sugar. Hops: Goldings, Fuggles. Late hops: Goldings. Dry hops: Goldings. Source: DL.

**XX Mild**: OG: 1041. Malt: Pale malt, Lager malt, Flaked maize, Glucose, Caramel. Hops: Spalt, Hallertau, Cluster. Yeast: Wyeast #1968/White Labs WLP002. Notes: Recipe from 1920. IBU: 33. SRM: 30. Source: VB.

**Honeydew**: OG: 1042. Malt: Alexis and Chariot pale malt, Honey. Hops: First Gold. Late hops: First Gold. IBU: 22. EBC: 19. Source: RP5.

**AK**: OG: 1045. Malt: Pale malt, Lager malt, Flaked maize, No.2 invert sugar, No.3 invert sugar. Hops: Fuggles, Goldings, Cluster. Yeast: Wyeast #1968/White Labs WLP002. Notes: Recipe from 1910. IBU: 49. SRM: 10. Source: VB.

**India Pale Ale**: OG: 1047. Malt: 96% Alexis pale malt, Crystal malt. Hops: Goldings. IBU: 42. EBC: 18. Source: RP4.

**Mr. Harry**: OG: 1048. Malt: 90% Pale malt, 10% Crystal malt. Hops: Target, Northdown, Challenger. IBU: 40-42. EBC: 42. Source: RP3/4.

**Old Winter Ale**: OG: 1048. Malt: 90% Alexis and Chariot pale malt, 10% Crystal malt. Hops: Target, Challenger, Northdown. IBU: 42. EBC: 52. Source: RP5.

**Porter**: OG: 1049. Malt: Pale malt, Lager malt, Brown malt, Black malt, Flaked maize, No.3 invert sugar. Hops: Fuggles, Goldings. Yeast: Wyeast #1098. Notes: Recipe from 1910. IBU: 44. SRM: 28. Source: VB.

**London Porter**: OG: 1053-56. Malt: 76% Alexis and Chariot pale, 10% Crystal malt, 12% Brown malt, 2% Chocolate malt. Hops: Fuggles. Late hops: Fuggles. IBU: 33. EBC: 140. Source: RP5/BC. Malt: Pale malt, Crystal malt, Patent black malt, Chocolate malt, Roast barley. Hops: Goldings. Late hops: Goldings. Source: 150.

**X**: OG: 1053. Malt: Lager malt, Mild malt, Flaked maize, No.3 invert sugar, Caramel. Hops: Fuggles, Cluster. Yeast: Wyeast #1968/White Labs WLP002. Notes: Recipe from 1910. IBU: 37. SRM: 18. Source: VB.

**ESB (Extra Special Bitter)**: OG: 1053-4. Malt: 90% Alexis and Chariot pale malt, 3% Crystal malt, 7% Flaked maize, Caramel. Hops: Target, Northdown, Challenger or Goldings. Late hops: Challenger, Northdown, Goldings. Dry hops: Yes. IBU: 35. EBC: 31. Source: RP/DL/JHF. OG: 1054-57. Malt: Pale malt, Flaked maize, Crystal malt, Amber malt, Aromatic malt, Sugar. Hops: Target. Late hops: Challenger, Northdown, Goldings. Dry hops: Goldings. Source: CB.

**ESB Export**: OG: 1060. Malt: Pale malt, Crystal malt, Flaked maize, Sugar. Hops: Target, Challenger. Late hops: Northdown, Goldings. Source: EBA/150.

**1845 Ale**: OG: 1062. Malt: Alexis and Chariot pale malt, Crystal malt, Amber malt. Hops: Goldings. Late hops: Goldings. IBU: 50. EBC: 50. Source: RP5.

**1845 Celebration Ale** (b-c): ABV: 6.3%. Malt: Pale malt, Crystal malt, Amber malt. Hops: Goldings. Source: JE1/2/3/4/5/6.

**OBE (Old Burton Extra)**: OG: 1068. Malt: Pale malt, Lager malt, Flaked maize, No.3 invert sugar, Glucose, Caramel. Hops: Fuggles, Brewers Gold. Yeast: Wyeast #1968/White Labs WLP002. Notes: Recipe from 1935. IBU: 79. SRM: 18. Source: VB.

**Brown Stout**: OG: 1070. Malt: Pale malt, Lager malt, Brown malt, Black malt, Flaked maize, No.3 invert sugar, No.4 invert sugar. Hops: Goldings. Yeast: Wyeast #1968/White Labs WLP002. Notes: Recipe from 1910. IBU: 51. SRM: 39. Source: VB.

**XXK**: OG: 1079. Malt: Pale malt, Crystal 40L malt, No.2 invert sugar. Hops: Fuggles, Goldings. Yeast: Wyeast #1968/White Labs WLP002. Notes: Recipe from 1887. IBU: 81. SRM: 12. Source: VB.

**Vintage Ale** (b-c): ABV: 8.5%. Malt: Pale malt, Crystal malt, Flaked maize. Hops: Target, Challenger, Northdown, Goldings oil. Source: JE1/2/3. Malt: Golden Promise pale malt. Hops: Goldings. Source: JE4. Malt: Optic pale malt. Hops: Target, Challenger, Northdown. Source: JE5. Malt: Optic pale malt. Hops: Fuggles. Source: JE6.

**Prize Old Ale** (b-c): ABV: 9%. Malt: Maris Otter pale malt, Black malt, Crystal malt. Hops: Fuggles, Goldings, Challenger. Source: JE6. Notes: Previously brewed by George Gale & Co.

### . *Fulstow, Louth*

**Fulstow Common**: ABV: 3.8%. Malt: Pearl pale malt, Crystal malt, Torrefied wheat. Hops: Northdown, Phoenix, Saaz. Source: JE6.

**Marsh Mild** (b-c): ABV: 3.8%. Malt: Pearl pale malt, Crystal malt, Dark chocolate malt. Hops: Northdown, Goldings. Source: JE6.

**Northway IPA** (b-c): ABV: 4.2%. Malt: Pearl pale malt, Crystal malt, Torrefied wheat. Hops: Saaz, Phoenix. Source: JE6.

**Pride of Fulstow** (b-c): ABV: 4.5%. Malt: Pearl pale malt, Crystal malt, Chocolate malt, Torrefied wheat. Hops: Challenger, Goldings. Source: JE6.

**Sledge Hammer Stout** (b-c): ABV: 8%. Malt: Pearl pale malt, Roast barley, Crystal malt, Chocolate malt, Brown malt. Hops: Phoenix, Goldings. Source: JE6.

### . *George Gale & Company, Horndean*

**XXXD Mild**: OG: 1030. Malt: 82% Maris Otter pale malt, 18% Sugar, Black malt, Caramel. Hops: Fuggles, Goldings, Challenger. IBU: 20. Source: RP1/2/3.

**XXXL Mild**: OG: 1030. Malt: 82% Maris Otter pale malt, 18% Sugar, Black malt. Hops: Fuggles, Goldings, Challenger. IBU: 20. Source: RP1/2.

**BBB / Butser Brew Bitter**: OG: 1036. Malt: 80-85% Maris Otter pale malt, 0-2.5% Crystal malt, 0-0.5% Black malt,5-18% Sugar, 2-7% Torrefied wheat. Hops: Challenger, Fuggles. Late hops: Goldings. Dry hops: Yes. IBU: 21-25. EBC: 26. Source: RP/JHF.

**Gold**: OG: 1040. Malt: 100% Maris Otter pale malt. Hops: Goldings. IBU: 24. Source: RP4.

**Best Bitter**: OG: 1040. Malt: 80-87% Maris Otter pale malt, 4.5-5% Crystal malt, 5-13% Sugar, 2-3% Torrefied wheat. Hops: Challenger, Fuggles. Late hops: Goldings. Dry hops: Yes. IBU: 23. EBC: 33. Source: RP.

**IPA**: OG: 1042. Malt: 93% Maris Otter pale malt, 3% Crystal malt, 4% Torrefied wheat. Hops: Goldings. Late hops: Goldings. Dry hops: Goldings. IBU: 30. EBC: 21. Source: RP5.

**Pompey Royal**: OG: 1044. Malt: 67.5% Pale malt, 7.5% Crystal malt, 12.5% Torrefied wheat, 12.5% Sugar. Hops: Hop extract, Styrian Goldings. Dry hops: Styrian Goldings. Source: RP2/3/4. Note: See **Pompey Royal**, Whitbread.

**XXXXX**: OG: 1044. Malt: 88% Maris Otter pale malt, 10% Sugar, 2% Torrefied wheat, Black malt, Caramel. Hops: Goldings, Challenger, Fuggles. IBU: 26. Source: RP1/2/3/4.

**Winterbrew**: OG: 1045. Notes: Varied blend of **Prize Old Ale** and **Butser** (occasionally **Best**), Sugar, Caramel. IBU: 25. EBC: 220. Source: RP5.

**GB Export Strength** (b-c): ABV: 4.5%. Malt: Maris Otter pale malt, Pale crystal malt. Hops: Fuggles, Challenger. Source: JE5.

**Nourishing Stout**: OG: 1048. Malt: 72.5% Maris Otter pale malt, 15% Torrefied wheat, 6.5% Black malt, 6% Glucose. Hops: 30% Goldings, 30% Challenger, 40% Fuggles. IBU: 22. EBC: 144. Source: EBA/GW.

**Horndean Special Bitter / HSB**: OG: 1050. Malt: 80-85% Maris Otter pale malt, 5-15% Sugar, 5-6% Torrefied wheat, 1% Black malt, 0-3% Crystal malt. Hops: Challenger, Fuggles. Late hops: Goldings. IBU: 26-31.5. EBC: 38. Source: RP1/2/3/4. OG: 1051. Malt: Pale malt, Crystal malt, Wheat malt, Sugar. Hops: Goldings, Bramling Cross. Late hops: Goldings. Dry hops: Goldings. Source: DL.

**HSB** (b-c): ABV: 4.8%. Malt: Maris Otter pale malt, Crystal malt, Black malt. Hops: Challenger, Fuggles, Goldings. Source: JE2/3/4/5.

**Strong Pale Ale**: OG: 1052. Malt: Maris Otter pale malt, Glucose, Torrefied wheat, Black malt. Hops: Goldings, Challenger, Fuggles. IBU: 30. Source: EBA.

**Festival Mild** (b-c): ABV: 4.8%. Malt: Maris Otter pale malt, Crystal malt, Black malt. Hops: Challenger, Fuggles, Goldings. Source: JE2/3/4/5.

**Festival Mild**: OG: 1054. Malt: 87% Maris Otter pale malt, 3% Black malt, 3% Crystal malt, 2% Torrefied wheat, 5% Sugar. Hops: Fuggles. Late hops: Fuggles, Goldings. IBU: 24. EBC: 140. Source: RP5/JHF/GW.

**Christmas Ale** (b-c): ABV: 7%. Malt: Maris Otter pale malt, Crystal malt. Hops: Fuggles, Goldings, Challenger. Source: JE1/2. ABV: 8.5%. Malt: Maris Otter pale malt, Crystal malt. Hops: Fuggles. Others: Cinnamon, Mace, Raisins. Source: JE4/5.

**Trafalgar Ale** (b-c): ABV: 9%. Malt: Maris Otter pale malt, Crystal malt. Hops: Fuggles, Challenger. Source: JE1/2/3/4. ABV: 10%. Malt: Maris Otter pale malt, Crystal malt. Hops: Goldings, Admiral. Source: JE5.

**Conquest Ale / Milestones Pale Ale** (b-c): ABV: 9%. Malt: Maris Otter pale malt. Hops: Fuggles. Source: JE3/4.

**Millennium Brew** (b-c): ABV: 10%. Malt: Maris Otter pale malt, Crystal malt. Hops: Challenger, Fuggles, Goldings. Source: JE2.

**Prize Old Ale** (b-c): OG: 1094-1110. Malt: 88-98% Maris Otter pale malt, optional Wheat, 2% Black malt, 0-10% Sugar, optional Crystal malt. Hops: Fuggles or Goldings. Late hops: Fuggles, Goldings. IBU: 47.5-53. EBC: 90. Source: RP/DL/JE1/2/3/4/5. Notes: Now brewed by **Fuller, Smith & Turner**.

**Jubilee Ale** (b-c): ABV: 12%. Malt: Maris Otter pale malt, Sugar. Hops: Fuggles. Source: JE4.

## Georges & Co., Bristol

**X**: OG: 1062. Malt: Pale malt, White sugar. Hops: Goldings. Notes: Recipe from 1867. Source: DP.

**Pale Ale**: OG: 1064. Malt: Pale malt. Hops: Fuggles. Dry hops: Goldings. Notes: Recipe from 1889. Source: DP.

**Brown Stout**: OG: 1076. Malt: Pale malt, Brown malt, Black malt. Hops: Fuggles. Notes: Recipe from 1867. Source: DP.

**Strong Ale**: OG: 1088. Malt: Pale malt. Hops: Fuggles. Notes: Recipe from 1896. Source: DP.

## Gibbs Mew, Salisbury

**Overlord**: OG: 1036. Malt: Pipkin pale malt, Crystal malt, Chocolate malt, 3% Torrefied wheat. Hops: Challenger, Fuggles, Goldings. EBC: 34. Source: RP4.

**Wiltshire Traditional Bitter**: OG: 1036. Malt: Pipkin pale malt, Crystal malt, Chocolate malt, 3% Torrefied wheat. Hops: Challenger, Target, Goldings. EBC: 34. Source: RP3/4.

**Timothy Chudley's Local Line**: OG: 1036. Malt: Pale malt, Crystal malt, Chocolate malt, 3% Torrefied wheat. Hops: Challenger, Fuggles, Goldings. EBC: 34. Source: RP3.

**Premium Bitter**: OG: 1042. Malt: Pale malt, Crystal malt, Chocolate malt, 3% Torrefied wheat. Hops: Challenger, Fuggles, Goldings. EBC: 37. Source: RP3.

**Salisbury Best Bitter**: OG: 1042. Malt: Pipkin pale malt, Crystal malt, Chocolate malt, 3% Torrefied wheat. Hops: Challenger, Fuggles, Goldings. Dry hops: Yes. EBC: 37. Source: RP3,4.

**Deacon**: OG: 1050. Malt: Golden Promise pale malt, Pipkin pale malt, 3-5% Torrefied wheat. Hops: Challenger, Fuggles, Goldings. EBC: 15. Source: RP.

**Wake Ale**: OG: 1051. Malt: Pipkin pale malt, Crystal malt, Chocolate malt, Torrefied wheat. Hops: Challenger, Fuggles, Goldings. EBC: 80. Source: RP4.

**The Bishop's Tipple**: OG: 1066. Malt: Pipkin pale malt, Crystal malt, optional Chocolate malt, 0-3% Torrefied wheat. Hops: Challenger, Fuggles, Goldings. EBC: 42. Source: RP. Malt: Pale malt, Crystal malt, Black malt, Golden syrup. Hops: Goldings. Source: DL. Notes: I brewed the Dave Line version of this brew many times and, in Sheffield, this brew was responsible for my brewing gaining a bit of a reputation for causing various "lost time" incidents. Personally, I blame the aliens...

## Glastonbury Ales, Somerton

**Mystery Tor** (b-c): ABV: 3.8%. Malt: Maris Otter pale malt, Crystal malt, Wheat malt. Hops: Fuggles, Cascade. Source: JE4.

**Lady of the Lake** (b-c): ABV: 4.2%. Malt: Maris Otter pale malt, Crystal malt, Wheat malt, Caramalt. Hops: Fuggles, Goldings, Mount Hood. Source: JE4.

**Golden Chalice** (b-c): ABV: 4.8%. Malt: Maris Otter pale malt, Caramalt, Wheat malt. Hops: Challenger, Mount Hood. Source: JE4.

**FMB** (b-c): ABV: 5%. Malt: Maris Otter pale malt, Crystal malt, Amber malt, Wheat malt. Hops: Challenger, Mount Hood. Source: JE4.

### . *Glenny Brewery Company, Witney*

**Witney Bitter**: OG: 1036. Malt: 89-95.5% Pale malt, 4% Crystal malt, 0.5% Chocolate malt, 0-6.5% Flaked barley. Hops: Progress. Dry hops: Hallertau. Source: RP. Note: The Glenny Brewery Company became the Wychwood Brewery Company in 1992.

**Dr. Thirsty's Draught**: OG: 1050. Malt: 90% Pale malt, 5% Crystal malt, 5% Chocolate malt. Hops: Progress. Dry Hops: Hallertau. Source: RP2/3. Note: This was a favourite brew of my Banbury friends and I on one of our infamous Oxford trips.

**Wychwood Best**: OG: 1044. Malt: 96% Pale malt, 3.75% Crystal malt, 0.25% Chocolate malt. Hops: Progress. Dry hops: Styrian Goldings. Source: RP1/2/3.

**Hobgoblin**: OG: 1058. Malt: 92.5-95.5% Pale malt, 4% Crystal malt, 0.5% Chocolate malt, 0-3% Flaked barley. Hops: Progress. Dry hops: Styrian Goldings, Hallertau. Source: RP.

Note: See Wychwood Brewery Company.

### . *P. & D.J. Goacher, Maidstone*

**Real Mild Maidstone Ale**: OG: 1033. Malt: 86.5-89% Halcyon and Maris Otter pale malt, 11-13.5% Crystal malt and Chocolate malt. Hops: Progress. Source: RP.

**Fine Light Chocolate Maidstone Ale**: OG: 1036. Malt: 96% Halcyon pale malt, 4% Crystal malt. Hops: Goldings, Progress. Source: RP1/2/3/4/5.

**Best Dark Maidstone Ale**: OG: 1040. Malt: 96% Halcyon pale malt, 6% Crystal malt and Chocolate malt, optional Black malt. Hops: Goldings, Progress. Source: RP.

**Gold Star Ale**: OG: 1050. Malt: 100% Halcyon pale malt. Hops: Goldings. Source: RP4/5.

**Maidstone Porter**: OG: 1050. Malt: 92% Halcyon pale malt, 8% Crystal malt and Chocolate malt. Hops: Progress. Late hops: Goldings. Source: RP4/5.

**Old Maidstone Ale**: OG: 1066. Malt: 94% Pale malt, 6% Crystal malt, Black malt, Chocolate malt. Hops: Goldings. Source: RP.

### . *Goddards Brewery, Ryde, Isle of Wight*

**Special Bitter**: OG: 1039. Malt: Maris Otter pale malt, Crystal malt, Roast barley, No.2 invert sugar or Pipkin pale malt, Crystal malt, Wheat malt, Chocolate malt, Sugar. Hops: Challenger, Fuggles, Goldings, USA Fuggles, Late hops: USA Fuggles. IBU: 30. Source: RP.

**Fuggle-Dee-Dum**: OG: 1045.5. Malt: 100% Maris Otter pale malt, Roast barley extract. Hops: Fuggles, USA Fuggles. Source: RP4/5.

### . Goff's Brewery, Winchcombe

**Jouster Ale**: OG: 1040. Malt: Pipkin pale malt, Crystal malt, Wheat malt. Hops: Challenger. Late hops: Fuggles. Source: RP5.

**Sudeley Ale** (b-c): ABV: 4.4%. Malt: Pipkin pale malt, Crystal malt, Wheat malt. Hops: Fuggles, Goldings. Source: JE2.

**White Knight**: OG: 1046. Malt: Pipkin pale malt, Wheat malt. Hops: Challenger, Fuggles. Source: RP5.

**Black Knight**: OG: 1053. Malt: Pipkin pale malt, Crystal malt, Chocolate malt, Wheat malt. Hops: Challenger, Fuggles, Goldings. Source: RP5.

### . Goldfinch Brewery, Dorchester

**Tom Brown's Best Bitter**: OG: 1039. Malt: 95% Pale malt. 5% Crystal malt. Hops: Goldings. Source: RP3/4/5.

**Flashman's Clout Strong Ale**: OG: 1043. Malt: 95% Pale malt, 5% Crystal malt. Hops: Goldings. Source: RP3/4/5/JHF.

**Midnight Blinder Premium Ale**: OG: 1050. Malt: 91% Pale malt, 8% Crystal malt, 1% Chocolate malt. Hops: Goldings. Source: RP3/4/5.

### . Goose Eye Brewery, Keighley

**Bitter**: OG: 1038. Malt: Maris Otter pale malt, small % Crystal malt. Hops: USA Fuggles. Late hops: Goldings. Dry hops: Goldings. Source: RP4/5.

**Brontë**: OG: 1040. Malt: Maris Otter pale malt, small % Crystal malt, Wheat malt and Chocolate malt. Hops: Fuggles. Late hops: Goldings. Dry hops: Yes. Source: RP5.

**Spellbound**: OG: 1040. Malt: Maris Otter pale malt, small % Crystal malt, Roast malt and Chocolate malt. Hops: Fuggles. Hops: Goldings, Bramling Cross. Dry hops: Yes. Source: RP5.

**Summer Jacks**: OG: 1042. Malt: Maris Otter pale malt, small % Crystal malt and Wheat malt. Hops: Fuggles. Late hops: Goldings. Dry hops: Yes. Source: RP5.

**Wharfedale**: OG: 1045. Malt: Maris Otter pale malt, small % Crystal malt. Hops: Fuggles, Goldings. Dry Hops: Yes. Source: RP4/5.

**Pommies Revenge**: OG: 1052. Malt: Maris Otter pale malt. Hops: Fuggles, Goldings. Dry hops: Yes. Source: RP4/5.

### . Grainstore, Davis'es Brewing Company, Oakham

**Ten Fifty** (b-c): ABV: 5%. Malt: Maris Otter pale malt. Hops: Fuggles, Northdown. Source: JE5/6.

. *Great Gable, Gosforth*

**Yewbarrow / Yulebarrow** (b-c): ABV: 5.5%. Malt: Pale malt, Crystal malt, Amber malt, Chocolate malt, Oat malt, Honey, Fruit syrup. Hops: Northdown. Source: JE5/6.

. *Green Dragon, Bungay*

**Wynnter Warmer** (b-c): ABV: 6%. Malt: Pale malt, Chocolate malt, Black malt, Wheat malt. Hops: Fuggles. Source: JE5.

. *Green Jack Brewing Company, Lowestoft. Www.green-jack.co.uk*

**Bitter**: OG: 1035. Malt: 95% Pale malt, 5% Crystal malt. Hops: Challenger, Styrian Goldings. Source: RP4/5.

**Canary**: ABV: 3.8%. Hops: Styrian Goldings. Source: Web.

**Honey Bunny**: ABV: 4%. Other: Honey. Source: Web.

**Summer Dream**: ABV: 4%. Other: Elderflowers. Source: Web.

**Grasshopper** (b-c): ABV: 4.2%. Malt: Halcyon pale malt, Crystal malt, Chocolate malt, optional Caramalt. Hops: Styrian Goldings, Challenger. Source: JE1/2/3.

**Best**: OG: 1043. Malt: 93% Pale malt, 7% Crystal malt. Hops: Challenger, Styrian Goldings. Source: RP4/5.

**Golden Sickle**: OG: 1047. Malt: 90% Pale malt, 9% Flaked maize, 1% Caramalt. Hops: Challenger, Styrian Goldings. Source: RP4/5.

**Golden Sickle** (b-c): ABV: 4.8%. Malt: Halcyon pale malt, Crystal malt, Caramalt, Flaked maize. Hops: Styrian Goldings, Challenger, First Gold. Source: JE1.

**Swallow** (b-c): ABV: 4.8%. Malt: Halcyon pale malt, Caramalt, Crystal malt, Sugar. Hops: Challenger, Styrian Goldings. Source: JE2.

**Norfolk Wolf Porter** (b-c): ABV: 5.2%. Malt: Halcyon pale malt, Crystal malt, Chocolate malt. Hops: Challenger, Styrian Goldings. Source: JE3.

**Lurcher**: OG: 1056. Malt: 95% Pale malt, 3% Crystal malt, 2% Chocolate malt. Hops: Challenger, Styrian Goldings. Source: RP4/5.

**Norfolk Wolf Porter**: OG: 1056. Malt: 90% Mild ale malt, 4.5% Crystal malt, 3% Chocolate malt, 2.5% Roast barley. Hops: Challenger, Styrian Goldings. Source: RP4/5.

**Ripper** (b-c): ABV: 8.5%. Malt: Halcyon pale malt, Caramalt, CaraPils malt, Sugar. Hops: Styrian Goldings, Challenger. Source: JE1/2/3.

. *Green Tye, Much Hadham*

**Shot in the Dark** (b-c): ABV: 3.6%. Malt: Maris Otter pale malt, Crystal malt, Wheat malt, Chocolate malt. Hops: Challenger, Goldings. Source: JE4/5/6.

**Union Jack**: ABV: 3.6%. Malt: Maris Otter pale malt, Crystal malt, Amber malt, Flaked maize. Hops: Challenger, Bramling Cross. Source: JE4/5/6.

**Mustang Mild** (b-c): ABV: 3.7%. Malt: Maris Otter pale malt, Crystal malt, Brown malt, Chocolate malt, Flaked maize. Hops: Fuggles. Source: JE4/5/6.

**Uncle John's Ferret** (b-c): ABV: 3.8%. Malt: Maris Otter pale malt, Crystal malt, Flaked maize, Chocolate malt. Hops: Jenny. Source: JE4/5.

**Snowdrop** (b-c): ABV: 3.9%. Malt: Maris Otter pale malt, Crystal malt. Hops: Goldings. Source: JE4/5/6.

**Smile for the Camera!** (b-c): ABV: 4%. Malt: Maris Otter pale malt, Flaked maize, Wheat malt, Honey. Hops: Susan or Northdown, Styrian Goldings, Goldings. Others: Elderflowers. Source: JE4/5/6.

**XBF** (b-c): ABV: 4%. Malt: Maris Otter pale malt, Crystal malt, Amber malt, Flaked barley. Hops: Pilgrim. Source: JE4/5/6.

**St. Margaret's** (b-c): ABV: 4.1%. Malt: Maris Otter pale malt, Cara Gold malt, Flaked maize. Hops: Willamette. Source: JE4/5.

**Autumn Rose** (b-c): ABV: 4.2%. Malt: Maris Otter pale malt, Crystal malt, Wheat malt, Chocolate malt, Flaked maize. Hops: Pilot or First Gold. Source: JE4/5/6.

**Ditch Diver** (b-c): ABV: 4.2%. Malt: Maris Otter pale malt, Dark Crystal malt, Amber malt. Hops: Challenger, Bramling Cross. Source: JE5/6.

**East Anglian Gold** (b-c): ABV: 4.2%. Malt: Maris Otter pale malt, Flaked maize. Hops: Sovereign. Source: JE6.

**Green Tiger** (b-c): ABV: 4.2%. Malt: Maris Otter pale malt, Crystal malt, Flaked maize. Hops: Goldings. Others: Ginger. Source: JE4/5/6.

**Mad Morris** (b-c): ABV: 4.2%. Malt: Maris Otter pale malt, Wheat malt. Hops: Susan or Northdown, Styrian Goldings, Goldings. Source: JE6.

**Wheelbarrow** (b-c): ABV: 4.3%. Malt: Maris Otter pale malt, Crystal malt, Wheat malt. Hops: Challenger. Source: JE4/5/6.

**Bowled Over!** (b-c): ABV: 4.5%. Malt: Maris Otter pale malt, Crystal malt, Wheat malt. Hops: Ruth or Northdown, Goldings. Source: JE5/6.

**Coal Porter** (b-c): ABV: 4.5%. Malt: Maris Otter pale malt, Chocolate malt, Wheat malt. Hops: Bramling Cross. Source: JE4/5/6.

**Merry Maker** (b-c): ABV: 4.6%. Malt: Maris Otter pale malt, Dark crystal malt, Wheat malt, Flaked maize. Hops: Challenger, Jenny. Source: JE4/5.

**Coal Ported** (b-c): ABV: 4.7%. Malt: Maris Otter pale malt, Chocolate malt, Wheat malt. Hops: Bramling Cross. Other: Port. Source: JE4/5.

**Conkerer** (b-c): ABV: 4.7%. Malt: Maris Otter pale malt, Crystal malt, Wheat malt. Hops: Hilary or Northdown, Styrian Goldings, Goldings. Source: JE4/5/6.

**Citrus Sin** (b-c): ABV: 4.8%. Malt: Maris Otter pale malt, Crystal malt, Wheat malt. Hops: Hilary. Others: Cinnamon, Orange oil. Source: JE4/5.

**Tumbledown Dick** (b-c): ABV: 5.3%. Malt: Maris Otter pale malt, Crystal malt, Wheat malt. Hops: Fuggles. Source: JE5.

## . Greene, King & Sons, Bury St. Edmunds

**Pale Ale** (bottled): ABV: 3.4%. Malt: Crystal malt, Sugar. Hops: Northern Brewer, Goldings. Source: DL.

**XX Dark**: OG: 1036. Malt: Halcyon pale malt, Pipkin pale malt, Puffin pale malt, Crystal malt, Black malt, Sugar, Caramel. Hops: Challenger, Northdown, Target. Late hops: Yes. IBU: 19. EBC: 65. Source: RP.

**Harvest Brown Ale** (bottled): ABV: 3.6%. Malt: Black malt, Crystal malt, Sugar. Hops: Northern Brewer, Fuggles. Source: DL.

**IPA**: OG: 1036. Malt: Halcyon pale malt, Pipkin pale malt, Puffin pale malt, Crystal malt, Sugar, Caramel. Hops: Challenger, Northdown, Target. Late hops: Yes. Dry hops: Hop oil. IBU: 26. EBC: 23. Source: RP.

**Rayments Special Bitter**: OG: 1040. Malt: Halcyon pale malt, Pipkin pale malt, Puffin pale malt, Crystal malt, Sugar, Caramel. Hops: Challenger, Northdown, Target. Late hops: Yes. IBU: 26-29. EBC: 29. Source: RP4.

**St. Edmunds**: ABV: 4.2%. Malt: Pale malt. Hops: Cascade. Source: WB.

**Abbot Ale**: OG: 1048. Malt: Halcyon pale malt, Pipkin pale malt, Puffin pale malt, Crystal malt, Sugar, optional Amber malt, Caramel. Hops: Challenger, Northdown, Target. Late hops: Yes. IBU: 36. EBC: 26. Source: RP/HB. OG: 1049. Malt: Pale malt, Crystal malt, Roast malt, Flaked maize, Sugar. Hops: Goldings, Northern Brewer. Late hops: Goldings. Dry hops: Goldings. Source: DL. OG: 1050. Malt: 83% Pale malt, 3.5% Crystal malt, 6% Flaked maize, 1% Black malt, 6.5% Light invert sugar. Hops: 50% Goldings, 50% Fuggles. Late hops: Goldings. Dry hops: Optional Goldings. IBU: 32. EBC: 28. Source: Anglian Craft Brewers. Notes: Abbot Ale was responsible for me acquiring the taste for real ale; I first encountered it in 1978 when it cost the princely sum of 35pence per pint. It has changed in character over the years from that life-changing pint.

**Kings Champion**: ABV: 4.2%. Malt: Halcyon pale malt, Pipkin pale malt, Amber malt. Hops: Fuggles, Goldings. Source: RP5.

**Mad Judge**: ABV: 4.2%. Malt: Halcyon pale malt, Pipkin pale malt, Amber malt. Hops: Fuggles, Goldings. Others: Cranberry juice. Source: RP5.

**Black Baron**: ABV: 4.3%. Malt: Halcyon pale malt, Pipkin pale malt, Puffin pale malt, Crystal malt, Black malt, Sugar, Caramel. Hops: Challenger, Northdown, Target. Late hops: Yes. IBU: 23. EBC: 80. Source: RP.

**The Sorcerer**: ABV: 4.5%. Malt: Halcyon pale malt, Pipkin pale malt, Puffin pale malt, CaraPils malt. Hops: Challenger, Northdown, Target. Late hops: Yes. IBU: 25. EBC: 17. Source: RP.

**St. Edmunds Ale**: ABV: 5.5%. Malt: Pale malt, Crystal malt. Hops: Target. Source: HB.

**Strong Pale Ale** (bottled): OG: 1060. Malt: Pale malt, Crystal malt, Sugar. Hops: Goldings, Northern Brewer. Source: DL.

**Suffolk Strong Ale** (bottled): OG: 1060. Malt: Pale malt, Black malt, Sugar. Hops: Goldings, Northern Brewer. Source: DL. Note: Blended with **Pale Ale**.

**Winter Ale**: ABV: 6.4%. Malt: Halcyon pale malt, Pipkin pale malt, Puffin pale malt, Crystal malt, Sugar. Hops: Challenger, Northdown, Target. IBU: 35. EBC: 105. Source: RP.

**Hen's Tooth** (b-c): ABV: 6.5%. Malt: Pipkin pale malt, Crystal malt, Maltose syrup. Hops: Challenger, Goldings. Source: JE3/4/5/6. Note: See **Hen's Tooth**, Morland & Company.

## . *Greenwood's Brewery, Wokingham*

**Mahogany Mild**: OG: 1036.5. Malt: Maris Otter pale malt, Crystal malt, Chocolate malt, Wheat malt. Hops: Challenger, Goldings. Source: RP5.

**Hop Pocket Bitter**: OG: 1038.5. Malt: 86% Maris Otter pale malt, 7% Crystal malt, 7% Wheat malt. Hops: Challenger, Goldings. Dry hops: Yes. Source: RP4/5.

**Temperance Relief**: OG: 1043.5. Malt: 85% Maris Otter pale malt, 7% Crystal malt, 7% Wheat malt, 1% Chocolate malt. Hops: Challenger, Goldings. Dry hops: Yes. Source: RP4/5.

**Prohibition**: OG: 1048.5. Malt: 84.5% Maris Otter pale malt, 8.5% Crystal malt, 5.5% Wheat malt, 1.5% Chocolate malt. Hops: Challenger, Goldings. Dry hops: Yes. Source: RP4/5.

**Amber Gambler**: OG: 1055.5. Malt: 88% Maris Otter pale malt, 7% Crystal malt, 5% Wheat malt. Hops: Challenger, Goldings. Dry hops: Yes. Source: RP4/5.

**Draught Excluder**: OG: 1060.5. Malt: Maris Otter pale malt, Crystal malt, Chocolate malt, Wheat malt. Hops: Challenger, Goldings. Dry hops: Yes. Source: RP5.

## . *Hadrian Brewery, Newcastle-upon-Tyne*

**Gladiator Bitter**: OG: 1039. Malt: 99% Pale malt, 1% Coloured malt. Hops: Fuggles, Goldings/Target. Source: RP.

**Legion Ale**: OG: 1041. Malt: 94% Pale malt, 6% Coloured malt. Hops: Fuggles, Goldings. Source: RP4.

**Emperor Ale**: OG: 1050. Malt: 98% Pale malt, 2% Coloured malt. Hops: Goldings or Fuggles, Target. Source: RP.

**Centurion Best Bitter**: OG: 1045. Malt: 99.5% Pale malt, 0.5% Coloured malt. Hops: Fuggles, Goldings/Target. Source: RP.

### . *Haggards, London*

**Imp Ale** (b-c): ABV: 4.7%. Malt: Pale malt, Crystal malt, Vienna malt, Sugar. Hops: Cascade, Goldings. Source: JE5.

### . *Hall & Woodhouse, Blandford St. Mary. Www.hall-woodhouse.co.uk*

**Cooper's WPA**: OG: 1036. Malt: Pale malt, Crystal malt. Hops: Challenger, Fuggles. Source: RP3.

**Badger Best Bitter**: OG: 1040-2. Malt: 97% Alexis pale malt, 3% Crystal malt, Sugar or 82% Prisma pale malt, 0-3% Crystal malt, 15-18% Sugar, optional Caramel. Hops: Challenger, Northdown, optional Goldings. IBU: 24-27. EBC: 30. Source: RP/JHF. Malt: Pale malt, Flaked maize, Wheat malt, Sugar. Hops: Goldings, Fuggles. Late hops: Goldings. Dry hops: Goldings. Source: DL. Note: I drank many pints of this beer during my time at university in Bristol.

**IPA**: OG: 1040-1. Malt: 82% Prisma pale malt, 18% Sugar. Hops: Challenger, Northdown, Styrian Goldings. Late hops: Styrian Goldings. Dry hops: Styrian Goldings. IBU: 23. EBC: 15. Source: RP5.

**Pickled Partridge**: ABV: 4.6%. Malt: Pale malt, Chocolate malt, Crystal malt. Hops: Admiral, Hallertau. Source: WB.

**Faygate Dragon** (b-c): ABV: 4.7%. Malt: Pale malt, Crystal malt, Enzymic malt. Hops: Liberty. Source: JE3. Note: See **Faygate Dragon**, King & Barnes.

**Tanglefoot**: OG: 1047. Malt: 82% Prisma or Alexis pale malt, 18% Sugar. Hops: Challenger, Northdown, optional Goldings. Dry hops: Styrian Goldings. IBU: 24-7. EBC: 18. Source: RP/JHF. Hops: Styrian Goldings. Source: W.

**Blandford Fly**: ABV: 5.2%. Others: Ginger. Source: Web/TBBK.

**Cornucopia** (b-c): ABV: 6.5%. Malt: Pale malt, Lager malt, Maize, Enzymic malt, Wheat malt. Hops: Goldings, WGV, Challenger. Source: JE3. Note: See **Cornucopia**, King & Barnes.

**Stinger**: Others: Nettles. Source: A,G&B.

**Poacher's Choice**: Others: Damsons. Source: A,G&B.

**Golden Champion**: Others: Elderflowers. Source: A,G&B.

**Golden Glory**: Others: Peach blossoms extract. Source: A,G&B.

### . *Hambleton Ales, Thirsk*

**Nightmare Porter**: OG: 1036. Malt: 84% Halcyon pale malt, 8% Crystal malt, 3% Pale chocolate malt, 3% Roast barley. Hops: Northdown. IBU: 25. Source: RP3/4/5. OG: 1053-54. Hops: Northdown. Late hops: Northdown. Source: BC.

**Best Bitter**: OG: 1036. Malt: Pale malt, Crystal malt and Chocolate malt. Hops: Challenger or Northdown. Source: RP.

**Goldfield**: OG: 1040. Malt: 99% Halcyon pale malt, 0.1% Pale chocolate malt. Hops: Northdown. Late hops: Styrian Goldings. IBU: 35. Source: RP4/5.

**Stallion**: OG: 1042. Malt: 93% Halcyon pale malt, 6% Crystal malt, 0.75% Roast barley. Hops:. Northdown. IBU: 40. Source: RP3/4/5.

**Thoroughbred**: OG: 1048. Malt: 99.9% Pale malt, 0.1% Pale chocolate malt. Hops: Northdown. Late hops: Styrian Goldings. Source: RP4/5.

## .  Hammerpot, Poling

**Red Hunter**: ABV: 4.3%. Malt: Pale malt, Roast barley, Chocolate malt, Crystal malt. Hops: Progress, Goldings. Source: JE6.

## .  Hammond's United Breweries, Bradford

**1903 Old Tom / XXXX**: OG: 1071. Malt: slightly less than 70% Pale malt, 15% Maize, slightly less than 15% Invert sugar, tiny amount, less than 1% Black malt. IBU: 72. Source: A,G&B.

**XXXXX**: OG: 1102. Malt: Pale malt, Black malt, Flaked maize, Barley sugar, Caramel. Hops: Fuggles. Dry hops: Goldings. Notes: Recipe from 1903. Source: DP.

## .  Hampshire Brewery, Andover / Romsey

**King Alfred's Hampshire Bitter**: OG: 1037. Malt: Pale malt, Crystal malt, Pale chocolate malt. Hops: Northdown or Challenger, Progress. IBU: 26. EBC: 20. Source: RP4/5.

**King Alfred's** (b-c): ABV: 3.8%. Malt: Maris Otter pale malt, Crystal malt. Hops: First Gold, Challenger, Goldings. Source: JE4/5/6.

**Strongs Best Bitter** (b-c): ABV: 3.8%. Malt: Maris Otter pale malt, Crystal malt, Black malt. Hops: Challenger, Progress, Goldings. Source: JE4/5/6.

**Ironside**: OG: 1042. Malt: Pale malt, Crystal malt, Pale chocolate malt. Hops: Progress. Late hops: Goldings. IBU: 30. EBC: 25. Source: RP5.

**Ironside Best** (b-c): ABV: 4.2%. Malt: Maris Otter pale malt, Crystal malt. Hops: Styrian Goldings, Progress, Goldings. Source: JE4/5/6.

**Richard the Lionheart Golden**: OG: 1044. Malt: Pale malt, Crystal malt, Flaked maize, Torrefied wheat. Hops: Northdown. IBU: 28. EBC: 11. Source: RP3.

**Lionheart**: OG: 1042. Malt: Pale malt, Crystal malt, Caramalt, Wheat malt. Hops: Challenger, Progress, Sticklebract. IBU: 28. EBC: 11. Source: RP4/5.

**Lionheart** (b-c): ABV: 4.5%. Malt: Maris Otter pale malt, Lager malt. Hops: First Gold, Northdown, Perle. Source: JE4/5/6.

**Penny Black**: ABV: 4.5%. Hops: Goldings. Source: W.

**Hampshire Porter**: OG: 1046. Malt: Pale malt, Crystal malt, Chocolate malt, Liquorice, Molasses. Hops: Northdown. Source: RP3.

**Gold Reserve** (b-c): ABV: 4.8%. Malt: Lager malt, Caramalt. Hops: First Gold, Styrian Goldings, Goldings. Source: JE4.

**King's Ransom** (b-c): ABV: 4.8%. Malt: Lager malt, Caramalt. Hops: First Gold, Goldings, Styrian Goldings. Source: JE5/6.

**Arthur Pendragon Strong Ale / Pendragon**: OG: 1047-8. Malt: Pale malt, Crystal malt, Chocolate malt, Pale chocolate malt. Hops: Northdown or Challenger, Progress. IBU: 33. EBC: 33. Source: RP.

**Arthur Pendragon** (b-c): ABV: 4.8%. Malt: Pipkin pale malt, Crystal malt, Pale chocolate malt. Hops: Challenger, Progress. Source: JE2/3.

**Pendragon** (b-c): ABV: 4.8%. Malt: Maris Otter pale malt, Crystal malt, Black malt. Hops: Challenger, Progress, Goldings. Source: JE4/5/6.

**Pride of Romsey** (b-c): ABV: 5%. Malt: Maris Otter pale malt, Crystal malt, Wheat malt, Chocolate malt. Hops: Cascade, Progress. Source: JE1. Malt: Maris Otter pale malt, Crystal malt. Hops: Challenger, Cascade, Goldings. Source: JE2/3/4/5/6.

**Pride of Romsey IPA**: OG: 1052-53. Malt: Pale malt, Crystal malt. Hops: Progress. Late hops: Challenger, Goldings. Source: BC.

**William the Conqueror**: OG: 1066. Malt: Pale malt, Crystal malt, Chocolate malt. Hops: Northdown. Source: RP3.

**1066** (b-c): ABV: 6%. Malt: Pipkin pale malt, Caramalt, Wheat malt. Hops: Progress, Challenger. Source: JE2. Malt: Lager malt, Caramalt, Wheat malt. Hops: Northern Brewer, Perle. Source: JE3. Malt: Maris Otter pale malt, Caramalt, Lager malt. Hops: Northdown, First Gold, Perle. Source: JE4/5/6.

**1066**: OG: 1066. Malt: 100% Pale malt. Hops: Challenger, Progress, Goldings. Dry hops: Yes. IBU: 42. EBC: 15. Source: RP4/5.

Note: This brewer relocated from Andover to Romsey in 1997.

## .  *Hanby Ales, Wem*

**Black Magic Mild**: OG: 1033. Malt: 88% Maris Otter pale malt, 10% Crystal malt, 2% Black malt. Hops: Fuggles. Source: RP2/3/4/5.

**Drawwell Bitter**: OG: 1039. Malt: 97% Maris Otter pale malt, 3% Crystal malt. Hops: Fuggles. Late hops: Goldings. Source: RP2/3/4/5.

**All Seasons Bitter**: OG: 1042. Malt: 100% Maris Otter pale malt. Hops: Fuggles. Late hops: Tettnang. Source: RP5/JHF.

**Rainbow Chaser**: OG: 1043. Malt: 100% Maris Otter pale malt. Hops: Fuggles, Pioneer. Late hops: Fuggles, Pioneer. Source: RP5/JE4/5.

**Shropshire Stout**: OG: 1044. Malt: 73% Maris Otter pale malt, 9% Crystal malt, 12% Black malt, 6% Chocolate malt. Hops: Fuggles. Source: RP3/4/5/JE2/3/4. ABV: 4.4%. Malt: Maris Otter pale malt, Crystal malt, Chocolate malt. Hops: Fuggles, Goldings. Source: JE5.

**Wem Special**: OG: 1044. Malt: 98% Maris Otter pale malt, 2% Crystal malt. Hops: Fuggles, small% Goldings. Late hops: Tettnang, Goldings. Source: RP5.

**Cascade**: OG: 1045. Malt: 100% Maris Otter pale malt. Hops: Fuggles, Cascade. Late hops: Fuggles, Cascade. Source: RP5.

**Scorpio Porter**: OG: 1045. Malt: 83% Maris Otter pale malt, 7% Crystal malt, 7% Black malt, 3% Chocolate malt. Hops: Fuggles. Source: RP5.

**Golden Honey** (b-c): ABV: 4.5%. Malt: Maris Otter pale malt, Honey. Hops: Fuggles, Cascade, optional Goldings. Source: JE4/5.

**Treacleminer Bitter / Premium Bitter**: OG: 1046. Malt: 97% Maris Otter pale malt, 3% Crystal malt. Hops: Fuggles, small % Goldings. Late hops: Goldings, optional Fuggles. Source: RP/JE1/2/3/4/5.

**Old Wemian**: OG: 1049. Malt: 96% Maris Otter pale malt, 4% Crystal malt. Hops: Fuggles, Goldings. Source: RP4/5.

**Taverners**: OG: 1053. Malt: 96% Maris Otter pale malt, 4% Crystal malt. Hops: Fuggles. Late hops: Goldings. Source: RP5.

**Nutcracker Bitter**: OG: 1060. Malt: 98% Maris Otter pale malt, 2% Crystal malt. Hops: Fuggles. Late hops: Goldings. Source: RP2/3/4/5.

**Cherry Bomb** (b-c): ABV: 6%. Malt: Maris Otter pale malt, Crystal malt. Hops: Fuggles, Goldings. Others: Cherry essence. Source: JE2/3/4/5.

## Hanseatic Trading Company, Leicester

**IPA** (b-c): OG: 1045. Malt: Pale malt, Wheat malt. Hops: Bramling Cross, Fuggles, Goldings, WGV. IBU: 45-50. EBC: 11. Source: RP3/4.

**Vussilenski's Black Russian**: OG: 1048. Malt: Pale malt, Black malt, Crystal malt, Brown malt. Hops: Fuggles, Goldings. IBU: 35. EBC: 140. Source: RP3/4.

## Thomas Hardy Brewery, Dorchester

**Pope's Traditional**: OG: 1038. Malt: 100% Pipkin pale malt. Hops: Northdown, Challenger, Target. IBU: 23. EBC: 20. Source: RP5.

**Thomas Hardy Country Bitter**: OG: 1040. Malt: 82% Pipkin pale malt, 8% Crystal malt, 10% Torrefied wheat. Hops: Challenger, Northdown. Late hops: Styrian Goldings. Dry hops: Styrian Goldings. IBU: 25. EBC: 32. Source: RP5.

**Royal Oak**: OG: 1048. Malt: 82% Pipkin pale malt, 8% Crystal malt, 10% Torrefied wheat. Hops: Challenger, Northdown. Late hops: Goldings. Dry hops: Goldings. IBU: 31. EBC: 40. Source: RP5.

**Thomas Hardy's Ale** (b-c): OG: 1125. Malt: 100% Pipkin pale malt. Hops: Challenger, Northdown. Late hops: Challenger, Goldings. Dry hops: Challenger, Goldings. IBU: 50-70. Source: RP5. Malt: Pipkin pale malt, Lager malt. Hops: Goldings. Source: JE1/2.

Notes: Formed from a management buy out of the Eldridge Pope brewery. See Eldridge Pope and O'Hanlon's.

### . Hardy's & Hanson's, Nottingham

**Kimberley Best Mild**: OG: 1035. Malt: Pipkin Mild ale malt, Crystal malt, Flaked maize, Maltose, Caramel. Hops: Challenger, Northdown, WGV/Target. Late hops: Goldings. IBU: 19. EBC: 90. Source: RP.

**Kimberley Best Bitter**: OG: 1039. Malt: Pipkin pale malt, Maltose, Flaked maize, Malt extract. Hops: Challenger, Northdown, WGV/Target. Late hops: Goldings. IBU: 19-26. EBC: 25. Source: RP.

**Olde Trip** (b-c): ABV: 4.3%. Malt: Maris Otter pale malt. Hops: Target, Challenger. Late hops: Goldings. Dry hops: Challenger. Source: JE6.

**Kimberley Classic**: OG: 1047. Malt: Pipkin pale malt, Crystal malt, Maltose. Hops: Challenger, Northdown, WGV/Target. Late hops: Goldings, optional Styrian Goldings. Dry hops: Goldings, optional Styrian Goldings. IBU: 31. EBC: 18. Source: RP.

### . Harp

**Harp Pilsner** (bottled): OG: 1034. Malt: Lager malt, Flaked maize. Hops: Hallertau. Source: DL.

### . Harris Browne, Hadley

**AK**: OG: 1055. Malt: Pale malt, Flaked rice, White sugar. Hops: Fuggles. Dry hops: Fuggles. Notes: Recipe from 1897. Source: DP.

### . Harvey & Son, Lewes

**XX Mild**: OG: 1030. Malt: Mild ale malt, Crystal malt, Black sugar, Caramel. Hops: Bramling Cross, Fuggles, Goldings. Source: RP1/2/3/4/5.

**Sussex Bitter / PA / Pale Ale**: OG: 1033. Malt: Pipkin pale malt, Maris Otter pale malt, Crystal malt, Flaked maize, Sugar. Hops: Bramling Cross, Fuggles, Goldings, Progress. Source: RP1/2/3/4/5.

**Sussex Best Bitter (BB)**: OG: 1040. Malt: Maris Otter pale malt, Pipkin pale malt, Crystal malt, Flaked maize, Sugar. Hops: Bramling Cross, Fuggles, Goldings, optional Progress. Source: RP. Malt: Pale malt, Flaked maize, Sugar. Hops: Goldings, Northern Brewer. Source: DL.

**Sussex Old / XXXX**: OG: 1043. Malt: Mild ale malt, Crystal malt, Black sugar, Caramel. Hops: Bramling Cross, Fuggles, Goldings. Source: RP1/2/3/4/5.

**Armada Ale**: OG: 1046. Malt: Pipkin pale malt, Maris Otter pale malt, Crystal malt, Flaked maize, Sugar. Hops: Bramling Cross, Fuggles, Goldings. Source: RP2/3/4/5.

**Harvey's Historic Porter**: OG: 1054-55. Malt: Pale malt, Crystal malt, Chocolate malt, Patent black malt, Treacle. Hops: Bramling Cross. Late hops: Goldings, Fuggles. Source: BC.

**Harvey's Elizabethan Ale**: OG: 1083-87. Malt: Maris Otter pale malt, Crystal malt, Treacle. Hops: Progress. Late hops: Goldings, Fuggles. Dry hops: Fuggles. Source: CB.

**Imperial Extra Double Stout**: ABV: 9%. Malt: Maris Otter pale malt, Amber malt, Brown malt, Black malt. Hops: Fuggles, Goldings. Source: WB/JE3/4/5/6. Note: Limited edition beer.

## Heritage, Salisbury

**Stonehenge** (b-c): ABV: 3.8%. Malt: Maris Otter pale malt, Crystal malt, Caramalt. Hops: Goldings, Cascade, Bramling Cross. Source: JE3.

**Avebury Ale** (b-c): ABV: 4.3%. Malt: Maris Otter pale malt, Crystal malt. Hops: Goldings, Bramling Cross, Cascade. Source: JE3.

**Old Warrior** (b-c): ABV: 5%. Malt: Maris Otter pale malt, Rye crystal malt, Roast barley. Hops: Goldings, Target. Source: JE3.

## Hesket Newmarket Brewery, Hesket Newmarket

**Great Cockup Porter**: OG: 1035. Malt: 37% Pale malt, 37% Glucose, 15% Crystal malt, 12% Chocolate malt. Hops: Fuggles, Goldings, Hallertau. Source: RP3/4/5.

**Skiddaw Special**: OG: 1035. Malt: 92% Pale malt, 8% Crystal malt. Hops: Fuggles, Goldings, Hallertau. Source: RP2/3/4/5.

**Blencathra Bitter**: OG: 1035. Malt: 83-84% Pale malt, 13-17% Crystal malt. 0-3% Chocolate malt. Hops: Fuggles, Goldings, Hallertau. Source: RP/JHF.

**Doris's 90th Birthday Ale**: OG: 1045. Malt: 92% Pale malt, 8% Crystal malt. Hops: Fuggles, Goldings, Hallertau. Source: RP2/3/4/5.

**Catbells Pale Ale**: OG: 1052. Malt: 100% Pale malt. Hops: Goldings. Source: RP4/5.

**Old Carrock Strong Ale**: OG: 1060. Malt: 83% Pale malt, 17% Crystal malt, Glucose. Hops: Goldings, Hallertau, optional Fuggles. Source: RP.

## Hexhamshire Brewery, Hexham

**Low Quarter Ale**: OG: 1035. Malt: Pale malt. Hops: Goldings, optional Styrian Goldings. Source: RP.

**Shire Bitter**: OG: 1037. Malt: Pale malt, Crystal malt. Hops: Goldings, Target, optional Styrian Goldings. Source: RP.

**Devil's Water**: OG: 1042. Malt: Pale malt, Crystal malt, Roast barley. Hops: Goldings, Target, optional Styrian Goldings. Source: RP.

**Whapweasel**: OG: 1048. Malt: Pale malt, Less than 5% Crystal malt. Hops: Goldings, Styrian Goldings, Target. Source: RP4/5.

## . *High Force Hotel Brewery, Barnard Castle*

**Forest XB** (b-c): ABV: 4.2%. Malt: Pale malt, Crystal malt, Chocolate malt, Torrefied wheat. Hops: Willamette. Source: JE2/3/4/5/6.

**Cauldron Snout** (b-c): ABV: 5.6%. Malt: Maris Otter pale malt, Crystal malt, Wheat malt, Roast barley. Hops: Fuggles, Goldings. Source: JE1. Malt: Pale malt, Crystal malt, Torrefied wheat, Roast barley. Hops: Fuggles, Goldings. Source: JE2/3. Malt: Pale malt, Crystal malt, Black malt. Hops: Challenger. Source: JE4/5/6.

## . *Highgate Brewery, Walsall. Www.highgatebrewery.com*

**Mild Ale / Dark Ale**: OG: 1035-1035.7. Malt: 93% Pale malt, 1% Crystal malt, 3.5% Maltose syrup, 2.5% Black malt, Caramel. Hops: Goldings or Challenger, WGV/Progress. Late hops: Challenger, WGV/Progress. IBU: 22. EBC: 62-78. Source: RP. ABV: 3.4%. Hops: Goldings, Fuggles, Progress. Source: Web. Malt: Halcyon pale malt, Crystal malt, Black malt, Sugar. Hops: Challenger and Goldings. Source: GW.

**Fox's Nob**: OG: 1035.7. Malt: 82% Halcyon pale malt, 3.5% Crystal malt, 0.5% Black malt, 14% Sugar. Hops: Challenger. Late hops: Challenger, Styrian Goldings. Dry hops: Yes. IBU: 24. EBC: 22. Source: RP5.

**Springfield Bitter**: OG: 1036. Malt: 82% Pale malt, 18% Maltose syrup. Hops: WGV. Late hops: Fuggles. IBU: 24. EBC: 19. Source: RP3.

**India Pale Ale**: OG: 1038. Malt: 85.4% Halcyon pale malt, 3.2% Crystal malt, 8.4% Amber malt, 3% Sugar, Caramel. Hops: Challenger, Goldings. Late hops: Fuggles, Styrian Goldings. Dry hops: Yes. IBU: 28. EBC: 29. Source: RP5.

**Special Bitter**: ABV: 3.8%. Malt: Pale malt, Crystal malt, Amber malt, Wheat malt, No.3 invert sugar. Hops: Goldings, Fuggles, Progress. Dry hops: Styrian Goldings. Source: Web.

**Davenports IPA**: ABV: 4%. Malt: Wheat malt, Maris Otter pale malt, Crystal malt, Lager malt. Source: Web.

**Davenports Original**: ABV: 4%. Malt: Pale malt, Crystal malt, Torrefied wheat, No.3 invert sugar. Hops: First Gold, Cascade, Styrian Goldings. Source: Web. Note: See **Traditional Bitter**, Davenports.

**Fat Catz**: ABV: 4%. Hops: Styrian Goldings, Cascade, First Gold. Source: W.

**Saddler Celebrated Best Bitter**: OG: 1042.8. Malt: 84.5% Halcyon pale malt, 3% Crystal malt, 7.5% Amber malt, 5% Sugar. Hops: Challenger, Goldings. Late hops: Challenger, Goldings, Styrian Goldings. Dry hops: Yes. IBU: 28. EBC: 24. Source: RP5.

**Davenports Knee Trembler**: ABV: 4.5%. Hops: Willamette, Cascade. Source: Web.

**Old Ale**: OG: 1053.5-1055.7. Malt: 91% Halcyon pale malt, 2% Crystal malt, 2.5% Black malt, 4.5% Fermentose syrup, optional Caramel. Hops: Challenger, WGV/Progress/Goldings. Late hops: Challenger, WGV. IBU: 30. EBC: 75-115. Source: RP.

.    *Highwood, Melton Ross. Www.tom-wood-com*

**Tom Wood's Hop and Glory**: ABV: 3.6%. Hops: UK Cascade. Source: Web.

**Tom Wood's Lincolnshire Legend**: ABV: 4.2%. Hops: Target. Source: Web.

**Tom Wood's Barn Dance**: ABV: 4.2%. Hops: First Gold. Source: Web.

**Tom Wood's Lincolnshire Longwool**: ABV: 4.4%. Hops: First Gold. Source: Web.

**Old Timber**: ABV: 4.5%. Hops: Challenger, Fuggles. Source: W.

.    *Higsons, Liverpool. Www.higsonsbrewery.co.uk*

**Mild**: OG: 1033. Malt: 71% Mild ale malt, 6% Crystal malt, 11% Wheat, 12% Invert sugar, Caramel. Hops: Bramling Cross, British Columbian, Fuggles, Goldings, WGV. Source: RP1.

**Pale Bitter**: ABV: 3.8%. Hops: Cascade. Source: Web.

**Bitter**: OG: 1038. Malt: 85.5% Pale malt, 3% Crystal malt, 3.5% Wheat, 8% Invert sugar, Caramel. Hops: Bramling Cross, British Columbian, Fuggles, Goldings, Styrian Goldings, WGV. Source: RP1.

**Lager**: ABV: 4.5%. Hops: Saaz. Source: Web.

**Dark Bitter**: ABV: 4.6%. Hops: Bramling Cross. Source: Web.

Notes: Since the closure of the original Higsons brewery in Liverpool, Higsons beers have been brewed by Whitbread in Sheffield and then the Castle Eden Brewery. Higsons was resurrected in 2005 brewing beers from the original recipes and has been brewed by the Liverpool Organic Brewery since 2011[23]. I had a few pints of Higsons Bitter during my formative years in Liverpool and I found that it had a distinctive character that, in the absence of any other frame of reference at the time, I could only describe as "beery" maybe because I thought that all normal beer should taste like this. On the rare occasions I have encountered a beer with this character since I've had to write down "beery" in my notes, because at least I know what I mean by it even if nobody else does. On one return visit to Liverpool I spent a happy afternoon supping several pints of Higsons Bitter (while it was still brewed in Liverpool), and not only was the beer wonderful but I was

---

[23] www.liverpoolecho.co.uk/news/liverpool-news/liverpools-famous-higsons-beer-making-3381549

entertained by the banter of a group of men at the next table whose sole topic of conversation over about 4 hours was footie[24].

### . *Historical recipes*

**Dr. Butler's Ale:** Others: Betony, Sage, Agrimony, Scurvy-grass, Roman wormwood, Elecampane, Horseradish. Note: 18th century purging ale. Source: A,G&B.

**Spruce Beer:** Malt: Roast oats, Molasses or Brown sugar. Others: Black spruce, optional Red wine. Notes: Recipe from 1838. Source: A,G&B.

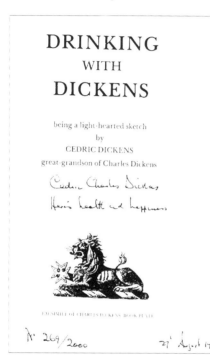

DRINKING
WITH
DICKENS

being a light-hearted sketch
by
CEDRIC DICKENS
great-grandson of Charles Dickens

*Cedric Charles Dickens*

*Harris health and happiness*

FACSIMILE OF CHARLES DICKENS BOOK PLATE

Nº 269/2000          27 April 19

**Charles Dickens' Beer**: Malt: 2oz Crystal malt, 2.5lb Malt extract, 3lb Brown sugar. Hops: 2oz Fuggles. Others: 5gal water, 1tsp salt. Notes: I have signed copy of this book and I am unsure how authentic the recipe is but it could originate from 1859. Source: Cedric Dickens (great grandson of Charles Dickens), *Drinking with Dickens*, 1980.

**X**: OG: 1055. Malt: Pale malt. Hops: Fuggles. Notes: Recipe from 1868. Source: DP.

**Porter India Export**: OG: 1058. Malt: Pale malt, Brown malt, Black malt. Hops: Fuggles. Dry hops: Dry. Notes: Recipe from 1868. Source: DP.

**Irish Porter**: OG: 1060. Malt: Pale amber malt, Amber malt, Brown malt, Chocolate malt. Hops: Fuggles, Saaz. Dry hops: Saaz. Notes: Recipe from 1898. Source: DP.

**East India Pale Ale**: OG: 1062. Malt: Pale malt. Hops: Goldings. Dry hops: Yes. Notes: Recipe from 1868. Source: DP.

**Windsor Ale**: OG: 1063. Malt: Pale malt, Honey. Hops: Fuggles. Notes: Recipe from 1796. Source: DP.

**Burton Pale Ale**: OG: 1070. Malt: Pale malt. Hops: Goldings. Notes: Recipe from 1871. Source: DP.

**London Mild Ale**: OG: 1070. Malt: Pale malt. Hops: Fuggles. Notes: Recipe from 1871. Source: DP.

---

[24] "footie" = football or soccer, which is taken very seriously in Liverpool. Even though I am not that interested in the game I do have to admit that I like to see Everton do well.

**Brown Stout (London)**: OG: 1075. Malt: Pale malt, Brown malt. Hops: Fuggles. Notes: Recipe from 1796. Source: DP.

**Irish Stout**: OG: 1075. Malt: Pale amber malt, Amber malt, Brown malt, Chocolate malt. Hops: Fuggles, Saaz. Dry hops: Yes. Notes: Recipe from 1899. Source: DP.

**Farmer's Beer**: OG: 1080. Malt: Pale malt. Hops: Fuggles. Notes: Recipe from 1743. Source: DP.

**Double Stout**: OG: 1080. Malt: Pale malt, Brown malt, Black malt. Hops: Fuggles. Notes: Recipe from 1868. Source: DP.

**Original Porter**: OG: 1081. Malt: Old style Brown malt. Hops: Fuggles. Notes: Recipe from 1743. Source: DP.

**London KXX**: OG: 1083. Malt: Pale malt. Hops: Fuggles. Notes: Recipe from 1868. Source: DP.

**Amber Ale**: OG: 1083. Malt: Pale malt, Amber malt. Hops: Fuggles. Others: Ground ginger. Notes: Recipe from 1796. Source: DP.

**London XXX Old Ale**: OG: 1086. Malt: Pale malt, Lager malt. Hops: Fuggles, Goldings. Dry hops: Dry. Notes: Recipe from 1868. Source: DP.

**Dorset XXX Old Ale**: OG: 1086. Malt: Pale malt. Hops: New Fuggles. Notes: Recipe from 1868. Source: DP.

**London Ale**: OG: 1090. Malt: Pale malt. Hops: Fuggles. Notes: Recipe from 1796. Source: DP.

**Imperial Ale**: OG: 1091. Malt: Pale malt. Hops: Goldings. Notes: Recipe from 1849. Source: DP.

**Dorchester Ale**: OG: 1100. Malt: Pale malt, Brown malt, Crystal malt, Diastatic malt syrup. Hops: Fuggles or Goldings. Notes: Recipe from ca. 1800. Source: DP.

**Sixpenny Ale**: OG: 1108. Malt: Pale malt. Hops: Fuggles. Notes: Recipe from 1796. Source: DP.

**October Pale Ale**: OG: 1110. **Small Beer**: OG: 1045. Malt: Pale malt. Hops: Fuggles. Notes: Parti-gyle recipes from 1743. Source: DP.

**London KXXXX Ale**: OG: 1111. Malt: Pale malt, Lager malt. Hops: Fuggles, Goldings. Dry hops: Yes. Notes: Recipe from 1868. Source: DP.

**Old Burton Ale**: OG: 1145. Malt: Pale malt. Hops: Fuggles. Dry hops: Goldings. Notes: Recipe from 1824. Source: DP.

## Hobsons Brewery & Company, Kidderminster

**Best Bitter**: OG: 1038. Malt: 92% Maris Otter pale malt, 8% Crystal malt. Hops: Challenger. Late hops: Progress. Dry hops: Progress. IBU: 35. Source: RP4/5.

**Steam No.9 / Manor Ale** (b-c): ABV: 4.2%. Malt: Maris Otter pale malt. Hops: Cascade, Challenger, Goldings. Source: JE5/6.

**Town Crier**: OG: 1043. Malt: 99% Maris Otter pale malt, 1% Crystal malt. Hops: Fuggles, Goldings, Progress. Hops: Fuggles, Goldings, Progress. Source: RP4/5.

**Town Crier** (b-c): ABV: 4.5%. Malt: Maris Otter pale malt, optional Wheat malt, optional Crystal malt. Hops: Progress, Goldings. Source: JE5/6.

**Old Henry**: OG: 1051. Malt: 90% Maris Otter pale malt, 10% Crystal malt. Hops: Challenger. Dry hops: Challenger. Source: RP4/5.

**Old Henry** (b-c): ABV: 5.2%. Malt: Maris Otter pale malt, Crystal malt. Hops: Goldings, Challenger. Source: JE4/5/6.

### . Hodges Brewhouse, Crook

**Original**: OG: 1040. Malt: Maris Otter pale malt, Crystal malt. Hops: Challenger, Fuggles. Source: RP4/5.

### . Hodgson's Kingston Brewery Company, Kingston-upon-Thames

**Bitter Ale**: OG: 1064. Malt: Pale malt. Hops: Fuggles. Yeast: Wyeast #1098/Wyeast #1099. Notes: Recipe from 1886. IBU: 150. SRM: 6. Source: VB. OG: 1062. Malt: Pale malt. Hops: Fuggles, Goldings. Notes: Recipe from 1896. Source: DP.

**XXXX**: OG: 1100. Malt: Pale malt, Black malt (added in boil), Crystal malt, White sugar. Hops: Fuggles. Notes: Recipe from 1896. Source: DP.

### . Hoggleys, Kislingbury

**Kislingbury Bitter** (b-c): ABV: 4%. Malt: Pale malt, Chocolate malt, Torrefied wheat. Hops: Goldings, Fuggles, Challenger. Source: JE6.

**Solstice Stout** (b-c): ABV: 5%. Malt: Pale malt, Roast barley, Chocolate malt, Torrefied wheat. Hops: Fuggles, Challenger, Molasses. Others: Cinnamon, Nutmeg. Source: JE6.

### . Hogs Back Brewery, Tongham

**Dark Mild**: OG: 1036. Malt: 70% Pipkin pale malt, 17% Crystal malt, 8% Chocolate malt, 5% Roast malt. Hops: Fuggles, Goldings. Source: RP4/5.

**APB (A-Pinta-Bitter)**: OG: 1037. Malt: 60% Pipkin pale malt, 15% Crystal malt, 10% Chocolate malt, 15% Roast malt. Hops: Fuggles, Goldings. Source: RP4/5.

**TEA (Traditional English Ale)**: OG: 1044. Malt: 92.5% Pipkin pale malt, 7.5% Crystal malt. Hops: Fuggles, Goldings. Source: RP3/4/5/JHF.

**TEA** (b-c): ABV: 4.2%. Malt: Maris Otter pale malt, Crystal malt. Hops: Fuggles, Goldings. Source: JE1/2/3/4/5/6.

**Friday 13th**: OG: 1044. Malt: 92% Pipkin pale malt, 8% Crystal malt. Hops: Fuggles. Hops: Fuggles, Goldings. Source: RP5/JHF.

**BSA (Burma Star Ale)** (b-c): ABV: 4.5%. Malt: Pipkin or Maris Otter pale malt, Crystal malt, optional Chocolate malt. Hops: Fuggles, Goldings. Source: JE1/2/4/5/6.

**Blackwater Porter**: OG: 1046. Malt: 60% Pipkin pale malt, 20% Crystal malt, 20% Chocolate malt. Hops: Fuggles, Goldings. Source: RP4/5.

**Hop Garden Gold**: OG: 1048. Malt: 100% Progress. Hops: Fuggles. Source: RP4/5.

**(RIP) Rip Snorter**: OG: 1052. Malt: 60% Pipkin pale malt, 30% Crystal malt, 10% Chocolate malt. Hops: Fuggles, Goldings. Source: RP4/5/JHF.

**Utopia**: OG: 1053. Malt: 65% Pipkin pale malt, 25% Crystal malt, 10% Chocolate malt. Hops: Fuggles, Goldings. Late hops: Fuggles, Goldings. Dry hops: Fuggles, Goldings. Source: RP5.

**YES (Your Every Success)**: OG: 1055. Malt: 90% Pipkin pale malt, 10% Wheat. Hops: Fuggles. Late hops: Goldings. Source: RP5.

**Fuggles Nouveau**: OG: 1055. Malt: 95% Pipkin pale malt, 5% Crystal malt. Hops: Fuggles. Late hops: Fuggles. Dry hops: Fuggles. Source: RP5.

**OTT** (b-c): ABV: 6%. Malt: Maris Otter pale malt, Crystal malt, Chocolate malt. Hops: Fuggles, Goldings. Source: JE3/4/5.

**OTT (Old Tongham Tasty / Over The Top)**: OG: 1066. Malt: 60-85% Pipkin pale malt, 9-15% Crystal malt, 6-25% Chocolate malt. Hops: Fuggles, Goldings. Source: RP.

**Vintage Ale** (b-c): ABV: 6.5%. Malt: Maris Otter pale malt, Crystal malt, Chocolate malt. Hops: Fuggles, Goldings. Source: JE3/4.

**Brewster's Bundle** (b-c): ABV: 7.4%. Malt: Pipkin or Maris Otter pale malt, Crystal malt. Hops: Fuggles, Goldings. Source: JE1/2/3/4/5/6.

**Brewsters Bundle**: OG: 1077. Malt: 100% Pipkin pale malt. Hops: Fuggles, Goldings. Source: RP4/5.

**Wobble in a Bottle / Santa's Wobble** (b-c): ABV: 7.5%. Malt: Pipkin or Maris Otter pale malt, Crystal malt, Chocolate malt. Hops: Fuggles, Goldings. Source: JE1/2/3/5/6.

**Santa's Wobble / Still Wobbling**: OG: 1077. Malt: 75-93% Pipkin pale malt, 7-15% Crystal malt, 0-10% Chocolate malt. Hops: Fuggles, Goldings. Source: RP.

**Millennium Ale** (b-c): ABV: 8.6%. Malt: Pipkin pale malt, Crystal malt. Hops: Fuggles, Goldings. Source: JE2.

**A Over T** (b-c): ABV: 9%. Malt: Pipkin or Maris Otter pale malt, Crystal malt, Chocolate malt. Hops: Fuggles, Goldings. Source: JE1/2/3/4/5/6.

**A Over T (Aromas Over Tongham)**: OG: 1091. Malt: 60% Pipkin pale malt, 28% Crystal malt, 12% Chocolate malt. Hops: Fuggles, Goldings. Source: RP4/5.

### . Holden's Brewery, Dudley

**Black Country Stout**: OG: 1036. Malt: 88% Maris Otter pale malt, 10% Dark malts, 2% Caramel. Hops: Fuggles. EBC: 270. Source: RP3/4/5.

**Black Country Mild**: OG: 1037. Malt: 92% Maris Otter pale malt, Brewing sugar, 8% Crystal malt and Dark malts. Hops: Fuggles, optional Goldings. IBU: 22. EBC: 50-54. Source: RP/JHF/GW.

**Black Country Bitter**: OG: 1039. Malt: 85-95% Maris Otter pale malt, 0-10% Crystal malt, 0-5% Torrefied wheat, 0-2% Brewing sugar. Hops: Fuggles, optional Goldings. Dry hops: Fuggles. EBC: 24-26. Source: RP.

**XB**: OG: 1042. Malt: 92% Maris Otter pale malt, 4% Crystal malt, 4% Brewing sugar. Hops: Fuggles. Late hops: Fuggles. EBC: 25-28. Source: RP3/4/5.

**Black Country Special Bitter / HSB**: OG: 1050. Malt: 90-95% Maris Otter pale malt, 5-10% Brewing sugar. Hops: Fuggles, optional Goldings. Dry hops: Fuggles. EBC: 28-32. Source: RP.

**XL Old Ale**: OG: 1092. Malt: 90-95% Maris Otter pale malt, 5-10% Sugar, Roast barley. Hops: Fuggles, optional Goldings. Dry hops: Fuggles. EBC: 40-45. Source: RP.

### . Joseph Holt, Manchester

**Mild**: OG: 1033. Malt: Halcyon, Pipkin, Alexis or Triumph pale malt, Crystal malt, Black malt, Flaked maize, Dark invert sugar. Hops: Goldings, Northdown. IBU: 30. Source: RP3/4/5.

**Bitter**: OG: 1039. Malt: Halcyon, Pipkin, Alexis or Triumph pale malt, Black malt, Flaked maize, Light invert sugar. Hops: Goldings, Northdown. IBU: 40. Source: RP3/4/5.

### . Holt, Plant & Deakin, Wolverhampton

**Holts Entire**: OG: 1043.5. Malt: Maris Otter pale malt, 8-10% Crystal malt, Wheat flour. Hops: Fuggles, Goldings. Source: RP4.

Note: Holt's **Bitter** and **Mild** were brewed by Tetley-Walker, Warrington.

### . Home Brewery, Nottingham

**Mild**: OG: 1036. Malt: 62% Pale malt, 8% Black malt, Crystal malt, Flaked maize, Caramel. Hops: Northdown, Target, Styrian Goldings, Fuggles. IBU: 22. Source: RP1/2/3.

**Bitter**: OG: 1038. Malt: 70% Pale malt, Flaked maize, Liquid sugar / Torrefied wheat, Caramel. Hops: Styrian Goldings or Northdown, Target, Styrian Goldings, Fuggles. Dry hops: Goldings. IBU: 32. EBC: 22. Source: RP.

### . Hook Norton Brewery Company, Hook Norton

**Best Mild**: OG: 1031-2. Malt: 94% Maris Otter pale malt, 6% Flaked maize, Caramel or Maris Otter Mild ale malt, Maris Otter pale malt, Crystal malt, Enzymic malt, Flaked maize, Brewing sugar, Caramel. Hops: Fuggles, Goldings, Challenger. Dry hops: Yes. IBU: 21-2. EBC: 50. Source: RP/GW.

**Best Bitter**: OG: 1035-6. Malt: 94% Maris Otter pale malt, 6% Flaked maize or Maris Otter Mild ale malt, Maris Otter pale malt, Crystal malt, Enzymic malt, Flaked maize, Brewing sugar, Caramel. Hops: Fuggles, Goldings, Challenger. Dry hops: Yes. IBU: 22. EBC: 21. Source: RP. Notes: I drank many pints of this fine brew when I lived in Banbury, mainly in Ye Olde Reine Deer Inn thanks to John and Hazel.

**303AD**: ABV: 4%. Malt: "small proportion of" Amber malt. Hops: First Gold. Source: WB.

**Old Hooky**: OG: 1049. Malt: 94% Maris Otter pale malt, 6% Flaked maize or Maris Otter Mild ale malt, Maris Otter pale malt, Crystal malt, Enzymic malt, Flaked maize, Brewing sugar, Caramel. Hops: Fuggles, Goldings, Challenger. Dry hops: Yes. IBU: 30. EBC: 32. Source: RP/W. OG: 1050. Malt: Pale malt, Black malt, Flaked barley, Sugar. Hops: Bramling Cross, Fuggles. Source: DL. Notes: I also drank many pints of this brew during my time in Banbury, mainly in the Wine Vaults.

**Double Stout**: OG: 1050. Malt: Maris Otter Mild ale malt, Maris Otter pale malt, Black malt, Brown malt, Enzymic malt, Brewing sugar. Hops: Fuggles, Goldings, Challenger. Dry hops: Yes. IBU: 34. EBC: 110. Source: RP5/W.

**Haymaker**: OG: 1052. Malt: Maris Otter Mild ale malt, Maris Otter pale malt,, CaraPils malt, Enzymic malt, Flaked maize, Brewing sugar. Hops: Fuggles, Goldings, Challenger. Dry hops: Yes. IBU: 22. EBC: 25. Source: RP4/5.

**Twelve Days**: OG: 1058. Malt: Maris Otter Mild ale malt, Maris Otter pale malt, Crystal malt, Chocolate malt, Enzymic malt, Flaked maize, Brewing sugar. Hops: Fuggles, Goldings, Challenger. Dry hops: Yes. IBU: 28. EBC: 60. Source: RP4/5. Notes: During the winter of 1995/6 I had an extended period in hospital after being hit by a car in Cambridge (I hadn't been drinking). Most of this was at the Horton General Hospital in Banbury, essentially waiting for bone to mend. While I was there a young lad from North-east England was admitted with various injuries and fractures. The details were a bit hazy, but it turned out that he had had a few beers with his friends and then, upon returning to where he was staying, had decided that it would be fun to play with a ladder that some builders had left lying around. However, he fell off the ladder when he was surprised by a priest! It sounded like a scene from *Fawlty Towers*![25] So I asked him what he had been drinking to get in to such a state. "Five pints of Twelve Days" was the reply. Some beers deserve respect and this is obviously one of them.

**XXX**: OG: 1063. Malt: Pale malt, Flaked rice, Invert sugar, Caramel. Hops: Fuggles. Notes: Recipe from 1899. Source: DP.

**XX (DPA)**: OG: 1070. Malt: Pale malt, White sugar, Demerara sugar, Glucose. Hops: Goldings. Notes: Recipe from 1889. Source: DP.

---

[25] *The Psychiatrist*: www.fawltysite.net/the-psychiatrist.htm

**Porter**: OG: 1070. Malt: Pale malt, Roast barley, Brown malt, Demerara sugar. Hops: Fuggles. Notes: Recipe from 1890. Source: DP.

### . *Hop Back Brewery, Salisbury*

**Mild**: OG: 1032. Malt: 90% Pipkin pale malt, 5% Crystal malt, 2.5% Chocolate malt, 2.5% Roast barley. Hops: Challenger. Late hops: Goldings. IBU: 25. EBC: 90. Source: RP3/4/5/GW.

**GFB**: OG: 1035. Malt: 95% Pipkin or Maris Otter pale malt, 5% Crystal malt. Hops: Challenger. Late hops: Goldings. IBU: 43. EBC: 30. Source: RP5.

**Special**: OG: 1041-2. Malt: 90% Pipkin pale malt, 9% Crystal malt, 1% Chocolate malt. Hops: Challenger, Goldings. Source: RP3/4.

**Wilt Alternative**: OG: 1041-2. Malt: 97% Pipkin pale malt, 3% Crystal malt. Hops: Challenger, Goldings. Late hops: Goldings. Source: RP3/4.

**Crop Circle** (b-c): ABV: 4.2%. Malt: Maris Otter or Optic pale malt, Flaked maize, Wheat malt. Hops: Pioneer, Tettnang, optional Goldings. Others: Coriander. Source: JE3/4/5/6.

**Taiphoon** (b-c): ABV: 4.2%. Malt: Maris Otter pale malt. Hops: Goldings, Progress/Pioneer. Others: Lemon grass. Source: JE2/3. Hops: Pioneer, Goldings. Others: Lemon grass, Coriander. Source: JE4/6. Malt: Optic pale malt. Source: JE5/6.

**Entire Stout**: OG: 1042-3. Malt: 88% Pipkin or Maris Otter pale malt, 4% Crystal malt, 4% Chocolate malt, 4% Roast barley. Hops: Challenger, optional Goldings. Late hops: Goldings. IBU: 33. EBC: 170. Source: RP.

**Entire Stout** (b-c): ABV: 4.5%. Malt: Maris Otter and/or Optic pale malt, Crystal wheat malt, Roast barley, Chocolate malt. Hops: Challenger, Goldings. Source: JE4/5/6.

**Wheat Beer**: OG: 1048-51. Malt: 50% Pipkin pale malt, 50% Wheat malt. Hops: Challenger, Goldings. Late hops: Goldings. Source: RP3/4.

**Thunderstorm**: OG: 1049. Malt: 50% Maris Otter pale malt, 50% Wheat malt. Hops: Progress. Late hops: Progress. EBC: 10. Source: RP5.

**Summer Lightning**: OG: 1049-50. Malt: 98% Pipkin pale malt, 2% Crystal malt or 100% Maris Otter pale malt. Hops: Challenger. Late hops: Goldings. IBU: 38. EBC: 14. Source: RP/JHF.

**Summer Lightning** (b-c): ABV: 5%. Malt: Maris Otter or Optic pale malt. Hops: Goldings. Source: JE1/2/3/4/6.

**Thunderstorm** (b-c): ABV: 5%. Malt: Maris Otter pale malt, Wheat malt. Hops: Progress, optional Goldings. Source: JE1/2/3. Hops: Progress, Goldings. Others: Coriander. Source: JE4.

### Hopdaemon, Canterbury

**Skrimshander IPA** (b-c): ABV: 4.5%. Malt: Pale malt, Crystal malt, Caramalt. Hops: Fuggles, Goldings, Bramling Cross. Source: JE4/5/6.

**Green Daemon** (b-c): ABV: 5%. Malt: Pale malt, Lager malt. Hops: New Zealand hops. Source: JE4/5/6.

**Leviathan** (b-c): ABV: 6%. Malt: Pale malt, Crystal malt, Chocolate malt, Wheat malt, Caramalt. Hops: Fuggles, Bramling Cross. Source: JE4/5/6.

### Tom Hoskins Brewery, Leicester

**Beaumanor Bitter**: OG: 1039. Malt: 69% Maris Otter pale malt, 3.5% Crystal malt, 0-4% Torrefied wheat, 23% No.1 invert sugar. Hops: Challenger. Dry hops: Challenger. IBU: 33. EBC: 19. Source: RP.

**Penn's Ale**: OG: 1045. Malt: 69% Maris Otter pale malt, 4.5% Crystal malt, 0-4% Torrefied wheat, 22% Black invert sugar. Hops: Challenger. IBU: 29. EBC: 33. Source: RP.

**Churchill's Pride**: OG: 1050. Malt: 69% Maris Otter pale malt, 4% Crystal malt, 4% Torrefied wheat, 23% No.1 invert sugar, Caramel. Hops: Challenger. IBU: 28. EBC: 88. Source: RP4/5.

**Premium**: OG: 1050. Malt: 69% Maris Otter pale malt, 4% Crystal malt, 4% Torrefied wheat, 23% No.1 invert sugar. Hops: Challenger. IBU: 28. EBC: 20. Source: RP4/5.

**Old Nigel**: OG: 1060. Malt: Maris Otter pale malt, Crystal malt, Invert sugar, optional Torrefied wheat. Hops: Challenger. Source: RP.

### Hoskins & Oldfield, Leicester

**HOB Best Mild**: OG: 1035. Malt: Pale malt, Crystal malt, Black malt. Hops: Goldings. Source: RP2/3/4/5.

**HOB Bitter**: OG: 1041. Malt: Pale malt, Crystal malt. Hops: Goldings. Source: RP2/3/4/5.

**White Dolphin**: OG: 1041. Malt: Pale malt, Wheat malt. Hops: Goldings. Source: RP4/5.

**Tom Kelly's Stout**: OG: 1043. Malt: Pale malt, Crystal malt, Black malt, Roast barley. Hops: Goldings. Source: RP2/3/4/5.

**EXS**: OG: 1051. Malt: Pale malt, Crystal malt. Hops: Goldings. Source: RP2/3/4/5.

**'04' Ale** (b-c): ABV: 5.2%. Malt: Maris Otter pale malt, Crystal malt, Wheat malt. Hops: Northdown, Mount Hood, Bramling Cross. Source: JE1.

**Old Navigation Ale**: OG: 1071. Malt: Pale malt, Crystal malt. Hops: Goldings. Source: RP2/3/4/5.

## . Sarah Hughes Brewery, Dudley

**Sedgley Surprise Bitter**: OG: 1048. Malt: Maris Otter pale malt, Invert sugar. Hops: Goldings. Dry hops: Goldings. Source: RP4/5.

**Dark Ruby Mild**: OG: 1058. Malt: 75% Maris Otter pale malt, 25% Crystal malt. Hops: Fuggles, Goldings. Source: RP1/2/3/4/5/GW/JE1/2/3/4/5.

## . Hull Brewery Company, Hull

**Brewery Mild**: OG: 1033. Malt: 80% Maris Otter pale malt, 15% Halcyon pale malt, 5% Black malt or 100% Maris Otter pale malt, Black malt, Sucramel. Hops: Fuggles. Source: RP2/3/4/5.

**Brewery Bitter**: OG: 1036-9. Malt: 100% Maris Otter pale malt, Chocolate malt. Hops: Goldings. Source: RP3/4/5.

**Ellwood's Best Bitter**: OG: 1038. Malt: 100% Maris Otter pale malt. Hops: Goldings. Source: RP4/5.

**Olde Traditional**: OG: 1042. Malt: 100% Maris Otter pale malt, Chocolate malt. Hops: Goldings. Source: RP4/5.

**Governer Strong Ale**: OG: 1048. Malt: 100% Maris Otter pale malt, Chocolate malt. Hops: Goldings. Source: RP3/4/5.

## . Humpty Dumpty, Reedham

**Nord Atlantic** (b-c): ABV: 3.7%. Malt: Pearl pale malt, Crystal malt, Caramalt, Wheat malt. Hops: Fuggles, Cascade. Source: JE4. Malt: Maris Otter pale malt, Crystal malt, Caramalt, Wheat malt. Hops: Fuggles, Challenger. Source: JE6.

**Little Sharpie** (b-c): ABV: 3.8%. Malt: Pearl pale malt, Caramalt, Wheat malt. Hops: Fuggles, Cascade. Source: JE4/5.

**Lemon & Ginger** (b-c): ABV: 4%. Malt: Pearl or Maris Otter pale malt, Caramalt, Wheat malt. Hops: Cascade, Bramling Cross. Others: Stem Ginger, Lemons. Source: JE5/6.

**Humpty Dumpty** (b-c): ABV: 4.1%. Malt: Pearl or Maris Otter pale malt, Crystal malt, Caramalt, Wheat malt. Hops: Fuggles, Challenger. Source: JE4/5/6.

**Claud Hamilton** (b-c): ABV: 4.1-4.3%. Malt: Pearl pale malt, Chocolate malt, Roast barley, Caramalt. Hops: Challenger. Source: JE4/5.

**Brief Encounter** (b-c): ABV: 4.3%. Malt: Maris Otter pale malt, Wheat malt. Hops: Goldings. Source: JE6.

**Golden Gorse** (b-c): ABV: 4.4%. Malt: Lager malt, Wheat malt. Hops: Fuggles, First Gold. Source: JE4/5.

**Reed Cutter** (b-c): ABV: 4.4%. Malt: Pearl or Maris Otter pale malt, Wheat malt. Hops: Fuggles, First Gold. Source: JE5/6.

**Cheltenham Flyer** (b-c): ABV: 4.6%. Malt: Pearl pale malt, Crystal malt, Wheat malt. Hops: Challenger, Mount Hood. Source: JE4/5.

**Peto's Porter** (b-c): ABV: 5%. Malt: Pearl or Maris Otter pale malt, Crystal malt, Amber malt, Wheat malt, Chocolate malt. Hops: First Gold. Source: JE5/6.

**Railway Sleeper** (b-c): ABV: 5%. Malt: Pearl or Maris Otter pale malt, Crystal malt, Amber malt, Wheat malt. Hops: First Gold. Source: JE4/5/6.

**Broadland Gold** (b-c): ABV: 6%. Malt: Pearl pale malt, Amber malt, Wheat malt. Hops: Challenger. Source: JE4/5.

## . *Hydes' Anvil Brewery, Manchester*

**Billy Westwood**: OG: 1031. Malt: Maris Otter pale malt, Crystal malt, Torrefied wheat. Hops: Fuggles, Challenger, First Gold. Dry hops: Yes. IBU: 23. EBC: 15. Source: RP5.

**Anvil Mild**: OG: 1032. Malt: 100% Maris Otter pale malt, 0.05% Caramel, optional Crystal malt, optional Chocolate malt. Hops: Fuggles. Dry hops: Yes. IBU: 21. Source: RP1/2/GW.

**Anvil Light**: OG: 1034-6. Malt: 100% Maris Otter pale malt, 0.025% Caramel, optional Crystal malt. Hops: Fuggles. Dry hops: Yes. IBU: 23. Source: RP.

**Anvil Bitter**: OG: 1036. Malt: 100% Maris Otter Pale malt, Caramel, optional Crystal malt. Hops: 50% Styrian Goldings. Late hops: 50% Fuggles. IBU: 28. Source: RP.

**Harem Scarem**: ABV: 4.7%. Hops: Styrian Goldings, Target, Fuggles. Source: W.

**Anvil Strong Ale / XXXX**: OG: 1076. Malt: 100% Maris Otter pale malt, 0.075% Caramel. Hops: Fuggles. Dry hops: Yes. IBU: 18. Source: RP1/2.

## . *Iceni Brewery, Mundford*

**Honey Mild** (b-c): ABV: 3.6%. Malt: Halcyon or Maris Otter pale malt, Crystal malt, Roast barley, Flaked barley, Honey. Hops: Fuggles, Challenger. Source: JE3/4/5/6.

**Star of the County Down** (b-c): ABV: 3.6%. Malt: Halcyon pale malt, Roast barley, Molasses. Hops: Fuggles, Challenger. Source: JE3.

**Thetford Forest Mild** (b-c): ABV: 3.6%. Malt: Halcyon pale malt, Torrefied wheat, Roast barley. Hops: Fuggles, Challenger. Source: JE3/4. Malt: Maris Otter pale malt, Crystal malt, Roast barley, Flaked barley. Hops: Fuggles, Challenger. Source: JE5/6.

**Boadicea Chariot Ale**: OG: 1038. Malt: 95% Pale malt, 5% Crystal malt, 0.3% Roast barley. Hops: Challenger, Fuggles. Source: RP4/5.

**Boadicea Chariot Ale** (b-c): ABV: 3.8%. Malt: Halcyon or Maris Otter pale malt. Hops: Fuggles, Challenger. Source: JE3/4/5/6.

**Brewer's Light** (b-c): ABV: 3.9%. Malt: Lager malt, Wheat. Hops: Brewers Gold. Source: JE5.

**Elveden Forest Gold** (b-c): ABV: 3.9%. Malt: Halcyon or Maris Otter pale malt, Caramalt. Hops: Fuggles, Challenger, Brewers Gold. Source: JE4/5/6.

**Celtic Queen** (b-c): ABV: 4%. Malt: Halcyon or Maris Otter pale malt, Caramalt. Hops: Fuggles, Challenger. Source: JE2/3/4/5/6.

**Fine Soft Day** (b-c): ABV: 4%. Malt: Halcyon or Maris Otter pale malt, Caramalt, Maple syrup. Hops: Fuggles, Challenger. Source: JE2/3/4/5/6.

**Lovely Day** (b-c): ABV: 4%. Malt: Maris Otter pale malt, Caramalt. Hops: Challenger, Fuggles, Boadicea. Source: JE6.

**Red, White & Blueberry** (b-c): ABV: 5%. Malt: Maris Otter pale malt, Caramalt. Hops: Cascade. Others: Blueberries. Source: JE5/6.

**Swaffham Pride** (b-c): ABV: 4%. Malt: Halcyon or Maris Otter pale malt, Caramalt, Fruit sugar. Hops: Fuggles, Challenger. Source: JE3/4/5/6.

**Cranberry Wheat** (b-c): ABV: 4.1%. Malt: Lager malt, Caramalt, Wheat malt. Hops: Cascade. Others: Cranberries. Source: JE4/5/6.

**Snowdrop** (b-c): ABV: 4.1%. Malt: Lager malt, Wheat. Hops: Fuggles, Cascade, Challenger. Source: JE3/4/5/6.

**Boadica Strong Ale** (b-c): ABV: 4.2%. Malt: Pale malt, Caramalt, Rye malt. Hops: Fuggles, Challenger. Source: JE2.

**Fen Tiger** (b-c): ABV: 4.2%. Malt: Halcyon or Maris Otter pale malt, Caramalt. Hops: Fuggles, Challenger. Others: Coriander. Source: JE2/3/4/5/6.

**On Target** (b-c): ABV: 4.2%. Malt: Halcyon or Maris Otter pale malt, Caramalt. Hops: Fuggles, Challenger, Target. Source: JE2/3/4/5/6.

**Thomas Paine Porter** (b-c): ABV: 4.2%. Malt: Halcyon or Maris Otter pale malt, Crystal malt, Flaked wheat, Torrefied wheat, Roast barley. Hops: Fuggles, Challenger. Source: JE3/4/5/6.

**Honey Stout** (b-c): ABV: 4.3%. Malt: Halcyon or Maris Otter pale malt, Crystal malt, Caramalt, Roast barley, Honey. Hops: Fuggles, Challenger. Source: JE3/4/5/6.

**Phoenix** (b-c): ABV: 4.3%. Malt: Lager malt, Wheat. Hops: Phoenix. Source: JE4/5/6.

**Dierdre of the Sorrows** (b-c): ABV: 4.4%. Malt: Halcyon or Maris Otter pale malt, Roast barley. Hops: Fuggles, Challenger. Source: JE2/3/4/5/6.

**Ported Porter** (b-c): ABV: 4.4%. Malt: Halcyon or Maris Otter pale malt, Torrefied wheat, Flaked barley, Roast barley. Hops: Fuggles, Challenger. Others: Port. Source: JE3/4/5/6.

**Roisin Dubh** (b-c): ABV: 4.4%. Malt: Halcyon or Maris Otter pale malt, Torrefied wheat, Roast barley. Hops: Fuggles, Challenger. Source: JE3/4/5/6.

**Good Night Out** (b-c): ABV: 4.5%. Malt: Halcyon or Maris Otter pale malt, Roast barley. Hops: Fuggles, Challenger. Others: Port. Source: JE3/4/5/6.

**It's a Grand Day** (b-c): ABV: 4.5%. Malt: Halcyon or Maris Otter pale malt. Hops: Fuggles, Challenger. Others: Stem ginger. Source: JE3/4/5/6.

**Iceni Gold** (b-c): ABV: 5%. Malt: Halcyon pale malt, Caramalt. Hops: Fuggles, Challenger. Source: JE2/3/4.

**L.A.D. (Lager Awareness Day) Lager / Norfolk Lager** (b-c): ABV: 5%. Malt: Lager malt, Wheat malt. Hops: Hersbrücker. Source: JE2/3/5.

**Norfolk Lager** (b-c): ABV: 5%. Malt: Lager malt, Wheat malt. Hops: Hersbrücker. Source: JE6.

**Norfolk Gold** (b-c): ABV: 5%. Malt: Halcyon or Maris Otter pale malt, Caramalt. Hops: Fuggles, Challenger. Source: JE3/4/5/6.

**Raspberry Wheat** (b-c): ABV: 5%. Malt: Halcyon or Maris Otter pale malt, Lager malt, Wheat malt. Hops: Hersbrücker. Others: Raspberries. Source: JE2/3/4/5/6.

**Swaffham Gold** (b-c): ABV: 5%. Malt: Halcyon or Maris Otter pale malt, Caramalt, Maple syrup. Hops: Fuggles, Challenger. Source: JE3/4/5/6.

**Winter Lightning** (b-c): ABV: 5%. Malt: Lager malt, Wheat malt. Hops: Hersbrücker. Source: JE2/3/4/5/6.

**Men of Norfolk** (b-c): ABV: 6.2%. Malt: Halcyon or Maris Otter pale malt, Crystal malt, Torrefied wheat, Flaked barley, Roast barley. Hops: Fuggles, Challenger. Source: JE3/4/5/6.

## Ind Coope Burton Brewery, Burton-upon-Trent

**Light Ale** (bottled): ABV: 3.5%. Malt: Crystal malt, Sugar. Hops: Fuggles. Source: DL.

**Long Life** (bottled): OG: 1041. Malt: Pale malt, Flaked maize, Wheat malt. Hops: Hallertau. Dry hops: Hop extract. Source: DL.

**Draught Burton Ale**: OG: 1047. Malt: 87.5% Pale malt, 1.5% Chocolate malt, 11% Maltose syrup. Hops: Target. Late hops: Styrian Goldings. Dry hops: Styrian Goldings. IBU: 35. Source: RP2/3/4/5/GW. OG: 1048. Malt: Pale malt, Crystal malt, Barley syrup, Sugar. Hops: Goldings, Fuggles. Late hops: Goldings. Dry hops: Goldings. Source: DL.

**Double Diamond**: OG: 1053. Malt: Pale malt, Crystal malt, Chocolate malt, High Maltose brewing sugar. Hops: Galena, Target. IBU: 35. Source: EBA. OG: 1054-57. Malt: Pale malt, Flaked maize, Crystal malt, Toasted pale malt, Amber malt, Sugar. Hops: Goldings. Late hops: Goldings, Challenger, Fuggles, Styrian Goldings. Source: CB. OG: 1040. Malt: Pale malt, Crystal malt, CaraPils malt, Munich malt. Hops: Goldings. Late hops: Fuggles. Yeast: Wyeast #1028. Source: Ronald J. Sup, MHF.

**Double Diamond** (keg): OG: 1038. Malt: Pale malt, Barley syrup, Sugar. Hops: Fuggles. Dry hops: Hop extract. Source: DL.

**Skol** (bottled): OG: 1034. Malt: Lager malt, Wheat malt, Flaked maize, Sugar. Hops: Hallertau, Goldings. Source: DL

### . Island Brewery, Newport, Isle of Wight

**Nipper Bitter**: OG: 1037-8. Malt: 96% Pipkin pale malt, 3% Crystal malt, 1% Chocolate malt. Hops: Challenger, Goldings, Target. Source: RP3/4.

**Newport Best Bitter**: OG: 1045. Malt: 96% Pipkin pale malt, 3% Crystal malt, 1% Chocolate malt. Hops: Challenger, Goldings, Target. Source: RP3.

Notes: Island was set up in 1991 and bought the Burts name and brands in 1993 after that brewery had stopped brewing. See Burts Brewery and Ventnor Brewery.

### . Isle of Man Breweries

**Castletown Bitter**: OG: 1035.8. Malt: Golden Promise or Triumph pale malt, Crystal malt. Hops: Fuggles, Goldings, Bramling Cross / Northern Brewer / Target. Source: RP1/2.

**Okells Mild**: OG: 1034. Malt: 95% Golden Promise, Pipkin and/or Triumph pale malt, 8% Black invert sugar, Caramel. Hops: Fuggles, Bramling Cross / Northern Brewer / Target. Late hops: Fuggles. IBU: 18. EBC: 55. Source: RP.

**Okells Bitter**: OG: 1035.8. Malt: Golden Promise, Pipkin or Triumph pale malt, Crystal malt. Hops: Bramling Cross / Northern Brewer / Target. Late hops: Fuggles, Goldings. IBU: 32. EBC: 25. Source: RP/JHF.

Note: Became Okell & Son in 1994.

### . Isle of Purbeck, Swanage

**IPA** (b-c): ABV: 4.8%. Malt: Maris Otter pale malt, Crystal malt. Hops: Bramling Cross, Pioneer, WGV. Source: JE6.

**Solar Power** (b-c): ABV: 5%. Malt: Lager malt, Wheat malt, Caramalt. Hops: First Gold, Perle. Source: JE6.

### . Itchen Valley, Alresford

**Godfathers** (b-c): ABV: 3.8%. Malt: Maris Otter pale malt, Crystal malt. Hops: Fuggles, Goldings, WGV, Progress. Source: JE3/4/5.

**Fagins** (b-c): ABV: 4.1%. Malt: Maris Otter pale malt, Crystal malt, Wheat malt. Hops: Fuggles, Goldings, First Gold. Source: JE3/4/5/6.

**Wykehams Glory** (b-c): ABV: 4.3%. Malt: Maris Otter pale malt, Crystal malt, Chocolate malt. Hops: First Gold. Source: JE3/4/5/6.

**Treacle Stout** (b-c): ABV: 4.4%. Malt: Maris Otter pale malt, Crystal malt, Chocolate malt, Roast barley, Treacle. Hops: Progress. Other: Liquorice. Source: JE5/6.

**Hambledon Bitter** (b-c): ABV: 4.5%. Malt: Maris Otter pale malt, Honey. Hops: Cascade. Other: Elderflowers. Source: JE5/6.

**Pure Gold** (b-c): ABV: 4.8%. Malt: Maris Otter pale malt, Lager malt. Hops: Cascade, Saaz. Source: JE3/4/5/6.

**Father Christmas** (b-c): ABV: 5%. Malt: Maris Otter pale malt, Crystal malt. Hops: Challenger. Source: JE3/4/5/6.

**Wat Tyler** (b-c): ABV: 5%. Malt: Maris Otter pale malt, Crystal malt. Hops: Progress. Source: JE3/4/5/6.

### . *Jennings Brothers, Cockermouth*

**Dark Mild**: OG: 1031. Malt: Pale malt, Wheat malt / Torrefied wheat, Invert sugar, Black malt. Hops: Challenger, Fuggles, Goldings, optional Bramling Cross. Source: RP/GW.

**Bitter**: OG: 1035. Malt: 85% Pale malt, 15% Wheat malt / Torrefied wheat, Black malt and/or Syrups. Hops: Challenger, Fuggles, Goldings, optional Bramling Cross. Source: RP.

**Cumberland Draught Bitter / Cumberland Ale**: OG: 1040. Malt: Pale malt, Wheat malt / Torrefied wheat, Invert sugar. Hops: Challenger, Fuggles, Goldings, optional Bramling Cross. Source: RP.

**Cocker Hoop**: ABV: 4.8%. Malt: Pale malt, Torrefied wheat. Hops: Challenger, Goldings. IBU: 35. EBC: 20. Source: RP5. OG: 1048-51. Malt: Pale malt, Crystal malt, Torrefied wheat. Hops: Goldings. Late hops: Challenger, Goldings. Source: BC.

**SL / Sneck Lifter**: OG: 1055. Malt: Pale malt, Wheat malt / Torrefied wheat, Invert sugar, small % Black malt. Hops: Challenger, Fuggles, Goldings, optional Bramling Cross. Source: RP.

### . *John O'Gaunt, Melton Mowbray*

**Robin a Tiptoe** (b-c): ABV: 3.9%. Malt: Maris Otter pale malt, Crystal malt. Hops: Fuggles, Willamette. Source: JE5.

**Duke of Lancaster** (b-c): ABV: 4.3%. Malt: Maris Otter pale malt. Hops: Willamette, Fuggles. Source: JE5.

**Coat o'Red** (b-c): ABV: 5%. Malt: Maris Otter pale malt, Crystal malt. Hops: Fuggles, Willamette. Source: JE5.

### . *Jolly Roger Brewing Group, Worcester*

**Jolly Roger Ale**: OG: 1038. Malt: Halcyon pale malt, Chocolate malt or 95% Maris Otter pale malt and Halcyon pale malt, 5% Crystal malt. Hops: Fuggles, Goldings, optional Challenger. Dry hops: Yes. Source: RP.

**Shipwrecked**: OG: 1040. Malt: 90% Maris Otter pale malt and/or Halcyon pale malt, 7% Crystal malt, 0-3% Roast malt. Hops: Fuggles, Goldings, Challenger. Late hops: Challenger, Fuggles, Goldings. Dry hops: Yes. Source: RP4.

**Goodness Stout**: OG: 1042. Malt: 90% Maris Otter pale malt and/or Halcyon pale malt, 10% Roast malt. Hops: Fuggles, Challenger. Late hops: Challenger, Fuggles. Dry hops: Yes. Source: RP4.

**Flagship**: OG: 1052. Malt: 90% Maris Otter pale malt and Halcyon pale malt, 7% Crystal malt, 1.5% Chocolate malt, 1.5% Roast malt. Hops: Goldings, Challenger. Late hops: Challenger, Goldings. Dry hops: Yes. Source: RP4.

### Jollyboat, Bideford

**Plunder** (b-c): ABV: 4.8%. Malt: Maris Otter pale malt, Crystal malt, Chocolate malt, Black malt, Wheat malt. Hops: Fuggles and 2 other varieties. Source: JE4/5.

**Privateer** (b-c): ABV: 4.8%. Malt: Maris Otter pale malt, Crystal malt, Chocolate malt, Wheat malt. Hops: Fuggles, Cascade. Source: JE2/3/4/5.

**Contraband** (b-c): ABV: 5.8%. Malt: Maris Otter pale malt, Amber malt, Black malt. Hops: Cascade, Fuggles. Source: JE5.

### Judges Brewery, Rugby

**Barrister's Bitter**: OG: 1037. Malt: 92% Halcyon pale malt, 2% Crystal malt, 6% Wheat malt. Hops: Challenger. Dry hops: Seedless. Source: RP3/4/5.

**Old Gavel Bender**: OG: 1050. Malt: 90% Halcyon pale malt, 3% Crystal malt, 7% Wheat malt. Hops: Challenger. Dry hops: Seedless. Source: RP3/4/5.

### Kelham Island Brewery, Sheffield

**Hallamshire Bitter**: OG: 1036. Malt: 90% Maris Otter pale malt, 5% Crystal malt, 5% Wheat malt. Hops: Challenger. Source: RP3.

**Bitter**: OG: 1038. Malt: 95% Maris Otter pale malt, 5% Crystal malt. Hops: Challenger. Source: RP3/4/5.

**Golden Eagle**: OG: 1042.5. Malt: 100% Lager malt. Hops: Liberty. Source: RP5.

**Gate Crasher**: OG: 1044.5. Malt: 85% Maris Otter pale malt, 5% Wheat malt. Hops: Willamette. Dry hops: Willamette. Source: RP5.

**Celebration Ale**: OG: 1046. Malt: 91% Maris Otter pale malt, 9% Crystal malt. Hops: Challenger. Source: RP3.

**Bete Noire**: OG: 1055. Malt: 83% Maris Otter pale malt, 7% Chocolate malt, 10% Wheat malt, Roast barley. Hops: Challenger. Source: RP3/4/5.

**Grande Pale**: OG: 1066.5. Malt: 85% Maris Otter pale malt, 15% Wheat malt. Hops: Mount Hood, Willamette. Dry hops: Yes. IBU: 25. Source: RP5.

Notes: This brewery was formed in 1990 in the back yard of the Fat Cat pub, where I used to drink on an occasional, but always enjoyable, basis between 1986-9 when I lived in Sheffield. After the ambulance men cut my Fat Cat sweatshirt off me after I suffered a serious road accident in 1994 I mentioned this to my sister, so she ordered a replacement from the pub. Not only did they send her a replacement sweatshirt, they returned her cheque and a letter to say they hoped I recovered soon. I really do appreciate this wonderful gesture. Not only are the people of the Fat Cat wonderful, but they brew some fine ale too.

### . Keltek, Lostwithiel

**King** (b-c): ABV: 5.1%. Malt: Pale malt, Crystal malt. Hops: Cascade, Hallertau. Source: JE3/4/5/6.

**Revenge / Lostwithiale** (b-c): ABV: 7%. Malt: Pale malt, Crystal malt, Chocolate malt. Hops: Cascade, Hallertau. Source: JE3/4/5.

**Beheaded '76'** (b-c): ABV: 7.6%. Malt: Pale malt, Wheat malt, Chocolate malt, Crystal malt. Hops: First Gold, Cluster. Source: JE6.

**Kripple Dick** (b-c): ABV: 8.5%. Malt: Pale malt, Crystal malt, Chocolate malt, Amber malt. Hops: First Gold, Hallertau. Source: JE3/4/5/6.

**Beheaded** (b-c): ABV: 10%. Malt: Pale malt, Crystal malt, Chocolate malt, Wheat malt. Hops: First Gold, Cluster. Source: JE5.

### . Kemptown Brewery Company, Brighton

**Bitter**: OG: 1040. Malt: 95% Pale malt, 5% Crystal malt. Hops: Challenger, Fuggles, Goldings. IBU: 38. Source: RP3/4/5.

**Celebrated Staggering Ale**: OG: 1050. Malt: 90% Pale malt, 10% Crystal malt. Hops: Fuggles, Goldings. IBU: 40. Source: RP3/4/5.

**SID (Staggering in the Dark)**: OG: 1052. Malt: 90% Pale malt, 8% Crystal malt, 2% Chocolate malt. Hops: Challenger, Goldings. IBU: 40. Source: RP3/4/5.

**Old Grumpy**: OG: 1060. Malt: 90% Pale malt, 9% Crystal malt, 1% Chocolate malt. Hops: Challenger, Fuggles, Goldings. Source: RP3/4/5.

### . Khean, Congleton

**Caught Behind** (b-c): ABV: 4.2%. Malt: Maris Otter pale malt, Chocolate malt, Roast barley. Hops: Fuggles, Goldings. Source: JE5.

**Fine Leg** (b-c): ABV: 4.2%. Malt: Maris Otter pale malt, Crystal malt. Hops: Fuggles, Goldings. Source: JE5.

**Leg Spinner** (b-c): ABV: 4.4%. Malt: Maris Otter pale malt, Pale crystal malt. Hops: Challenger. Source: JE5.

**Jingle Balls** (b-c): ABV: 5.2%. Malt: Maris Otter pale malt, Crystal malt. Hops: Fuggles, Goldings, Challenger. Source: JE5.

## C.N. Kidd & Sons, Dartford

**X**: OG: 1031. Malt: Pale malt, Mild malt, Crystal malt, Flaked maize, Cane sugar, Caramel. Hops: Fuggles, Goldings, Bramling Cross. Yeast: Wyeast #1098/Wyeast #1099. Notes: Recipe from 1934. IBU: 35. SRM: 25. Source: VB.

## W.J. King & Company (Brewers), Horsham

**Five Generations** (b-c): ABV: 4.4%. Malt: Maris Otter pale malt, Crystal malt, Wheat malt, Chocolate malt. Hops: Goldings, Cascade. Source: JE6.

**King's Old Ale** (b-c): ABV: 4.5%. Malt: Maris Otter pale malt, Crystal malt, Chocolate malt, Wheat malt. Hops: optional Goldings, WGV, Challenger. Source: JE5/6.

**Red River Ale** (b-c): ABV: 5%. Malt: Maris Otter pale malt, Crystal malt, Chocolate malt, Enzymic malt. Source: JE6.Hops: WGV, Goldings, Challenger. Source: JE4/5/6.

**Mallard Ale** (b-c): ABV: 5%. Malt: Maris Otter pale malt. Hops: Goldings. Source: JE6.

**Cereal Thriller** (b-c): ABV: 6.3%. Malt: Pale malt, Enzymic malt, Flaked maize. Hops: WGV. Source: JE5. Malt: Maris Otter pale malt, Crystal malt, Chocolate malt, Enzymic malt, Flaked maize. Hops: WGV. Source: JE6.

**Merry Ale** (b-c): ABV: 6.5%. Malt: Pale malt, Crystal malt, Chocolate malt. Hops: WGV, Goldings, Challenger. Source: JE5. Malt: Maris Otter pale malt, Crystal malt, Chocolate malt, Enzymic malt. Hops: Goldings, WGV. Source: JE6.

## King & Barnes, Horsham

**Sussex Mild**: OG: 1032-4. Malt: Puffin pale malt, Crystal malt, Flaked maize, optional Chocolate malt, Enzymic malt, Caramel, Invert sugar and/or Roast barley extract. Hops: Challenger, Goldings, optional WGV. Late hops: Yes. IBU: 21-25. EBC: 80-100. Source: RP.

**Mild Ale**: OG: 1033. Malt: Pale malt, Flaked maize, Black malt, Sugar. Hops: WGV, Fuggles. Source: DL.

**Sussex Bitter**: OG: 1034. Malt: Puffin pale malt, Crystal malt, Flaked maize, optional Chocolate malt, Caramel, Enzymic malt and/or Invert sugar. Hops: Challenger, Goldings, optional WGV. Late hops: Yes. IBU: 31.5-32. Source: RP.

**Sussex Pale Ale**: OG: 1035. Malt: Pale malt, Flaked maize, Sugar. Hops: Goldings, Fuggles. Late hops: Goldings. Dry hops: Goldings. Source: DL.

**Wealdman**: OG: 1035. Malt: Alexis Pilsner Lager malt, CaraPils malt, Wheat malt. Hops: Challenger, Goldings, WGV. Dry hops: Yes. Source: RP4/5.

**Broadwood**: OG: 1040-1. Malt: Puffin pale malt, Crystal malt, Enzymic malt, Invert sugar, Caramel, optional Flaked maize. Hops: Challenger, WGV. Late hops: Goldings. IBU: 37. Source: RP.

**King's Crystal** (b-c): ABV: 4.3%. Malt: Pale malt, Crystal malt. Hops: Challenger, WGV, Goldings. Source: JE1/2.

**Old Ale**: OG: 1045-6. Malt: Puffin pale malt, Crystal malt and Torrefied barley, Flaked barley, Chocolate malt, Caramel, Invert sugar and/or Wheat malt. Hops: Challenger, Goldings / WGV. IBU: 27-33. Source: RP.

**Faygate Dragon** (b-c): ABV: 4.7%. Malt: Pale malt, Crystal malt, Enzymic malt. Hops: Liberty. Source: JE1/2. Also see **Faygate Dragon**, Hall & Woodhouse.

**Harvest Ale** (b-c): ABV: 4.7%. Malt: Pale malt, Crystal malt, Enzymic malt, Flaked maize. Hops: Goldings. Source: JE1/2.

**Single Hop Ale / Challenger Ale** (b-c): ABV: 4.7%. Malt: Pale malt, Crystal malt, Enzymic malt. Hops: Challenger. Source: JE1/2.

**Sussex Old Ale**: OG: 1048. Malt: Pale malt, Black malt, Sugar. Hops: WGV, Fuggles. Source: DL.

**Festive**: OG: 1050. Malt: Puffin pale malt, Crystal malt, Flaked maize and Enzymic malt, Chocolate malt and/or Caramel. Hops: Challenger and Goldings and/or WGV. Late hops: Yes. IBU: 41.5-45. Source: RP/JE1/2.

**IPA** (b-c): ABV: 5%. Malt: Pale malt, Crystal malt, Enzymic malt. Hops: Challenger, WGV, Goldings. Source: JE1/2.

**India Pale Ale**: OG: 1054-55. Malt: Pale malt, Crystal malt, Invert sugar. Hops: Challenger. Late hops: WGV, Goldings. Source: BC.

**Coppercast** (b-c): ABV: 5.5%. Malt: Pale malt, Rye crystal malt, Rye malt, Chocolate malt. Hops: Challenger, Styrian Goldings, WGV, Goldings. Source: JE1/2.

**Old Porter** (b-c): ABV: 5.5%. Malt: Pale malt, Crystal malt, Chocolate malt, Wheat malt. Hops: WGV, Challenger, Goldings. Source: JE1/2.

**Worthington White Shield** (b-c): ABV: 5.6%. Malt: Pale malt, Crystal malt, Roast barley. Hops: WGV, Challenger, Goldings. Source: JE1/2. Notes: See **Worthington White Shield**, Bass Mitchells & Butlers, **Worthington White Shield**, Bass, Sheffield, **Worthington White Shield**, Museum Brewing Company and **Worthington White Shield**, Coors, Burton-on-Trent.

**Cornucopia** (b-c): ABV: 6.5%. Malt: Pale malt, Lager malt, Enzymic, Wheat malt, Maize. Hops: WGV, Challenger, Goldings. Source: JE1. Note: See **Cornucopia**, Hall & Woodhouse.

**Christmas Ale** (b-c): ABV: 8%. Malt: Pale malt, Crystal malt, Enzymic malt, Flaked maize. Hops: WGV, Challenger, Goldings. Source: JE1.

**Christmas Ale**: OG: 1083-87. Malt: 100% Maris Otter pale malt, Flaked maize, Dextrin malt, Crystal malt. Hops: Bramling Cross. Late hops: Goldings, Fuggles, Progress. Source: CB.

**Millennium Ale** (b-c): ABV: 9.5%. Malt: Maris Otter pale malt. Hops: Goldings, Early Bird. Source: JE1.

### . King's Head, Bildeston

**First Gold** (b-c): ABV: 4.3%. Malt: Maris Otter pale malt, Crystal malt. Hops: First Gold. Source: JE4.

**Apache** (b-c): ABV: 4.5%. Malt: Maris Otter pale malt, Crystal malt. Hops: Fuggles, Challenger. Source: JE4.

**Crowdie** (b-c): ABV: 5%. Malt: Maris Otter pale malt, Crystal malt, Black malt, Oats. Hops: Fuggles, First Gold. Source: JE4.

**Dark Vader** (b-c): ABV: 5.4%. Malt: Maris Otter pale malt, Crystal malt, Chocolate malt. Hops: Fuggles, Goldings. Source: JE4.

### . Kitchen, Huddersfield

**Carrot Cruncher** (b-c): ABV: 4.4%. Malt: Maris Otter pale malt, Crystal malt, Amber malt, Black malt. Hops: Fuggles, Goldings. Others: Carrots. Source: JE2.

**Tormented Turnip** (b-c): ABV: 4.5%. Malt: Maris Otter pale malt, Crystal malt, Amber malt, Black malt. Hops: Fuggles, Goldings. Others: Turnips. Source: JE2.

**Mystic Nutmeg** (b-c): ABV: 5%. Malt: Maris Otter pale malt, Amber malt. Hops: Cascade, Goldings. Others: Nutmeg. Source: JE2.

### . Lakeland, Kendal

**Amazon** (b-c): ABV: 4.5%. Malt: Pale malt, Crystal malt. Hops: Willamette, Mount Hood. Source: JE1/2.

**Great Northern** (b-c): ABV: 5%. Malt: Pale malt, Crystal malt. Hops: Mount Hood, Willamette. Source: JE1/2.

**Winter Holiday** (b-c): ABV: 5%. Malt: Pale malt, Crystal malt, Chocolate malt. Hops: Mount Hood, Willamette. Source: JE1.

**Damson Ale** (b-c): ABV: 5.5%. Malt: Maris Otter pale malt, Crystal malt, Chocolate malt, Sugar. Hops: Mount Hood, Willamette. Others: Damsons. Source: JE1/2.

### . Larkins Brewery, Edenbridge

**Traditional**: OG: 1034-7. Malt: 90% Halcyon pale malt, 10% Crystal malt, small % Chocolate malt. Hops: Fuggles, WGV. Late hops: Goldings. IBU: 39. Source: RP3/4/5.

**Sovereign Bitter / Chiddingstone Bitter**: OG: 1038-42. Malt: 90% Halcyon pale malt, 10% Crystal malt, dash of Chocolate malt. Hops: Fuggles, WGV, optional Progress. Late hops: Goldings. IBU: 36. Source: RP.

**Best Bitter**: OG: 1044-7. Malt: 90% Halcyon pale malt, 10% Crystal malt, Chocolate malt. Hops: Fuggles, Goldings, optional Progress, WGV. IBU: 45. Source: RP.

**Porter**: OG: 1052-4. Malt: 88% Halcyon pale malt, 7% Crystal malt, 5% Chocolate malt. Hops: Fuggles, Goldings, optional Progress, WGV. IBU: 59. Source: RP.

## . *Lastingham Brewery Company, Pickering*

**Church Bitter**: OG: 1038. Malt: Halcyon pale malt, Crystal malt, Pale chocolate malt. Hops: Fuggles, Goldings. Source: RP4/5.

**Curate's Downfall**: OG: 1043. Malt: Halcyon pale malt, Crystal malt, small % Wheat. Hops: Fuggles, Goldings. Source: RP4/5.

**Royal Oui**: OG: 1044. Malt: Halcyon pale malt, Crystal malt, small % Wheat. Hops: Liberty, Yeoman. Source: RP4/5.

## . *Leatherbritches Brewery, Ashbourne*

**Belter**: OG: 1040. Malt: 99% Pale malt, 1% Crystal malt. Hops: Progress, Fuggles. EBC: 15. Source: RP4/5.

**Ashbourne Ale**: OG: 1045. Malt: 96% Pale malt, 4% Crystal malt. Hops: Progress, Fuggles. EBC: 20. Source: RP4/5.

**Hairy Helmet**: ABV: 4.7%. Malt: 100% Maris Otter pale malt. Hops: Fuggles. Late hops: Goldings. Dry hops: Goldings. EBC: 15. Source: RP5.

**Ale Conner's Tipple / Hairy Helmet** (b-c): ABV: 4.9%. Malt: Maris Otter pale malt. Hops: Progress, Styrian Goldings. Source: JE4/5/6.

**Bespoke**: OG: 1050. Malt: 96.5% Pale malt, 3.5% Crystal malt. Hops: Progress, Fuggles. EBC: 20. Source: RP4/5.

**Ale Conner's Bespoke** (b-c): ABV: 5.2%. Malt: Maris Otter pale malt, Crystal malt. Hops: Progress, Styrian Goldings. Source: JE4/5/6.

**Ale Conner's Porter** (b-c): ABV: 5.4%. Malt: Maris Otter pale malt, Chocolate malt, Crystal malt. Hops: Progress. Source: JE4/5/6.

**Blue** (b-c): ABV: 9%. Malt: Maris Otter pale malt, Crystal malt, Torrefied wheat. Hops: Vary. Others: Cinnamon, Berries, e.g. Blackberries, Aronia berries. Source: JE6.

## . *Leek Brewing Company, Leek*

**Staffordshire Gold** (b-c): ABV: 3.8%. Malt: Maris Otter pale malt, Lager malt, Wheat malt. Hops: Cascade. Source: JE5/6.

**Dovd Ale** (b-c): ABV: 4%. Malt: Pale malt, Wheat malt, Crystal malt. Hops: Cascade. Source: JE6.

**Danebridge IPA** (b-c): ABV: 4.1%. Malt: Maris Otter pale malt. Hops: Fuggles, Cascade. Source: JE5/6.

**Staffordshire Bitter** (b-c): ABV: 4.2%. Malt: Maris Otter pale malt, Crystal malt. Hops: Challenger. Source: JE5/6.

**Black Grouse** (b-c): ABV: 4.4%. Malt: Maris Otter pale malt, Crystal malt, Chocolate malt, Wheat malt, Roast barley. Hops: Fuggles, Bramling Cross. Source: JE5/6.

**Hen Cloud** (b-c): ABV: 4.5%. Malt: Maris Otter pale malt, Lager malt, Wheat malt. Hops: Goldings. Source: JE5/6.

**St. Edwards** (b-c): ABV: 4.7%. Malt: Maris Otter pale malt, Crystal malt, Wheat malt. Hops: Target, First Gold. Source: JE5/6.

**Rudyard Ruby** (b-c): ABV: 4.8%. Malt: Maris Otter pale malt, Crystal malt, Chocolate malt. Hops: Fuggles, First Gold. Source: JE5/6.

**Blackcurrant Sunset** (b-c): ABV: 5%. Malt: Maris Otter pale malt, Wheat malt. Hops: Fuggles. Others: Blackcurrants. Source: JE5.

**Cherry Sunset** (b-c): ABV: 5%. Malt: Maris Otter pale malt, Wheat malt. Hops: Fuggles. Others: Cherries. Source: JE5.

**Raspberry Sunset** (b-c): ABV: 5%. Malt: Maris Otter pale malt, Wheat malt. Hops: Fuggles. Others: Raspberries. Source: JE5.

**Strawberry Sunset** (b-c): ABV: 5%. Malt: Maris Otter pale malt, Wheat malt. Hops: Fuggles. Others: Strawberries. Source: JE5/6.

**Peach Sunset** (b-c): ABV: 5%. Malt: Maris Otter pale malt, Wheat malt. Hops: Fuggles. Others: Peaches. Source: JE6.

**Double Sunset** (b-c): ABV: 5.2%. Malt: Maris Otter pale malt, Wheat malt. Hops: First Gold, Fuggles. Source: JE5/6.

**Leek Abbey Ale** (b-c): ABV: 5.8%. Malt: Maris Otter pale malt, Wheat malt, Chocolate malt. Hops: Fuggles, Challenger. Source: JE5/6.

**Cleddleton Steamer** (b-c): ABV: 6%. Malt: Pale malt, Wheat malt. Source: JE6.

**Tittesworth Tipple** (b-c): ABV: 6.5%. Malt: Maris Otter pale malt, Wheat malt. Hops: Fuggles, Cascade. Source: JE5/6.

## . *J. W. Lees & Company, Manchester*

**GB Mild**: OG: 1032. Malt: 90% Maris Otter pale malt, 10% No.3 invert sugar. Hops: Goldings, optional Fuggles. IBU: 23. EBC: 45. Source: RP.

**Bitter**: OG: 1037-1037.8. Malt: 100% Maris Otter pale malt, Caramel. Hops: Goldings, optional Fuggles. Late hops: Goldings. IBU: 27-8. EBC: 17. Source: RP/MO. OG: 1054. Malt: Pale malt, No.1 invert sugar. Hops: Fuggles. Yeast: Wyeast #1318. Notes: Recipe from 1909. IBU: 70. SRM: 6.3. OG: 1047. Malt: Pale malt, No.1 invert sugar. Hops: Saaz, Brewers Gold. Yeast: Wyeast #1318. Notes: Recipe from 1933. IBU: 34. SRM: 5. Source: VB.

**John Willie's Premium**: ABV: 4.5%. Hops: Northdown, Goldings. Source: W.

**C**: OG: 1052. Malt: Pale malt, Black malt, No.3 invert sugar, Glucose, Caramel. Hops: Goldings, Fuggles, Northern Brewer. Yeast: Wyeast #1318. Notes: Recipe from 1946. IBU: 51. SRM: 20. Source: VB.

**Moonraker**: OG: 1073. Malt: 100% Maris Otter pale malt, Caramel. Hops: Goldings, optional Fuggles. Late hops: Goldings. IBU: 30. EBC: 80. Source: RP/MO. OG: 1077-79. Malt: Maris Otter pale malt, Crystal malt, Aromatic malt, Chocolate malt. Hops: Goldings. Late hops: Goldings. Source: BC.

**Vintage Harvest Ale**: OG: 1120. Malt: 100% Maris Otter pale malt. Hops: Goldings. IBU: 34. EBC: 30. Source: RP3/4/5/BBB/WB. Malt: Maris Otter pale malt, Crystal malt, Golden syrup. Hops: Goldings. Late hops: Goldings. Dry hops: Goldings. Source: CB.

## . Leyland Breweries, Wellingborough

**Old Cock Up Bitter**: ABV: 3.4%. Malt: Maris Otter pale malt, 7.5% Crystal malt, Caramel. Hops: Fuggles, Goldings. Source: RP5.

**This Bitter**: ABV: 3.6%. Malt: Maris Otter pale malt, 7.5% Crystal malt, Roast barley. Hops: Fuggles, Goldings. Source: RP5.

**Two Henry's Bitter**: ABV: 4.2%. Malt: Maris Otter pale malt, 7.5% Crystal malt, Roast barley. Hops: Fuggles, Goldings. Source: RP5.

**Winky's Winter Warmer**: ABV: 4.7%. Malt: Maris Otter pale malt, 5% Crystal malt, 5% Roast barley. Hops: Fuggles, Goldings. Source: RP5.

**That**: ABV: 5%. Malt: Maris Otter pale malt, 7.5% Crystal malt, 2.5% Wheat malt. Hops: Fuggles, Goldings. Source: RP5.

**Winky Wobbler**: ABV: 7.5%. Malt: Maris Otter pale malt, 10% Crystal malt. Hops: Fuggles, Goldings. Source: RP5.

## . Lichfield Brewery, Lichfield

**Steeple Chase**: OG: 1037. Malt: 98% Maris Otter pale malt, 2% Amber malt. Hops: Styrian Goldings, 60% Challenger. Source: RP4/5.

**Inspired**: OG: 1040. Malt: 95% Maris Otter pale malt, 5% Crystal malt. Hops: 50% Goldings, 50% Challenger. Late hops: 50% Goldings, 50% Challenger. Source: RP3/4/5.

**Resurrection**: OG: 1043. Malt: 100% Maris Otter pale malt. Hops: Styrian Goldings. Source: RP5.

**Steeplejack**: OG: 1045. Malt: 98% Maris Otter pale malt, 2% Chocolate malt. Hops: Styrian Goldings, 70% Challenger. Source: RP4/5.

**Xpired**: OG: 1050. Malt: 90% Maris Otter pale malt, 10% Crystal malt. Hops: 40% Goldings, 60% Challenger. Late hops: 40% Goldings, 60% Challenger. Source: RP3/4/5.

### . *Linfit Brewery, Huddersfield*

**Mild**: OG: 1032. Malt: 87% Pale malt, 12% Roast barley, 1% Flaked barley. Hops: Challenger. Source: RP1/2/3/4/5.

**Bitter**: OG: 1035. Malt: 87% Pale malt, 12% Crystal malt, 1% Flaked barley. Hops: Challenger. Source: RP1/2/3/4/5.

**Special**: OG: 1041. Malt: 88% Pale malt, 11% Crystal malt, 1% Flaked barley. Hops: Challenger. Source: RP1/2/3/4/5.

**English Guineas Stout**: OG: 1050. Malt: 87% Pale malt, 12% Roast barley, 1% Flaked barley. Hops: Challenger. Source: RP1/2/3/4/5.

**English Guineas** (b-c): ABV: 5.5%. Malt: Pale malt, Roast barley. Hops: Challenger. Source: JE1/2.

**Old Eli**: OG: 1050. Malt: 90% Pale malt, 9% Crystal malt, 1% Flaked barley. Hops: Challenger. Source: RP1/2/3/4/5.

**Leadboiler**: OG: 1063. Malt: 92% Pale malt, 7% Crystal malt, 1% Flaked barley. Hops: Challenger. Source: RP1/2/3/4/5.

**Enoch's Hammer**: OG: 1080. Malt: 99% Pale malt, 1% Flaked barley. Hops: Challenger. Source: RP1/2/3/4/5.

**Xmas Ale**: OG: 1080. Malt: 99% Pale malt, 1% Flaked barley. Hops: Challenger. Source: RP1/2/3/4/5.

### . *Little Valley, Hebden Bridge*

**Withens IPA** (b-c): ABV: 3.9%. Malt: Cellar pale malt, Wheat malt, Caramalt. Hops: Cascade, First Gold. Source: JE6.

**Cragg Vale** (b-c): ABV: 4.2%. Malt: Cellar pale malt, Wheat malt, Crystal malt. Hops: Challenger, Goldings. Source: JE6.

**Hebden's Wheat** (b-c): ABV: 4.5%. Malt: Cellar pale malt, Wheat malt. Hops: Hallertau, Hersbrücker. Others: Coriander seeds, Lemon peel. Source: JE6.

**Stoodley Stout** (b-c): ABV: 4.8%. Malt: Cellar pale malt, Chocolate malt, Crystal malt, Oats. Hops: Pacific Gem, First Gold. Source: JE6.

**Tod's Blonde** (b-c): ABV: 5%. Malt: Cellar lager malt, Wheat malt. Hops: Pacific Gem, Hersbrücker. Source: JE6.

**Moor Ale** (b-c): ABV: 5.5%. Malt: Cellar pale malt, Munich malt, Peat-smoked malt. Hops: Pacific Gem, First Gold. Others: Heather. Source: JE6.

. Liverpool Organic Brewery, Liverpool. Www.liverpoolorganicbrewery.com

**Styrian**: ABV: 4.2%. Hops: Styrian Goldings. Source: Web.

**24 Carat Gold**: ABV: 4.2%. Hops: 100% Brewers Gold. Source: Web.

**William Roscoe**: ABV: 4.3%. Hops: Fuggles. Source: Web.

**Jade**: ABV: 4.4%. Hops: Pacific Jade. Source: Web.

**Josephine Butler**: ABV: 4.5%. Others: Organic Elderflowers. Source: Web.

**Honey Blond**: ABV: 4.5%. Malt: Organic Wildflower honey. Source: Web.

. *Lloyds Country Beers, Ingleby*

**Classic**: OG: 1038. Malt: 100% Triumph or Maris Otter pale malt. Hops: Challenger. Late hops: Challenger. Dry hops: Challenger. Source: RP2/3/4/5.

**Country Gold**: OG: 1040. Malt: 100% Maris Otter pale malt. Hops: Challenger. Source: RP4/5.

**JTS XXX / Bitter**: OG: 1042. Malt: Pale malt, Barley syrup. Hops: Challenger. Dry hops: Challenger. Source: RP1.

**Derby or Country Bitter**: OG: 1042. Malt: 99% Maris Otter pale malt, 1% Chocolate malt, Barley syrup. Hops: Challenger. Late hops: Challenger. Dry hops: Challenger. Source: RP.

**Vixen Velvet / Derby Porter**: OG: 1045. Malt: 90% Maris Otter pale malt, 10% Chocolate malt. Hops: Challenger. Late hops: Challenger. Source: RP3/4/5.

**Scratching Dog**: OG: 1046. Malt: 95% Maris Otter pale malt, 5% Crystal malt. Hops: Target. Late hops: Willamette. Dry hops: Willamette. Source: RP5.

**VIP**: OG: 1048. Malt: Pale malt, Barley syrup, Chocolate malt. Hops: Challenger. Dry hops: Challenger. Source: RP1/2.

**Skullcrusher**: OG: 1065. Malt: Maris Otter pale malt, Barley syrup, Chocolate malt. Hops: Challenger. Late hops: Challenger. Dry hops: Challenger. Source: RP1/2/3/4/5.

**Overdraft**: OG: 1065. Malt: 100% Maris Otter pale malt. Hops: Challenger. Late hops: Challenger. Source: RP3/4/5.

. *Loddon, Dunsden. Www.loddonbrewery.com*

**Hoppit**: ABV: 3.5%. Hops: Goldings. Source: web.

**Dragonfly**: ABV: 4%. Hops: Challenger. Source: Web.

**Rin Tin Tin**: ABV: 4.1%. Hops: Fuggles, Progress. Source: Web.

**Hullabaloo**: ABV: 4.2%. Hops: Fuggles. Source: Web.

**Flight of Fancy**: ABV: 4.2%. Malt: 40% Wheat malt. Hops: First Gold. Source: Web.

**Chantry Cheer**: ABV: 4.2%. Malt: Chocolate malt, Crystal malt. Hops: Goldings, Fuggles. Source: Web.

**Hornets Nest**: ABV: 4.3%. Malt: Orange blossom honey. Hops: Goldings. Source: Web.

**Mumbojumbo**: ABV: 4.3%. Hops: Amarillo, WGV, Hallertau. Source: Web.

**Razzle Dazzle**: ABV: 4.3%. Hops: Cascade. Source: Web.

**Whirlwind**: OG: ABV: 4.4%. Hops: Cascade, Willamette. Source: Web.

**Russet**: ABV: 4.5%. Malt: Wheat malt, Crystal rye malt, Oats. Hops: Styrian Goldings, Fuggles. Source: Web.

**Life of Riley**: ABV: 4.5%. Hops: Goldings, Fuggles, Cascade. Source: Web.

**Hocus Pocus**: ABV: 4.6%. Hops: Styrian Goldings, First Gold, Goldings, Fuggles. Source: W.

**Green Bullet**: ABV: 4.6%. Hops: Green Bullet. Source: Web.

**Check-Mate**: ABV: 4.8%. Malt: Pale Caramalt. Hops: Saaz. Source: Web.

**Ferryman's Gold** (b-c): ABV: 4.8%. Malt: Maris Otter pale malt, Caramalt, Wheat malt, Torrefied wheat. Hops: Fuggles, Styrian Goldings. Source: Web/JE6.

### . *Longstone Brewery Company, Belford*

**Bitter**: OG: 1040. Malt: 99% Halcyon pale malt, 1% Crystal malt. Hops: Challenger, Mount Hood. Source: RP4.

### . *Henry Lovibond and Son, London*

**XB**: OG: 1053. Malt: Pale malt. Hops: Goldings. Yeast: Wyeast #1098/Wyeast #1099. Notes: Recipe from 1864. IBU: 83. SRM: 5. Source: VB.

**XX**: OG: 1064. Malt: Mild malt. Hops: Goldings, Cluster. Yeast: Wyeast #1968/White Labs WLP002. Notes: Recipe from 1865. IBU: 40. SRM: 7. Source: VB.

### . *Thomas McGuinness Brewing Company, Rochdale*

**Feather Plucker Mild**: OG: 1034. Malt: 96% Pipkin pale malt, 3% Roast barley, 1% Torrefied wheat. Hops: Fuggles, Challenger. Source: RP4/5/JHF.

**McGuinness Best Bitter**: OG: 1038. Malt: 94% Pipkin pale malt, 4% Torrefied wheat, 2% Crystal malt. Hops: Fuggles. Source: RP3/4/5.

**McGuinness Stout**: OG: 1039. Malt: 91% Pipkin pale malt, 7% Roast barley, 2% Torrefied wheat. Hops: Fuggles, Challenger. Source: RP4/5.

**Junction Best Bitter**: OG: 1042. Malt: 94% Pipkin pale malt, 4% Torrefied wheat, 2% Roast malt. Hops: Fuggles, Challenger. Source: RP3/4/5.

**Tommy Dodd Porter**: OG: 1050. Malt: 92% Pipkin pale malt, 3% Torrefied wheat, 5% Roast barley. Hops: Fuggles, Challenger. Source: RP3/4/5.

## . *McMullen & Sons, Hertford*

**Original AK**: OG: 1033. Malt: 79-84% Halcyon pale malt, 1% Chocolate malt, 10-14% Maltose syrup, 5-6% Flaked maize. Hops: WGV, optional Goldings. IBU: 22. EBC: 24. Source: RP/MO/GW. OG: 1037-38. Malt: Pale malt, Crystal malt, Flaked maize, Chocolate malt, Invert sugar. Hops: Goldings. Late hops: Goldings. Source: BC.

**Country Best Bitter**: OG: 1041.Malt: 76% Halcyon pale malt, 3-4% Crystal malt, 9-14% Maltose syrup, 6-8% Flaked maize. Hops: Progress or WGV, optional Goldings. Dry hops: WGV. IBU: 30. EBC: 19. Source: RP/GW/MO.

**Gladstone**: ABV: 4.3%. Malt: 90% Halcyon pale malt, 4% Crystal malt, 6% Torrefied wheat / Flaked maize. Hops: Fuggles. IBU: 28. EBC: 20. Source: RP.

**Christmas Ale / Stronghart**: OG: 1070. Malt: 74% Halcyon pale malt, 4% Crystal malt, 18-19% Maltose syrup, 4-6% Flaked maize. Hops: WGV, optional Goldings. IBU: 33. EBC: 50. Source: RP/MO.

## . *Mallard Brewery, Nottingham*

**Duck and Dive**: OG: 1036. Malt: 100% Maris Otter pale malt. Hops: First Gold. Dry hops: First Gold. Source: RP5.

**Duck 'n' Dive** (b-c): ABV: 3.7%. Malt: Maris Otter pale malt. Hops: First Gold. Source: JE3.

**Waddler's Mild** (b-c): ABV: 3.7%. Malt: Maris Otter pale malt, Crystal malt, Chocolate malt. Hops: Liberty. Source: JE3.

**Bitter**: OG: 1038. Malt: 92% Maris Otter pale malt, 4% Crystal malt, 4% Amber malt. Hops: 75% Challenger, 25% Liberty. Late hops: Liberty. Source: RP5.

**Duckling**: OG: 1039. Malt: 100% Maris Otter pale malt, 5% Honey. Hops: 83% Challenger, 17% Pioneer. Dry hops: Pioneer. Source: RP5.

**Duckling** (b-c): ABV: 4.2%. Malt: Maris Otter pale malt, Honey. Hops: Challenger, Pioneer. Source: JE3.

**Spittin' Feathers** (b-c): ABV: 4.4%. Malt: Maris Otter pale malt, Crystal malt, Amber malt, Chocolate malt. Hops: Challenger, Liberty. Source: JE3.

**Drake**: OG: 1044. Malt: 80% Maris Otter pale malt, 20% Crystal malt, 4% Sugar. Hops: Challenger. Late hops: Challenger. Dry hops: Challenger. Source: RP5/JHF.

**Drake** (b-c): ABV: 4.5%. Malt: Pale malt, Crystal malt. Hops: First Gold, Challenger. Source: JE2/3.

**Owd Duck**: OG: 1047. Malt: 82% Maris Otter pale malt, 14% Amber malt, 4% Chocolate malt. Hops: Challenger. Late hops: Liberty. Source: RP5/JE2.

**Owd Duck** (b-c): ABV: 4.8%. Malt: Maris Otter pale malt, Amber malt. Hops: Liberty, Challenger. Source: JE3.

**Friar Duck**: OG: 1048. Malt: 97% Maris Otter pale malt, 3% Crystal malt, Sugar. Hops: 50% Challenger, 50% Liberty. Dry hops: Liberty. Source: RP5.

**Friar Duck** (b-c): ABV: 5%. Malt: Maris Otter pale malt, Crystal malt. Hops: Challenger, Liberty. Source: JE2/3.

**D.A.**: OG: 1057. Malt: 78% Maris Otter pale malt, 15% Crystal malt, 5% Amber malt, 2% Chocolate malt. Hops: Challenger. Late hops: Liberty. Source: RP5/JE2/3.

**Quismas Quacker**: OG: 1061. Malt: 80% Maris Otter pale malt, 9% Crystal malt, 7% Amber malt, 3% Chocolate malt, 1% Black malt. Hops: Challenger. Late hops: First Gold. Source: RP5.

**Quismas Quacker** (b-c): ABV: 6%. Malt: Maris Otter pale malt, Crystal malt, Chocolate malt, Amber malt. Hops: First Gold, Challenger. Source: JE2/3.

## . *Malton Brewery Company, Malton*

**Pale Ale**: OG: 1032.9-1033.8. Malt: 98% Halcyon pale malt, 2% Crystal malt. Hops: Goldings or Challenger. IBU: 30. EBC: 15. Source: RP/MO.

**Dark**: OG: 1034.9. Malt: 85.5% Halcyon pale malt, 8% Wheat malt, 0.5% Black malt, 1% Crystal malt, 5% Chocolate malt. Hops: Goldings. EBC: 90. Source: RP5.

**Double Chance Bitter**: OG: 1036.9-1037.8. Malt: 98% Halcyon pale malt, 2% Crystal malt. Hops: Goldings or Challenger. IBU: 27-34. EBC: 17. Source: RP/MO.

**Pickwick's Porter**: OG: 1041.8-1041.9. Malt: 80-82% Halcyon pale malt, 3.5-4.5% Crystal malt, 13.5% Black malt, 0-3% Oat malt. Hops: Goldings or Challenger. IBU: 28-42. EBC: 230. Source: RP/MO.

**Golden Chance** (b-c): ABV: 4.2%. Malt: Optic pale malt, Crystal malt, Torrefied wheat. Hops: Challenger, Styrian Goldings. Source: JE4.

**Crown Bitter**: OG: 1043.9. Malt: 93% Halcyon pale malt, 4% Crystal malt, 3% Wheat malt. Hops: Challenger. Late hops: Hersbrücker. IBU: 40. EBC: 40. Source: RP5.

**Owd Bob**: OG: 1053.9-1054.9. Malt: 94-94.5% Halcyon pale malt, 3-3.25% Crystal malt, 2.5-2.75% Black malt. Hops: Goldings or Challenger. IBU: 46-50. EBC: 80-81. Source: RP/MO.

## . *Mann, Crossman & Paulin, London*

**KKK**: OG: 1080. Malt: Pale malt. Hops: Fuggles. Notes: Recipe from 1860. Source: DP.

**KKKK**: OG: 1086. Malt: Pale malt. Hops: Fuggles. Notes: Recipe from 1860. OG: 1094. Malt: Pale malt. Hops: Fuggles. Notes: Recipe from 1872. Source: DP.

**XXX**: OG: 1095. Malt: Pale malt. Hops: Fuggles. Notes: Recipe from 1850. Source: DP.

## . *Mansfield Brewery Company, Mansfield*

**Riding Dark Mild**: OG: 1035. Malt: 75% Maris Otter or Halcyon pale malt, 5-10% Crystal malt, 0-20% Invert sugar. Hops: Fuggles. IBU: 22-23. EBC: 100. Source: RP.

**Riding Traditional Bitter**: OG: 1036. Malt: 80% Maris Otter pale malt, 20% Invert sugar. Hops: Fuggles. Dry hops: Styrian Goldings. IBU: 26. Source: RP1/2.

**Riding Bitter**: OG: 1035. Malt: 82% Halcyon pale malt, 18% Invert sugar. Hops: Fuggles. Late hops: Styrian Goldings. Dry hops: Styrian Goldings. IBU: 24. EBC: 21. Source: RP3/4/5/MO.

**Bitter**: OG: 1038. Malt: 82% Halcyon pale malt, 18% Invert sugar. Hops: Fuggles, Progress. IBU: 26. EBC: 25. Source: RP4/5.

**Deakins Red Admiral**: OG: 1042. Malt: 75% Halcyon pale malt, 25% Maltose. Hops: Challenger, Hersbrücker, Target. IBU: 22. EBC: 12. Source: RP4.

**Deakins White Rabbit**: OG: 1042. Malt: 95% Halcyon pale malt, 5% Crystal malt. Hops: Target, Progress. Dry hops: Yes. IBU: 24. EBC: 20. Source: RP4.

**Old Bailey**: OG: 1045. Malt: 80-82% Maris Otter or Halcyon pale malt, 18-20% Invert sugar. Hops: Fuggles. Dry hops: Fuggles or Styrian Goldings. IBU: 29-30. EBC: 28. Source: RP/MO.

**Deakins Wild Boar**: OG: 1057. Malt: 80% Halcyon pale malt, 20% Invert sugar. Hops: Fuggles, Progress, Target. Dry hops: Yes. IBU: 35. EBC: 36. Source: RP4.

## . *Marches Ales, Leominster*

**Best Bitter**: OG: 1036. Malt: 92% Maris Otter pale malt, 6% Crystal malt, 2% Wheat malt. Hops: Challenger, Fuggles, Goldings. IBU: 35. Source: RP4/5.

**Forever Autumn**: OG: 1040. Malt: 92% Maris Otter pale malt, 6% Amber malt, 2% Wheat malt. Hops: Goldings. Source: RP5.

**First Gold** (b-c): ABV: 4%. Malt: Pale malt, Amber malt. Hops: First Gold. Source: JE2.

**Corn Spirit** (b-c): ABV: 4.4%. Malt: Pale malt, Crystal malt, Wheat malt. Hops: Goldings. Source: JE2.

**Priory Ale**: OG: 1045. Malt: 93% Maris Otter pale malt, 4% Amber malt, 3% Crystal malt. Hops: Challenger, Goldings. Source: RP4/5.

**Priory Ale** (b-c): ABV: 4.5%. Malt: Pale malt, Crystal malt. Hops: Fuggles, Goldings. Source: JE2.

**Jenny Pipe's Summer Ale**: OG: 1050. Malt: 88% Lager malt, 12% Maris Otter pale malt. Hops: Challenger, Saaz. Source: RP4/5.

**Earl Leofrick's Winter Ale**: OG: 1070. Malt: 90% Maris Otter pale malt, 8% Crystal malt, 2% Black malt. Hops: Challenger. Source: RP4/5.

### . *Marston Moor Brewery, York*

**Cromwell Bitter**: OG: 1037. Malt: 95% Maris Otter pale malt, 2.5% Wheat malt, 2,5% Crystal malt. Hops: Challenger. Late hops: Styrian Goldings. IBU: 26. Source: RP2/3/4/5/MO.

**Brewers Pride**: OG: 1042. Malt: 95% Maris Otter pale malt, 2.5% Wheat malt, 2,5% Crystal malt. Hops: Challenger. Late hops: Styrian Goldings. Source: RP2/3/4/5/MO.

**Porter**: OG: 1042. Malt: 87% Maris Otter pale malt, 8% Roast barley, 2.5% Wheat malt, 2.5% Crystal malt. Hops: Challenger. Late hops: Styrian Goldings. Source: RP2/3/4/5/MO.

**Brewers Droop**: OG: 1048. Malt: 95% Maris Otter pale malt, 2.5% Wheat malt, 2.5% Crystal malt. Hops: Challenger. Late hops: Styrian Goldings. Source: RP2/3/4/5/JE4/5.

**Brewers Pride** (b-c): ABV: 5%. Malt: Maris Otter pale malt, Crystal malt, Wheat malt. Hops: Challenger, Styrian Goldings. Source: JE4/5.

### . *Marston, Thompson & Evershed, Burton-upon-Trent*

**Border Mild**: OG: 1030. Malt: 92% Pale malt, 5% Glucose, 3% Sucrose, Caramel. Hops: Fuggles, Goldings, optional WGV. Source: RP.

**Mercian Mild**: OG: 1032. Malt: 83% Pale malt, 17% Glucose, Caramel. Hops: Fuggles, Goldings optional WGV. Source: RP.

**Border Bitter**: OG: 1034. Malt: 95% Pale malt, 5% Glucose. Hops: Fuggles, Goldings optional WGV. Source: RP.

**Burton Best Bitter**: OG: 1037. Malt: 83% Pale malt, 17% Glucose. Hops: Fuggles, Goldings, optional WGV. Source: RP.

**Bitter**: OG: 1037. Malt: 92% Pale malt, 8% Glucose. Hops: Fuggles, Goldings, WGV. EBC: 27. Source: RP3/4/5.

**Merrie Monk**: OG: 1043. Note: This was **Pedigree** with added Caramel for colour. Source: RP2/3.

**Pedigree Bitter**: OG: 1043-4. Malt: 83% Maris Otter pale malt, 17% Glucose. Hops: Fuggles, Goldings, optional WGV. Source: RP/DL/HB/BBB. Notes: This is the only remaining beer brewed by the "Burton Union" system. I acquired the taste for this beer when on a visit to the brewery and it became a favourite of mine. The beer at the brewery had a wonderful bread-like flavour. Another of its features is a sulphurous nose due to the high levels of sulphate in the water supply used for brewing. Initially this can be somewhat off-putting but if you leave the pint standing for a few minutes it will evaporate off. Eventually, it will become appreciated as an essential feature of the brew and can be easily replicated with homebrew by increasing the amount of calcium sulphate in the brewing water (or "liquor"). On the evening of our visit to the Marston's brewery, my good friend Neil and I boarded a bus home in Banbury. The bus driver proclaimed, "Blimey, you stink of beer! Have you been to a brewery or something?" "Yes", was all that we replied.

**Oyster Stout**: OG: 1048-51. Malt: Maris Otter and Pipkin pale malt, Black malt, Roast barley. Hops: Fuggles, Goldings. Source: JE1/2/W. Malt: Pale malt, Dextrin malt, Crystal malt, Roast barley, Chocolate malt, Maltodextrin. Hops: Fuggles, Goldings. Late hops: Styrian Goldings, Hersbrücker. Source: CB.

**Tesco Stout** (b-c): ABV: 4.5%. Malt: Pale malt, Wheat malt, Roast barley, Malt extract, Black malt, Caramel. Hops: Fuggles, Goldings, Challenger. Source: JE2.

**Tesco India Pale Ale** (b-c): ABV: 5%. Malt: Maris Otter pale malt. Hops: Fuggles, Goldings. Source: JE1/2.

**Old Empire**: ABV: 5.7%. Hops: Cascade, Goldings, Fuggles. Source: W.

**Owd Rodger**: OG: 1080. Malt: 73% Pale malt, 10% Crystal malt, 17% Glucose, Caramel. Hops: Fuggles, Goldings, optional WGV. Source: RP2/3/4/5.

### . *Martin Brewery, Lincoln*

**Stanley Bitter**: OG: 1037. Malt: Pale malt, Crystal malt. Hops: Fuggles, Goldings. Source: RP1.

### . *Martin Ales, Martin*

**Johnson's Bitter**: OG: 1042. Malt: Pale malt, Wheat malt, Crystal malt, Flaked barley, Flaked maize. Hops: Northdown, Goldings. Dry hops: Northdown, Goldings. Source: RP1.

### . *Mauldons Brewery, Sudbury*

**Best Bitter**: OG: 1037. Malt: 48.5% Maris Otter pale malt, 48.5% Halcyon pale malt, 3% Crystal malt. Hops: Challenger. Late hops: Goldings. IBU: 28. EBC: 24. Source: RP1/2/3/4/5.

**May Bee** (b-c): ABV: 3.9%. Malt: Maris Otter pale malt, Honey. Hops: Fuggles, Styrian Goldings. Source: JE6.

**Porter**: OG: 1042. Malt: 47% Maris Otter pale malt, 47% Halcyon pale malt, 3% Crystal malt, 3% Black malt. Hops: Challenger. Late hops: Goldings. IBU: 23. EBC: 170. Source: RP1/2/3/4/5.

**Old XXXX / Eatanswill Old**: OG: 1042. Malt: 95% Halcyon pale malt, 5% Crystal malt. Hops: Challenger, optional Goldings. IBU: 25. Source: RP.

**Squires Bitter**: OG: 1044. Malt: 48.5% Maris Otter pale malt, 48.5% Halcyon pale malt, 3% Crystal malt. Hops: Challenger. Late hops: Goldings. Dry hops: Yes. IBU: 33. EBC: 26. Source: RP1/2/3/4/5.

**Suffolk Pride** (b-c): ABV: 4.8%. Malt: Maris Otter pale malt, Pearl pale malt, Crystal malt. Hops: Goldings, Fuggles. Source: JE6.

**Bah Humbug** (b-c): ABV: 4.9%. Malt: Maris Otter pale malt, Pearl pale malt. Hops: Fuggles, Styrian Goldings. Source: JE6.

**Suffolk Punch**: OG: 1050. Malt: 97% Halcyon pale malt, 3% Crystal malt. Hops: Challenger. Late hops: Goldings. IBU: 37. EBC: 30. Source: RP1/2/3/4/5.

**Black Adder**: OG: 1053-5. Malt: 46% Maris Otter pale malt, 46% Halcyon pale malt, 3% Crystal malt, 5% Black malt. Hops: Challenger, optional Goldings. IBU: 27-37. EBC: More than 300. Source: RP.

**Black Adder** (b-c): ABV: 5.3%. Malt: Maris Otter and/or Pearl pale malt, Crystal malt, Black malt. Hops: Fuggles. Source: JE4/5/6.

**White Adder**: OG: 1053-5. Malt: 100% Maris Otter pale malt, optional Crystal malt. Hops: Goldings. IBU: 37. EBC: 20. Source: RP/JHF/W.

**Suffolk Comfort**: OG: 1065. Malt: 48.5% Maris Otter pale malt, 48.5% Halcyon pale malt, 3% Crystal malt. Hops: Challenger. Late hops: Goldings. Dry hops: Goldings. IBU: 45. EBC: 45. Source: RP3/4/5.

### .    *Mayflower Brewery, Up Holland*

**Mild**: ABV: 3.5%. Malt: Maris Otter pale malt, Wheat malt, Chocolate malt. Hops: Pilgrim, Challenger, Fuggles. Late hops: Styrian Goldings. Source: PP.

**Bitter / Best Bitter**: ABV: 3.7%. Malt: Maris Otter pale malt, Chocolate malt, Crystal malt. Hops: Pilgrim, Challenger, Fuggles. Late hops: Pilgrim, Goldings. Source: PP.

**Pale Ale / IPA**: ABV: 3.9%. Hops: Citra. Source: PP.

**Douglas Valley**: ABV: 4%. Malt: Maris Otter pale malt. Hops: English. Source: PP.

**Light Oak**: ABV: 4%. Malt: Maris Otter pale malt, Wheat malt, Crystal malt. Hops: Pilgrim, Challenger, Fuggles. Late hops: Styrian Goldings. Source: PP.

**Special Branch**: ABV: 4.5%. Malt: Pale malt, Lager malt. Hops: Challenger. Late hops: Challenger. Source: PP.

**A Winters Ale**: ABV: 4.5%. Malt: Maris Otter pale malt. Hops: Goldings. Source: Web.

**Hic Bibi**: ABV: 5%. Hops: Goldings, Fuggles. Source: Web.

### .    *Maypole Brewery, Eakring. Www.maypolebrewery.co.uk*

**Mayday Mild**: ABV: 3.5%. Malt: Roast malt, Crystal malt. Hops: Challenger. Source: Web.

**Lions Pride**: OG: 1038. Malt: 87% Maris Otter pale malt, 13% Crystal malt. Hops: Challenger. Hops: Challenger. Source: RP5.

**Celebration**: OG: 1040. Malt: 90% Maris Otter pale malt, 10% Crystal malt. Hops: Challenger. Late hops: Challenger. Source: RP5.

**BXA**: ABV: 4%. Hops: Bramling Cross. Source: Web.

**Centenary Ale**: OG: 1041. Malt: 85% Maris Otter pale malt, 7.5% Crystal malt, 7.5% Wheat malt. Hops: Challenger. Late hops: Challenger. Source: RP5.

**Mayfair**: ABV: 4.1%. Hops: Saaz. Source: Web.

**Cockchafer**: ABV: 4.1%. Other: Ginger. Source: Web.

**Mae West**: OG: 1043. Malt: 83% Maris Otter pale malt, 1% Crystal malt, 16% Wheat malt. Hops: Challenger. Late hops: Challenger. Source: RP5/JHF.

**Mayday**: OG: 1045. Malt: 80% Maris Otter pale malt, 20% Crystal malt. Hops: Challenger. Late hops: Challenger. Source: RP5.

**Poleaxed**: OG: 1046. Malt: Maris Otter pale malt, 10% Crystal malt, 27% Wheat malt, 3% Roast barley. Hops: Challenger. Late hops: Challenger. Source: RP5.

**Old Homewrecker Porter**: OG: 1048. Malt: 92% Maris Otter pale malt, 8% Crystal malt. Hops: Challenger. Late hops: Challenger. Source: RP5.

### . *Meads of Mercia, Willenhall*

**The Bee's Knees** (b-c): ABV: 6.2%. Malt: Pale malt, Black malt, Crystal malt, Chocolate malt, Honey. Hops: Goldings. Source: JE1. Malt: Pale malt, Chocolate malt, Black malt, Honey. Hops: Fuggles. Source: JE3. Malt: Pale malt, Chocolate malt, Black malt, Wheat malt, Honey. Hops: Fuggles. Source: JE4/5.

### . *Meantime, London. Www.meantimebrewing.com*

**Strawberry** (b-c): ABV: 4%. Malt: Pale malt, Wheat malt. Hops: Variable. Others: Strawberries. Source: JE5.

**London Pale Ale**: ABV: 4.3%. Malt: Pale malt. Hops: Cascade, Goldings, Centennial. Source: Web.

**London Stout**: ABV: 4.5%. Malt: Brown malt, Black malt. Hops: Goldings. Source: Web.

**Pilsner**: ABV: 4.7%. Malt: Lager malt. Hops: Perle, Hallertau. Source: Web.

**Union**: ABV: 4.9%. Hops: Spalt, Perle, Cascade. Source: Web.

**Taste the Difference Raspberry Wheat Beer** (b-c): ABV: 5%. Malt: 50% Pale malt, 50% Wheat malt. Hops: Perle, Northern Brewer. Others: Raspberry extract/Raspberries. Source: JE4/5/6.

**Taste the Difference Bavarian Style Wheat Beer** (b-c): ABV: 5%. Malt: Pale malt, Wheat malt. Hops: Perle, Northern Brewer. Yeast: Bavarian wheat. Source: JE4/5/6/Web.

**Coffee Beer** (b-c): ABV: 6%. Malt: Pale malt, Brown malt, Chocolate malt, Black malt, Other malts. Hops: Fuggles. Others: Coffee. Source: JE6.

**Wheat Grand Cru** (b-c): ABV: 6.3%. Malt: Pale malt, Wheat malt. Hops: Perle, Northern Brewer. Source: JE6.

**Raspberry Grand Cru** (b-c): ABV: 6.5%. Malt: Pale malt, Wheat malt. Hops: Perle, Northern Brewer. Others: Raspberry extract. Source: Web/JE6.

**Chocolate** (b-c): ABV: 6.5%. Malt: Pale malt, Chocolate malt, Other dark malts. Hops: Fuggles. Others: Dark bitter chocolate. Source: Web/JE6.

**London Porter**: ABV: 6.5%. Malt: Seven malts including Pale malt, Chocolate malt, Brown malt, Black malt. Hops: Fuggles. Source: Web/JE6.

**India Pale Ale** (b-c): ABV: 7.5%. Malt: Maris Otter pale malt. Hops: 2 lbs per barrel of Goldings, Fuggles. Source: Web/JE6.

**Hospital Porter**: ABV: 8%. Others: Oak aged for 12 months and blended with a younger beer. Source: Web.

### . *Merivales Ales, Banbury*

**Edgcote Ordinary Bitter**: OG: 1037. Malt: 90% Pale malt, 8% Crystal malt, 2% Wheat malt. Hops: Challenger, Goldings. Source: RP4/5.

**Edgcote Best Bitter**: OG: 1045. Malt: 90% Pale malt, 8% Crystal malt, 2% Wheat malt. Hops: Challenger. Source: RP4/5.

### . *Merrimans Brewing Company, Leeds*

**Old Fart**: OG: 1050. Malt: Halcyon pale malt, Crystal malt, Wheat malt, Pale chocolate malt, Roast barley. Hops: Liberty, Progress. IBU: 32. Source: RP5.

### . *Mersea Island, Colchester*

**Island Pale Ale** (b-c): ABV: 3.9%. Malt: Maris Otter pale malt, Caramalt, Black malt. Hops: Fuggles, Phoenix, Challenger, Cascade. Source: JE6.

**Island Gold** (b-c): ABV: 4.5%. Malt: Lager malt, Wheat malt, Crystal malt. Hops: Perle, Hersbrücker. Source: JE6.

**Island Monkeys** (b-c): ABV: 4.5%. Malt: Maris Otter pale malt, Caramalt, Wheat malt, Roast barley, Crystal malt. Hops: Goldings, Fuggles. Source: JE6.

**Island Stout** (b-c): ABV: 5%. Malt: Maris Otter pale malt, Caramalt, Chocolate malt, Crystal malt, Black malt. Hops: Fuggles. Source: JE6.

### . *Mew Langton, Newport, Isle of Wight*

**B Porter**: OG: 1052. Malt: Pale malt, Brown malt, Black malt. Hops: Fuggles. Dry hops: Yes. Notes: Recipe from 1891. Source: DP.

**India Ale**: OG: 1056. Malt: Pale malt, White sugar. Hops: Goldings. Notes: Recipe from 1885. Source: DP.

**Gibraltar Porter**: OG: 1062. Malt: Pale malt, Brown malt, Black malt, Demerara sugar. Hops: Fuggles. Notes: Recipe from 1889. Source: DP.

### . *Mildmay Brewery, Holbeton*

**Colours Best Bitter**: OG: 1040. Malt: 95% Pipkin pale malt, 5% Crystal malt. Hops: Target. Late hops: Styrian Goldings. IBU: 34. Source: RP4/5. Malt: Pale malt, Crystal malt, Wheat flour, Flaked barley. Hops: Target, Styrian Goldings. Late hops: Styrian Goldings. Dry hops: optional Styrian Goldings. Source: MO.

**SP Ale (Starting Price)**: OG: 046. Malt: 4% Pipkin pale malt, 5% Crystal malt, 1% Chocolate malt. Hops: Target. Late hops: Challenger. IBU: 31. Source: RP5.

**50/1 Porter**: OG: 1052. Malt: 94% Pipkin pale malt, 5% Crystal malt, 0.25% Chocolate malt, 0.5% Black malt. Hops: Styrian Goldings. Late hops: Target. IBU: 35. Source: RP5.

**Old Horse Whip**: OG: 1054. Malt: Pale malt, 2% Flaked barley or 100% Pipkin pale malt. Hops: Saaz. Late hops: Saaz. IBU: 30-38. Source: RP/MO.

### . *Mill Brewery, Newton Abbot*

**Janner's Ale / Janner's Bitter**: OG: 1038. Malt: 95% Pale malt, 4.5% Crystal malt, 0.5% Chocolate malt. Hops: Challenger, optional Fuggles. IBU: 30. Source: RP.

**Janner's Old Dark**: OG: 1040. Malt: Pale malt, Black malt. Hops: Challenger, Fuggles. Source: RP1.

**Janner's Old Original**: OG: 1045. Malt: 96.5% Pale malt, 3.5% Crystal malt. Hops: Challenger. IBU: 30. Source: RP1/2/3/4/5.

**Janner's Christmas Ale**: OG: 1050. Malt: Pale malt, Crystal malt. Hops: Challenger. Source: RP1.

**Black Bushel**: OG: 1059. Malt: 91% Pale malt, 4.5% Crystal malt, 4.5% Roast barley. Hops: Challenger. IBU: 27. Source: RP4/5.

### . *Millstone, Mossley*

**Three Shires Bitter** (b-c): ABV: 4%. Malt: Golden Promise pale malt. Hops: First Gold, Liberty, Goldings. Source: JE6.

**Windy Miller** (b-c): ABV: 4.1%. Malt: Golden Promise pale malt, Rye malt. Hops: Green Bullet, Pilot. Source: JE6.

**Grain Storm** (b-c): ABV: 4.2%. Malt: Golden Promise pale malt, Crystal wheat malt. Hops: Green Bullet, Pacific Hallertau. Source: JE6.

**Autumn Leaves** (b-c): ABV: 4.3%. Malt: Golden Promise pale malt, Dark crystal malt. Hops: Hilary, Cascade. Source: JE6.

**Millstone Edge** (b-c): ABV: 4.4%. Malt: Golden Promise pale malt, Crystal malt. Hops: First Gold, Goldings, Fuggles. Source: JE6.

**True Grit** (b-c): ABV: 5%. Malt: Golden Promise. Hops: Chinook. Source: JE6.

## . Miners Arms Brewery, Westbury sub Mendip

**Light**: OG: 1035. Malt: Pale malt, Crystal malt. Hops: Fuggles. Source: RP2.

**Own Ale**: OG: 1040. Malt: Pale malt, Crystal malt. Hops: Fuggles. Source: RP1/2.

**Guv'nor's Special Brew**: OG: 1048. Malt: Pale malt, Crystal malt. Hops: Goldings. Source: RP1/2.

## . Mitchell's of Lancaster, Lancaster

**Dark Mild**: OG: 1033. Malt: Maris Otter pale malt, Pipkin pale malt, Crystal malt, Roast barley / Torrefied wheat, Black invert sugar. Hops: Challenger, Progress, optional Goldings. Late hops: Yes. EBC: 80-90. Source: RP.

**Best Bitter**: OG: 1035. Malt: Maris Otter pale malt, Pipkin pale malt, Roast barley / Torrefied wheat, Invert sugar. Hops: Challenger, Progress, optional Goldings. Dry hops: Yes. EBC: 11-13. Source: RP.

**Olde Priory Porter**: OG: 1035. Malt: Maris Otter pale malt, Pipkin pale malt, Crystal malt, Torrefied wheat, Roast malt extract, Black invert sugar. Hops: Challenger, Progress, Goldings. EBC: 120. Source: RP3/4.

**Country Mild**: OG: 1035. Malt: 91% Maris Otter pale malt, 5% Crystal malt, 3% Chocolate malt, 1% Roast malt. Hops: Progress. IBU: 25. EBC: 75. Source: RP5.

**Original Bitter**: OG: 1035.7. Malt: 95% Maris Otter pale malt, 5% Crystal malt. Hops: Progress. Late hops: Styrian Goldings. IBU: 31. EBC: 23. Source: RP5.

**William Mitchell's Original Bitter**: OG: 1036. Malt: 86.5% Maris Otter pale malt, 2% Crystal malt, 2.5% Wheat malt, 9% No.2 invert sugar. Hops: Challenger, Progress, Goldings. IBU: 26. EBC: 20. Source: RP4.

**Fortress**: OG: 1042. Malt: Maris Otter pale malt, Pipkin pale malt, Crystal malt, Torrefied wheat, Invert sugar. Hops: Challenger, Goldings, Progress. EBC: 32-36. Source: RP3,4.

**Lancaster Bomber**: OG: 1044. Malt: 91% Maris Otter pale malt, 9% Wheat malt Hops: Challenger, Progress, Styrian Goldings. IBU: 34. EBC: 21. Source: RP4. Malt: 90% Maris Otter pale malt, 90% Lager malt. Hops: Progress. Late hops: Styrian Goldings. IBU: 38. EBC: 18. Source: RP5

**Olde Clog**: OG: 1045. Malt: Maris Otter pale malt, Pipkin pale malt, Crystal malt, Torrefied wheat, Roast malt extract, Invert sugar. Hops: Challenger, Progress, Goldings. EBC: 120. Source: RP3/4.

**Reverend William Spooner**: OG: 1045. Malt: Maris Otter pale malt, 5% Crystal malt, 9% Invert sugar. Hops: Progress. Dry hops: Styrian Goldings. IBU: 30. EBC: 31. Source: RP5.

**ESB**: OG: 1050. Malt: Maris Otter pale malt, Pipkin pale malt, Crystal malt, optional Torrefied wheat, Invert sugar. Hops: Challenger, Progress, optional Goldings. Late hops: Yes. EBC: 40-44. Source: RP.

**Conqueror**: OG: 1050. Malt: 90% Maris Otter pale malt, 10% Amber malt. Hops: Progress. EBC: 41. Source: RP5.

**Brewers Pride**: OG: 1050.5. Malt: 100% Maris Otter pale malt, 9% Invert sugar. Hops: Progress. Late hops: Cascade. IBU: 29. EBC: 20. Source: RP5.

**Christmas Cracker**: OG: 1056. Malt: 88% Maris Otter pale malt, 12% Crystal malt. Hops: Progress. Dry hops: Goldings. IBU: 30. EBC: 52. Source: RP5.

**Old Faithful**: ABV: 5.2%. Malt: 92.8% Maris Otter pale malt, 7% Crystal malt, 0.2% Roast malt, 6% Invert sugar. Hops: Progress, Styrian Goldings, Perle. IBU: 38. EBC: 40. Source: RP5.

## . *Mitchells & Butler, Birmingham*

**DPA Bitter (Dunkirk Pale Ale / Derby Pale Ale)**: OG: 1033. Malt: Pale malt, Flaked maize, Sugar. Hops: Fuggles. Source: DL.

## . *Mole's Brewery, Melksham*

**Tap Bitter**: OG: 1035. Malt: 92% Maris Otter pale malt, 8% Crystal malt. Hops: Fuggles, Progress, WGV or Bramling Cross, WGV. Late hops: Fuggles. Source: RP.

**Cask Bitter / Best Bitter**: OG: 1040. Malt: 90% Maris Otter pale malt, 10% Crystal malt. Hops: Progress, Goldings or Progress, WGV or WGV, Bramling Cross. Late hops: Fuggles. Source: RP.

**Barley Mole**: OG: 1042. Malt: 100% Maris Otter pale malt. Hops: Bramling Cross. Late hops: Fuggles. Source: RP5/JHF.

**Mole's Brew 97**: OG: 1050. Malt: 88% Maris Otter pale malt, 12% Crystal malt. Hops: Fuggles, WGV or WGV, Bramling Cross. Late hops: Fuggles. Source: RP.

## . *Moor Beer Company, Ashcott*

**Withy Cutter**: OG: 1041. Malt: 80% Maris Otter pale malt, 10% Crystal malt, 5% Dark malt, 5% Wheat malt. Hops: Target. Late hops: Goldings. Source: RP5.

**Merlins Magic** (b-c): ABV: 4.3%. Malt: Maris Otter pale malt, Crystal malt, Lager malt. Hops: Fuggles, Liberty. Source: JE2/3/4. Malt: Maris Otter pale malt, Crystal malt, Amber malt. Hops: Fuggles, Liberty. Source: JE5/6.

**Merlins Magic**: OG: 1045. Malt: 70% Maris Otter pale malt, 10% Torrefied wheat, 20% Lager malt. Hops: Fuggles. Late hops: Target. Source: RP5/JHF.

**Peat Porter** (b-c): ABV: 4.5%. Malt: Maris Otter pale malt, Crystal malt, Chocolate malt, Amber malt. Hops: Bramling Cross, Fuggles. Source: JE5/6.

**Chandos Gold**: OG: 1056. Malt: 45% Maris Otter pale malt, 10% Wheat malt, 45% Lager malt. Hops: Fuggles, Target. Source: RP5.

**Old Freddy Walker** (b-c): ABV: 7.3%. Malt: Maris Otter pale malt, Crystal malt, Dark Lager malt / Black malt. Hops: Nugget, Liberty. Source: JE2/3/4/5/6.

### . Moorhouses Brewery, Burnley

**Black Cat Mild**: OG: 1034. Malt: 80.5% Maris Otter pale malt, 1% Chocolate malt, 9.5% Flaked maize, 9% Invert sugar or 60% Halcyon pale malt, 10% Chocolate malt, 13% Flaked maize, 17% Invert sugar. Hops: Fuggles. Source: RP. OG: 1033-35. Malt: Pale malt, Flaked maize, Crystal malt, Peat-smoked malt, Chocolate malt, Invert sugar. Hops: Fuggles. Late hops: Fuggles. Source: BC.

**Premier Bitter**: OG: 1036. Malt: 80-96% Halcyon or Maris Otter pale malt, 4-5% Crystal malt, 5% Flaked maize, 0-10% Invert sugar. Hops: Bramling Cross, Challenger, Fuggles, Goldings or Fuggles. Late hops: Fuggles or 15% Willamette. Source: RP.

**Pride of Pendle**: ABV: 4.1%. Late hops: Fuggles, Willamette. Source: BBB.

**Pendle Witches Brew**: OG: 1050-52. Malt: 80-96% Maris Otter or Halcyon pale malt, 4-5% Crystal malt, 0-4% Flaked maize, 0-5% Torrefied wheat, 0-10% Invert sugar. Hops: Fuggles, optional Bramling Cross, Challenger, Goldings. Source: RP/BC.

**Owd Ale**: OG: 1065. Malt: 71-88% Halcyon or Maris Otter pale malt, 6-7.5% Crystal malt, 4.5-6.5% Flaked maize, 14% Invert sugar, 0.5% Caramel. Hops: Fuggles. Source: RP.

### . Mordue Brewery, Shiremoor

**Five Bridge Bitter**: ABV: 3.8%. Malt: Halcyon pale malt, Pale chocolate malt, Torrefied wheat. Hops: Challenger, Fuggles, Goldings. Source: RP5.

**Workie Ticket**: ABV: 4.5%. Malt: Halcyon pale malt, Pale chocolate malt, Torrefied wheat. Hops: Challenger, Fuggles, Goldings. Source: RP5/BC.

**Radgie Gadgie**: ABV: 4.8%. Malt: Halcyon pale malt, Crystal malt, Roast barley. Hops: Challenger, Willamette. Source: RP5. OG: 1052-53. Malt: Pale malt, Crystal malt, Aromatic malt, Roast barley. Hops: Challenger. Late hops: Challenger, Willamette. Source: BC.

**Geordie Pride**: ABV: 4.2%. Malt: Halcyon pale malt, Crystal malt, Torrefied wheat. Hops: Challenger, Liberty. Source: RP5.

### . Morland & Company, Abingdon

**Mild Ale**: OG: 1033. Malt: Pale malt, Roast barley, Sugar. Hops: Fuggles. Source: DL.

**Independent IPA**: OG: 1034.5. Malt: Pipkin pale malt, Crystal malt, optional Brewing sugar. Hops: Challenger. Late hops: Challenger. IBU: 35-41. EBC: 27-31. Source: RP.

**Original Bitter**: OG: 1035. Malt: Pipkin pale malt, Crystal malt, Sugar. Hops: Challenger. Late hops: Goldings. IBU: 33-37. EBC: 21-25. Source: RP1/2/3/4/5.

**Old Masters**: OG: 1040. Malt: Pipkin pale malt, Crystal malt, Wheat, Sugar. Hops: Challenger. Late hops: Goldings. IBU 31-40. EBC: 26-31. Source: RP2/3/4/5.

**Best Bitter**: OG: 1043. Malt: Pale malt, Crystal malt, Sugar. Hops: Bramling Cross, Goldings, Fuggles. Late hops: Goldings. Dry hops: Goldings. Source: DL.

**The Tanners Jack**: OG: 1043.5. Malt: Pale malt, Crystal malt, Sugar. Hops: Challenger. Late hops: Goldings. IBU: 32-38. EBC: 29-33. Source: RP4.

**Old Speckled Hen**: OG: 1050. Malt: Pipkin pale malt, Crystal malt, Sugar. Hops: Challenger. Late hops: Goldings. IBU: 30-35. EBC: 32-37. Source: RP2/3/4/5. OG: 1051-53. Malt: Pale malt, Wheat malt, Crystal malt, Sugar. Hops: Challenger. Late hops: Goldings, Challenger. Source: CB. Notes: When I visited Morland Brewery in 1995 I was told that they used Pipkin pale malt although they previously used to use Maris Otter pale malt.

**Hen's Tooth**: OG: 1064-66. Malt: Pale malt, Torrefied wheat, Crystal malt, Aromatic malt, Invert sugar. Hops: Target, Challenger. Late hops: Challenger, Styrian Goldings, Fuggles. Source: BC.

**Hen's Tooth** (b-c): ABV: 6.5%. Malt: Pipkin pale malt, Crystal malt, Maltose syrup. Hops: Challenger, Goldings. Source: JE1/2. Note: See **Hen's Tooth**, Greene, King & Sons.

## . *Morrells Brewery, Oxford*

**Light Ale**: OG: 1032. Malt: 82-87% Maris Otter pale malt, 6-8% Crystal malt, 7-10% Torrefied wheat. Hops: Challenger, optional Goldings, Target. Late hops: Goldings. IBU: 26. Source: RP.

**Dark Mild**: OG: 1033. Malt: 82-87% Maris Otter pale malt, 6-8% Crystal malt, 7-10% Torrefied wheat. Hops: Challenger, optional Target. Late hops: Goldings. IBU: 26. Source: RP.

**Dark Mild / Oxford Mild**: OG: 1037-8. Malt: 80% Pipkin pale malt, 8% Crystal malt, 0-4% Roast barley, Torrefied wheat. Hops: Challenger. Late hops: Goldings. IBU: 26-28. Source: RP.

**Best Bitter**: OG: 1036. Malt: 81-86% Pipkin or Maris Otter pale malt, 7-9% Crystal malt, 7-10% Torrefied wheat. Hops: Challenger, optional Target. Late hops: Goldings. IBU: 26-30. Source: RP.

**Oxford Bitter**: OG: 1039. Malt: Pipkin pale malt, Crystal malt as required, Torrefied wheat. Hops: Challenger, Goldings. IBU: 30. Source: RP5.

**Strong Country Bitter**: OG: 1037. Malt: 65% Pale malt, 7.5% Crystal malt, 15% Torrefied wheat, 12.5% Invert sugar. Hops: 90% extract, Target. Late hops: Target. Source: RP2/3/4.

**Varsity**: OG: 1041. Malt: 80-85% Piplin pale malt, 7-10% Crystal malt, 8-10% Torrefied wheat. Hops: Challenger, optional Target. Late hops: Goldings. IBU: 29-32. Source: RP/GW. Malt: Pale malt, Crystal malt, Roast barley, Sugar. Hops: Fuggles. Source: DL.

**Graduate**: OG: 1048. Malt: 78-83% Maris Otter or Pipkin pale malt, 9-12% Crystal malt, 8-10% Torrefied wheat. Hops: Challenger. Late hops: Goldings. IBU: 28-33. Source: RP.

**BB (Best Bitter)**: OG: 1055. Malt: Pale malt. Hops: Fuggles. Notes: Recipe from 1909. Source: DP.

**College Ale**: OG: 1072. Malt: 78-89% Pipkon or Maris Otter pale malt, 6-12% Crystal malt, 5-10% Torrefied wheat. Hops: Challenger, optional Target. Late hops: Goldings. IBU: 28-33. Source: RP.

**XXXX**: OG: 1080. Malt: Pale malt. Hops: Fuggles. Notes: Recipe from 1899. Source: DP.

## . *E. & G. Morse, Lowestoft*

**Mild Ale**: OG: 1068. Malt: Pale amber malt. Hops: Fuggles. Notes: Recipe from 1849. Source: DP.

**XXX**: OG: 1100. Malt: Pale malt, Pale amber malt. Hops: Fuggles. Notes: Recipe from 1846. Source: DP.

## . *Museum Brewing Company, Burton-on-Trent*

**Masterpiece IPA** (b-c): ABV: 5.4%. Malt: Halcyon pale malt, Crystal malt. Hops: Fuggles, Goldings. Source: JE1/2/3. Note: Apparently "very reminiscent of [Bass] **Red Triangle**".

**Wulfric** (b-c): ABV: 5.5%. Malt: Halcyon pale malt, Crystal malt. Hops: Fuggles, Challenger. Others: Ginger essence. Source: JE3.

**Worthington White Shield** (b-c): ABV: 5.6%. Malt: Halcyon pale malt, Crystal malt. Hops: Goldings, Challenger. Source: JE3. Notes: See **Worthington White Shield**, Bass, Sheffield, **Worthington White Shield**, Bass Mitchells & Butlers, **Worthington White Shield**, King & Barnes, **Worthington White Shield**, Coors, Burton-on-Trent.

**P2** (b-c): ABV: 8%. Malt: Halcyon pale malt, Chocolate malt. Hops: Fuggles, Goldings. Source: JE1/2. Malt: Halcyon pale malt, Crystal malt, Black malt. Hops: Fuggles, Goldings. Source: JE3.

**No. 1 Barley Wine** (b-c): ABV: 10.5%. Malt: Halcyon pale malt. Hops: Fuggles, Goldings. Source: JE1/2/3. Note: See **No. 1 Barley Wine**, Coors, Burton-on-Trent.

## . *Nene Valley Brewery, Higham Ferrers*

**Trojan Bitter**: OG: 1038. Malt: 95% Pale malt, 5% Crystal malt, Roast barley. Hops: 33% Challenger, 33% Fuggles, 33% Goldings. Source: RP3/4/5.

**Rawhide**: OG: 1050. Malt: 91% Pale malt, 7.5% Crystal malt, 2% Wheat malt, Roast barley. Hops: Fuggles, Goldings. Source: RP3/4/5.

## Nethergate Brewery Company, Clare

**Casks IPA / IPA**: OG: 1035-6. Malt: 89.98% Maris Otter pale malt, 5.01% Wheat, 5.01% Crystal malt, 1.43% Black malt. Hops: WGV / Goldings / Challenger. Late hops: Fuggles. IBU: 26-27. EBC: 28. Source: RP.

**Umbel Ale**: OG: 1038. Malt: 90% Maris Otter pale malt, 5% Torrefied wheat, 5% Crystal malt. Hops: Fuggles, Challenger. Others: Coriander seeds. IBU: 28. EBC: 27. Source: RP4/5.

**Bitter**: OG: 1039-40. Malt: 88.63-88.71% Maris Otter pale malt, 4.92-4.93% Wheat, 4.92-4.93% Crystal malt, 1.43-1.53% Black malt. Hops: Goldings, Fuggles or WGV. Late hops: Fuggles. IBU: 36. EBC: 40. Source: RP.

**Golden Gate**: OG: 1045. Malt: 90% Maris Otter pale malt, 4.5% Torrefied wheat, 5.5% Crystal malt. Hops: Challenger, Target. Late hops: Fuggles. EBC: 29. Source: RP5.

**Augustinian Ale**: ABV: 4.8%. Malt: Maris Otter pale malt, Crystal malt. Hops: Styrian Goldings. Source: HB.

**Augustinian Ale** (b-c): ABV: 5.2%. Malt: Maris Otter pale malt, Crystal malt. Hops: Styrian Goldings / Fuggles. Others: Coriander seeds. Source: HB/JE3/4/5.

**Old Growler**: OG: 1055. Malt: 85.3-85.35% Maris Otter pale malt, 3.41% Torrefied wheat, 8.53% Crystal malt, 2.71-2.76% Black malt / Chocolate malt. Hops: Fuggles, Goldings / WGV / Fuggles, Challenger / Fuggles, WGV. Late hops: Fuggles. IBU: 27. EBC: 70. Source: RP/EBA. Malt: Maris Otter pale malt, Crystal malt, Black malt. Hops: Fuggles, Challenger. Source: JE2/3/W.

**Umbel Magna**: OG: 1055. Malt: 85.3% Maris Otter pale malt, 3.41% Torrefied wheat, 8.53% Crystal malt, 2.76% Black malt. Hops: Challenger. Late hops: Fuggles. Others: Coriander seeds. IBU: 27. EBC: 70. Source: RP4/5.

## Newale Brewing Company, Andover

**New Tun Mild**: OG: 1035. Malt: 82.5% Maris Otter pale malt, 8% Crystal malt, 2% Chocolate malt, 1.5% Roast barley, 5% Torrefied wheat. Hops: Bramling Cross. Late hops: Styrian Goldings. EBC: 42. Source: RP5.

**Amber Ale**: OG: 1037. Malt: 90% Maris Otter pale malt, 10% Torrefied wheat. Hops: Bramling Cross. Late hops: Styrian Goldings. EBC: 17. Source: RP5.

**Anna Valley Ale**: OG: 1038. Malt: 92% Halcyon pale malt, 6% Crystal malt, 2% Torrefied wheat. Hops: Bramling Cross, Styrian Goldings. EBC: 21. Source: RP4/5.

**Balksbury Bitter**: OG: 1043.5. Malt: 87% Halcyon pale malt, 10% Crystal malt, 1% Chocolate malt, 2% Torrefied wheat. Hops: Bramling Cross, Styrian Goldings. EBC: 40. Source: RP4/5.

**Clatford Clout**: OG: 1047.5. Malt: 98% Halcyon pale malt, 2% Torrefied wheat. Hops: Bramling Cross, Styrian Goldings. EBC: 9.2. Source: RP4/5.

**Old Hatch Ale**: OG: 1058. Malt: 88% Halcyon pale malt, 8% Crystal malt, 2.5% Torrefied wheat, 1.5% Roast barley. Hops: Bramling Cross, Styrian Goldings. EBC: 48. Source: RP4/5.

## . *Nix Wincott Brewery, Turvey*

**Old Cock Up Mild**: OG: 1033. Malt: 91% Maris Otter pale malt, 9% Crystal malt, Sugar, Caramel. Hops: Fuggles, Goldings. Source: RP4.

**Turvey Bitter**: OG: 1033. Malt: 91% Maris Otter pale malt, 9% Crystal malt. Hops: Fuggles, Goldings. Source: RP4.

**Two Henrys Bitter**: OG: 1039. Malt: 90% Pale malt, 10% Crystal malt. Hops: Fuggles, Goldings. Source: RP1/2/3/4.

**That**: OG: 1048. Malt: 90% Pale malt, 10% Crystal malt. Hops: Fuggles, Goldings. Source: RP3/4.

**Old Nix**: OG: 1056.5. Malt: 94.4% Pale malt, 5.6% Crystal malt. Hops: Fuggles, Goldings. Source: RP1/2/3/4.

**Winky's Winter Warmer**: OG: 1058. Malt: 94.2% Pale malt, 5.8% Crystal malt, Caramel. Hops: Fuggles, Goldings. Source: RP2/3/4.

**Winky Wobbler**: OG: 1070. Malt: 90% Pale malt, 10% Crystal malt. Hops: Fuggles, Goldings. Source: RP3/4.

## . *Noakes & Co., London*

**LBA**: OG: 1045. Malt: Pale malt, Lager malt, Flaked rice, No.1 invert sugar. Hops: Fuggles, Goldings. Yeast: Wyeast #1098/Wyeast #1099. Notes: Recipe from 1915. IBU: 52. SRM: 6. Source: VB.

**X**: OG: 1045. Malt: Pale malt, Black malt, Crystal 40L malt, No.3 invert sugar, Caramel. Hops: Fuggles, Goldings, Bramling Cross. Yeast: Wyeast #1098/Wyeast #1099. Notes: Recipe from 1915. IBU: 35. SRM: 20. Source: VB.

## . *North & East Riding Brewers, Scarborough*

**William Clark's Thistle Mild**: OG: 1034. Malt: Maris Otter pale malt, Chocolate malt, Crystal malt, Black malt, Flaked maize, Torrefied wheat. Hops: Challenger, Styrian Goldings. Source: RP1/2.

**William Clark's EXB**: OG: 1040. Malt: Maris Otter pale malt, Crystal malt, Flaked maize, Torrefied wheat. Hops: Challenger, Styrian Goldings. Source: RP1/2.

**William Clark's Thistle Bitter**: OG: 1040. Malt: Maris Otter pale malt, Crystal malt, Flaked maize, Torrefied wheat. Hops: Challenger, Styrian Goldings. Source: RP1/2.

**William Clark's 68**: OG: 1050. Malt: Maris Otter pale malt, Chocolate malt, Crystal malt, Black malt, Flaked maize, Torrefied wheat. Hops: Challenger, Styrian Goldings. Source: RP1/2.

## North Cotswold Brewery, Moreton-in-Marsh

**Summer Solstice** (b-c): ABV: 4.5%. Malt: Lager malt, Wheat. Hops: Saaz, Hersbrücker. Others: Coriander. Source: JE6.

**Hung Drawn n'Portered** (b-c): ABV: 5%. Malt: Maris Otter pale malt, Wheat malt, Chocolate malt, Crystal malt, Black malt, Wheat, Black treacle. Hops: Bramling Cross, Fuggles. Source: JE6.

**Stour Stout** (b-c): ABV: 5%. Malt: Maris Otter pale malt, Wheat, Chocolate malt, Crystal malt, Dark roast malt. Hops: Goldings, Fuggles. Source: JE6.

**Blitzen** (b-c): ABV: 6%. Malt: Maris Otter pale malt, Wheat, Roast malt, Crystal malt, Treacle. Hops: Goldings, Fuggles. Others: Dried fruit, Cloves, Nutmeg, Cinnamon, Root ginger, Allspice. Source: JE6.

## North Yorkshire Brewing Company, Middlesborough/Guisborough
www.nybrewery.co.uk

**Best Bitter**: OG: 1036. Malt: 90% Maris Otter pale malt, 10% Crystal malt. Hops: Northdown. Late hops: Styrian Goldings. Source: RP.

**Best Bitter** (b-c): ABV: 3.6%. Malt: Pale malt, Crystal malt. Hops: Hallertau. Source: JE4/5. Malt: Maris Otter pale malt. Hops: First Gold. Source: JE6.

**Prior's Ale** (b-c): ABV: 3.6%. Malt: Pale malt. Hops: Hallertau, First Gold. Source: JE4. Malt: Maris Otter pale malt. Hops: First Gold. Source: JE6.

**Golden Ginseng**: ABV: 3.6%. Others: Ginseng. Source: Web.

**XXB / IPA / Yorkshire Brown**: OG: 1040. Malt: Maris Otter pale malt, Crystal malt, Chocolate malt. Hops: Northdown. Source: RP2/3/4.

**Archbishop Lee's Ruby Ale** (b-c): ABV: 4%. Malt: Pale malt, Crystal malt, Chocolate malt. Hops: Hallertau, First Gold. Source: JE4/5. Malt: Maris Otter pale malt, Chocolate malt. Hops: First Gold. Source: JE6.

**Boro Best**: OG: 1040. Malt: 75% Maris Otter pale malt, 25% Crystal malt. Hops: Northdown. Source: RP5/JHF.

**Boro Best** (b-c): ABV: 4%. Malt: Pale malt, Crystal malt. Hops: Hallertau, First Gold. Source: JE4/5. Malt: Maris Otter pale malt, Chocolate malt. Hops: First Gold. Source: JE6.

**Yorkshire Porter**: OG: 1040. Malt: Maris Otter pale malt, Roast barley. Hops: Northdown. Source: RP3/4.

**Erimus Dark**: OG: 1040-6. Malt: Maris Otter pale malt, Crystal malt, Chocolate malt, Roast barley. Hops: Northdown. Source: RP2/3/4.

**Cereal Killer** (b-c): ABV: 4.5%. Malt: Maris Otter pale malt, Wheat malt. Hops: First Gold. Source: JE6.

**Fools Gold**: OG: 1045. Malt: 100% Maris Otter pale malt. Hops: Northdown. Late hops: Styrian Goldings. Source: RP.

**Fools Gold** (b-c): ABV: 4.6%. Malt: Maris Otter pale malt. Hops: First Gold. Source: JE4/5/6.

**Golden Ale** (b-c): ABV: 4.6%. Malt: Pale malt, Crystal malt. Hops: Hallertau, First Gold. Source: JE4/5. Malt: Maris Otter pale malt. Hops: First Gold. Source: JE6.

**Flying Herbert**: OG: 1048. Malt: Maris Otter pale malt, 5% Crystal malt, 1% Chocolate malt. Hops: Northdown. Source: RP2/3/4/5/JHF.

**Flying Herbert** (b-c): ABV: 4.7%. Malt: Pale malt, Crystal malt, Chocolate malt. Hops: Hallertau, First Gold. Source: JE4/5. Malt: Maris Otter pale malt, Chocolate malt. Hops: First Gold. Source: JE6.

**Lord Lee's** (b-c): ABV: 4.7%. Malt: Pale malt, Crystal malt, Chocolate malt. Hops: Hallertau, First Gold. Source: JE4/5. Malt: Maris Otter pale malt, Chocolate malt. Hops: First Gold. Source: JE6.

**Dizzy Dick** (b-c): ABV: 4.8%. Malt: Maris Otter pale malt, Chocolate malt. Hops: First Gold. Source: JE6.

**Dizzy Dick**: OG: 1080. Malt: 65% Maris Otter pale malt, 30% Crystal malt, 5% Chocolate malt, optional Roast barley. Hops: Northdown. Source: RP3/4/5.

## . *Northern Clubs Federation Brewery, Dunston*

**Buchanan Best Bitter**: OG: 1034.5. Malt: 76% Halcyon pale malt, 12% Torrefied wheat, 12% Glucose, Caramel. Hops: Bramling Cross, Target, Styrian Goldings, Goldings (pellets and oils). Dry hops: Yes. IBU: 20. EBC: 23. Source: RP4/5.

**Best Bitter**: OG: 1034-6. Malt: 75-76% Pale malt, 10% Flaked maize / 12% Torrefied wheat, 12-15% Glucose. Hops: Bramling Cross, Target, Challenger. Late hops: Goldings. IBU: 21. EBC: 27. Source: RP.

**Buchanan Special**: OG: 1039.5. Malt: 75% Halcyon pale malt, 12% Torrefied wheat, 13% Maltose syrup, Caramel. Hops: Bramling Cross, Target, Styrian Goldings, Goldings. Dry hops: Yes. IBU: 22. EBC: 17. Source: RP4/5.

**Special Ale**: OG: 1041. Malt: 75-76% Pale malt, 10% Flaked maize / 12% Torrefied wheat, 15% Maltose syrup / 12% Glucose. Hops: Bramling Cross, Target, Challenger. Late hops: Goldings. Dry hops: Yes. IBU: 23. EBC: 17. Source: RP3.

**Buchanan Original**: OG: 1042-4. Malt: 75-79% Halcyon pale malt, 11-11.5% Torrefied wheat, 9% Glucose / 13.5% Maltose syrup, optional Caramel. Hops: Bramling Cross, Target, Goldings, Challenger / Styrian Goldings. Dry hops: Yes. IBU: 24. EBC: 45. Source: RP.

### The Northumberland Brewery, Ashington

**Best Bitter**: OG: 1045. Malt: Maris Otter pale malt, Crystal malt, Pale chocolate malt, Torrefied wheat. Hops: Challenger. Late hops: Styrian Goldings. IBU: 34. Source: RP5.

**Duke of Northumberland Premium Ale**: OG: 1049. Malt: Maris Otter pale malt, Crystal malt, Roast barley, Pale chocolate malt, Torrefied wheat. Hops: Challenger. Late hops: Styrian Goldings. IBU: 34. Source: RP5.

**Castles Bitter**: OG: 1038. Malt: Maris Otter pale malt, Crystal malt, Brown malt, Torrefied wheat. Hops: Challenger. Late hops: Styrian Goldings. IBU: 38. Source: RP5.

### O'Hanlon's, Whimple

**Wheat Beer / Double Champion Wheat Beer** (b-c): ABV: 4%. Malt: Optic pale malt, Wheat malt, Caramalt. Hops: Challenger. Late hops: First Gold, Cascade. Others: Coriander. Source: JE3/5/6.

**Organic Rye Beer** (b-c): ABV: 4.5%. Malt: Pale malt, Crystal malt, Flaked rye. Hops: Hallertau. Source: JE4/5.

**Red Ale** (b-c): ABV: 4.5%. Malt: Optic pale malt, Crystal malt, Caramalt, Roast barley. Hops: Phoenix, Styrian Goldings. Source: JE4.

**Yellowhammer** (b-c): ABV: 4.5%. Malt: Optic pale malt, Caramalt. Hops: First Gold, Cascade. Source: JE4/5. Malt: Optic pale malt, Caramalt. Hops: First Gold. Late hops: Cascade. Dry hops: First Gold. Source: JE6.

**Original Port Stout**: ABV: 4.8%. Malt: Optic pale malt, Crystal malt, Caramalt, Roast barley, Flaked barley. Hops: Phoenix. Late hops: Styrian Goldings. Other: Ferreira Port at rate of 2 bottles per barrel (36 gal). Source: WB/JE3/4/5/6.

**Good Will** (b-c): ABV: 5%. Malt: Optic pale malt, Crystal malt, Torrefied wheat. Hops: Northdown, Challenger, Amarillo, Styrian Goldings. Source: JE6.

**Royal Oak** (b-c): ABV: 5%. Malt: Optic pale malt, Crystal malt, Torrefied wheat. Hops: Challenger, Northdown, Goldings. Source: JE5/6. Notes: See **Royal Oak**, Eldridge Pope and **Royal Oak**, Thomas Hardy Brewery.

**Thomas Hardy's Ale** (b-c): ABV: 11.7%. Malt: Low colour pale malt, Crystal malt. Hops: Northdown, Challenger, Styrian Goldings, Goldings. Source: JE5/6. Malt: Pale malt, Maltose syrup, "touch of" Crystal malt. Hops: Northdown, Challenger, Styrian Goldings, Goldings. Source: WB. Notes: See **Thomas Hardy's Ale**, Eldridge Pope and **Thomas Hardy's Ale**, Thomas Hardy Brewery.

### Oak Brewing Company, Heywood

**Best Bitter**: OG: 1038. Malt: Pale malt, Crystal malt, Black malt. Hops: Challenger, Goldings, WGV. Dry hops: Yes. Source: RP2/3/4/5.

**Old Oak Ale**: OG: 1044. Malt: Pale malt, Crystal malt, Black malt. Hops: Challenger, Goldings, WGV. Dry hops: Yes. Source: RP2/3/4/5.

**Double Dagger**: OG: 1050. Malt: Pale malt, Crystal malt, Black malt. Hops: Challenger, Goldings, WGV. Source: RP2/3/4/5.

**Wobbly Bob**: OG: 1060. Malt: Pale malt, Crystal malt, Black malt. Hops: Challenger, Goldings, WGV. Source: RP2/3/4/5.

### . *Oakham Ales, Oakham*

**Inferno**: ABV: 4%. Hops: Sterling, Amarillo, Centennial, Cascade, Chinook. Source: W.

**Hunky-Dory**: OG: 1045. Malt: 91% Low colour Maris Otter pale malt, 9% Amber malt. Hops: Challenger. Late hops: Mount Hood or Cascade. IBU: 34. Source: RP/MO.

**Bishops Farewell**: OG: 1046. Malt: 92% Low colour Maris Otter pale malt, 8% Wheat malt. Hops: Challenger. Late hops: Cascade. IBU: 34. Source: RP5.

**Mompessons Gold**: OG: 1050. Malt: 98% Low colour Maris Otter pale malt, 2% Crystal malt. Hops: Challenger. Late hops: Styrian Goldings. IBU: 33. Source: RP5/JHF.

**Old Tosspot**: OG: 1052. Malt: 92% Low colour Maris Otter pale malt, 7.85% Crystal malt, 0.15% Chocolate malt. Hops: Challenger. Late hops: Mount Hood. IBU: 35. Source: RP4/5/MO.

**Jeffrey Hudson Bitter (JHB)**: OG: 1038. Malt: 95% Low colour Maris Otter pale malt, 5% Wheat malt. Hops: Challenger. Late hops: Mount Hood. IBU: 33. Source: RP4/5/MO.

### . *Oakhill Brewery, Oakhill*

**Somer Ale**: OG: 1036. Malt: 95% Halcyon pale malt, up to 5% Crystal malt, 2-4% Flour. Hops: Willamette, Challenger, Fuggles, Goldings. Source: RP4/5.

**Farmers Ale**: OG: 1038. Malt: Pale malt, Crystal malt. Hops: Bramling Cross, Challenger, Fuggles, Goldings. Source: RP1.

**Bitter / Best Bitter**: OG: 1039. Malt: 93.5% Halcyon / Triumph pale malt, 6.5% Crystal malt. Hops: Bramling Cross, Challenger, Fuggles, Goldings. Source: RP.

**Black Magic Stout**: OG: 1044. Malt: 80% Halcyon or Triumph pale malt, 10% Chocolate malt, 10% Roast barley. Hops: Bramling Cross, Challenger, Fuggles, Goldings. Source: RP3/4/5.

**Yeoman Ale / Yeoman Strong Ale / Yeoman Strong 1767 Ale**: OG: 1049-1050. Malt: 91.5% Triumph or Halcyon pale malt, 8.5% Crystal malt. Hops: Bramling Cross, Challenger, Fuggles, Goldings. Source: RP.

**Mendip Tickler**: OG: 1060-2. Malt: 88% Halcyon pale malt, 9% Crystal malt, 3% Roast barley, 4% Flour. Hops: Willamette, Fuggles. Source: RP4/5.

### . *Oakleaf, Gosport*

**Maypole Mild** (b-c): ABV: 3.8%. Malt: Optic pale malt, Roast barley, Chocolate malt, Crystal malt. Hops: First Gold, Fuggles, Styrian Goldings. Source: JE6.

**Bitter** (b-c): ABV: 3.8%. Malt: Optic pale malt, Crystal malt. Hops: First Gold, Fuggles, Styrian Goldings. Source: JE6.

**Heart of Oak** (b-c): ABV: 4.5%. Malt: Optic pale malt, Chocolate malt, Crystal malt. Hops: Brewers Gold, Bramling Cross, Cascade. Source: JE6.

**It's Not Bitter** (b-c): ABV: 4.9%. Malt: Lager malt. Hops: Saaz. Source: JE6.

**Hole Hearted** (b-c): ABV: 4.7%. Malt: Pale malt, Caramalt, Wheat malt. Hops: Cascade. Source: JE4. Malt: Optic pale malt, Caramalt, Torrefied wheat. Hops: Cascade. Source: JE5/6.

**Blake's Gosport Bitter** (b-c): ABV: 5.2%. Malt: Optic pale malt, Crystal malt, Chocolate malt, Flaked barley. Hops: Fuggles, Goldings. Source: JE4/6.

**Eichenblatt Bitte** (b-c): ABV: 5.4%. Malt: Smoked malt, Wheat malt. Hops: Saaz, Styrian Goldings. Source: JE6.

**Blake's Heaven** (b-c): ABV: 7%. Malt: Optic pale malt, Chocolate malt, Crystal malt, Flaked barley. Hops: Goldings, Fuggles. Source: JE6.

## .   *Okell & Son, Douglas, Isle of Man*

**Okells Mild**: OG: 1034. Malt: 85% Golden Promise or Triumph pale malt, 5% Crystal malt, Invert sugar. Hops: Target, Fuggles. Late hops: Fuggles. IBU: 18. EBC: 60. Source: RP5.

**Okells Bitter**: OG: 1037. Malt: 90% Golden Promise or Triumph pale malt, 5% Crystal malt, Invert sugar. Hops: Target, Fuggles. Late hops: Challenger. IBU: 33. EBC: 26. Source: RP5.

**Old Skipper**: OG: 1045. Malt: 80% Golden Promise or Triumph pale malt, 10% Crystal malt, Invert sugar. Hops: Progress, Target. Late hops: Hallertau. IBU: 37. EBC: 37. Source: RP5.

**Aile**: ABV: 4.8%. Hops: Styrian Goldings, Cascade, Willamette. Source: W.

**St. Nick**: OG: 1050. Malt: 89% Golden Promise or Triumph pale malt, 9% Crystal malt, Invert sugar. Hops: Fuggles, Target. Late hops: Goldings. IBU: 44. EBC: 62. Source: RP5.

Note: Formerly Isle of Man Breweries.

## .   *Old Barn, Bishop Auckland*

**Sheepdog** (b-c): ABV: 4.7%. Malt: Maris Otter pale malt, Crystal malt, Wheat malt. Hops: Challenger, Mount Hood. Source: JE1.

**Collie Wobbles** (b-c): ABV: 4.7%. Malt: Maris Otter pale malt, Crystal malt, Wheat malt. Hops: Challenger, Mount Hood. Source: JE1.

**2000 Special Reserve** (b-c): ABV: 10%. Malt: Dark malt extract, Sugar. Hops: Challenger, Mount Hood. Source: JE1.

## Old Bear, Keighley

**Best Bitter / Original** (b-c): ABV: 3.9%. Malt: Maris Otter pale malt, Pale chocolate malt, Crystal malt, Flaked barley, Black malt, Torrefied wheat. Hops: Goldings, Fuggles, Saaz, Progress. Source: JE6.

**Goldilocks** (b-c): ABV: 4.5%. Malt: Lager malt, Wheat malt, Roast barley, Torrefied wheat. Hops: Goldings, Northern Brewer, Fuggles, Crystal. Source: JE6.

**Hibernator** (b-c): ABV: 5%. Malt: Maris Otter pale malt, Crystal malt, Black malt, Torrefied wheat, Flaked barley. Hops: Pioneer. Source: JE5. Malt: Maris Otter pale malt, Chocolate malt, Crystal malt, Black malt, Torrefied wheat, Flaked barley. Hops: Pioneer, Northern Brewer. Source: JE6.

## Old Chimneys Brewery, Diss

**Meadow Brown Ale** (b-c): ABV: 3.4%. Malt: Pale malt, Crystal malt, Roast barley, optional Wheat malt. Hops: Fuggles, Challenger. Source: JE5/6.

**Swallowtail IPA**: OG: 1036. Malt: 93% Pale malt, 7% Crystal malt. Hops: Mount Hood, Willamette. Late hops: UK hops. IBU: 25. EBC: 24. Source: RP4/5.

**Victorian Brown Ale** (b-c): ABV: 3.8%. Malt: Pale malt, Crystal malt, Amber malt, Roast barley, Lactose. Hops: Challenger. Source: JE4.

**Leading Porter** (b-c): ABV: 4.2%. Malt: Pale malt, Crystal malt, Roast barley, Lactose. Hops: Fuggles, Challenger. Source: JE4.

**Great Raft Bitter**: OG: 1042. Malt: 88% Pale malt, 12% Crystal malt. Hops: Mount Hood, Willamette. Late hops: UK hops. IBU: 29. EBC: 36. Source: RP4/5.

**Great Raft Bitter** (b-c): ABV: 4.3%. Malt: Pearl pale malt, Crystal malt, Caramalt. Hops: optional Fuggles, Challenger, Target. Source: JE4/5/6.

**Hairy Canary** (b-c): ABV: 4.2%. Malt: Lager malt, Wheat malt, Sugar, Lactose. Hops: Hallertau. Others: Lemons. Source: JE6.

**Black Rat Stout** (b-c): ABV: 4.5%. Malt: Pale malt, Crystal malt, Roast barley, optional Wheat malt, Lactose. Hops: Fuggles, Challenger. Source: JE5/6.

**Golden Pheasant** (b-c): ABV: 4.9%. Malt: Pearl pale malt, Caramalt. Hops: Target, Challenger. Source: JE4/5/6.

**Natterjack Premium Ale**: OG: 1050. Malt: 80% Pale malt, 20% Crystal malt. Hops: Mount Hood, Willamette. Late hops: UK hops. IBU: 35. EBC: 50. Source: RP4/5.

**Natterjack** (b-c): ABV: 5.4%. Malt: Pearl pale malt, Crystal malt, Caramalt. Hops: Fuggles, optional Challenger. Source: JE4/5/6.

**Lord Kitchener's India Pale Ale / India Pale Ale** (b-c): ABV: 5.7%. Malt: Pale malt, Caramalt, Amber malt. Hops: Target, Challenger. Source: JE4/5/6.

**Brimstone** (b-c): ABV: 6.5%. Malt: Lager malt, Sugar. Hops: Hallertau, Northern Brewer. Source: JE3/4/5. Malt: Lager malt, Wheat malt, Sugar. Hops: Hallertau. Source: JE6.

**Greenshank** (b-c): ABV: 7%. Malt: Pale malt, Caramalt, Unrefined sugar. Hops: Hallertau. Source: JE4/5.

**Redshank** (b-c): ABV: 8.7%. Malt: Halcyon pale malt, Crystal malt, optional Caramalt. Hops: Fuggles, Challenger. Source: JE3/4/5/6.

**Good King Henry Special Reserve** (b-c): ABV: 9.6%. Malt: Halcyon pale malt, Crystal malt, Roast barley. Hops: Fuggles, Challenger. Source: JE3/4/5/6.

### . *Old Luxters Farm Brewery, Henley-on-Thames*

**Vintage Ale** (b-c): ABV: 4.5%. Malt: Halcyon pale malt, Crystal malt, Chocolate malt. Hops: Fuggles, Goldings. Source: JE1.

**Fortnum & Mason Summer Ale** (b-c): ABV: 4.5%. Malt: Maris Otter pale malt, Crystal malt, Chocolate malt. Hops: Fuggles, Goldings. Other: Elderflowers. Source: JE5/6.

**Old Windsor Gold Ale** (b-c): ABV: 4.5%. Malt: Maris Otter pale malt, Crystal malt. Hops: Fuggles, Goldings. Source: JE5/6.

**Dark Roast** (b-c): ABV: 5%. Malt: Halcyon or Maris Otter pale malt, Crystal malt, Chocolate malt. Hops: Fuggles, Goldings. Source: JE1/2/3/4/5/6.

**Luxters Gold** (b-c): ABV: 5%. Malt: Maris Otter pale malt. Hops: Fuggles, Goldings. Source: JE2/3/4/5/6.

**Fortnum's Ale** (b-c): ABV: 5%. Malt: Maris Otter pale malt, Crystal malt, Chocolate malt. Hops: Fuggles, Goldings. Source: JE3/4/5/6.

**Traders Ale** (b-c): ABV: 5%. Malt: Pale malt, Crystal malt. Hops: Fuggles, Goldings. Source: JE3.

**Old Windsor Dark Ale** (b-c): ABV: 5%. Malt: Maris Otter pale malt, Crystal malt, Chocolate malt. Hops: Fuggles, Goldings. Source: JE5/6.

**Barn Ale**: OG: 1042.5-1052. Malt: 94% Halcyon pale malt, 5% Crystal malt, 1% Chocolate malt. Hops: Fuggles. Late hops: Goldings. Source: RP2/4/5.

**Barn Ale** (b-c): ABV: 5.4%. Malt: Maris Otter pale malt, Crystal malt, Chocolate malt. Hops: Fuggles, Goldings. Source: JE1/2/3/4/5/6.

**Winter Warmer** (b-c): ABV: 6%. Malt: Maris Otter pale malt, Crystal malt, Chocolate malt. Hops: Fuggles, Goldings. Others: Cinnamon, Other Spices. Source: JE5.

**Damson Ale** (b-c): ABV: 7%. Malt: Maris Otter pale malt, Crystal malt, Chocolate malt. Hops: Fuggles, Goldings. Others: Damson juice. Source: JE5/6.

### Old Mill Brewery, Snaith

**Traditional Mild**: OG: 1034. Malt: Halcyon pale malt, Crystal malt, Pale chocolate malt, Black malt. Hops: Fuggles, Goldings, Styrian Goldings or Target. Late hops: Styrian Goldings. Source: RP3/4/5.

**Nellie Dene**: OG: 1034.5. Malt: Maris Otter pale malt, Crystal malt, Wheat malt. Hops: Northdown, Willamette. Source: RP5.

**Traditional Bitter**: OG: 1037. Malt: Halcyon pale malt, Crystal malt. Hops: Styrian Goldings and Fuggles, Goldings, Target and/or Northdown. Source: RP.

**Old Curiosity**: OG: 1043. Malt: Halcyon pale malt, Crystal malt, Pale chocolate malt, Black malt. Hops: Target, Northdown, Styrian Goldings. Source: RP5.

**Bullion**: OG: 1044. Malt: Halcyon pale malt, Crystal malt, Pale chocolate malt. Hops: Styrian Goldings and Fuggles, Goldings, Target and/or Northdown. Source: RP.

### Oldershaw, Grantham

**Caskade** (b-c): ABV: 4.2%. Malt: Optic pale malt, Crystal malt. Hops: Cascade. Source: JE6.

**Grantham Stout** (b-c): ABV: 4.3%. Malt: Optic pale malt, Wheat malt, Roast barley, Chocolate malt, Crystal malt. Hops: First Gold, Willamette, Goldings. Source: JE6.

**Regal Blonde** (b-c): ABV: 4.4%. Malt: Lager malt, Wheat malt. Hops: Saaz, Hersbrücker, Cascade. Source: JE6.

**Isaac's Gold** (b-c): ABV: 4.5%. Malt: Optic pale malt. Hops: First Gold. Source: JE6.

**Old Boy** (b-c): ABV: 4.8%. Malt: Optic pale malt, Wheat malt, Chocolate malt, Crystal malt. Hops: First Gold, Fuggles, Willamette, Cascade. Source: JE6.

**Alchemy** (b-c): ABV: 5.3%. Malt: Optic pale malt. Hops: First Gold. Source: JE6.

### Orange Brewery, London

**SW1**: OG: 1039-41. Malt: Pale malt, Crystal malt. Hops: Goldings. Late hops: Goldings. Source: BC.

### Organic, Helston

**Lizard Point** (b-c): ABV: 4%. Malt: Pale malt, Crystal malt. Hops: Hallertau. Source: JE4/5/6.

**Serpentine** (b-c): ABV: 4.5%. Malt: Pale malt, Crystal malt, Chocolate malt, Wheat malt. Hops: Hallertau, optional First Gold. Source: JE3/4/5/6.

**Black Rock Stout** (b-c): ABV: 4.7%. Malt: Pale malt, Crystal malt, Chocolate malt, Wheat malt. Hops: Hallertau. Source: JE4/5/6.

**Wolf Rock** (b-c): ABV: 5%. Malt: Pale malt, Crystal malt, Wheat malt. Hops: Hallertau. Source: JE4/5/6.

### . *Otter Brewery, Honiton. Www.otterbrewery.com*

**Otter Bitter**: OG: 1036. Malt: 92% Halcyon and Maris Otter pale malt, 8% Crystal malt. Hops: Challenger, optional Fuggles. Source: RP.

**Otter Dark**: OG: 1046. Malt: 45% Halcyon pale malt, 45% Maris Otter pale malt, 4% Crystal malt, 4% Chocolate malt, 2% Torrefied wheat. Hops: Fuggles, Goldings. Source: RP4/5/JHF.

**Otter Head**: OG: 1054-62. Malt: 47% Halcyon pale malt, 47% Maris Otter pale malt, 6% Crystal malt. Hops: Challenger, optional Fuggles. Source: RP4/5/BC.

**Otter Bright**: OG: 1039. Malt: 98% Maris Otter pale malt Lager malt, 2% Torrefied wheat. Hops: Fuggles. Source: RP4/5.

**Witch Otter / Otter Claus / MacOtter / Cupids Otter**: ABV: 5%. Hops: Fuggles, Challenger. Source: Web.

### . *Oulton Ales, Oulton Broad*

**Sunrise** (b-c): ABV: 4%. Malt: Pearl pale malt, Crystal malt, Caramalt, Maize. Hops: Styrian Goldings, Challenger. Source: JE5. Malt: Maris Otter pale malt, Caramalt, Crystal malt, Maize. Hops: Challenger, Styrian Goldings. Others: Elderflowers. Source: JE6.

**Nautilus** (b-c): ABV: 4.2%. Malt: Pearl or Maris Otter pale malt, Crystal malt, Chocolate malt, Caramalt. Hops: Challenger, Styrian Goldings. Source: JE4/5/r.

**Gone Fishing** (b-c): ABV: 5%. Malt: Pearl or Maris Otter pale malt, Crystal malt, Chocolate malt, Caramalt. Hops: Fuggles. Source: JE4/5/6.

**Cormorant Porter** (b-c): ABV: 5.2%. Malt: Optic pale malt, Caramalt, Roast chocolate malt, Crystal malt, Chocolate malt. Hops: Challenger, Styrian Goldings. Source: JE6.

**Roaring Boy** (b-c): ABV: 8.5%. Malt: Pearl pale malt, Caramalt, Maize, Sugar. Hops: Challenger, Styrian Goldings. Source: JE4/5. Malt: Maris Otter pale malt, Caramalt, Maize, Candi sugar. Hops: Challenger, Cascade. Source: JE6.

### . *Paine, St. Neots*

**E.G. Bitter (Eynesbury Giant / Extra Gravity)**: OG: 1049. Malt: Pale malt, Sugar. Hops: Goldings, Fuggles. Source: DL.

### . *J. C. & R. H. Palmer, Bridport*

**Bridport Bitter / BB**: OG: 1031-2. Malt: 100% Pale malt or 90% Pipkin pale malt, 5% Crystal malt, 5% No.3 invert sugar, optional Caramel. Hops: Goldings, optional Styrian Goldings. Late hops: Goldings, Styrian Goldings. IBU: 26. EBC: 26. Source: RP/JHF.

**Extra Stout** (bottled): OG: 1036. Malt: Pale malt, Crystal malt, Black malt, Sugar. Hops: Fuggles. Source: DL.

**IPA**: OG: 1039. Malt: 100% Pale malt or 90% Pipkin pale malt, 5% Crystal malt, 5% No.3 invert sugar, Caramel. Hops: Goldings, optional Styrian Goldings. Late hops: Goldings, Styrian Goldings. IBU: 20. Source: RP.

**Best Bitter / IPA**: OG: 1039. Malt: 90% Pipkin pale malt, 5% Crystal malt, 5% No.3 invert sugar. Hops: Goldings, Styrian Goldings / Mount Hood. Late hops: Goldings, Mount Hood, Styrian Goldings. IBU: 28. EBC: 27. Source: RP.

**Draught IPA**: OG: 1040. Malt: Pale malt, Roast barley, Sugar. Hops: Goldings, Fuggles. Late hops: Goldings. Dry hops: Goldings. Source: DL.

**Tally Ho!**: OG: 1047. Malt: 100% Pale malt or 87-93% Pipkin pale malt, 6-7% Crystal malt, 0-6% No.3 invert sugar, 0-1% Caramel. Hops: Goldings, optional Styrian Goldings / Mount Hood. Late hops: Goldings, Mount Hood, Styrian Goldings. IBU: 40. EBC: 80. Source: RP.

**200**: OG: 1052. Malt: 90% Pipkin pale malt, 10% Crystal malt. Hops: Goldings, Mount Hood optional Styrian Goldings. Late hops: Styrian Goldings optional Goldings, Mount Hood. IBU: 30. EBC: 31. Source: RP.

## . *Paradise, Nantwich*

**Mild** (b-c): ABV: 3.6%. Malt: Maris Otter pale malt, Crystal malt, Chocolate malt. Hops: First Gold, Goldings. Source: JE5.

**Old Creamery Mild** (b-c): ABV: 3.6%. Malt: Maris Otter pale malt, Chocolate malt. Hops: Goldings. Source: JE6.

**Farmer's Favourite** (b-c): ABV: 4%. Malt: Maris Otter pale malt, Crystal malt. Hops: Northdown. Source: JE6.

**Dabbers** (b-c): ABV: 5%. Malt: Maris Otter pale malt, Wheat malt. Hops: Styrian Goldings. Source: JE5/6.

**Nantwich Ale** (b-c): ABV: 5.6%. Malt: Maris Otter pale malt, Crystal malt. Hops: optional First Gold, Fuggles. Source: JE5/6.

Notes: This brewery closed in 2006, relocated and became the North Wales Brewery (q.v. Wales).

## . *Parish Brewery, Somerby*

**Mild**: OG: 1033. Malt: Pale malt, Crystal malt, Wheat, Sugar. Hops: Fuggles, Goldings, Bramling Cross. Source: RP2.

**Bitter**: OG: 1038. Malt: 90% Pale malt, 4% Crystal malt, 4% Wheat, Sugar. Hops: Fuggles, Goldings, Bramling Cross. Source: RP1.

**Special Bitter (PSB)**: OG: 1038. Malt: 85-90% Maris Otter pale malt, 2-8% Crystal malt, 5% Wheat, 2-3% of a "secret" malt / Black malt. Hops: Fuggles, Goldings, Bramling Cross or Goldings or Willamette, Mount Hood. Late hops: Challenger. IBU: 24-32. Source: RP/MO.

**PSB** (b-c): ABV: 4.3%. Malt: Maris Otter pale malt, Crystal malt, Wheat malt. Hops: Fuggles, Goldings. Source: JE5.

**Burrough Bitter** (b-c): ABV: 4.8%. Malt: Maris Otter pale malt, Crystal malt, Wheat malt. Hops: Fuggles, Goldings. Source: JE5.

**Poachers Ale**: OG: 1060. Malt: 85-90% Maris Otter pale malt, 4-8% Crystal malt, 4-5% Wheat malt, 0-2% Black malt, optional Dark sugar. Hops: Goldings, optional Fuggles, Bramling Cross. Late hops: Fuggles. IBU: 24. Source: RP/MO.

**Baz's Bonce Blower**: OG: 1110. Malt: 85-90% Halcyon pale malt, 4-7% Crystal malt, 4-5% Wheat malt, 2% Black malt, 1% Secret ingredient / Black syrup, Dark sugar. Hops: Goldings. Late hops: Bramling Cross, Fuggles. IBU: 38-42. Source: RP/JHF.

**Baz's Bonce Blower** (b-c): ABV: 11.5%. Malt: Maris Otter pale malt, Crystal malt, Black malt. Hops: Fuggles, Goldings, Willamette. Source: JE5/6.

### . *Phoenix, Manchester*

**Navvy**: ABV: 3.8%. Hops: Styrian Goldings, Green Bullet, Goldings, Willamette, Hallertau. Source: W.

### . *Pilgrim Ales, Reigate*

**Surrey Pale Ale / Surrey Bitter**: OG: 1038. Malt: 85-97% Pale malt, 0-8% Crystal malt, 3-7% Torrefied wheat. Hops: Goldings. Dry hops: Goldings. Source: RP.

**Dark XXXX**: OG: 1040. Malt: Pale malt, 3-4% Torrefied wheat, Roast malt extract, optional Crystal malt. Hops: Goldings. Source: RP.

**Porter**: OG: 1041. Malt: 80% Pale malt, 4% Crystal malt, 4% Torrefied wheat, 4% Roast barley. Hops: Goldings. Source: RP3/4/5.

**Progress**: OG: 1041. Malt: Pale malt, 3-4% Torrefied wheat, optional Crystal malt. Hops: Goldings. Source: RP.

**Progress** (b-c): ABV: 4.3%. Malt: Maris Otter pale malt, Crystal malt, Chocolate malt. Hops: Styrian Goldings, Goldings. Source: JE1/2/3.

**Saracen Stout**: OG: 1048. Malt: Pale malt, Roast malt, Crystal malt, optional Chocolate malt. Hops: Goldings. Source: RP.

**Talisman / Talisman Winter Warmer**: OG: 1048. Malt: 82% Pale malt, 11% Crystal malt, 3-4% Torrefied wheat, 2% Roast barley, 2% Molasses. Hops: Goldings. Source: RP.

**Springbock** (b-c): ABV: 5.2%. Malt: Maris Otter pale malt, Wheat malt. Hops: Tettnang, Goldings. Source: JE1/2/3.

**Pudding** (b-c): ABV: 6.8%. Malt: Maris Otter pale malt, Crystal malt, Chocolate malt. Hops: Goldings. Others: Cherry brandy. Source: JE1/2/3.

**Organic Lager** (b-c): ABV: 3.7%. Malt: Maris Otter pale malt. Hops: Hallertau. Source: JE3.

**Bitter**: OG: 1038. Malt: 90% Pale malt, 7% Crystal malt, 3% Wheat. Hops: Goldings. Source: RP1.

**Bitter / Original Bitter** (b-c): ABV: 3.7%. Malt: Maris Otter pale malt, Crystal malt, Wheat malt. Hops: Fuggles, Goldings, Challenger. Source: JE1/2/3/4/5/6.

**Golden Otter Ale** (b-c): ABV: 4%. Malt: Maris Otter pale malt. Hops: Goldings. Source: JE1/2.

**Harvest Ale** (b-c): ABV: 4%. Malt: Maris Otter pale malt, Crystal malt, Caramalt. Hops: First Gold, Goldings. Source: JE1/2.

**Shoreditch Stout** (b-c): ABV: 4%. Malt: Maris Otter pale malt, Roast barley, Flaked barley. Hops: Fuggles, Target, Challenger. Source: JE1/2/3/4/5/6.

**Amber Ale** (b-c): ABV: 4.2%. Malt: Maris Otter pale malt, Crystal malt, Amber malt, Wheat malt, Torrefied wheat. Hops: Fuggles, Goldings, Challenger. Source: JE1/2.

**East Kent Goldings** (b-c): ABV: 4.2%. Malt: Maris Otter pale malt, Crystal malt, Wheat malt, Flaked maize. Hops: Goldings. Source: JE2/3/4/5/6.

**Eco Warrior** (b-c): ABV: 4.5%. Malt: Chariot pale malt, Sugar. Hops: Hallertau. Source: JE1/2/3/4/5/6.

**Jack Frost** (b-c): ABV: 4.5%. Malt: Maris Otter pale malt, Crystal malt, Amber malt, Chocolate malt, Flaked barley. Hops: Fuggles, Challenger. Source: JE1/2.

**1998 Ale** (b-c): ABV: 4.5%. Malt: Maris Otter pale malt, Crystal malt, Amber malt, Chocolate malt, Torrefied wheat, Wheat malt, Sugar. Hops: Goldings. Source: JE1.

**Hoxton Best Bitter**: OG: 1048. Malt: Pale malt, Crystal malt, Wheat. Hops: Goldings. Source: RP1.

**Hoxton Heavy / Hoxton Best Bitter** (b-c): ABV: 4.8%. Malt: Maris Otter pale malt, Crystal malt, Roast barley, Dried pale malt. Hops: Northdown, Goldings, Challenger. Source: JE1/2/3/4/5/6.

**Dark Star**: OG: 1048. Malt: Pale malt, Crystal malt, Wheat, Roast barley. Hops: Goldings. Source: RP.

**Black Eagle** (b-c): ABV: 5%. Malt: Maris Otter pale malt, Crystal malt, Wheat malt, Black malt. Hops: Fuggles, Styrian Goldings, Challenger. Source: JE1/2/3/4/5/6.

**Honey Ale** (b-c): ABV: 5%. Malt: Maris Otter pale malt, Crystal malt, Caramalt, Black malt, Flaked barley, Wheat malt, Honey. Hops: First Gold, Goldings. Others: Ginseng. Source: JE2.

**Liquorice Porter** (b-c): ABV: 5%. Malt: Maris Otter pale malt, Crystal malt, Black malt. Hops: Goldings. Others: Liquorice. Source: JE1/2.

**Pumpkin Porter** (b-c): ABV: 5%. Malt: Maris Otter pale malt, Crystal malt, Black malt. Hops: First Gold, Goldings, Challenger. Source: JE1/2.

**Trafalgar Ale** (b-c): ABV: 5%. Malt: Maris Otter pale malt, Crystal malt, Black malt, Torrefied wheat, Flaked maize. Hops: Fuggles, Goldings, Challenger. Source: JE1/2.

**N1** (b-c): ABV: 5%. Malt: Pale malt, Wheat malt. Hops: Hallertau. Others: Coriander. Source: JE5/6.

**1850 London Porter** (b-c): ABV: 5%. Malt: Maris Otter pale malt, Brown malt, Roast barley. Hops: Goldings. Source: JE5/6.

**Valentine Ale** (b-c): ABV: 5%. Malt: Maris Otter pale malt, Crystal malt, Caramalt, Torrefied wheat, Wheat malt, Honey. Hops: First Gold, Goldings. Others: Ginger, Damiana, Ginseng, Coriander, Saw palmetto berries, Blackberry leaves. Source: JE1/2.

**1830 Amber Ale** (b-c): ABV: 5%. Malt: Maris Otter pale malt, Amber malt, Chocolate malt. Hops: Fuggles, Goldings, Styrian Goldings. Source: JE4/5/6.

**21st Anniversary Ale** (b-c): ABV: 5.5%. Malt: Maris Otter pale malt, Crystal malt, Wheat malt. Hops: Challenger, Goldings. Source: JE4.

**London Porter**: OG: 1058. Malt: Pale malt, Crystal malt, Black malt. Hops: Goldings. Source: RP1.

**1824 Mild Ale** (b-c): ABV: 6.5%. Malt: Maris Otter pale malt, Black malt, Wheat malt. Hops: Goldings. Source: JE4/5/6.

**1837 India Pale Ale** (b-c): ABV: 7%. Malt: Maris Otter pale malt, Roast barley. Hops: Northdown, Goldings. Source: JE5/6.

**1792 Imperial Stout** (b-c): ABV: 9.3%. Malt: Maris Otter pale malt, Roast barley, Wheat malt. Hops: Northdown. Source: JE4/5/6.

**1896 XXXX Stock Ale** (b-c): ABV: 10%. Malt: Maris Otter pale malt, Crystal malt. Hops: Northdown. Source: JE5/6.

**Millennium 2000 Ale** (b-c): ABV: 10.5%. Malt: Maris Otter pale malt, Amber malt, Brown malt. Hops: Goldings, Challenger. Source: JE1/2.

Notes: See Premier Ales and Wiltshire Brewery Company.

## *Plympton Brewery, Plymouth*

**Plympton Best / Dartmoor Best Bitter**: OG: 1038. Malt: 86% Pale malt, 14% Crystal malt. Hops: Fuggles, Goldings. Source: RP1.

**Dartmoor Best Bitter:** OG: 1038. Malt: 86% Maris Otter or Pipkin pale malt, 14% Crystal malt. Hops: Fuggles, Progress / Goldings. Late hops: Goldings. IBU: 30. Source: RP.

**Dartmoor Strong / Dartmoor Legend**: OG: 1044. Malt: 93% Maris Otter or Pipkin pale malt, 7% Crystal malt. Hops: Fuggles, Goldings / Progress. Late hops: Goldings. IBU: 32. Source: RP.

**Cockleroaster**: OG: 1060. Malt: 100% Pipkin. Hops: Fuggles, Goldings. IBU: 30. EBC: 15-18. Source: RP3/4.

.    *Poachers, Swinderby / North Hykeham* www.poachersbrewery.co.uk

**Trembling Rabbit Mild** (b-c): ABV: 3.4%. Malt: Maris Otter pale malt, Crystal malt, Chocolate malt. Hops: Goldings. Source: JE4. Hops: Cascade, Mount Hood. Source: JE5/6. Others: Local honey. Source: Web.

**Shy Talk Bitter** (b-c): ABV: 3.7%. Malt: Maris Otter pale malt, Crystal malt. Hops: Challenger, Cascade, Mount Hood. Source: JE5/6.

**Poachers Pride** (b-c): ABV: 4%. Malt: Maris Otter pale malt, Crystal malt. Hops: Cascade, Mount Hood. Source: JE5/6. Hops: Chinook, Challenger. Source: Web.

**Poachers Den** (b-c): ABV: 4.2%. Malt: Maris Otter pale malt, Roast barley. Hops: Styrian Goldings, Goldings, Hersbrücker. Source: JE4. Hops: Challenger, Cascade, Mount Hood. Source: JE5.

**Poachers Trail** (b-c): ABV: 4.2%. Malt: Maris Otter pale malt, Roast barley. Hops: Styrian Goldings, Goldings. Source: JE5/6.

**Billy Boy** (b-c): ABV: 4.4%. Malt: Maris Otter pale malt, Crystal malt. Hops: Mount Hood, Fuggles. Source: JE6/Web.

**Black Crow Stout** (b-c): ABV: 4.5%. Malt: Maris Otter pale malt, Roast barley. Hops: Challenger, Goldings. Source: JE4. Hops: Challenger, Chinook, Styrian Goldings. Source: JE5/6.

**Poachers Dick** (b-c): ABV: 4.5%. Malt: Maris Otter pale malt, Crystal malt. Hops: Styrian Goldings, Goldings. Source: JE4. Hops: Goldings, Cascade, Mount Hood, Challenger, Styrian Goldings. Source: JE5/6.

**Monkey Hanger**: ABV: 4.5%. Hops: Hersbrücker, Styrian Goldings. Source: Web.

**Jock's Trap** (b-c): ABV: 5%. Malt: Maris Otter pale malt, Roast barley. Hops: Cascade, Mount Hood. Source: JE4/5/6/Web.

**Der Wilderer** (b-c): ABV: 5.1%. Malt: Maris Otter pale malt, Crystal malt, Chocolate malt, Smoked malt. Hops: Hersbrücker, Styrian Goldings. Source: JE4.

**Trout Tickler** (b-c): ABV: 5.5%. Malt: Maris Otter pale malt, Roast barley. Hops: Mount Hood, Cascade. Source: JE5. Malt: Maris Otter pale malt, Crystal malt, Chocolate malt. Hops: Mount Hood, Cascade. Source: JE6.

### . Points West, Plymouth

**Medieval Porter / Kitchen Porter** (b-c): ABV: 4.4%. Malt: Lager malt, Black malt, Roast barley. Hops: Goldings. Source: JE5.

**Drake's Drum** (b-c): ABV: 4.8%. Malt: Lager malt. Hops: Tettnang, Saaz. Source: JE5.

### . Poole Brewery, Poole

**Poole Best Bitter / Dolphin Bitter**: OG: 1038. Malt: 87.5% Pale malt, 12.5% Crystal malt, Caramel, optional Cane sugar. Hops: 30% Goldings, 50% Fuggles. Late hops: 10% Goldings. Dry hops: 0-10% Goldings. IBU: 35. Source: RP/MO.

**Bosun Best Bitter**: OG: 1049. Malt: 85-92.5% Pale malt, 7.5-15% Crystal malt, Caramel, optional Roast barley, optional Chocolate malt, optional Cane sugar syrup. Hops: 100% Goldings. Late hops: Goldings. Dry hops: Goldings. IBU: 40. Source: RP/MO.

### . Potton Brewery Company, Potton

**John Cunningham Night Fighter** (b-c): ABV: 4%. Malt: Pearl pale malt, Caramalt, Roast barley, Crystal malt. Hops: Target, First Gold. Source: JE6.

**Butler's Ale** (b-c): ABV: 4.3%. Malt: Halcyon pale malt, Crystal malt. Hops: Target, Styrian Goldings. Source: JE3. Malt: Pearl pale malt, Crystal malt. Hops: Target, First Gold. Source: JE4/5/6.

**Shambles Bitter** (b-c): ABV: 4.3%. Malt: Halcyon or Pearl pale malt, Crystal malt. Hops: Target, Styrian Goldings. Source: JE3/4/5/6.

**No-Ale Spiced** (b-c): ABV: 4.8%. Malt: Pearl pale malt, Crystal malt, Roast barley, CaraPils malt. Hops: Target, First Gold. Others: Ginger, Cinnamon, Mace, Cloves. Source: JE4/5/6.

### . Premier Ales, Stourbridge

**Old Merlin Mild**: OG: 1037-9. Malt: Pale malt, Dark sugars, Caramel. Hops: Goldings, Styrian Goldings. Source: RP1/2.

**Pitfield Bitter**: OG: 1038. Malt: 90% Pale malt, 7% Crystal malt, 3% Wheat malt. Hops: Goldings. Source: RP2.

**Knight Porter**: OG: 1040. Malt: Pale malt, Roast barley, Flaked barley, Dark sugar. Hops: Goldings. Source: RP1.

**Knightly Bitter**: OG: 1044. Malt: Pale malt, Lager malt, Crystal malt. Hops: Challenger, Target, Hallertau Styrian. Source: RP1/2.

**Pitfield Hoxton Heavy**: OG: 1048. Malt: Pale malt, Crystal malt, Wheat malt. Hops: Goldings. Source: RP2.

**Pitfield Dark Star**: OG: 1049. Malt: Pale malt, Crystal malt, Wheat malt, Roast barley. Hops: Goldings. Source: RP2.

**Black Knight Stout**: OG: 1050. Malt: Pale malt, Roast barley, Flaked barley, Dark sugars. Hops: Challenger. Source: RP1/2.

**Pitfield London Porter**: OG: 1058. Malt: Pale malt, Crystal malt, Black malt. Hops: Goldings. Source: RP2.

**Maiden's Ruin**: OG: 1074-5. Malt: Pale malt, Wheat malt, Light sugars. Hops: Challenger, Target, Styrian Goldings. Source: RP1/2.

Notes: See Pitfield Brewery and Wiltshire Brewery Company.

### . *Preston Brewing Company, Preston*

**Pride Dark Mild**: ABV: 3.6%. Malt: Maris Otter pale malt, Crystal malt, Torrefied wheat, Chocolate malt. Hops: Challenger, Fuggles, Northdown, Target. Source: RP3.

**Pride Ale**: OG: 1036. Malt: Maris Otter pale malt, Crystal malt, Torrefied wheat. Hops: Challenger, Fuggles, Northdown, Target. IBU: 25-30. EBC: 10. Source: RP3.

**Atlas Really Strong Export**: OG: 1060. Malt: Maris Otter pale malt, Crystal malt, Torrefied wheat, Chocolate malt. Hops: Challenger, Fuggles, Northdown, Target. IBU: 30-40. EBC: 60. Source: RP3.

### . *Princetown Breweries, Princetown*

**Jail Ale** (b-c): ABV: 4.8%. Malt: Pipkin pale malt, Crystal malt, Wheat malt. Hops: Progress, Challenger. Source: JE1/2/3/4/5/6.

### . *Quay Brewery, Weymouth*

**SOS**: OG: 1038. Malt: 89% Maris Otter pale malt, 6% Crystal malt, 5% Barley. Hops: Fuggles, Bramling Cross. Source: RP5.

**Weymouth Special Pale Ale**: OG: 1040. Malt: 88% Maris Otter pale malt, 3% Crystal malt, 9% Wheat malt. Hops: Challenger. Late hops: Goldings, Willamette. Dry hops: Yes. Source: RP5.

**Weymouth JD 1742**: OG: 1041. Malt: 96% Maris Otter pale malt, 4% Crystal malt. Hops: Challenger. Late hops: Bramling Cross. Source: RP5.

**Weymouth JD 1742** (b-c): ABV: 4.2%. Malt: Maris Otter pale malt. Hops: Challenger, Mount Hood. Source: JE4.

**Steam Beer** (b-c): ABV: 4.5%. Malt: Lager malt, Black malt, Wheat malt. Hops: Cascade. Source: JE3/4.

**Bombshell Bitter**: OG: 1045. Malt: 80% Maris Otter pale malt, 15% Crystal malt, 1% Chocolate malt, 4% Barley. Hops: Fuggles. Late hops: Goldings, Bramling Cross. Dry hops: Yes. Source: RP5.

**Jurassic** (b-c): ABV: 4.7%. Malt: Pale malt, Crystal malt. Hops: Hallertau, Saaz. Source: JE4.

**Old Rott**: OG: 1048. Malt: 75% Maris Otter pale malt, 15% Crystal malt, 1% Chocolate malt, 10% Wheat malt. Hops: Challenger. Late hops: Bramling Cross. Source: RP5.

**Organic Gold** (b-c): ABV: 4.8%. Malt: Pale malt. Hops: Hallertau. Source: JE3/4.

**Groves Oatmeal Stout** (b-c): ABV: 4.8%. Malt: Pale malt, Chocolate malt, Amber malt, Black malt, Flaked oats. Hops: Fuggles, Bramling Cross. Source: JE1/2/3.

**Groves Oatmeal Stout**: OG: 1052. Malt: 58% Maris Otter pale malt, 10% Amber malt, 8% Black malt, 24% Flaked oats. Hops: Fuggles. Late hops: Goldings. Dry hops: Yes. Source: RP5.

**Santa's Blotto** (b-c): ABV: 4.9%. Malt: Maris Otter pale malt, Crystal malt, Black malt, Rolled barley. Hops: Bramling Cross. Others (optional): Cassia bark, Ginger. Source: JE1/2.

**Old Rott** (b-c): ABV: 5.4%. Malt: Pale malt, Crystal malt. Hops: Bramling Cross, Challenger. Source: JE1/2/3/4.

**Silent Knight** (b-c): ABV: 5.9%. Malt: Maris Otter pale malt, Chocolate malt, Wheat malt. Hops: Bramling Cross. Source: JE1/2/3/4.

Note: Became Dorset Brewing Company in 2004.

## . *RCH, Weston-super-Mare*

**PG Steam**: OG: 1039. Malt: 92% Pale malt, 8% Crystal malt. Hops: Fuggles, Progress. Source: RP4/5.

**On the Tiles** (b-c): Bottled version of **PG Steam**. Source: JE2/3/4/5/6.

**Pitchfork**: OG: 1043. Malt: 100% Pale malt. Hops: Fuggles, Goldings. Source: RP4/5/JE1/2/3/4/5/6/JHF.

**Wheat Beer**: OG: 1044. Malt: 57% Pale malt, 8% Crystal malt, 35% Wheat. Hops: Target, Goldings. Source: RP4/5.

**Old Slug Porter**: OG: 1046. Malt: 86% Pale malt, 6% Crystal malt, 8% Black malt. Hops: Fuggles, Goldings. Source: RP4/5/JE1/2/3/4/5/6.

**East Street Cream**: OG: 1050. Malt: 89% Pale malt, 10% Crystal malt, 0.75% Chocolate malt, 0.25% Black malt. Hops: Fuggles, Progress. Source: RP4/5.

**Double Header** (b-c): ABV: 5.3%. Malt: Pale malt. Hops: Goldings. Source: JE5/6.

**Ale Mary** (b-c): ABV: 6%. Malt: Pale malt, Chocolate malt. Hops: Progress, Target. Others: Ginger, Cloves, Cinnamon, Coriander, Nutmeg, Pimento. Source: JE3/4/5/6/TBBK.

**Firebox**: OG: 1060. Malt: 99% Pale malt, 1% Chocolate malt. Hops: Target, Progress. Source: RP4/5/JE1/2/3/4/5/6.

**Santa Fe**: OG: 1071. Malt: 89% Pale malt, 10% Crystal malt, 0.75% Chocolate malt, 0.25% Black malt. Hops: Fuggles, Progress, Goldings. Source: RP4/5.

Notes: Formerly the Royal Clarence brewery but moved from the Royal Clarence Hotel and became the RCH Brewery in 1993.

### . Rebellion Beer Company, Marlow

**Rebellion IPA**: OG: 1039. Malt: 92% Halcyon or Maris Otter pale malt, 8% Crystal malt and Dark malts. Hops: Target or Challenger. Late hops: Goldings. IBU: 28. Source: RP.

**Rebellion Smuggler**: OG: 1041. Malt: 92% Halcyon pale malt, 8% Crystal malt/Chocolate malt. Hops: Target, First Gold. Late hops: First Gold. Dry hops: First Gold. IBU: 36. Source: RP5.

**White** (b-c): ABV: 4.5%. Malt: Pale malt, Wheat malt. Hops: First Gold, Cascade. Others: Coriander, Orange peel, Lemon peel. Source: JE4/5/6.

**Rebellion Mutiny**: OG: 1046. Malt: Halcyon or 90% Maris Otter pale malt, 10% Crystal malt/Chocolate malt. Hops: Target. Late hops: Goldings. IBU: 32-38. Source: RP5.

### . Red Rose. Blackburn

**Accrington Stanley Ale** (b-c): ABV: 3.6%. Malt: Maris Otter pale malt, Crystal malt, Black malt. Hops: Target, Goldings, Fuggles, Challenger. Source: JE6.

**Bowley Best** (b-c): ABV: 3.7%. Malt: Maris Otter pale malt, Crystal malt, Black malt. Hops: Target, Goldings, Fuggles, Challenger. Source: JE6.

**Quaffing Ale** (b-c): ABV: 3.8%. Malt: Maris Otter pale malt, Crystal malt, Black malt. Hops: Goldings, Challenger. Source: JE6.

**Treacle Miner's Tipple** (b-c): ABV: 3.9%. Malt: Maris Otter pale malt, Crystal malt, Black malt. Hops: Goldings, Fuggles. Source: JE6.

**Felix** (b-c): ABV: 4.2%. Malt: Maris Otter pale malt. Hops: Goldings, Fuggles, Challenger. Source: JE6.

**Old Ben** (b-c): ABV: 4.3%. Malt: Maris Otter pale malt. Hops: Goldings. Others: Coriander. Source: JE6.

**Lancashire & Yorkshire Aleway** (b-c): ABV: 4.5%. Malt: Maris Otter pale malt, Crystal malt, Black malt. Hops: Target, Goldings, Fuggles, Challenger. Source: JE6.

**Care Taker of History** (b-c): ABV: 6%. Malt: Maris Otter pale malt, Crystal malt, Black malt. Hops: Target, Fuggles, Challenger. Source: JE6.

### . Redburn, Hexham

**Haltwhistle Pride** (b-c): ABV: 4.3%. Malt: Maris Otter pale malt, Crystal malt. Hops: Perle. Source: JE6.

**Fortis** (b-c): ABV: 4.4%. Malt: Maris Otter pale malt, Roast barley. Hops: Perle. Source: JE6.

**Solis** (b-c): ABV: 4.4%. Malt: Maris Otter pale malt, Wheat malt. Hops: Perle. Source: JE6.

**Bishop Ridley Ale** (b-c): ABV: 4.8%. Malt: Maris Otter pale malt, Crystal malt, Black malt. Hops: Perle. Source: JE6.

**Twice Brewed IPA** (b-c): ABV: 5.3%. Malt: Maris Otter pale malt, Wheat malt. Hops: Perle. Source: JE6.

**Special** (b-c): ABV: 6%. Malt: Maris Otter pale malt, Crystal malt, Amber malt, Black malt. Hops: Perle. Source: JE6.

## . *Reepham Brewery, Reepham*

**Summer Velvet**: OG: 1040. Malt: 97% Pale malt, 3% Crystal malt. Hops: Fuggles, Hallertau, WGV. Source: RP4. Malt: 84% Maris Otter pale malt, 6% Lager malt, 2% Crystal malt, 8% Cane sugar. Hops: Goldings. Late hops: Fuggles. Source: RP5.

**Velvet Stout**: OG: 1043. Malt: 84-85% Maris Otter pale malt, 6% Crystal malt, 1% Black malt, 5-6% Cane sugar, 1-4% Caramel. Hops: Goldings, Fuggles or WGV. Late hops: Fuggles. Source: RP.

**Old Bircham Ale**: OG: 1043-6. Malt: 86-88% Maris Otter pale malt, 5-6% Crystal malt, 0-1% Black malt, 7% Barley syrup, 0-1% Caramel. Hops: Goldings or WGV. Late hops: Fuggles. Source: RP.

**Rapier Pale Ale** (b-c): ABV: 4.2%. Malt: Maris Otter pale malt, Crystal malt, Barley syrup. Hops: Fuggles, WGV. Source: JE4. Malt: Maris Otter pale malt, Crystal malt. Hops: Fuggles, WGV, Bramling Cross. Source: JE5. Malt: Maris Otter pale malt, Barley syrup. Hops: Fuggles, Bramling Cross. Source: JE6.

**Rapier Pale Ale**: OG: 1044. Malt: 88-95% Maris Otter pale malt, 4-5% Crystal malt, 0-1% Wheat, 4-8% Barley syrup. Hops: Fuggles, Goldings or WGV. Late hops: Fuggles. Source: RP.

**Norfolk Wheaten**: OG: 1045. Malt: 30% Wheat malt, 46% Lager, 24% Maris Otter pale malt. Hops: WGV. Late hops: Fuggles. Source: RP5.

**Smugglers Stout**: OG: 1047. Malt: 84% Pale malt, 8% Crystal malt, 4% Black and Chocolate malt, 4% Wheat. Hops: Fuggles, Goldings. Source: RP1/2.

**Bittern**: OG: 1050. Malt: 86-7% Maris Otter pale malt, 4% Crystal malt, 9% Barley syrup. Hops: WGV. Late hops: Fuggles. Source: RP.

**Brewhouse Ale**: OG: 1055. Malt: 90% Pale and Crystal malt, 5% Wheat, 5% Barley syrup. Hops: Fuggles, Goldings. Source: RP1/2.

*.  Refresh UK, Trowbridge / Witney*

**Brakspear Live Organic** (b-c): ABV: 4.6%. Malt: Optic pale malt, Crystal malt. Hops: Target, Hallertau, Goldings. Source: JE4/5.

*.  Reid and Company, London*

**BPA**: OG: 1056. Malt: Pale malt. Hops: Goldings. Yeast: Wyeast #1098/Wyeast #1099. Notes: Recipe from 1839. IBU: 158. SRM: 5. Source: VB.

**IPA**: OG: 1057. Malt: Pale malt. Hops: Goldings. Yeast: Wyeast #1098/Wyeast #1099. Notes: Recipe from 1839. IBU: 177. SRM: 5. Source: VB.

**RG (Running Porter)**: OG: 1058. Malt: Pale malt, Brown malt, Black malt. Hops: Fuggles. Dry hops: Goldings. Notes: Recipe from 1877. Source: DP.

**Keeping Brown Stout**: OG: 1072. Malt: Pale malt, Roast barley, Brown malt. Hops: Fuggles. Dry hops: Goldings. Notes: Recipe from 1838. Source: DP.

**Stout No. 448**: OG: 1075. Malt: Pale malt, Brown malt, Black malt. Hops: Fuggles. Dry hops: Goldings. Notes: Recipe from 1878. Source: DP.

**KKKK**: OG: 1114. Malt: Pale malt. Hops: Fuggles. Dry hops: Goldings. Notes: Recipe from 1867. Source: DP.

*.  Nevile Reid & Co., Windsor*

**Double Stout**: OG: 1080. Malt: Pale malt, Roast barley, Brown malt. Hops: Fuggles. Dry hops: Goldings. Notes: Recipe from 1858. Source: DP.

*.  Reindeer Brewery, Norwich*

**Mild**: OG: 1034. Malt: 75% Maris Otter pale malt, 22% Crystal malt, 2% Chocolate malt, 1% Wheat malt. Hops: Goldings. Source: RP3.

**Bevy**: OG: 1037. Malt: 87% Maris Otter pale malt, 8% Crystal malt, 5% Wheat malt. Hops: Goldings. Late hops: Goldings. Source: RP3.

**Gnu Brew**: OG: 1042. Malt: 96% Maris Otter pale malt, 2% Crystal malt, 2% Wheat malt. Hops: Goldings. Late hops: Goldings. Source: RP3.

**Bitter**: OG: 1047. Malt: 87% Maris Otter pale malt, 9% Crystal malt, 4% Wheat malt. Hops: Goldings. Late hops: Goldings. Source: RP3.

**Rednose**: OG: 1057. Malt: 86% Maris Otter pale malt, 13% Crystal malt, 1% Chocolate malt. Hops: Goldings. Source: RP3.

*.  Ridgeway, South Stoke*

**Bitter** (b-c): ABV: 4%. Malt: Maris Otter pale malt, Crystal malt. Hops: Challenger, Boadicea. Source: JE5/6.

**Blue** (b-c): ABV: 5%. Malt: Maris Otter pale malt, Optic pale malt. Hops: Fuggles, Challenger, Styrian Goldings. Source: JE6.

**Ivanhoe** (b-c): ABV: 5.2%. Malt: Maris Otter pale malt, Chocolate malt. Hops: Goldings, Admiral. Source: JE6.

**IPA** (b-c): ABV: 5.5%. Malt: Maris Otter pale malt, Optic pale malt. Hops: Target, Fuggles, Challenger, Cascade. Source: JE6.

## . T. D. Ridley & Sons, Chelmsford

**Mild / XXXX**: OG: 1034-5. Malt: 78% Pipkin pale malt, 10.5% Crystal malt, 0-0.1% Chocolate malt, 0-10.5% Torrefied wheat, 8.5% No.3 invert sugar, Caramel. Hops: Fuggles, Goldings. Dry hops: Yes. IBU: 24. EBC: 150. Source: RP/JHF.

**Bitter / PA / IPA Bitter**: OG: 1035. Malt: 78% Pipkin pale malt, 10.5% Crystal malt, 0-0.1% Chocolate malt, 0-10.5% Torrefied wheat, 8.5% No.3 invert sugar. Hops: Styrian Goldings. Late hops: Fuggles, Goldings. Dry hops: Fuggles, Goldings. IBU: 28-35. EBC: 30. Source: RP/JHF.

**Witchfinder Porter**: OG: 1045. Malt: 88% Pipkin pale malt, 7-7.4% Crystal malt, 3.7-5% Chocolate malt, 12% Invert sugar. Hops: Fuggles, Goldings, Styrian Goldings. IBU: 44. EBC: 100-115. Source: RP.

**ESX Best**: OG: 1047. Malt: 79-83% Pipkin pale malt, 6.9-7.2% Crystal malt, 0.2% Chocolate malt, 8.8-12% Torrefied wheat, 7-9% Invert sugar. Hops: Fuggles, Goldings, Styrian Goldings. IBU: 34. EBC: 31-34. Source: RP.

**Spectacular**: OG: 1047-8. Malt: 100% Pipkin pale malt. Hops: Fuggles, Goldings, optional Styrian Goldings. Late hops: Fuggles, Goldings. EBC: 8.2-15. Source: RP.

**Rumpus**: OG: 1049. Malt: 76% Pipkin pale malt, 10% Crystal malt, 13% Torrefied wheat, 9% No.3 invert sugar. Hops: Fuggles, Goldings, Styrian Goldings. Dry hops: Yes. Source: RP5/JHF.

**Winter Ale**: OG: 1050-5. Malt: 81% Pipkin pale malt, 6% Crystal malt, 0.2% Chocolate malt, 4% Torrefied wheat, 8% Invert sugar. Hops: Fuggles, Goldings. IBU: 31. EBC: 120-175. Source: RP.

## . W.E. & J. Rigden, Faversham

**Mild Beer**: OG: 1058. Malt: Pale malt, Brown malt. Hops: Fuggles. Notes: Recipe from 1836. Source: DP.

**Beer**: OG: 1062. Malt: Pale malt. Hops: Fuggles. Notes: Recipe from 1859. Source: DP.

## . Ringwood Brewery, Ringwood

**Best Bitter**: OG: 1038-9. Malt: 89-94% Maris Otter pale malt, 0-7% Crystal malt, Chocolate malt, 4% Torrefied wheat / Wheat flour. Hops: Goldings, Progress and/or Challenger. Late hops: Goldings. IBU: 24-30. EBC: 24-26. Source: RP.

**Bold Forrester** (b-c): ABV: 4.2%. Malt: Maris Otter pale malt, Crystal malt, Amber malt. Hops: Challenger, Goldings/Progress. Source: JE4/5/6.

**True Glory**: OG: 1043. Malt: 92% Maris Otter pale malt, 8% Crystal malt and Chocolate malt. Hops: Goldings, Fuggles. Late hops: Goldings, Fuggles. IBU: 28. EBC: 40. Source: RP5.

**Huffkin** (b-c): ABV: 4.4%. Malt: Maris Otter pale malt, Chocolate malt, Crystal malt. Hops: Goldings, Fuggles. Source: JE6.

**XXXX Porter** (b-c): ABV: 4.7%. Malt: Maris Otter pale malt, Crystal malt, Chocolate malt, optional Roast barley extract. Hops: Challenger, Progress, Goldings. Source: JE3/4/5/6.

**XXXX Porter**: OG: 1048. Malt: 80-92% Maris Otter pale malt, 8.5-13% Crystal malt, Chocolate malt, 7-8% Torrefied wheat / Wheat flour, Caramel. Hops: Goldings, Challenger and/or Progress. Late hops: Goldings. IBU: 30-35. EBC: 75. Source: RP.

**Fortyniner**: OG: 1048. Malt: 90-94% Maris Otter pale malt, 0-5% Crystal malt, Chocolate malt, 2-5% Torrefied wheat / Wheat flour. Hops: Goldings, Challenger and/or Progress. Late hops: Goldings. IBU: 28-37. EBC: 20-22. Source: RP/JHF/W.

**Fortyniner** (b-c): ABV: 4.9%. Malt: Maris Otter pale malt, Crystal malt, optional Chocolate malt. Hops: Progress, Goldings, Challenger. Source: JE1/2/3/4/5/6.

**Old Thumper**: OG: 1058. Malt: 90-92% Maris Otter pale malt, 4% Crystal malt, Chocolate malt, 6% Torrefied wheat / Wheat flour. Hops: Goldings, Challenger and/or Progress. Late hops: Goldings. IBU: 32-42.5. EBC: 28-30. Source: RP.

## . *Rising Sun Inn & Brewery, Audley*

**Sunlight**: OG: 1036. Malt: 96% Halcyon pale malt, 1% Crystal malt, 3% Flaked wheat. Hops: Challenger, Fuggles, Goldings. Late hops: Goldings. Source: RP3/4/5.

**Rising**: OG: 1040. Malt: 90% Halcyon pale malt, 4% Crystal malt, 6% Flaked wheat. Hops: Challenger, Fuggles, Goldings. Late hops: Challenger. Source: RP3/4/5.

**Setting**: OG: 1045. Malt: 89% Halcyon pale malt, 5% Crystal malt, 5% Flaked wheat, 1% Chocolate malt. Hops: Challenger, Fuggles, Goldings. Late hops: Goldings. Source: RP3/4/5.

**Sunstroke**: OG: 1056. Malt: 87% Halcyon pale malt, 8% Crystal malt, 5% Flaked wheat. Hops: Challenger, Fuggles, Goldings. Late hops: Goldings. Source: RP3/4/5.

**Total Eclipse**: OG: 1072. Malt: 83% Halcyon pale malt, 10% Crystal malt, 5% Flaked wheat, 1.5% Chocolate malt. Hops: Fuggles, Goldings. Late hops: Goldings. Source: RP3/4/5.

**Solar Flare**: OG: 1100. Malt: 82% Halcyon pale malt, 11% Crystal malt, 5% Flaked wheat, 1.5% Chocolate malt. Hops: Fuggles, Goldings. Source: RP3/4/5.

### . Riverside, Sunderland

**New Age Millennium** (b-c): ABV: 10%. Malt: Light Malt extract. Hops: Fuggles, Challenger. Others: Ginger. Source: JE1.

### . Frederic Robinson, Stockport

**Best Mild / Dark Mild / Hatters Mild**: OG: 1032. Malt: Halcyon pale malt, Pipkin pale malt, Crystal malt, small % Flaked maize, Torrefied wheat, optional Wheat malt, Caramel. Hops: Goldings, small % Northdown, optional Fuggles. Dry hops: Goldings. IBU: 22. EBC: 34. Source: RP.

**Bitter / Old Stockport Bitter**: OG: 1035. Malt: Halcyon or Pipkin pale malt, Crystal malt, Caramel, small % Flaked maize and Torrefied wheat. Hops: Goldings, small % Northdown, optional Fuggles. Hops: Goldings. IBU: 24. EBC: 26. Source: RP.

**Hartleys XB**: OG: 1040. Malt: Mild ale malt or Halcyon pale malt, Crystal malt, small % Flaked maize, Invert sugar. Hops: Goldings, optional Styrian Goldings. IBU: 18. EBC: 23. Source: RP.

**Best Bitter**: OG: 1041. Malt: Halcyon or Pipkin pale malt, Crystal malt, Caramel, small % Flaked maize and Torrefied wheat. Hops: Goldings, small % Northdown, optional Fuggles. Dry hops: Goldings. IBU: 28. EBC: 19. Source: RP.

**Tempus Fugit**: ABV: 4.2%. Hops: Progress. Source: W.

**Frederic's**: OG: 1050. Malt: Pale malt, Wheat malt. Hops: Goldings, optional Fuggles. Dry hops: Goldings. IBU: 32. EBC: Less than 17. Source: RP.

**Old Tom**: OG: 1080. Malt: Halcyon pale malt, optional Pipkin pale malt, Crystal malt, Caramel, optional small % Flaked maize, optional Torrefied wheat, optional small % Chocolate malt. Hops: Goldings, optional small % Northdown. Dry hops: Goldings. IBU: 35. EBC: 100. Source: RP. OG: 1085-86. Malt: Pale malt, Crystal malt, Torrefied wheat, Chocolate malt, Treacle. Hops: Goldings. Late hops: Goldings. Dry hops: Goldings. Source: BC.

### . Robinwood Brewers & Vintners, Todmorden

**Best Bitter**: OG: 1035-6. Malt: 94-5% Halcyon or Maris Otter pale malt, 4-6% Crystal malt, 0-1% Chocolate malt. Hops: WGV or Challenger. IBU: 32. Source: RP.

**IPA**: OG: 1040. Malt: 94% Maris Otter pale malt, 6% Crystal malt. Hops: WGV. IBU: 36. Source: RP.

**XB**: OG: 1046. Malt: 93.8-95% Halcyon or Maris Otter pale malt, 5% Crystal malt, 0-1.2% Pale chocolate malt. Hops: WGV or Challenger. IBU: 34. Source: RP.

**Old Fart / Old XXXX Ale**: OG: 1060. Malt: 74% Maris Otter or Halcyon pale malt, 6% Crystal malt, 3-4% Roast barley, 0-1% Pale chocolate malt, 16% Malt extract. Hops: WGV or Challenger. IBU: 30-40. Source: RP.

## . Rooster's Brewery, Harrogate

**Jak's**: OG: 1039. Malt: Pipkin pale malt, Crystal malt. Hops: Challenger, Fuggles, Goldings, Styrian Goldings. Source: RP4/5.

**Special**: OG: 1039. Malt: Pipkin pale malt, Crystal malt. Hops: Challenger, Fuggles, Goldings, Styrian Goldings. Source: RP4/5.

**Yankee**: OG: 1042. Malt: Pipkin pale malt, Crystal malt. Hops: Challenger, Fuggles, Goldings, Styrian Goldings. Source: RP3/4/5.

**Rooster's Bitter**: OG: 1047. Malt: Pale malt, Crystal malt. Hops: Challenger, Fuggles, Goldings, Styrian Goldings. Source: RP3/4/5.

## . Ross Brewing Company, Bristol

**Best Bitter / Hartcliffe Bitter** (bottled): OG: 1045. Malt: 95% Pale malt, 5% Crystal malt. Hops: Goldings. Source: RP3.

**Clifton Dark Ale**: OG: 1045. Malt: 90% Pale malt, 5% Black malt, 5% Crystal malt. Hops: Goldings. Source: RP3.

**Medieval Porter**: OG: 1055. Malt: 90% Pale malt, 10% Black malt. Hops: Goldings. Others: Ginger, Liquorice, Coriander. Source: RP3.

**Saxon Strong Ale**: OG: 1055. Malt: 100% Pale malt, Honey. Hops: Goldings. Others: Apple juice.

## . Rother Valley Brewery Company, Northiam

**Lighterman**: OG: 1035. Malt: 48% Puffin pale malt, 48% Alexis pale malt, 4% Flaked maize. Hops: Yeoman. Late hops: WGV. Source: RP5.

**Level Best**: OG: 1040. Malt: 83% Puffin pale malt, 7% Crystal malt, 10% Torrefied wheat. Hops: Goldings. Source: RP4. Malt: 48% Puffin pale malt, 48% Alexis pale malt, 5% Crystal malt. Hops: Yeoman. Late hops: WGV. Source: RP5.

**Blues**: OG: 1050. Malt: 40% Puffin pale malt, 40% Alexis pale malt, 5% Crystal malt, 5% Brown malt. Hops: Yeoman. Late hops: WGV. Source: RP5.

## . Royal Clarence, Burnham-on-Sea

**Clarence Pride**: OG: 1036. Malt: 89-95% Pale malt, 5-10% Crystal malt, Roast barley or 1% Black malt. Hops: Fuggles, Goldings. Dry hops: Yes. Source: RP.

**Clarence Regent**: OG: 1050. Malt: 87-95% Pale malt, 5-10% Crystal malt, Roast barley or 3% Black malt. Hops: Fuggles, Goldings. Dry hops: Yes. Source: RP.

Notes: Moved from the Royal Clarence Hotel and became the RCH brewery in 1993.

### Ruddles Brewery, Langham

**Best Bitter**: OG: 1037. Malt: 86-90% Halcyon pale malt, 1-4% Crystal malt, 9-10% Sugar. Hops: Fuggles, Goldings, Challenger, Bramling Cross. Source: RP1/2/3/4/ Malt: 90% Halcyon pale malt, 1%Crystal malt, 9% Sugar. Hops: 91% Bramling Cross, Northdown, Fuggles and Goldings, 9% Northdown. IBU: 35. EBC: 26. Source: RP5.

**Bob's Gold**: OG: 1047. Malt: 90% Halcyon pale malt, 10% Sugar. Hops: First Gold. IBU: 29. EBC: 29. Source: RP5.

**County**: OG: 1050. Malt: 85-90% Halcyon pale malt, 3-4% Crystal malt, 7-11% Syrup. Hops: Goldings, Challenger, Bramling Cross, Northdown / Fuggles. IBU: 38. Source: RP/GW/BC. Malt: Pale malt, Crystal malt, Sugar. Hops: WGV, Fuggles. Late hops: WGV. Source: DL.

### Rudgate Brewery, York

**Viking**: OG: 1039. Malt: 90% Halcyon pale malt, 10% Crystal malt. Hops: Fuggles, Northdown or Challenger, Goldings. Late hops: Goldings. IBU: 24. EBC: 24-30. Source: RP.

**Battleaxe**: OG: 1044. Malt: 90% Halcyon pale malt, 9-10% Crystal malt, 0-1% Chocolate malt. Hops: Fuggles, Northdown or Challenger, Goldings. Late hops: Goldings. IBU: 28. EBC: 30. Source: RP.

### Russell's Gravesend Brewery, Gravesend

**LDA (Light Dinner Ale)**: OG: 1047. Malt: Pale malt, Lager malt, Flaked maize, No.1 invert sugar. Hops: Fuggles. Yeast: Wyeast #1098/Wyeast #1099. Notes: Recipe from 1911. IBU: 36. SRM: 5. Source: VB.

### Thomas Russell, Wolverhampton

**Export Pale Ale**: OG: 1088. Malt: Pale malt. Hops: Fuggles. Notes: Parti-gyle with **Burton Bitter**. Recipe from 1906. Source: DP.

**Burton Bitter**: OG: 1051. Malt: Pale malt. Hops: Fuggles. Notes: Parti-gyle with **Export Pale Ale**. Recipe from 1801. Source: DP.

### Ryburn Brewery, Sowerby Bridge

**Best Mild**: OG: 1033. Malt: Halcyon Mild ale malt, Roast barley, Chocolate malt, Pale chocolate malt, Wheat, Flaked barley. Hops: Fuggles. Source: RP3/4/5.

**Best Bitter**: OG: 1038. Malt: Halcyon pale malt, Crystal malt, Wheat. Hops: Goldings. Late hops: Fuggles. Dry hops: Fuggles. Source: RP3/4/5.

**Rydale Bitter**: OG: 1044. Malt: Halcyon pale malt, Crystal malt, Wheat. Hops: Goldings. Late hops: Fuggles. Dry hops: Fuggles. Source: RP3/4/5.

**Old Stone Troff Bitter**: OG: 1047. Malt: Halcyon pale malt, Crystal malt, Wheat. Hops: Goldings, Fuggles. Late hops: Northdown. Source: RP5.

**Strong Mild / Luddite**: OG: 1048. Malt: Halcyon Mild ale malt, Roast barley, Chocolate malt, Pale chocolate malt, Wheat, Flaked barley. Hops: Fuggles. Source: RP3/4/5.

**Stabbers Bitter**: OG: 1050. Malt: Halcyon pale malt, Crystal malt, Wheat. Hops: Goldings. Late hops: Fuggles. Dry hops: Fuggles. Source: RP3/4/5.

**Coiners**: OG: 1060. Malt: Halcyon pale malt, Crystal malt, Wheat. Hops: Goldings, Fuggles. Late hops: Northdown. Source: RP4/5.

### . *Sadlers Ales, Stourbridge. Www.sadlersales.co.uk*

**Honey Fuggle**: ABV: 3.7%. Malt: Honey. Hops: Fuggles. Source: Web.

**Red House**: ABV: 4%. Hops: Goldings. Source: Web.

**Solar Bear**: ABV: 4%. Malt: Maris Otter pale malt. Source: Web.

**Pumpkin Eater**: ABV: 4.5%. Others: Fresh pumpkin. Source: Web.

**Cheeky Elf**: ABV: 4.5%. Malt: Chocolate malt. Source: Web.

**Hop Bomb**: ABV: 5%. Hops: Citra, Amarillo. Source: Web.

**Mud City Stout**: ABV: 6.6%. Malt: Flaked oats, Flaked wheat, Dark malts. Others: Raw cocoa, Vanilla pods. Source: Web.

### . *St. Austell Brewery Company, St. Austell* www.staustellbrewery.co.uk

**Bosun's Bitter**: OG: 1034. Malt: Pale malt, Crystal malt, optional Torrefied wheat. Hops: British Fuggles, Goldings, optional Bramling Cross. EBC: 25. Source: RP.

**Dartmoor Best Bitter**: ABV: 3.5%. Malt: Maris Otter pale malt, Black malt. Hops: Willamette. Source: Web.

**XXXX Mild**: OG: 1037. Malt: Pale malt, Crystal malt, Caramel, optional Torrefied wheat. Hops: British Fuggles, Goldings, optional Bramling Cross. EBC: 95. Source: RP.

**Trelawny**: ABV: 3.8%. Hops: Goldings, Galaxy. Source: Web.

**Tinners Bitter**: OG: 1038. Malt: Pale malt, Crystal malt, Torrefied wheat. Hops: Fuggles, Goldings. Dry hops: Yes. EBC: 28. Source: RP3/4/5.

**Strawberry Blonde**: ABV: 4%. Malt: Cornish lager malt, Crystal malt, Flaked maize. Hops: Hop extract. Others: Strawberries. Source: Web.

**Black Prince**: ABV: 4%. Malt: Maris Otter pale malt, Crystal malt, Black malt. Hops: Goldings, Fuggles. Source: Web.

**Tribute**: ABV: 4.2%. Malt: CaraPils malt, Munich malt, Wheat malt. Late hops: Willamette. Source: BBB. Malt: Maris Otter pale malt, Cornish Gold malt. Hops: Fuggles, Willamette, Styrian Goldings. Source: Web.

**Trelawny's Pride**: OG: 1044. Malt: Alexis pale malt, Crystal malt, 15% Wheat malt. Hops: Fuggles, Bramling Cross. Dry hops: Styrian Goldings. Source: RP5.

**Proper Job**: ABV: 4.5%. Malt: Maris Otter pale malt. Hops: Chinook, Willamette, Cascade. Source: Web.

**Korev**: ABV: 4.8%. Malt: Cornish lager malt, Cara Gold malt, Flaked maize. Hops: Perle, Saaz, Hersbrücker. Source: Web.

**Smuggler's Ale / Admiral's Ale** (b-c): ABV: 5%. Malt: Cornish Gold malt. Hops: Cascade, Styrian Goldings. Source: JE6/Web.

**HSD / Hicks Special**: OG: 1050. Malt: Pale malt, Crystal malt, Torrefied wheat. Hops: Fuggles, Goldings. Dry hops: Yes. EBC: 33. Source: RP3/4/5. Malt: Maris Otter pale malt, Crystal malt, Black malt. Hops: Goldings, Fuggles. Source: Web.

**Clouded Yellow** (b-c): ABV: 4.8-5%. Malt: Maris Otter pale malt, Wheat malt, Maple syrup. Hops: Willamette. Others: Vanilla pods, Cloves, Coriander. Source: JE3/4/5/6/TBBK/Web.

**1013 Cornish Stout**: ABV: 5.2%. Malt: Maris Otter pale malt, Roast barley, Chocolate malt, Smoked malt, Crystal malt, Oat malt. Hops: Fuggles. Source: Web.

**Proper Job** (b-c): ABV: 5.5%. Malt: Maris Otter pale malt. Hops: Willamette, Chinook, Cascade. Source: JE6/Web.

**Smugglers** (b-c): ABV: 6%. Malt: Maris Otter pale malt, Roast malt, Crystal malt. Hops: Fuggles, Styrian Goldings. Others: Coriander. Source: Web.

**Cardinal Syn**: ABV: 8%. Malt: Pilsner malt, Crystal malt, Roast malt, Demerara sugar, Dark caramel. Hops: Perle, Hersbrücker, Styrian Celeia. Dry hops: Dana. Others: Coriander. Yeast: Trappist ale. Source: Web.

**Bad Habit**: ABV: 8.5%. Malt: Pilsner malt, Wheat malt, Oat malt, Light sugar. Hops: Citra, Dana. Others: Coriander, Orange peel, Grains of Paradise. Source: Web.

**Big Job**: ABV: 9%. Hops: Citra, Centennial. Source: Web.

. *St. Peter's Brewery Company, Bungay. Www.StPetersBrewery.co.uk*

**Mild**: OG: 1035. Malt: 95% Halcyon pale malt, 5% Chocolate malt. Hops: Challenger. Late hops: Goldings. IBU: 20. Source: RP5/Web.

**Fruit Beer**: OG: 1035. Malt: 85% Halcyon pale malt, 15% Torrefied wheat. Hops: Challenger. Late hops: Goldings. Others: Raspberries or Elderberries. IBU: 18. Source: RP5.

**Wheat Beer**: OG: 1035. Malt: 70% Halcyon pale malt, 20% Wheat malt, 10% Torrefied wheat. Hops: Challenger. Late hops: Goldings. IBU: 18. Source: RP5.

**Best Bitter**: OG: 1036. Malt: 85% Halcyon pale malt, 15% Crystal malt. Hops: Challenger. Late hops: Goldings. IBU: 25. Source: RP5/Web.

**Dark G-Free**: ABV: 3.9%. Malt: Gluten-free. Hops: Sovereign. Source: Web.

**Organic Best Bitter**: ABV: 4.1%. Malt: Chariot pale malt. Hops: Goldings. Source: Web.

**G-Free**: ABV: 4.2%. Malt: Gluten-free. Hops: Amarillo. Source: Web.

**Extra**: OG: 1043. Malt: 85% Halcyon pale malt, 12.5% Crystal malt, 2.5% Roast malt. Hops: Challenger. Late hops: Goldings. Source: RP5/JHF.

**Ruby Red Ale**: ABV: 4.3%. Hops: Cascade. Source: Web.

**Golden Ale**: OG: 1044. Malt: Halcyon pale malt, Lager malt, Torrefied wheat. Hops: Goldings/Challenger. Late hops: Goldings. Source: RP5/Web.

**Wheat Beer**: ABV: 4.7%. Yeast: Bavarian Weiss ale. Source: Web.

**Grapefruit**: ABV: 4.7%. Other: **Wheat Beer** and Grapefruits. Source: Web.

**Honey Porter**: OG: 1048. Malt: 85% Halcyon pale malt, 12% Crystal malt, 3% Chocolate malt, Honey. Hops: Challenger. Late hops: Goldings. Source: RP5/JHF.

**Suffolk Smokey**: ABV: 4.8%. Malt: Peat-smoked malt. Source: Web.

**The Saints Whisky Beer**: ABV: 4.8%. Malt: Peat-smoked malt. Other: St. George's Distillery Whisky. Source: Web.

**Strong Ale**: OG: 1049. Malt: 85% Halcyon pale malt, 15% Crystal malt. Hops: Challenger. Late hops: Goldings. Source: RP5/Web.

**Suffolk Gold**: ABV: 4.9%. Hops: First Gold. Source: Web.

**King Cnut™ Ale**: ABV: 5%. Malt: Halcyon pale malt, Roast barley. Hops: None. Other: Juniper berries, Stinging nettles. Source: HB.

**Old Style Porter**: ABV: 5.1%. Blend of a "mature old ale and a younger light beer". Source: JE6.

**English Lager**: ABV: 5.2%. Hops: Styrian Goldings, Hallertau. Yeast: Lager. Source: Web.

**Cream Stout**: ABV: 6.5%. Malt: 5 malts. Hops: Challenger, Fuggles. Source: Web.

## Salopian Brewing Company, Shrewsbury

**Bitter**: OG: 1035. Malt: Maris Otter pale malt, Crystal malt, Black malt. Hops: Fuggles, Goldings. Source: RP5.

**Choir Porter**: OG: 1045. Malt: Maris Otter pale malt, Crystal malt, Black malt. Hops: Fuggles. Source: RP5.

**Minsterley Ale / Proud Salopian** (b-c): ABV: 4.5%. Malt: Maris Otter pale malt, Crystal malt. Hops: Fuggles, Goldings, Styrian Goldings. Source: JE1/2/3/4/5.

**Gingersnap** (b-c): ABV: 4.7%. Malt: Pale malt, Crystal malt, Pale chocolate malt, Wheat malt. Hops: Goldings, Hersbrücker, Styrian Goldings, Saaz. Others: Root Ginger. Source: JE2/3/4/5.

**Cerise de Salop** (b-c): ABV: 4.8%. Malt: Pale malt, Crystal malt, Lager malt, Wheat malt, Maize. Hops: Fuggles. Others: Cherries. Source: JE2.

**Entire Butt** (b-c): ABV: 4.8%. Malt: Maris Otter pale malt, Crystal malt, Dark crystal malt, Amber malt, Pale chocolate malt, Chocolate malt, Brown malt, Black malt, Lager malt, CaraPils malt, Wheat malt, Oat malt, Roast barley, Torrefied wheat. Hops: Fuggles, Styrian Goldings, Goldings. Source: JE2/3/4/5/6.

**Jigsaw** (b-c): ABV: 4.8%. Malt: Maris Otter pale malt, Crystal malt, Coloured malt, Oat malt, Wheat malt. Hops: Fuggles, Styrian Goldings. Source: JE1.

**Puzzle** (b-c): ABV: 4.8%. Malt: Lager malt, Wheat malt. Hops: Saaz,Hersbrücker. Others: Ginger, Coriander, Orange peel. Source: JE1/3/4/5.

**Answer** (b-c): ABV: 4.8%. Malt: Lager malt, Caramel malt, Wheat malt. Hops:Hersbrücker, Goldings, Styrian Goldings, Cascade. Others: Coriander, Lemons. Source: JE1.

**Goodalls Gold** (b-c): ABV: 4.8%. Malt: Maris Otter pale malt, Crystal malt. Hops: Cascade, Goldings. Source: JE3.

**Firefly** (b-c): ABV: 5%. Malt: Maris Otter pale malt, Dark crystal malt, Peat-smoked malt. Hops: Goldings, Styrian Goldings. Source: JE2/3/4/5.

### . Sambrook's Brewery, London. Www.sambrooksbrewery.co.uk

**Junction Ale**: ABV: 4.5%. Malt: Crystal malt, Roast barley. Hops: English. Source: Web.

### . Scarecrow, Arreton, Isle of Wight

**Best Bitter** (b-c): ABV: 4.2%. Malt: Pale malt, Crystal malt, Wheat malt. Hops: Bramling Cross. Source: JE4/5/6.

### . Scott's Brewing Company, Lowestoft

**Golden Best Bitter**: OG: 1033-8. Malt: 98% Pipkin or Maris Otter pale malt, 2% Crystal malt. Hops: Fuggles, Challenger / Goldings. Source: RP.

**Blues & Bloater Bitter**: OG: 1035-8. Malt: 93% Maris Otter pale malt, 6% Crystal malt, 1% Chocolate malt. Hops: Fuggles, Goldings / Challenger. Source: RP.

**William French**: OG: 1047-51. Malt: 90% Maris Otter pale malt, 9% Crystal malt, 0-1% Chocolate malt. Hops: Fuggles, Goldings / Challenger. Source: RP.

**Dark Oast**: OG: 1048-51. Malt: 88% Maris Otter pale malt, 9% Crystal malt, 2% Chocolate malt, 1% Roast barley. Hops: Fuggles, Goldings. Source: RP4/5.

### . Scottish & Newcastle Breweries, Newcastle-upon-Tyne

**Newcastle Amber Ale** (bottled): ABV: 3.2%. Malt: Crystal malt, Sugar. Hops: Fuggles. Dry hops: Hop extract. Source: DL. OG: 1031. Malt: Pale malt, Crystal malt, Flaked maize, Roast barley. Hops: Challenger. Source: 150.

**Theakston Best Bitter**: OG: 1038. Malt: Pale malt, Crystal malt, Unmalted cereal, Sugar. Hops: Fuggles, others. Late hops: Fuggles. Dry hops: Yes. IBU: 24. EBC: 15. Source: RP1/2/3/4/5. Note: See **Best Bitter**, T&R Theakston.

**Exhibition**: OG: 1040. Malt: White malt, Crystal malt, Flaked maize, Torrefied wheat. Hops: Styrian Goldings. IBU: 24. EBC: 18. Source: RP4/5.

**Newcastle Brown Ale** (bottled): OG: 1044. Malt: Pale malt, Crystal malt, Brewing sugar, optional Chocolate malt. Hops: Hallertau, Northdown, Northern Brewer, Target or Fuggles. Dry hops: Northern Brewer hop extract. Source: EBA/DL. Note: 2:3 by volume blend of **Old Ale** and **Amber Ale**. Source: 150. OG: 1048-1051. Malt: Pale malt, Crystal malt, Chocolate malt, Black malt. Hops: Target. Dry hops: Late hops: Goldings. Source: CB.

**John Courage Amber**: OG: 1045. Malt: Pale malt, Biscuit malt, Crystal malt. Hops: Northern Brewer. Late hops: Fuggles. Source: 150.

**Theakston XB**: OG: 1044. Malt: Pale malt, Crystal malt, Unmalted cereal, Sugar. Hops: Fuggles, Others. Late hops: Fuggles. Dry hops: Yes. IBU: 26. EBC: 26. Source: RP3/4/5. Note: See **XB**, T&R Theakston.

**Old Ale**: OG: 1064. Malt: Pale malt, Crystal malt, Flaked maize, Roast barley, Chocolate malt. Hops: Fuggles. Late hops: Goldings. Source: 150.

## Selby (Middlebrough) Brewery, Selby

**Best Bitter**: OG: 1036. Malt: 95% Pale malt, 5% Crystal malt. Hops: Sunshine, Goldings. Source: RP1/2.

**Strong Ale**: OG: 1045. Malt: 90% Maris Otter pale malt, 10% Crystal malt. Hops: WGV. Source: RP3/4/5.

**Old Tom**: OG: 1065-6. Malt: 90-95% Maris Otter pale malt, 5-10% Crystal malt. Hops: WGV, optional Sunshine. Source: RP.

## Shakespeare's, Bidford-on-Avon

**Noble Fool** (b-c): ABV: 3.9%. Malt: Maris Otter pale malt, Wheat malt, Crystal malt, Rye malt. Hops: First Gold. Source: JE6.

**Taming of the Brew** (b-c): ABV: 4.3%. Malt: Maris Otter pale malt, Wheat malt, Chocolate malt, Crystal malt, Rye malt. Hops: Goldings, Challenger. Source: JE6.

**The Scottish Ale** (b-c): ABV: 4.6%. Malt: Maris Otter pale malt, Wheat malt, Chocolate malt, Crystal malt. Hops: Goldings, Fuggles. Source: JE6.

**The Tempest** (b-c): ABV: 5.5%. Malt: Maris Otter pale malt, Wheat malt, Chocolate malt, Crystal malt, Rye malt. Hops: Challenger. Source: JE6.

### Shardlow Brewery, Shardlow

**Session**: OG: 1036. Malt: 91% Maris Otter pale malt, 9% Crystal malt. Hops: Willamette. Source: RP4/5.

**Best Bitter / Special Bitter** (b-c): ABV: 3.9%. Malt: Maris Otter pale malt, Crystal malt. Hops: Goldings, Phoenix. Source: JE5/6.

**Golden Hop** (b-c): ABV: 4.1%. Malt: Maris Otter pale malt. Hops: Goldings, Phoenix. Source: JE6.

**Bitter**: OG: 1042. Malt: Maris Otter pale malt, Crystal malt. Hops: Willamette, Mount Hood. Late hops: Styrian Goldings. Source: RP4/5.

**Cavendish Gold** (b-c): ABV: 4.5%. Malt: Maris Otter pale malt. Hops: Goldings, Phoenix. Source: JE5.

**Narrowboat** (b-c): ABV: 4.5%. Malt: Maris Otter pale malt, Crystal malt. Hops: Phoenix. Source: JE5/6.

**Reverend Eaton's** (b-c): ABV: 4.5%. Malt: Maris Otter pale malt. Hops: Goldings, Phoenix. Source: JE5/6.

**Cavendish 47 Bridge**: OG: 1047. Malt: 85.8% Maris Otter pale malt, 14.2% Crystal malt. Hops: Willamette. Source: RP4/5.

**Five Bells** (b-c): ABV: 5%. Malt: Maris Otter pale malt, Black malt. Hops: Phoenix. Source: JE6.

**Whistlestop** (b-c): ABV: 5%. Malt: Maris Otter pale malt. Hops: Phoenix. Source: JE5/6.

**Stedman Tipple** (b-c): ABV: 5.1%. Malt: Maris Otter pale malt, Crystal malt, Dark crystal malt. Hops: Cascade. Source: JE5.

**Sleighed**: OG: 1060. Malt: 85.7% Maris Otter pale malt, 7.15% Crystal malt, 7.15% Chocolate malt. Hops: Willamette. Source: RP4/5.

### Sharp's, Rock. www.sharpsbrewery.co.uk

**Summer Honey Gold**: ABV: 4.2%. Malt: Honey. Hops: 5 varieties. Others: Spices, Ginger. Source: Web.

**Winter Cornish Stout**: ABV: 4.3%. Others: Chestnuts. Source: Web.

**Sharp's Own / Original**: ABV: 4.4%. Malt: Crystal malt, Roast malt. Late hops: Northdown. Source: Web.

**Chalky's Bark**: ABV: 4.5%. Others: Ginger. Source: Web.

**Chalky's Bite**: ABV: 6.8%. Others: Fennel seeds. Source: TBBK/Web/WB.

**Master Brew Bitter**: OG: 1034-6. Malt: 75% Pale malt, 8% Crystal malt, 5% Amber malt, 4% Wheat malt, 8% Torrefied wheat, Glucose sugar. Hops: Omega, Target, Zenith, Goldings oil. Source: RP1/2/3. Malt: 83% Halcyon pale malt, 7% Crystal malt, 10% Cereal adjuncts. Hops: Target, Goldings. Dry hops: Yes. IBU: 37. EBC: 25. Source: RP4/5.

**Master Brew Best Bitter**: OG: 1037-9. Malt: 75% Pale malt, 8% Crystal malt, 5% Amber malt, 4% Wheat malt, 8% Torrefied wheat, Glucose syrup. Hops: Omega, Target, Zenith, Goldings oil. Source: RP1/2/3. Malt: 83% Halcyon pale malt, 7% Crystal malt, 10% Cereal adjuncts. Hops: Target, Goldings. Dry hops: Yes. IBU: 41. EBC: 28. Source: RP4/5.

**Best Bitter**: OG: 1040. Malt: Pale malt, Flaked maize, Amber malt, Sugar. Hops: WGV, Goldings. Late hops: Goldings. Dry hops: Goldings. Source: DL.

**Stock Ale**: Note: **Master Brew Best Bitter** with added colour. Source: RP1/2/3/4/5.

**Masons Dark Ale**: OG: 1039. Malt: 80% Halcyon pale malt, 7% Crystal malt, 3% Chocolate malt, 10% Cereal adjuncts. Hops: Target, Goldings. Dry hops: Yes. IBU: 35. EBC: 48. Source: RP4/5.

**Spitfire Ale**: OG: 1043-5. Malt: 75% Pale malt, 8% Crystal malt, 5% Amber malt, 4% Wheat malt, 8% Torrefied wheat, Glucose syrup. Hops: Omega, Target, Zenith, Goldings oil. Source: RP2/3. Malt: 83% Halcyon pale malt, 7% Crystal malt, 10% Cereal adjuncts. Hops: Target, Goldings. Dry hops: Yes. IBU: 41. EBC: 31. Source: RP4/5/JHF.

**Spitfire** (b-c): ABV: 4.7%. Malt: Halcyon pale malt, Lager malt. Hops: Goldings. Source: JE1.

**Bishops Finger**: OG: 1047-52. Malt: 75% Pale malt, 8% Crystal malt, 5% Amber malt, 4% Wheat malt, 8% Torrefied wheat, Glucose syrup. Hops: Omega, Target, Zenith, Goldings oil. Source: RP2/3. Malt: 83% Halcyon pale malt, 7% Crystal malt, 10% Cereal adjuncts. Hops: Target, Goldings. Dry hops: Yes. IBU: 43. EBC: 41. Source: RP4/5. OG: 1052-55. Malt: Pale malt, Crystal malt, Torrefied wheat, Amber malt, Sugar. Hops: Target. Late hops: Challenger, Goldings, Styrian Goldings. Source: CB. Hops: First Gold, Target. Source: W.

**Original Porter**: OG: 1047-9. Malt: 65-77% Halcyon pale malt, 7-12% Crystal malt, 6-7% Chocolate malt, 8-10% Torrefied wheat, Glucose. Hops: Target, Goldings. IBU: 33. EBC: 70. Source: RP/WB.

**Kaltenberg Prinzregent Luitpold Weissbier** (b-c): ABV: 5%. Malt: Halcyon pale malt, Wheat malt. Hops: Challenger. Source: JE1. Note: See **Prinzregent Luitpold Weissbier**, Schlossbrauerei Kaltenberg, Germany.

**IPA**: OG: 1055-57. Malt: Pale malt, Amber malt, Crystal malt, Torrefied wheat. Hops: Target. Late hops: Goldings. Dry hops: Goldings. Source: CB.

**1698** (b-c): ABV: 6.5%. Malt: Pearl pale malt, Crystal malt. Hops: Target. Late hops: Goldings. Source: JE6.

### . *James Shipstone & Sons, Nottingham*

**Mild Ale**: OG: 1034. Malt: 85% Maris Otter or Triumph pale malt, 15% Sugar, Crystal malt, Caramel. Hops: Fuggles, Goldings. Dry hops: Goldings. Source: RP1.

**Bitter**: OG: 1037. Malt: 93% Maris Otter or Triumph pale malt, 7% Invert sugar, Crystal malt. Hops: Fuggles, Goldings. Dry hops: Goldings. Source: RP1.

### . *Shoes, Norton Cannon*

**Norton Ale** (b-c): ABV: 3.6%. Malt: Malt extract. Hops: Goldings. Source: JE6.

**Cannon Bitter** (b-c): ABV: 4.2%. Malt: Malt extract. Hops: Fuggles. Source: JE6.

**Peplowe's Tipple** (b-c): ABV: 6%. Malt: Malt extract. Hops: Goldings. Source: JE6.

**Farrier's Beer** (b-c): ABV: 13.9-15.1%. Malt: Malt extract, Sugar. Hops: Fuggles. Source: JE3/4/5.

### . *H. & G. Simonds, Reading*

**SB**: OG: 1057. Malt: Pale malt. Hops: Goldings, Cluster. Yeast: Wyeast #1275/White Labs WLP023. Notes: Recipe from 1869. IBU: 85. SRM: 5. Source: VB.

**Bitter**: OG: 1062. Malt: Pale malt, Pale amber malt. Hops: Fuggles. Late hops: Goldings. Dry hops: Yes. Notes: Recipe from 1880. Source: DP.

**Double Stout**: OG: 1081. Malt: Pale malt, Brown malt, Black malt. Hops: Fuggles. Notes: Recipe from 1878. Source: DP.

**Bottling Stout**: OG: 1082. Malt: Pale malt, Brown malt, Black malt. Hops: Fuggles. Notes: Recipe from 1870. Source: DP.

### . *Simpson's Brewery, Baldock*

**March Beer**: OG: 1061 and 1100. Malt: Pale malt. Hops: Fuggles. Notes: Parti-gyle recipes from 1854. Source: DP.

### . *Skinner's, Truro*

**Cornish Knocker** (b-c): ABV: 4.5%. Malt: Pale malt, Other malts. Hops: Northdown, Styrian Goldings. Source: JE3.

**Figgy's Brew** (b-c): ABV: 4.5%. Malt: Optic pale malt, Crystal malt, Dark malts. Hops: Northdown. Source: JE4.

**Who Put The Lights Out?** (b-c): ABV: 5%. Malt: Pale malt, Other malts. Hops: Challenger. Source: JE3.

**Jingle Knockers** (b-c): ABV: 5.5%. Malt: Pale malt, Other malts. Hops: Challenger. Source: JE3.

## . *Smiles Brewing Company, Bristol*

**Brewery Bitter**: OG: 1037. Malt: 90% Pale malt, 10% Amber malt / Wheat malt. Hops: Goldings. Late hops: Goldings. IBU: 28. Source: RP/GW.

**Golden**: OG: 1039. Malt: Halcyon pale malt, Crystal malt, Amber malt. Hops: Challenger, Styrian Goldings. Late hops: Willamette. Dry hops: Willamette. IBU: 27. Source: RP5.

**Best Bitter**: OG: 1041. Malt: Halcyon pale malt, Crystal malt, Chocolate malt, Wheat malt. Hops: Goldings or Styrian Goldings. Late hops: Willamette. Dry hops: Willamette. IBU: 22. EBC: 26. Source: RP.

**Bristol Stout**: OG: 1046. Malt: Halcyon pale malt, Wheat malt, Roast barley. Hops: Goldings or Styrian Goldings. Late hops: Willamette. Dry hops: Willamette. IBU: 26. EBC: 25. Source: RP.

**Heritage**: OG: 1051. Malt: Halcyon pale malt, Crystal malt, Chocolate malt, Wheat malt. Hops: Styrian Goldings. Late hops: Willamette. Dry hops: Willamette. EBC: 44. Source: RP5.

**Exhibition**: OG: 1052. Malt: Pale malt, Crystal malt, Chocolate malt. Hops: Goldings. Source: RP. Notes: I enjoyed supping this superb beer during my time in Bristol (mainly in the Highbury Vaults). I also chose it as a guest beer for my leaving celebration from Banbury (held in the Swan, thank you Stuart) that resulted in me being in what was later described as "a rare state of total drunkenness". It was a very good night. This beer is now brewed at the Bristol Beer Factory (q.v.) and, having tasted this beer too, I'd say that it is about as close as I've got in my many attempts to clone this fine ale, so I'll give my current version here: OG: 1052. Malt: 74% Pale malt, 25% Crystal malt, 1% Chocolate malt. Hops: Goldings. Late hops: Goldings. AAU: 9-11. Yeast: Safale S-04. I think that this is quite close to the Smiles version of this brew and maybe even closer to the Bristol Beer Factory version. I'd recommend mashing this at a somewhat hot temperature in order to get nearer the necessary body for this ale. However, I have now received further information about this brew from the Bristol Beer Factory (q.v.) which I intend to use as I tweak this recipe further. I am encouraged that I've got about as close as a former Smiles brewer has managed in a new brewery. I guess that it is some unknown factor in the processing and/or yeast that is necessary to get this recipe those few more percentage points closer to the real thing (or at least my memory of it). Even if my recipe is not quite a 100% Smiles Exhibition clone, it was good enough be awarded runner up in a Scottish Craft Brewers National Competition in 2004!

**Holly Hops**: OG: 1052. Malt: Halcyon pale malt, Crystal malt, Wheat malt. Hops: Target. Late hops: Willamette. Dry hops: Willamette. IBU: 28. EBC: 32. Source: RP5.

**Old Vic**: OG: 1065. Malt: Pale malt, Crystal malt, Chocolate malt. Hops: Goldings. Source: RP1/2.

## John Smith's Brewery, Tadcaster

**Websters Yorkshire Bitter**: OG: 1034.8. Malt: 74% Pale malt, 5% Torrefied wheat, 1% Black malt, 20% Sugar, Caramel. Hops: Target. IBU: 35. EBC: 26. Source: RP5.

**Bitter / Yorkshire Bitter**: OG: 1036. Malt: Pale malt, Brewing sugar, Black malt. Hops: Target, Yeoman. Source: RP1/2.

**Yorkshire Bitter** (keg): OG: 1037. Malt: Pale malt, Wheat malt, Sugar. Hops: Goldings, Bramling Cross. Late hops: Goldings. Source: DL.

Notes: See Webster's Fountain Head Brewery and Samuel Webster & Wilsons.

**Cask Bitter**: OG: 1036. Malt: 78.8-89% Pale malt, 10-20% Concentrated sugar, 1-1.2% Black malt, Caramel. Hops: Target. IBU: 32.5. EBC: 26. Source: RP.

**Magnet**: OG: 1040. Malt: 78.6-83.7% Pale malt, 1.3-1.4% Black malt, 15-20% Concentrated sugar, Caramel. Hops: Target, optional Yeoman. IBU: 32.5. EBC: 37. Source: RP/JHF.

**Imperial Russian Stout**: OG: 1102. Malt: 59.8% Pale malt, 21.4% Amber malt, 16% Concentrated sugar, 2.8% Black malt, Caramel. Hops: Target. IBU: 50. EBC: 235. Source: RP4/5/JHF/JE2. Notes: See **Imperial Russian Stout**, Scottish & Newcastle Beer Production, Scotland and **Imperial Russian Stout**, Courage, Staines.

## Samuel Smith Old Brewery, Tadcaster

**Old Brewery Bitter**: OG: 1037. Malt: 91% Pale malt, 9% Crystal malt. Hops: Fuggles. Late hops: Goldings. IBU: 27. Source: GW/RP1/2/3/4/5/JHF. OG: 1040. Malt: Pale malt, Crystal malt, Torrefied barley, Sugar. Hops: Goldings, Fuggles. Source: DL.

**Museum Ale**: OG: 1048. Malt: 90% Pale malt, 10% Crystal malt. Hops: Fuggles. Hops: Goldings. IBU: 30. EBC: 20. Source: RP1/2/3/4/.

**Old Brewery Pale Ale**: OG: 1048. Malt: Pale malt, Crystal malt. Hops: Fuggles, Goldings. IBU: 30. Source: EBA.

**Oatmeal Stout**: OG: 1048-51. Malt: Pale malt, Flaked oats, Roast barley, Crystal malt, Chocolate malt. Hops: Goldings. Source: CB.

**Nut Brown Ale**: OG: 1051-53. Malt: Pale malt, Chocolate malt, Crystal malt. Hops: Fuggles, Goldings. Late hops: Goldings. Source: BC.

**Taddy Porter**: OG: 1052-54. Malt: Pale malt, Black malt, Crystal malt, Chocolate malt, Black Treacle. Hops: Goldings. Late hops: Fuggles, Goldings. Source: CB.

**India Ale**: OG: 1060. Malt: Pale malt, Toasted pale malt, Crystal malt, Wheat malt. Hops: Northdown. Late hops: Goldings, Bramling Cross. Dry hops: Fuggles. Source: 150.

**Winter Welcome**: OG: 1068-70. Malt: Pale malt, Crystal malts. Hops: Goldings. Late hops: Fuggles, Goldings. Source: CB.

## . *South Hams, Stokenham*

**Devon Pride** (b-c): ABV: 3.8%. Malt: Maris Otter pale malt, Chocolate malt, Crystal malt. Hops: Bramling Cross, Cascade. Source: JE6.

**Devon Porter** (b-c): ABV: 5%. Malt: Maris Otter pale malt, Crystal malt, Black malt. Hops: Bramling Cross, Styrian Goldings. Source: JE6.

## . *Spikes Brewery, Portsmouth*

**Impaled Ale**: OG: 1036. Malt: 90-95% Pale malt, 5-10% Crystal malt. Hops: USA Challenger, Fuggles or Goldings. Late hops: Fuggles. Source: RP.

**Stinger**: OG: 1045. Malt: 100% Pale malt, Honey. Hops: USA Challenger, Fuggles. Source: RP4.

**Gold**: OG: 1049. Malt: 100% Pale malt. Hops: Goldings. Late hops: No. Dry hops: No. Source: RP5.

## . *Spinning Dog,Hereford*

**Hereford Organic Bitter** (b-c): ABV: 3.7%. Malt: Maris Otter pale malt. Hops: Spalt. Source: JE6.

**Organic Oatmeal Stout** (b-c): ABV: 4.4%. Malt: Maris Otter pale malt, Roast barley, Oats. Hops: Hallertau. Source: JE6.

**Celtic Gold**: ABV: 4.5%. Hops: Challenger. Source: W.

## . *Springhead Brewery, Sutton on Trent*

**Hersbrucker Weizenbier**: OG: 1034. Malt: 66% Halcyon pale malt, 33% Wheat malt. Hops: Northdown. Late hops: Saaz. Source: RP5.

**Bitter**: OG: 1040. Malt: 98.5% Halcyon pale malt, 1.5% Crystal malt. Hops: Northdown. Late hops: Northdown. IBU: 23. Source: RP3/4/5/MO.

**Roundhead's Gold**: OG: 1040. Malt: 100% Halcyon pale malt, Honey. Hops: Northdown. Source: RP5/JHF.

**Roundhead's Gold** (b-c): ABV: 4.4%. Malt: Pale malt, Wild honey. Hops: Northdown, Saaz. Source: JE3/5.

**Hole-in-Spire Porter**: OG: 1040. Malt: 92.3% Halcyon pale malt, 7.6% Roast barley. Hops: Northdown. Source: RP5.

**Leveller**: OG: 1048. Malt: 82% Halcyon pale malt, 18% Dark amber malt. Hops: Northdown. Source: RP4/5/JHF.

**The Leveller** (b-c): ABV: 5%. Malt: Pale malt, Amber malt, Roast malt. Hops: Northdown. Source: JE3/5.

**1661**: OG: 1050. Malt: 93.75% Halcyon pale malt, 6.25% Crystal malt. Hops: Northdown. Source: RP5.

**Roaring Meg**: OG: 1052. Malt: 100% Halcyon pale malt. Hops: Northdown. Source: RP4/5.

**Roaring Meg** (b-c): ABV: 5.7%. Malt: Pale malt. Hops: Northdown. Source: JE3/5.

**Cromwell's Hat**: OG: 1058. Malt: 90-94.74% Halcyon pale malt, 5.26-10% Crystal malt. Hops: Northdown. Others: Cinnamon, Juniper berries. Source: RP.

**Cromwell's Hat** (b-c): ABV: 6.2%. Malt: Pale malt, Crystal malt. Hops: Northdown. Others: Cinnamon, Juniper berries. Source: JE3/5.

## Steam Packet Brewery, Knottingley

**Mellor's Gamekeeper**: OG: 1036. Malt: 88% Maris Otter pale malt, 12% Crystal malt. Hops: Challenger. Source: RP3/4/5.

**Bit O'Black**: OG: 1040. Malt: Halcyon pale malt, Crystal malt, Black malt. Hops: Challenger, Fuggles. Others: Fruit and Nuts. Source: RP3/4/5.

**Bargee**: OG: 1048. Malt: Halcyon pale malt, Maris Otter pale malt, Wheat, Black malt. Hops: Challenger, Fuggles, Goldings. Dry hops: Yes. Others: Fruit and Nuts. Source: RP3/4/5.

**Poacher's Swag**: OG: 1050. Malt: Maris Otter pale malt, Pipkin pale malt, Crystal malt, Flaked maize. Hops: Challenger. Dry hops: Challenger. Source: RP3/4/5.

**Giddy Ass**: OG: 1080. Malt: Halcyon pale malt, Maris Otter pale malt, Crystal malt, Wheat, Flaked maize. Hops: Challenger, Fuggles. Source: RP3/4/5.

## Stocks Brewery, Doncaster

**Best Bitter**: OG: 1037.7. Malt: 98.65% Pale malt, 1.35% Chocolate malt. Hops: Fuggles, Goldings. Source: RP1/2/3/4/5.

**Golden Wheat**: OG: 1044. Malt: Pale malt, Crystal malt, Wheat malt. Hops: Goldings. Late hops: Fuggles. Source: RP4/5.

**Select**: OG: 1044.7. Malt: 98.15% Pale malt, 1.85% Chocolate malt. Hops: Fuggles, Goldings. Source: RP1/2/3/4/5.

**St. Leger Porter**: OG: 1050. Malt: Pale malt, Crystal malt, Chocolate malt. Hops: Goldings. Source: RP4/5.

**Old Horizontal**: OG: 1054. Malt: 97% Pale malt, 3% Chocolate malt. Hops: Fuggles, Goldings. Source: RP1/2/3/4/5.

## Storm, Macclesfield

**Bosley Cloud** (b-c): ABV: 4.1%. Malt: Pale malt, Lager malt, Wheat malt. Hops: Cluster, Fuggles. Source: JE5/6.

**Ale Force** (b-c): ABV: 4.2%. Malt: Pale malt, Crystal malt, Chocolate malt. Hops: Fuggles. Source: JE5/6.

**Silk of Amnesia** (b-c): ABV: 4.7%. Malt: Pale malt, Crystal malt, Chocolate malt. Hops: Cluster, Fuggles. Source: JE5/6.

### . *Strawberry Bank, Grange-over-Sands*

**Damson Beer** (b-c): ABV: 7%. Malt: Pale malt, Crystal malt, Dark malt, Sugar. Hops: Willamette, Cluster. Others: Damson juice. Source: JE1/2/3.

### . *Summerskills Brewery, Plymouth*

**Best Bitter**: OG: 1042. Malt: 92% Pale malt, 7-8% Crystal malt, 0-1% Black malt. Hops: Fuggles or Styrian Goldings, Goldings or Willamette, Goldings. Late hops: Fuggles. Source: RP.

**Best Bitter** (b-c): ABV: 4.3%. Malt: Triumph pale malt, Crystal malt, Black malt. Hops: Willamette, Goldings. Source: JE1/2/3.

**Whistle Belly Vengeance**: OG: 1046. Malt: 91-3% Pale malt, 6-8% Crystal malt, 1% Black malt. Hops: Goldings, Styrian Goldings / Willamette. Source: RP.

**Ninja Beer**: OG: 1049. Malt: 94.5-95% Pale malt, 5-5.5% Crystal malt. Hops: Goldings, optional Styrian Goldings. Source: RP.

**Indiana's Bones**: OG: 1056. Malt: 93% Pale malt, 6% Crystal malt, 1% Black malt. Hops: Willamette, Goldings. Source: RP4/5.

**Indiana's Bones** (b-c): ABV: 5.6%. Malt: Triumph pale malt, Crystal malt, Black malt. Hops: Willamette, Goldings. Source: JE1/2.

**BBB**: ABV: 3.7%. Malt: Pale malt, Crystal malt, Black malt. Hops: Goldings, Willamette. Source: RP5.

**Tamar BB**: ABV: 4.3%. Malt: Pale malt, Crystal malt, Black malt. Hops: Willamette, Goldings. Source: RP5.

**Menacing Dennis**: ABV: 4.5%. Malt: Pale malt, Crystal malt, Black malt. Hops: Goldings. Source: RP5.

### . *Sussex Brewery, Emsworth*

**Wyndham Bitter**: OG: 1037. Malt: 95% Pale malt, 5% Crystal malt. Hops: Challenger, Goldings. Source: RP1.

**Hermitage Best Bitter**: OG: 1047. Malt: 94% Pale malt, 6% Crystal malt. Hops: Challenger, Goldings. Source: RP1/2.

**Warrior Ale**: OG: 1057. Malt: 93% Pale malt, 7% Crystal malt. Hops: Challenger, Goldings. Source: RP1/2.

## . Suthwyk Ales, Fareham

**Bloomfields** (b-c): ABV: 3.8%. Malt: Optic pale malt, Crystal malt. Hops: Challenger, Fuggles, Goldings. Source: JE4/5/6.

**Liberation** (b-c): ABV: 4.2%. Malt: Optic pale malt, Crystal malt. Hops: Liberty. Source: JE5/6.

**Skew Sunshine Ale** (b-c): ABV: 4.6%. Malt: Optic pale malt. Hops: Challenger. Source: JE3/4/5/6.

## . Sutton, Plymouth

**Madiba Stout** (b-c): ABV: 5%. Malt: Maris Otter pale malt, Crystal malt, Chocolate malt, Black malt, Roast malt, Wheat malt. Hops: Bramling Cross. Source: JE3/4/5.

## . Swale, Sittingbourne

**Whistable Oyster Stout**: OG: 1048-49. Malt: Maris Otter pale malt, Chocolate malt, Roast barley, optional Brown malt. Hops: Challenger. Source: BC/JE2/3.

**Kentish Gold** (b-c): ABV: 5%. Malt: Maris Otter pale malt, CaraPils malt. Hops: Goldings. Source: JE1/2/3.

**Indian Summer** (b-c): ABV: 5%. Malt: Maris Otter pale malt, CaraPils malt. Hops: Willamette, Chinook, Cascade. Source: JE2/3.

**Indian Summer Pale Ale**: OG: 1052-54. Malt: Pale malt, Dextrin malt, Crystal malt. Hops: Chinook. Late hops: Cascade, Willamette. Source: BC.

**Old Dick** (b-c): ABV: 5.2%. Malt: Maris Otter pale malt, Crystal malt, Barley. Hops: Challenger. Source: JE1/2/3.

**Spiced Christmas Ale** (b-c): ABV: 6%. Malt: Maris Otter pale malt, Caramalt, Crystal malt, Chocolate malt, Torrefied wheat, Molasses. Hops: Challenger. Others: Cinnamon, Nutmeg. Source: JE2.

**Millennium Ale** (b-c): ABV: 8%. Malt: Maris Otter pale malt, Crystal malt, Chocolate malt. Hops: Fuggles, Goldings, Pioneer. Source: JE2.

## . Tally Ho! Country Inn & Brewery, Hatherleigh

**Potboiler's Brew**: OG: 1036. Malt: Pale malt, Crystal malt, Chocolate malt. Hops: Goldings. Source: RP3/4/5.

**Nutters**: OG: 1048. Malt: Pale malt, Crystal malt, Chocolate malt, Black malt. Hops: Goldings. Source: RP3/4/5.

**Tarka Tipple**: OG: 1048. Malt: Pale malt, Crystal malt, Chocolate malt. Hops: Styrian Goldings, Goldings. Source: RP3/4/5.

**Hunter's Ale** (b-c): ABV: 5.1%. Malt: Pale malt, Crystal malt, Chocolate malt. Hops: Goldings. Source: JE1/2.

**Thurgia** (b-c): OG: 1056. Malt: Pale malt, Crystal malt, Black malt. Hops: Goldings, Styrian Goldings. Source: RP3/4/5/JE1.

## . Tamar, Brewery Devonport

**High Gravity Mild Ale**: OG: 1075. Malt: Pale malt. Hops: Fuggles. Notes: Recipe from 1844. Source: DP.

**Eightpenny Ale**: OG: 1093. Malt: Pale malt. Hops: Fuggles. Notes: Recipe from 1839. Source: DP.

## . H.H. Tebbutt, Cambridge

**XXX**: OG: 1077. Malt: Pale malt, Demerara sugar. Hops: Fuggles. Notes: Recipe from 1887. Source: DP.

## . Timothy Taylor, Keighley

**Bitter**: OG: 1033. Malt: 100% Golden Promise pale malt. Hops: Fuggles. Late hops: Goldings. Source: RP1/2.

**Golden Mild**: OG: 1033. Note: **Bitter** with added Caramel. EBC: 20-23. Source: RP1/2/3/4.

**Best Dark Mild**: OG: 1033. Note: **Golden Mild** with extra Caramel. Source: RP1/2/3/4.

**Golden Best**: OG: 1033. Malt: 100% Golden Promise pale malt. Hops: Fuggles, Goldings, Styrian Goldings. EBC: 20. Source: RP5.

**Dark Mild**: OG: 1033. Note: **Golden Best** with added Caramel. Source: RP5.

**Best Bitter**: OG: 1037. Malt: 95% Golden Promise pale malt, 5% Roast crystal malt. Hops: Fuggles, Goldings. Late hops: Styrian Goldings. EBC: 27-9. Source: RP.

**Landlord**: OG: 1042. Malt: 100% Golden Promise pale malt. Hops: Fuggles. Late hops: Styrian Goldings, Goldings. Source: RP1/2/3/4/5. OG: 1045-46. Malt: Golden Promise pale malt, Crystal malt, Aromatic malt. Hops: Fuggles, Goldings. Late hops: Goldings, Styrian Goldings. Source: BC. Hops: WGV. Source: BBB. Notes: This is one of my favourite beers. It is a demonstration that a complex recipe is not required in order to brew a classic beer and that the skill of the brewer is an important factor.

**Ram Tam**: OG: 1042. Note: This is **Landlord** with caramel added. Source: RP1/2/3/4/5.

**Porter**: OG: 1043. Malt: Golden Promise pale malt, Roast barley / Roast crystal malt. Hops: Fuggles. Source: RP. Malt: 100% Golden Promise pale malt, 10% Sugar, 1% Caramel. Hops: Fuggles, Goldings, Styrian Goldings. EBC: 80. Source: RP5.

## . Teignworthy Brewery, Newton Abbot

**Reel Ale**: OG: 1038-40. Malt: 90% Triumph or Maris Otter pale malt , 10% Crystal malt. Hops: Omega, Goldings. Source: RP4/5.

**Reel Ale / Edwin Tucker's Devonshire Prize Ale** (b-c): ABV: 4%. Malt: Maris Otter pale malt, Crystal malt. Hops: Willamette, Goldings, Bramling Cross, Omega/Challenger. Source: JE1/2/3/4/5. Hops: Goldings, Fuggles, Bramling Cross, Challenger. Source: JE6.

**Spring Tide** (b-c): ABV: 4.3%. Malt: Maris Otter pale malt, Crystal malt. Hops: Willamette, Bramling Cross, Goldings, Omega/Challenger. Source: JE1/2/3/4/5. Hops: Goldings, Fuggles, Bramling Cross, Challenger. Source: JE6.

**Old Moggie** (b-c): ABV: 4.4%. Malt: Maris Otter pale malt, Crystal malt, Wheat malt, Torrefied wheat. Hops: Fuggles, Goldings, Bramling Cross. Source: JE3/4/5/6.

**Beachcomber** (b-c): ABV: 4.5%. Malt: Maris Otter pale malt. Hops: Willamette, Bramling Cross, Goldings, Omega/Challenger. Source: JE1/2/3/4/5/6.

**Harvey's Special Brew** (b-c): ABV: 4.6%. Malt: Pale malt, Crystal malt, Wheat malt. Hops: Fuggles, Goldings. Source: JE3/4/5/6.

**Amy's Ale** (b-c): ABV: 4.8%. Malt: Pale malt, Crystal malt, Wheat malt. Hops: Goldings, Bramling Cross. Source: JE4/5/6.

**Maltster's Ale** (b-c): ABV: 5%. Malt: Maris Otter pale malt, Crystal malt. Hops: Willamette, Goldings, Bramling Cross, Omega/Challenger. Source: JE1/2/3/4/5. Hops: Goldings, Fuggles, Bramling Cross, Challenger. Source: JE6.

**Martha's Mild** (b-c): ABV: 5.3%. Malt: Pale malt, Crystal malt, Amber malt, Chocolate malt, Wheat malt. Hops: Goldings, Fuggles. Source: JE4/5/6.

**Edwin Tucker's Maris Otter** (b-c): ABV: 5.5%. Malt: Maris Otter pale malt, Crystal malt, Wheat malt. Hops: Willamette, Goldings, Bramling Cross, Omega/Challenger. Source: JE1/2/4/5/6.

**John Parnell Tucker Centennial Ale** (b-c): ABV: 5.8%. Malt: Maris Otter pale malt, Amber malt, Flaked maize. Hops: Challenger, Goldings. Source: JE3.

**Edwin Tucker's 175 Ale** (b-c): ABV: 5.8%. Malt: Westminster pale malt, Wheat malt, Crystal malt. Hops: Goldings, Fuggles. Source: JE6.

**Edwin Tucker's Eclipse Double Celebratory Ale** (b-c): ABV: 5.9%. Malt: Pipkin pale malt, Crystal malt, Wheat malt. Hops: Goldings, Willamette. Source: JE2.

**Christmas Cracker** (b-c): ABV: 6%. Malt: Maris Otter pale malt, Crystal malt. Hops: Willamette, Goldings, Bramling Cross, Omega/Challenger. Source: JE1/2/3/4/5/6.

**Edwin Tucker's Choice Old Walnut Brown Ale** (b-c): ABV: 6%. Malt: Maris Otter pale malt, Brown malt, Wheat malt, Chocolate malt, Amber malt. Hops: Goldings, Fuggles. Source: JE6.

**Edwin Tucker's East India Pale Ale** (b-c): ABV: 6.5%. Malt: East India malt (specially kilned malt to match the colour of malt used in the days of the Empire – close to Lager malt), Wheat malt. Hops: Bramling Cross, Goldings. Source: JE3/4/5/6.

**Edwin Tucker's Devonshire Strong Ale** (b-c): ABV: 8%. Malt: Maris Otter pale malt, Crystal malt. Hops: Willamette, Goldings, Bramling Cross, Omega/Challenger. Source: JE1/2/3.

**Edwin Tucker's Celebrated Arctic Ale** (b-c): ABV: 9%. Malt: Maris Otter pale malt, Crystal malt. Hops: Bramling Cross, Goldings, Challenger. Source: JE4/5.

**Edwin Tucker's Empress Russian Porter** (b-c): ABV: 10.5-12%. Malt: Maris Otter pale malt, Oat malt, Chocolate malt, Roast barley. Hops: Willamette, Bramling Cross, Goldings, Challenger. Source: JE2/3/4/5/6.

**Edwin Tucker's Victorian Stock Ale** (b-c): ABV: 12%. Malt: Pale or Lager malt. Hops: Willamette, Goldings, Bramling Cross, Omega/Challenger. Source: JE1/2/3.

### . *Teme Valley, Knightwick*

**This** (b-c): ABV: 3.7%. Malt: Maris Otter pale malt, Chocolate malt, Wheat malt. Hops: Goldings, Fuggles, Challenger. Source: JE4/5./6

**The Hop Neuvelle** (b-c): ABV: 4.1%. Malt: Maris Otter pale malt, Wheat malt. Hops: optional fresh Goldings, fresh First Gold. Source: JE4/5/6.

**Lulsley Court** (b-c): ABV: 4.1%. Malt: Pale malt, Chocolate malt, Wheat malt. Hops: Pilgrim, Goldings. Source: JE5.

**Northdown Neuvelle** (b-c): ABV: 4.1%. Malt: Pale malt, Crystal malt, Wheat malt. Hops: Northdown. Source: JE5.

**That** (b-c): ABV: 4.1%. Malt: Maris Otter pale malt, Chocolate malt, Wheat malt, Roast barley. Hops: Challenger, Fuggles. Source: JE4. Malt: Maris Otter pale malt, Crystal malt, Wheat malt, Roast barley. Hops: Fuggles, Challenger. Source: JE5/6.

**Wotever Next?** (b-c): ABV: 5%. Malt: Maris Otter pale malt, Crystal malt, Chocolate malt, Wheat malt. Hops: Northdown, Fuggles. Source: JE4/5/6.

**Hearth Warmer** (b-c): ABV: 6%. Malt: Maris Otter pale malt, Crystal malt, Chocolate malt, Wheat malt, Roast barley. Hops: Northdown, Fuggles. Source: JE5/6.

### . *Joshua Tetley & Son, Leeds*

**Mild**: OG: 1032. Malt: Pale malt, 14% Cane sugar, 10% Micronised Barley, Caramel. Hops: Goldings, Zenith, Challenger, Northdown, Northern Brewer. Late hops: Northdown. Dry hops: Northdown. Source: RP1/2/3/4/5.

**Bitter**: OG: 1036. Malt: Pale malt, 14% Cane sugar, 10% Torrefied barley, Caramel. Hops: Goldings, Zenith, Challenger, Northdown, Northern Brewer. Late hops: Northdown. Dry hops: Northdown. Source: RP1/2. Malt: Pale malt, Crystal malt, Wheat malt, Sugar. Hops: Bramling Cross, Fuggles. Source: DL.

**Imperial**: OG: 1042. Malt: Pale malt, 14% Cane sugar, 10% Torrefied barley, Caramel. Hops: Goldings, Zenith, Challenger, Northdown, Northern Brewer. Source: RP1.

**EIPA**: OG: 1062. Malt: Pale malt. Hops: Goldings. Yeast: Wyeast #1469. Notes: Recipe from 1868. IBU: 146. SRM: 6. Source: VB.

**A**: OG: 1063. Malt: Pale malt. Hops: Goldings. Yeast: Wyeast #1469. Notes: Recipe from 1858. IBU: 122. SRM: 6. Source: VB.

**Keeping Pale Ale**: OG: 1063. Malt: Pale malt. Hops: Goldings. Notes: Recipe from 1873. Source: DP.

**Pale Ale**: OG: 1064. Malt: Pale malt. Hops: Fuggles. Notes: Recipe from 1886. Source: DP.

**Amber Ale**: OG: 1068. Malt: Pale malt, Pale amber malt, Dark amber malt. Hops: Fuggles. Notes: Recipe from 1844. Source: DP.

**Stout**: OG: 1070. Malt: Pale malt, Brown malt, Black malt. Hops: Fuggles. Notes: Recipe from 1847. Source: DP.

**XX**: OG: 1072. Malt: Pale malt. Hops: Goldings, Saaz. Yeast: Wyeast #1469. Notes: Recipe from 1868. IBU: 74. SRM: 6. Source: VB.

**XX Porter**: OG: 1072. Malt: Pale malt, Brown malt, Black malt. Hops: Fuggles. Notes: Recipe from 1844. Was renamed to **Stout** in 1847. Source: DP.Source:

**XXX**: OG: 1100. Malt: Pale malt. Hops: Fuggles. Notes: Recipe from 1844. Source: DP.

## Tetley Walker, Warrington

**Tetley Dark Mild**: OG: 1032. Malt: Pale malt, Crystal malt, Dark liquid sugar, Micronised Wheat, Caramel. Hops: Northdown. Dry hops: Northdown. Source: RP3/4.

**Walker Mild**: OG: 1032. Malt: Pale malt, Crystal malt, Dark liquid sugar, Caramel. Hops: Northdown. Dry hops: Northdown. Source: RP3/4.

**Greenalls Cask Mild**: OG: 1033. Malt: Pale malt, Crystal malt, Torrefied wheat, Maltose sugar, Caramel. Hops: Fuggles, Goldings. Dry hops: Yes. IBU: 17. EBC: 105. Source: RP3/4.

**Walker Bitter**: OG: 1033. Malt: Pale malt, Crystal malt, Wheat, Liquid sugar. Hops: Northdown. Dry hops: Northdown. Source: RP3/4.

**Walker Best Bitter**: OG: 1033-6. Malt: Pale malt, Micronised Wheat, Dark liquid sugar, optional Crystal malt. Hops: Northdown. Dry hops: Northdown. Source: RP.

**Greenalls Cask Bitter**: OG: 1036. Malt: Pale malt, Torrefied wheat, Maltose sugar. Hops: Fuggles, Goldings. Dry hops: Yes. IBU: 27. EBC: 21. Source: RP3/4.

**Thomas Greenall's Original Bitter**: OG: 1045. Malt: Maris Otter pale malt, Crystal malt, Maltose syrup. Hops: Fuggles, Goldings. IBU: 33. EBC: 30. Source: RP3/4.

**Wild Rover**: OG: 1055. Malt: 70% White, 6% Crystal malt, 24% Maltose syrup. Hops: Fuggles, Goldings, Styrian Goldings. Dry hops: Styrian Goldings. IBU: 35. EBC: 39. Source: RP4.

**Walker Winter Warmer**: OG: 1060. Malt: Pale malt, Crystal malt, Micronised Wheat, Dark liquid sugar, Liquid sugar. Hops: Northdown. Dry hops: Northdown. Source: RP3/4.

## . T. & R. Theakston, Masham

**Traditional Mild**: OG: 1034. Malt: Pale malt, Crystal malt, Black malt, Unmalted cereal, Sugar. Hops: Fuggles, Others. Dry hops: Yes. IBU: 22. EBC: 70. Source: RP3/4/5.

**Black Bull Bitter**: OG: 1037. Malt: Pale malt, Crystal malt. Hops: Goldings, Others. Dry hops: Yes. IBU: 29. EBC: 23. Source: RP4/5.

**Best Bitter**: OG: 1038. Malt: Pale malt, Flaked maize, Sugar. Hops: Goldings, Fuggles. Late hops: Goldings. Dry hops: Goldings. Source: DL. Note: See **Theakston Best Bitter**, Scottish & Newcastle, Newcastle-upon-Tyne.

**XB**: OG: 1046. Malt: Pale malt, Crystal malt, Flaked maize, Sugar. Hops: Fuggles, Others. Dry hops: Yes. IBU: 26. Source: RP1/2. Note: See **Theakston XB**, Scottish & Newcastle, Newcastle-upon-Tyne.

**Old Peculier**: OG: 1058. Malt: Pale malt, Crystal malt, Flaked maize, Sugar. Hops: Fuggles, Others. Dry hops: Yes. IBU: 29. EBC: 95. Source: RP1/2/3/4/5. ABV: 6%. Malt: Crystal malt, Roast barley, Dark brown sugar, Treacle. Hops: Fuggles. Source: DL. OG: 1060. Malt: Pale malt, Torrefied wheat / Flaked wheat, Crystal malt, Chocolate malt, Sugar. Hops: Northern Brewer. Late hops: Fuggles. Dry hops: Fuggles. Source: 150. OG: 1061-64. Malt: Pale malt, Crystal malt, Chocolate malt, Torrefied wheat, Candi sugar, Golden syrup, Dark brown sugar. Hops: Northern Brewer. Late hops: Fuggles. Dry hops: Fuggles. Yeast: Wyeast #1084. Source: CB. ABV: 5.7%. Malt: Pale malt, Crystal malt, Sugar. Hops: Fuggles. Source: HB. OG: 1058. Malt: Pale malt, Crystal malt, Chocolate malt. Hops: Challenger, Fuggles. Late hops: Goldings. Malt: Pale malt, Crystal malt, Black malt, Maltose, Invert sugar. Hops: Challenger, Fuggles. Late hops: Fuggles. Source: GW.

## . Thompsons, Ashburton

**Best Bitter**: OG: 1040. Malt: 94% Pale malt, 6% Crystal malt. Hops: WGV. Source: RP2/3/4/5.

**IPA**: OG: 1044-5. Malt: 99% Pale malt, 1% Black malt. Hops: WGV. Source: RP2/3/4/5.

**Yuletide Tipple**: OG: 1050. Malt: 96% Pale malt, 3% Crystal malt, 1% Black malt. Hops: WGV. Source: RP2.

**Figurehead**: OG: 1050. Malt: 96% Pale malt, 3% Crystal malt, 1% Black malt. Hops: WGV. Source: RP3/4/5.

## . Thornbridge, Ashford-in-the-Water

**Jaipur IPA** (b-c): ABV: 5.9%. Malt: Maris Otter pale malt. Hops: Chinook, Cascade. Source: JE6.

**Saint Petersburg** (b-c): ABV: 7.7%. Malt: Maris Otter pale malt, Roast barley, Chocolate malt. Hops: Galena, Bramling Cross. Source: JE6.

### . *Three B's, Blackburn*

**Tackler's Tipple** (b-c): ABV: 4.3%. Malt: Maris Otter pale malt, Chocolate malt, Crystal malt, Flaked maize, Torrefied wheat. Hops: Progress, Goldings, Challenger. Source: JE6.

**Doff Cocker** (b-c): ABV: 4.5%. Malt: Maris Otter pale malt, Wheat malt, Flaked maize. Hops: Progress, Hallertau, Challenger. Source: JE6.

**Knocker Up** (b-c): ABV: 4.8%. Malt: Maris Otter pale malt, Roast barley, Chocolate malt, Black malt, Flaked barley, Torrefied wheat. Hops: Progress, Goldings. Source: JE6.

**Shuttle Ale** (b-c): ABV: 5.2%. Malt: Maris Otter pale malt, Crystal malt, Flaked maize. Hops: Fuggles. Source: JE6.

### . *Three Tuns, Bishop's Castle*

**Little Tun** (b-c): ABV: 4.1%. Malt: Maris Otter pale malt, Crystal malt, Wheat malt. Hops: Fuggles, Goldings. Source: JE2.

**Chocolate Stout** (b-c): ABV: 4.5%. Malt: Maris Otter pale malt, Crystal malt, Roast barley. Hops: Goldings. Others: 15kg per 5 barrels Cocoa powder. Source: JE3.

**Cleric's Cure** (b-c): ABV: 5%. Malt: Maris Otter pale malt, optional Wheat malt. Hops: Fuggles, Goldings. Source: JE1/2/3.

**Bellringer** (b-c): ABV: 6.3%. Malt: Maris Otter pale malt, Crystal malt, Wheat malt. Hops: Fuggles, Goldings. Source: JE2.

**Old Scrooge** (b-c): ABV: 6.5%. Malt: Maris Otter pale malt, Crystal malt, Black malt, Wheat malt. Hops: Fuggles, Goldings. Source: JE1/2/3.

### . *Daniel Thwaites, Blackburn*

**Mild**: OG: 1031. Malt: 85% Pale malt and Crystal malt, 15% Sugar. Hops: Fuggles, Goldings. Source: RP1/2/3.

**Best Mild**: OG: 1034. Malt: 85% Pipkin pale malt, 10% Crystal malt, 5-15% Sugar. Hops: Fuggles, Goldings / Challenger. IBU: 22. EBC: 100. Source: RP/GW.

**Bitter**: OG: 1036. Malt: 45% Pipkin pale malt, 45% Maris Otter pale malt, 10% Sugar. Hops: Fuggles, Goldings, Challenger. IBU: 30. EBC: 24. Source: RP4/5.

**Chairman's Premium Select Ale**: OG: 1039. Malt: 90% Maris Otter pale malt, 3% Crystal malt, 8% Sugar. Hops: Goldings, Fuggles. Hops: Fuggles. IBU: 30. EBC: 20. Source: RP5.

**Craftsman**: OG: 1042. Malt: Maris Otter pale malt, 3% Crystal malt, 8% Sugar. Hops: Fuggles, Goldings, WGV. IBU: 32. EBC: 20. Source: RP4/5.

**Daniel's Hammer**: OG: 1048. Malt: 100% Maris Otter pale malt. Hops: Goldings, Fuggles. IBU: 28. EBC: 16. Source: RP4/5.

### . *Tindall, Bungay / Seething*

**Summer Loving** (b-c): ABV: 3.6%. Malt: Maris Otter and Fanfare pale malt. Hops: Mount Hood. Source: JE3/4/5/6.

**Best Bitter** (b-c): ABV: 3.7%. Malt: Maris Otter and Halcyon pale malt. Hops: Goldings. Source: JE3/4/5/6.

**Mild** (b-c): ABV: 3.7%. Malt: Halcyon and Maris Otter pale malt, Crystal malt, Chocolate malt. Hops: Fuggles, Goldings. Source: JE3/4/5/6.

**Liberator** (b-c): ABV: 3.8%. Malt: Maris Otter and Pearl pale malt. Hops: Cascade. Source: JE4/5/6.

**Resurrection** (b-c): ABV: 3.8%. Malt: Halcyon pale malt. Hops: Cascade. Source: JE3/4/5/6.

**Alltime** (b-c): ABV: 4%. Malt: Maris Otter and Halcyon pale malt. Hops: Goldings. Source: JE3/4/5/6.

**Christmas Cheers** (b-c): ABV: 4%. Malt: Maris Otter and Halcyon pale malt, Crystal malt. Hops: Goldings. Source: JE3/4/5/6.

**Ditchingham Dam** (b-c): ABV: 4.2%. Malt: Maris Otter pale malt, Roast malt, Chocolate malt. Hops: Mount Hood, Goldings. Others: Liquorice, Ginger. Source: JE3/4/5/6.

**Extra** (b-c): ABV: 4.5%. Malt: Maris Otter and Halcyon pale malt. Hops: Goldings. Source: JE3/4/5/6.

**Norfolk 'n' Good** (b-c): ABV: 4.6%. Malt: Halcyon pale malt. Hops: Cascade. Source: JE3/4/5/6.

**Norwich Dragon** (b-c): ABV: 4.6%. Malt: Halcyon pale malt. Hops: Goldings, Cascade. Source: JE4/5/6.

**Honeydo** (b-c): ABV: 5%. Malt: Halcyon pale malt, Honey. Hops: Cascade. Source: JE5/6.

### . *Tipples Brewery, Acle*

**Longshore** (b-c): ABV: 3.6%. Malt: Maris Otter pale malt, Crystal malt. Hops: Goldings, Bramling Cross, Cascade. Source: JE6.

**Ginger** (b-c): ABV: 3.8%. Malt: Maris Otter pale malt, Crystal malt. Hops: Bramling Cross, Cascade. Others: Root ginger. Source: JE6.

**The Hanged Monk** (b-c): ABV: 3.8%. Malt: Mild ale malt, Crystal malt. Hops: Bramling Cross, Willamette, Goldings. Source: JE6.

**Lady Evelyn** (b-c): ABV: 4.1%. Malt: Maris Otter pale malt. Hops: Bramling Cross, Goldings, Cascade. Source: JE6.

**Redhead** (b-c): ABV: 4.2%. Malt: Maris Otter pale malt, Crystal malt. Hops: Bramling Cross, Goldings, Cascade. Source: JE6.

**Battle** (b-c): ABV: 4.3%. Malt: Maris Otter pale malt, Crystal malt. Hops: Bramling Cross, Goldings, Cascade. Source: JE6.

**Topper Stout** (b-c): ABV: 4.5%. Malt: Maris Otter pale malt, Chocolate malt, Crystal malt, Black malt. Hops: Bramling Cross, Goldings, Cascade. Source: JE6.

**Moon Rocket** (b-c): ABV: 5%. Malt: Maris Otter pale malt, Crystal malt. Hops: Bramling Cross, Goldings, Cascade. Source: JE6.

**Jack's Revenge** (b-c): ABV: 5.8%. Malt: Maris Otter pale malt, Chocolate malt, Crystal malt. Hops: Bramling Cross, Willamette. Source: JE6.

### . *Tisbury Brewery, Tisbury*

**Fanfare** (b-c): ABV: 4.5%. Malt: Maris Otter pale malt. Hops: Progress, Goldings. Source: JE2.

**Real Nut Ale** (b-c): ABV: 4.5%. Malt: Maris Otter pale malt, Rye malt, Wheat malt. Hops: Progress, Hersbrücker, Target, Bramling Cross. Others: Chestnuts. Source: JE2.

### . *Titanic Brewery, Burslem, Stoke-on-Trent*

**Best Bitter**: OG: 1036. Malt: 97% Maris Otter pale malt, 3% Flaked wheat. Hops: Goldings, Fuggles. Dry hops: Yes. Source: RP1/2/3. Hops: Goldings, Fuggles, Willamette, Yakima. Source: RP4. Malt: 97% Maris Otter pale malt, 3% Wheat malt. Hops: Fuggles, Northdown, Yakima Galena. Late hops: Goldings, Willamette. Source: RP5.

**Lifeboat Ale**: OG: 1040. Malt: 85% Maris Otter pale malt, 14% Crystal malt, 1% Black malt. Hops: Goldings, Fuggles, optional Willamette, Yakima, Late hops: Goldings. Source: RP2/3/4. Malt: 85% Maris Otter pale malt, 10% Crystal malt, 3% Chocolate malt, 2% Wheat malt, 1% Raw Barley. Hops: Fuggles, Yakima Galena. Late hops: Goldings, Willamette. Source: RP5/JHF.

**Premium**: OG: 1042. Malt: 90-95% Maris Otter pale malt, 0-5% Crystal malt, 5% Flaked wheat. Hops: Goldings, Fuggles. Dry hops: Yes. Source: RP1/2. Malt: 90% Maris Otter pale malt, 5% Crystal malt, 0.5% Black malt, 4.5% Flaked wheat. Hops: Goldings, Fuggles. Source: RP3. Hops: Goldings, Willamette, Yakima. Source: RP4. Malt: 90% Maris Otter pale malt, 4% Crystal malt, 0.5% Chocolate malt, 5.5% Wheat malt. Hops: Fuggles, Yakima Galena. Late hops: Goldings, Willamette. Source: RP5.

**Red Cap** (b-c): ABV: 4.3%. Malt: Maris Otter pale malt, CaraPils malt, Wheat malt, Roast barley. Hops: Northdown, Admiral. Source: JE2.

**Saddleback** (b-c): ABV: 4.3%. Malt: Maris Otter pale malt, Crystal malt, Wheat malt, Pale chocolate malt, Roast barley. Hops: Northdown, Fuggles, Bramling Cross. Source: JE2.

**Full Steam Ahead**: ABV: 4.4%. Hops: Cascade, Yakima Galena, Goldings. Source: W.

**Horse Power** (b-c): ABV: 4.5%. Malt: Maris Otter pale malt, Crystal malt, Wheat malt, Amber malt. Hops: Goldings, Admiral. Source: JE2.

**Stout**: OG: 1046. Malt: 90% Maris Otter pale malt, 8% Roast barley, 2% Wheat malt. Hops: Goldings, Willamette, Yakima. Source: RP4. Hops: Northdown, Yakima Galena. Late hops: Willamette, Goldings. Source: RP5.

**Stout** (b-c): ABV: 4.5%. Malt: Maris Otter pale malt, Wheat malt, Roast barley, optional Crystal malt. Hops: Northdown, Willamette, Goldings. Source: JE1/2/3/5. Malt: Maris Otter pale malt, Wheat malt, Roast barley. Hops: Northdown, Goldings, Yakima Galena. Source: JE4. Hops: Goldings, Fuggles, Northdown. Source: JE6.

**Shugborough Horse Power**: OG: 1046. Malt: 90% Maris Otter pale malt, 2% Amber malt, 8% Wheat malt. Hops: Northdown, Yakima Galena. Late hops: Goldings, Willamette. Source: RP5.

**White Star**: OG: 1050. Malt: 94% Maris Otter pale malt, 1% Crystal malt, 5% Wheat. Hops: Goldings, Willamette, Yakima. Source: RP4.

**Captain Smith's Strong Ale**: OG: 1050. Malt: 80-90% Maris Otter pale malt, 0-10% Crystal malt. 5% Flaked wheat, 5% Glucose syrup. Hops: Goldings. Source: RP1/2/3. Malt: 80% Maris Otter pale malt, 10% Crystal malt, 5% Flaked wheat, 5% Glucose syrup. Hops: Goldings, Willamette, Yakima. Source: RP4. Malt: 80% Maris Otter pale malt, 10% Crystal malt, 7% Wheat malt, 3% Roast barley. Hops: Fuggles, Yakima Galena. Late hops: Willamette, Goldings. Source: RP5.

**Captain Smith's Strong Ale** (b-c): ABV: 5.2%. Malt: Maris Otter pale malt, Crystal malt, Wheat malt. Hops: Willamette, Goldings, Yakima/Yakima Galena. Source: JE1/2.

**Longhorn** (b-c): ABV: 5.5%. Malt: Maris Otter pale malt, Crystal malt, Wheat malt. Hops: Northdown, Willamette, Yakima Galena. Source: JE2.

**Shugborough Longhorn**: OG: 1057. Malt: 85% Maris Otter pale malt, 5% Crystal malt, 10% Wheat malt. Hops: Northdown, Yakima Galena. Late hops: Willamette. Source: RP5.

**Christmas Ale** (b-c): ABV: 7.2%. Malt: Maris Otter pale malt, Crystal malt, Wheat malt, Invert sugar. Hops: Goldings, Galena. Source: JE2/3/4/5/6.

**Christmas Ale**: OG: 1080. Malt: 85% Maris Otter pale malt, 5% Flaked wheat, 10% Glucose syrup. Hops: Fuggles. Source: RP1.

**Wreckage**: OG: 1080. Malt: 80-85% Maris Otter pale malt, 0-8% Crystal malt, 4-5% Flaked wheat, 0-2% Black malt, 6-10% Glucose syrup. Hops: Fuggles. Source: RP2/3. Malt: 80% Maris Otter pale malt, 8% Crystal malt, 2% Black malt, 4% Flaked wheat, 6% Glucose syrup. Hops: Goldings, Fuggles, Willamette, Yakima. Source: RP4. Malt: 80%

Maris Otter pale malt, 8% Crystal malt, 2% Roast barley, 4% Sugar, 6% Wheat malt. Hops: Yakima Galena. Late hops: Willamette, Goldings. Source: RP5.

### Tolly Cobbold, Tollemache & Cobbold Brewery, Ipswich

**Mild**: OG: 1032. Malt: 85% Pipkin pale malt, 10% Crystal malt, 5% Chocolate malt. Hops: Challenger, Northdown, Target or Challenger, Goldings. IBU: 18. EBC: 120. Source: RP.

**Bitter**: OG: 1034-5. Malt: 75% Pipkin pale malt, 10% Amber malt, 15% Crystal malt. Hops: Goldings. IBU: 26-28. EBC: 30. Source: RP2/3/4/5/GW. Malt: Pale malt, Wheat flour, Crystal malt, Sugar. Hops: Goldings, Fuggles. Late hops: Goldings. Source: DL.

**Original**: OG: 1038-1038.5. Malt: Pipkin pale malt, Invert sugar, Crystal malt. Hops: Challenger, Goldings, optional Northdown, Target. IBU: 28-30. EBC: 40. Source: RP.

**Cobbolds IPA**: OG: 1040-2. Malt: Pipkin pale malt, Crystal malt. Hops: Goldings. IBU: 30. EBC: 20. Source: RP4/5.

**Old Strong**: OG: 1047. Malt: Pipkin pale malt, Crystal malt, Chocolate malt. Hops: Challenger, Northdown, Target. IBU: 24. Source: RP2/3. OG: 1050.5. Malt: Pipkin pale malt, Crystal malt, Chocolate malt. Hops: Challenger, Goldings. IBU: 35-43. EBC: 180-90. Source: RP4/5.

**Tollyshooter**: OG: 1049.5. Malt: Pipkin pale malt, Crystal malt, Invert sugar. Hops: Challenger, Goldings. Dry hops: Yes. IBU: 33. EBC: 55-60. Source: RP4/5.

### Tomlinson's Old Castle Brewery, Pontefract

**Sessions**: OG: 1038. Malt: Maris Otter pale malt, Crystal malt, Pale chocolate malt. Hops: Challenger. Late hops: Styrian Goldings. Source: RP4/5.

**Hermitage Mild**: OG: 1038. Malt: Pale malt, Crystal malt, Pale chocolate malt, Roast barley, Flaked barley. Hops: Goldings. Source: RP5.

**Down With It**: OG: 1042. Malt: Maris Otter pale malt, Crystal malt. Hops: Goldings. Source: RP4/5.

**De Lacy**: OG: 1044. Malt: Maris Otter pale malt, Amber malt, Flaked maize. Hops: Challenger. Late hops: Styrian Goldings. Source: RP4/5.

**Fractus XB**: OG: 1045. Malt: Maris Otter pale malt, Crystal malt, Pale chocolate malt. Hops: Challenger. Source: RP4.

**Deceitful Rose**: OG: 1048. Malt: 100% Maris Otter pale malt. Hops: Challenger. Late hops: Styrian Goldings. Source: RP4/5.

**Richard's Defeat**: OG: 1050. Malt: Maris Otter pale malt, Crystal malt, Pale chocolate malt, Flaked barley. Hops: Challenger. Late hops: Styrian Goldings. Source: RP4/5.

**Three Sieges**: OG: 1058. Malt: Maris Otter pale malt, Crystal malt, Pale chocolate malt. Hops: Challenger. Late hops: Styrian Goldings. Others: Liquorice. Source: RP4/5.

**Liquorice Stout** (b-c): ABV: 6%. Malt: Maris Otter pale malt, Crystal malt, Pale chocolate malt, Roast barley. Hops: Challenger. Others: Liquorice. Source: JE1/2.

### . *Tomson & Wotton, Ramsgate*

**XXXX**: OG: 1110. Malt: Pale malt. Hops: Fuggles. Dry hops: Fuggles. Notes: Recipe from 1863. Source: DP.

### . *Townes Brewery, Chesterfield*

**Muffin Ale**: OG: 1035. Malt: 87% Halcyon pale malt, 3.5-5% Crystal malt, 4.5-5% Amber malt, 1.5-2% Black malt, 0-1% Roast barley, 0-2.5% Wheat malt. Hops: Bramling Cross, optional Challenger. IBU: 25. Source: RP.

**Sunshine**: OG: 1035. Malt: 95.25% Maris Otter pale malt, 4.75% Wheat malt or 95% Halcyon pale malt, 2.5% Wheat malt, 2.5% Pale crystal malt. Hops: Bramling Cross. Late hops: Bramling Cross. IBU: 28. Source: RP/MO.

**Best Lockoford Bitter**: OG: 1040. Malt: 92.6% Maris Otter pale malt, 4.1% Crystal malt, 3.3% Wheat malt or 95% Halcyon pale malt, 2.5% Pale crystal malt, 2.5% Wheat malt. Hops: Challenger, optional Styrian Goldings. Late hops: Goldings. IBU: 33. Source: RP/MO.

**GMT**: OG: 1042. Malt: 90% Halcyon pale malt, 10% Wheat malt. Hops: Challenger. Late hops: Cascade. Source: RP5.

**Staveley Cross** (b-c): ABV: 4.3%. Malt: Halcyon pale malt, Crystal malt, Wheat malt. Hops: Styrian Goldings. Source: JE4.

**Pynot Porter**: OG: 1045. Malt: 87.5% Halcyon pale malt, 3% Crystal malt, 3% Black malt, 2.5% Roast barley, 4% Wheat malt. Hops: Northdown, Styrian Goldings. IBU: 40. Source: RP4/MO.

**IPA**: OG: 1045. Malt: 96.15% Maris Otter pale malt, 3.85% Wheat malt. Hops: Willamette. IBU: 40. Source: RP4/MO.

**India Pale Ale** (b-c): ABV: 4.5%. Malt: Halcyon pale malt, Wheat malt. Hops: Cascade. Source: JE4.

**Pynot Porter** (b-c): ABV: 4.5%. Malt: Halcyon pale malt, Crystal malt, Black malt, Roast barley, Wheat malt. Hops: Bramling Cross, Styrian Goldings. Source: JE4.

**Muffin Man** (b-c): ABV: 4.6%. Malt: Halcyon pale malt, Crystal malt, Amber malt, Black malt, Wheat malt, Roast barley. Hops: Northern Brewer, Bramling Cross. Source: JE4.

**Oatmeal Stout** (b-c): ABV: 4.7%. Malt: Halcyon pale malt, Crystal malt, Black malt, Oat malt, Roast barley, Wheat malt. Hops: Challenger. Source: JE4.

**Mellow Yellow**: OG: 1048. Malt: 90% Halcyon pale malt, 2.5% Pale crystal malt, 7.5% Wheat malt. Late hops: First Gold. Source: RP5.

**Staveleyan** (b-c): ABV: 4.9%. Malt: Halcyon pale malt, Crystal malt, Wheat malt. Hops: Styrian Goldings. Source: JE4.

**Double Dagger**: OG: 1050. Malt: 91.5% Maris Otter pale malt, 3.5% Crystal malt, 1.5% Black malt, 3.5% Wheat malt. Hops: Northdown, Willamette. IBU: 44. Source: RP4/MO.

**Essence** (b-c): ABV: 5.1%. Malt: Halcyon pale malt, Lager malt, Wheat malt. Hops: Liberty. Source: JE4.

## . Tring Brewery Company, Tring

**Finest Summer Ale**: OG: 1037. Malt: Maris Otter pale malt, Crystal malt, Wheat malt. Hops: Goldings. Source: RP4/5.

**Ridgeway Bitter**: OG: 1039. Malt: Maris Otter pale malt, Crystal malt, Chocolate malt. Hops: Challenger, Goldings. Source: RP3/4/5.

**Legless Lal's Winter Ale**: ABV: 4.5%. Hops: Goldings. Source: W.

**Old Icknield Ale**: OG: 1049. Malt: Maris Otter pale malt, Crystal malt, Chocolate malt, Wheat malt. Hops: Challenger, Goldings. Source: RP4/5.

**Death or Glory Ale**: OG: 1070. Malt: Maris Otter pale malt, Chocolate malt, Malt extract. Hops: Challenger, Goldings. Source: RP4/5.

**Death or Glory Ale** (b-c): ABV: 7.2%. Malt: Pale malt, Chocolate malt. Hops: Goldings, Challenger. Source: JE1/2.

## . Trough Brewery, Bradford

**Bitter**: OG: 1035.5. Malt: 46% Halcyon pale malt, 46% Triumph pale malt, 8% Sugar. Hops: Fuggles, Progress, WGV. Source: RP2/3.

**Wild Boar**: OG: 1039.5. Malt: 46% Halcyon pale malt, 46% Triumph pale malt, 8% Sugar. Hops: Fuggles, Progress, WGV. Source: RP2/3.

**Hogshead**: OG: 1044.5. Malt: 46% Halcyon pale malt, 46% Triumph pale malt, 8% Sugar. Hops: Fuggles, Progress, WGV. Source: RP2.

**Festival**: OG: 1047. Malt: 47.5% Halcyon pale malt, 47.5% Maris Otter pale malt, 5% Sugar. Hops: Northdown. Late hops: Goldings. Source: RP3.

**Blind Pugh**: OG: 1052. Malt: 35% Halcyon pale malt, 35% Maris Otter pale malt, 15% Crystal malt, 15% Chocolate malt. Hops: Northdown, Goldings. Source: RP3.

## . Sam Trueman's Brewery, Medmenham

**Northdown Ale** (b-c): ABV: 4.7%. Malt: Pale malt, Crystal malt, Chocolate malt. Hops: Northdown, Goldings, Fuggles. Source: JE1.

**True Gold Lager** (b-c): ABV: 5.9-6%. Malt: Lager malt. Hops: Saaz. Source: JE1/2/3.

**Percy's Downfall** (b-c): ABV: 6.5%. Malt: Pale malt. Hops: Fuggles, Goldings. Source: JE2/3.

## . *Truman's, London*

**Ben Trumans Export** (keg): OG: 1036. Malt: Pale malt, Wheat malt, Flaked maize, Sugar. Hops: Fuggles. Dry hops: Hop extract. Source: DL.

**P2**: OG: 1042. Malt: Pale malt, Flaked oats, No.1 invert sugar. Hops: Goldings, Cluster, Northern Brewer. Yeast: Wyeast #1028/White Labs WLP013. Notes: Recipe from 1943. IBU: 37. SRM: 4. Source: VB.

**P1B**: OG: 1051. Malt: Pale malt, Flaked maize, No.1 invert sugar. Hops: Fuggles, Goldings. Yeast: Wyeast #1028/White Labs WLP013. Notes: Recipe from 1953. IBU: 40. SRM: 5. Source: VB.

**Keeping**: OG: 1059. Malt: Pale malt, Brown malt, Black malt. Hops: Goldings. Yeast: Wyeast #1098/Wyeast #1099. Notes: Recipe from 1831. IBU: 116. SRM: 24.

**Runner**: OG: 1063. Malt: Pale malt, Brown malt, Black malt. Hops: Goldings. Yeast: Wyeast #1098/Wyeast #1099. Notes: Recipe from 1840. IBU: 70. SRM: 27. OG: 1059. Malt: Pale malt, Brown malt, Black malt. Hops: Strisselspalt. Yeast: Wyeast #1098/Wyeast #1099. Notes: Recipe from 1870. IBU: 57. SRM: 29. OG: 1055. Malt: Pale malt, Brown malt, Black malt, Flaked maize, No.3 invert sugar. Hops: Goldings, Fuggles. Yeast: Wyeast #1098/Wyeast #1099. Notes: Recipe from 1900. IBU: 50. SRM: 40. Source: VB.

**P1**: OG: 1064. Malt: Pale malt. Hops: Goldings, Fuggles, Cluster. Yeast: Wyeast #1028/White Labs WLP013. Notes: Recipe from 1877. IBU: 170. SRM: 6. Source: VB.

**Keeping Stout**: OG: 1073. Malt: Pale malt, Brown malt, Black malt. Hops: Goldings. Yeast: Wyeast #1098/Wyeast #1099. Notes: Recipe from 1821. IBU: 130. SRM: 25. Source: VB.

**Running Stout**: OG: 1078. Malt: Pale malt, Brown malt, Black malt. Hops: Goldings. Yeast: Wyeast #1098/Wyeast #1099. Notes: Recipe from 1840. IBU: 92. SRM: 26. Source: VB.

**Double Stout**: OG: 1079. Malt: Pale malt, Brown malt, Black malt. Hops: Goldings. Yeast: Wyeast #1098/Wyeast #1099. Notes: Recipe from 1860. IBU: 130. SRM: 28. Source: VB.

**4**: OG: 1079. Malt: Pale malt. Hops: Goldings, Cluster. Yeast: Wyeast #1028/White Labs WLP013. Notes: Recipe from 1877. IBU: 125. SRM: 6. Source: VB.

**XXX**: OG: 1087. Malt: Pale malt, Mild malt. Hops: Goldings. Yeast: Wyeast #1098/Wyeast #1099. Notes: Recipe from 1860. IBU: 120. SRM: 10. Source: VB.

**Double Export**: OG: 1092. Malt: Pale malt, Brown malt, Black malt. Hops: Goldings, Cluster. Yeast: Wyeast #1098/Wyeast #1099. Notes: Recipe from 1870. IBU: 188. SRM: 37. Source: VB.

**Imperial**: OG: 1099. Malt: Pale malt, Brown malt, Black malt. Hops: Goldings. Yeast: Wyeast #1098/Wyeast #1099. Notes: Recipe from 1850. IBU: 174. SRM: 31. Source: VB.

**S1 Barley Wine**: OG: 1105. Malt: Pale malt, Lager malt, Mild malt, No.2 invert sugar, Caramel. Hops: Goldings, Fuggles, Brewers Gold. Yeast: Wyeast #1028/White Labs WLP013. Notes: Recipe from 1931. IBU: 137. SRM: 25. Source: VB.

**XXXK**: OG: 1106. Malt: Pale malt. Hops: Goldings. Yeast: Wyeast #1098. Notes: Recipe from 1835. IBU: 112. SRM: 7.5. Source: VB.

**XXXX Mild**: OG: 1114. Malt: Mild malt. Hops: Goldings. Yeast: Wyeast #1098/Wyeast #1099. Notes: Recipe from 1832. IBU: 73. SRM: 10. Source: VB.

**XXXXK**: OG: 1118. Malt: Pale malt. Hops: Goldings. Yeast: Wyeast #1098/Wyeast #1099. Notes: Recipe from 1846. IBU: 136. SRM: 9. Source: VB.

## . *Tunnel Brewery, Nuneaton*

**Linda Lear Beer** (b-c): ABV: 3.7%. Malt: Maris Otter pale malt, Chocolate malt, Crystal malt, Black malt. Hops: Galena, Bullion. Source: JE6.

**Ghost** (b-c): ABV: 4%. Malt: Maris Otter pale malt, Lager malt. Hops: Pacific Gem, Cluster, Styrian Goldings. Source: JE6.

**Light at the End of the Tunnel / Late OTT** (b-c): ABV: 4%. Malt: Maris Otter pale malt, Crystal malt. Hops: Pacific Gem, First Gold, Styrian Goldings. Source: JE6.

**Legend** (b-c): ABV: 4.3%. Malt: Maris Otter pale malt, Chocolate malt, Crystal malt, Wheat malt. Hops: Bullion, Goldings, Saaz. Source: JE6.

**Trade Winds** (b-c): ABV: 4.6%. Malt: Maris Otter pale malt, Wheat malt. Hops: Cascade. Source: JE6.

**Sweet Parish Ale** (b-c): ABV: 4.7%. Malt: Maris Otter pale malt, Chocolate malt, Crystal malt. Hops: Goldings, Styrian Goldings. Source: JE6.

**Stranger in the Mist** (b-c): ABV: 5%. Malt: Maris Otter pale malt, Wheat malt, Torrefied wheat. Hops: Perle, Saaz. Source: JE6.

**Nelson's Column** (b-c): ABV: 5.2%. Malt: Maris Otter pale malt, Crystal malt. Hops: Goldings, Cascade. Source: JE6.

**Boston Beer Party** (b-c): ABV: 5.6%. Malt: Maris Otter pale malt, Wheat malt, Crystal malt. Hops: Cascade. Source: JE6.

## . *Uley Brewery, Dursley*

**Bitter / Hogshead / UB40**: OG: 1040. Malt: Pale malt, Crystal malt. Hops: Fuggles, Goldings. Source: RP1/2/3/4/5.

**Old Ric**: OG: 1045. Malt: Pale malt, Crystal malt. Hops: Fuggles, Goldings. Source: RP4/5.

**Pig's Ear IPA**: OG: 1050. Malt: 100% Lager malt. Hops: Fuggles, Goldings. Source: RP1/2/3.

**Old Spot Prize Ale**: OG: 1050. Malt: 85% Pale malt, 15% Crystal malt. Hops: Fuggles, Goldings. Source: RP1/2/3/4/5/JHF.

**Pig's Ear Strong Beer**: OG: 1050. Malt: 100% Pale malt. Hops: Fuggles, Goldings. Source: RP4/5.

**Pigor Mortis**: OG: 1058. Malt: 80% Pale malt, 20% Crystal malt. Hops: Fuggles, Goldings. Source: RP2/3/4.

### . *Uncle Stuart's Brewery, Norwich*

**Brew No. 1 / Pack Lane** (b-c): ABV: 4%. Malt: Pale malt, Crystal malt, Black malt, Chocolate malt. Hops: Goldings, Progress. Source: JE4/5/6.

**Excelsior** (b-c): ABV: 4.5%. Malt: Pale malt, Crystal malt. Hops: Goldings, Progress. Source: JE5/6.

**Brew No. 9 / Church View** (b-c): ABV: 4.7%. Malt: Pale malt, Crystal malt. Hops: Goldings, Progress. Source: JE4/5.

**Brew No. 3** (b-c): ABV: 5.6%. Malt: Pale malt, Crystal malt. Hops: Goldings, Progress. Source: JE4.

**Buckenham Woods** (b-c): ABV: 5.6%. Malt: Pale malt, Crystal malt, Flaked maize. Hops: Goldings, Progress. Source: JE5/6.

**Brew No. 2** (b-c): ABV: 5.7%. Malt: Pale malt, Crystal malt, Flaked maize. Hops: Goldings, Progress. Source: JE4.

**Strumpshaw Fen** (b-c): ABV: 5.7%. Malt: Pale malt, Crystal malt. Hops: Goldings, Progress. Source: JE5/6.

**Christmas Ale** (b-c): ABV: 7%. Malt: Pale malt, Crystal malt, Black malt. Hops: Progress, Goldings. Source: JE4/5/6.

### . *Ushers, Trowbridge*

**January Sale**: OG: 1031. Malt: Halcyon pale malt, Crystal malt. Hops: Target. Late hops: Target. IBU: 26. EBC: 28. Source: RP5.

**P.A.**: OG: 1032. Malt: Pale malt, Flaked maize, Sugar. Hops: Fuggles. Source: DL.

**Best Bitter**: OG: 1037-8. Malt: 81% Pipkin pale malt, 4% Crystal malt, 15% Syrup. Hops: Target. Late hops: Goldings. Source: RP2. Malt: 96% Halcyon and optional Pipkin pale malt, 4% Crystal malt. Hops: Target. Late hops: Styrian Goldings. IBU: 27. Source: RP3/4/5/MO.

**Spring Fever**: OG: 1040. Malt: Halcyon pale malt, Crystal malt, Oat malt. Hops: Styrian Goldings. Late hops: Styrian Goldings. IBU: 30. EBC: 20. Source: RP4/5.

**Summer Madness**: OG: 1040. Malt: Halcyon pale malt, Wheat malt, Crystal malt. Hops: Styrian Goldings. IBU: 36. EBC: 18. Source: RP4/5.

**Autumn Frenzy**: OG: 1041. Malt: Halcyon pale malt, Crystal malt, Rye malt. Hops: Target, Styrian Goldings. IBU: 30. EBC: 45. Source: RP4/5.

**Winter Storm**: OG: 1042. Malt: Halcyon pale malt, Crystal malt. Hops: Target. Late hops: Styrian Goldings. IBU: 32. EBC: 29. Source: RP5.

**Founders Ale**: OG: 1045. Malt: 93% Halcyon and optional Pipkin pale malt, 7% Crystal malt. Hops: Target. Late hops: Styrian Goldings. IBU: 34. EBC: 30. Source: RP/MO.

**1824 Particular**: OG: 1060. Malt: 92% Halcyon and optional Pipkin pale malt, 8% Crystal malt. Hops: Target. Late hops: Styrian Goldings. IBU: 33. EBC: 60-63. Source: RP/MO.

**Ruby Ale**: OG: 1069. Malt: Pale malt, Crystal malt, Vienna malt, Patent black malt. Hops: Fuggles. Late hops: Styrian Goldings. Source: BC.

### . *Vale, Haddenham*

**Black Swan Dark Mild** (b-c): ABV: 3.3%. Malt: Maris Otter pale malt, Crystal malt, Roast barley. Hops: Fuggles, Goldings. Source: JE3/4/5/6.

**Wychert Ale** (b-c): ABV: 3.9%. Malt: Halcyon and/or Maris Otter pale malt, Crystal malt. Hops: Fuggles, Challenger. Source: JE3/4/5/6.

**VPA**: ABV: 4.2%. Hops: Amarillo, Challenger. Source: W.

**Black Beauty Porter** (b-c): ABV: 4.3%. Malt: Maris Otter pale malt, Roast barley. Hops: Fuggles, Goldings. Source: JE3/4/5/6.

**Edgar's Golden Ale / Halcyon Daze** (b-c): ABV: 4.3%. Malt: Halcyon or Maris Otter pale malt. Hops: Fuggles, Goldings. Source: JE3/4/5/6.

**Grumpling Old Ale / Grumpling Premium** (b-c): ABV: 4.6%. Malt: Maris Otter pale malt, Crystal malt, Roast barley. Hops: Challenger, Goldings. Source: JE3/4/5/6.

**Hadda's Headbanger** (b-c): ABV: 5%. Malt: Maris Otter pale malt, Crystal malt, optional Roast barley. Hops: Fuggles, Challenger. Source: JE3/4/5/6.

**Good King Senseless** (b-c): ABV: 5.2%. Malt: Maris Otter pale malt, Crystal malt, Chocolate malt. Hops: Goldings, Fuggles. Source: JE5. Hops: Mount Hood. Source: JE6.

### . *Vaux Breweries, Sunderland*

**Lorimer's Best Scotch**: OG: 1036. Malt: 85% Triumph pale malt, 12% Glucose / Invert sugar, 3% Roast barley or Blend of Halcyon and Pipkin pale malt, Black malt, 10% Wheat. Hops: Fuggles, Challenger, optional Target. EBC: 38. Source: RP.

**Best Bitter / Bitter**: OG: 1037. Malt: 100% Triumph pale malt or Blend of Halcyon and Pipkin pale malt, 10% Wheat. Hops: Challenger, Fuggles, Target. Source: RP.

**Samson Ale**: OG: 1042. Malt: 85% Triumph pale malt, 15% Glucose / Invert sugar or Blend of Halcyon and Pipkin pale malt, Crystal malt, 10% Wheat, Caramel. Hops: Challenger, Fuggles, Target. Source: RP.

**Double Maxim**: OG: 1044.5. Malt: Blend of pale malt or Halcyon and Pipkin pale malt, Crystal malt, 10% Wheat, Caramel. Hops: Challenger, Fuggles, Target. Source: RP.

## . *Ventnor Brewery, Ventnor, Isle of Wight*

**Oyster Stout** (b-c): ABV: 4.5%. Malt: Pale malt, Crystal malt, Wheat malt, Chocolate malt. Hops: Fuggles, WGV. Others: Fresh Oysters. Source: JE2/3.

**Old Ruby Bitter** (b-c): ABV: 4.7%. Malt: Pale malt, Crystal malt, Wheat malt. Hops: Goldings, Challenger. Source: JE4/5/6.

Notes: See Burts Brewery and Island Brewery.

## . *Wadworth & Company, Devizes*

**Devizes Bitter**: OG: 1030. Malt: 89% Triumph pale malt, 3% Crystal malt, 8% Sugar, Caramel. Hops: Fuggles. Dry hops: Goldings. Source: RP1.

**Henry Wadworth IPA**: OG: 1034-5. Malt: 89% Triumph pale malt / 47-94% Pipkin and 0-47% Halcyon pale malt, 3-4% Crystal malt, 2-8% Sugar, Caramel. Hops: Fuggles. Dry hops: Goldings. IBU: 22. Source: RP/MO.

**6X**: OG: 1040. Malt: 89% Triumph pale malt / 47-94% Pipkin and 0-47% Halcyon pale malt, 2-3% Crystal malt, 4-8% Sugar, Caramel. Hops: Fuggles. Dry hops: Goldings. IBU: 22. Source: RP/MO/JHF. Malt: Pale malt, Crystal malt, Flaked maize, Sugar. Hops: Goldings, Bramling Cross. Source: DL.

**Easter Ale**: OG: 1043. Malt: 46.5-93% Pipkin pale malt, 0-46.5% Halcyon pale malt, 7% Crystal malt. Hops: Fuggles, Progress, Goldings. Dry hops: Styrian Goldings. IBU: 26. EBC: 32. Source: RP.

**Malt & Hops**: OG: 1043. Malt: 98.7% Pipkin pale malt, 1.3% Crystal malt. Hops: Goldings. Late hops: Goldings. IBU: 30. EBC: 17. Source: RP4/5.

**Summersault**: OG: 1043. Malt: 100% Pipkin pale malt. Hops: Fuggles, Styrian Goldings, Saaz. Dry hops: Saaz. IBU: 28. EBC: 13. Source: RP4/5.

**Valentines Oat Malt Ale**: OG: 1044. Malt: 32.5% Pipkin pale malt, 32.5% Halcyon pale malt, 3% Crystal malt, 10% Amber malt, 11% Oat malt, 6% Oatmeal, 5% Dark unrefined sugar. Hops: 40% Fuggles, 30% WGV, 30% Progress. Late hops: WGV. Dry hops: First Gold. IBU: 30. EBC: 50. Source: RP5.

**Farmer's Glory**: OG: 1046. Malt: 89-90% Triumph pale malt / 47-94% Pipkin pale malt, 0-47% Halcyon pale malt, 2-3% Crystal malt, 4-8% Sugar, optional Roast malt extract, Caramel. Hops: Fuggles. Late hops: Goldings. Dry hops: Goldings. IBU: 22. Source: RP.

**Old Timer**: OG: 1055. Malt: 89% Triumph pale malt / 47-90% Pipkin pale malt, 0-47% Halcyon pale malt, 2-3% Crystal malt, 4-8% Sugar, optional Caramel. Hops: Fuggles. Dry hops: Goldings. IBU: 22. Source: RP/GW/MO. OG: 1054. Malt: Pale malt, Crystal malt, Flaked barley, Sugar. Hops: Goldings, Fuggles. Late hops: Goldings. Dry hops: Goldings. Source: DL.

**Strongest Ale** (b-c): ABV: 11%. Malt: Pipkin pale malt, Crystal malt, Sugar. Hops: Fuggles, Goldings. Source: JE3.

**JCB**: Malt: plenty of Crystal malt. Late hops: 25% added as hop tea. Source: BBB.

## . S.H. Ward & Company, Sheffield

**Darley Dark Mild**: OG: 1032. Malt: 89% Maris Otter and Triumph pale malt, Chocolate malt, Crystal malt, Torrefied wheat, Invert sugar. Hops: Fuggles, Goldings. Source: RP1.

**Mild**: OG: 1032. Malt: 80% Maris Otter, Triumph and optional Pipkin pale malt, Chocolate malt, Crystal malt, Torrefied wheat, 10% Invert sugar, Caramel. Hops: Target, Progress or Challenger, Fuggles. Late hops: Fuggles or Progress. IBU: 17. EBC: 80. Source: RP.

**Thorne Best Bitter**: OG: 1037. Malt: 85-94% Maris Otter, Pipkin, Triumph and/or Halcyon pale malt, Crystal malt, up to 15% Torrefied wheat, Invert sugar, Caramel. Hops: Challenger, optional Fuggles. Late hops: Fuggles, Goldings or Progress. Dry hops: Fuggles, Goldings or Progress. IBU: 29. EBC: 27. Source: RP.

**Sheffield Best Bitter / Best Bitter**: OG: 1038. Malt: 89-94% Maris Otter, Triumph, Halcyon and/or Pipkin pale malt, Enzymic malt, up to 10% Invert sugar, optional Crystal malt, optional Torrefied wheat, Caramel. Hops: Challenger, optional Fuggles / Target. Late hops: Fuggles optional Goldings / Progress. Dry hops: Fuggles, optional Goldings. IBU: 24-31. EBC: 23. Source: RP.

**Kirby Strong Beer**: OG: 1045. Malt: 89% Maris Otter, Halcyon and optional Pipkin pale malt, Enzymic malt, Crystal malt, Invert sugar, Torrefied wheat, Caramel. Hops: Challenger. Late hops: Fuggles, Goldings. IBU: 31. Source: RP.

**Vaux Waggle Dance**: OG: 1047. Malt: Pipkin and Halcyon pale malt, Honey. Hops: Challenger. Late hops: Fuggles. IBU: 26. EBC: 15. Source: RP4/5.

**Vaux Extra Special Bitter**: OG: 1049. Malt: 85% Pipkin pale malt, Halcyon pale malt, Enzymic malt and Crystal malt, 15% Invert sugar and Torrefied wheat. Hops: Challenger, Target. Hops: Fuggles, Progress. IBU: 31. EBC: 31. Source: RP4.

## . Warwickshire, Leamington Spa

**Best Bitter** (b-c): ABV: 3.9%. Malt: Maris Otter pale malt, Crystal malt, Torrefied wheat. Hops: First Gold, Goldings. Source: JE5/6.

**Lady Godiva** (b-c): ABV: 4.2%. Malt: Maris Otter pale malt, Amber malt, Torrefied wheat. Hops: Cascade, Styrian Goldings. Source: JE5/6.

**Churchyard Bob** (b-c): ABV: 4.9%. Malt: Maris Otter pale malt, Amber malt, Chocolate malt, Torrefied wheat. Hops: Fuggles. Source: JE5/6.

**Warwick Market Ale** (b-c): ABV: 4.9%. Malt: Maris Otter pale malt, Crystal malt, Torrefied wheat. Hops: Goldings, First Gold. Source: JE6.

**Kingmaker** (b-c): ABV: 5.5%. Malt: Maris Otter pale malt, Crystal malt, Torrefied wheat. Hops: Challenger, Goldings. Source: JE5/6.

## . *Watney Mann, London*

**Special Mild** (keg): OG: 1031. Malt: Pale malt, Flaked barley, Sugar. Hops: Fuggles. Dry hops: Hop extract. Source: DL.

**Starlight Bitter** (keg): OG: 1032. Malt: Pale malt, Flaked maize, Flaked barley, Sugar. Hops: Fuggles. Dry hops: Hop extract. Source: DL.

**Manns Brown Ale** (bottled): ABV: 3.2%. Malt: Black malt, Sugar. Hops: Northern Brewer. Dry hops: Hop extract. Source: DL.

**Special Bitter** (keg): OG: 1035. Malt: Crystal malt, Sugar. Hops: Fuggles. Dry hops: Hop extract. Source: DL.

**Watney's Cream Label** (bottled): ABV: 3.5%. Malt: Crystal malt, Black malt, Sugar. Hops: Fuggles. Source: DL.

**Watney's Cream Stout**: OG: 1047-48. Malt: Pale malt, Dextrin malt, Crystal malt, Chocolate malt, Flaked barley, Roast barley, Maltodextrin. Hops: Fuggles. Source: CB.

## . *Samuel Webster & Wilsons, Halifax*

**Wilsons Original Mild**: OG: 1030.8. Malt: Pale malt, Crystal malt, Flaked barley, Maize syrup. Hops: Goldings, Northern Brewer, Northdown, Challenger, Target. IBU: 24. Source: RP1/2.

**Websters Green Label Best**: OG: 1032. Malt: Pale malt, Flaked barley, Maize syrup. Hops: Goldings, Northern Brewer, Northdown, Challenger, Target. IBU: 26. Source: RP1/2.

**Wilsons Original Bitter**: OG: 1035.8. Malt: Pale malt, Flaked barley, Crystal malt, Maize syrup. Hops: Goldings, Northern Brewer, Northdown, Challenger, Target. IBU: 33. Source: RP1/2.

**Websters Yorkshire Bitter**: OG: 1035.8. Malt: Pale malt, Flaked barley, Maize syrup, Caramel. Hops: Goldings, Northern Brewer, Northdown, Challenger, Target. IBU: 32. Source: RP1/2. OG: 1038. Malt: Pale malt, Crystal malt, Wheat malt, Sugar. Hops: Fuggles. Late hops: Bramling Cross. Source: DL.

Notes: See John Smith's Brewery and Webster's Fountain Head Brewery.

**Websters Choice**: OG: 1045. Malt: Pale malt, Flaked barley, Maize syrup, Caramel. Hops: Goldings, Northern Brewer, Northdown, Challenger, Target. IBU: 36. Source: RP1/2.

## Webster's Fountain Head Brewery, Halifax

**Wilsons Original Mild**: OG: 1031. Malt: Pale malt, Crystal malt, 20% Syrup. Hops: Northdown, Challenger, Target. EBC: 80. Source: RP3.

**Green Label Best**: OG: 1031.8-1033. Malt: 70-80% Pale malt, 20% Syrup, 0-10% Torrefied wheat. Hops: Target, optional Northdown, Challenger. Late hops: Styrian Goldings (pellets and oil). IBU: 26. EBC: 17.5. Source: RP.

**Pennine Bitter**: OG: 1034.8. Malt: 70% White malt, 10% Torrefied wheat, 20% Syrup. Hops: Target. IBU: 32. EBC: 21. Source: RP4.

**Wilsons Original Bitter**: OG: 1036. Malt: 70-73% Pale malt, 7-10% Crystal malt, 20% Syrup. Hops: Target, optional Northdown, Challenger. IBU: 33. EBC: 21. Source: RP.

**Websters Yorkshire Bitter**: OG: 1034.8-1036. Malt: 70-80% Pale malt, 20% Wheat syrup, 0-10% Torrefied wheat. Hops: Target, optional Northdown, Challenger. IBU: 33-35. EBC: 26. Source: RP.

Notes: See John Smith's Brewery and Samuel Webster & Wilsons.

## Weetwood Ales, Tarporley

**Best Cask Bitter / Best Bitter**: OG: 1039.5-1040.5. Malt: 90% Maris Otter pale malt, 5% Crystal malt, 5% Wheat malt, 0.5% Chocolate malt. Hops: Challenger, Goldings. IBU: 33. EBC: 20. Source: RP3/4/5.

**Old Dog Premium Bitter**: OG: 1045. Malt: 90% Maris Otter pale malt, 5% Crystal malt, 5% Wheat malt, 0.5% Chocolate malt. Hops: Challenger, Goldings. IBU: 40. EBC: 25. Source: RP4/5.

**Oasthouse Gold Bitter**: OG: 1050. Malt: 83% Maris Otter pale malt, 17% Wheat malt. Hops: Goldings. IBU: 25. EBC: 12. Source: RP5/JHF.

## Charles Wells, Bedford

**Eagle Bitter / Eagle IPA**: OG: 1035. Malt: 80-85% Pale malt, Crystal malt. Hops: Challenger, Goldings. IBU: 28. Source: RP1/2/3/4/5.

**Bombardier**: OG: 1042-4. Malt: Almost 100% pale malt, Crystal malt. Hops: Challenger, Goldings. IBU: 34-6. Source: RP1/2/3/4/5/W.

**Fargo Strong Ale**: ABV: 5%. Malt: Pale malt, Crystal malt. Hops: Challenger, Goldings. Source: RP4/5.

Notes: Merged with Young & Co. (qv) in 2006 to form Wells and Young's (qv).

## Wells and Young's Brewing Co., Bedford. www.wellsandyoungs.co.uk

**Champion Live Golden Beer** (b-c): ABV: 5%. Malt: Lager malt. Hops: Styrian Goldings. Source: JE6.

**Special London Ale** (b-c): ABV: 6.4%. Malt: Maris Otter pale malt, Crystal malt. Hops: Goldings, Fuggles. Source: JE6.

**Wells Banana Bread Beers**: ABV: 5.2%. Others: Bananas. Source: TBBK.

Notes: Formed by merger of Charles Wells (qv) and Young & Co. (qv) in 2006.

## .  Wentworth, Rotherham

**Wentworth Pale Ale** (b-c): ABV: 4%. Malt: Maris Otter pale malt, Lager malt, Wheat malt. Hops: Fuggles, Cascade. Source: JE3/4/5.

**Oatmeal Stout** (b-c): ABV: 4.8%. Malt: Maris Otter pale malt, Black malt, Wheat malt, Roast barley, Oatmeal. Hops: Goldings. Source: JE3/4/5.

**Moore's Magic** (b-c): ABV: 5.5%. Malt: Maris Otter pale malt, Wheat malt. Hops: Cascade. Source: JE4.

**Rampant Gryphon** (b-c): ABV: 6.2%. Malt: Maris Otter pale malt, Crystal malt, Wheat malt. Hops: Challenger, Goldings. Source: JE3/4/5.

## .  West Berkshire, Thatcham

**Full Circle** (b-c): ABV: 4.6%. Malt: Maris Otter pale malt, Crystal malt, Wheat malt. Hops: Northdown, optional others. Source: JE4/5.

## .  West Coast Brewing Company, Manchester

**Dark Mild**: OG: 1032. Malt: 95% Pale malt, 5% Roast barley, 5% Roast malt. Hops: Fuggles, Goldings, New Zealand. Dry hops: Yes. IBU: 18. EBC: 100. Source: RP3.

**Kangaroo XXXX Pale Ale**: OG: 1038. Malt: 100% Maris Otter pale malt. Hops: Pride of Ringwood. Dry hops: Yes. IBU: 40. EBC: 10. Source: RP3.

**Dobbins Ginger Beer**: OG: 1050. Malt: 80% Maris Otter pale malt, 20% Sugar syrup. Hops: New Zealand. Others: Dry ground ginger added in boil and Sliced fresh ginger added to casks. IBU: 20. EBC: 6. Source: RP3.

**Yakima Grande Porter**: OG: 1050. Malt: 80% Maris Otter pale malt, Roast barley, Roast malt, Wheat malt, Chocolate malt. Hops: Yakima, New Zealand. IBU: 20. EBC: 100. Source: RP3.

**Old Soporific Barley Wine**: OG: 1086. Malt: 70% Maris Otter pale malt, 6% Crystal malt, 0.1% Black malt. Hops: New Zealand. Dry hops: Goldings. IBU: 50. EBC: 24. Source: RP3.

## .  Westerham, Edenbridge

**British Bulldog** (b-c): ABV: 4.3%. Malt: Maris Otter pale malt, Crystal malt. Hops: Northdown, Goldings. Source: JE6.

. *Wheal Ale, Hayle*

**Speckled Parrot** (b-c): ABV: 5.5%. Malt: Maris Otter pale malt, Crystal malt. Hops: Fuggles, Goldings. Source: JE5.

. *Whim Ales, Buxton*

**Hartington Bitter**: OG: 1039.5. Malt: Maris Otter pale malt, Crystal malt. Hops: Goldings. IBU: 28. Source: RP5.

**Black Bear Stout** (b-c): ABV: 6.5%. Malt: Maris Otter pale malt, Crystal malt, Roast barley. Hops: Fuggles. Source: JE1.

. *Whitbread*

**Mackeson** (bottled): ABV: 3.3%. Malt: Chocolate malt, Sugar, Caramel, Saccharin. Hops: Fuggles, Northern Brewer. Source: DL. OG: 1056-57. Malt: Pale malt, Dextrin malt, Crystal malt, Chocolate malt, Black malt, Lactose, Maltodextrin. Hops: Target. Source: CB.

**Heineken Pilsner Lager** (bottled): OG:1034. Malt: Lager malt, Flaked rice, Crystal malt. Hops: Hallertau. Source: DL.

**Light Ale** (bottled): OG:1034. Malt: Pale malt, Flaked barley, Crystal malt. Hops: Goldings, Northern Brewer. Late hops: Northern Brewer. Source: DL.

**Tankard** (keg): OG: 1039. Malt: Pale malt, Torrefied barley, Sugar. Hops: Bramling Cross, Fuggles. Late hops: Bramling Cross. Source: DL.

**Pompey Royal**: OG: 1047. Malt: Pale malt, Crystal malt, Barley syrup, Sugar. Hops: Goldings, Fuggles, Bramling Cross. Late hops: Goldings. Source: DL. Note: See **Pompey Royal**, George Gale & Co.

. *Whitbread, Cheltenham*

**West Country Pale Ale**: OG: 1030.5. Malt: 65% Pale malt, 7.5% Crystal malt, 15% Torrefied wheat, 12.5% Sugar or 96% Pale malt, 4% Crystal malt. Hops: 90% Hop extract, 10% Target / WGV. Late hops: 5% Styrian Goldings, optional Target oil. Dry hops: Target or Goldings. IBU: 25. EBC: 23. Source: RP/MO.

**Fremlins Bitter**: OG: 1035. Malt: 70-82% Pale malt, 4-5% Crystal malt, 0-12% Torrefied wheat, 13-14% Sugar. Hops: 94-100% Hop extract, 0-5% Target. Dry hops: Styrian Goldings. IBU: 24. EBC: 24. Source: RP/MO.

**Wethereds Bitter**: OG: 1035. Malt: 65% Pale malt, 7.5% Crystal malt, 15% Torrefied wheat, 12.5% Sugar. Hops: 90% Hop extract, 10% Target. Dry hops: Target. IBU: 32. Source: RP1/2.

**Flowers IPA**: OG: 1036. Malt: 65-80% Pale malt, 7.5% Crystal malt, 0-15% Torrefied wheat, 12.5% Sugar. Hops: 90-5% Hop extract, 0-10% Target, 0-10% Styrian Goldings. Dry hops: Target or Styrian Goldings. IBU: 24. EBC: 24. Source: RP/MO.

**Whitbread Best Bitter**: OG: 1036. Malt: 87-96% Pale malt, 4-5% Crystal malt, 0-8% Torrefied wheat. Hops: 85-95% Hop extract, 0-10% WGV. Late hops: 5% Styrian Goldings or Goldings, Target. Dry hops: Target oil. IBU: 26-29. EBC: 29. Source: RP/MO.

**Strong Country Bitter**: OG: 1037. Malt: 65% Pale malt, 7.5% Crystal malt, 15% Torrefied wheat, 12.5% Sugar. Hops: 90% Hop extract, 10% Target. Dry hops: Target. Source: RP1.

**Trophy**: OG: 1037. Malt: Pale malt, Flaked barley, Barley syrup, Sugar. Hops: Goldings, Fuggles. Late hops: Goldings. Dry hops: Goldings. Source: DL. Note: See **Trophy**, Whitbread, Sheffield.

**Wethered SPA**: OG: 1040. Malt: 65% Pale malt, 7.5% Crystal malt, 15% Torrefied wheat, 12.5% Sugar. Hops: 90% Hop extract, 10% Target. Dry hops: Target. Source: RP1.

**Flowers Original**: OG: 1044. Malt: 65-80% Pale malt, 7.5% Crystal malt, 0-15% Torrefied wheat, 12.5% Sugar. Hops: 90-95% Hop extract or Target, 5-10% Styrian Goldings. Dry hops: Target or Target oil, Styrian Goldings. IBU: 30. EBC: 27. Source: RP/MO/BC.

## . *Whitbread, London*

**Best Ale**: OG: 1031. Malt: Pale malt, Mild malt, Crystal 40L malt, No.3 invert sugar, Caramel. Hops: Fuggles, Goldings. Yeast: Wyeast #1098/Wyeast #1099. Notes: Recipe from 1950. IBU: 28. SRM: 28. Source: VB.

**Forest Brown**: OG: 1033. Malt: Pale malt, Crystal 60L malt, No.3 invert sugar, Caramel. Hops: Brewers Gold, Northern Brewer. Yeast: Wyeast #1098/Wyeast #1099. Notes: Recipe from 1955. IBU: 38. SRM: 24. Source: VB.

**TA**: OG: 1036. Malt: Pale malt, Lager malt, Crystal 40L malt, No.1 invert sugar. Hops: Goldings, Fuggles. Yeast: Wyeast #1098/Wyeast #1099. Notes: Recipe from 1931. IBU: 35. SRM: 6. Source: VB.

**IPA**: OG: 1050. Malt: Pale malt, Lager malt, No.1 invert sugar. Hops: Goldings. Yeast: Wyeast #1098/Wyeast #1099. Notes: Recipe from 1902. IBU: 71. SRM: 5. Source: VB.

**FA**: OG: 1053. Malt: Pale malt, No.1 invert sugar. Hops: Fuggles, Cluster. Yeast: Wyeast #1098/Wyeast #1099. Notes: Recipe from 1880. IBU: 122. SRM: 7. Source: VB.

**DB**: OG: 1055. Malt: Pale malt, Lager malt, Chocolate malt, No.3 invert sugar, Caramel. Hops: Fuggles, Goldings. Yeast: Wyeast #1098/Wyeast #1099. Notes: Recipe from 1933. IBU: 50. SRM: 23. Source: VB.

**PA**: OG: 1060. Malt: Pale malt, No.1 invert sugar. Hops: Goldings, Cluster. Yeast: Wyeast #1098/Wyeast #1099. Notes: Recipe from 1875. IBU: 148. SRM: 7. OG: 1057. Malt: Pale malt, Lager malt, No.1 invert sugar. Hops: Fuggles. Yeast: Wyeast #1098/Wyeast #1099. Notes: Recipe from 1916. IBU: 50. SRM: 7. Source: VB.

**Porter**: OG: 1060. Malt: Pale malt, Brown malt, Black malt. Hops: Goldings/Fuggles. Notes: Recipe from 1850. Malt: Pale malt, Pale amber malt, Brown malt, Black malt. Hops: Fuggles. Notes: Recipe from 1896. Source: DP. OG: 1055. Malt: Pale malt, Brown malt, Black malt. Hops: Spalt, Fuggles, Cluster. Yeast: Wyeast #1098/Wyeast #1099. Notes: Recipe from 1880. IBU: 37. SRM: 29. OG: 1058. Malt: Pale malt, Brown malt, Black malt, No.3 invert sugar. Hops: Fuggles, Goldings, Cluster. Yeast: Wyeast #1098. Notes: Recipe from 1892. IBU: 49. SRM: 38. OG: 1028. Malt: Pale malt, Lager malt, Brown malt, Black malt, Flaked oats, No.3 invert sugar. Hops: Cluster. Yeast: Wyeast #1098/Wyeast #1099. Notes: Recipe from 1922. IBU: 26. SRM: 27. OG: 1029. Malt: Pale malt, Lager malt, Brown malt, Chocolate malt, Flaked oats, No.3 invert sugar. Hops: Fuggles, Goldings. Yeast: Wyeast #1098/Wyeast #1099. Notes: Recipe from 1940. IBU: 25. SRM: 21. Source: VB.

**X**: OG: 1060. Malt: Pale malt, Mild malt, No.2 invert sugar. Hops: Spalt, Fuggles, Cluster. Yeast: Wyeast #1098/Wyeast #1099. Notes: Recipe from 1890. IBU: 58. SRM: 8. Source: VB.

**KKK**: OG: 1070. Malt: Pale malt, Mild malt, No.3 invert sugar, Caramel. Hops: Goldings. Yeast: Wyeast #1098/Wyeast #1099. Notes: Recipe from 1916. IBU: 74. SRM: 22. Source: VB.

**India Export Pale Ale**: OG: 1070. Malt: Pale malt. Hops: Goldings. Notes: Recipe from 1864. Source: DP.

**XL**: OG: 1071. Malt: Pale malt. Hops: Fuggles. Notes: Recipe from 1864. Source: DP.

**Export Stout**: OG: 1071. Malt: Pale malt, Brown malt, Black malt. Hops: Fuggles. Notes: Recipe from 1864. Source: DP.

**Export XX**: OG: 1078. Malt: Mild malt, No.2 invert sugar. Hops: Fuggles, Goldings. Yeast: Wyeast #1098/Wyeast #1099. Notes: Recipe from 1880. IBU: 113. SRM: 11. Source: VB. OG: 1086. Malt: Pale malt. Hops: Fuggles. Notes: Recipe from 1864. Source: DP.

**KXX**: OG: 1081. Malt: Pale malt. Hops: Goldings. Yeast: Wyeast #1098/Wyeast #1099. Notes: Recipe from 1850. IBU: 111. SRM: 6.2. Source: VB.

**SSS (Triple Stout)**: OG: 1093. Malt: Pale malt, Brown malt, Black malt, No.3 invert sugar. Hops: Fuggles, Goldings, Cluster. Yeast: Wyeast #1098/Wyeast #1099. Notes: Recipe from 1892. IBU: 80. SRM: 43. Source: VB. OG: 1096. Malt: Pale malt, Brown malt, Black malt. Hops: Fuggles. Notes: Recipe from 1838. Source: DP.

**KXXXX**: OG: 1113. Malt: Pale malt. Hops: Fuggles. Notes: Recipe from 1836. Source: DP.

### .   *Whitbread, Sheffield*

**Chester's Best Mild**: OG: 1032. Malt: 70% Pale malt, 5% Chocolate malt, 15% Torrefied wheat, 10% Sugar. Hops: 75% Hop extract, 25% Target. IBU: 23. Source: RP1/2.

**Higson's Best Mild**: OG: 1032. Malt: Pale malt, Crystal malt, Torrefied wheat, Sugar, Caramel. Hops: British Columbian Bramling Cross, Challenger, Fuggles, Styrian Goldings. IBU: 22. Source: RP2. Notes: See **Mild**, Higsons and **Higson Mild**, Castle Eden.

**Chester's Best Bitter**: OG: 1033. Malt: 72% Pale malt, 3% Crystal malt, 15% Torrefied wheat, 10% Sugar. Hops: 85% Hop extract, 15% Target. IBU: 25. Source: RP1/2.

**Trophy**: OG: 1036. Malt: 70% Pale malt, 5% Crystal malt, 10% Torrefied wheat, 15% Sugar. Hops: 80% Hop extract, 20% Target. Dry hops: Goldings. IBU: 24. Source: RP1/2. Note: See **Trophy**, Whitbread, Cheltenham.

**Higson's Best Bitter**: OG: 1037. Malt: 75% Pale malt, 5% Crystal malt, 10% Torrefied wheat, 10% Brewing sugar. Hops: British Columbian Bramling Cross, Challenger, Fuggles, Styrian Goldings. IBU: 32. Source: RP2. Notes: See **Bitter**, Higsons and **Higsons Bitter**, Castle Eden.

. *White Horse, Stanford in the Vale*

**Giant**: ABV: 4.3%. Hops: Bramling Cross. Source: W.

. *White Star, Southampton*

**UXB** (b-c): ABV: 3.8%. Malt: Maris Otter pale malt. Source: JE6.

**Crafty Shag** (b-c): ABV: 4.1%. Hops: Saaz, Hersbrücker. Source: JE6.

**Majestic** (b-c): ABV: 4.2%. Malt: Optic pale malt. Hops: Northdown. Source: JE6.

**Dark Destroyer** (b-c): ABV: 4.7%. Malt: Pale malt, Roast malt. Source: JE6.

**Capstan Full Strength** (b-c): ABV: 6%. Hops: Fuggles. Source: JE6.

. *Whittingtons, Newent*

**Cats Whiskers** (b-c): ABV: 4.2%. Malt: Maris Otter pale malt, Crystal malt, Chocolate malt, Sugar. Hops: Cascade, First Gold. Source: JE5/6.

. *Why Not Brewery, Norwich*

**Wally's Revenge** (b-c): ABV: 4%. Malt: Maris Otter pale malt, Crystal malt. Hops: Goldings, Fuggles. Source: JE6.

**Cavalier Red** (b-c): ABV: 4.7%. Malt: Maris Otter pale malt, Chocolate malt, Crystal malt. Hops: Goldings, Fuggles. Source: JE6.

**Chocolate Nutter** (b-c): ABV: 5.5%. Malt: Maris Otter pale malt, Chocolate malt, Crystal malt. Hops: Goldings, Fuggles. Source: JE6.

. *Wicked Hathern, Loughborough*

**Doble's Dog** (b-c): ABV: 3.5%. Malt: Maris Otter pale malt, Crystal malt, Chocolate malt, Wheat malt. Hops: Fuggles, Goldings. Source: JE5/6.

**Hawthorn Gold** (b-c): ABV: 3.5-4.8%. Malt: Maris Otter pale malt, Wheat malt. Hops: Fuggles, Goldings. Source: JE5/6.

**WHB (Wicked Hathern Bitter)** (b-c): ABV: 3.8-4.1%. Malt: Maris Otter pale malt, Crystal malt, Chocolate malt, Wheat malt. Hops: Fuggles, Goldings. Source: JE5/6.

**Hathern Cross** (b-c): ABV: 4%. Malt: Maris Otter pale malt, Amber malt, Wheat malt. Hops: Fuggles. Source: JE6.

**Cockfighter** (b-c): ABV: 4.2-4.5%. Malt: Maris Otter pale malt, Crystal malt. Hops: Goldings. Source: JE5/6.

**Albion Special** (b-c): ABV: 4.3%. Malt: Maris Otter pale malt, Crystal malt, Wheat. Hops: Fuggles, Goldings. Source: JE5/6.

**Soar Head** (b-c): ABV: 4.8-5.1%. Malt: Maris Otter pale malt, Crystal malt, Chocolate malt, Wheat malt. Hops: Fuggles, Goldings. Source: JE5/6.

**Derby Porter** (b-c): ABV: 5%. Malt: Maris Otter pale malt, Wheat malt, Chocolate malt, Crystal malt. Hops: Goldings, Fuggles. Source: JE6.

**Gladstone Tidings** (b-c): ABV: 5.4%. Malt: Maris Otter pale malt, Chocolate malt, Crystal malt. Hops: Goldings. Source: JE6.

## . *Wickwar Brewing Company, Wickwar*

**Coopers WPA (Wickwar Pale Ale)**: OG: 1035-7. Malt: Halcyon pale malt, Crystal malt. Hops: Challenger, Fuggles. Late hops: Yes. Source: RP4/5.

**Brand Oak Bitter / BOB / Dog's Hair** (b-c): OG: 1038-40. Malt: Halcyon pale malt, Crystal malt, Chocolate malt. Hops: Challenger, Fuggles. Late hops: Yes. Source: RP2/3/4/5. ABV: 4%. Malt: Maris Otter pale malt, Crystal malt, Chocolate malt/Black malt, optional Torrefied wheat. Hops: Fuggles, Challenger. Source: JE3/4/5/6.

**Cotswold Way** (b-c): ABV: 4.2%. Malt: Maris Otter pale malt, Crystal malt, Chocolate malt. Hops: Fuggles, Challenger. Source: JE4. Malt: Maris Otter pale malt, Crystal malt, Black malt. Hops: Fuggles. Source: JE5.

**Severn Bore**: ABV: 4.2%. Hops: Fuggles. Source: W.

**Infernal Brew** (b-c): ABV: 4.8%. Malt: Maris Otter pale malt, Crystal malt, Chocolate malt. Hops: Challenger, Fuggles. Source: JE4/5.

**Old Merryford Ale / Old Arnold** (b-c): OG: 1048-1050. Malt: Halcyon pale malt, Chocolate malt, optional Crystal malt. Hops: Challenger, Fuggles. Late hops: Yes. Source: RP. ABV: 4.8%. Malt: Maris Otter or Halcyon pale malt, Crystal malt, Chocolate malt. Hops: Fuggles, Challenger. Source: JE2/3/4. Malt: Maris Otter pale malt, Black malt. Hops: Fuggles, Challenger. Source: JE5.

**Mr. Perrett's** (b-c): ABV: 5.9%. Malt: Maris Otter pale malt, Crystal malt, Chocolate malt. Hops: Challenger, Fuggles. Source: JE4. Malt: Maris Otter pale malt, Crystal malt, Black malt. Hops: Fuggles. Source: JE5.

**Station Porter** (b-c): ABV: 6.1%. Malt: Maris Otter or Halcyon pale malt, Crystal malt, Chocolate malt. Hops: Fuggles, Goldings. Source: JE3/4. Malt: Maris Otter pale malt, Crystal malt, Black malt. Hops: Fuggles. Source: JE5.

## . *Wild's Brewery, Huddersfield*

**Wild Oats**: OG: 1041. Malt: 94% Maris Otter pale malt, 5% Amber malt, 1% Chocolate malt. Hops: Challenger, Fuggles. Source: RP4/5.

**Wild Blonde**: OG: 1045. Malt: 100% Maris Otter pale malt. Hops: Challenger, Fuggles. Source: RP4/5.

**Wild Redhead**: OG: 1045. Malt: 90% Maris Otter pale malt, 9% Crystal malt, 1% Chocolate malt. Hops: Challenger, Cascade. Source: RP4/5.

## . *Wiltshire Brewery Company, Stourbridge*

**Stonehenge Mild / Pitfield Mild**: OG: 1035. Malt: Maris Otter pale malt, Pipkin pale malt, Crystal malt, Roast barley, Dark cane sugar, Caramel. Hops: Challenger, Northdown, Goldings. Source: RP3.

**Pitfield Bitter / Stonehenge Bitter**: OG: 1036. Malt: Maris Otter pale malt, Pipkin pale malt, Crystal malt, Roast barley. Hops: Challenger, Northdown, Goldings. Source: RP3.

**Pitfield ESB**: OG: 1044. Malt: Maris Otter pale malt, Pipkin pale malt, Light muscovado cane sugar. Hops: Challenger, Goldings. Dry hops: Goldings. Source: RP3.

**Olde Grumble**: OG: 1048. Malt: Maris Otter pale malt, Pipkin pale malt, Crystal malt, Wheat malt, Malt extract. Hops: Northdown, Goldings. Dry hops: Goldings. Source: RP3.

**Pitfield Hoxton Heavy**: OG: 1048-50. Malt: Maris Otter pale malt, Pipkin pale malt, Crystal malt, Wheat malt, Malt extract. Hops: Northdown, Goldings. Source: RP3.

**Pitfield Dark Star**: OG: 1049-1050. Malt: Maris Otter pale malt, Pipkin pale malt, Crystal malt, Wheat malt, Roast barley, Malt extract. Hops: Goldings. Source: RP3.

**Pitfield Black Knight Stout**: OG: 1050. Malt: Maris Otter pale malt, Pipkin pale malt, Roast barley, Wheat malt, Dark cane sugar, Malt extract. Hops: Challenger, Goldings. Source: RP3.

**Pitfield London Porter**: OG: 1058. Malt: Maris Otter pale malt, Pipkin pale malt, Black malt, Malt extract. Hops: Northdown, Goldings. Source: RP3.

**Pitfield Maiden's Ruin**: OG: 1075. Malt: Maris Otter pale malt, Pipkin pale malt, Light muscovado cane sugar, Malt extract. Hops: Challenger, Northdown. Dry hops: Yes. Source: RP3.

**Pitfield Santa's Downfall**: OG: 1078. Malt: Maris Otter pale malt, Pipkin pale malt, Malt extract, Light muscovado cane sugar. Hops: Challenger, Northdown. Others: Raspberries. Source: RP3.

Notes: Premier Ales merged with the Pitfield Brewery in 1989 and production of all the beers moved to Stourbridge. The Wiltshire Brewery Company bought the Pitfield brand names and stopped brewing in Tisbury. Then it became the Chainmaker Beer Company, which was bought by United Breweries of India in 1992. Then it became complex and involved the Brewery on Sea in Lancing, the London Beer Company and others… E&OE.

### . Wiltshire Brewery Company, Tisbury

**Local Bitter**: OG: 1035. Malt: 92% Pale malt, 4% Crystal malt, 4% Amber malt. Hops: Fuggles, Goldings. Source: RP1.

**Stonehenge Best Bitter**: OG: 1040-1. Malt: 90% Pale malt, 5% Crystal malt, 5% Amber malt. Hops: Fuggles, Goldings. Late hops: Goldings. Source: RP1/2/GW.

**Olde Grumble**: OG: 1049-1050. Malt: 83-97% Pale malt, 1.5-2% Crystal malt, 0-0.5% Black malt, 1-15% Sugar. Hops: Fuggles, Goldings. Source: RP. Note: See Wiltshire Brewing Company, Stourbridge.

**Old Devil**: OG: 1059-1060. Malt: 74-91% Pale malt, 3-4% Crystal malt, 3-4% Amber malt, 1-19.5% Sugar. Hops: Fuggles, Goldings. Source: RP/GW.

### . Edward Winch & Sons, Chatham

**Amber Ale**: OG: 1041. Malt: Pale malt, Amber malt. Hops: Fuggles. Notes: Recipe from 1814. Source: DP.

### . Wissey Valley, King's Lynn

**WVB (Wissey Valley Bitter)** (b-c): ABV: 3.6%. Malt: Pale malt, Crystal malt, Caramalt. Hops: Fuggles, Target. Source: JE5.

**Ratty Bob** (b-c): ABV: 3.7%. Malt: Pale malt, Caramalt. Hops: Fuggles. Source: JE5.

**Captain Grumpy's Best Bitter** (b-c): ABV: 3.9%. Malt: Pale malt, Crystal malt, Caramalt. Hops: Target, Challenger. Source: JE5.

**Bodger Brown** (b-c): ABV: 4%. Malt: Pale malt, Crystal malt, Caramalt. Hops: Target, Challenger. Source: JE5.

**Old Wobbly** (b-c): ABV: 4.2%. Malt: Pale malt, Crystal malt, Caramalt, Chocolate malt, Roast barley. Hops: Target, Phoenix. Source: JE5.

**Wissey Dawn** (b-c): ABV: 4.3%. Malt: Pale malt, Caramalt. Hops: Bramling Cross. Source: JE5.

**Busted Flush** (b-c): ABV: 4.4%. Malt: Pale malt, Crystal malt, Caramalt. Hops: Phoenix, Challenger. Source: JE5.

**Stoked Up** (b-c): ABV: 4.4%. Malt: Pale malt, Caramalt. Hops: Phoenix. Source: JE5.

**Old Faithful** (b-c): ABV: 4.5%. Malt: Pale malt, Crystal malt, Caramalt. Hops: Bramling Cross. Source: JE5.

**Old Grumpy** (b-c): ABV: 4.5%. Malt: Pale malt, Crystal malt, Caramalt, Chocolate malt, Roast barley. Hops: Target, Challenger. Source: JE5.

**Eel Catcher** (b-c): ABV: 4.8%. Malt: Pale malt, Crystal malt, Caramalt, Chocolate malt, Roast barley. Hops: Fuggles, Target, Phoenix. Source: JE5.

**Wissey Sunset** (b-c): ABV: 5%. Malt: Pale malt, Crystal malt, Caramalt. Hops: Phoenix. Source: JE5. Note: Hops added in 3 stages.

**Golden Rivet** (b-c): ABV: 5.1%. Malt: Pale malt, Crystal malt, Caramalt. Hops: Challenger. Late hops: Bramling Cross. Source: JE5.

**Khaki Sergeant** (b-c): ABV: 6.7%. Malt: Pale malt, Crystal malt, Caramalt, Chocolate malt, Roast barley. Hops: Target, Challenger. Source: JE5.

### .   *Wolf, Attleborough*

**Edith Cavell / Cavell Ale 9503** (b-c): ABV: 3.7%. Malt: Pearl or Halcyon pale malt, Crystal malt, Wheat malt. Hops: Fuggles, Challenger. Source: JE3/4/5/6.

**Festival Ale** (b-c): ABV: 3.7%. Malt: Halcyon pale malt, Crystal malt, Wheat malt, Lavender honey. Hops: Fuggles, Challenger. Source: JE3. Malt: Pearl pale malt, Crystal malt, Wheat malt, optional Lavender honey. Hops: Challenger, Fuggles. Others: Optional Blackcurrants. Source: JE4/5/6.

**Norfolk Lavender** (b-c): ABV: 3.7%. Malt: Optic pale malt, Crystal malt, Wheat malt, Lavender honey. Hops: Goldings, Styrian Goldings, Cascade. Source: JE4/5/6.

**Wolf in Sheep's Clothing** (b-c): ABV: 3.7%. Malt: Pearl pale malt, Crystal malt, Wheat malt, Chocolate malt. Hops: Goldings, Cascade. Source: JE4/5/6.

**99** (b-c): ABV: 3.7%. Malt: Halcyon pale malt, Crystal malt, Chocolate malt, Wheat malt. Hops: Fuggles, Challenger. Others: Vanilla essence. Source: JE3.

**Best Bitter** (b-c): ABV: 3.9%. Malt: Pearl or Halcyon pale malt, Crystal malt, Amber malt. Hops: Fuggles, Goldings. Source: JE3/4.

**Wolf Ale** (b-c): ABV: 3.9%. Malt: Pearl pale malt, Crystal malt, Wheat malt. Hops: Styrian Goldings, Goldings, Challenger. Source: JE4/5/6.

**Coyote Bitter** (b-c): ABV: 4.3%. Malt: Pearl or Halcyon pale malt, Crystal malt, Wheat malt. Hops: Cascade, Styrian Goldings, Goldings. Source: JE3/4/6.

**Big Red** (b-c): ABV: 4.5%. Malt: Pearl pale malt, Crystal malt, Amber malt, Wheat malt, Chocolate malt. Hops: Challenger, Styrian Goldings, Goldings. Source: JE4.

**Lupine** (b-c): ABV: 4.5%. Malt: Pearl pale malt, Crystal malt, Amber malt, Wheat malt. Hops: Styrian Goldings, Goldings. Source: JE4/5.

**Straw Dog** (b-c): ABV: 4.5%. Malt: Lager malt, Wheat malt. Hops: Saaz, Hallertau. Source: JE5/6.

**Granny Wouldn't Like It!!!** (b-c): ABV: 4.8%. Malt: Pearl or Halcyon pale malt, Crystal malt, Chocolate malt, Wheat malt. Hops: Challenger, Goldings. Source: JE3/4/5/6.

**Woild Moild** (b-c): ABV: 4.8%. Malt: Pearl pale malt, Crystal malt, Chocolate malt, Wheat malt. Hops: Fuggles, Challenger, Goldings. Source: JE5/6.

**Prairie** (b-c): ABV: 5%. Malt: Pearl pale malt, Wheat malt. Hops: Goldings, Styrian Goldings. Source: JE4.

**Timber Wolf** (b-c): ABV: 5.8%. Malt: Pearl pale malt, Crystal malt, Chocolate malt, Wheat malt. Hops: Challenger, Goldings. Source: JE4/5/6.

**Ported Timber Wolf** (b-c): ABV: 5.8%. Malt: Halcyon or Pearl pale malt, Crystal malt, Wheat malt, Chocolate malt. Hops: Challenger, Goldings. Others: Port. Source: JE3/5/6.

## .   *Wood Brewery, Craven Arms*

**Sam Powell Best Bitter**: OG: 1031-5. Malt: 86% Pale malt, 5.5% Crystal malt, 1% Chocolate malt, 7.5% Wheat flour / Torrefied wheat. Hops: Fuggles, Goldings. Source: RP.

**Parish Bitter**: OG: 1037-41. Malt: 96% Pale malt, 4% Crystal malt. Hops: Fuggles. Dry hops: Goldings. Source: RP1/2/3/4/5.

**Sam Powell Original Bitter**: OG: 1035-9. Malt: 86% Pale malt, 5.5% Crystal malt, 1% Chocolate malt, 7.5% Wheat flour / Torrefied wheat. Hops: Fuggles, Goldings. Source: RP.

**Armada** (b-c): ABV: 4%. Malt: Halcyon pale malt, Crystal malt, Torrefied wheat. Hops: Fuggles, Goldings. Source: JE3.

**Shropshire Lass**: ABV: 4.1%. Hops: Crystal, Mount Hood, Fuggles. Source: W.

**Woodcutter**: OG: 1040-4. Malt: 86% Pale malt, 5.5% Crystal malt, 1% Chocolate malt. Hops: Fuggles, Goldings. Dry Hops: Yes. Source: RP4/5/JHF.

**Special Bitter**: OG: 1040-44. Malt: 91% Pale malt, 9% Crystal malt. Hops: Fuggles. Source: RP1/2/3/4/5.

**Shropshire Lad**: OG: 1043-7. Malt: 91% Pale malt, 4% Crystal malt, 1% Chocolate malt, 4% Torrefied wheat. Hops: Fuggles, Goldings. Dry hops: Yes. Source: RP4/5/JHF.

**Shropshire Lad Spring Bitter** (b-c): ABV: 5%. Malt: Pale malt, Crystal malt, Chocolate malt, Torrefied wheat. Hops: Fuggles, Goldings. Source: JE1/2/3/4.

**Wonderful**: OG: 1046-50. Malt: 92% Pale malt, 7% Crystal malt, 1% Chocolate malt. Hops: Fuggles. Dry hops: Goldings. Source: RP1/2/3/4/5.

**Hopping Mad** (b-c): ABV: 4.7%. Malt: Halcyon pale malt, Crystal malt, Torrefied wheat. Hops: Progress. Source: JE1/2/3/4.

**Sam Powell Old Sam**: OG: 1048. Malt: 86.5% Pale malt, 5.5% Crystal malt, 1% Chocolate malt, 7% Wheat flour / Torrefied wheat. Hops: Fuggles, Goldings. Source: RP.

**Christmas Cracker**: OG: 1058-62. Malt: 83% Pale malt, 16% Crystal malt, 1% Chocolate malt. Hops: Fuggles. Dry hops: Goldings. Source: RP1/2/3/4/5.

**Christmas Cracker** (b-c): ABV: 6%. Malt: Halcyon pale malt, Crystal malt, Chocolate malt. Hops: Fuggles, Goldings. Source: JE1/2/3/4.

### . *Woodforde's Norfolk Ales, Norwich*

**Mardlers Mild**: OG: 1035. Malt: Halcyon or Maris Otter pale malt, Crystal malt, Chocolate malt. Hops: Fuggles, Goldings. IBU: 20. Source: RP3/4/5.

**Broadsman Bitter**: OG: 1035-6. Malt: 100% Halcyon, Maris Otter and/or Pipkin pale malt and Crystal malt. Hops: Goldings, Styrian Goldings / Fuggles. Dry hops: Yes. IBU: 30-32. Source: RP.

**Wherry Best Bitter**: OG: 1039. Malt: Halcyon, Maris Otter or Triumph pale malt, Crystal malt. Hops: Goldings, Styrian Goldings / Fuggles. IBU: 29-30. Source: RP/JE1/2/3/4/5/6.

**Norfolk Porter**: OG: 1042. Malt: Triumph or Halcyon pale malt, Crystal malt, Chocolate malt, optional Roast barley. Hops: Goldings, Styrian Goldings / Fuggles. Dry hops: Yes. IBU: 22. Source: RP.

**Emerald Ale / Norfolk Stout**: OG: 1042. Malt: 85% Halcyon or Maris Otter pale malt and Chocolate malt, 15% Roast barley. Hops: Fuggles. IBU: 36. Source: RP.

**Old Bram**: OG: 1042. Malt: Halcyon or Maris Otter pale malt, Crystal malt, Chocolate malt. Hops: Fuggles, Goldings. IBU: 19. Source: RP.

**Great Eastern Ale**: OG: 1043. Malt: Maris Otter or Halcyon pale malt, Alexis pale malt. Hops: Fuggles, Goldings. IBU: 33. Source: RP/JE1/2.

**Great Eastern Ale** (b-c): ABV: 4.3%. Malt: Maris Otter pale malt, Lager malt. Hops: Fuggles, Goldings. Source: JE3. Hops: Progress. Source: JE4/5/6.

**Nelson's Revenge**: OG: 1045. Malt: Maris Otter or Halcyon pale malt, Crystal malt. Hops: Goldings, optional Fuggles. IBU: 29. Source: RP/JE1/2/3/4/5. Hops: Goldings, Styrian Goldings. Source: JE6.

**Phoenix XXX**: OG: 1047. Malt: Triumph pale malt, Crystal malt, Chocolate malt. Hops: Goldings, optional Styrian Goldings. IBU: 25. Source: RP.

**Norfolk Nog**: OG: 1049. Malt: Halcyon, Maris Otter or Triumph pale malt, Crystal malt, Chocolate malt. Hops: Fuggles, Goldings. IBU: 18. Source: RP/JE1/2/3/4/5. Hops: Goldings, Styrian Goldings. Source: JE6.

**Admiral's Reserve** (b-c): ABV: 5%. Malt: Maris Otter pale malt, Crystal malt, Rye crystal malt. Hops: Goldings. Source: JE4/5/6.

**Baldric**: OG: 1052. Malt: Maris Otter or Halcyon pale malt, Caramalt. Hops: Goldings. Dry hops: Goldings. IBU: 27. Source: RP/JE1/2. Notes: The pump clip/label states that this is a "A strong evil brew with the pungent essence of old socks" but I found it to be absolutely delicious!

**Headcracker**: OG: 1069. Malt: Halcyon, Maris Otter or Triumph pale malt, optional Wheat malt, optional Caramalt. Hops: Goldings, optional Styrian Goldings. IBU: 24. Source: RP.

**Headcracker** (b-c): ABV: 7%. Malt: Maris Otter pale malt, Caramalt. Hops: Goldings. Source: JE1/2/3/4/5. Hops: Goldings, Styrian Goldings. Source: JE6.

**Norfolk Nips** (b-c): ABV: 8.2%. Malt: Maris Otter pale malt, Chocolate malt. Hops: Goldings. Source: JE1. Malt: Maris Otter pale malt, Crystal malt, Chocolate malt, Roast barley. Hops: Goldings. Source: JE2/3/4/5/6.

### . *Woodlands, Wrenbury*

**Old Willow** (b-c): ABV: 4.1%. Malt: Maris Otter pale malt, Golden Promise pale malt, Pale crystal malt. Hops: Target, Challenger, Cascade. Source: JE6.

**Oak Beauty** (b-c): ABV: 4.2%. Malt: Maris Otter pale malt, Halcyon pale malt, Crystal malt, Pale crystal malt, Black malt. Hops: Goldings, Fuggles, Cascade, Northdown. Source: JE6.

**India Pale Ale** (b-c): ABV: 4.3%. Malt: Maris Otter pale malt, Torrefied wheat. Hops: Target, Fuggles, Challenger. Source: JE6.

**Midnight Stout** (b-c): ABV: 4.4%. Malt: Maris Otter pale malt, Halcyon pale malt, Roast barley, Black malt. Hops: Goldings, WGV. Source: JE6.

**Bitter** (b-c): ABV: 4.4%. Malt: Maris Otter pale malt, Halcyon pale malt, Crystal malt. Hops: Challenger, Northdown. Source: JE6.

**Gold Brew** (b-c): ABV: 5%. Malt: Halcyon pale malt, Golden Promise pale malt, Pale crystal malt. Hops: Goldings, Fuggles, Target, Cascade. Source: JE6.

### . *Worldham Brewery, Alton*

**Old Dray Bitter**: OG: 1043. Malt: Maris Otter pale malt, Halcyon pale malt, Crystal malt, Roast malt. Hops: Goldings. Source: RP4/5.

**Barbarian**: OG: 1053. Malt: Maris Otter pale malt, Halcyon pale malt, Crystal malt, Roast malt. Hops: Goldings. Source: RP4/5.

### . *Wychwood Brewery Company, Witney*

**Shires Bitter**: OG: 1034-6. Malt: 95.5-98% Pipkin pale malt, 0.5-2% Chocolate malt, 0-4% Crystal malt. Hops: Progress, optional Styrian Goldings. Dry hops: Hallertau. IBU: 32. EBC: 18. Source: RP.

**Fiddlers Elbow**: OG: 1040. Malt: 100% Pipkin pale malt or 80% Maris Otter pale malt, 20% Wheat malt. Hops: Styrian Goldings, optional Challenger. IBU: 40. EBC: 12-22. Source: RP/JHF.

**Dirty Tackle**: ABV: 4%. Malt: Crystal malt, Wheat malt. Hops: Northdown, Challenger, Target. Source: W/WB.

**Special**: OG: 1042. Malt: 98% Maris Otter pale malt, 2% Black malt. Hops: Progress. Late hops: Styrian Goldings. IBU: 22. EBC: 25. Source: RP5.

**Wychwood Best**: OG: 1044. Malt: 98% Pipkin pale malt, 2% Chocolate malt. Hops: Progress, Styrian Goldings. Late hops: Yes. IBU: 30. EBC: 24. Source: RP4.

**Old Devil**: OG: 1047. Malt: 89% Maris Otter pale malt, 9.5% Amber malt, 1.5% Wheat. Hops: Target. Late hops: Challenger. IBU: 30. EBC: 24. Source: RP5.

**Duchy Originals Summer Ale** (b-c): ABV: 4.7%. Malt: Pale malt, Wheat malt, Crystal malt. Hops: Goldings, Fuggles, Target. Source: JE6.

**Black Wych Stout**: OG: 1050. Malt: 90% Pipkin pale malt, 10% Roast malt. Hops: Progress. IBU: 80. EBC: 100. Source: RP4.

**Dog's Bollocks**: OG: 1050. Malt: 100% Maris Otter pale malt. Hops: Styrian Goldings. IBU: 28. EBC: 20. Source: RP5.

**Dr. Thirsty's Draught**: OG: 1052. Malt: 97% Pipkin pale malt, 3% Chocolate malt. Hops: Progress, Styrian Goldings. IBU: 28. EBC: 40. Source: RP4.

**Hobgoblin**: OG: 1053. Malt: 98% Maris Otter or Pipkin pale malt, 2% Black / Chocolate malt. Hops: Progress. Late hops: Styrian Goldings. IBU: 28-35. EBC: 41-5. Source: RP. OG: 1059. Malt: Maris Otter pale malt, Crystal malt, Chocolate malt, Patent black malt. Hops: Progress. Late hops: Styrian Goldings. Source: BC.

Note: See Glenny Brewery Company.

## Wye Valley Brewery, Hereford

**Hereford Bitter / Bitter**: OG: 1036-7. Malt: 78.5-92% Maris Otter or Golden Promise pale malt, 5-8% Crystal malt, 0-7.2% Wheat malt, 0-7.1% Flaked barley. Hops: Target, optional Goldings. Source: RP.

**HPA**: OG: 1040. Malt: 90-97% Golden Promise pale malt, 0-3% Crystal malt, 0-10% Wheat malt. Hops: Target, optional Goldings. Source: RP/JHF.

**Summer Stinger**: ABV: 4%. Others: Nettles. Source: WB.

**Dorothy Goodbody's Golden Ale** (b-c): ABV: 4.2%. Malt: Maris Otter or Optic pale malt, Pale crystal malt, Wheat malt. Hops: Fuggles, Goldings. Source: JE3/4/5/6.

**Supreme**: OG: 1043. Malt: 71.7-88% Golden Promise or Maris Otter pale malt, 12-15.6% Crystal malt, 0-8% Wheat malt, 0-5.9% Flaked barley. Hops: Target. Source: RP/JHF.

**Dorothy Goodbody's Wholesome Stout**: ABV: 4.6%. Malt: Maris Otter pale malt, Crystal malt, Chocolate malt, Roast barley, Flaked barley. Hops: Northdown. Source: WB.

**Dorothy Goodbody's Wholesome Stout** (b-c): ABV: 4.6%. Malt: Maris Otter or Optic pale malt, Roast barley, Flaked barley. Hops: Northdown. Source: JE1/2/3/4/5. Malt: Maris Otter pale malt, Roast barley, Chocolate malt, Crystal malt, Flaked barley. Hops: Northdown. Source: JE6.

**Butty Bach** (b-c): ABV: 4.8%. Malt: Maris Otter pale malt, Wheat malt. Hops: Fuggles, Bramling Cross, Goldings. Source: JE2. ABV: 4.5%. Malt: Maris Otter or Optic pale malt, Crystal malt. Hops: Goldings, Fuggles. Source: JE4. Malt: Maris Otter pale malt, Crystal malt, Wheat malt, Flaked barley. Hops: Fuggles, Bramling Cross, Goldings. Source: JE5/6.

**Dorothy Goodbody's Winter Tipple** (b-c): ABV: 5.3%. Malt: Maris Otter pale malt, Crystal malt. Hops: Fuggles, Challenger. Source: JE1/2.

**Brew 69**: OG: 1055. Malt: 87-95% Golden Promise or Maris Otter pale malt, 3.5-5% Crystal malt, 0-9.5% Wheat malt. Hops: Target. Source: RP.

**Brew 69** (b-c): ABV: 5.6%. Malt: Maris Otter pale malt, Crystal malt, Wheat malt. Hops: Target. Source: JE1/2/3.

**Dorothy Goodbody's Country Ale / Christmas Ale** (b-c): ABV: 6%. Malt: Maris Otter or Optic pale malt, Crystal malt, Amber malt, Wheat malt, Flaked barley, Roast barley. Hops: Bramling Cross, Fuggles. Source: JE4/5/6.

**Dorothy Goodbody's Christmas Ale** (b-c): ABV: 6%. Malt: Maris Otter pale malt, Crystal malt, Wheat malt, Roast barley, Flaked barley. Hops: Bramling Cross, Fuggles. Source: JE3.

**Dorothy Goodbody's Father Christmas Ale** (b-c): ABV: 8%. Malt: Maris Otter pale malt, Crystal malt, Wheat malt, Roast barley, Dark brown Molasses. Hops: Target. Source: JE1/2.

## . *Wylye Valley Brewery, Warminster*

**Goldings Crystal Bitter**: OG: 1046. Malt: 80% Maris Otter pale malt, 10% Crystal malt, 10% Torrefied wheat. Hops: Goldings, Northern Brewer. IBU: 28. Source: RP4/5.

## . *Wyre Piddle, Evesham*

**Piddle in the Hole** (b-c): ABV: 4.6%. Malt: Pale malt, Roast barley. Hops: Fuggles, Challenger. Source: JE2/3.

## . *XT Brewing Company, Long Crendon* www.xtbrewing.com

**Alehoof**: ABV: 4.0%. Others: Ground-ivy. Source: Web.

**Fresh Hop 1**: ABV: 4.2%. Hops: Fresh hops. Source: Web.

**2**: ABV: 4.2%. Malt: Pale malt, Munich malt. Source: Web.

**3**: ABV: 4.2%. Malt: Maris Otter pale malt, Vienna malt. Hops: Styrian Celeia, Columbus, Cluster. Source: Web.

**4**: ABV: 4.2%. Malt: Maris Otter pale malt, Belgian malt. Hops: English and American. Source: Web.

**γ**: ABV: 4.3%. Hops: Columbus. Source: Web.

**APA**: ABV: 4.4%. Others: Apricots. Source: Web.

**13**: ABV: 4.5%. Malt: Amber malts. Hops: Galaxy, Riwaka, Columbus, Pacific Gem. Source: Web.

**Animal Brewing Company Oink!**: ABV: 4.6%. Malt: Rye malt. Hops: Amarillo. Source: Web.

**δ**: ABV: 4.6%. Others: Raw chocolate, Vanilla pods. Source: Web.

**α**: ABV: 4.7%. Others: Raw chocolate, Blackberries. Source: Web.

**25**: ABV: 4.7%. Hops: Wakatu, Goldings. Source: Web.

**99 - Roast Cacao**: ABV: 5%. Others: Roast cacao nibs, Vanilla pods. Source: Bottle label.

**80**: ABV: 5.2%. IBU: 80. Source: Web.

**9**: ABV: 5.5%. Malt: Nine malts including Aromatic malt, Swedish Gotland Birch-smoked malt. Hops: Nine hop varieties. Yeast: Two varieties. Source: Web.

**Cock Ale**: ABV: 6.0%. Others: Roast chicken, Raisins, White wine. Source: Web.

### . *Yates', Ventnor, Isle of Wight*

**Undercliff Experience** (b-c): ABV: 4.1%. Malt: Optic pale malt, Crystal malt, Chocolate malt, Torrefied wheat. Hops: Cascade. Others: Coriander. Source: JE4. Hops: Goldings. Late hops: Fuggles. Source: JE5/6.

**Blonde Ale** (b-c): ABV: 4.5%. Malt: Optic pale malt, Torrefied wheat. Hops: Fuggles, Cascade. Source: JE6.

**Holy Joe** (b-c): ABV: 4.9%. Malt: Optic pale malt, Crystal malt, Torrefied wheat. Hops: Cascade. Others: Coriander. Source: JE4/5/6.

**Wight Winter** (b-c): ABV: 5%. Malt: Optic pale malt, Roast malt, Torrefied wheat, Crystal malt/Chocolate malt. Hops: Northdown. Source: JE4/5/6.

**Broadway Blitz** (b-c): ABV: 5.5%. Malt: Optic pale malt, Torrefied wheat. Hops: Fuggles, Cascade. Source: JE4.

**YSD (Yates' Special Draught)** (b-c): ABV: 5.5%. Malt: Optic pale malt, Crystal malt. Hops: Fuggles, Cascade. Source: JE5/6.

### . *The York Brewery, York*

**Guzzler**: ABV: 3.6%. Hops: Styrian Goldings. Source: W.

**Stonewall** (b-c): ABV: 3.7%. Malt: Halcyon pale malt, Crystal malt. Hops: Fuggles, Challenger. Source: JE1.

**Last Drop Bitter** (b-c): ABV: 4.5%. Malt: Halcyon pale malt, Pale chocolate malt, Roast malt. Hops: Challenger, Fuggles. Source: JE1.

### . *Young & Company's Brewery, London*

**Bitter**: OG: 1036. Malt: 90-93% Maris Otter pale malt, 3-4% Torrefied wheat, optional Sugar, optional Crystal malt. Hops: Fuggles, Goldings. IBU: 30-36. EBC: 13-15. Source: RP.

**Porter**: OG: 1040. Malt: Maris Otter pale malt, Chocolate malt, Crystal malt, Brewing sugar. Hops: Fuggles, Goldings. IBU: 30. EBC: 100. Source: RP3.

**Special Bitter**: OG: 1046. Malt: 90-93% Maris Otter pale malt, 3-4% Torrefied wheat, 0-5% Sugar, optional Crystal malt. Hops: Fuggles, Goldings. Dry hops: Target. IBU: 30-34. EBC: 20-27. Source: RP. OG: 1047. Malt: Pale malt, Crystal malt, Sugar. Hops: Goldings, Fuggles. Late hops: Goldings. Dry hops: Goldings. Source: DL.

**Oatmeal Stout**: OG: 1049-51. Malt: Maris Otter pale malt, Toasted Flaked oats, Crystal malt, Chocolate malt, Torrefied wheat, Roast barley, Brown sugar. Hops: Fuggles. Late hops: Goldings. Source: BC.

**Champion Live Golden Beer** (b-c): ABV: 5%. Malt: Lager malt. Hops: Styrian Goldings. Source: JE4/5.

**Ram Rod**: OG: 1050. Malt: 98% Maris Otter pale malt, 2% Crystal malt. Hops: Fuggles, Goldings. Dry hops: Goldings. IBU: 30-34. EBC: 23-27. Source: RP5.

**Double Chocolate Stout**: OG: 1053. Malt: Pale malt, Crystal malt, Chocolate malt, Lactose, Sugar, Cocoa powder, Chocolate extract. Hops: Fuggles. Lage hops: Goldings. Source: 150.

**Winter Warmer**: OG: 1055. Malt: 70% Maris Otter pale malt, 7% Crystal malt, optional Torrefied wheat / Torrefied barley, 0-20% Dark sugar, 0-3% Enzymic malt. Hops: Fuggles, Goldings. IBU: 26-30. EBC: 65. Source: RP.

**Special London Ale**: OG: 1064. Malt: Maris Otter pale malt, Crystal malt. Hops: Fuggles. Late hops: Goldings. Dry hops: Goldings, Target. Source: 150/JE2. OG: 1066-67. Malt: Maris Otter pale malt, Crystal malt, Torrefied wheat. Hops: Goldings, Fuggles. Late hops: Goldings. Source: BC.

**Special London Ale** (b-c): ABV: 6.4%. Malt: Maris Otter pale malt, Crystal malt. Hops: Goldings, Fuggles. Source: JE3/4/5.

**Old Nick**: OG: 1083-84. Malt: Maris Otter pale malt, Crystal malt, Chocolate malt, Dark brown sugar. Hops: Fuggles, Goldings. Late hops: Fuggles, Goldings. Source: BC.

Notes: Merged with Charles Wells (qv) in 2006 to form Wells and Young's (qv).

## Estonia

. *Saku Brewery, Saku*

**Saku Estonian Porter**: OG: 1076-79. Malt: Lager malt, Crystal malt, Munich malt. Hops: Northern Brewer. Late hops: Hersbrücker. Source: CB.

## Finland

. *Oy Hartwall, Helsinki*

**Kulta**: OG: 1049. Malt: Pale malt, Unmalted cereals. Hops: Hallertau, Saaz. Source: EBA.

. *Oy Sinebrychoff Brewery, Helsinki*

**Sinebrychoff Porter**: OG: 1074-77. Malt: Pale malt, Dextrin malt, Vienna malt, Munich malt, Chocolate malt, Crystal malt. Hops: Northern Brewer. Late hops: Hersbrücker, Saaz. Source: CB.

## France

. *Grande Brasserie Alsacienne d'Adelshoffen, Schiltigheim*

**Adelshoffen Export**: OG:. 1044. Malt: Pale malt, Flaked maize. Hops: Hallertau, Styrian Goldings. IBU: 18-22. Source: EBA

**Adelscott Bière au Malt a Whisky**: OG: 1065. Malt: 81.5% Peat-smoked malt, 18.5% Flaked maize. Hops: Brewers Gold, Hallertau, Styrian Goldings. IBU: 18. EBC: 18. Source: EBA/GW.

. *Bailleux, Bavay*

**Saison St. Médard**: ABV: 7%. Malt: Pale malt, Amber malt, Dark malts. Hops: Brewers Gold, Hersbrücker, Spalt. Source: HB.

. *Brasserie Castelain, Bénifontaine*

**Castelain Blond Bière de Garde**: OG: 1066-68. Malt: Pilsner malt, CaraVienne malt. Hops: Brewers Gold. Late hops: Brewers Gold, Hersbrücker. Source: CB.

**Sint Arnoldus**: ABV: 7.5%. Malt: Pale malts. Hops: Hallertau. Source: HB.

. *La Choulette, Hourdain*

**Bière des Sans Culottes**: OG: 1072-73. Malt: Pilsner malt, Aromatic malt, Biscuit malt, Crystal malt. Hops: Styrian Goldings. Late hops: Styrian Goldings, Strisselspalt, Tettnang. Source: BC.

**L'Abbaye de Vaucelles**: ABV: 7.5%. Malt: Pale malt. Hops: Hallertau. Source: HB.

. *Brasserie Duyck, Jenlain*

**Jenlain Bière de Garde**: OG: 1065-68. Malt: Pilsner malt, CaraMunich malt, Crystal malt. Hops: Brewers Gold. Late hops: Saaz. Source: CB.

. *Brasseries Kronenbourg*

**Kronenbourg Export Lager**: OG: 1052. Malt: Lager malt, Flaked maize, Honey. Hops: Goldings, Saaz. Late hops: Saaz. Source: DL.

. *Brasserie Nouvelle de Lutèce, Bonneuil*

**Lutèce Bière de Paris**: OG: 1063. Malt: Munich malt, Crystal malt, CaraAmber® malts. Hops: Spalt, Saaz. IBU: 23. Source: EBA.

. *Brasserie de St. Sylvestre, Saint Sylvestre-Cappel*

**Trois Monts**: OG: 1080. Malt: 94% Pilsner malt, 6% Sugar. Hops: Brewers Gold, Tettnang. IBU: 27. EBC: 6. Source: EBA/GW. OG: 1084-87. Malt: Lager malt, Pilsner malt, CaraMunich malt, Candi sugar. Hops: Brewers Gold. Late hops: Tettnang. Source: CB.

**Bière des Templiers**: ABV: 8.5%. Malt: Pilsner malt, Amber malt. Hops: Brewers Gold, Hallertau. Source: HB.

**Flanders Winter Ale**: OG: 1089-90. Malt: Pilsner malt, Munich malt, Aromatic malt, CaraMunich malt, Biscuit malt, Chocolate malt, Dark candi sugar. Hops: Brewers Gold. Late hops: Tettnang. Source: BC.

# Germany

. *Allgäuer Brauhaus, Allgäu*

**Oberdorfer Weissbier**: OG: 1052. Malt: Pilsner malt, Wheat malt. Hops: Hallertau. Late hops: Hallertau. Source: 150.

. *Klosterbräu Andechs, Andechs*

**Helles Bock**: ABV: 6.8%. Malt: Lager malt. Hops: Hallertau. Source: HB.

**Doppelbock Dunkel**: ABV: 7%. Malt: Lager malt, Munich malt. Hops: Hallertau. Source: HB.

. *Brauerei Aying, Aying*

**Bräu Weisse**: OG: 1049. Malt: 55% Pale malt, 45% Wheat malt. Hops: Hallertau, Spalt, Hersbrücker. IBU: 15. EBC: 8. Source: EBA/GW.

**Jahrhundertbier**: OG: 1053. Malt: Pilsner malt. Hops: 18% Hallertau, 54.5% Saaz, Spalt, Hersbrücker. IBU: 25. EBC: 4. Source: EBA/GW.

**Ayinger Oktober Fest-Märzen**: OG: 1055-56. Malt: Pilsner malt, Dextrin malt, CaraMunich malt, Crystal malt, Munich malt, CaraVienne malt, Maltodextrin. Hops: Tettnang. Late hops: Hersbrücker. Source: CB.

**Altbairisch Dunkel**: OG: 1057-58. Malt: Pilsner malt, CaraMunich malt, Munich malt, Crystal malt, Chocolate malt. Hops: Hersbrücker. Source: BC.

**Ayinger Maibock**: OG: 1070-72. Malt: Lager malt, Dextrin malt, Crystal malt, Munich malt, Aromatic malt, Maltodextrin. Hops: Hersbrücker. Late hops: Hersbrücker. Source: CB.

**Ayinger Celebrator Doppelbock**: OG: 1073. Malt: Pilsner malt, Munich malt, Carafa® Special II malt. Hops: Hallertau. Source: 150. OG: 1080-83. Malt: Pilsner malt, Dextrin malt, Munich malt, Crystal malt, Chocolate malt, Maltodextrin. Hops: Hersbrücker, Northern Brewer. Late hops: Hersbrücker. Source: CB.

### .   *Bayer Staats, Freising*

**Weihenstephaner Hefeweissbier**: OG: 1053. Malt: Pilsner malt, Wheat malt. Hops: Hersbrücker. Source: BC.

### .   *Bitburger, Bitburg*

**Bitburger Premium**: OG: 1045. Malt: Pilsner malt, CaraPils malt. Hops: Perle, Hallertau. Source: 150. OG: 1048-50. Malt: Pilsner malt, Munich malt, Crystal malt. Hops: Northern Brewer. Late hops: Perle, Hallertau Mittelfrüh, Tettnang. Source: CB.

### .   *Dortmunder Actien-Brauerei (DAB), Dortmund*

**Dortmunder Original**: OG: 1051-53. Malt: Pilsner malt, Munich malt, Crystal malt. Hops: Northern Brewer. Source: BC.

### .   *Dortmunder Union Brauerei (DUB), Dortmund*

**Siegel Pils**: OG: 1046. Malt: Pale malt. Hops: Hallertau. IBU: 30. Source: EBA.

**Hansa Export**: OG: 1053. Malt: Lager malt. Hops: Saaz. Source: DL.

### .   *Eichbaum Brauereien, Mannheim*

**Ureich Pils**: OG: 1045. Malt: Pale malt. Hops: Hallertau, Tettnang. Source: EBA.

### .   *Einbecker Brauhaus, Einbeck*

**Ür-Bock Dunkel**: OG: 1069-71. Malt: Pilsner malt, Munich malt, CaraMunich malt, Biscuit malt. Hops: Northern Brewer. Late hops: Perle, Hersbrücker. Source: BC.

### .   *Privatbrauerei Erdinger Weissbräu, Erding*

**Erdinger Hefe-Weissbier**: OG: 1051. Malt: Brauweizen Wheat malt, Pale malt. Hops: Hallertau. IBU: 18. EBC: 9. Source: EBA/GW.

**Kristallklar**: OG: 1051. Malt: Brauweizen Wheat malt, Pale malt. Hops: Hallertau. Source: EBA.

**Erdinger Pinkantus Weizenbock**: OG: 1071. Malt: Brauweizen Wheat malt, Pale malt. Hops: Hallertau. Source: EBA.

### . Hacker-Pschorr Bräu, Munich

**Münchener Hell**: OG: 1045. Malt: Pilsner malt. Hops: 28.6% Hallertau, 71.4% Tettnang. IBU: 20. EBC: 4. Source: EBA/GW.

**Pschorr-Bräu Weisse**: OG: 1051. Malt: Pale malt, Wheat malt. Hops: Hallertau. IBU: 17. Source: EBA.

**Edelhell Export**: OG: 1051. Malt: Pilsner malt. Hops: 27% Hallertau, 73% Tettnang. IBU: 24. EBC: 4. Source: EBA/GW.

**Oktoberfest Amber Märzen**: OG: 1055. Malt: Pale malt. Hops: 42% Hallertau, 58% Tettnang. IBU: 20. EBC: 25. Source: EBA/GW. OG: 1059-61. Malt: Pilsner malt, Munich malt, CaraMunich malt, Biscuit malt, Aromatic malt. Hops: Tettnang, Hersbrücker. Source: BC.

**Dunkel Weizen**: OG: 1055-56. Malt: Pilsner malt, Wheat malt, Munich malt, CaraMunich malt, Chocolate malt. Hops: Tettnang. Source: BC.

### . Heller, Bamburg

**Aecht Schlenkerla Rauchbier Märzen**: OG: 1057-58. Malt: Pilsner malt, CaraMunich malt, Munich malt, Rauchmalz, Chocolate malt. Hops: Tettnang. Late hops: Tettnang, Hersbrücker. Source: BC.

### . Brauerei Felsenkeller Herford, Herford

**Herforder Pils**: OG: 1046. Malt: Pilsner malt. Hops: 60% Hallertau Northern Brewer. Late hops: 40% Perle and Tettnang. IBU: 32. Source: EBA.

### . Historical beers

**Broyan**: OG: 1054. Malt: Pilsner malt, optional Wheat malt, optional Oats. Hops: None. Others: Optional Cloves, Cinnamon or Coriander seeds. Yeast: Kölsch/Lactobacillus. Notes: Recipe from 1850. IBU: 0. SRM: 3.5. Source: VB.

**Kotbusser**: OG: 1057. Malt: Pilsner malt, Pale wheat malt, Oats, Sugar, Honey. Hops: Spalt. Yeast: Kölsch/Lactobacillus. Notes: Recipe from 1850. IBU: 13. SRM: 5. Source: VB.

### . Hofbräuhaus, Munich

**Berchtesgadener Hell**: OG: 1052-54. Malt: Pilsner malt, Munich malt, Crystal malt, Aromatic malt. Hops: Spalt, Hersbrücker. Source: BC.

### Holsten Brauerei, Hamburg

**Holsten Pilsner Lager**: OG: 1046. Malt: Lager malt, Wheat malt, Crystal malt. Hops: Hallertau. Late hops: Goldings. Source: DL.

### Kaiserdom Privatbrauerei, Bamberg

**Kaiserdom Rauchbier**: OG: 1052-54. Malt: Pilsner malt, Smoked malt, CaraMunich malt. Hops: Tettnang, Hersbrücker. Late hops: Hersbrücker. Source: CB.

### Kulmbacher Brauerei, Kulmbach

**EKU Kulminator 28**: OG: 1121. Malt: Pilsner malt, Crystal malt. Hops: Northern Brewer. Late hops: Styrian Goldings, Hersbrücker. Source: BC.

### Kulmbacher Mönchshof, Kulmbach

**Mönchshof Schwarzbier**: OG: 1052-53. Malt: Pilsner malt, CaraMunich malt, Chocolate malt. Hops: Northern Brewer. Late hops: Hersbrücker. Source: BC.

### Friesiches Bräuhaus zu Jever, Jever

**Jever Pils**: OG: 1046. Malt: Pale malt. Hops: 26% Hallertau, 74% Tettnang. IBU: 44. EBC: 12. Source: EBA/GW.

### Schlossbrauerei Kaltenberg, Geltendorf

**Kaltenberg**: ABV: 4.9%. Malt: Pale malt. Hops: Hallertau. IBU: 28-30. Source: EBA.

**König Ludwig Dunkel**: OG: 1055. Malt: 97% Pale malt, 3% Chocolate malt. Hops: Hallertau. IBU: 25. EBC: 75. Source: EBA/GW.

**Prinzregent Luitpold Weissbier**: ABV: 5.6%. Malt: 50% Pale malt, 50% Wheat malt. Hops: Hallertau. IBU: 14-16. Source: EBA. Note: See **Kaltenberg Prinzregent Luitpold Weissbier**, Shepherd Neame, England.

### Krombacher Brauerei, Kreuztal-Krombach

**Krombacher Pils**: ABV: 4.8%. Malt: Pale malt. Hops: Hallertau, Tettnang. IBU: 24-26. Source: EBA.

### Kronen Brauerei, Dortmund

**Kronen Pils**: OG: 1045. Malt: Pale malt. Hops: Hallertau. IBU: 32. Source: EBA.

**Kronen Classic**: OG: 1046. Malt: Pale malt. Hops: Hallertau. IBU: 26. Source: EBA.

### Löwenbräu, Munich

**Hefe-Weissbier**: OG: 1049. Malt: Pale malt, more than 50% Wheat malt. Hops: Hallertau. IBU: 15. Source: EBA.

**Löwenbräu Special Export**: OG: 1051. Malt: Pale malt. Hops: Hallertau. IBU: 24. Source: EBA.

**Löwenbräu Premium Dark**: OG: 1051-53. Malt: Pilsner malt, CaraMunich malt, Munich malt, Chocolate malt. Hops: Tettnang, Northern Brewer. Source: BC.

**Löwenbräu Light Blonde Special**: OG: 1060. Malt: Lager malt, Crystal malt. Hops: Hallertau, Saaz. Late hops: Saaz. Dry hops: Saaz. Source: DL.

### . *Paulaner, Munich*

**Hefe-Weizen**: OG: 1053. Malt: Pilsner malt, Wheat malt. Hops: Hersbrücker. Source: 150. OG: 1053-54. Malt: Pale malt, Wheat malt, Munich malt. Hops: Hersbrücker. Source: CB.

**Salvator**: ABV: 7.5%. Malt: Lager malt, Caramalt, Munich malt. Hops: Hallertau. Source: HB. OG: 1079-81. Malt: Pilsner malt, Munich malt, CaraMunich malt, Aromatic malt. Hops: Northern Brewer, Hersbrücker. Source: BC. OG: 1075. Malt: Munich 20L malt. Hops: Hallertau. Yeast: Wyeast #2308. Notes: Recipe from 1890. IBU: 46. SRM: 22. Source: VB.

### . *Brauerei Pinkus Müller, Münster*

**Pinkus Homebrew Münster Alt**: OG: 1050-51. Malt: Lager malt, Wheat malt, Munich malt. Hops: Saaz. Late hops: Saaz. Source: CB.

**Pinkus Alt**: ABV: 5.1%. Malt: 60% Bioland Pilsner malt, 40% Wheat malt. Hops: Hallertau. Source: EBA.

**Pinkus Hefe Weizen**: ABV: 5.2%. Malt: 60% Bioland Wheat malt, 40% Gersten barley malt. Hops: Hallertau. Source: EBA.

**Pinkus Special**: ABV: 5.2%. Malt: Pilsner Bioland Gerstenbräu malt. Hops: Hallertau. Source: EBA.

### . *St. Pauli Brauerei, Bremen*

**St. Pauli Girl Dark**: OG: 1047-50. Malt: Lager malt, Munich malt, Crystal malt, Chocolate malt. Hops: Spalt. Late hops: Tettnang, Hersbrücker. Source: CB.

### . *Heinrich Reissdorf, Cologne*

**Reissdorf Kölsch**: OG: 1048-51. Malt: Pilsner malt, Wheat malt, Munich malt. Hops: Tettnang. Late hops: Spalt, Saaz. Source: BC.

### . *Privatbrauerei Georg Schneider & Sohn, Kelheim*

**Aventinus Wheat-Doppelbock**: OG: 1075-76. Malt: Pale malt, Wheat malt, Munich malt, Crystal malt, Chocolate malt, Melanoidin malt. Hops: Hersbrücker. Late hops: Hersbrücker. Source: CB.

### . *Spaten-Franziskaner, Munich*

**Franziskaner Hefe-Weisse**: OG: 1052-54. Malt: Wheat malt, Pilsner malt, Aromatic malt, Acid malt. Hops: Hersbrücker. Late hops: Spalt, Perle. Source: BC.

**Ür-Märzen Oktoberfestbier**: OG: 1061-62. Malt: Pilsner malt, Munich malt, Vienna malt, CaraMunich malt, Aromatic malt. Hops: Northern Brewer, Hersbrücker. Source: BC.

**Optimator**: OG: 1077-79. Malt: Pilsner malt, Munich malt, Aromatic malt, Chocolate malt, CaraMunich malt. Hops: Tettnang. Source: BC.

### . *Thurn & Taxis, Regensburg*

**Roggen Bier**: OG: 1049-51. Malt: Pilsner malt, CaraMunich malt, Crystal malt, Chocolate malt, Rye malt. Hops: Perle. Late hops: Saaz. Source: BC.

### . *Warsteiner Brauerei, Warstein*

**Warsteiner Premium**: OG: 1046. Malt: Pilsner malt, CaraPils malt. Hops: Magnum. Late hops: Tettnang, Hersbrücker. Source: 150. OG: 1048-50. Malt: Pilsner malt, Munich malt, Crystal malt. Hops: Tettnang. Late hops: Hersbrücker. Source: CB.

### . *Weihenstephan, Munich*

**Original**: ABV: 5.4%. Malt: Lager malt. Hops: Hallertau. Source: HB.

**Pils**: ABV: 5.4%. Malt: Lager malt. Hops: Hallertau. Source: HB.

**Hefeweissenbier Dunkel**: ABV: 5.3%. Malt: Wheat malt, Dark Wheat malt, Barley malt. Hops: Hallertau. Source: HB.

**Hefeweissenbier**: ABV: 5.4%. Malt: Wheat malt, Barley malt. Hops: Hallertau. Source: HB.

### . *Klosterschenke Weltenberg, Weltenberg*

**Asam Doppelbock**: ABV: 6.5%. Malt: Lager malt, Munich malt, Caramalt. Hops: Hallertau. Source: HB.

### . *Würtzburger Hofbräu, Würtzburg*

**Würtzburger Oktoberfest**: OG: 1058-59. Malt: Pilsner malt, Vienna malt, Munich malt, CaraMunich malt. Hops: Saaz, Tettnang. Source: BC.

# *Ghana*

### . *Guinness, Kumasi*

**Foreign Extra Stout**: Others: Guinness flavour extract. Source: BY.

# Greece

### . Athenian Brewery, Athens

**Marathon**: OG: 1052-54. Malt: Pilsner malt, Dextrin malt, Crystal malt, Maltodextrin. Hops: Hersbrücker. Late hops: Hersbrücker. Source: CB.

# Guatemala

### . Cerveceria Centro, Guatemala City

**Famosa Lager**: OG: 1040-41. Malt: Lager malt, Crystal malt. Hops: Tettnang. Late hops: Saaz. Source: CB.

# Iceland

### . Stedji, Brugghús Steðja. Www.stedji.com

**Hvalur**: ABV: 5.2%. Others: Milled whale bones. Source: Web.

**Hvalur 2**: ABV: 5.2%. Others: Fin whale testicles smoked using dried sheep excrement. Source: Web.

# Ireland

### . Beoir: www.beoir.org

### . Beamish & Crawford, Cork

**Beamish Stout**: OG: 1039. Malt: Pale malt, Stout malt, Roast barley, Wheat malt, Wheat syrup. Hops: Hallertau, Northdown, Perle. Late hops: Styrian Goldings. IBU: 38-44. Source: EBA. Malt: Pale malt, Wheat malt, Crystal malt, Chocolate malt, Patent black malt, Roast barley, Sugar. Hops: Challenger, Goldings. Late hops: Hersbrücker. Source: 150. OG: 1042-44. Malt: Pale malt, Roast barley, Flaked wheat, Patent black malt. Hops: Northdown. Late hops: Styrian Goldings. Source: BC.

### . Celtic Brew, Enfield

**Finian's Irish Stout**: ABV: 4.3%. Malt: Pale malt, Crystal malt, Roast malt, Stout malt. Hops: Northdown. Source: HB.

**Finian's Irish Red Ale**: ABV: 4.6%. Malt: Pale malt, Crystal malt, Roast malt. Hops: Hersbrücker, Northdown. Source: HB.

### . Arthur Guinness, Son & Company, Dublin

**Guinness Draught**: IBU: 42. Source: BY (see Notes).

**Guinness Extra / Original** (b-c): OG: 1038-40. Malt: 80% Pale malt, 10% Flaked barley, 10% Roast barley. Hops: Galena, Nugget, Target, Goldings or Bullion, Northern Brewer.

IBU: 44-5. Source: RP1/2/GW/EBA/DL/150. OG: 1042-45. Malt: Pale malt, Flaked barley, Roast barley, Crystal malt, optional Acid malt. Hops: Target, Goldings. Source: CB.

**Guinness Export Stout**: OG: 1048. Malt: 66% Pale malt, 25.5% Flaked barley, 8.5% Roast barley. Hops: Galena, Nugget, 40% Target. IBU: 49. EBC: 200. Source: EBA/GW.

**Guinness Foreign Extra Stout**: OG: 1078. Malt: Pale malt, Flaked barley, Roast barley. Hops: Challenger. Source: 150. IBU: 65. Source: BY (see Notes).

**Extra Stout**: OG: 1076. Malt: Pale malt, Amber malt, Black malt. Hops: Fuggles, Goldings. Yeast: Wyeast #1098/Wyeast #1099. Notes: Recipe from 1883. IBU: 94. SRM: 31. Source: VB.

Notes: Some information on the Guinness brewing process in given in *Guinness® - The 250-year quest for the perfect pint*[BY], but it is not always clear which product is being referred to. It would appear that Guinness may use roast malt, rather than roast barley, and chooses its hops based on high α-acid content rather than variety. The Guinness yeast ferments the wort very rapidly at the unusually high temperature of 25 °C and the beer is blended with a parallel brew that has been fermented and stored in a different way.

### . *Harp, Dundalk*

**Harp Lager**: OG: 1051-54. Malt: Lager malt, Crystal malt. Hops: Hersbrücker. Late hops: Hersbrücker, Saaz. Source: CB.

### . *Murphy, Cork. Www.murphys.com*

**Murphy's Irish Stout**: OG: 1038. Malt: Pale malt, Crystal malt, Chocolate malt, Roast barley, Sugar. Hops: Target. Late hops: Goldings. IBU: 34. EBC: 120. Source: 150. OG: 1040-43. Malt: Pale malt, Crystal malt, Chocolate malt, Roast barley, Sugar. Hops: Target. Late hops: Goldings. Source: CB.

**Murphy's Irish Red**: ABV: 5%. Malt: Pale malt, Chocolate malt. IBU: 23. EBC: 24. Source: Web.

### . *Porterhouse Brewing Co., Dublin. Www.porterhousebrewco.com*

**TSB (Turner's Sticklebract Bitter)**: ABV: 3.7%. Malt: Pale malt, Crystal malt, Wheat malt, Flaked barley, Vienna malt, Munich malt. Hops: Sticklebract. Source: Web.

**Chiller**: ABV: 4.2%. Malt: Lager malt. Hops: Galena, Nugget, Cascade, Tettnang. Source: Web.

**Temple Brau**: ABV: 4.3%. Malt: Lager malt, Caramalt. Hops: Galena, Nugget, Perle, Hersbrücker. Source: Web.

**Porterhouse Red**: ABV: 4.4%. Malt: Pale malt, Crystal malt, Wheat malt, Chocolate malt. Hops: Galena, Nugget, Goldings. Source: Web.

---

[BY] Bill Yenne, *Guinness® - The 250-year quest for the perfect pint*, Wiley, Hoboken (2007).

**Hersbrucker**: ABV: 5%. Malt: Lager malt, Caramalt. Hops: Galena, Nugget, Hersbrücker. Source: Web.

**Bohemia Freak Out**: ABV: 5%. Malt: Lager malt, Crystal malt, Roast malt, Chocolate malt. Hops: Saaz. Yeast: Pilsner Urquell. Source: Web.

**Plain Porter**: ABV: 5%. Malt: Pale malt, Crystal malt, Black malt, Flaked barley, Roast barley. Hops: Galena, Nugget, Goldings. Source: Web.

**Oyster Stout**: Malt: Pale malt, Black malt, Flaked barley, Roast barley. Hops: Galena, Nugget, Goldings. Others: Fresh oysters. Source: Web.

**Wrasslers XXXX**: ABV: 5%. Malt: Pale malt, Black malt, Flaked barley, Roast barley. Hops: Galena, Nugget, Goldings. Source: Web.

**Hop Head**: Malt: Pale malt, Black malt, Flaked barley, Roast barley. Hops: Galena, Nugget, Goldings. Source: Web.

**An Brain Blasta**: ABV: 7%. Malt: Pale malt, Black malt, Flaked barley, Roast barley. Hops: Galena, Nugget, Goldings. Source: Web.

### . *E. Smithwick & Son, Kilkenny*

**Smithwick's Draught**: ABV: 3.5%. Malt: Pale malt, Roast barley, Maltose syrup. Hops: Goldings, Challenger, Target, Northdown. Source: HB.

**Smithwick's Ale / Kilkenny Irish Beer**: ABV: 4% or 5%. Malt: Pale malt, Roast barley, Maltose syrup. Hops: Goldings, Challenger, Target, Northdown. Source: HB.

**Kilkenny Ale**: OG: 1052. Malt: 91% Pale malt, 9% Crystal malt. Hops: Fuggles, Goldings, Northdown, Northern Brewer. IBU: 33. EBC: 30. Source: EBA/GW.

# Israel

### . *Temp Beer Industries, Netanya*

**Maccabee Premium Beer**: OG: 1067-70. Malt: Lager malt, Dextrin malt, Crystal malt, Aromatic malt. Hops: Tettnang. Late hops: Tettnang. Source: CB.

# Italy

### . *Birra Forst, Lagundo*

**Forst Pils**: OG: 1047. Malt: Pale malt, Flaked maize. Hops: Hallertau. IBU: 28-32. Source: EBA.

### . *Birra Moretti, Udine*

**Birra Friulana**: ABV: 4.5%. Malt: Pale malt, 30% Flaked maize. Hops: Hallertau. IBU: 21. Source: EBA.

**La Rossa**: ABV: 7.5%. Malt: 10% Pale malt, 90% Dark malt. Hops: Hallertau, Spalt. IBU: 24. Source: EBA.

**Doppio Malto**: OG: 1080-83. Malt: Pilsner malt, Dextrin malt, Crystal malt, Chocolate malt, Munich malt. Hops: Styrian Goldings. Late hops: Styrian Goldings. Source: CB.

. *Birra Peroni Industriale, Rome*

**Peroni Birra**: OG: 1044. Malt: Lager malt, Crystal malt, Flaked rice. Hops: Saaz. Late hops: Saaz. Source: DL.

**Nastro Azzuro**: OG: 1050. Malt: Alexis and Prisma pale malt, 20% Flaked maize. Hops: Saaz. Source: EBA.

## India

. *Mohan Meakin, Ghaziabad*

**Golden Eagle Lager Beer**: OG: 1050-52. Malt: Rice, Lager malt, Crystal malt, Peat-smoked malt, Munich malt, Rice syrup. Others: Kosher salt. Hops: Tettnang. Late hops: Hersbrücker. Source: CB.

## Indonesia

. *PT Multi Bintang, Tangerang*

**Bintang Pilsner Lager**: OG: 1042-43. Malt: Lager malt, Crystal malt, Kosher salt. Hops: Saaz. Late hops: Saaz. Source: CB (which for some reason states that Tangerang is in China).

## Ivory Coast

. *Solibra Brewery, Abidjan*

**Mamba Malt Liquor**: OG: 1055-6. Malt: Lager malt, Flaked maize, Crystal malt, Aromatic malt. Hops: Saaz. Late hops: Saaz. Source: CB.

## Jamaica

. *Desnoes & Geddes, Kingston*

**Dragon Stout**: OG: 1073-75. Malt: Lager malt, Flaked maize, Crystal malt, Chocolate malt, Black malt, Roast barley, Sugar. Hops: Yakima Magnum. Source: CB.

**Guinness Foreign Extra Stout**: Others: Guinness flavour extract. Source: BY.

# Japan

### . Asahi, Tokyo

**Asahi Dry Draft Beer**: OG: 1040-41. Malt: Rice, Pale malt, Crystal malt, Rice syrup. Hops: Saaz. Late hops: Saaz. Source: CB.

### . Kirin, Tokyo

**Kirin Lager**: OG: 1045-46. Malt: Rice, Pale malt, Crystal malt, Rice syrup. Hops: Saaz, Hersbrücker. Late hops: Saaz, Hersbrücker. Source: CB.

### . Sapporo, Tokyo

**Sapporo Black Stout Draft**: OG: 1055-57. Malt: Pale malt, Crystal malt, Munich malt, Black malt. Hops: Northern Brewer. Late hops: Saaz. Source: CB.

# Kenya

### . Kenya Breweries, Nairobi

**Tusker Premium Lager**: OG: 1044. Malt: Pilsner malt, Crystal malt, Sugar. Hops: Hersbrücker. Late hops: Styrian Goldings. Source: BC.

### . Guinness, Mombasa / Nairobi

**Foreign Extra Stout**: Others: Guinness flavour extract. Source: BY.

# Lebanon

### . Brasserie et malterie Almaza, Beirut

**Almaza Pilsener Beer**: OG: 1040. Malt: Lager malt, Flaked maize, Crystal malt, Munich malt. Hops: Tettnang. Late hops: Saaz, Tettnang. Source: CB.

# Luxembourg

### . Diekirch

**Diekirch Lager**: OG: 1045. Malt: Lager malt, Crystal malt. Hops: Saaz. Late hops: Saaz. Source: DL.

### . Brasserie Reunies de Luxembourg Mousel et Clausen

**Mousel Premium Pils**: OG: 1047. Malt: 90% Pale malt, 10% Rice. Hops: 25% Hallertau, 75% Saaz. IBU: 28.5. EBC: 3. Source: EBA/GW.

## Malaysia

. *Guinness, Sungei Way New Village*

**Ginis Setaut / Foreign Extra Stout**: Others: Guinness flavour extract. Source: BY.

## Mexico

. *Cervecaria Cuauhtemoc, Monterrey*

**Bohemia Beer**: OG: 1054-57. Malt: Pilsner malt, Crystal malt. Hops: Spalt. Late hops: Tettnang. Source: CB.

**Noche Buena**: OG: 1060-61. Malt: Pale malt, Flaked rice, Flaked maize, Crystal malt, CaraMunich malt, Munich malt, Chocolate malt. Hops: Tettnang. Late hops: Tettnang. Source: BC.

. *Cerveceria Moctezuma, Veracruz*

**Dos Equis**: OG: 1049-50. Malt: Pilsner malt, Black malt, Crystal malt, Vienna malt. Hops: Tettnang. Late hops: Tettnang, Saaz. Source: CB.

. *Cerveceria Modelo, Mexico City*

**Negra Modelo**: OG: 1050-51. Malt: Pilsner malt, Crystal malt, Vienna malt, Chocolate malt. Hops: Hersbrücker, Tettnang. Late hops: Tettnang. Source: CB.

## Namibia

. *Hansa Breweries, Swakopmund*

**Tafel Pilsner Lager**: OG: 1045-8. Malt: Pilsner malt, Crystal malt, Aromatic malt. Hops: Tettnang. Late hops: Saaz. Source: CB.

. *Namibia Breweries, Windhoek*

**Windhoek Special**: OG: 1054-5. Malt: Pilsner malt, Crystal malt. Hops: Hersbrücker. Late hops: Saaz, Hersbrücker. Source: CB.

## Netherlands

. *Alfa Bierbrowerij, Schinnen*

**Alfa Beer**: OG: 1048. Malt: Pale malt, Munich malt. Hops: Hallertau, Saaz, Tettnang. IBU: 19. Source: EBA.

. *De Arcense Bierbrouwerij, Arcen*

**Arcener Stoom Bier**: ABV: 5%. Malt: Pale malt, Wheat malt. Hops: Hallertau Northern Brewer. Late hops: Hersbrücker Spät. IBU: 22. Source: EBA.

**Arcener Tarwe**: ABV: 5%. Malt: 50% Pale malt, 50% Wheat malt. Hops: Hallertau Northern Brewer, Hersbrücker Spät. IBU: 17. Source: EBA.

**Arcener Stout**: ABV: 6.5%. Malt: 72% Pale, 22% Light Munich malt, 6% Chocolate malt, Coloured malts. Hops: Hallertau Northern Brewer, Hersbrücker Spät. IBU: 27. Source: EBA/GW.

### . Koninklijke Brand Bierbrouwerij, Wijlre

**Brand Pils**: OG: 1048. Malt: 90% Pale malt, 10% Flaked maize. Hops: 50% Hallertau Northern Brewer, 50% Perle. Late hops: Hersbrücker. IBU: 26-28. EBC: 7. Source: EBA/GW.

**Brand Up**: OG: 1050. Malt: 100% Pale malt. Hops: Hersbrücker, Spalt, 43% Tettnang. IBU: 36-38. EBC: 9. Source: EBA/GW.

### . Grolsch Bierbrouwerij, Groenlo / Enschede

**Grolsch Premium Lager**: OG: 1048. Malt: Pilsner malt, small % Flaked maize. Hops: 54.5% Saaz, 45.5% Hallertau. IBU: 27. EBC: 3. Source: EBA/GW. Malt: Lager malt, Crystal malt. Hops: Hallertau. Source: DL. OG: 1055-57. Malt: Pilsner malt, Crystal malt, Munich malt. Hops: Northern Brewer. Late hops: Hersbrücker, Saaz. Source: CB.

### . Gulpener Bierbrouwerij, Gulpen

**Mestreechs Aajt**: OG: 1034. Malt: Pale malt, Sugar. Hops: Hallertau. IBU: 10. Source: EBA.

**Gulpener Dort**: OG: 1065. Malt: Pale malt, Flaked maize. Hops: Hallertau. IBU: 20. Source: EBA.

### . Heineken Brouwerijen, Zoerterwoude / 's-Hertogenbosch / Wijlre

**Heineken**: OG: 1045. Malt: Pilsner malt, Acid malt, CaraPils malt, Corn grits. Hops: Magnum. Late hops: Saaz. Source: 150. OG: 1051-54. Malt: Pilsner malt, Crystal malt. Hops: Northern Brewer, Hersbrücker. Late hops: Hersbrücker. Source: CB.

### . Jopen, Haarlem

**Grätzer**: OG: 1032. Malt: 100% Smoked wheat malt, optional rice hulls. Hops: Lublin, Fuggles. Yeast: White Labs WLP029. Notes: This a recreation of a historical beer style brewed in Poland and Germany. IBU: 20-40. SRM: 3. Source: VB.

**Grodziskie**: Same recipe as **Grätzer** with the addition of Willow bark. Source: VB.

### . Brouwhuis Maximiliaan, Amsterdam

**Bethaniën**: ABV: 4.5%. Malt: 100% Pale malt. Hops: Saaz, Perle. Source: HB.

**Meibock**: ABV: 6.5%. Malt: Pale malt, Caramalt. Hops: Saaz. Source: HB.

**Maximator Wheatbock**: ABV: 6.5%. Malt: Wheat malt, Barley malt. Hops: Saaz. Source: HB.

**Caspers Max Tripel**: ABV: 7.5%. Malt: Pale malt, Amber malt. Hops: Saaz. Source: HB.

. *Brouwerij Museum Raaf, Heumen*

**Witbier**: ABV: 5%. Malt: Pilsner malt, Wheat malt. Hops: Hersbrücker, Perle. Source: EBA.

**Tripel**: ABV: 8.5%. Malt: Pilsner malt. Hops: Hersbrücker, Perle. Source: EBA.

. *Trappist Brewery de Schaapskooi, Tilburg*

**La Trappe Enkel**: ABV: 5.5%. Malt: Pale malt, Munich malt. Hops: Hallertau, Northern Brewer. Source: HB.

**La Trappe Dubbel**: ABV: 6.5%. Malt: Pale malt, Munich malt, Coloured malts. Hops: Hallertau, Northern Brewer. Source: HB.

**La Trappe Tripel**: ABV: 8%. Malt: Pale malt, Munich malt. Hops: Goldings. Source: HB.

**La Trappe Quadrupel**: OG: 1096-1110. Malt: Pilsner malt, Pale malt, Crystal malt, Biscuit malt, Aromatic malt, Candi sugar. Hops: Brewers Gold. Late hops: Styrian Goldings. Others: Curaçao Bitter orange peel, Coriander seeds. Source: CB. ABV: 10%. Malt: Pale malt, Munich malt. Hops: Hallertau, Northern Brewer. Source: HB.

# New Zealand

. *New Zealand Breweries, Auckland. Www.steinlager.com*

**Steinlager**: OG: 1048-51. Malt: Pilsner malt, Crystal malt. Hops: Sticklebract. Late hops: Tettnang, Styrian Goldings. Source: CB. Hops: Green Bullet. Source: Web.

# Nigeria

. *Guinness, Lagos / Ogba*

**Foreign Extra Stout**: Others: 2-8% Guinness flavour extract. Source: BY.

. *Nigerian Breweries, Igamnu, Aba, Kaduna, Ibadan and Ama*

**Gulda Export Premium**: OG: 1049-51. Malt: Lager malt, Flaked maize, Crystal malt, Vienna malt. Hops: Saaz. Late hops: Saaz. Source: CB.

# Northern Ireland

. *Hilden, Lisburn*

**Hilden Ale**: OG: 1038-40. Malt: Pale malt, Crystal malt. Hops: Goldings, Hallertau. Source: RP1/2/3/4/5.

**Special Reserve**: OG: 1040-4. Malt: Pale malt, Crystal malt, Black malt. Hops: Goldings, Hallertau. Source: RP1/2/4.

**Hilden Original Ale** (b-c): ABV: 4.6%. Malt: Halcyon pale malt, Crystal malt, Chocolate malt, Black malt. Hops: First Gold, Northdown, optional Hersbrücker, Goldings. Source: JE2/3/5/6.

**Molly Malone / Molly Malone Single X** (b-c): ABV: 4.6%. Malt: Halcyon pale malt, Chocolate malt, Black malt. Hops: Goldings, Nothdown, Hallertau. Source: JE3/5/6.

.   *Strangford Lough, Killyleagh*

**St. Patrick's Best** (b-c): ABV: 3.8%. Malt: Pale malt, Crystal malt, Black malt. Hops: First Gold, Goldings. Source: JE6.

**Barelegs Brew** (b-c): ABV: 4.5%. Malt: Pale malt, Lager malt, Caramalt, Flaked maize. Hops: First Gold, Northern Brewer, Perle. Source: JE5/6.

**Legbiter** (b-c): ABV: 4.8%. Malt: Lager malt, Caramalt, Flaked maize. Hops: Goldings, Northern Brewer, First Gold, Styrian Goldings. Source: JE5/6.

**St. Patrick's Gold** (b-c): ABV: 4.8%. Malt: Pale malt, Lager malt, Wheat malt. Hops: Cascade. Others: Orange peel, Lemon peel. Source: JE6.

**St. Patrick's Ale** (b-c): ABV: 6%. Malt: Pale malt, Crystal malt, Black malt. Hops: Progress, Challenger. Source: JE6.

.   *Whitewater Brewing Company, Kilkeel*

**Mountain Ale**: OG: 1043. Malt: 93% Pale malt, 7% Crystal malt. Hops: Fuggles, Phoenix. IBU: 29. Source: RP5.

**Eireann Stout**: OG: 1044. Malt: 70% Pale malt, 9% Crystal malt, 2% Black malt, 10% Roast barley. Hops: Fuggles, Galena. IBU: 37. Source: RP5.

**Bee's Endeavour**: OG: 1048. Malt: 100% Pale malt, Honey. Hops: Phoenix. Others: Root ginger. IBU: 33. Source: RP5.

# Panama

.   *Cervecerias Del Barú, David*

**Cerveza Panama Lager Alemania style**: OG: 1048-49. Malt: Lager malt, Flaked maize, Crystal malt, Sugar. Hops: Tettnang. Late hops: Saaz. Source: CB.

# Peru

.   *Compania Cerveceria del Sur del Peru, Cuzco*

**Cuzco Dark Premium**: OG: 1065-66. Malt: Pale malt, Dextrin malt, Crystal malt, Chocolate malt. Hops: Willamette. Others: Chocolate powder. Source: CB.

# Poland

### . Cobra Beer, Kielce

**King Cobra** (b-c): ABV: 8%. Malt: Maize, Rice. Hops: German. Source: JE6. Notes: This beer is brewed by Browar Belgia, bottled and dosed with yeast in Belgium before shipping to the UK.

### . Elbrewery, Elbag

**Hevelius Kaper**: OG: 1091-92. Malt: Pilsner malt, Flaked maize, CaraMunich malt, Munich malt, Crystal malt. Hops: Lublin. Late hops: Lublin. Source: BC.

### . Okocim Brewery, Okocim

**Malt Liquor**: OG: 1075. Malt: Pilsner malt, Pale malt, Flaked maize, Aromatic malt, Crystal malt. Hops: Lublin. Late hops: Styrian Goldings, Lublin. Source: BC.

**Okocim Porter**: OG: 1087-91. Malt: Pilsner malt, Dextrin malt, Crystal malt, Black malt, Chocolate malt, Munich malt. Hops: Polishner Lublin. Late hops: Polishner Lublin. Source: CB.

### . Żywiec Brewery, Żywiec

**Żywiec Tatra / Żywiec Beer**: OG: 1052. Malt: Lager malt, Wheat malt, Sugar. Hops: Saaz. Late hops: Saaz. Source: DL. Malt: Pilsner malt, Crystal malt, Munich malt. Hops: Polishner Lublin. Late hops: Hersbrücker. Source: CB.

**Porter**: OG: 1096-97. Malt: Pilsner malt, CaraMunich malt, Dark crystal malt, Chocolate malt, Patent black malt. Hops: Lublin. Source: BC.

# Portugal

### . Unicer Uniao cervejeria, Leca do Balio

**Unicer Super Bock**: OG: 1052-54. Malt: Pilsner malt, Dextrin malt, Crystal malt, Munich malt. Hops: Hallertau Northern Brewer. Late hops: Spalt, Tettnang. Source: CB.

# Puerto Rico

### . Medalla, San Juan

**Medalla Light Cerveza**: OG: 1039-40. Malt: Rice, Pale malt, Flaked maize, Crystal malt, Sugar. Hops: Hersbrücker. Source: CB.

# Russia

### . Baltika, Chelyabinsk

**Urals Master Lager**: ABV: 4%. Malt: Pale malt. Source: eng.baltika.ru

**Chelyabinkoye Zhivoye**: ABV: 4.4%. Malt: Pale malt. Source: eng.baltika.ru

**Chelyabinkoye Lager**: ABV: 4.5%. Malt: Pale malt. Source: eng.baltika.ru

**Urals Master Classic**: ABV: 5.1%. Malt: Rice. Source: eng.baltika.ru

**Urals Master Extra**: ABV: 8%. Malt: Rice. Source: eng.baltika.ru

. *Baltika, Khabarovsk*

**DV Lager**: ABV: 4%. Malt: Pale malt, Caramel malt, Barley. Source: eng.baltika.ru

**DV Zhivoye**: ABV: 4.4%. Malt: Pale malt, Caramel malt, Barley. Source: eng.baltika.ru

**DV Classic**: ABV: 5.1%. Malt: Pale malt, Caramel malt, Barley. Source: eng.baltika.ru

**DV Extra**: ABV: 7%. Malt: Pale malt, Barley, Maltose syrup. Source: eng.baltika.ru

. *Baltika, Novosibirsk*

**Sibirskiy Bochonok Classic**: ABV: 5.1%. Malt: Pale malt, Rice. Source: eng.baltika.ru

**Bolshaya Kruzhka Extra**: ABV: 7%. Malt: Pale malt, Barley, Maltose syrup. Source: eng.baltika.ru

**Sibirskiy Bochonok Extra**: ABV: 8%. Malt: Pale malt, Rice. Source: eng.baltika.ru

. *Baltika, Pikra*

**Kupecheskoye Zhivoye**: ABV: 4%. Malt: Pale malt, Rice, Barley. Source: eng.baltika.ru

**Kupecheskoye Classic**: ABV: 4.5%. Malt: Pale malt, Barley. Source: eng.baltika.ru

**Kupecheskoye Extra**: ABV: 8%. Malt: Pale malt, Barley. Source: eng.baltika.ru

. *Baltika, Rostov*

**Don Zhivoye**: ABV: 4%. Malt: Pale malt, Rice, Barley, Maltose syrup. Source: eng.baltika.ru

**Don Lager**: ABV: 4.4%. Malt: Pale malt, Barley, Maltose syrup. Source: eng.baltika.ru

**Don Classic**: ABV: 4.5%. Malt: Pale malt, Barley, Maltose syrup. Source: eng.baltika.ru

**Don Southern**: ABV: 6%. Malt: Pale malt, Barley, Maltose syrup. Source: eng.baltika.ru

. *Baltika, St. Petersburg*

**Zhigulevskoye**: ABV: 4%. Malt: Pale malt, Barley. Source: eng.baltika.ru

**No.1 Light (Legkoye)**: ABV: 4.4%. Malt: Pale malt, Maltose syrup. Source: eng.baltika.ru

**Nevskoe Lager**: ABV: 4.6%. Malt: Pale malt. Source: eng.baltika.ru

**Cooler**: ABV: 4.7%. Malt: Pale malt, Caramel malt, Flaked maize, Maltose syrup. Source: eng.baltika.ru

**No.2 Pale**: ABV: 4.7%. Malt: Pale malt, Rice. Source: eng.baltika.ru

**Nevskoe Ice**: ABV: 4.7%. Malt: Pale malt. Source: eng.baltika.ru

**No.3 Classic**: ABV: 4.8%. Malt: Pale malt. Source: eng.baltika.ru

**Nevskoe Classic**: ABV: 5%. Malt: Pale malt. Source: eng.baltika.ru

**No.8 Wheat**: ABV: 5%. Malt: Pale malt, Caramel malt, Wheat malt syrup. Source: eng.baltika.ru

**No.5 Gold**: ABV: 5.3%. Malt: Pale malt, Caramel malt, Maltose syrup. Source: eng.baltika.ru

**No.7 Export**: ABV: 5.4%. Malt: Pale malt. Source: eng.baltika.ru

**No.4 Original**: ABV: 5.6%. Malt: Pale malt, Caramel malt, Rye malt, Maltose syrup. Source: eng.baltika.ru

**Nevskoe Original**: ABV: 5.7%. Malt: Pale malt. Source: eng.baltika.ru

**No.6 Porter**: OG: 1072-73. Malt: Pilsner malt, CaraMunich malt, Crystal malt, Chocolate malt, Patent black malt. Hops: Northern Brewer. Late hops: Hersbrücker. Source: BC. ABV: 7%. Malt: Pale malt, Caramel malt, Roast malt, Maltose syrup. Source: eng.baltika.ru

**Nine Extra**: ABV: 8%. Malt: Maltose syrup. Source: eng.baltika.ru

### *. Baltika, Samara*

**Samara Light**: ABV: 4%. Malt: Pale malt, Barley, Maltose syrup. Source: eng.baltika.ru

**Samara Zhivoye**: ABV: 4%. Malt: Pale malt, Rice, Barley, Maltose syrup. Source: eng.baltika.ru

**Samara Classic**: ABV: 5%. Malt: Pale malt, Rice, Barley, Maltose syrup. Source: eng.baltika.ru

**Samara Extra**: ABV: 6.5%. Malt: Pale malt, Rice, Barley, Maltose syrup. Source: eng.baltika.ru

### *. Baltika, Tula*

**Arsenalnoe Zhivoye**: ABV: 4%. Malt: Pale malt, Maltose syrup. Source: eng.baltika.ru

**Arsenalnoe Classic**: ABV: 4.5%. Malt: Pale malt, Maltose syrup. Source: eng.baltika.ru

**Arsenalnoe Traditional**: ABV: 5.1%. Malt: Pale malt, Caramel malt, Maltose syrup. Source: eng.baltika.ru

**Arsenalnoe Extra**: ABV: 7%. Malt: Pale malt, Maltose syrup. Source: eng.baltika.ru

**Arsenalnoe Extra Strong**: ABV: 8.2%. Malt: Pale malt, Maltose syrup. Source: eng.baltika.ru

. *Baltika, Yaroslavl*

**Yarpivo Lager**: ABV: 4.2%. Malt: Pale malt. Source: eng.baltika.ru

**Yarpivo Original**: ABV: 4.7%. Malt: Pale malt. Source: eng.baltika.ru

**Yarpivo Ledyanoe**: ABV: 4.9%. Malt: Pale malt, Rice. Source: eng.baltika.ru

**Volga Yantarnoye Special**: ABV: 5%. Malt: Pale malt. Others: Natural "tonic" flavour. Source: eng.baltika.ru

**Yarpivo Yantarnoye**: ABV: 5.3%. Malt: Pale malt, Rice. Source: eng.baltika.ru

**Yarpivo Extra**: ABV: 7.2%. Malt: Pale malt, Rice. Source: eng.baltika.ru

Notes: Baltika brew a wide range of beers at their various breweries in Russia. Many of the brands are brewed in more than one location. I have attempted to capture the main brands associated with the main locations above.

. *Kiev Obolon Brewery, Kiev*

**Zhiguli**: OG: 1044. Malt: Pale malt, Brewing sugar, less than 5% Rice. Hops: Klon. IBU: 17. Source: EBA.

# *Scotland*

. *Scottish Craft Brewers: www.scottishcraftbrewers.org*

. *Craft Brewing Association: www.craftbrewing.org.uk*

. *Aberdeenshire Ales, Ellon*

**Buchan Gold**: ABV: 4%. Malt: Pale malt, Crystal malt. Hops: Mount Hood, Styrian Goldings, Yeoman. Source: RP4.

. *Arran Brewery, Brodick, Isle of Arran*

**Fireside**: ABV: 4.7%. Hops: Cascade, Challenger, Mount Hood, Hersbrücker. Source: W.

. *Atlas, Kinlochleven*
  *www.scottishbrewing.com/breweries/orkneyandshetland/atlas-range.php*

**Latitude**: ABV: 3.6%. Malt: Maris Otter pale malt, Lager malt. Hops: Styrian Goldings. Source: Web.

**3 Sisters**: ABV: 4.2%. Malt: Chocolate malt. Source: Web.

**Wayfarer**: ABV: 4.4%. Malt: small additions of Caramalt, Wheat malt, Crystal malt. Hops: Bramling Cross. Source: Web.

**Nimbus**: ABV: 5%. Malt: 5% Wheat malt. Source: Web.

Notes: Atlas Brewery closed in 2010 but some of its beers are now brewed by the Orkney Brewery.

### . *Bass, Glasgow*

**Tennent Lager** (bottled): OG: 1037. Malt: Lager malt, Flaked maize, Honey. Hops: Hallertau, Goldings. Source: DL.

### . *Belhaven Brewing Company, Dunbar*

**60/-**: OG: 1030.5. Malt: 89% Golden Promise or Pipkin pale malt, 2 - 4% Black malt, 0 – 2% Crystal malt, 7% Liquid sugar. Hops: WGV / Bramling Cross. Late hops: Fuggles, Goldings. IBU: 21. EBC: 43. Source: RP/MO/GW.

**70/-**: OG: 1035.5. Malt: 89% Golden Promise pale malt, 1% Black malt, 1.5% Crystal malt, 8.5% Liquid sugar. Hops: Fuggles, Goldings, British Columbian Bramling Cross. IBU: 23. Source: RP1/2. Malt: 92% Pipkin pale malt, 1% Black malt, 2% Crystal malt, 5% Liquid sugar. Hops: WGV. Late hops: Fuggles, Goldings. IBU: 23. EBC: 23. Source: RP3/4/5/MO.

**Sandy Hunter's Traditional Ale**: OG: 1038. Malt: 92% Pipkin pale malt, 1% Black malt, 2% Crystal malt, 5% Liquid sugar. Hops: WGV. Late hops: Fuggles, Goldings. IBU: 25. EBC: 25. Source: RP4/5/MO.

**Festival Gold**: OG: 1039. Malt: 100% Chariot pale malt. Hops: British Columbian Bramling Cross, Challenger. Late hops: Styrian Goldings. IBU: 24. EBC: 10. Source: RP4/5.

**Belhaven Scottish Ale**: OG: 1041. Malt: Pale malt, Black malt, Crystal malt, Brewing sugar. Hops: British Columbian Bramling Cross, Fuggles, Goldings, WGV. IBU: 28. Source: EBA.

**80/-**: OG: 1041.5. Malt: 86% Pipkin or Golden Promise pale malt, 2.5% Black malt, 2.5% Crystal malt, 10% Liquid sugar. Hops: Fuggles, Goldings, British Columbian Bramling Cross or WGV. Late hops: Fuggles, Goldings. IBU: 29. EBC: 33. Source: RP/MO.

**Belhaven Export Ale**: OG: 1044. Malt: 79% Pale malt, 1% Black malt, 15% Crystal malt, 5% Sucrose. Hops: British Columbian Bramling Cross, Fuggles, Goldings, WGV. IBU: 28. EBC: 60. Source: EBA/GW.

**St. Andrew's Ale**: OG: 1046. Malt: 86% Pipkin pale malt, 1.5% Black malt, 2.5% Crystal malt, 10% Liquid sugar. Hops: WGV. Late hops: Fuggles, Goldings. Dry hops: Fuggles, Goldings. IBU: 36. EBC: 35. Source: RP3/4/5/MO/HB.

**90/-**: OG: 1070. Malt: 84% Pipkin or Golden Promise pale malt, 4% Black malt, 12% Liquid sugar. Hops: Fuggles, Goldings, British Columbian Bramling Cross or WGV. Late hops: Fuggles, Goldings. IBU: 34. EBC: 75. Source: RP/MO.

**XXX**: OG: 1070. Malt: Pale malt. Hops: Goldings. Dry hops: Yes.. Notes: Recipe from 1871. Source: DP.

**Belhaven Scottish Ale**: OG: 1074-77. Malt: Golden Promise pale malt, Crystal malt, Toasted pale malt, Peat-smoked malt, Treacle, Sugar. Hops: Goldings. Late hops: Goldings. Source: CB.

**Wee Heavy**: OG: 1075-76. Malt: Pale malt, Crystal malt, Biscuit malt, Aromatic malt, Peat-smoked malt, Patent black malt, Roast barley, Invert sugar. Hops: WGV. Late hops: Fuggles, Goldings. Source: BC.

## William Black & Company, Aberdeen

**X**: OG: 1075. Malt: Pale malt. Hops: Goldings. Dry hops: Yes. Notes: Recipe from 1849. Source: DP.

**Brown Stout**: OG: 1077. Malt: Pale malt, Amber malt, Brown malt, Black malt. Hops: Fuggles. Dry hops: Yes. Notes: Recipe from 1835. Source: DP.

**Best Ale**: OG: 1110. Malt: Pale malt. Hops: Goldings. Dry hops: Goldings. Notes: Recipe from 1835. Source: DP.

## Black Isle, Munlochy

**Organic Blonde** (b-c): ABV: 4.5%. Malt: Pale malt, Wheat malt. Hops: Hersbrücker. Source: JE4. Challenger, Hallertau. Source: JE5.

**Organic Porter** (b-c): ABV: 4.5%. Malt: Pale malt, Crystal malt, Chocolate malt, Wheat malt, Flaked oats. Hops: Hallertau, Goldings. Source: JE4. Malt: Pale malt, Crystal malt, Pale chocolate malt, Oat malt, Wheat malt. Hops: Challenger, Goldings, optional Styrian Goldings. Source: JE5/6.

**Organic Scotch Ale** (b-c): ABV: 4.5%. Malt: Pale malt, Crystal malt, Peat-smoked malt, Wheat malt. Hops: Hallertau, Styrian Goldings. Others: Sweet Gale (Bog Myrtle). Source: JE4. Hops: Challenger, Goldings. Others: Sweet Gale (Bog Myrtle). Source: JE5/6.

**Organic Wheat Beer** (b-c): ABV: 4.5%. Malt: Pale malt, Wheat malt. Hops: Hersbrücker. Others: Coriander, Orange peel. Source: JE4. Hops: Hallertau, optional Challenger. Others: Coriander, Orange peel, Lemon peel. Source: JE5/6.

## Borve Brew House, Ruthven

**Borve Ale**: OG: 1040. Malt: 97% Pale malt, 1.5% Crystal malt, 0.5% Chocolate malt, 1% Roast barley. Hops: Goldings or Target, Omega. Late hops: Optional Omega. IBU: 26. Source: RP/MO.

**Borve Ale** (b-c): ABV: 4%. Malt: Pale malt, Crystal malt, Chocolate malt, Roast barley. Hops: Target. Source: JE1/2/3/4.

**Aberdeen Union Street 200**: OG: 1050. Malt: 94% Pale malt, 2% Crystal malt, 4% Roast barley. Hops: Target. Late hops: Hersbrücker. IBU: 20. Source: RP4/5/MO.

**Tall Ships India Pale Ale**: OG: 1050. Malt: 99% Pale malt, 0.75% Crystal malt, 0.25% Chocolate malt. Hops: Omega or Target. Late hops: Hersbrücker. IBU: 20. Source: RP/MO.

**Tall Ships** (b-c): ABV: 5%. Malt: Pale malt, Crystal malt, Chocolate malt. Hops: Target, Hersbrücker. Source: JE1/2/3/4.

**Elphinstone Ale**: OG: 1053, Malt: 97% Blenheim pale malt, 1% Crystal malt, 2% Roast barley. Hops: Omega. Late hops: Hallertau. IBU: 20. Source: RP2.

**Borve Extra Strong Ale**: OG: 1085. Malt: 92% Pale malt, 8% Crystal malt, 0.5% Chocolate malt. Hops: Goldings. Source: RP1.

**Grampian Extra Strong**: OG: 1085. Malt: 90% Blenheim pale malt, 10% Crystal malt. Hops:. Omega. Late hops: Hersbrücker. Dry hops: Yes. IBU: More than 30. Source: RP1/2.

**Borve Ale Extra Strong** (b-c): ABV: 10%. Malt: Pale malt, Crystal malt. Hops: Target, Hersbrücker. Source: JE1/2/3/4.

. *Brewdog, Ellon. www.brewdog.com*

**Dead Pony Club**: ABV: 3.8%. Malt: Caramalt, Crystal malt. Hops: Simcoe, Citra, Mosaic. Source: Web.

**5 a.m. Saint**: OG: 1048. Malt: Maris Otter pale malt, Caramalt, Munich malt, Crystal malt, Dark crystal malt. Hops: Nelson Sauvin, Amarillo. Dry hops: Simcoe, Centennial, Ahtanum, Nelson Sauvin, Cascade. IBU: 25. Source: Web.

**Punk IPA**: OG: 1053. Malt: Low colour Maris Otter pale malt. Hops: Chinook, Simcoe, Nelson Sauvin, Ahtanum. IBU: 45. Source: BA/Web. OG: 1060. Malt: Maris Otter pale malt. Hops: Columbus. Late hops: Ahtanum. Dry hops: Amarillo. Yeast: White Labs WLP007. IBU: 62. SRM: 8. Source: BYO.

**Libertine Black Ale**: OG: 1069. Malt: Maris Otter pale malt, Caramalt, Carafa® malt, Munich malt, Dark crystal malt. Hops: Simcoe. IBU: 65. Source: Web.

**Dogma**: OG: 1082. Malt: Munich malt, Crystal malt, Chocolate malt, Dark chocolate malt, Brown malt, Heather honey. Hops: First Gold, Saaz. Source: Web.

**Hardcore IPA**: OG: 1083. Malt: Maris Otter pale malt, Caramalt, Crystal malt. Hops: Simcoe, Centennial, Columbus. Dry hops: Centennial, Columbus, Simcoe. IBU: 150. Source: Web. OG: 1084. Malt: Maris Otter pale malt. Hops: Simcoe, Warrior. Late hops: Chinook. Dry hops: Amarillo. Yeast: Wyeast #1056/White Labs WLP001/Safale US-05. SRM: 11. Source: BYO.

**AB:01**: ABV: 10.2%. Others: Vanilla beans. Source: Web.

**AB:03**: ABV: 10.5%. Others: Raspberries, Strawberries. Source: Web.

**AB:05**: ABV: 12.5%. Others: Toasted coconut, Cacao. Source: Web.

**AB:11**: ABV: 12.8%. Others: Ginger, Black raspberries, Chipotle chillies. Source: Web.

**Tokyo**: OG: 1142. Malt: Maris Otter pale malt, Caramalt, Roast barley, Chocolate malt, Dark crystal malt. Hops: Galena. Dry hops: Galena. Others: Jasmine flowers, Cranberries, Oak chips. IBU: 90. Source: Web.

**AB:04**: ABV: 15%. Others: Coffee, Cacao, Chillies. Source: Web.

### . Bridge of Allan Brewery, Bridge of Allan

**Brig O'Allan** (b-c): ABV: 4.1%. Malt: Maris Otter pale malt, Crystal malt, Chocolate malt, Wheat malt. Hops: Goldings, Hallertau. Source: JE3/4/5/6.

**Sporran Warmer** (b-c): ABV: 4.8%. Malt: Maris Otter pale malt, Crystal malt, Chocolate malt, Torrefied wheat. Hops: Goldings, Sterling. Source: JE6.

**Organic Blonde** (b-c): ABV: 5%. Malt: Pale malt, Crystal malt, Wheat malt. Hops: Hallertau. Source: JE6.

**Beerjolais Neuveau** (b-c): ABV: 5%. Malt: Maris Otter pale malt, Crystal malt, Caramalt, Torrefied wheat. Hops: Saaz. Source: JE6.

**Scottish Bramble Ale** (b-c): ABV: 5%. Malt: Maris Otter pale malt, Crystal malt, Amber malt, Chocolate malt, Wheat malt. Hops: First Gold. Others: Blackberries. Source: JE6.

### . Broughton Ales, Biggar

**IPA**: OG: 1036. Malt: Maris Otter pale malt, Crystal malt. Hops: Willamette. IBU: 35. EBC: 15. Source: RP5.

**Greenmantle Ale**: OG: 1038. Malt: Maris Otter pale malt, small % Roast barley, optional Flaked maize. Hops: Fuggles, Goldings or Target. Dry hops: Fuggles, Goldings. IBU: 24. EBC: 34-40. Source: RP.

**Special Bitter**: OG: 1038. Malt: Maris Otter pale malt, Flaked maize, Roast barley. Hops: Target. Late hops: Fuggles, Goldings. Dry hops: Fuggles, Goldings. IBU: 24. EBC: 40. Source: RP5.

**Scottish Oatmeal Stout**: OG: 1040. Malt: Maris Otter pale malt, Pinhead Oatmeal, Roast barley, optional Black malt. Hops: Fuggles, Goldings or Target. Late hops: Fuggles, Goldings. IBU: 28-30. EBC: 130-170. Source: RP.

**Merlin's Ale**: OG: 1044. Malt: Pipkin pale malt, Roast barley. Hops: Fuggles, Goldings or Target or Target, Goldings. Late hops: Fuggles and Goldings or Styrian Goldings. IBU: 30. EBC: 15. Source: RP. OG: 1044-45. Malt: Maris Otter pale malt, Crystal malt, Peat-smoked malt, Roast barley. Hops: Target, Goldings. Late hops: Styrian Goldings, Fuggles. Source: BC.

**Tate Chillie**: OG: 1043. Malt: Maris Otter pale malt, Crystal malt. Hops: Fuggles, Target. Late hops: Goldings, Hallertau. IBU: 35-40. EBC: 28. Source: RP5.

**Black Douglas**: OG: 1053. Malt: Maris Otter pale malt, Crystal malt, Black malt. Hops: Target. Late hops: Goldings. IBU: 25. EBC: 75. Source: RP5.

**Old Jock**: OG: 1070. Malt: Maris Otter pale malt, Roast barley, optional Flaked maize. Hops: Fuggles, Goldings or Target. Late hops: Fuggles, Goldings. IBU: 32. EBC: 48. Source: RP. Malt: Golden Promise pale malt, Dextrin malt, Crystal malt, Aromatic malt, Roast barley, Maltodextrin. Hops: Fuggles, Goldings. Late hops: Fuggles, Goldings. Source: CB.

**Greenmantle 80/-**: OG: 1042. Malt: Pale malt, small % Roast barley. Hops: Fuggles, Goldings. IBU: 29. Source: RP2.

**80/-**: OG: 1042. Malt: Pipkin or Maris Otter pale malt, Crystal malt, Roast barley. Hops: Target and optional Goldings. Late hops: Fuggles and Goldings or Styrian Goldings. IBU: 30. EBC: 40-50.

### . *Burntisland Brewing Company, Burntisland*

**Alexander's Downfall** (b-c): ABV: 4.3%. Malt: Pale malt, Crystal malt. Hops: Fuggles, Goldings. Source: JE1.

**Dockyard Rivets** (b-c): ABV: 5.1%. Malt: Lager malt, Wheat malt. Hops: Saaz. Source: JE1.

### . *Cairngorm Brewery Company, Aviemore. www.cairngormbrewery.com*

**Winter Flurry**: ABV: 4%. Malt: Crystal malt. Hops: Goldings. Source: Web.

**Stag**: ABV: 4.1%. Hops: Fuggles, Challenger. Source: Web.

**Trade Winds**: ABV: 4.3%. Hops: Perle. Others: Elderflowers. Source: Web.

**Mountain Blue**: ABV: 4.3%. Hops: Chinook. Source: Web.

**Cairngorm Gold**: ABV: 4.5%. Hops: Saaz, Styrian Goldings. Source: Web.

**Blessed Thistle**: ABV: 4.5%. Others: Blessed thistle. Source: Web.

**Ginger Rodent**: ABV: 4.5%. Hops: Saaz, Styrian Goldings. Source: Web.

**White Lady**: ABV: 4.7%. Others: Orange peel, Coriander. Source: Web.

**Highland IPA**: ABV: 5%. Hops: Amarillo, Centennial, Perle. Source: Web.

### . *Caledonian Brewing Company, Edinburgh. www.caledonian-brewery.co.uk*

**60/-**: OG: 1032. Malt: Pipkin pale malt, Crystal malt, Amber malt, Black malt, Wheat malt, Enzymic malt. Hops: Fuggles, Goldings. IBU: 30-2. EBC: 44-46. Source: RP4/5.

**70/-**: OG: 1036. Malt: Golden Promise or Pipkin pale malt, Crystal malt, Amber malt, Chocolate malt, Black malt, Wheat malt and/or Enzymic malt. Hops: Fuggles, Goldings. IBU: 28-30. EBC: 40-42. Source: RP.

**Murray's Summer Ale**: OG: 1036. Malt: Pipkin pale malt, Crystal malt, Amber malt. Hops: Fuggles, Goldings. IBU: 38-40. EBC: 14-16. Source: RP4/5. Note: See Maclay & Company.

**R & D Deuchars IPA**: OG: 1038. Malt: Golden Promise or Pipkin pale malt pale malt, Crystal malt, Wheat malt. Hops: Fuggles. Late hops: Goldings. IBU: 34-6. EBC: 15-17. Source: RP2/3/4/5. Hops: Styrian Goldings. Source: W.

**Tempus Fugit** (b-c): ABV: 3.8%. Malt: Pipkin pale malt, Crystal malt, Wheat malt. Hops: Fuggles, Goldings. Source: JE1. Note: This is the 1998 version based on Deuchars IPA.

**Murrays Heavy**: OG: 1044. Malt: Pipkin pale malt, Crystal malt, Amber malt, Wheat malt. Hops: Fuggles, Goldings. IBU: 38-40. EBC: 41-43. Source: RP4/5. Note: See Maclay & Company.

**Porter**: OG: 1042. Malt: Golden Promise or Pipkin pale malt, Crystal malt, Amber malt, Chocolate malt, Black malt, Wheat malt. Hops: Fuggles, Goldings. IBU: 34-6. EBC: 70. Source: RP1/2/3/4/5.

**Edinburgh Real Ale**: OG: 1042. Malt: Pipkin pale malt, Crystal malt, Chocolate malt, Wheat malt, Roast barley. Hops: Fuggles, Goldings. IBU: 36-8. EBC: 36-38. Source: RP3/4/5.

**80/-**: OG: 1043. Malt: Golden Promise or Pipkin pale malt, Crystal malt, Amber malt, Chocolate malt, Black malt, Wheat malt. Hops: Fuggles, Goldings. IBU: 34-6. EBC: 25-27. Source: RP/W. Note: "Caley 80" is the favourite beer of my good friend Akis.

**XPA**: ABV: 4.3%. Hops: Northdown, Cascade. Source: Web.

**Campbell Hope & King Double Amber**: OG: 1045. Malt: Pipkin pale malt, Crystal malt, Amber malt, Black malt. Hops: Fuggles, Goldings. IBU: 44-6. EBC: 50-52. Source: RP4/5.

**Caledonian 125**: OG: 1046. Malt: Pipkin pale malt, Crystal malt, Amber malt, Wheat malt. Hops: Fuggles, Goldings. EBC: 16-18. Source: RP4/5.

**Burns Ale** (b-c): ABV: 4.7%. Malt: Golden Promise pale malt, Crystal malt, Rye malt. Hops: Goldings. Source: JE2.

**Golden Promise**: OG: 1048. Malt: 100% Atem pale malt. Hops: Hersbrücker, Pride of Ringwood or Progress. IBU: 50-52. Notes: Organic. Source: RP.

**Merman XXX**: OG: 1049-52. Malt: Golden Promise or Pipkin pale malt, Crystal malt, Amber malt, Chocolate malt, Black malt, Wheat malt. Hops: Fuggles. IBU: 48-50. EBC: 43-45. Source: RP1/2/3/4/5.

**Tempus Fugit** (b-c): ABV: 5.5%. Malt: Chariot pale malt. Hops: Target. Source: JE2. Note: This is the 1999 version based on **Golden Promise IPA**.

**Edinburgh Strong Ale**: OG: 1063-78. Malt: Golden Promise or Pipkin pale malt, Crystal malt, Amber malt, Chocolate malt, Black malt, Wheat malt. Hops: Fuggles, Goldings. IBU: 62-64. EBC: 30-33. Source: RP.

### Carlsberg-Tetley Alloa, Alloa

**Archibald Arrol's 80/-**: OG: 1041. Malt: 90% Halcyon and Puffin pale malt, 10% Crystal malt. Hops: Galena, Northdown, Target. Dry hops: Goldings. IBU: 23. EBC: 35. Source: RP4/5.

### Clockwork Beer Company, Glasgow www.clockworkbeercompany.co.uk

**Amber Ale**: ABV: 3.8%. Malt: Pale malt, Crystal malt. Hops: American and New Zealand hops. Source: Web.

**Red Alt**: ABV: 4.4%. Malt: Wheat malt. Hops: American hops. Source: Web.

### Devon Ales, Sauchie www.devonales.com

**Devon Original**: ABV: 3.8%. Hops: Goldings. Source: Web.

### Fyfe Brewing Company, Kirkcaldy

**Rope of Sand**: ABV: 3.5%. Malt: 90% Pale malt, 5% Crystal malt, 5% Torrefied wheat. Hops: First Gold. Late hops: Cascade. Source: RP5/JHF.

**Auld Alliance**: ABV: 4%. Malt: 89% Pale malt, 5% Crystal malt, 1% Roast malt, 5% Torrefied wheat. Hops: Target. Late hops: Cascade. Source: RP5.

### Glashu Brewery, Glasgow

**Best Bracken**: OG: 1044. Malt: 90% Pale malt, 4% Caramalt, 4% Crystal malt, 2% Wheat malt. Hops: Fuggles, Goldings. Source: RP4.

**IPA**: OG: 1048. Malt: 90% Pale malt, 9% Caramalt, 1% Wheat malt. Hops: Fuggles, Goldings. Source: RP4.

**Double Whammy**: OG: 1063. Malt: 90% Pale malt, 6% Caramalt, 3% Chocolate malt, 1% Wheat malt. Hops: Fuggles, Goldings. Source: RP4.

### Harviestoun Brewery, Dollar/Alva. www.harviestoun.com

**Dragonfly**: ABV: 3.6%. Malt: Oat malt, Roast malt. Source: Web.

**Waverley 70/-**: OG: 1037. Malt: 92-96% Pipkin or Halcyon pale malt, 4-8% Crystal malt, 1-2% Roast barley, 5-6% Brown sugar. Hops: Progress. Late hops: Goldings. Dry hops: Styrian Goldings or Hop oil. IBU: 21-25. Source: RP/MO.

**Bitter & Twisted**: ABV: 3.8%. Hops: Styrian Goldings, Hersbrücker, Challenger. Source: Web.

**Late Harvest**: ABV: 3.8%. Hops: Goldings. Late hops: Cascade. Source: Web.

**Gold Rush**: ABV: 3.9%. Hops: Admiral, Herald, WGV. Source: Web.

**Original 80/-**: OG: 1040. Malt: 85-92% Pipkin or Halcyon pale malt, 6-9% Crystal malt, 3-6% Brown sugar, 0-9% Wheat. Hops: Fuggles. Late hops: Goldings. Dry hops: Styrian Goldings or Hop oil. IBU: 20-33. EBC: 25. Source: RP/MO.

**Top Dollar**: ABV: 4%. Malt: Roast malt. Hops: Styrian Goldings, Pilot, Cascade, Glacier. Source: Web.

**Natural Blonde**: ABV: 4%. Malt: Lager malt, Wheat malt. Hops: Styrian Goldings, Pilot, Cascade, Glacier. Source: Web.

**Hoptober Fest**: ABV: 4%. Hops: Fresh hops. Source: Web.

**Game Burd**: ABV: 4.1%. Malt: Crystal rye malt. Hops: Liberty, Willamette, Pioneer.. Source: Web.

**Montrose Ale**: OG: 1042. Malt: 90% Pipkin pale malt, 8% Crystal malt, 2% Chocolate malt, 1% Molasses. Hops: USA Fuggles, Goldings. Dry hops: Hop oil. IBU: 28. EBC: 46. Source: RP4/5/MO.

**Haggis Hunter**: ABV: 4.3%. Malt: Pale malt, Crystal malt. Hops: Fuggles, Goldings, Styrian Goldings. Source: Web.

**Ptarmigan**: OG: 1045. Malt: 91-2% Pipkin or Halcyon pale malt, 3-4% Crystal malt, 2-4% Wheat, 3-4% White sugar. Hops: Saaz or Challenger. Late hops: Saaz. Dry hops: Pioneer or Hop oil. IBU: 26-34. EBC: 18. Source: RP/MO/JHF/Web.

**Mr Sno'Balls**: ABV: 4.5%. Malt: Crystal malt, Chocolate malt. Hops: Styrian Goldings, Challenger. Source: Web.

**Schiehallion**: OG: 1048. Malt: 95% Prizum lager malt, 5% Wheat malt. Hops: Challenger, Hersbrücker, optional Styrian Goldings, IBU: 28 or 37.5. EBC: 12.5. Source: RP4/5/MO/JHF/Web.

**Old Manor**: OG: 1050. Malt: 93-5% Pipkin pale malt, 4-6% Crystal malt, 1% Chocolate malt, 0-5% Wheat, optional Brown sugar. Hops: Northern Brewer. Late hops: Goldings. Dry hops: Styrian Goldings or Hop oil. IBU: 24-32. EBC: 35. Source: RP/MO.

**Old Engine Oil**: ABV: 6%. Malt: Pale malt, Oats, "masses of" Roast barley. Hops: Galena, Fuggles, Goldings. Source: Web.

**Ola Dubh**: ABV: 8%. Notes: Based on **Old Engine Oil** and aged in 12-, 16- or 30-year old Highland Park malt whiskey casks. Source: Web.

### . *Heather Ale Brewery, Taynult / Strathaven / Alloa*

**Fraoch Heather Ale**: OG: 1041. Malt: Scotch pale malt, 5% Wheat, 3% Caramalt. Hops: Brewers Gold. Others: Flowering heather, Root ginger, Sweet Gale (Bog Myrtle). IBU: 22-24. EBC: 19. Source: RP4/5. OG: 1048. Malt: Maris Otter pale malt, CaraPils malt, Crystal malt, Chocolate malt. Hops: Fuggles. Late hops: Fuggles. Others: Heather flowers. Source: 150. OG: 1050-53. Malt: Golden Promise pale malt, Crystal malt. Hops: Brewers Gold. Late hops: Goldings. Others: Heather blossoms. Source: CB. Notes: This is one of my favourite ales. A well-kept pint of draught Fraoch is delicious and the bottled version is also very good. I believe that flowering heather may be added to the mash as well as during/after the boil. This recipe is a recreation of an ancient Pictish ale.

**Pictish Heather Ale**: OG: 1051. Malt: Scotch pale malt, 5% Caramalt, 5% Wheat malt. Hops: Brewers Gold. Others: Flowering heather, Root ginger, Sweet Gale (Bog Myrtle). IBU: 27-29. EBC: 24. Source: RP4/5.

Note: This brewery has moved as it has grown and has now been renamed William Bros. (qv).

### . Highland Brewing Company, Evie, Orkney
www.highlandbrewingcompany.co.uk

**Orkney Best**: ABV: 3.6%. Malt: Maris Otter pale malt. Hops: American, Polish and New Zealand hops. Source: Web.

**Scapa Special**: ABV: 4.2%. Malt: Maris Otter pale malt. Hops: American, German, New Zealand and Slovakian hops. Source: Web.

**St. Magus Ale**: ABV: 5.2%. Malt: Maris Otter pale malt, dash of Chocolate malt. Hops: 2 English hops. Source: Web.

### . Hillside, Corse

**Macbeth** (b-c): ABV: 4.2%. Malt: Pale malt, Wheat malt, Crystal malt. Hops: Fuggles, Cascade. Source: JE6.

### . Houston Brewing Company, Houston. Www.houston-brewing.co.uk

**Texas**: OG: 1045. Malt: Pale malt, Pale chocolate malt. Hops: Cascade. Source: Web.

### . Innis & Gunn, Edinburgh www.innisandgunn.com

**Lager Beer**: ABV: 4.6%. Malt: Lager malt, Naked golden oats. Hops: Super Styrian Goldings, Styrian Goldings. Source: Web.

**Blonde**: ABV: 6%. Malt: Roast barley. Hops: Goldings. Notes: Matured for 37 days over Bourbon-infused heartwood. Source: Web.

**Original**: ABV: 6.6%. Malt: Wheat, Crystal malt. Hops: Super Styrian Goldings. Notes: Matured for 77 days over Bourbon-infused heartwood. Source: Web.

**Rum Finish**: ABV: 6.8%. Malt: Roast barley, Chocolate malt, Crystal malt. Hops: Super Styrian Goldings. Notes: Matured for 57 days over Rum-infused heartwood. Source: Web.

**Treacle Porter**: ABV: 7.4%. Malt: Wheat, Chocolate malt, Crystal malt, Treacle. Hops: Super Styrian Goldings. Notes: Matured for 39 days over Bourbon-infused heartwood. Source: Web.

**Canadian Cherrywood Finish**: ABV: 8.3%. Malt: Optic pale malt, Roast barley, Crystal malt, Aromatic malt, Roast wheat, Maple syrup. Hops: Goldings, Styrian Goldings. Notes: Matured for 49 days over Bourbon-infused Canadian black cherrywood. Source: Web.

### . Inveralmond, Perth. Www.inveralmond-brewery.co.uk

**Independence**: ABV: 3.8%. Hops: Pilgrim, Saaz. Source: Web.

**Ossians Ale**: ABV: 4.1%. Hops: First Gold, Perle, Cascade. Source: Web. Hops: Perle, Cascade, Fuggles, First Gold. Source: W.

**Thrappledouser**: ABV: 4.3%. Hops: Pilgrim, Goldings, Cascade. Source: Web.

**Santa's Swallie**: ABV: 4.3%. Hops: Fuggles. Others: Nutmeg, Cinnamon. Source: Web.

**Lia Fail**: ABV: 4.7%. Hops: Fuggles, Challenger, Cascade. Source: web.

**Sunburst Pilsner**: ABV: 4.8%. Hops: Hersbrücker. Source: Web.

. *Islay Ales, Bridgend, Isle of Islay* www.islayales.com

**Finlaggan Ale** (b-c): ABV: 3.7%. Malt: Pale malt, Crystal malt. Hops: Goldings. Late hops: Mount Hood, Styrian Goldings. Source: JE6/Web.

**Black Rock Ale** (b-c): ABV: 4.2%. Malt: Pale malt, Roast barley, Crystal malt. Hops: Goldings. Late hops: Fuggles, Mount Hood. Source: JE6/Web.

**Dun Hogs Head Ale** (b-c): ABV: 4.4%. Malt: Pale malt, Wheat malt, Roast barley, Chocolate malt, Crystal malt. Hops: Fuggles, Bramling Cross. Source: JE6. Hops: Goldings, Bramling Cross. Late hops: Bramling Cross. Source: Web.

**Saligo Ale** (b-c): ABV: 4.4%. Malt: Pale malt, Lager malt, Wheat malt. Hops: Goldings, Mount Hood. Source: JE6. Hops: Goldings. Late hops: Bramling Cross. Source: Web.

**Angus Og Ale** (b-c): ABV: 4.5%. Malt: Pale malt, Crystal malt. Hops: Goldings, Mount Hood, Styrian Goldings. Source: JE6/Web.

**Ardnave Ale** (b-c): ABV: 4.6%. Malt: Pale malt, small amount of Crystal malt. Hops: Goldings, Fuggles, Mount Hood, Styrian Goldings. Source: JE6.Web.

**Nerabus Ale** (b-c): ABV: 4.8%. Malt: Pale malt, Dark crystal malt, Wheat malt, Chocolate malt, Caramalt. Hops: Amarillo, Bramling Cross. Source: JE6/Web.

**Single Malt Ale** (b-c): ABV: 5%. Malt: Pale malt. Hops: Amarillo, Bramling Cross. Source: JE6/Web.

**Ballinby Ale** (b-c): ABV: 7.1%. Malt: Pale malt, Caramalt, Chocolate malt, Crystal malt. Hops: Challenger, Northdown, Bramling Cross. Source: JE6.

. *Isle of Skye, Uig* www.kyebrewery.co.uk

**Cuillin Gorm**: ABV: 4%. Others: Blueberries. Source: Web.

**Witchwand**: ABV: 4%. Others: Rowanberries. Source: Web.

**Tarasgeir**: ABV: 4%. Malt: Peat-smoked malt. Source: Web.

**Misty Isle** (b-c): ABV: 4.3%. Malt: Maris Otter pale malt, CaraPils malt, Wheat malt. Hops: Hersbrücker. Others: Organic Lemon juice. Source: JE5/6.

**Black Cuillin**: ABV: 4.5%. Malt: Roast barley, Roast oatmeal, Scottish heather honey. Source: Web.

**Am Basteir** (b-c): ABV: 7%. Malt: Maris Otter pale malt, Crystal malt, Amber malt, Torrefied wheat, Organic demerara sugar. Hops: Fuggles. Source: JE6.

### . *Kelburn, Barrhead www.kelburnbrewery.com*

**Kracker**: ABV: 6.0%. Malt: Munich malt. Source: Web.

### . *Luckie Ales, Auchtermuchty www.luckie-ales.com*

**Eighty Shilling**: ABV: 5%. Malt: 6 different malts. Yeast: Scottish. IBU: 23. Source: Web.

**Midnycht Myld Ale**: ABV: 5%. Malt: 4 malts including Roast barley, Chocolate malt. Yeast: London ale. IBU: 23. Source: Web.

**Amber Ale**: ABV: 5%. Malt: Amber malt. Yeast: English. IBU: 27. Source: Web.

**Edinburgh Export Stout**: ABV: 6.7%. Malt: Pale malt, Crystal malt, CaraPils malt, Black malt. Hops: Goldings/Fuggles. IBU: 78. Notes: A copy of an Export Stout brewed by Youngers of Edinburgh in 1897. Source: Web/DP.

**Edinburgh 68/-**: ABV: 8.1%. IBU: 48. Source: Web. Notes: A reincarnation of the 68/- brewed by J. & T. Usher of Edinburgh in 1885.

### . *Maclay & Company, Alloa*

**60/-**: OG: 1030. Malt: Pale malt, No.1 invert sugar, No.3 invert sugar, Caramel. Hops: Fuggles, Northern Brewer. Yeast: White Labs WLP028. Notes: Recipe from 1951. IBU: 37. SRM: 12. Source: VB.

**60/- Pale Ale**: OG: 1034. Malt: 100% Golden Promise pale malt, Caramel. Hops: Fuggles. Source: RP1/2. Or Malt: 90% Maris Otter pale malt or 45% Golden Promise pale malt, 45% Camargue and 5% Crystal malt, 5% Wheat malt. Hops: Fuggles. Late hops: Brewers Gold. IBU: 30. EBC: 80. Source: RP3/4/5.

**70/- / Special**: OG: 1036. Malt: 100% Golden Promise pale malt, Caramel or 90% Maris Otter pale malt, 5% Crystal malt, 5% Wheat malt. Hops: Fuggles. Late hops: Brewers Gold. IBU: 30. EBC: 30. Source: RP/MO.

**Murray's Summer Ale**: OG: 1036. Malt: 90% Pale malt, 5% Crystal malt, 5% Wheat malt. Hops: Fuggles. Late hops: Brewers Gold. Dry hops: Yes. IBU: 50. EBC: 15. Source: RP3. Note: See Caledonian Brewing Company.

**Broadsword**: OG: 1038. Malt: 71% Maris Otter pale malt, 29% Caramalt / CaraPils. Hops: Fuggles. Late hops: Styrian Goldings. EBC: 10. Source: RP4/5/MO.

**80/- / Export**: OG: 1039-40. Malt: 100% Golden Promise pale malt, Caramel or 90% Maris Otter pale malt, 5% Crystal malt, 5% Wheat malt. Hops: Fuggles. Late hops: Brewers Gold. EBC: 25. Source: RP. Notes: This used to my favourite 80 shilling style beer before the Maclay's brewery closed and production of this beer was moved to Belhaven. It had a wonderful subtle smoky character, which I am told came from the yeast rather than any smoked ingredients.

**Kane's Amber Ale**: OG: 1040. Malt: 90% Maris Otter pale malt or 45% Golden Promise pale malt, 45% Camargue pale malt and 5% Crystal malt, 5% Wheat malt. Hops: Fuggles. Late hops: Brewers Gold / Fuggles. Source: RP/MO.

**Porter**: OG: 1040. Malt: 100% Golden Promise pale malt, Caramel or 90% Maris Otter pale malt, 5% Crystal malt, 5% Wheat malt. Hops: Fuggles, optional Goldings. Late hops: Brewers Gold. EBC: 80. Source: RP.

**Oat Malt Stout**: OG: 1045. Malt: 40% Golden Promise pale malt, 40% Camargue pale malt, 15% Oat malt, 4% Roast barley, 1% Chocolate malt or 70% Maris Otter pale malt, 22% Oat malt, 6% Roast barley, 2% Chocolate malt. Hops: Fuggles. IBU: 35. EBC: 50. Source: RP.

**Wallace IPA**: OG: 1045. Malt: 75% Maris Otter pale malt, 7.5% Amber malt, 7.5% Caramalt, 10% Wheat malt. Hops: Fuggles. Late hops: Styrian Goldings. EBC: 25. Source: RP4/5.

**Maclay Scotch Ale**: OG: 1050. Malt: 95% Golden Promise pale malt, 5% Crystal malt or 47.5% Golden Promise pale malt, 47.5% Camargue pale malt, 5% Caramalt or 90% Maris Otter pale malt, 5% Caramalt, 5% Wheat malt. Hops: Fuggles, optional Goldings. IBU: 35. EBC: 12. Source: RP/MO.

**PI 60/-**: OG: 1051. Malt: Pale malt, Lager malt, Flaked maize, No.1 invert sugar. Hops: Fuggles, Hallertau, Cluster. Yeast: White Labs WLP028. Notes: Recipe from 1903. IBU: 47. SRM: 3. Source: VB.

**56/-**: OG: 1062. Malt: Pale malt, Amber malt, Black malt, Wheat malt. Hops: Fuggles, Dry hops: Yes. Notes: Mild ale recipe from 1909. Source: DP.

**63/- Oatmeal Stout**: OG: 1050. Malt: Pale malt, Amber malt, Black malt, Flaked oats. Hops: Fuggles. Dry hops: Yes. Notes: Recipe from 1909. Source: DP.

**Old Alloa Ale**: OG: 1070. Malt: 100% Pale malt. Hops: Fuggles. EBC: 25. Source: RP3/4/5.

**Murrays Amber Heavy**: OG: 1040. Malt: 90% Pale malt, 5% Crystal malt, 5% Wheat malt. Hops: Brewers Gold, Fuggles, Goldings. Dry hops: Yes. EBC: 35. Source: RP3. Note: See Caledonian Brewing Company.

**SA**: OG: 1089. Malt: Pale malt, Lager malt, Flaked maize, No.2 invert sugar, Caramel. Hops: Fuggles, Styrian Goldings, Northern Brewer. Yeast: White Labs WLP028. Notes: Recipe from 1939. IBU: . SRM: . Source: VB.

## . *Moulin Hotel & Brewery, Moulin*

**Ale of Atholl** (b-c): ABV: 4.5%. Malt: Maris Otter pale malt, Crystal malt, Chocolate malt, optional Roast malt. Hops: Fuggles. Source: JE1/2/3/4/5/6.

## . *Old Worthy Brewing Company, Isle of Skye* www.isleofskye.co.uk

**Scottish Pale Ale**: ABV: 5%. Malt: Maris Otter pale malt, Peat-smoked malt, Crystal malt. Heather honey. Source: Web.

### Orkney Brewery, Sandwick, Orkney Islands
*www.sinclairbreweries.co.uk*

**Raven Ale**: OG: 1038. Malt: 92-3% Golden Promise pale malt, 4-7% Torrefied wheat, Roast barley, 0-3% Crystal malt, 0-1% Chocolate malt, Hops: WGV or Goldings, Fuggles. Late hops: Goldings. IBU: 18. Source: RP/MO/W. Malt: Pale malt, Amber malt, Crystal malt. Hops: Goldings, Fuggles. Source: Web.

**Dragonhead Stout**: OG: 1040. Malt: 90% Golden Promise pale malt, 2% Crystal malt, 1% Black malt, 3% Torrefied barley, 3% Roast barley. Hops: Omega. Late hops: Goldings. IBU: 29. Source: RP3/4/5/MO/JHF/Web.

**Red McGregor**: OG: 1040. Malt: 92% Pipkin pale malt, 4% Crystal malt, 1% Chocolate malt, 3% Torrefied wheat. Hops: Omega. Late hops: Cascade. IBU: 25. Source: RP5. Malt: Chocolate malt, Crystal malt. Hops: Cascade. Source: Web.

**Northern Light**: ABV: 4%. Hops: Saaz, Hersbrücker, Liberty. Source: Web.

**Clootie Dumpling**: ABV: 4.3%. Hops: Bramling Cross, First Gold, Fuggles. Source: Web.

**Dark Island**: OG: 1045. Malt: 85-90% Golden Promise pale malt, 3% Crystal malt, 3% Chocolate malt, 3-4% Torrefied wheat, 0-6% Cane sugar. Hops: Omega. Late hops: Challenger. IBU: 22. Source: RP/MO/JHF. Hops: First Gold, Goldings. Source: Web.

**Skullsplitter**: OG: 1080. Malt: 88% Golden Promise pale malt, 3% Crystal malt, 1% Chocolate malt, 3% Torrefied wheat, 5% Cane sugar. Hops: WGV. Late hops: Goldings. IBU: 20. Source: RP2/3/4/5/MO/Web. OG: 1085-88. Malt: Golden Promise pale malt, Wheat malt, Aromatic malt, Crystal malt, Roast barley, Peat-smoked malt. Hops: Goldings. Others: Steamed Oak chips. Source: CB.

**White Christmas**: ABV: 6%. Malt: 90% Pipkin pale malt, 5% Crystal malt, 2% Torrefied wheat, 3% Cane sugar. Hops: Challenger. Late hops: Goldings. IBU: 18. Source: RP5.

**Dark Island Reserve**: ABV: 10%. Notes: **Dark Island** ale matured in Orkney whisky casks. Source: Web.

### Plockton Brewery. Plockton *www.theplocktonbrewery.com*

**Hitched/Plockton Gold**: ABV: 4.1% Late hops: Cascade, Styrian Goldings. Source: Web.

**Ciste Dhubh/Plockton Dark**: Hops: Goldings. Source: Web.

**Plockton Bay/Plockton Tawny**: ABV: 4.6% Hops: Styrian Goldings. Source: Web.

**Fiddler's Fancy**: ABV: 4.6% Hops: Amarillo or Cascade, Summit. Source: Web.

**Starboard!/Plockton Light**: ABV: 5.1% Malt: Maris Otter pale malt, Torrefied wheat. Hops: Styrian Goldings. Source: Web.

## . Scottish & Newcastle Beer Production, Edinburgh

**McEwans Export / Export IPA** (bottled): OG: 1046. Malt: Pale malt, Roast barley / Black malt, Flaked barley. Hops: Fuggles, Yeoman, Target or Hallertau. Dry hops: Hop extract. IBU: 24. Source: EBA/DL. Malt: Golden Promise pale malt, Flaked maize, Crystal malt, Roast barley, Peat-smoked malt, Sugar. Hops: Goldings. Late hops: Goldings, Fuggles. Source: CB.

**McEwan's No. 1 Champion Ale**: OG: 1079. Malt: Golden Promise pale malt, Torrefied wheat, Crystal malt, Roast barley, Peat-smoked malt, Invert sugar. Hops: Goldings. Late hops: Styrian Goldings, Hersbrücker. Source: BC.

**Gordons Highland Ale**: OG: 1090. Malt: Pale malt, Roast barley, Cereal adjunct. Hops: Fuggles, Target, Yeoman. IBU: 43. Source: EBA.

**Imperial Russian Stout** (b-c): ABV: 10%. Malt: Pale malt, Black malt, Amber malt. Hops: Target. Source: JE1/2. Notes: See **Imperial Russian Stout**, John Smith's Brewery, Tadcaster, England and **Imperial Russian Stout**, Courage, Staines, England.

## . Stewart Brewing, Edinburgh www.stewartbrewing.co.uk

**Zymic**: ABV: 3.5%. Malt: Low colour Maris Otter pale malt, Maris Otter pale malt, Wheat malt. Hops: Magnum, Centennial, Amarillo, Cascade. IBU: 23. EBC: 4. Source: Web.

**Edinburgh Festival**: ABV: 3.9%. Malt: Maris Otter pale malt, Wheat malt. Hops: Magnum, Nelson Sauvin, Challenger, Styrian Goldings. IBU: 25. EBC: 7. Source: Web.

**Forth Mist**: ABV: 3.9%. Malt: Maris Otter pale malt, Wheat malt. Hops: Tettnang, Styrian Goldings. IBU: 24. EBC: 7. Source: Web.

**Pentlan IPA**: ABV: 3.9%. Malt: Maris Otter pale malt, Wheat malt. Hops: Magnum, Challenger, Styrian Goldings. IBU: 21. EBC: 7. Source: Web.

**SRA (Stewart's Rugby Ale)**: ABV: 4%. Malt: Maris Otter pale malt, Wheat malt, Crystal malt. Hops: Chinook, Challenger, Styrian Goldings. IBU: 30. EBC: 16. Source: Web.

**Copper Cascade**: ABV: 4.1%. Malt: Maris Otter pale malt, Wheat malt, Chocolate malt, Crystal malt. Hops: Magnum, Challenger, Cascade, Styrian Goldings. IBU: 23. EBC: 42. Source: Web.

**Pumpkin Ale**: ABV: 4.3%. Malt: Maris Otter pale malt, Wheat malt, Chocolate malt. Hops: Southern Cross, Magnum. Others: Pumpkins, Cloves. IBU: 25. EBC: 25. Source: Web.

**No. 3**: ABV: 4.3%. Malt: Maris Otter pale malt, Wheat malt, Chocolate malt, Crystal malt. Hops: Challenger. IBU: 16. EBC: 84. Source: Web.

**80/-**: ABV: 4.4%. Malt: Maris Otter pale malt, Wheat malt, Chocolate malt, Crystal malt, CaraPils malt. Hops: Magnum, Tettnang, Challenger, Styrian Goldings. IBU: 18. EBC: 59. Source: Web.

**Coconut Porter**: ABV: 4.5%. Malt: Pale malt, Wheat malt, Chocolate malt, Crystal malt. Hops: Magnum, Challenger. Others: Toasted coconut. IBU: 45. EBC: 156. Source: Web.

**Three Wise Men**: ABV: 4.5%. Malt: Maris Otter pale malt, Wheat malt, Chocolate malt, Crystal malt, CaraPils malt. Hops: Magnum, Challenger. Others: Christmas seasonal fruits, Cinnamon. IBU: 26. EBC: 60. Source: Web.

**Edinburgh Gold**: ABV: 4.8%. Malt: Maris Otter pale malt, Wheat malt, CaraPils malt. Hops: Magnum, Tettnang, Challenger, Styrian Goldings. IBU: 23. EBC: 11. Source: Web.

**Embra**: ABV: 5%. Malt: Maris Otter pale malt, Wheat malt, Crystal malt. Hops: Magnum, Chinook. IBU: 37. EBC: 26. Source: Web.

**Hollyrood**: ABV: 5%. Malt: Maris Otter pale malt, Wheat malt. Hops: Magnum, Amarillo. IBU: 31. EBC: 10. Source: Web.

**St. Giles**: ABV: 5%. Malt: Maris Otter pale malt, Wheat malt, Chocolate malt, Crystal malt, Oats. Hops: Magnum, Cascade. IBU: 30. EBC: 80. Source: Web.

**Black IPA**: ABV: 5%. Malt: Maris Otter pale malt, Wheat malt, Chocolate malt. Hops: Magnum, Galaxy. IBU: 45. EBC: 132. Source: Web.

**Ka Pai**: ABV: 5.2%. Malt: Low colour Maris Otter pale malt, Wheat malt. Hops: Pacifica, Wakatu, Green Bullet, NZ Cascade. Source: Web.

**Hefeweizen**: ABV: 5.5%. Malt: Maris Otter pale malt, Wheat malt, Oats, CaraPils malt. Hops: Tettnang, Crystal. Others: Blueberries. IBU: 16. EBC: 11. Source: Web.

**Cauld Reekie**: ABV: 6.2%. Malt: Maris Otter pale malt, Wheat malt, Chocolate malt, Crystal malt. Hops: Magnum, Northern Brewer. IBU: 65. EBC: 210. Source: Web.

**Chilli Reekie**: ABV: 6.2%. Malt: Maris Otter pale malt, Wheat malt, Chocolate malt, Crystal malt. Hops: Magnum, Northern Brewer. Others: Chillies. IBU: 65. EBC: 210. Source: Web.

**8**: ABV: 8%. Malt: Concerto lager malt, Aromatic malt. Hops: Magnum, Galaxy, Nelson Sauvin, Cascade. Others: Ground coriander, Sweet orange peel. IBU: 38. EBC: 16. Source: Web.

## Strathaven Ales, Strathaven

**Duchess Anne**: ABV: 3.9%. Malt: Lager malt, Wheat malt. Others: Meadowsweet. Source: Web.

**Ginger Jock**: ABV: 4%. Others: Root ginger, Lemon juice, Lime juice. Source: Web.

**Line Out**: ABV: 4%. Malt: Pale malt, Crystal malt, Roast malt. Hops: 3 varieties. Source: Web.

**Trumpeter**: ABV: 4.2%. Malt: Roast malt, Oats. Others: Root ginger. Source: Web.

**Claverhouse**: ABV: 4.5%. Malt: Crystal malt, Red malt. Source: Web.

**Aleberry**: ABV: 4.6%. Others: Damsons. Source: Web.

**Lord Kelvin**: ABV: 4.7%. Malt: Maris Otter pale malt, Crystal malt. Others: Root ginger. Source: Web.

**Winter Glow**: ABV: 5%. Others: Cinnamon, Tangerine zest. Source: Web.

### . *Sulwath Brewers, Castle Douglas www.sulwathbrewers.co.uk*

**Black Galloway**: ABV: 4.4%. Malt: Maris Otter pale malt, Chocolate malt. Source: Web.

**Reinbeer**: ABV: 4.5%. Malt: Maris Otter pale malt, Chocolate malt. Others: Christmas spices. Source: Web.

**Criffel**: ABV: 4.6%. Malt: Maris Otter pale malt, Roast barley. Hops: 3 varieties. Source: Web.

**Galloway Gold**: ABV: 5%. Malt: Lager malt, Wheat malt. Hops: Saaz. Source: Web.

**Solway Mist**: ABV: 5.5%. Malt: Wheat malt, Rolled oats. Others: Seville orange peel. Source: Web.

### . *Tennent Caledonian Breweries, Glasgow*

**Aitken's 80/- Cask Ale**: OG: 1041. Malt: Ale malt, Wheat flour, Maltose syrup, Caramel. Hops: Challenger, Northdown. IBU: 26. EBC: 32. Source: RP4.

### . *Tomintoul Brewery Company, Tomintoul*

**Tomintoul Caillie**: OG: 1036. Malt: 94% Halcyon pale malt, 6% Crystal malt. Hops: Challenger. Late hops: Goldings. IBU: 40. EBC: 30. Source: RP4/MO.

**Laird's Ale**: OG: 1038. Malt: 90% Pipkin pale malt, 9% Crystal malt, 1% Chocolate malt. Hops: Challenger. Late hops: Goldings. IBU: 20-24. Source: RP5.

**Stag**: OG: 1039.5. Malt: 93% Pipkin or Halcyon pale malt, 5% Crystal malt, 2% Chocolate malt. Hops: Challenger, optional Northdown. Late hops: Fuggles. IBU: 24-36. EBC: 45-55. Source: RP/MO.

**80/-**: OG: 1041. Malt: 94.5% Maris Otter pale malt or Pipkin pale malt, 5.5% Crystal malt. Hops: Northdown, Goldings. IBU: 26. Source: RP4/MO.

**Stillman's 80/-**: OG: 1040. Malt: 93% Pipkin pale malt, 7% Crystal malt. Hops: Challenger, Goldings. IBU: 20. EBC: 30. Source: RP5.

**Black Gold**: OG: 1048.5. Malt: 80% Pipkin pale malt, 8% Crystal malt, 4% Chocolate malt, 8% Roast barley. Hops: Challenger. Late hops: Fuggles. Source: RP5.

**Wild Cat**: OG: 1049.5. Malt: 90-5% Pipkin or Halcyon pale malt, 4-8% Crystal malt, 1-2% Chocolate malt. Hops: Northdown or Challenger. Late hops: Fuggles. IBU: 25-28. EBC: 40-45. Source: RP/MO.

### . Traditional Scottish Ales, Stirling www.tsabrewingco.co.uk

**Turkey Stuffing**: ABV: 3.8%. Malt: Maris Otter pale malt, Crystal malt, Torrefied wheat. Source: Web.

**Golden Harvest**: ABV: 4%. Hops: Fresh hops. Source: Web.

**Scottish Bramble Ale**: ABV: 4.2%. Others: Blackberries. Source: Web.

**Ginger Explosion**: ABV: 5%. Others: Root ginger. Source: Web.

**Red Mist**: ABV: 5%. Others: Raspberries. Source: Web.

### . Traquair House Brewery, Innerleithen

**Bear Ale**: OG: 1050. Malt: 99-100% Pale malt, small-1% Roast barley/Hops: Goldings, optional Red Sell. IBU: 34. Source: RP.

**Traquair House Ale**: OG: 1075. Malt: 98.1-100% Pale malt, small-1.9% Roast barley / Black malt. Hops: Goldings, optional Red Sell. IBU: 35. Source: RP/EBA/150. Malt: Golden Promise pale malt, Dextrin malt, Aromatic malt, Crystal malt, Peat-smoked malt, Roast barley, Maltodextrin. Hops: Goldings. Late hops: Fuggles, Goldings. Dry hops: Fuggles. Source: CB.

**Jacobite Ale**: OG: 1077. Malt: 93% Halcyon pale malt, 2% Roast barley, 5% Crystal malt. Hops: Goldings. Others: Coriander seeds. Source: RP5.

### . Traquair House Brewery, Innerleithen

**Bear Ale**: OG: 1050. Malt: 99-100% Pale malt, small-1% Roast barley/Hops: Goldings, optional Red Sell. IBU: 34. Source: RP.

**Traquair House Ale**: OG: 1075. Malt: 98.1-100% Pale malt, small-1.9% Roast barley / Black malt. Hops: Goldings, optional Red Sell. IBU: 35. Source: RP/EBA/150. Malt: Golden Promise pale malt, Dextrin malt, Aromatic malt, Crystal malt, Peat-smoked malt, Roast barley, Maltodextrin. Hops: Goldings. Late hops: Fuggles, Goldings. Dry hops: Fuggles. Source: CB.

**Jacobite Ale**: OG: 1077. Malt: 93% Halcyon pale malt, 2% Roast barley, 5% Crystal malt. Hops: Goldings. Others: Coriander seeds. Source: RP5.

### . Tryst Brewery, Larbert. Www.trystbrewery.co.uk

**Brockville Dark** (b-c): ABV: 3.8%. Malt: Optic pale malt, Roast barley, Chocolate malt, Crystal malt, Amber malt. Hops: Goldings, Challenger. Source: JE6.

**Brockville Pale** (b-c): ABV: 3.8%. Malt: Optic pale malt, Crystal malt. Hops: Goldings, Challenger. Source: JE6.

**Blàthan**: ABV: 4%. Hops: Challenger. Others: Elderflowers. Source: Web/WB.

**Festival Red** (b-c): ABV: 4%. Malt: Optic pale malt, Crystal malt. Hops: Columbus, Goldings, Cascade. Source: JE6.

**Carronade India Pale Ale**: ABV: 4.2%. Malt: 100% Optic pale malt. Hops: Columbus, Cascade. Source: Web/JE6.

**Buckled Wheel**: ABV: 4.2%. Malt: Optic pale malt. Hops: Goldings, Fuggles, Challenger. Source: Web/JE6.

**Zetland Wheatbier**: ABV: 4.5%. Malt: Pale malt, Munich malt, Wheat malt. Source: Web.

Notes: When I published the first edition of this book I donated a signed copy to a Scottish Craft Brewers raffle and it was won by John McGarva who later went on to set up the Tryst Brewery.

### . J. & T. Usher, Edinburgh

**Stout**: OG: 1051. Malt: Pale malt, Pale amber malt, Amber malt, Brown malt, Black malt, Crystal malt. Hops: Fuggles. Dry hops: Goldings. Notes: Recipe from 1885. Source: DP.

**Brown Ale**: OG: 1055. Malt: Pale malt, Lager malt, Crystal 40L malt, No.3 invert sugar, Caramel. Hops: Fuggles, Goldings. Yeast: White Labs WLP028. Notes: Recipe from 1931. IBU: 38. SRM: 21. Source: VB.

**60/- Pale Ale**: OG: 1060. Malt: Pale malt. Notes: Recipe from 1886. Source: DP.

**100/-**: OG: 1068. Malt: Pale malt, Lager malt, No.1 invert sugar. Hops: Fuggles, Cluster. Yeast: White Labs WLP028. Notes: Recipe from 1894. IBU: 50. SRM: 9. Source: VB.

**68/-**: OG: 1080. Malt: Pale malt, Pale amber malt. Hops: Goldings. Dry hops: Yes. Notes: Mild recipe from 1885. Source: DP.

**Old Scotch Ale**: OG: 1085. Malt: Pale malt, Lager malt, Flaked maize, No.2 invert sugar, Caramel. Hops: Fuggles, Goldings, Cluster. Yeast: White Labs WLP028. Notes: Recipe from 1928. IBU: 56. SRM: 34. Source: VB.

### . Valhalla Brewery, Haroldswick, Unst, Shetland
### www.valhallabrewery.co.uk

**Old Scatness**: ABV: 4%. Malt: Bere, Wheat, Oats, Heather honey. Source: Web.

**Island Bere**: ABV: 4.2%. Malt: Bere. Hops: Cascade. Source: Web.

Note: Bere is an ancient type of 6-row barley.

**Sjolmet Stout**: ABV: 5%. Malt: Pale malt, Wheat malt, Roast barley, Crystal malt, Oat malt. Hops: Goldings, Challenger. Source: Web.

### . William Bros. Brewing Company, Alloa. www.williambrosbrew.com

**Ginger**: ABV: 3.8%. Malt: Wheat malt, Organic cane sugar. Hops: None. Others: Lemon juice, Lemon peel, Root ginger. Source: Web.

**Róisin**: ABV: 4.2%. Others: Tayberries. Source: Web.

**Kelpie**: ABV: 4.4%. Malt: Roast barley. Others: Seaweed (Bladder wrack). Source: Web/TBBK.

**Fraoch Heather Ale**: ABV: 5%. Others: Flowering heather, Sweet Gale (Bog Myrtle). Source: Web/TBBK. Notes: See Heather Ale Brewery.

**Grozet**: ABV: 5%. Malt: Lager malt, Wheat. Others: Sweet Gale (Bog Myrtle), Meadowsweet, Gooseberries. Source: Web/TBBK.

**Good Times**: ABV: 5%. Malt: Oats. Others: Meadowsweet, Elderflowers. Source: Web.

**Birds and Bees**: ABV: 5%. Malt: Belgian pale malt, Wheat. Hops: Bobek, Cascade. Others: Elderflowers, Lemon zest. Source: Web.

**Rooster**: ABV: 5%. Malt: Crystal malt, Wheat malt. Hops: Bobek, Cascade. Source: Web.

**Seven Giraffes**: ABV: 5.1%. Malt: 7 varieties including Wheat malt. Others: Elderflowers, Lemon zest. Source: Web.

**Midnight Sun**: ABV: 5.6%. Malt: Oats, Roast barley, Chocolate malt. Others: Root ginger. Source: Web.

**Ebulum**: ABV: 6.5%. Malt: Roast oats. Others: Elderberries. Source: Web/TBBK.

**Alba**: ABV: 7.5%. Others: Scots pine, Spruce. Source: Web/TBBK.

**Fraoch 20**: ABV: 11%. Others: Flowering heather, Sweet Gale (Bog Myrtle). Source: Web. Notes: Matured in sherry/malt whisky casks.

## .  *W. Youngers, Edinburgh*

**Wee Willie Pale Ale** (bottled): OG:1036. Malt: Pale malt, Flaked barley, Caramel. Hops: Fuggles, Northern Brewer. Source: DL.

**Tartan Keg** (keg): OG: 1036. Malt: Pale malt, Flaked barley, Sugar. Hops: Northern Brewer, Fuggles. Source: DL.

**XP**: OG: 1058. Malt: Pale malt. Hops: Goldings. Yeast: Wyeast #1098/Wyeast #1099. Notes: Recipe from 1853. IBU: 196. SRM: 5. OG: 1054. Malt: Pale malt. Hops: Spalt, Goldings, Cluster. Yeast: White Labs WLP028. Notes: Recipe from 1885. IBU: 92. SRM: 5. Source: VB.

**80/-**: OG: 1064. Malt: Pale malt. Hops: Spalt, Fuggles, Cluster. Yeast: White Labs WLP028. Notes: Recipe from 1885. IBU: 42. SRM: 6. Source: VB. OG: 1072. Malt: Pale malt. Hops: Goldings. Dry hops: Yes. Notes: Recipe from 1872. Source: DP.

**Export Stout**: OG: 1067. Malt: Pale malt, Black malt, Crystal malt. Hops: Fuggles. Dry hops: Goldings. Notes: Recipe from 1897. Source: DP.

**Porter**: OG: 1070. Malt: Pale malt, Brown malt, Black malt. Hops: Goldings. Dry hops: Yes. Notes: Recipe from 1848. Source: DP.

**No. 3**: OG: 1074. Malt: Pale malt. Hops: Fuggles, Cluster. Yeast: White Labs WLP028. Notes: Recipe from 1879. IBU: 115. SRM: 6. OG: 1055. Malt: Pale malt, Lager malt, Flaked maize. Hops: Fuggles, Cluster. Yeast: White Labs WLP028. Notes: Recipe from 1933. IBU: 32. SRM: 4. Source: VB. OG: 1076. Malt: Pale malt, Lager malt. Hops: Goldings. Dry hops: Yes. Notes: Recipe from 1896. Source: DP.

**120/-**: OG: 1093. Malt: Pale malt. Hops: Goldings. Dry hops: Goldings. Notes: Recipe from 1872. Source: DP.

**No. 2**: OG: 1095. Malt: Pale malt. Hops: Goldings. Dry hops: Goldings. Notes: Recipe from 1872. Source: DP.

**100/-**: OG: 1099. Malt: Pale malt. Hops: Goldings, Cluster. Yeast: White Labs WLP028. Notes: Recipe from 1848. IBU: 84. SRM: 9. Source: VB.

**No. 1**: OG: 1099. Malt: Pale malt. Hops: Goldings. Yeast: White Labs WLP028. Notes: Recipe from 1868. IBU: 75. SRM: 7. Source: VB. OG: 1102. Malt: Pale malt. Hops: Goldings. Dry hops: Goldings. Notes: Recipe from 1872. Source: DP.

**160/-**: OG: 1099. Malt: Pale malt, Flaked maize, No.2 invert sugar, No.3 invert sugar. Hops: Fuggles, Cluster. Yeast: White Labs WLP028. Notes: Recipe from 1913. IBU: 76. SRM: 10. Source: VB. OG: 1126. Malt: Pale malt. Hops: Goldings. Dry hops: Goldings. Notes: Recipe from 1872. Source: DP.

**140/-**: OG: 1114. Malt: Pale malt. Hops: Goldings. Yeast: White Labs WLP028. Notes: Recipe from 1858. IBU: 67. SRM: 8. Source: VB.

# Singapore

### . Asia Pacific Breweries

**Tiger Lager**: OG: 1035. Malt: Lager malt, Flaked rice. Hops: Hallertau. Source: DL. OG: 1050-52. Malt: Pale malt, Flaked rice, Flaked maize, Crystal malt. Hops: Hersbrücker. Late hops: Hersbrücker. Source: BC.

### . Archipelago Brewer Company

**ABC Extra Stout**: OG: 1081-82. Malt: Pale malt, Flaked maize, Crystal malt, Roast barley, Sugar. Hops: Northern Brewer. Late hops: Hersbrücker. Source: CB.

# South Africa

### . South African Breweries, Johannesburg

**Castle Milk Stout**: OG: 1037. Malt: Pale malt, Black malt, Flaked maize, Sugar. Hops: Saaz. Source: DL.

**Lion Lager**: OG: 1046. Malt: Pale malt, Flaked maize, Sugar, Caramel. Hops: Saaz. Source: DL. OG: 1049-51. Malt: Lager malt, Flaked maize, Crystal malt. Hops: Saaz, Tettnang. Late hops: Tettnang. Source: CB.

**Castle Lager**: OG: 1050-1. Malt: Pilsner malt, Flaked maize, Crystal malt, Vienna malt. Hops: Spalt. Late hops: Tettnang, Hersbrücker. Source: CB

**Guinness Foreign Extra Stout**: Others: Guinness flavour extract. Source: BY.

## South Korea

. *Oriental Brewing Company, Seoul*

**O.B. Lager Beer**: OG: 1044-45. Malt: Pale malt, Flaked maize, Crystal malt, Sugar. Hops: Tettnang. Late hops: Hersbrücker. Source: CB.

## Spain

. *Cerveceros Caseros Españolas: www.cerveceroscaseros.es*

. *SA El Aguila, Madrid*

**Aguila Pilsener**: OG: 1045. Malt: Pale malt, Corn grits. Hops: Northern Brewer, Brewers Gold. IBU: 23. Source: EBA.

**Adlerbräu**: OG: 1053. Malt: Pale malt, Caramel malt, Corn grits. Hops: Northern Brewer, Brewers Gold. IBU: 28. Source: EBA.

**Aguila Reserva Extra**: OG: 1062. Malt: Pale malt, Roast malts, Corn grits. Hops: Northern Brewer, Brewers Gold. IBU: 28. Source: EBA.

. *Estrella Galicia Brewery, Galicia*

**Estrella Galicia Especial**: OG: 1049-51. Malt: Pilsner malt, Flaked maize, Munich malt, Crystal malt. Hops: Tettnang. Late hops: Styrian Goldings, Saaz. Source: CB.

. *San Miguel Fabricas de Cerveza y Malta, Madrid*

**San Miguel Premium Lager**: ABV: 5.4%. Malt: Pale malt. Hops: Hallertau Northern Brewer, Perle, Styrian Goldings. IBU: 23-25. Source: EBA. ABV: 5.5%. Malt: Sugar. Hops: Hallertau. Source: DL.

**Selecta XV**: ABV: 5.4%. Malt: Pale malt. Hops: Hallertau Northern Brewer, Perle, Styrian Goldings. IBU: 23-25. Source: EBA.

## Sweden

. *Pripps, Sundsvall*

**D. Carnegie & Co. Porter**: OG: 1062-63. Malt: Pale malt, Chocolate malt, Crystal malt, Black malt, Kiln Coffee malt. Hops: Northern Brewer. Late hops: Styrian Goldings. Source: CB.

# Switzerland

### . Brauerei Hürlimann, Zürich

**Löwenbräu Lager**: OG: 1045. Malt: Pale malt. Hops: Hallertau, Hersbrücker. IBU: 21. Source: EBA.

**Sternbräu**: OG: 1057. Malt: Pale malt. Hops: Hallertau, Saaz. IBU: 28. Source: EBA. OG: 1047. Malt: Lager malt, Sugar. Hops: Saaz. Late hops: Saaz. Source: DL.

**Caesarus Imperator Heller Bock**: OG: 1072-75. Malt: Pilsner malt, Munich malt, Dextrin malt, Vienna malt, Aromatic malt, Crystal malt. Hops: Spalt. Late hops: Hersbrücker. Source: CB.

**Samichlaus**: OG: 1122. Malt: Pale malt, Dark malt. Hops: Hallertau, Hersbrücker, Styrian Goldings. IBU: 30. Source: EBA. OG: 1138-1144. Malt: Pilsner malt, Vienna malt, Crystal malt, Candi sugar. Hops: Northern Brewer. Late hops: Tettnang, Hallertau Mittelfrüh. Source: CB.

### . Schützengarten, St. Gallen

**St. Galler Landbier**: ABV: 5%. Malt: Pale malt, Wheat malt. Hops: Hallertau, Saaz. Source: HB.

**St. Galler Klosterbräu**: ABV: 5.2%. Malt: Pale malt, Amber malt. Hops: Hallertau, Saaz. Source: HB.

# Thailand

### . Boon Rawd Brewing Company, Bangkok

**Sinhga Malt Liquor**: OG: 1063. Malt: Pale malt, Flaked maize, Dextrin malt, Crystal malt, Munich malt, Maltodextrin, Sugar. Hops: Northern Brewer. Late hops: Saaz, Hersbrücker. Source: CB. Notes: Bangkok was previously called Krungthep Mahanakhon Bovorn Ratanakosin Mahintharayutthaya Mahadilokpop Noparatratchathani Burirom Udomratchanivet Mahasathan Amornpiman Avatarnsathit Sakkathattiyavisnukarmprasit. Try saying that after a few too many Singhas!

# Togo

### . Brasserie BB, Lomé

**Ngoma Togo Pils**: OG: 1057-60. Malt: Crystal malt, Pilsner malt, Vienna malt. Hops: Spalt. Late hops: Hersbrücker, Tettnang. Source: CB.

**Ngoma Malt Liquor Tiger Lager**: OG: 1061-63. Malt: CaraMunich malt, Pilsner malt. Hops: Northern Brewer. Late hops: Hersbrücker. Source: CB.

Notes: Also brewed in South Africa, Kenya, Mozambique and Nigeria.

## Trinidad

. *Carib Brewery, Champs Fleurs*

**Carib Ginger Shandy**: OG: 1014. Malt: Pale malt, Flaked maize, Crystal malt, Sugar, Lactose. Others: Fresh ginger, Ginger. Source: CB.

## Turkey

. *Efes, Istanbul, Izmir and Adana*

**Efes Pilsener**: OG: 1051-52. Malt: Rice, Pale malt, Munich malt, Crystal malt. Hops: Tettnang. Late hops: Tettnang. Source: CB.

## United Kingdom Islands

. *Ann Street Brewery Company, St. Helier, Jersey*

**Old Jersey Ale**: OG: 1035. Malt: 95% Pipkin pale malt, 2.5% Chocolate malt, 1% Wheat malt, 1.5% Sugars. Hops: Challenger, Fuggles, Goldings, Hallertau. Dry hops: Yes. IBU: 33. EBC: 40. Source: RP3. Note: See The Jersey Brewery.

**Winter Ale**: OG: 1068. Malt: 94% Pipkin pale malt, 2% Chocolate malt, 1.5% Wheat malt, 2.5% Sugars. Hops: Challenger, Fuggles, Goldings, Hallertau. Dry hops: Yes. IBU: 50.2. EBC: 87.5. Source: RP3. Note: See The Jersey Brewery.

. *The Jersey Brewery, St. Helier, Jersey.*
*Www.genuinejersey.com/member pages/jerseybrewery.htm*

**Mary Ann Best Bitter**: ABV: 3.6%. Malt: Chocolate malt. Source: Web.

**Old Jersey Ale**: OG: 1035. Malt: 95% Pipkin pale malt, 2.5% Chocolate malt, 1% Wheat malt, 1.5% Sugars. Hops: Challenger, Fuggles, Goldings. Dry hops: Yes. IBU: 33. EBC: 40. Source: RP4/5. Note: See the Ann Street Brewery Company.

**Mary Ann Special**: ABV: 4.5%. Malt: Maris Otter pale malt. Hops: Fuggles, Goldings. Source: Web.

**Ann's Treat**: OG: 1050. Malt: 90% Pipkin pale malt, 1.2% Crystal malt, 0.7% Chocolate malt, 2.4% Wheat malt, 5.7% Sugars. Hops: Challenger, Fuggles, Goldings. Late hops: Yes. IBU: 27. EBC: 36. Source: RP4/5.

**Winter Ale**: OG: 1068. Malt: 94% Pipkin pale malt, 2% Chocolate malt, 1.5% Wheat malt, 2.5% Sugars. Hops: Challenger, Fuggles, Goldings. Dry hops: Yes. IBU: 50.2. EBC: 87.5. Source: RP4/5. Note: See the Ann Street Brewery Company.

### Guernsey Brewery Company, St. Peter Port, Guernsey

**LBA Mild**: OG: 1038. Malt: 98% Pale malt, 1.5% Flaked barley, 0.5% Wheat malt, Caramel. Hops: Bavarian hops, Fuggles, Northern Brewer. Dry hops: Goldings. Source: RP1/2/3.

**Braye Ale**: OG: 1038. Malt: 98% Maris Otter pale malt, 1% Flaked barley, 1% Wheat malt, Caramel. Hops: 80% Fuggles, 10% WGV, 10% Hallertau. Dry hops: 10% Goldings. Source: RP4/5.

**Sunbeam Bitter**: OG: 1045. Malt: 97% Maris Otter pale malt, 1% Flaked barley, 1% Wheat malt, 1% Crystal malt. Hops: Fuggles, WGV. Late hops: Fuggles, WGV, Goldings. Dry hops: Goldings. Source: RP.

**Real Draught Bitter**: OG: 1046. Malt: 98% Pale malt, 1.5% Flaked barley, 0.5% Wheat malt, Caramel. Hops: Fuggles, Hallertau, Goldings/WGV. Dry hops: Goldings. Source: RP.

**Britannia Bitter**: ABV: 4%. Note: Blend of **Sunbeam** and **Braye**. Source: RP4/5.

### R. W. Randall, Guernsey

**Best Mild**: OG: 1033. Malt: 93% Pale malt, 3% Wheat malt, 4% Sugar. Hops: Fuggles, optional Hop oil. Source: RP.

**Best Bitter / Bitter**: OG: 1046. Malt: 94% Pale malt, 3% Wheat malt, Sugar. Hops: Fuggles, Hallertau, optional Hop oil. Source: RP.

**Patois**: OG: 1046. Malt: 94% Pale malt, 3% Wheat malt, Sugar, Caramel. Hops: Fuggles, Hallertau. Dry hops: Yes. Source: RP5.

**Stout** (b-c): ABV: 5.5%. Malt: Maris Otter pale malt, Crystal malt, Chocolate malt, Sugar. Hops: Fuggles. Source: JE1/2.

### Ales of Scilly, St. Marys, Isles of Scilly

**Scuppered** (b-c): ABV: 4.6%. Malt: Maris Otter pale malt, Crystal malt, Black malt. Hops: Challenger. Source: JE6.

# USA

### American Homebrewers Association: www.beertown.org or www.homebrewersassociation.org.

### Abita Brewing Company, Abita Springs, LA. Www.abita.com

**Wheat**: OG: 1040. Hops: Mount Hood. Source: GAM.

**Golden**: OG: 1040. Malt: Lager malt. Hops: Mount Hood. Source: Web/GAM.

**Abita Amber**: OG: 1048. Malt: Lager malt, Munich malt, Vienna malt, Crystal malt. Hops: Tettnang. Late hops: Tettnang. Source: NACB. OG: 1043-44. Malt: Pale malt,

Crystal malt, Chocolate malt, Munich malt. Hops: Chinook. Late hops: Crystal, Perle. Source: BC/Web. OG: 1044. Malt: Caramel malt. Hops: Perle, Crystal. Source: GAM.

**Red Ale**: Malt: Pale malt, Crystal malt. Hops: Liberty. Source: GAM.

**Fall Fest**: OG: 1050. Malt: Pale malt, Chocolate malt, Crystal malt. Hops: Hersbrücker. Source: Web/GAM.

**Turbodog**: OG: 1054. Malt: Pale malt, Crystal malt, Chocolate malt. Hops: Chinook. Late hops: Willamette. Source: 150/Web. OG: 1056. Malt: Pale malt, Caramel malt, Chocolate malt. Hops: Willamette. Source: GAM.

**Bock**: OG: 1054. Malt: Pale malt, Caramel malt. Hops: Perle. Source: Web/GAM.

**Andygator**: Malt: Pale malt. Hops: Liberty. Source: Web.

**Purple Haze**: Others: Raspberry puree. Source: Web.

**Restoration Ale**: Malt: Pale malt, Lager malt, Crystal malt, CaraPils malt. Hops: Cascade. Source: Web.

### . *Alaskan Brewing, Juneau, AK. Www.alaskanbeer.com*

**Pale Ale**: OG: 1048. Malt: Pale malt, Munich malt. Hops: Willamette, Tettnang, Chinook. Source: GAM/Web.

**Summer Ale**: OG: 1048. Malt: Pale malt, Wheat malt, Munich malt, Vienna malt. Hops: Hallertau. Source: Web.

**Autumn Ale**: OG: 1048. Malt: Pale malt, Crystal malt. Hops: Cascade, Centennial. Source: GAM.

**Amber Beer**: OG: 1054. Malt: Pilsner malt, Munich malt. Hops: Mount Hood. Late hops: Spalt. Source: NACB. Malt: Pale malt, Crystal malts. Hops: Cascade. Late hops: Saaz. Source: 150/Web. OG: 1057. Malt: Pale malt, Munich malt. Hops: Cascade, Saaz. Source: GAM.

**ESB**: OG: 1054. Malt: Pale malt, Crystal malt. Hops: Cascade, Centennial. Source: Web.

**Smoked Porter**: OG: 1065. Malt: Smoked pale malt, Crystal malt, Black malt, Chocolate malt. Hops: Goldings. Late hops: Willamette, Goldings. Source: NACB. Malt: Pale malt, Crystal malt, Chocolate malt, Patent black malt, optional Munich malt, Hops: Chinook. Late hops: Willamette. Source: 150/GAM. Malt: Alder-smoked malt. Source: Web.

**Stout**: OG: 1065. Malt: Pale malt, Wheat malt, Roast barley, Black malt, Oats, Vienna malt. Hops: Goldings. Source: Web.

**Winter Ale**: OG: 1066. Malt: Pale malt, Caramel malt, Wheat malt, Munich malt. Hops: Saaz. Others: Sitka spruce tips. Source: Web.

### Acadian Brewing Company, New Orleans, LA

**Acadian Pilsner**: OG: 1050. Malt: Lager malt, Vienna malt, CaraPils malt. Hops: Saaz. Late hops: Saaz. Source: NACB.

### Ale Asylum, Madison, WI

**Bedlam! Trappist IPA**: Hops: Citra. Source: BA.

### AleSmith Brewing Company, San Diego, CA

**AleSmith IPA**: OG: 1073. Malt: Pale malt, CaraPils malt, Crystal malt, Honey malt, Munich malt, Wheat malt. Hops: Columbus, Simcoe. Late hops: Amarillo, Simcoe, Columbus, Cascade. Dry hops: Columbus, Amarillo, Cascade, Simcoe, Chinook. Source: 150.

### Allagash Brewing Company, Portland, ME www.Allegash.com

**Allagash White**: ABV: 5%. Others: Coriander, Curaçao orange peel. Source: Web.

**Big Little Beer**: ABV: 5.5%. Malt: 2 Pilsner malts, Red wheat malt, Victory malt. Demerara sugar. Hops: Northern Brewer, Mount Hood, Nelson Sauvin. Note: Aged in wine and bourbon casks. Source: Web.

**Allagash Grand Cru**: OG: 1060. Malt: Belgian pale malt, CaraVienne malt, Wheat malt, Peat-smoked malt, Candi sugar. Hops: Brewers Gold. Others: Dried sweet Orange peel, Star Anise. Source: NACB. ABV: 7.2%. Malt: Peat-smoked malt. Others: Coriander, Anise, Sweet orange peel. Source: Web.

**Blonde**: ABV: 7.1%. Malt: Pilsner malt. Hops: Hallertau, Saaz. Source: Web.

**Allagash Black**: ABV: 7.5%. Malt: Pale malt, Chocolate malt, Torrefied wheat, Roast malt, Oats, Dark candi sugar. Source: Web.

**Allagash Confluence**: ABV: 7.5%. Malt: Pale malt, Pilsner malt, Caramel malt. Hops: Goldings, Tettnang. Dry hops: Glacier. Source: Web.

**Fluxus 2012**: ABV: 7.7%. Malt: Spelt. Hops: Northern Brewer, Saaz, Cascade. Others: Green peppercorns, Pink peppercorns. Source: Web.

**Hugh Malone Ale**: Hops: Simcoe, Sorachi Ace, Teamaker. Source: BA. ABV: 7.8%. Malt: Pilsner malt, Wheat malt. Hops: Chinook. Late hops: Centennial, Amarillo. Dry hops: Centennial, Amarillo. Source: Web.

**Respect Your Elderberries**: ABV: 7.9%. Others: Elderberries. Source: Web.

**Saison Mihm**: ABV: 8%. Malt: Maine honey. Others: Juniper, Lemon grass. Source: Web.

**Fluxus 2011**: ABV: 8%. Malt: Pilsner malt, Light Munich malt, Wheat malt, Aromatic malt, Coloured malts. Hops: Brewers Gold. Source: Web.

**Old HLT**: ABV: 8%. Malt: Pilsner malt, Wheat malt, Munich malt, Candi sugar. Others: Montmorency cherries. Source: Web.

**Fedeltá**: ABV: 8.2%. Malt: Pale malt, Pilsner malt, 15% Wheat malt, Cane sugar, Honey. Hops: Cascade, Amarillo. IBU: 35. Source: Web.

**Fluxus 2009**: ABV: 8.3%. Hops: Centennial. Others: Sweet potatoes, Black pepper. Source: Web.

**Allagash 11th Anniversary Ale**: ABV: 9%. Malt: Aromatic malt. Hops: Northern Brewer, Cascade. Yeast: Champagne. Source: Web.

**Victoria Ale**: ABV: 9%. Others: Chardonnay grapes. Source: Web.

**Victor Ale**: ABV: 9%. Malt: Pilsner malt. Hops: Fuggles, Hallertau. Others: Cabernet Franc grapes. Yeast: Wine. Source: Web.

**Yakuza**: ABV: 9%. Hops: Sorachi Ace, Cascade. Source: Web.

**BAM**: ABV: 9%. Malt: Rye malt, Honey. Hops: Northern Brewer, Mount Hood, Saaz. Note: Aged in mead casks. Source: Web.

**BAT**: ABV: 9%. Malt: Rye malt, Honey. Hops: Northern Brewer, Mount Hood, Saaz. Note: Aged in Tequila casks. Source: Web.

**Gargamel**: ABV: 9.2%. Malt: Pale malt, Wheat malt, Caramel malt, Wheat. Others: Raspberries. Aged in wine casks. Source: Web.

**Smoke and Beards**: ABV: 9.2%. Malt: Pale malt, Smoked malt. Hops: Northern Brewer, Hallertau, Saaz. Source: Web.

**Vrienden**: ABV: 9.3%. Others: Elderberries, Dandelion leaves. Source: Web.

**Victor Francenstein**: ABV: 9.7%. Others: Cabernet Franc grapes. Source: Web.

**Allagash Four**: ABV: 10%. Malt: 4 malts. Hops: 4 hops. Yeast: 4 yeast strains. Source: Web.

**Fluxus 2007**: ABV: 10%. Malt: Pilsner malt, 25% Rye malt. Hops: Warrior, Brewers Gold. Others: Yarrow. Source: Web.

**Fluxus 2008**: ABV: 10%. Malt: Wheat malt, Wheat. Others: Spices, Ginger. Source: Web.

**Fluxus 2010**: ABV: 10.3%. Malt: 3 roast malts, Oats. Hops: Saaz, Glacier. Others: Cacao nibs. Source: Web.

**Allagash Odyssey**: ABV: 10.4%. Malt: Pale malt, Wheat malt, Roast barley, Candi sugar. Source: Web.

**Avancé**: ABV: 10.8%. Others: Strawberries. Aged in and bourbon casks. Source: Web.

**Les Deux Brasseurs**: Malt: Pilsner malt, small amount of Torrefied wheat. Hops: Hallertau. Dry hops: Saaz. Source: Web.

### Alpine Beer Company, Alpine, CA AlpineBeerCo.WordPress.com

**Mandarin Nectar**: OG: 1060. Malt: Orange blossom honey. Others: Coriander seeds, Orange peel. IBU: 6. Source: Web.

**Duet**: OG: 1065. Hops: Simcoe, Amarillo. Source: Web.

**Nelson**: OG: 1065. Malt: Rye malt. Hops: Nelson Sauvin. Others: Oak chips. Source: BA/Web.

**Ichabod Ale**: ABV: 6-7%. Others: Pumpkins, Cinnamon, Nutmeg. Source: Web.

### Anchor Brewing Company, San Francisco, CA

**Anchor Steam**: OG: 1051. Malt: Pale malt, Crystal malt. Hops: Northern Brewer. Late hops: Northern Brewer. Source: 150/CB/Dan Morris, HF.

**Anchor Porter**: OG: 1055. Malt: Pale malt, Crystal malt, Patent black malt, Munich malt. Hops: Northern Brewer. Late hops: Northern Brewer. Source: NACB. OG: 1068-69. Malt: Pale malt, Dextrin malt, Crystal malt, Chocolate malt, Black malt, Roast barley. Hops: Cascade, Northern Brewer. Source: BC.

**Liberty Ale**: OG: 1057. Malt: Pale malt, Toasted pale malt, Crystal malt. Hops: Cascade. Late hops: Cascade. Dry hops: Cascade. Source: NACB. Malt: Light dry malt extract, Crystal malt, Pale malt. Hops: Galena. Late hops: Cascade. Dry hops: Cascade. Yeast: Wyeast #1056. Source: Frank Tutzauer, HF. Malt: Pale malt, CaraPils malt. Hops: Chinook, Cascade. Late hops: Cascade. Dry hops: Cascade. Source: Darren Evans-Young, HF. OG: 1060-63. Malt: Pale malt, Crystal malt. Hops: Northern Brewer. Late hops: Northern Brewer, Cascade. Dry hops: Cascade. Source: BC.

**Our Special Ale**: OG: 1068-69. Malt: Pale malt, Chocolate malt, Crystal malt. Hops: Northern Brewer. Late hops: Northern Brewer. Others: Vanilla bean, Nutmeg, Anise. Source: BC. Note: 1995 version.

### Anderson Valley Brewing Company, Boonville, CA

**High Roller's Wheat**: OG: 1051. Malt: Pale malt, Wheat malt. Hops: Northern Brewer, Mount Hood. Source: GAM.

**Deep Ender's Dark Porter**: OG: 1052. Malt: Pale malt, Caramel 40L malt, Caramel 80L malt, Chocolate malt. Hops: Nugget, Cluster, Liberty. Source: GAM.

**Poleko Gold**: OG: 1052. Malt: Pale malt, Caramel 40L malt. Hops: Eroica, Nugget, Northern Brewer, Cascade. Source: GAM.

**Boont Amber**: OG: 1059. Malt: Pale malt, Crystal malts. Hops: Eroica. Late hops: Cluster, Liberty. Source: BC. OG: 1055. Malt: Pale malt, Caramel 40L malt, Caramel 80L malt. Hops: Eroica, Cluster, Liberty. Source: GAM.

**Belk's Extra Special Bitter Ale**: 1052. Malt: Pale malt, Caramel 40L malt, Munich 20L malt. Hops: Eroica, Northern Brewer, Nugget, Mount Hood. Source: GAM.

**Barney Flats Oatmeal Stout**: OG: 1055. Malt: Pale malt, Crystal malt, Flaked oats, Chocolate malt, Roast barley. Hops: Goldings. Late hops: Willamette. Source: NACB. OG: 1063. Malt: Pale malt, Caramel 40L malt, Caramel 80L malt, Munich 20L malt, Chocolate malt, Wheat malt, Roast barley, Oats. Hops: Eroica, Northern Brewer, Cascade. Source: GAM.

**Winter Solstice**: OG: 1064. Malt: Pale malt, Caramel 40L malt, Caramel 80L malt, Munich 20L malt. Hops: Northern Brewer, Mount Hood. Source: GAM.

### . *Anheuser-Busch, St. Louis, MO*

**Budweiser**: OG: 1046. Malt: Lager malt, Flaked rice. Hops: Hallertau. Source: DL.

### . *Appleton Brewing Company, Appleton, WI*

**Adler Brau Oatmeal Stout**: OG: 1050. Malt: Pale malt, Lager malt, Flaked oats, Roast barley, Patent black malt, Caramel 60L malt. Hops: Willamette. Source: GAM.

**Adler Brau Mosquito Pilsner**: OG: 1050. Malt: Pale malt, Lager malt, Wheat malt, Caramel 20L malt, CaraPils malt. Hops: Saaz, Hallertau. Source: GAM.

**Adler Brau Tailgate Amber**: OG: 1052. Malt: Pale malt, Lager malt, Chocolate malt, Caramel 20L malt, Caramel 60L malt, Munich malt. Hops: Northern Brewer, Cascade, Hallertau. Source: GAM.

**Erich Weiss Beer**: OG: 1054. Malt: Pale malt, Wheat malt, Munich malt. Hops: Northern Brewer, Cascade, Hallertau. Source: GAM.

**Classic Porter**: OG: 1055. Malt: Pale malt, Lager malt, Chocolate malt, Caramel 40L malt, Munich malt. Hops: Northern Brewer, Willamette. Source: GAM.

### . *Arrowhead, Chambersburg, PA*

**Red Feather Pale Ale**: OG: 1047. Malt: Pale malt. Hops: Cascade, Northern Brewer, Willamette. Source: GAM.

### . *Atlantic Brewing Company, Bar Harbor, ME*

**Bar Harbor Real Ale**: OG: 1048. Malt: Pale malt, Crystal malt, Patent black malt. Hops: Willamette. Source: GAM.

**Lompoc's Pale Ale**: OG: 1048. Malt: Pale malt, Munich malt. Hops: Perle, Chinook. Source: GAM.

**Coal Porter**: OG: 1050. Malt: Pale malt, Roast barley. Hops: Willamette, Chinook. Source: GAM.

**Lompoc's Bar Harbor Blueberry Ale**: OG: 1052. Malt: Pale malt, Munich malt. Hops: Willamette. Others: Blueberries. Source: GAM.

**Lompoc's Ginger Wheat**: OG: 1056. Malt: Pale malt, Munich malt. Hops: Willamette. Others: Root ginger. Source: GAM.

### Atlantic Coast Brewing, Boston, MA

**Tremont IPA**: OG: 1067. Malt: Pale malt, Crystal malt, Torrefied wheat. Hops: Fuggles. Late hops: Styrian Goldings, Fuggles, Cascade. Dry hops: Cascade. Source: BC.

### Atlas Brewing Company, Chicago, IL www.atlasbeercompany.com

**Elusive Spring Wheat Ale**: ABV: 5.8%. Others: Orange blossom, Chamomile, Lemon grass, Coriander. Source: Web.

### Avery Brewing Company, Boulder, CO. Www.averybrewing.com

**Joe's Pilsner**: OG: 1041. Malt: 100% Pale malt. Hops: 12.5% Bravo. Late hops: 87.5% Hersbrücker. Yeast: Weihenstephan. Source: Web.

**14'er ESB**: OG: 1048. Malt: Pale malt, Caramel 120L malt. Hops: Bullion, Fuggles. IBU: 37. Source: Web.

**Karma**: OG: 1048. Malt: 85.8% Pale malt, 0.8% Special B malt, 7.6% Caramel 45L malt, 5.8% Aromatic malt. Hops: 12.2% Sterling. Late hops: 87.8% Sterling. Yeast: Rochefort. IBU: 10. Source: Web.

**White Rascal**: OG: 1050. Malt: 50% Pale malt, 50% Wheat malt. Hops: Saaz or 51.1% Bravo. Late hops: 3.4% Sterling, 19.6% Hersbrücker. Others: Coriander, Bitter orange peel, Sweet orange peel. Yeast: Hoegaarden. IBU: 10. Source: Web.

**Redpoint**: OG: 1052. Malt: Pale malt, Munich 100L malt, Caramel 75L malt, Caramel 120L malt. Hops: Columbus, Crystal, Sterling. IBU: 22. Source: Web.

**Out of Bounds**: OG: 1054. Malt: 80% Pale malt, 7.2% Roast barley, 3.6% Caramel 120L malt, 3.6% Black malt, 0-2% Wheat malt. Hops: Fuggles or 89% Bullion. Late hops: 11% Bullion. Yeast: California. IBU: 51. Source: Web.

**Ellie's Brown**: OG: 1056. Malt: 80.5% Pale malt, 6.4% Munich 10L malt, 4.2% Caramel 120L malt, 6.6% Chocolate malt, 0-2.3% Honey malt. Hops: Cascade, Fuggles, 8.9% Bullion, 21.9% Sterling. Late hops: 69.2% Sterling. Yeast: California. IBU: 17. Source: Web.

**Avery IPA**: OG: 1058. Malt: 94% Pale malt, 4% Munich 10L malt, 2% Caramel 120L malt. Hops: 9.4% Columbus. Late hops: 30.2% Cascade, 30.2% Centennial, 30.2% Chinook, optional Simcoe, optional Crystal. Yeast. California. IBU: 69. Source: Web.

**Fifteen**: OG: 1064. Malt: Pale malt, Wheat malt. Hops: Sterling. Others: Black mission figs, Hibiscus flowers, White pepper. IBU: 19.2. Source: Web.

**New World Porter**: OG: 1067. Malt: Pale malt, Munich malt, Crystal malt, CaraPils malt, Chocolate malt, Patent black malt. Hops: Columbus. Late hops: Columbus, Fuggles. Source: 150. OG: 1065. Malt: Pale malt, Munich 10L malt, Chocolate malt, Black malt, Caramel 120L malt. Hops: Columbus, Fuggles. IBU: 45. Source: Web. OG: 1065. Malt: 66.3% Pale malt, 3% Black malt, 4% CaraPils malt, 7.3% Caramel 120L malt, 3.8%

Chocolate malt, 15.6% Munich malt. Hops: 8% Columbus. Late hops: 34.4% Columbus, 34.4% Centennial. Dry hops: 23.3% Cascade. Yeast: California. Source: Web.

**Old Jubilation**: OG: 1074. Malt: 88.3% Pale malt, 4.7% Special Roast malt, 4.7% Victory malt, 0.7% Black malt, 1.6% Chocolate malt, optional Sugar. Hops: 46% Bullion. Late hops: 54% Bullion. Yeast: California. IBU: 30. Source: 150/Web.

**Twelve**: ABV: 7.6%. Malt: Pale malt, Wheat malt. Hops: Columbus, Sterling, Styrian Goldings. Others: Sweet Orange peel, Lemon peel, Grains of Paradise, Chamomile, Lavender. Source: Web.

**Collaboration not Litigation Ale**: OG: 1079. Notes: Blend of **Salvation** and Russian River **Salvation** (ABV:9%). Not a 50:50 blend. Source: Web/Basic Brewing Radio (February 15, 2007).

**Salvation**: OG: 1080. Malt: 91.8% Pale malt, 4.1% Caramel 8L malt, 4.1% Caramel 20L malt, Light candi sugar. Hops: Styrian Goldings or 21% Sterling. Late hops: 20% Sterling, 52.1% Fuggles. Yeast: Wyeast #3787/Westmalle. IBU: 25-28. Source: BLAM/Web.

**The Maharaja**: OG: 1080. Malt: Pale malt, Caramel 120L malt, Victory malt. Hops: Magnum, Crystal, Centennial, Simcoe. IBU: 102. Source: Web. OG: 1090. Malt: 93.8% Pale malt, 3.1% Caramel 120L malt, 3.1% Victory malt. Hops: 14.3% Columbus. Late hops: 14.3% Centennial, 14.3% Simcoe. Dry hops: 28.7% Simcoe, 14.3% Centennial, 14.3% Chinook. Yeast: California. Source: Web.

**The Kaiser**: OG: 1080. Malt: Pale malt, Vienna malt, Munich 10L malt, Aromatic malt. Hops: Magnum, Sterling, Tettnang, Hersbrücker. IBU: 24. Source: Web. OG: 1085. Malt: 64.7% Pale malt, 11.8% Vienna malt, 11.8% Munich malt, 7.9% Dark Munich malt, 3.8% Aromatic malt. Hops: 27.3% Hallertau, 9.1% Magnum, 18.2% Sterling. Late hops: 22.7% Hersbrücker, 22.7% Tettnang. Yeast: Weihenstephan. Source: Web.

**Hog Heaven**: OG: 1085. Malt: 87.4% Pale malt, 12.6% Caramel 75L malt. Hops: 20% Columbus. Late hops: 34.3% Columbus. Dry hops: 45.7% Columbus. Yeast: California. IBU: 104. Source: Web.

**Thirteen**: OG: 1089. Malt: Wheat malt. Source: Web.

**Fourteen**: OG: 1089. Malt: Numerous. Hops: Styrian Goldings. Dry hops: Yes. IBU: 60. Source: Web.

**The Reverend**: OG: 1093. Malt: Pale malt, Caramel 8L malt, Caramel 20L malt, Caramel 15L malt, Caramel 40L malt, Special B malt. Hops: Styrian Goldings. IBU: 10. Source: Web; Malt: 90.6% Pale malt, 1.9% Caramel 45L malt, 1.9% Caramel 20L malt, 1.9% Special B malt, 3.7% Aromatic malt, Dark candi sugar. Hops: 42.3% Sterling. Late hops: 57.7% Sterling. Yeast: Westmalle. Source: Web.

**The Czar**: OG: 1100. Malt: Pale malt, Black malt, Chocolate malt, Carafa® III malt, Caramel 8L malt, Caramel 45L malt, Honey malt. Hops: Magnum, Hallertau. IBU: 60. Source: Web. OG: 1104. Malt: 86.8% Pale malt, 1.9% Caramel 8L malt, 1.2% Chocolate malt, 3.7% Caramel 45L malt, 1.2% De-bittered black malt, 1.5% Carafa® III malt, 3.7% Honey malt. Hops: 63.8% Magnum. Late hops: 18.1% Hallertau, 18.1% Sterling. Yeast: California. Source: Web.

**Samael's Ale**: OG: 1140. Malt: Pale malt, Caramel 150L malt. Hops: Columbus, Fuggles. IBU: 41. Source: Web.

**Mephistopheles' Stout**: OG: 1145. Malt: Pale malt, Black malt, Roast barley, Special B malt, Aromatic malt. Hops: Magnum, Styrian Goldings. IBU: 107. Source: Web.

**The Beast**: OG: 1148. Malt: Pale malt, Special B malt, Honey malt, Aromatic malt, Wheat malt, Roast wheat malt. Hops: Magnum, Galena, Saaz, Hallertau, Tettnang, Hersbrücker. IBU: 68. Source: Web.

### . *BJ's Restaurant Brewhouse. Www.bjsrestaurants.com*

**BJ's Brewhouse Blonde**: OG: 1044. Malt: Pale malt, Wheat malt, Vienna malt. Hops: Perle, Hallertau. IBU: 15. Source: Web.

**Harvest Hefeweizen**: OG: 1048. Malt: Pale malt, Wheat malt, Vienna malt. Hops: Perle, Hallertau. IBU: 15. Source: Web.

**Piranha® Pale Ale**: OG: 1056. Malt: Pale malt, Wheat malt, Crystal malt. Hops: Chinook, Cascade. IBU: 45. Source: Web.

**Nutty Brunette®**: OG: 1061. Malt: Pale malt, Crystal malt, Victory malt, Special Roast malt, Chocolate malt. Hops: Magnum, Fuggles, Willamette. IBU: 35. Source: Web.

**PM Porter**: OG: 1064. Malt: Pale malt, Dark caramel malt, Chocolate malt, Black malt. Hops: Perle, Willamette. IBU: 30. Source: Web.

**Tatonka Stout**: OG: 1068. Malt: Pale malt, Crystal malt, Chocolate malt, Black malt, Roast barley, Oats, Brown sugar, Molasses. Hops: Magnum, Centennial. IBU: 60. Source: Web.

**Jeremiah Red Ale**: OG: 1070. Malt: Pale malt, Munich malt, Crystal malt, Chocolate malt. Hops: Northern Brewer. IBU: 25. Source: Web.

**BJ's Grand Cru**: OG: 1075. Malt: Pale malt, Crystal malt, Candi sugar. Hops: Saaz. Late hops: Saaz. Others: Curaçao Orange peel, Coriander seeds. Source: 150.

**BJ's Millennium Ale**: OG: 1090. Malt: Pale malt, Orange blossom honey, Candi sugar. Hops: Hersbrücker. Others: Curaçao Orange peel, Ginger root, Coriander seeds. Source: 150.

### . *Ballast Point, San Diego, CA. Www.ballastpoint.com*

**Wahoo**: ABV: 4.5%. Malt: Wheat, Oats. Others: Orange peel, Coriander. IBU: 12. Source: Web.

**Homework Series Batch #4**: ABV: 5.8%. Malt: 75.6% Maris Otter pale malt, 6.3% Crystal 40L malt, 1.3% Roast barley, 4.2% Crystal 120L malt, 4.2% Melanoidin malt,

4.2% Dark Munich 20L malt. Hops: 50% Goldings. Late hops: 50% Fuggles. Others: Roast pumpkin puree, Cinnamon, Nutmeg, Cloves. Yeast: White Labs WLP013. IBU: 22. Source: Web.

**Piper Down**: ABV: 5.8%. Malt: Maris Otter pale malt, Roast barley. Hops: UK hops. IBU: 22. Source: Web.

**Homework Series Batch #3**: ABV: 6.5%. Malt: 80.8% Pale malt, 9.6% Munich malt, 5.8% Crystal 40L malt, 3.8% Crystal 20L malt. Hops: 26.8% Willamette. Late hops: 24.4% Willamette. Dry hops: 48.8% Willamette. Yeast: White Labs WLP002. IBU: 53. Source: Web.

**Homework Series Batch #5**: ABV: 6.8%. Malt: 74.5% Pale malt, 12.8% Flaked oats, 8.5% Wheat malt, 6.4% Crystal 10L malt, 6.4% Acid malt. Hops: 25% Belma. Late hops: 25% Belma. Dry hops: 50% Belma. Yeast: White Labs WLP575. IBU: 39. Source: Web.

**Homework Series Batch #1**: ABV: 7%. Malt: 73.3% Pale malt, 9.2% Munich malt, 5.9% CaraMunich, 5.9% CaraVienne malt, 5.2% Crystal 80L malt, 0.5% Blackprinz® malt. Hops: 13.4% CTZ. Late hops: 19.6% Centennial. Dry hops: 67% Centennial. Yeast: White Labs WLP001. IBU: 70. Source: Web.

**Habanero Sculpin**: ABV: 7%. Others: Habanero peppers. IBU: 70. Source: Web.

**Big Eye**: ABV: 7%. Hops: Columbus, Centennial. IBU: 71. Source: Web.

**Homework Series Batch #2**: ABV: 10%. Malt: 75.2% Pale malt, 8.4% Flaked wheat, 5.6% Munich 10L malt, 4.2% Caramel 20L malt, 2.8% Honey malt, 0.6% Acid malt, 3.3% Clear Belgian candi sugar. Mash hops: 5.8% Mount Hood. Hops: 12.5% Galena, 10% Nugget, 4.2% Chinook. Late hops: 4.2% Palisade. Dry hops: 31.7% Crystal, 15.8% Palisade, 15.8% El Dorado. Yeast: White Labs WLP410. IBU: 118. Source: Web.

### . *Baltimore Brewing Company, Baltimore, MD*

**DeGroen's Märzen**: OG: 1054. Malt: Lager malt, Munich malt, CaraPils malt. Hops: Perle. Late hops: Hallertau, Tettnang. Source: NACB.

### . *Bank Brewing Co., Hendricks, MN, Www.bankbrewing.com*

**Sour Bomb**: OG: 1043. Malt: Pilsner malt, Wheat malt. Hops: Citra. Yeast: Kolsch. IBU: 8. Source: Web.

**Wanted**: OG: 1045. Malt: Pale malt, Caramalt, Red wheat malt. Hops: Amarillo. Yeast: Kolsch. IBU: 40. Source: Web.

**Hop Bandit**: OG: 1050. Malt: Pale malt, Munich malt, Dextrin malt, Caramalt. Hops: Simcoe. Yeast: Kolsch. IBU: 20. Source: Web.

**Hop Lab - Blue**: OG: 1068. Malt: Pale malt, Caramalt. Hops: Citra. Yeast: American. IBU: 88. Source: Web.

**Hop Lab - Green**: OG: 1068. Malt: Pale malt, Caramalt. Hops: Simcoe, Citra, Amarillo. Yeast: American. IBU: 88. Source: Web.

**Smoke Bomb**: OG: 1070. Malt: Pale malt, Smoked malt, Dextrin malt, Carafa® Special III malt, Patent black malt. Hops: Northern Brewer. Yeast: English ale. IBU: 34. Source: Web.

**Into The Black**: OG: 1101. Malt: Pale malt, Carafa® Special III malt, Crystal malt, Pale chocolate malt, Dark candi sugar. Hops: Citra, Amarillo. Yeast: American. IBU: 98. Source: Web.

### . Bar Harbor Brewing Company, Bar Harbor, ME

**Bar Harbor Ginger Mild Brew**: OG: 1036. Malt: Pale malt, Mild ale malt, Chocolate malt, Crystal malt. Hops: Cascade, Willamette, Cluster. Others: Root ginger. Source: GAM.

**Harbor Lighthouse Ale**: OG: 1036. Malt: Pale malt, Mild ale malt, Chocolate malt, Crystal malt. Hops: Cascade, Willamette, Cluster. Source: GAM.

**Thunder Hole Ale**: OG: 1060. Malt: Pale malt, Mild ale malt, Chocolate malt, Crystal malt. Hops: Cascade, Willamette, Cluster. Source: GAM.

**Cadillac Mtn. Stout**: OG: 1075. Malt: Pale malt, Mild ale malt, Roast barley, Chocolate malt, Crystal malt. Hops: Cascade, Willamette, Cluster. Source: GAM.

### . Barley Boys Brewing, Omaha, NE

**Phil's Pils**: OG: 1048. Malt: Lager malt, CaraPils malt, Vienna malt. Hops: Hallertau. Late hops: Saaz. Source: NACB.

### . Bear Republic Brewing Company, Healdsburg, CA

**Racer 5**: OG: 1071. Malt: Pale malt, Wheat malt, Crystal malt, CaraPils malt, Dextrose. Hops: Chinook. Late hops: Cascade. Dry hops: Cascade, Centennial, Amarillo, Columbus. Source: 150.

### . Bell's Brewery, Galesburg, MI

**Oberon**: OG: 1057. Malt: Pale malt, White wheat, Crystal 20L malt. Hops: Hersbrücker. Late hops: Hersbrücker, Saaz. Dry hops: Saaz. Other: Coriander. IBU: 20.5. SRM: 4.7. Source: BYO.

**Two Hearted Ale**: OG: 1058. Malt: Pale malt, Vienna malt, Crystal malt, CaraPils malt. Hops: Centennial. Late hops: Centennial. Dry hops: Centennial. Source: 150.

**Bell's Best Brown Ale**: OG: 1064. Malt: Pale malt, Victory malt, Special roast malt, Crystal malt, Chocolate malt. Hops: Cascade, Nugget. Late hops: Fuggles. Source: 150.

Note: Formerly Kalamazoo Brewing Company.

### . Belmont Brewing Company, Long Beach, CA

**Marathon**: ABW: 3.6%. Malt: Special roast malts. Hops: Mount Hood. Source: GAM.

**Top Sail**: ABW: 4.6%. Malt: Crystal 90L malt, Victory malt. Hops: Mount Hood, Hallertau. Source: GAM.

**Long Beach Crude**: ABW: 4.6%. Malt: Victory malt, Caramel malt, Chocolate malt, Roast barley. Hops: Cascade, Mount Hood. Source: GAM.

### . *Bend Brewing Company, Bend, OR. Www.bendbrewingco.com*

**High Desert Hefeweizen**: Malt: Pale malt, 50% Wheat malt, Munich malt, Crystal malt. Source: Web.

**Pinnacle Porter**: Malt: Crystal malt, Black malt. Source: Web.

**Hophead Imperial IPA**: OG: 1073. Malt: Pale malt, Crystal malt. First wort hops: Saaz, Hops: Chinook. Late hops: Northern Brewer, Cascade. Dry hops: Cascade. Yeast: Wyeast #1968 or White Labs WLP002. Source: BYO.

### . *Bent River Brewing Company, Moline, IL*

**Bohemian Pilsner**: OG: 1044. Malt: Lager malt, CaraPils malt. Hops: Saaz. Late hops: Saaz. Source: NACB.

### . *H.C.Berger Brewing Company, Fort Collins, CO*

**Mountain Kölsch Ale**: OG: 1042. Malt: Lager malt, CaraPils malt. Hops: Spalt. Late hops: Spalt. Source: NACB. Malt: Pale malt, Crystal malt, Wheat malt. Hops: Cascade, Perle, Willamette. Source: GAM.

**Chocolate Stout**: Malt: Dry roast English Dark malt, Chocolate malt. Source: GAM.

**Indego Pale Ale**: Malt: Pale malt, Patent black malt, Wheat malt, Roast barley, Vienna malt. Hops: Cluster, Tettnang, Hersbrücker. Source: GAM.

**Red Raspberry Wheat Ale**: Malt: Pale malt, Crystal malt, Wheat malt. Others: Raspberries. Source: GAM.

**Colorado Golden Ale**: Hops: Cascade, Willamette, Perle. Source: GAM.

**Dunkel**: Malt: Pale malt, Wheat malt, Munich malt, Vienna malt. Hops: Spalt, Hersbrücker. Source: GAM.

**Red Banshee Ale**: Malt: Pale malt, Crystal malt, Roast barley. Hops: Cluster, Chinook, Tettnang. Source: GAM.

**Whistlepin Wheat ale**: Malt: Pale malt, Wheat malt. Hops: Cascade, Perle. Source: GAM.

### . *Berkshire Brewing Company, South Deerfield, MA*

**Steel Rail Extra Pale Ale**: OG: 1054. Malt: Pale malt. Hops: Willamette, Goldings. Source: GAM.

**Berkshire Ale**: OG: 1064. Malt: Pale malt, Caramel malt, Crystal malt. Hops: Bullion, Cascade, Fuggles. Source: GAM.

**Drayman's Porter**: OG: 1064. Malt: Pale malt, Chocolate malt, Crystal malt, Patent black malt, CaraPils malt. Hops: Northern Brewer, Fuggles. Source: GAM.

**Private Stock Imperial Stout**: OG: 1072. Malt: Pale malt, Crystal malt, Roast barley, Chocolate malt, Molasses. Hops: Styrian Goldings. Late hops: Cascade, Styrian Goldings. Source: NACB.

### . Big Hole Brewing Company, Belgrade, MT

**Wisdom Cream Ale**: OG: 1053. Malt: Pale malt. Hops: Tettnang. Late hops: Saaz. Source: 150.

### . Big Sky Brewing Company, Missoula, MT. Www.bigskybrew.com

**Scape Goat**: ABV: 4.7%. Malt: Pale malt, Crystal malt. Hops: Goldings, Crystal. Source: Web.

**Big Sky Crystal Ale**: ABV: 4.7%. Hops: Hallertau, Liberty, Crystal. Source: Web.

**Moose Drool**: OG: 1052. Malt: 87% Pale malt, 10% Crystal malt, "handful" of Black malt, 3% Chocolate malt. Hops: Goldings. Late hops: Liberty, Willamette. Yeast: Fullers. IBU: 26. SRM: 38. Notes: Mash temperature = 152°F, Final gravity = 3°P. Source: CYBI/Web.

**Slow Elk Oatmeal Stout**: OG: 1055. Malt: Pale malt, Crystal malt, Patent black malt, Flaked oats. Hops: Goldings. Source: 150.

**Powder Hound Winter Ale**: OG: 1060. Malt: Pale malt, Crystal malt, Chocolate malt, Flaked barley. Hops: Challenger. Late hops: Challenger, Goldings. Source: 150.

### . Big Time, Seattle, WA

**Prime Time Pale Ale**: OG: 1048. Malt: Pale malt, Light dextrin malt, Crystal malt. Hops: Yakima Chinook, Cascade, Hersbrücker. Source: GAM.

**Atlas Amber Ale**: OG: 1056. Malt: Pale malt, Light dextrin malt, Crystal malt, Munich malt. Hops: Cascade, Chinook, Centennial. Source: GAM.

**Coal Creek Porter**: OG: 1060. Hops: Centennial. Source: GAM.

### . Bird Creek Brewing Company, Anchorage, AK

**Iliamna Wheat Raspberry Wheat Beer**: OG: 1044. Malt: Pale malt, Wheat malt, Munich malt. Hops: Saaz. Source: GAM.

**Anchorage Ale**: OG: 1045. Malt: Pale malt. Hops: Cascade. Source: GAM.

**Denali Style Ale**: OG: 1045. Malt: Pale malt. Hops: Chinook, Cascade. Others: Wild flowers. Source: GAM.

**Brewed in Alaska Festival Beer**: OG: 1048. Malt: Pale malt, Munich malt. Hops: Saaz.Source: GAM.

**Old 55 Pale Ale**: OG: 1050. Malt: Pale malt, Lager malt. Hops: Chinook, Cascade. Source: GAM.

### . *Birmingham Brewing Company. Birmingham, AL*

**Red Mountain Golden Lager**: OG: 1045. Malt: Pale malt. Hops: Noble hops. Source: GAM.

**Red Mountain Golden Ale**: OG: 1046. Malt: Pale malt. Hops: Cascade. Source: GAM.

**Red Mountain Red Ale**: OG: 1050. Malt: Pale malt, Roast barley. Hops: Cascade, Willamette. Source: GAM.

**Red Mountain Wheat Beer**: OG: 1050. Malt: Pale malt, Crystal malt, Roast barley. Hops: Cluster, Willamette. Source: GAM.

### . *Black Moon, St. Paul, MN*

**Coyote Amber Lager**: Malt: Pale malt, Caramel malt, Mesquite-smoked malt. Hops: Mount Hood, Cascade. Source: GAM.

### . *Black Mountain Brewing Company, Cave Creek, AZ*

**Crazy Ed's Original Cave Creek Chili Light Beer**: ABW: 3.5%. Hops: Saaz. Source: GAM.

**Crazy Ed's Original Cave Creek Chili Beer**: OG:1046. Malt: Lager malt, CaraPils malt, Vienna malt, Flaked maize. Hops: Hallertau. Late hops: Mount Hood. Others: Dried Chilli peppers. Source: NACB. OG: 1044. Malt: Lager malt, Corn syrup. Hops: Hop extract. Others: Serrano chillies. Source: GAM.

**Crazy Ed's Original Cave Creek Amber**: OG: 1044. Malt: Lager malt, Patent black malt. Hops: Hop extract. Source: GAM.

**Crazy Ed's Original Cave Creek Black Mountain Gold**: ABW: 4.7%. Hops: Saaz. Source: GAM.

### . *Blue Hen Brewing Company, Newark, DE*

**Lager Beer**: OG: 1047. Malt: Pale malt, Lager malt. Hops: Saaz, Mount Hood, Cascade, Hersbrücker. Source: GAM.

**Black & Tan**: OG: 1051. Note: Blend of **Lager Beer** and **Porter**. Source: GAM.

**Porter**: OG: 1056. Malt: Pale malt, Lager malt, Chocolate malt, Caramel malt. Hops: Cascade, Goldings. Source: GAM.

### Blue Moon Brewing Company, Golden, CO.
*Www.bluemoonbrewingcompany.com*

**Belgian White/Bellyside Belgian White**: OG: 1049. Malt: Pale malt, Wheat, Flaked oats. Hops: Hallertau, Saaz. Others: Bitter orange peel, Coriander. Source: SMB/Web.

**Rising Moon**: Others: Fresh Kaffir lime leaves. Source: Web.

**Honey Moon/Summer Ale**: Malt: Clover honey. Source: Web.

Note: Part of the Molson Coors Brewing Company.

### Blue Ridge Brewing Company, Frederick, MD

**Subliminator Dopplebock**: OG: 1073. Malt: Lager malt, CaraPils malt, Munich malt. Hops: Tettnang. Late hops: Hallertau, Mount Hood. Source: NACB.

### Boston Beer Company, Boston, MA. *Www.samueladams.com*

**Boston Lightship**: OG: 1032. Malt: Pale malt, Caramel 60L malt. Hops: Hallertau Mittelfrüh, Tettnang, Saaz. Source: GAM.

**Samuel Adams® Light**: ABV: 4.05%. Malt: Pale malt, Caramel 60L malt. Hops: Spalt. Source: Web.

**Samuel Adams® Dark Wheat**: OG: 1046. Malt: Pale malt, Caramel 60L malt. Hops: Saaz, Tettnang. Source: GAM.

**Samuel Adams® Boston Lager**: OG: 1049-1052. Malt: Pale malt, Caramel 60L malt. Hops: Tettnang. Late hope: Hallertau Mittelfrüh, Tettnang. Dry hops: Hallertau Mittelfrüh. Source: Web/CB/GAM.

**Samuel Adams® Cream Stout**: ABV: 4.9%. OG: 1054-55. Malt: Pale malt, Caramel 60L malt, Wheat malt, Roast barley, Chocolate malt. Hops: Goldings, Fuggles. Late hops: Goldings. Source: Web/BC/GAM.

**Samuel Adams® Black Lager**: ABV: 4.9%. Malt: Pale malt, Carafa® Special malt, Munich malt. Hops: Spalt. Source: Web.

**Samuel Adams® Boston Ale**: ABV: 5.1%. Malt: Pale malt, Caramel 60L malt. Hops: Spalt / Saaz, Fuggles, Goldings. Source: Web/GAM. OG: 1056. Malt: Crystal malt. Hops: Cascade. Late hops: Cascade. Yeast: Wyeast #1007 or Cooper's ale. Source: Steve Rogers, MHF.

**Samuel Adams® Hallertau 24**: ABV: 5.1%. Malt: Pilsner malt. Hops: Hallertau Mittelfrüh. Source: Web.

**Samuel Adams® Brown Ale**: ABV: 5.35%. Malt: Maris Otter pale malt, Carafa® malt, Caramel malt, Munich malt. Hops: Spalt, Goldings. Source: Web.

**Samuel Adams® Scotch Ale**: OG: 1052. Malt: Pale malt, Peat-smoked malt, Roast barley, Crystal malt, Munich malt. Hops: Galena. Source: NACB. ABV: 5.4%. Malt: Pale malt, Caramel 60L malt, Munich 10L malt, Chocolate malt, Peat-smoked malt. Hops: Fuggles, Goldings. Source: Web/GAM.

**Samuel Adams® Pale Ale**: ABV: 5.4%. Malt: Pale malt, Munich 10L malt. Hops: Goldings, Fuggles. Source: Web.

**Samuel Adams® Hefeweizen**: ABV: 5.4%. Malt: Pale malt, Wheat malt. Hops: Spalt. Source: Web.

**Samuel Adams® Cherry Wheat**: ABV: 5.4%. Malt: Pale malt, Wheat malt, Munich malt, Honey. Hops: Tettnang. Others: Cherries. Source: Web. OG: 1051. Malt: Pale malt, Caramel 60L malt, Wheat malt, Munich malt, Honey. Hops: Tettnang. Others: Cherries. Source: GAM.

**Samuel Adams® White Ale**: ABV: 5.4%. Malt: Pale malt, Munich malt, Wheat malt. Hops: Tettnang. Others: Orange peel, Lemon peel, Grains of Paradise, Coriander, Anise, Hibiscus, Vanilla, Dried plums, Rosehips, Tamarind. Source: Web.

**Samuel Adams® Octoberfest**: ABV: 5.4%. Malt: Pale malt, Caramel 60L malt, Munich 10L malt, 2-row Moravian malt. Hops: Tettnang, Hallertau Mittelfrüh. Source: Web. OG: 1056. Malt: Pale malt, Caramel 60L malt, Munich malt. Hops: Saaz, Tettnang, Hallertau. Source: GAM.

**Samuel Adams® Honey Porter**: ABV: 5.45%. Malt: Pale malt, Caramel 60L malt, Carafa® malt, Munich 10L malt, Scottish heather honey. Hops: Spalt, Fuggles, Goldings. Source: Web. OG: 1059. Malt: Pale malt, Caramel 60L malt, Chocolate malt. Hops: Saaz, Goldings, Fuggles. Source: GAM.

**Samuel Adams® Summer Ale**: OG: 1055. Malt: Pilsner malt, CaraPils malt, Wheat malt, Flaked wheat. Hops: Hallertau. Late hops: Hallertau. Others: Grains of Paradise, Lemon zest. Source: NACB. Malt: Pale malt, Wheat malt. Hops: Tettnang. Source: Web.

**Samuel Adams® Chocolate Bock**: ABV: 5.5%. Malt: Pale malt, Caramel 60L malt, Munich 10L malt, Chocolate malt. Hops: Tettnang, Spalt. Others: Chocolate. Source: Web.

**Samuel Adams® Winter Lager**: ABV: 5.8%. Malt: Pale malt, Caramel 60L malt, Wheat malt, Munich malt. Hops: Tettnang, Hallertau, Goldings. Source: Web. OG: 1064. Malt: Pale malt, Caramel 60L malt, Wheat malt. Hops: Saaz, Goldings, Tettnang. Source: GAM.

**Samuel Adams® Holiday Porter**: ABV: 5.8%. Malt: Pale malt, Caramel 60L malt, Munich 10L malt, Carafa® malt, Flaked oats. Hops: Fuggles, Goldings, Spalt. Source: Web.

**Samuel Adams® Old Fezziwig® Ale**: ABV: 5.9%. Malt: Pale malt, Caramel 60L malt, Munich 10L malt, Chocolate malt. Hops: Tettnang, Hallertau Mittelfrüh. Source: Web.

**Samuel Adams® Cranberry Lambic**: ABV: 5.9%. Malt: Pale malt, Wheat malt. Hops: Spalt. Others: Cranberries. Source: Web. OG: 1040. Malt: Pale malt, Wheat malt, Maple syrup. Hops: Saaz, Tettnang. Others: Cranberries. Source: GAM.

**Winter Brew**: OG: 1069. Malt: Pale malt, Munich malt, Wheat malt, Crystal malt. Hops: Goldings. Late hops: Tettnang, Hersbrücker. Others: Curaçao Orange peel, Cinnamon, Ginger root. Source: 150.

**Samuel Adams® Imperial Pilsner 2005 Harvest**: ABV: 8.7%. Malt: Pale malt, Munich malt. Hops: Hallertau Mittelfrüh. Source: Web.

**Samuel Adams® Double Bock**: ABV: 8.8%. Malt: Pale malt, Caramel 60L malt. Hops: Tettnang, Hallertau. Source: Web. OG: 1083-84. Malt: Pale malt, CaraMunich malt, Munich malt, Crystal malt, Chocolate malt. Hops: Tettnang, Hallertau Mittelfrüh. Late hops: Saaz, Hallertau Mittelfrüh. Source: BC. Malt: Pale malt, Caramel 60L malt. Hops: Saaz, Tettnang. Source: GAM.

**Samuel Adams® Triple Bock**: ABV: 18%. Malt: Pale malt, Caramel 60L malt. Hops: Hallertau. Source: Web. ABW: 14%. Malt: Pale malt, Chocolate malt. Hops: Tettnang, Hallertau. Source: GAM.

**Samuel Adams® Millennium**: ABV: 20%. Malt: Pale malt, Caramel 60L malt, Vienna malt. Hops: Saaz, Tettnang, Spalt, Hallertau Mittelfrüh. Source: Web.

**Samuel Adams® Utopias**: ABV: 25.6%. Malt: Pale malt, Caramel 60L malt, Munich malt, 2-row Moravian malt, Bavarian Smoked malt. Hops: Spalt, Tettnang, Hallertau, Hallertau Mittelfrüh, Saaz. Source: Web.

### *Boulevard Brewing Co., Kansas City, MO. Www.boulevard.com*

**Tenpenny American Bitter**: OG: 1038. Malt: Pale malt, Carastan 13-17L malt, Black malt, Munich malt. Hops: Nugget, Liberty. Source: GAM.

**Unfiltered Wheat Beer**: OG: 1046. Malt: Pale malt, Crystal 50-60L malt, Wheat malt. Hops: Nugget, Liberty. Source: GAM. °P: 11.2. IBU: 14. EBC: 7.3. Source: Web.

**Pale Ale**: OG: 1049. Malt: Pale malt, Carastan 30-37L malt, Crystal 50-60L malt. Hops: Nugget, Cascade. Source: GAM. °P: 12.2. IBU: 30. EBC: 23. Source: Web.

**Bob's '47 Oktoberfest**: OG: 1054. Malt: Pale malt, Crystal 50-60L malt, Munich malt. Hops: Nugget, Hersbrücker. Source: GAM. °P: 13.5. IBU: 27. EBC: 30. Source: Web.

**Irish Ale**: OG: 1054. Malt: Pale malt, Crystal 50-60L malt, Wheat malt, Chocolate malt, Munich malt. Hops: Nugget, Goldings. Source: GAM. °P: 13.5. Malt: "Six kinds of pale and roast barley malts". IBU: 30. EBC: 51.5. Source: Web.

**Bully! Porter**: OG: 1055. Malt: Pale malt, Black malt, Wheat malt, Crystal malt, Chocolate malt. Hops: Nugget, Willamette. Late hops: Mount Hood. Source: NACB. OG: 1058. Malt: Pale malt, Crystal 50-60L malt, Wheat malt, Chocolate 500-550L malt. Hops: Nugget, Cascade, Liberty. Source: GAM. °P: 14.2. IBU: 49. EBC: 131. Source: Web.

**Nutcracker Ale**: OG: 1063. Malt: Pale malt, Wheat malt, Crystal 50L malt, CaraMunich, CaraPils malt, Brown sugar. Hops: Magnum, Cascade. Late hops: Chinook, Cascade. Yeast: Wyeast #1028/White Labs WLP002. IBU: 32. SRM: 23. Source: BYO. °P: 16. Hops: Chinook. IBU: 38. EBC: 61.8. Source: Web.

## Breckenridge Brewery, Denver, CO. Www.breckenbridgebrewery.com

**Proper**: ABV: 4.0%. Malt: Pale malt, 50% Wheat malt, Caramel malt, CaraPils malt, Torrefied wheat. Hops: Fuggles, Cascade. IBU: 9. Source: Web.

**Summerbright Ale**: ABV: 4.5%. Malt: Pale malt, Wheat malt, Munich malt, CaraPils malt. Hops: Fuggles, Cascade, Willamette. IBU: 15. Source: Web.

**Vanilla Porter**: ABV: 4.7%. Malt: Pale malt, Chocolate malt, Caramel malt, Black malt, Roast barley. Hops: Chinook, Tettnang, Perle, Goldings. Others: Vanilla. IBU: 16. Source: Web.

**Oatmeal Stout**: ABV: 4.95%. Malt: Pale malt, Chocolate malt, Caramel malt, Black malt, Flaked oats, Roast barley. Hops: Perle, Chinook. IBU: 31. Source: Web.

**Avalanche Ale**: ABV: 5.41%. Malt: Pale malt, Chocolate malt, Munich malt, Roast barley. Hops: Willamette, Chinook, Tettnang, Hallertau. IBU: 19. Source: Web. OG: 1054. Malt: Pale malt, Munich malt, Crystal malt, Chocolate malt, Roast barley. Hops: Chinook, Willamette. Late hops: Tettnang, Hallertau. Source: 150.

**Trademark Pale Ale**: ABV: 5.7%. Malt: Pale malt, Munich malt, Caramel malt. Hops: Fuggles, Saaz, Perle, Willamette, Bramling Cross. IBU: 40. Source: Web.

**Autumn Ale**: ABV: 6.7%. Malt: Pale malt, Munich malt, Chocolate malt, Roast barley. Hops: Perle, Hallertau. IBU: 21. Source: Web.

**Christmas Ale**: OG: 1078. Malt: Pale malt, Crystal malt, Chocolate malt, Patent black malt. Hops: Chinook. Late hops: Mount Hood. IBU: 22. Source: 150/Web.

## Brewery Hill Brewery, Wilkes-Barre, PA

**Honey Amber**: OG: 1051. Malt: Pale malt, Caramel 60L malt, Honey. Hops: Saaz, Mount Hood, Goldings, Hersbrücker. Source: GAM.

**Black & Tan**: OG: 1052. Malt: Pale malt, Caramel 60L malt, Chocolate malt. Hops: Saaz, Mount Hood, Goldings, Tettnang, Hersbrücker. Source: GAM.

**Cherry Wheat**: OG: 1052. Malt: Pale malt, Caramel 60L malt, Wheat malt. Hops: Northern Brewer, Cascade. Source: GAM.

**Pale Ale**: OG: 1052. Malt: Pale malt, Caramel 60L malt, CaraPils malt. Hops: Cascade, Mount Hood. Source: GAM.

**Caramel Porter**: OG: 1055. Malt: Pale malt, Crystal malt, Chocolate malt, Black malt, Roast barley. Hops: Target. Late hops: Goldings. Source: NACB.

## BridgePort Brewing Company, Portland, OR

**Coho Pacific Extra Pale Ale**: OG: 1044. Malt: Pale malt. Hops: Nugget, Fuggles. Source: GAM.

**Nut Brown Ale**: OG: 1048. Malt: Pale malt. Hops: Nugget, Northern Brewer, Willamette. Source: GAM.

**Blue Heron Pale Ale**: OG: 1050. Malt: Pale malt, Crystal malt, Wheat malt. Hops: Willamette. Late hops: Willamette, Cascade. Dry hops: Willamette. Source: NACB. OG: 1052. Malt: Pale malt, Patent black malt, Chocolate malt. Hops: Willamette, Nugget. Source: GAM.

**BridgePort Porter**: OG: 1056. Malt: Pale malt, Crystal malt, Chocolate malt, Roast barley. Hops: Goldings. Source: 150.

**Pintail Extra Special Bitter Ale**: OG: 1056. Malt: Scottish Pale malt. Hops: Goldings. Source: GAM.

**BridgePort IPA**: OG: 1056-57. Malt: Pale malt, Crystal malt. Hops: Chinook. Late hops: Goldings, Cascade, Crystal. Dry hops: Cascade. Source: BC.

**XX Dublin Extra Stout**: OG: 1064. Malt: Pale malt, Crystal malt, Patent black malt. Hops: Northern Brewer, Fuggles. Source: GAM.

**Old Knucklehead Barley Wine Style Ale**: OG: 1096. Malt: Pale malt, Scottish Crystal malt. Hops: Nugget, Goldings. Source: GAM.

### . *Broadway Brewing Company, Denver, CO*

**Road Dog Ale**: OG: 1048. Malt: Pale malt, Wheat malt, Crystal malt, Roast barley. Hops: Target. Source: NACB.

### . *Brooklyn Brewery, Brooklyn and Utica, NY. Www.brooklynbrewery.com*

**Brooklyn ½ Ale**: ABV: 3.4%. Malt: Pilsner malt, Munich malt. Hops: Simcoe, Sorachi Ace, Perle, Amarillo. Yeast: Belgian. Source: Web.

**Scorcher IPA**: °P: 10. Malt: Pale malt, Caramel malt. Hops: Bravo, Pilgrim, Cascade, Amarillo, Willamette. Yeast: Ale. Source: Web.

**Scorcher #366**: °P: 10. Malt: Pale malt, Crystal malt. Hops: Willamette. Late hops: HBC #366. Yeast: Ale. Source: Web.

**American Ale**: °P: 10.5. Malt: Maris Otter pale malt, Pale malt, Crystal malt. Hops: Cascade, Amarillo, Willamette. Yeast: Ale. Source: Web.

**Summer Ale**: °P: 11. Malt: Pale malts. Hops: Fuggles, Cascade, Perle, Amarillo. IBU: 18. Source: Web.

**Shackmeister Ale**: °P: 11.6. Malt: Pale malt, Lager malt, Caramalt, Crystal malt. Hops: Glacier, Perle, Willamette. Yeast: Ale. Source: Web.

**Best Bitter**: °P: 11.6. Malt: Maris Otter pale malt, Pale malt, Caramel malt, Aromatic malt, Crystal malt. Hops: Goldings, Fuggles, Palisade, Cascade, Willamette. Yeast: Ale. Source: Web.

**Brooklyn Greenmarket Wheat**: °P: 12. Malt: Pale malt, Wheat malt, Honey. Hops: Willamette. Yeast: Weisse. Source: Web.

**Brooklyn Pilsner**: °P: 12. Malt: Pale malt. Hops: Hallertau Mittelfrüh, Saaz, Perle, Vanguard. IBU: 33. Source: Web.

**Lager**: OG: 1052. Malt: Pale malt, Caramel malt, CaraPils malt. Hops: Cascade, Hallertau. Source: GAM. ABV: 5.2%. Malt: Pale malt. Hops: Hallertau Mittelfrüh, Vanguard, Cascade. IBU: 33. Source: Web.

**Post Road Pumpkin Ale**: °P: 13.5. Malt: Pale malt, Crystal malt, Aromatic malt, Biscuit malt, Wheat malt. Hops: Fuggles, Willamette. Others: Pumpkins, Nutmeg. IBU: 24. Source: Web.

**Insulated Lager**: °P: 13.5. Malt: Pilsner malt, Carafa® malt, Munich malt. Hops: Hallertau Mittelfrüh, Perle. Yeast: Lager. Source: Web.

**Brooklyn Oktoberfest**: °P: 13.7. Malt: Pilsner malt, Munich malt. Hops: Hallertau Mittelfrüh, Perle. IBU: 25. Source: Web.

**Red Sumac Wit**: °P: 14.5. Malt: Pale malt, Wheat. Hops: Perle. Others: Red Sumac. Yeast: Belgian. Source: Web.

**Brooklyn Gold Standard Export Kellerbier**: °P: 14.6. Malt: 100% Hanka lager malt. Hops: Hallertau Mittelfrüh, Saaz, Perle. Yeast: New Glarus lager. IBU: 44.5. Source: Web.

**Fiat Lux**: ABV: 6.1%. Malt: Pale malt, Wheat. Hops: Chinook, Centennial, Columbus, Cascade, Perle. Others: Lime peel, Coriander. Yeast: Levure Belgique. Source: Web.

**Brown Ale**: OG: 1060-61. Malt: Pale malt, Wheat malt / Roast barley, Chocolate malt, Crystal malt, Biscuit malt. Hops: Northern Brewer. Late hops: Cascade, Willamette. Source: BC/GAM. °P: 15.5. Malt: Pale malt, Belgiam aromatic malts, Roast malts. Hops: Fuggles, Cascade, Willamette. IBU: 30. Source: Web.

**Main Engine Start**: ABV: 6.2%. Malt: Pale malt, Crystal malt, Aromatic malt, Honey malt. Hops: Goldings, Perle, Styrian Aurora. Source: Web.

**Defender IPA**: °P: 16. Malt: Pilsner malt, CaraRed® malt, Crystal malt. Hops: Mosaic, Cascade, Pilgrim, Amarillo, Willamette. Yeast: Ale. Source: Web.

**Wild Horse Porter**: ABV: 6.5%. Malt: Pale malt, Caramel malt, Black barley, Spelt, Black malt, Chocolate malt, Dark candi sugar. Hops: Goldings, Willamette. Yeast: Wyeast #3522 and Brettanomyces. Source: Web.

**East India Pale Ale**: OG: 1067. Malt: Caramel malt, Wheat malt, Pipkin pale malt, Halcyon pale malt, Pilsner malt. Hops: Cascade, Willamette, Goldings. Source: GAM. °P: 17. Malt: Pale malts, Wheat malt. Hops: Goldings, Centennial, Northdown, Willamette. IBU: 47. Source: Web.

**Brooklyn Sorachi Ace**: °P: 15.7. Malt: Pilsner malt. Hops: Sorachi Ace. Yeast: Belgian and Champagne. IBU: 34. Source: Web.

**I Wanna Rye-It**: °P: 16.2. Malt: Pale malt, Rye malt, Crystal 150L malt. Hops: Centennial, Willamette. Yeast: Ale. Source: Web.

**Brooklyn Winter Ale**: °P: 16.5. Malt: Maris Otter pale malt, Crystal malt, Aromatic malt. Hops: Willamette. IBU: 25. Source: Web.

**Black Chocolate Stout**: OG: 1075. Malt: Pale malt, Crystal malt, Roast barley, Chocolate malt, Black malt, Kiln Coffee malt. Hops: Northern Brewer. Late hops: Fuggles. Source: NACB. OG: 1088-90. Malt: Pale malt, Wheat malt, Chocolate malt, Roast barley, Flaked wheat, Patent black malt. Hops: Goldings. Late hops: Goldings, Willamette, Cascade. Source: BC. OG: 1084. Malt: Pale malt, Caramel malt, Wheat malt, Roast barley, Chocolate malt, Black malt. Hops: Willamette, Fuggles. Source: GAM. °P: 21.7. Malt: Pale malt, Caramel malt, Wheat malt, Roast barley. Hops: Fuggles, Willamette. IBU: 51. Source: Web.

**The Concoction**: ABV: 7.6%. Malt: Pale malt, Pilsner malt, Peat-smoked malt, Wildflower honey. Hops: Simcoe, Goldings, Fuggles, Citra, Sorachi Ace, Cascade, Amarillo, Willamette. Others: Dried lemon peel, Minced ginger, Organic lemon juice. Source: Web.

**Buzz Bomb**: °P: 17.2. Malt: Pilsner malt, Crystal malt, Wildflower honey, Acacia honey. Hops: Perle. Others: Sweet orange peel. Source: Web.

**There Will Be Black**: °P: 17.2. Malt: Pale malt, Lager malt, Black malt, Black barley, Chocolate malt, Crystal malt. Hops: Motueka, Pacific Gem, Willamette. Yeast: Ale. Source: Web.

**Cuvée Noire**: °P: 17.3-7. Malt: Pilsner malt, Black barley, Black malt, Chocolate malt, Demerara sugar. Hops: Perle, Styrian Aurora. Others: Sweet orange peel, Aged in Bourbon casks. Yeast: Belgian. Source: Web.

**Fire & Ice**: °P: 17.5. Malt: Pale malt, Rauchmalz, Flaked oats, Crystal malt, Roast malts. Hops: Fuggles, Goldings, Willamette. Yeast: Ale. Source: Web.

**Ridgy-Didge**: °P: 17.5. Malt: Pilsner malt, Dark candi sugar. Hops: Perle, Pride of Ringwood. Others: Lemon myrtle, Tasmanian pepperberry. Yeast: Belgian. Source: Web.

**Weizenhammer**: °P: 17.8. Malt: Pilsner malt, Wheat malt. Hops: Mosaic, Perle. Yeast: Weisse. Source: Web.

**Brooklyn Cuvée La Boîte**: °P: 17.9. Malt: Pale malt, Wheat malt, Wildflower honey. Hops: Perle. Others: La Boîte's Mishmash N.33 (Lemon, Saffron, Crystallised ginger), Lemon peel, Kaffir lime leaves, Espelette peppers. Yeast: Belgian. Source: Web.

**Hammarby Syndrome**: °P: 18. Malt: Maris Otter pale malt, Pale malt, Crystal malt, Spelt malt. Hops: Willamette. Others: Spruce fronds. Yeast: Ale. Source: Web.

**Brooklyn Local 1**: °P: 18.5. Malt: Pilsner malt, Demerara sugar. Hops: Styrian Goldings, Perle. Yeast: Belgian. IBU: 26. Source: Web.

**Brooklyn Local 2**: °P: 18.5. Malt: Pilsner malt, Chocolate malt, Wildflower honey, Dark candi sugar. Hops: Goldings, Perle, Styrian Aurora. Others: Sweet orange peel. Yeast: Belgian and Champagne. IBU: 21. Source: Web.

**Wild Streak:** °P: 18.5. Malt: Pilsner malt. Hops: Styrian Celeia, Perle, Styrian Aurora. Others: aged in Bourbon oak casks. Yeast: Belgian, Champagne and Brettanomyces Lambicus. Source: Web.

**Mary's Maple Porter**: °P: 18.5. Malt: Pale malt, Crystal malt, Roast malts, Dark amber maple syrup, Light amber maple syrup. Hops: Goldings, Willamette. Yeast: Ale. Source: Web.

**K is for Kriek**: °P: 18.5. Malt: Pilsner malt, Chocolate malt, Dark candi sugar. Wildflower honey. Hops: Goldings, Perle, Styrian Aurora. Others: Sweet orange peel, Dried Montmorency cherries. Yeast: Belgian, Champagne and Brettanomyces bruxellensis. Source: Web.

**Brooklyn Blast!**: °P: 18.8. Malt: Maris Otter pale malt, Pilsner malt. Hops: Simcoe, Fuggles, Magnum, Centennial, Cascade, Willamette. IBU: 53. Source: Web.

**The Companion**: ABV: 9.1%. Malt: Pilsner malt, Dark malt, Wheat malt, Pale wheat malt. Hops: Styrian Goldings, Perle, Willamette. Source: Web.

**Detonation**: ABV: 9.2%. Malt: Maris Otter pale malt, Pilsner malt, Crystal malt, Demerara sugar. Hops: Sorachi Ace, Goldings, Simcoe, Palisade, Cascade, Amarillo, Willamette. Source: Web.

**Quadraceratops**: °P: 21. Malt: Pilsner malt, Abbey malt, Special B malt, Dark candi sugar. Hops: Goldings, Perle, Styrian Aurora. Yeast: Belgian. Source: Web.

**Quintaceratops**: °P: 21. Malt: Pale malt, Abbey malt, Special B malt, Dark candi syrup. Hops: Goldings, Perle, Styrian Aurora. Yeast: Belgian and Champagne. Source: Web.

**Intensified Coffee Porter**: °P: 21.5. Malt: Maris Otter pale malt, Aromatic malt, Black barley, Chocolate malt, Crystal 150L malt, Demerara sugar. Hops: Goldings, Willamette. Others: Cold brewed coffee. Yeast: Ale. Source: Web.

**Hand & Seal**: °P: 29. Malt: Maris Otter pale malt, Pale malt, Chocolate malt. Hops: Goldings, Magnum, Willamette. Yeast: Ale. Source: Web.

## . *BruRm @ BAR, New Haven, CT*

**Raven Hair Beauty**: OG: 1043. Malt: Mild ale malt, Pale malt, Munich malt, Crystal malt, Special B malt, Extra Special malt, Vienna malt, Black malt. Hops: Mount Hood. Late hops: Willamette, Liberty. Source: 150.

**BAR Pale Ale**: OG: 1050. Malt: Pale malt, Crystal malt. Hops: Centennial. Late hops: Mount Hood. Dry hops: Willamette, Goldings. Source: 150.

## . *Buffalo Bill's Brewery, Hayward, CA. Www.buffalobillsbrewery.com*

**Pumpkin Ale**: OG: 1052. Malt: Lager malt, Crystal malt, Patent black malt. Hops: Cascade, Northern Brewer. Others: Pumpkins, Allspice. Source: GAM. OG: 1048. Malt: Pale malt, Crystal malt. Hops: Cascade. Others: Pumpkins, Pumpkin pie spices. Source: SMB. Others: Baked pumpkin, Roast pumpkin, Cloves, Cinnamon, Nutmeg. Source: Web.

**Tasmanian Devil**: OG: 1052. Malt: Lager malt, Wheat malt, Demerara sugar. Hops: Southern Brewer, Green Bullet. Source: GAM. Hops: Cascade, Pride of Ringwood. Source: Web.

**Alimony Ale**: OG: 1072. Malt: Lager malt, Crystal malt, Patent black malt. Hops: Cascade, Northern Brewer. IBU: 72. Source: GAM. OG: 1046. Malt: Pale malt, Crystal malt. Hops: Cascade. Source: SMB.

**Billy Bock**: OG: 1082. Malt: Lager malt, Patent black malt, Crystal malt. Hops: Cascade, Northern Brewer. Source: GAM.

**Diaper Pale Ale**: Malt: Lager malt, Crystal malt, Patent black malt. Hops: Cascade, Northern Brewer. Source: GAM.

**Blue Christmas**: Others: Blueberries. Source: Web.

**Ricochet Red**: Hops: Nugget, Cascade. Source: Web.

**Johnny Midnite Oatmeal Stout**: Malt: Oatmeal. Hops: Goldings. Dry hops: Cascade. Source: Web.

### . *Butte Creek Brewing Company, Chico, CA*

**Winter Ale**: OG: 1055-61. Malt: Pale malt, Chocolate malt, Munich malt. Hops: Perle. Late hops: Fuggles. Source: 150.

### . *Buzzards Bay Brewing Company, Westport, MA*

**Buzzards Bay Stock Ale**: OG: 1060. Malt: Pale malt, Crystal malt, Black malt, Wheat malt. Hops: Fuggles. Late hops: Cascade. Source: NACB.

### . *Cambridge Brewing Company, Cambridge, MA*

**Cambridge Amber**: OG: 1048. Malt: Pale malt, Crystal malt, Patent black malt, Chocolate malt. Hops: Willamette. Late hops: Willamette, Yakima Goldings. Source: 150.

### . *Cape Ann Brewing, Gloucester, MA*

**Fisherman's IPA**: ABV: 6%. Hops: Sorachi Ace, Chinook. Source: BA.

### . *Capital Brewing, Middleton and Stevens Point, WI*

**Special Garten Bräu**: OG: 1045. Malt: Caramel malt, Caramel malt, Munich malt. Hops: Saaz, Cluster, Northern Brewer. Source: GAM.

**Capital Brown Ale**: OG: 1048. Malt: Maris Otter pale malt, Crystal malt, Caramalt, Patent black malt. Hops: Fuggles. Source: 150.

**Liam Mahooney's Brown Ale**: OG: 1050. Malt: Crystal malt. Hops: Brewers Gold, Fuggles. Source: GAM.

**Wild Rice Garten Bräu**: OG: 1050. Malt: Wild rice. Hops: Cluster, Cascade, Northern Brewer, Willamette. Source: GAM.

**Wisconsin Amber Garten Bräu**: OG: 1051. Hops: Mount Hood. Source: GAM.

**Capital Summerfest**: OG: 1052. Malt: Lager malt, CaraPils malt, Wheat malt, Munich malt. Hops: Saaz. Late hops: Spalt, Hallertau. Source: NACB.

**Winterfest Garten Bräu**: OG: 1058. Malt: Caramel malt. Hops: Spalt. Source: GAM.

### . *Carolina Beer & Beverage Company, Mooresville, NC*

**Cottonwood Frostbite**: OG: 1050. Malt: Pale malt, Crystal malt, Munich malt. Hops: Centennial. Late hops: Centennial, Columbus. Source: 150.

### . *Castle Springs Brewing Company, Moultenborough, NH*

**Lucknow Munich-Style Lager**: OG: 1046. Malt: Pilsner malt, CaraMunich malt, Munich malt. Hops: Hallertau. Source: NACB.

**Lucknow IPA**: OG: 1059. Malt: Pale malt, Crystal malt, Munich malt. Hops: Chinook, Centennial. Late hops: Columbus, Cascade. Dry hops: Cascade. Source: BC.

### . *Catamount, White River Junction / Windsor, VT*

**Amber**: ABW: 4%. Malt: Lager malt, Caramel 40L malt, CaraPils malt. Hops: Galena, Willamette. Source: GAM.

**American Wheat**: OG: 1042. Malt: Pale malt, Wheat malt. Hops: Goldings, Hallertau. Source: GAM.

**Porter**: OG: 1044. Malt: Pale malt, Chocolate malt, Patent black malt, Crystal malt. Hops: Galena. Late hops: Cascade. Source: NACB. OG: 1053. Malt: Lager malt, Roast barley, Caramel malt, Black malt, CaraPils malt. Hops: Galena, Cascade. Source: GAM.

**Gold**: OG: 1045. Malt: Lager malt, Caramel 40L malt, CaraPils malt. Hops: Willamette. Source: GAM.

**Pale Ale**: OG: 1049. Malt: Pale malt, Caramel 40L malt, Patent black malt, CaraPils malt. Hops: Cascade, Goldings. Source: GAM.

**Octoberfest**: OG: 1056. Malt: Pale malt, Caramel malt, Munich malt. Hops: Northern Brewer, Tettnang. Source: GAM.

**Christmas Ale**: OG: 1058. Malt: Lager malt, Wheat malt, Patent black malt, Caramel malt, Munich malt, CaraPils malt. Hops: Cascade. Source: GAM.

**Bock**: OG: 1064. Malt: Pale malt, Caramel 90L malt, Caramel 40L malt, Munich 10L malt. Hops: Northern Brewer, Hallertau. Source: GAM.

### . *Celis, Austin, TX*

**Raspberry**: OG: 1048. Malt: Wheat malt, Wheat. Hops: Willamette, Goldings. Others: Raspberry juice. Source: GAM.

**Golden**: OG: 1049. Malt: Pale malt. Hops: Saaz. Source: GAM.

**White**: OG: 1050. Malt: Wheat malt, CaraPils malt, Pilsner malt, Sugar. Hops: Cascade, Willamette. Late hops: Willamette, Cascade. Others: Coriander seeds, Dried curaçao Orange peel. Source: NACB. OG: 1048-49. Malt: Pilsner malt, Wheat malt, Aromatic malt, Flaked wheat. Hops: Willamette. Late hops: Willamette, Cascade. Others: Bitter orange peel, Coriander seeds. Source: BC. OG: 1048. Malt: Wheat. Hops: Willamette, Cascade. Source: GAM.

**Pale Bock**: OG: 1050. Malt: Caramel malt. Hops: Saaz, Willamette, Cascade. Source: GAM.

**Grand Cru**: OG: 1080. Malt: Pale malt. Hops: Saaz, Cascade. Source: GAM.

### . *Cisco, Nantucket, MA*

**Moor Porter**: OG: 1059. Malt: Pale malt, Special B malt, Flaked rye, Rye chocolate malt, Chocolate malt, Roast barley, Patent black malt. Hops: Northern Brewer. Late hops: Northern Brewer. Source: BC.

### . *Champion, Denver, CO*

**Norm Clarke Sports Ale**: OG: 1048. Malt: Pale malt, CaraPils malt, Wheat malt, Caramel malt, Munich malt. Hops: Spalt, Tettnang, Hersbrücker. Source: GAM.

**Home Run Ale**: OG: 1054. Malt: Roast barley, Chocolate malt. Hops: Nugget, Willamette, Cascade. Source: GAM.

**Larimer Red**: OG: 1059. Malt: Caramel malt, Roast barley, Munich malt, CaraPils malt, Vienna malt. Hops: Cascade, Centennial. Source: GAM.

### . *Cherryland, Sturgeon Bay, WI*

**Door County Weiss**: OG: 1042. Malt: Pale malt, Wheat malt, Crystal malt. Hops: Perle, Cascade. Source: GAM.

**Raspberry Bier**: OG: 1042. Malt: Pale malt. Hops: Cascade. Others: Raspberry juice. Source: GAM.

**Cherry Rail**: OG: 1044. Malt: Pale malt. Hops: Cascade. Others: Cherry juice. Source: GAM.

**Silver Rail**: OG: 1046. Malt: Pale malt. Hops: Hallertau. Source: GAM.

**Golden Rail**: OG: 1050. Malt: Pale malt, Crystal malt, Munich malt. Hops: Tettnang. Source: GAM.

**Apple Bach**: OG: 1052. Malt: Roast crystal malt. Hops: Cascade, Tettnang. Source: GAM.

### . *Chicago Brewing Company, Chicago, IL*

**Heartland Weiss**: OG: 1046. Malt: Lager malt, Wheat malt. Hops: Chinook. Source: GAM.

**Legacy Red Ale**: OG: 1050. Malt: Pale malt, Caramel malt, Victory malt. Hops: Chinook, Willamette. Source: GAM.

**Chicago's Legacy Lager**: OG: 1050. Malt: Pale malt, Caramel malt, Dextrin malt, Munich malt. Hops: Mount Hood, Chinook. Source: GAM.

**Chicago's Big Shoulders Porter**: OG: 1054. Malt: Pale malt, Caramel malt, Special roast malt, Chocolate malt, Roast barley. Hops: Chinook, Willamette. Source: GAM.

### . Clown Shoes Beer, Ipswich, MA

**Eagle Claw Fist Imperial Amber Ale**: Hops: Simcoe, Centennial, Citra. Source: BA.

### . Clipper City Brewing Company, Baltimore, MD

**Clipper City Pale Ale**: OG: 1050. Malt: Pale malt, Crystal malt. Hops: Goldings. Late hops: Goldings. Dry hops: Fuggles. Source: NACB.

### . Cold Spring Brewing Company, Cold Spring, MN

**Honey Almond**: OG: 1044. Malt: Lager malt. Hops: Hop extract. Source: GAM.

**River Road Red**: OG: 1048. Malt: Lager malt, Caramel 60L malt, Caramel 80L malt. Hops: Cascade, Willamette, Chinook. Source: GAM.

**Blackberry Bramble**: OG: 1054. Malt: Lager malt, Caramel malt. Hops: Cascade, Willamette. Others: Blackberries. Source: GAM.

**Pale Ale**: OG: 1054. Malt: Lager malt, Caramel 60L malt. Hops: Cascade, Willamette. Source: GAM.

Notes: Cold Spring contract brews for many microbreweries, including J&L Brewing Company, San Rafael, CA.

### . Commonwealth Brewing Company, New York, NY

**Porter**: OG: °P: 13.2. Malt: Pale malt, Roast barley, Chocolate malt, Roast barley, Crystal 60-80L malt, Black malt, Flaked barley, Black barley. Hops: Goldings. Late hops: Cascade, Goldings, Challenger. Source: SMB.

### . Cottrell Brewing, Pawcatuck, CT

**Old Yankee Ale**: OG: 1048. Malt: Pale malt, Crystal malt. Hops: Fuggles. Late hops: Goldings. Source: NACB.

### . Crane River, Lincoln, NE

**Homestead Pale Ale**: OG: 1040. Malt: Pale malt, Crystal malt. Hops: Bullion, Willamette, Cascade. Source: GAM.

**Platte River ESB**: OG: 1040. Malt: Pale malt, Crystal malt. Hops: Bullion, Willamette, Cascade. Source: GAM.

**Whooping Wheat**: OG: 1042. Malt: Pale malt, Wheat malt. Hops: Cascade, Hallertau. Source: GAM.

**Zlate Pivo**: OG: 1042. Malt: Pale malt, Pilsner malt. Hops: Saaz. Source: GAM.

**Good Life Stout**: OG: 1044. Malt: Pale malt, Amber malt, Roast barley, Chocolate malt, Munich malt, Rolled oats, Flaked barley. Hops: Bullion, Willamette. Source: GAM.

**Sodhouse Altbier**: OG: 1046. Malt: Wheat malt, Crystal malt, Pilsner malt, Munich malt, Black malt, Vienna malt. Hops: Hallertau. Source: GAM.

### . *Crested Butte Brewery & Pub, Crested Butte*

**Buck's Wheat**: OG: 1048. Malt: Pale malt, Wheat malt. Hops: Saaz, Hallertau. Source: GAM.

**Three-Pin Grin Porter**: OG: 1049. Malt: Pale malt, Caramel malt, Roast barley, Chocolate malt. Hops: Perle, Saaz, Fuggles. Source: GAM.

**White Buffalo Peace Ale**: OG: 1050. Malt: Pale malt, Caramel malt, Chocolate malt, Munich malt. Hops: Perle, Cascade, Oregon Fuggles. Source: GAM.

**Red Lady Ale**: OG: 1050. Malt: Pale malt, Caramel malt, Chocolate malt. Hops: Chinook, Perle, Willamette, Tettnang. Source: GAM.

**Rodeo Stout**: OG: 1052. Malt: Pale malt, Caramel malt, Oats, Roast barley, Chocolate malt, Black malt. Hops: Perle, Chinook. Source: GAM.

**India Pale Ale**: OG: 1056. Malt: Pale malt, Caramel malt, Munich malt. Hops: Saaz, Cascade, Fuggles, Willamette. Source: GAM.

### . *Crooked River Brewing Company, Cleveland, OH*

**Crooked River ESB**: OG: 1063. Malt: Pale malt, Crystal malt, Aromatic malt. Hops: Horizon. Late hops: Goldings, Cascade. Source: 150.

### . *Crystal Lake Brewing, Crystal Lake, IL. Www.CrystalLakeBrew.com*

**Wake Maker**: ABV: 4.8%. Malt: Pale malt, Munich malt. Hops: Centennial, Cascade, Amarillo. IBU: 53. Source: Web.

**Sea How It Goze**: ABV: 4.5%. Others: Coriander, Kosher salt. Yeast: Lactobacillus. IBU: 12. Source: Web.

### . *Dark Horse Brewing Company, Marshall, MI*

**Thirsty Trout Porter**: OG: 1064. Malt: Pale malt, Crystal malt, Munich malt, Chocolate malt, Black malt. Hops: Columbus. Late hops: Cascade. Source: 150.

### . *Deschutes Brewery, Bend, OR. Www.deschutesbrewery.com*

**River Ale**: ABV: 3.9%. Malt: Pale malt, Munich malt, Crystal malt, CaraPils malt. Hops: Crystal, Nugget, Cascade. IBU: 28. Source: Web.

**Mirror Pond Pale Ale**: OG: 1044. Malt: Pale malt, Crystal malt. Hops: Cascade. Late hops: Cascade. Dry hops: Cascade. Source: NACB. OG: 1052. Malt: Pale malt, Munich malt, Crystal malt. Hops: Centennial. Late hops: Cascade. Source: 150; ABV: 5%. Malt: Pale malt, Crystal malt, Munich malt, CaraPils malt. Hops: Cascade. IBU: 40. Source: Web.

**Bachelor Bitter**: OG: 1050. Malt: Pale malt, Crystal malt, CaraPils malt. Hops: Galena, Willamette, Goldings. Source: GAM.

**Twighlight**: ABV: 5%. Malt: Pale malt, Munich malt, Crystal malt, CaraPils malt. Hops: Tettnang, Amarillo, Cascade, Northern Brewer. IBU: 38. Source: Web.

**Black Butte Porter**: OG: 1053-56. Malt: Pale malt, Chocolate malt, Crystal malt. Hops: Galena. Late hops: Cascade, Tettnang. Source: 150./GAM. ABV: 5.2%. Malt: Pale malt, Wheat malt, Chocolate malt, Crystal malt, CaraPils malt. Hops: Bravo, Tettnang, Cascade. IBU: 30. Source: Web.

**Cascade Golden Ale**: OG: 1054. Malt: Pale malt, Crystal malt, CaraPils malt. Hops: Galena, Cascade, Tettnang. Source: GAM.

**Chainbreaker White IPA**: ABV: 5.6%. Malt: Pilsner malt, Wheat malt, Wheat. Hops: Bravo, Centennial, Amarillo, Cascade. Others: Sweet orange peel, Coriander. IBU: 55. Source: Web.

**Hop Trip**: ABV: 5.8%. Malt: Pale malt, Extra Special malt, Munich malt, CaraMunich malt, CaraPils malt. Hops: Centennial, Nugget, fresh Crystal. IBU: 38. Source: Web.

**Armory XPA**: ABV: 5.9%. Malt: Pale malt, Crystal malt. Hops: Nugget, Centennial, Citra, Cascade, Northern Brewer. IBU: 55. Source: Web.

**Red Chair NWPA**: ABV: 6.2%. Malt: Pale malt, Pilsner malt, Munich malt, Crystal malt, CaraPils malt. Hops: Centennial, Cascade. IBU: 60. Source: Web.

**Zarabanda**: ABV: 6.3%. Malt: Pilsner malt, Munich malt, Crystal malt, Spelt malt, Vienna malt, Flaked oats. Hops: Saaz. Others: Dried lime, Sumac, Pink peppercorns, Lemon Verbena, Sour wort. Yeast: French Saison. IBU: 18. Source: Web.

**Fresh Squeezed IPA**: ABV: 6.4%. Malt: Pale malt, Crystal malt, Munich malt. Hops: Citra, Nugget, Mosaic. IBU: 60. Source: Web.

**Obsidian Stout**: OG: 1065-68. Malt: 79-80.5% Pale malt, 6-7% Caramel 70-80L malt, 8.5+% Black malt, 1% Roast barley, 4% combined of Wheat malt, CaraPils malt and Munich malt. Hops (90 minutes): Galena, Nugget. Late hops: Willamette (30 minutes), Northern Brewer (5 minutes). IBU:52-57. SRM: 120+. Notes: Mash temperature = 150-1°F, Final gravity = 1017-20. Source: CYBI. ABV: 6.4%. Malt: Pale malt, Wheat malt, Roast barley, Munich malt, Crystal malt, CaraPils malt, Black malt. Hops: Bravo, Nugget, Delta, Northern Brewer. IBU: 55. Source: Web.

**Pinedrops IPA**: ABV: 6.5%. Malt: Pale malt, Pilsner malt, Munich malt, Crystal malt, CaraPils malt. Hops: Nugget, Centennial, Chinook, Equinox, Northern Brewer. IBU: 70. Source: Web.

**Foray IPA**: ABV: 6.5%. Malt: Pilsner malt, CaraPils malt. Hops: Nugget, Amarillo, Mosaic, Galaxy. IBU: 60. Source: Web.

**Jubelale**: ABV: 6.7%. Malt: Pale malt, Roast barley, Crystal malt, CaraPils malt, Extra Special malt. Hops: Nugget, Goldings, Tettnang, Delta, Cascade. IBU: 65. Source: Web.

**Inversion IPA**: ABV: 6.8%. Malt: Pale malt, Caramel malt, Munich malt. Hops: Delta, Millennium, Bravo, Centennial, Cascade, Northern Brewer. IBU: 80. Source: Web.

**Chasin' Freshies IPA**: ABV: 7.2%. Malt: Pilsner malt, Flaked oats. Hops: Bravo, fresh Lemondrop. IBU: 65. Source: Web.

**Hop Henge IPA**: ABV: 9.5%. Malt: Pale malt, Munich malt. Hops: Millennium, Mandarina Bavaria, Experimental. IBU: 90. Source: Web.

**Jubel 2015**: ABV: 10.5%. Malt: Pale malt, Roast barley, Chocolate malt, Crystal malt, Special B malt, Flaked barley. Hops: Millennium, Goldings, Tettnang, Nugget, Cascade, Willamette. Others: Aged in Pinot Noir and Oregon oak. IBU: 55. Source: Web.

**The Dissident**: ABV: 10.7%. Malt: Pilsner malt, Munich malt, Crystal 20L malt, Dark crystal malt, Special B malt, Acid malt, Dark candi sugar. Hops: Hallertau, Saaz, Hersbrücker. Others: Montmorncey cherries, Oak aged. IBU: 18. Source: Web.

**The Stoic**: ABV: 10.9%. Malt: Pilsner malt, Beet sugar, Belgian candi sugar, Date sugar, Pomegranate molasses. Hops: Hallertau Mittelfrüh, Saaz, Northern Brewer. Others: Aged in Pinot Noir and Rye Whiskey casks. IBU: 20. Source: Web.

**The Abyss**: ABV: 11%. Malt: Pale malt, Roast barley, Chocolate malt, Wheat malt, Black malt, Black barley, Molasses. Hops: Millennium, Styrian Goldings, Nugget, Northern Brewer. Others: Liquorice, Vanilla beans, Cherry bark, aged in Pinot Noir, Bourbon and Oregon oak. IBU: 86. Source: Web.

**Black Butte XXVII**: ABV: 11.6%. Malt: Pale malt, Wheat malt, Chocolate malt, Crystal malt, Midnight wheat malt, Pomegranate molasses. Hops: Millennium, Tettnang, Cascade. Others: Theo Chocolate cocoa nibs, Apricot puree, aged in Bourbon casks. IBU: 60. Source: Web.

### . *Devil Mountain Brewing Company, Cincinnati, OH*

**Railroad Gold Ale**: OG: 1048. Malt: Pale malt, Caramel malt. Hops: Liberty, Chinook. Source: GAM.

**Five Malt Ale**: OG: 1053. Malt: Pale malt, Caramel malt, Chocolate malt, Crystal malt, Patent black malt. Hops: Liberty, Cascade. Source: GAM.

**Black Honey Ale**: OG: 1050. Malt: Pale malt, Crystal malt, Black malt, Chocolate malt. Hops: Willamette. Late hops: Willamette. Source: NACB. OG: 1061. Malt: Pale malt, Caramel malt, Chocolate malt, African black honey, New England Buckwheat honey. Hops: Liberty, Northern Brewer. Source: GAM.

### . Dick's Brewing Company, Centralia, WA

**Bottleworks IPA**: OG: 1080. Malt: Pale malt, Crystal malt, Chocolate malt. Hops: Columbus. Late hops: Columbus. Source: 150.

### . Dixie Brewing Company, New Orleans, LA

**Crimson Voodoo Ale**: ABW: 3.96%. Malt: Caramel malt, Chocolate malt. Hops: Cascade, Mount Hood. Source: GAM.

**Jazz Amber Light Beer**: ABW: 4.12%. Malt: Rice. Hops: Cascade, Cluster. Source: GAM.

**Dixie Blackened Voodoo Lager**: OG: 1053-56. Malt: Rice, Lager malt, Pale malt, Black malt / Patent black malt, Crystal malt / Caramel malt, Chocolate malt. Hops: Mount Hood. Late hops: Cascade, Mount Hood. Source: CB/GAM.

### . Dock Street Brewing Company, Philadelphia, PA

**Amber Beer**: OG: 1050. Malt: Pale malt, Caramel malt. Hops: Cascade. Source: GAM.

**Bohemian USA**: OG: 1055-57. Malt: Pilsner malt, Dextrin malt, Munich malt, Crystal malt. Hops: Saaz, Hersbrücker. Late hops: Saaz. Source: BC. OG: 1050. Malt: Pale malt, Munich malt, CaraPils malt. Hops: Saaz, Hallertau. Source: GAM.

**Illuminator USA**: OG: 1071-72. Malt: Pilsner malt, Dextrin malt, Munich malt, Crystal malt, CaraMunich malt, Chocolate malt. Hops: Tettnang. Late hops: Tettnang, Hersbrücker. Source: BC. Malt: Pale malt, Caramel malt, Munich malt, CaraPils malt. Hops: Tettnang, Hallertau. Source: GAM.

### . Dogfish Head Brewing Company, Lewes, DE. Www.dogfish.com

**60-Minute IPA**: OG: 1064. Malt: Pale malt, Amber malt. Hops: Warrior. Late hops: Simcoe, Palisade. Dry hops: Amarillo, Simcoe, Glacier. Yeast: Wyeast #1187. IBU: 60. SRM: 6. Source: BYO/150.

**Indian Brown Ale**: OG: 1070. Malt: Pilsner malt, Crystal malt, Flaked maize, Amber malt, Roast barley, Coffee malt, Sugar. Hops: Warrior. Late hops: Goldings, Liberty. Dry hops: Goldings, Liberty. Source: 150.

**Midas Touch**: OG: 1079. Malt: Pale malt, Honey, Muscat grape juice concentrate. Hops: Willamette. Late hops: Willamette. Others: Saffron. Source: 150.

**Chateau Jiahu**: OG: 1088. Malt: Pale malt, Orange blossom honey, Rice syrup, Muscat grape juice concentrate. Hops: Simcoe. Others: Hawthorn berry powder. Source: BYO[26]. ABV: 8%. Malt: Pre-gelatinized Flaked rice, Wildflower honey, Muscat grapes, barley malt. Others: Hawthorn berries, Chrysanthemum flowers. Yeast: Sake. Source: Web.

**90-Minute IPA**: OG: 1088. Malt: Pilsner malt, Amber malt. Hops: Amarillo, Simcoe, Warrior. Dry hops: Amarillo, Simcoe, Warrior. Source: 150.

---

[26] http://byo.com/recipe/1709.html

**Immortale**: OG: 1105. Malt: Pale malt, Biscuit malt, Crystal malt, Wheat malt, Roast barley, Peat-smoked malt. Hops: Northern Brewer. Late hops: Centennial. Source: NACB.

. *Elysian Brewing Company, Seattle, WA. Www.elysianbrewing.com*

**Elysian Fields Pale Ale**: OG: 1048. Malt: Pale malt, Crystal malt, CaraMunich malt, CaraVienne malt, Biscuit malt. Hops: Simcoe. Late hops: Simcoe, Amarillo. IBU: 36. Source: Web.

**Zephyrus Pilsner**: OG: 1050. Hops: Northern Brewer. Late hops Saaz. IBU: 38. Source: Web.

**Loki Lager**: OG: 1052. Malt: Pale malt, Caramalt, Munich malt. Hops: Northern Brewer. Late hops. Styrian Goldings. Source: Web/SMB.

**The Wise ESB**: OG: 1058. Malt: Pale malt, Crystal 80L malt, Crystal 120L malt, Munich malt. Hops: Chinook. Late hops: Cascade, Centennial. IBU: 39. Source: SMB. Malt: 79.1% Pale malt, 8.8% Crystal 77L malt, 8.8% Munich malt, 2.2% CaraHell® malt, 1.1% Special B malt. Hops: Chinook. Late hops: 50% Cascade, 50% Centennial. Yeast: Wyeast #1056 or Siebel BR96. Source: Web.

**Perseus Porter**: OG: 1058. Malt: Pale malt, Crystal 80L malt, Chocolate malt, Munich malt, Black malt. Hops: Centennial. Late hops: Northern Brewer. IBU: 25. Source: SMB/Web.

**Night Owl Pumpkin Ale**: OG: 1060. Malt: Pale malt, Crystal malt, Munich malt. Hops: Horizon. Others: Pumpkins, Pumpkin seeds (roast and green), Nutmeg, Cloves, Cinnamon, Ginger, Allspice. Source: Web.

**Saison Elysée**: OG: 1061. Malt: Pale malt, Munich malt. Hops: Magnum. Late hops: Saaz. Others: Cumin seeds. Source: Web.

**Avatar Jasmine IPA**: OG: 1062. Malt: Pale malt, Munich malt, small amount Crystal malt, small amount CaraHell® malt. Hops: Chinook. Late hops: Glacier, Amarillo. Others: Dried Jasmine flowers. Source: Web.

**The Immortal IPA**: OG: 1063. Malt bill for 5 US gal: 10.5lb (91.3%) Pale malt, 4oz (2.2%) Crystal 70-80L malt, 4oz (2.2%) Light dextrin malt such as CaraHell® malt, 8oz (4.3%) Munich malt. Mash at 153-154°F. Hops: Chinook. AAU: 7.5. Boil for 90 minutes. Late hops (2 minutes before end of boil): 1oz Amarillo, 0.5oz Centennial. Late hops (End of boil): 0.25oz Centennial. Yeast: Attenutive American ale yeast such as Wyeast #1056. IBU: 42. Source: Web.

**Ambrosia Maibock**: OG: 1068. Malt: Pale malt, CaraHell® malt, Munich malt. Hops: Northern Brewer. Late hops: Styrian Goldings. Source: Web.

**Pandora's Bock**: OG: 1070. Malt: Pale malt, Caramalt, Munich malt, Dark crystal malt, Black malt, Chocolate malt. Hops: Northern Brewer. Late hops: Northern Brewer, Styrian Goldings. Source: Web.

**Pandora's Wild Fling**: Malt: Pale malt, Munich malt, Caramalt, Wild rice. Hops: Northern Brewer. Late hops: Styrian Goldings. Source: SMB.

**Bête Blanche**: OG: 1075. Malt: Pale malt, Candi sugar. Hops: Northern Brewer. Late hops: Styrian Goldings. IBU: 31. Source: Web.

**BiFröst Winter Ale**: OG: 1078. Malt: Pale malt, small amount Crystal malt, small amount Munich malt. Hops: Centennial. Late hops: Amarillo, Styrian Goldings. IBU: 42. Source: Web.

**Dragonstooth Stout**: OG: 1080. Malt: Pale malt, 10% Flaked oats, Roast barley, Chocolate malt. Hops: Magnum. Late hops: Cascade, Centennial. IBU: 36. Source: Web.

**Evacutinus**: Malt: Pale malt, Wheat malt, Carafa® malt/Dark crystal malt, Caramalt, Munich malt. Hops: Northern Brewer. Late hops: Northern Brewer. Source: SMB.

### Estes Park Brewery, Estes Park, CO

**Long Peaks Raspberry Wheat**: OG: 1043. Malt: Pale malt, Wheat malt, Crystal malt. Hops: Northern Brewer. Late hops: Fuggles. Source: BC.

### Falstaff Brewing Company, Milwaukee, WI

**Ballantine XXX Ale**: OG: 1045. Malt: Pale malt, Crystal malt. Hops: Nugget, Cascade. Late hops: Cascade. Source: NACB.

### Firestone & Walker Brewing Company, Los Olivos, CA

**Firestone Double Barrel Ale**: OG: 1055-56. Malt: Pale malt, Crystal malt, CaraMunich malt, Victory malt. Hops: Goldings. Late hops: Styrian Goldings, Goldings, Fuggles. Other: Oak chips. Source: BC. ABV: 5%. Malt: 42% US 2-row pale malt, 17% Maris Otter pale malt, 25% English pale malt, 7% Munich 10L malt, 6% Caramel 77L malt, 2% Caramel 120L malt, 1% Chocolate malt. Hops: Magnum, Goldings, Styrian Goldings. Late hops: Styrian Goldings, Goldings. Other: Fermented in oak using the Union system. Yeast: British or London ale. Notes: Possible substitutions for the Styrian Goldings are either US Fuggles or Willamette and Tradition. IBU: 27.5-31. Source: CYBI.

### Fish Brewing Company, Olympia, WA. Www.fishbrewing.com

**Fish Tale Blonde Ale**: ABV: 4%. Malt: Pale malt, Rye malt. Hops: Tettnang. Source: Web.

**Wild Salmon Organic Pale Ale**: OG: 1048. Hops: Yakima Cascade. Source: Web.

**Fish Tale Organic Amber Ale**: OG: 1056. Malt: Pale malt, Munich malt, Crystal malt. Hops: Hallertau. Source: Web.

**Thornton Creek Pale Ale**: OG: 1056. Malt: Pale malt, Carastan malt, Crystal malt. Hops: Cascade, Willamette, Chinook. Source: Web.

**Fish Tale Trout Stout**: OG: 1059. Malt: Pale malt, CaraPils malt, Munich malt, Crystal malt, Black malt, Roast malt. Hops: Chinook, Cascade. Late hops: Cascade. Source: 150.

OG: 1058. Malt: Carastan malt, Crystal malt, Black malt, Munich malt. Hops: Chinook. Late hops: Cascade. Source: Web.

**Fish Tale Organic India Pale Ale**: OG: 1060. Malt: Pale malt, Crystal malt. Hops: Pacific Gem. Source: Web.

**Mudshark Porter**: OG: 1060. Malt: Pale malt, CaraPils malt, Munich malt, Crystal malt, Black malt, Roast malt. Hops: Chinook, Cascade. Late hops: Cascade. Source: 150. OG: 1058. Malt: Carastan malt, Crystal malt, Black malt, Munich malt. Hops: Chinook. Late hops: Cascade. Source: Web.

**Winterfish Ale**: OG: 1072. Malt: Pale malt, Honey malt. Hops: 100% Yakima Chinook. Source: Web.

**Detonator Doppelbock**: OG: 1080. Malt: Pale malt, Chocolate malt, Munich malt. Hops: Hallertau, Columbus. Source: Web.

**Leviathan Barleywine**: OG: 1084. Malt: Pale malt, Carastan malt, Chocolate malt. Hops: Chinook. Late hops: Cascade. Source: Web.

**Poseidon's Imperial Stout**: ABV: 10%. Malt: ESB pale malt, Caramel malt, Chocolate malt. Hops: Columbus. Late hops: Cascade. Source: Web.

### . *Florida Beer Brands, Orlando, FL*

**Flying Aces Light Beer**: ABW: 3.7%. Malt: Lager malt. Source: GAM.

**Gator Light**: OG: 1040. Malt: Lager malt. Source: GAM.

**Growlin' Gator Lager**: OG: 1045. Malt: Pale malt, Corn syrup. Hops: Saaz, Yakima. Source: GAM.

**Famous Old West John Wesley Hardin Amber Beer / Famous Old West Etta Place Amber Beer**: OG: 1050. Malt: Pale malt, Caramel malt. Hops: Cascade, Mount Hood. Source: GAM.

Note: Beers brewed by August Schell.

### . *Flossmoor Station, Flossmoor, IL. Www.flossmoorstation.com*

**Gandy Dancer Honey Ale**: Malt: Orange blossom honey. Source: Web.

**Station Master Wheat Ale**: Malt: 33% Wheat malt. Source: Web.

**Iron Horse Stout**: Malt: Baked oats. Source: Web.

**Pullman Brown Ale**: OG: 1065-7. Malt: 62-4% Golden Promise pale malt, 5-10% Golden naked oats, 5% Brown malt, 5% Chocolate malt, 5% Honey malt, 5% Caramel 30-37L malt, 4-5% Munich malt, 4-5% Red wheat malt, Molasses. Hops: Northern Brewer. Late hops: Cascade. IBU: 25-30. Yeast: Wyeast #1318. Source: CYBI.

*Flying Dog, Denver, CO. Www.flyingdogales.com*

**Tire Biter Golden Ale**: OG: 1046. Malt: Pale malt, Wheat malt, Munich malt. Hops: Perle. Late hops: Hallertau. Source: 150.

**Woody Creek White**: OG: 1047. Malt: Pilsner malt, Wheat, Oat malt. Hops: Hallertau. IBU: 14. Source: Web.

**Doggie Style Ale**: OG: 1048. Malt: Pale malt, Caramel malt. Hops: Yakima Chinook, Yakima Cascade. Source: GAM.

**Dogtoberfest**: OG: 1056. Malt: Vienna malt, Munich malt. Hops: Perle, Hersbrücker. Source: Web.

**Heller Hound Maibock**: OG: 1062. Malt: Vienna malt, CaraHell® malt, Munich malt. Hops: Perle, Hersbrücker, Saaz. IBU: 22. Source: Web.

**K-9 Cruiser Winter Ale**: OG: 1064. Malt: Crystal malt, Chocolate malt, Oat malt, Munich malt. Hops: Millennium, Saaz. IBU: 30. Source: Web.

**Gonzo Imperial Porter**: OG: 1093. Malt: Crystal malt, Chocolate malt, Black malt. Hops: Warrior, Northern Brewer, Cascade. IBU: 80. Source: Web.

**Wild Dog Gonzo Imperial Porter**: Note: This is **Gonzo Imperial Porter** aged in used whiskey barrels. Source: Web.

**Horn Dog Barley Wine**: OG: 1100. Malt: Crystal malt, Carastan malt, Munich malt. Hops: Perle, Northern Brewer, Cascade. IBU: 44. Source: Web.

**Double Dog Double Pale Ale**: OG: 1102. Malt: Carastan malt, Chocolate malt. Hops: Columbus, Millennium, Cascade. IBU: 85. Source: Web.

*Flying Fish Brewing Company, Cherry Hill, NJ. Www.flyingfish.com*

**Farmhouse Summer Ale**: °P: 11.5. ABV: 4.6%. Malt: 2-row pale malt, Wheat malt, CaraPils malt, Acid malt. Hops: Magnum, Styrian Goldings. Source: Web. OG: 1045-48. Malt: Pale malt, Wheat malt, Dextrin malt. Hops: Magnum, Styrian Goldings. Late hops: Styrian Goldings. Source: 150.

**Extra Pale Ale**: °P: 12.2. ABV: 4.8%. Malt: 2-row pale malt, Munich malt, Aromatic malt. Hops: Magnum, Mount Hood. Source: Web.

**BlackFish**: °P: 13.3. ABV: 5.2%. Malt: 2-row pale malt, Munich malt, Aromatic malt, CaraPils malt, Caramel 60L malt, Chocolate malt. Hops: Magnum, Mount Hood. Source: Web.

**ESB Ale**: °P: 14.3. ABV: 5.5%. Malt: 2-row pale malt, Munich malt, Aromatic malt, Crystal malt. Hops: Magnum, Fuggles, Yakima Goldings. Source: Web.

**OktoberFish**: °P: 14.3. ABV: 5.5%. Malt: 2-row pale malt, Munich malt, Aromatic malt, De-bittered black malt. Hops: Horizon, Crystal. Source: Web.

**Hopfish India Pale Ale**: °P: 15. ABV: 6.2.8%. Malt: 2-row pale malt, Munich malt, Crystal malt. Hops: Magnum, Nugget, Ahtanum. Source: Web.

**Belgian Abbey Dubbel**: °P: 16.4. ABV: 7%. OG: 1067. Malt: 2-row malt, Munich malt, CaraPils malt, Special B malt, Chocolate malt, Candi sugar. Hops: Styrian Goldings. IBU: 18. Source: BLAM/Web. OG: 1064. Malt: Belgian pale malt, Crystal malt, Special B malt, Wheat malt. Hops: Northern Brewer. Late hops: Goldings. Source: NACB.

**Belgian Grand Cru Golden Winter Ale**: °P: 16.6. ABV: 7.2%. Malt: 2-row pale malt, CaraPils malt, Wheat malt, Acid malt. Hops: Magnum, Styrian Goldings. Source: Web.

**Imperial Espresso Porter**: °P: 18. ABV: 8%. Malt: 2-row pale malt, Munich malt, Chocolate malt, Crystal malt, Caramalt. Hops: Magnum, Mount Rainier. Source: Web.

**Exit 16 Wild Rice Double IPA**: ABV: 8.2%. Malt: Wild rice, Brown rice, White rice. Hops: Citra, Chinook. Source: BA.

**Big Fish Barleywine**: °P: 21.5. ABV: 10%. Malt: 2-row pale malt, Munich malt, Crystal malt. Hops: Magnum, Simcoe. Late hops: Simcoe. Source: Web.

### Forrest Williams Brewing Company, Martha's Vineyard, MA

**Martha's Vineyard Extra Stout**: OG: 1052. Malt: Pale malt, Crystal malt, Roast barley, Wheat malt. Hops: Northern Brewer. Late hops: Willamette. Source: NACB.

### Fort Spokane Brewery, Spokane, WA

**Blonde Alt**: OG: 1052. Malt: Pale malt, Caramel malt, Wheat malt, Munich malt. Hops: Willamette, Tettnang. Source: GAM.

**Red Alt**: OG: 1052. Malt: Pale malt, Caramel malt, Chocolate malt, Munich malt. Hops: Willamette. Source: GAM.

**Border Run**: OG: 1056. Malt: Pale malt, Wheat malt, Munich malt. Hops: Willamette, Tettnang. Source: GAM.

**Bulldog Stout**: OG: 1056. Malt: Pale malt, Caramel malt, Roast barley, Patent black malt, Flaked barley. Hops: Willamette. Source: GAM.

### Frankenmuth Brewery, Frankenmuth, MI

**Pilsener**: OG: 1046. Malt: Lager malt. Hops: Cluster, Perle. Source: GAM.

**Oktoberfest**: OG: 1050. Malt: Lager malt, Munich malt, CaraPils malt. Hops: Cluster, Perle. Source: GAM.

**Old Detroit Red Lager**: OG: 1050. Malt: Lager malt, Caramel 60L malt, Munich malt, CaraPils malt. Hops: Cluster, Perle. Source: GAM.

**Dark**: OG: 1054. Malt: Lager malt, Patent black malt, Caramel 60L malt, Munich malt. Hops: Perle, Cluster. Source: GAM.

**Old Detroit Amber Ale**: OG: 1055. Malt: Lager malt, Caramel 60L malt, Munich malt, CaraPils malt. Hops: Cluster, Perle. Source: GAM.

**Bock**: OG: 1066. Malt: Lager malt, Caramel 60L malt, Munich malt, Patent black malt, Munich malt, CaraPils malt. Hops: Cluster, Perle. Source: GAM.

### . *Frederick Brewing Company, Frederick, MD*

**Hempen Ale**: OG: 1045. Malt: Mild ale malt, Crystal malt, Brown malt, Toasted Hemp seeds, Sugar. Hops: Cascade. Others: Hemp seeds. Source: NACB.

### . *Fredericksburg Brewing Company, Fredericksburg, TX*

**Frederiscksburg Porter**: OG: 1054. Malt: Pale malt, Carastan malt, Crystal malt, Munich malt, Chocolate malt, Roast barley. Hops: Northern Brewer. Late hops: Willamette, Goldings. Source: 150.

### . *Full Sail Brewing Company, Hood River, OR. Www.fullsailbrewing.com*

**Nut Brown Ale**: ABV: 4.3%. Malt: Pale malt, Chocolate malt, Crystal malt. Source: GAM.

**Equinox ESB**: ABV: 4.5%. Malt: Crystal malt. Hops: Saaz, Target. Source: GAM.

**Golden Ale**: OG: 1048. Malt: Pale malt, Crystal malt, Barley. Hops: Mount Hood, Tettnang. Source: GAM.

**India Pale**: ABV: 5%. Malt: Triumph pale malt. Hops: Challenger, Goldings. Source: GAM.

**Amber Ale**: OG: 1055-59. Malt: Pale malt, Crystal malt, Chocolate malt. Hops: Hallertau, Cascade. Late hops: Hallertau, Cascade. Source: 150. Hops: Mount Hood, Cascade. Source: Web/GAM.

**Wassail**: OG: 1070. Malt: Pale malt, Malt extract, Crystal malt, Chocolate malt, Roast barley, Patent black malt. Hops: Northern Brewer, Styrian Goldings. Late hops: Hersbrücker, Styrian Goldings. Source: 150.

**Mercator Doppelbock**: OG: 1076. Malt: Lager malt, CaraVienne malt, Munich malt, Vienna malt, Crystal malt. Hops: Tettnang. Late hops: Spalt, Hallertau. Source: NACB.

### . *D. L. Geary Brewing, Portland, ME*

**London Porter**: OG: 1045. Malt: Pale malt, Patent black malt, Chocolate malt, Crystal malt. Hops: Cascade, Willamette, Goldings. Source: GAM.

**Geary's Pale Ale**: OG: 1046-48. Malt: Pale malt, Crystal malt, Chocolate malt. Hops: Cascade, Mount Hood. Late hops: Tettnang, Fuggles. Dry hops: Cascade. Source: CB/GAM.

**Hampshire Special Ale**: OG: 1070. Malt: Pale malt, Crystal malt, Chocolate malt. Hops: Cascade, Mount Hood. Late hops: Goldings. Source: NACB/GAM.

**Tic Wit Tic**: °P: 10.5. Malt: 44.8% Pilsner malt, 13.8% Acid malt, 17.2% Wheat malt, 12.1% Flaked wheat, 12.1% Rolled oats. Late hops: 70% Willamette, 30% Crystal. Others: Bitter orange peel, Sweet orange peel, Crushed coriander, Cardamom. Yeast: Wyeast #3463 and Wyeast #5335. IBU: 18. Source: Web.

**Ume Umai**: °P: 11. Malt: 89.4% Pilsner malt, 10.6% Cooked black rice. Hops: Summit. Others: Plums. Yeast: Wyeast #1728. IBU: 12. Source: Web.

**Lo-Fi Pale**: °P: 11. Malt: 88% Pale malt, 12% Vienna malt. Hops: 2.3% Magnum, 15.3% Centennial. Late hops: 48.9% Cascade, 15.3% Simcoe. Dry hops: 9.2% Mosaic, 9.2% Simcoe. Yeast: Wyeast #1728. IBU: "A few". Source: Web.

**Bang On!**: °P: 13. Malt: 93.8% Maris Otter pale malt, 3.1% Caramel 30-37L malt, 3.1% Crystal 50-60L malt. Hops: 5.1% Magnum, 40.7% Willamette. Late hops: 27.1% Brewers Gold, 27.1% Willamette. Yeast: Wyeast #1728. IBU: 35. Source: Web.

**Most Interesting Beer In The World**: °P: 13.3. Malt: 93.9% Pale malt, 6.1% CaraHell® malt. Hops: Magnum. Late hops: Fresh Cascade. Yeast: Wyeast #1728. IBU: "Lots". Source: Web.

**Firebird Smoked Hefeweizen**: °P: 13.5. Malt: 30.5% Pilsner malt, 22.9% Wheat malt, 38.1% Rauchmalz, 5.7% Dark wheat malt, 2.9% Acid malt. Hops: 14.4% Willamette, 85.6% Mount Hood. Yeast: Wyeast #3068. IBU: 26. Source: Web.

**High Fidelity Pale**: °P: 13.5. Malt: 93.8% Pale malt, 6.2% Crystal 15L malt. Hops: 2% Magnum. Late hops: 50% Mount Hood, 20.4% Simcoe. Dry hops: 28.6% Simcoe. Yeast: Wyeast #1728. IBU: 35. Source: Web.

**Time Traveler**: °P: 13.5. Malt: 83.3% Pale malt, 7.6% Caramel 42-50L malt, 3.4% Caramel 80L malt, 3.8% Black malt, 1.9% Carafa® II malt. Hops: 9.3% Magnum, 16.1% Cascade, 75.3% Willamette. Yeast: Wyeast #1728. IBU: 40. Source: Web.

**Axes of Evil**: °P: 14. Malt: 94% Maris Otter pale malt, 6% Caramel 30-37L malt. Hops: 2.6% Magnum. Late hops: 44.9% Crystal, 15% Motueka, 7.5% Sterling. Dry hops: 30% Pacific Jade. Yeast: Wyeast #1728. IBU: 40. Source: Web.

**Dark Meddle Vienna Lager**: °P: 14. Malt: 37% Pilsner malt, 32.5% Vienna malt, 22.2% Munich II malt, 3% Crystal 42-50L malt, 0.2% Carafa® Special III malt, 5.2% Piloncillo sugar. Hops: 11.1% Willamette. Late hops: 44.4% Mount Hood, 44.4% Sterling. Yeast: Wyeast #3470. IBU: 30. Source: Web.

**The Future Is Now**: °P: 14.5. Malt: 81.9% Pale malt, 10.9% CaraMunich II malt, 4.1% Crystal 70-80L malt, 0.3% Carafa® Special II malt, 2.7% Raw sugar. Hops: 2.6% Magnum, 13.9% Cascade, 13.9% Mount Hood. Late hops: 27.8% Cascade, 19.1% Crystal. Dry hops: 8.7% Cascade, 13.9% Mosaic. Yeast: Wyeast #1728. IBU: 70. Source: Web.

**Rauchweizen and the Bandit**: °P: 14.5. Malt: 31.4% Pilsner malt, 21.4% Wheat malt, 39.3% Smoked malt, 7.9% Dark wheat malt. Hops: 100% Willamette. Yeast: Wyeast #3068. IBU: 22. Source: Web.

**N Juice IPA**: °P: 15. Malt: 100% Pale malt. Hops: 4.9% Simcoe. Late hops: 24.4% Cascade, 48.8% Simcoe. Dry hops: 7.3% Cascade, 14.6% Simcoe. Others: Pineapple juice, Grapefruit juice, Tangerine juice. Yeast: Wyeast #1728. IBU: "Lots". Source: Web.

**Sodbusted Simcoe**: °P: 15. Malt: 93.3% Pale malt, 6.7% Crystal 15L malt. Hops: 0.4% Magnum. Late hops: 99.6% Fresh Simcoe. Yeast: Wyeast #1728. IBU: "Lots". Source: Web.

**The Royale**: °P: 15. Malt: 91.2% Pilsner malt, 5.9% Munich malt, 2.9% Crystal 42-50L malt. Hops: 1.2% Magnum. Late hops: 12% Willamette, 24.1% Cascade, 16.9% Mount Hood, 16.9% Crystal. Dry hops: 21.7% Pacific Jade, 7.2% Simcoe. Yeast: Wyeast #1214. IBU: 45. Source: Web.

**Gigantic IPA**: °P: 16. Malt: 93.7% Pale malt, 6.3% Munich I malt. Hops: 2.3% Magnum, 8.9% Cascade, 8.9% Centennial, 8.9% Crystal. Late hops: 8.9% Centennial, 13.6% Cascade, 17.8% Crystal, 9.8% Simcoe. Dry hops: 14% Cascade, 7% Simcoe. Yeast: Wyeast #1728. IBU: "Lots". Source: Web.

**Kiss The Goat Black Bock**: °P: 16.5. Malt: 69.8% Pilsner malt, 18.6% Vienna malt, 5.8% Melanoidin malt, 5.8% Carafa® Special III malt. Hops: 9.4% Sterling, 31.3% Mount Hood. Late hops: 9.4% Sterling, 50% Mount Hood. Yeast: Wyeast #3479. IBU: 35. Source: Web.

**Geezers Need Excitement Chocolate IPA**: °P: 17. Malt: 97.7% Pale malt, 2.3% Crystal 50-60L malt. Hops: 2.9% Magnum, 13.3% Cascade, 13.3% Centennial. Late hops: 22.9% Cascade, 9.5% Centennial, 9.5% Crystal, 9.5% Amarillo. Dry hops: 9.5% Cascade, 4.8% Simcoe, 4.8% Amarillo. Others: Cocoa nibs. Yeast: Wyeast #1728. IBU: "Lots". Source: Web.

**The Scut Farkus Affair**: °P: 17.5. Malt: 85% Maris Otter pale malt, 10.2% Crystal 50-60L malt, 2.8% Crystal 70-80L malt, 0.6% Carafa® II malt, 4% Raw sugar. Hops: 1.9% Magnum, 14.3% Cascade, 14.3% Crystal. Late hops: 14.3% Simcoe, 21% Cascade, 21% Crystal. Dry hops: 13.3% Mosaic. Others: 0.8% Haribo Gummi bears. Yeast: Wyeast #1728. IBU: 70. Source: Web.

**Hellion Dry Hopped Belgian Golden**: °P: 17.5. Malt: 87.1% Pilsner malt, 4.7% Crystal 15L malt, 8.2% Raw sugar. Late hops: 13.9% Mount Hood, 50% Sterling. Dry hops: 13.9% Simcoe, 22.2% Sorachi Ace. Yeast: Wyeast #3522. IBU: 23. Source: Web.

**Too Much Coffee Man**: °P: 17.7. Malt: 62.6% Pilsner malt, 9.1% Melanoidin malt, 6.3% Crystal 70-80L malt, 6.3% Special B malt, 5.7% Wheat malt, 0.9% Smoked malt, 9.1% Raw sugar. Hops: 41% Sterling, 59% Willamette. Others: Coava coffee. Yeast: Wyeast #3787. IBU: 25. Source: Web.

**Old Man Gower's Holiday Tipple**: °P: 18. Malt: 59.8% Golden Promise pale malt, 20.6% Pale malt, 3.1% Caramel 40L malt, 4.1% Crystal 42-50L malt, 4.1% Special B malt, 4.1% Especial malt, 3.1% Raw sugar. Others: Grated fresh ginger, Grated nutmeg. Hops: 52.2% Willamette. Late hop: 21.7% Bramling Cross. Dry hops: 26.1% Bramling Cross. Yeast: Wyeast #1718. IBU: 50. Source: Web.

**The City Never Sleeps**: °P: 18.6. Malt: 63% Pilsner malt, 9.7% Melanoidin malt, 4% Crystal 70-80L malt, 5.2% Special B malt, 0.9% Smoked malt, 5.7% Black malt, 11.5% Raw sugar. Hops: 25% Willamette. Late hops: 37.5% Sterling, 37.5% Willamette. Yeast: Wyeast #3522. IBU: 26. Source: Web.

**Black Friday Imperial CDA**: °P: 18.8. Malt: 85.6% Pale malt, 4.3% Crystal II 65L malt, 5.3% Blackprinz® malt, 1.1% Chocolate malt, 3.7% Raw sugar. Hops: 3% Magnum,7.5% Willamette. Late hops: 24.1% Cascade, 7.5% Mount Hood, 9% Willamette, 16.5% Centennial, 3.8% Summit, 3.8% Amarillo. Dry hops: 13.5% Cascade, 3.8% Motueka, 3.8% Amarillo, 3.8% Summit. Yeast: Wyeast #1728. IBU: 80. Source: Web.

**Whole in the Head Imperial IPA**: °P: 19. Malt: 85.7% Pale malt, 4.1% Munich malt, Raw sugar. Hops: 1.7% Magnum, 5.6% Willamette. Late hops: 17.9% Cascade, 19% Centennial, 10.1% Simcoe, 10.1% Crystal. Dry hops: 22.3% Cascade, 22.3% Simcoe. Yeast: Wyeast #1728. IBU: "Lots". Source: Web.

**End of Reason**: °P: 19. Malt: 33.7% Pale malt, 33.7% Vienna malt, 10.9% Melanoidin malt, 4% Crystal 80L malt, 7.9% Special B malt, 9.9% Raw sugar. Hops: 5.3% Magnum, 31.6% Mount Hood, 31.6% Sterling, 31.6% Willamette. Yeast: Wyeast #3787. IBU: 36. Source: Web.

**Dyn-o-mite!**: °P: 20.5. Malt: 91.2% Pale malt, 8.8% Dextrose. Hops: 2.9% Magnum, 7.2% Willamette, 7.2% Centennial, 7.2% Crystal. Late hops: 7.2% Centennial, 14.5% Cascade, 7.2% Simcoe, 14.5% Crystal. Dry hops: 14.5% Cascade, 8.7% Simcoe, 1.4% Motueka. Yeast: Wyeast #1728. IBU: "Lots". Source: Web.

**Most Premium Russian Imperial Stout**: °P: 22.5. Malt: 57.7% Pale malt, 8.5% Vienna malt, 3.1% Crystal 42-50L malt, 3.1% Crystal 75-85L malt, 3.1% Crystal 120L malt, 6.2% Chocolate malt, 3.8% Black malt, 3.1% Roast barley, 11.5% Raw sugar. Hops: 13.8% Magnum, 58.6% Willamette. Late hops: 27.6% Cascade. Yeast: Wyeast #1728. IBU: 55. Source: Web.

**MASSIVE!**: °P: 26.5. Malt: 100% Halcyon pale malt. Hops: 2% Magnum. Late hops: 34.3% Cascade, 2.5% Willamette. Dry hops: 39.2% Mosaic. Yeast: Wyeast #1728. IBU: 30. Source: Web.

## *Golden Pacific Brewing Company, Berkeley, CA*

**Golden Bear Lager**: OG: 1048. Malt: Pale malt, Caramel malt, CaraPils malt, Wheat malt, Munich malt. Hops: Mount Hood, Tettnang. Source: GAM.

**Black Bear Lager**: OG: 1048. Malt: Patent black malt. Hops: Perle, Cascade. Source: GAM.

**Golden Gate Original Ale**: OG: 1056. Malt: Pale malt, Caramel malt, Chocolate malt, Munich malt. Hops: Perle, Tettnang, Willamette, Centennial. Source: GAM.

**Hibernator Winter Ale 1995**: OG: 1064. Malt: Pale malt, Belgian malt, Brown malt. Hops: Perle, Columbus, Goldings. Source: GAM.

### . Goose Island Beer Company, Chicago, IL

**Hex Nut Brown Ale**: OG: 1044. Malt: Pale malt, Crystal malt, Brown malt, Chocolate malt. Hops: Willamette. Source: NACB.

**Honker's Ale**: OG: 1049-51. Malt: Pale malt, Crystal malt, CaraMunich malt, Munich malt. Hops: Northern Brewer. Late hops: Cascade, Willamette. Source: BC.

### . Gordon Biersch, San Jose, CA. Www.gordonbiersch.com

**Hefeweizen**: ABV: 5.4%. Malt: 45% Pale malt, 55% Wheat malt. Source: Web.

**Festbier**: Malt: Pilsner malt, Munich malt. Late hops: Hallertau. Source: Web.

**Winterbock**: ABV: 7.5%. IBU: 24. Source: Web.

### . Grand Teton Brewing Company, Wilson, WY and Victor, ID. Www.grandtetonbrewing.com

**Workhorse Wheat**: OG: 1042. Malt: Pale malt, CaraHell® malt, Wheat malt, Wheat. Hops: Liberty, Mount Hood. IBU: 10.4. Source: Web.

**Au Naturale**: OG: 1052. Malt: Pilsner malt, CaraHell® malt, Vienna malt. Hops: Hallertau. IBU: 23. Source: Web.

**Old Faithful Ale**: OG: 1052. Malt: Pale malt, CaraHell® malt, Vienna malt. Hops: Goldings, Willamette, Hallertau. IBU: 23. Source: Web.

**Teton Ale**: OG: 1053. Malt: Pale malt, CaraAmber® malt, CaraAroma® malt. Hops: Goldings, Willamette, Saaz, Harsduucher. IBU: 24. Source: Web.

**Bitch Creek ESB**: OG: 1061. Malt: Pale malt, CaraAroma® malt, Crystal malt, Melanoidin malt, CaraAmber® malt. Hops: Galena, Chinook, Centennial. Late hops: Galena, Chinook, Centennial. Dry hops: Centennial. IBU: 51. Source: 150/Web.

**Sweetgrass IPA**: OG: 1062. Malt: Pale malt, CaraVienne malt, CaraAmber® malt, Vienna malt. Hops: Goldings, Willamette, Galena, Amarillo, Saaz, Cascade. Dry hops: Cascade. IBU: 58. Source: Web.

Note: Formerly Otto Brothers Brewing Company.

### . Bert Grant's Real Ales, Yakima, WA

**Bert Grant's Imperial Stout**: OG: 1071-74. Malt: Pale malt, Black malt, Crystal malt, Clover honey. Hops: Galena. Late hops: Cascade. Dry hops: Goldings, Cascade. Source: CB.

### Gray's Brewing Company, Janesville, WI

**Gray's Oatmeal Stout**: OG: 1045. Malt: Pale malt, Flaked oats, Crystal malt, Roast barley. Hops: Goldings. Late hops: Northern Brewer. Source: NACB.

**Gray's Imperial Stout**: OG: 1070. Malt: Pale malt, Black malt, Crystal malt, Munich malt, Roast barley. Hops: Willamette, Tettnang. Late hops: Willamette. Source: NACB.

### Great Divide Brewing Company, Denver, CO

**Hibernation Ale**: OG: 1080. Malt: Pale malt, Crystal malt, Brown malt, Roast barley, Wheat malt. Hops: Magnum. Late hops: Goldings. Source: NACB.

### Great Lakes Brewing Company, Cleveland, OH

**Moon Dog Ale**: ABW: 4%. Malt: Pale malt, Crystal malt, Wheat malt, Dextrin malt. Hops: Northern Brewer, Goldings. Source: GAM.

**Dortmunder Gold**: ABW: 4.3%. Malt: Pale malt, Caramel malt. Hops: Cascade, Hallertau. Source: GAM.

**Edmund Fitzgerald Porter**: OG: 1057. Malt: Pale malt, Crystal malt, Chocolate malt, Roast barley. Hops: Northern Brewer. Late hops: Fuggles, Cascade. Source: NACB. ABW: 4.7%. Malt: Pale malt, Crystal malt, Roast barley, Chocolate malt. Hops: Northern Brewer, Willamette, Cascade. Source: GAM.

**Burning River Pale Ale**: OG: 1061-63. Malt: Pale malt, Crystal malt, Biscuit malt. Hops: Cascade, Northern Brewer. Late hops: Cascade. Dry hops: Cascade. Source: BC. ABW: 4.8%. Malt: Pale malt, Crystal malt, Victory malt. Hops: Cascade. Source: GAM.

**Oktoberfest**: ABW: 5%. Malt: Pale malt, Caramel malt. Hops: Liberty, Hallertau. Source: GAM.

**Rockefeller Bock**: ABW: 5.3%. Malt: Pale malt, Caramel malt, Chocolate malt. Hops: Tettnang, Hallertau. Source: GAM.

**Commodore Perry India Pale Ale**: ABW: 5.7%. Malt: Pale malt, Caramel malt. Hops: Galena, Goldings. Source: GAM.

**Elliot Ness Lager**: OG: 1063-65. Malt: Lager malt, Crystal malt, Munich malt. Hops: Tettnang, Hersbrücker. Late hops: Tettnang, Hersbrücker. Source: CB. ABW: 5%. Malt: Pale malt, Caramel malt, Munich malt. Hops: Tettnang, Hallertau. Source: GAM.

Notes: On my first visit to Cleveland my good friend Brian Asquith had taken me on a very enjoyable tour of the city and we ended up in the Great Lakes Brewing Company with a number of his friends. The group was sufficiently large (I think there were about 20 of us) that we relocated to the basement of the pub and monopolised the tables in the centre of the room. Good beer and good conversation was had, during which Lisa, a friend of Brian's, related how when Brian stayed with them on his first arrival in the USA she used to do his laundry for him. On one occasion, while Brian was out at the pub, she was doing his laundry and discovered a pair of his underpants having a pattern of balloons on them. She decided to wear these on her head and paraded around the room while Tom, her husband, asked her to stop playing with them... Lisa then told how her father used to sit in the corner wearing her mother's bra on his head for some unexplained reason... Lisa then told a story of how her grandmother went to the toilet and after some delay returned with a large bowel movement in her hand and proclaimed "This goddam thing nearly killed me!"... Lisa then told how the family dog had once been told off by the grandmother and while she was away to the toilet the dog took the opportunity to run into her room and defecate on her bed...and the dog was taken to the vet where it was judged to be suffering from some sort of mental illness... At this point I put my hand up and say "So let me get this straight: your Dad is sat in the corner with a bra on his head, you are mincing around with Brian's undercrackers on your head and your Grandma comes in with a turd in her hand? And you wonder why the dog has got mental problems?!" The whole room collapsed with laughter! I didn't think it was that funny, but I guess you had to be there. It was certainly a good moment.

### . Great Northern Brewing Company, Whitefish, MT

**Minott's Black Star Premium Lager Beer**: OG: 1049. Malt: Pale malt, Caramel 60L malt. Hops: Saaz, Mount Hood. Source: GAM.

**Wold Huckleberry Wheat Lager**: ABV: 5.8%. Malt: Pale malt, Wheat malt. Hops: Cascade. Others: Huckleberry juice. Source: GAM.

### . Green Flash Brewing Company, Vista, CA. Www.greenflashbrew.com

**Summer Saison**: ABV: 4.3%. Others: Ginger, Grains of Paradise, Curaçao Orange peel. IBU: 20. Source: Web.

**Hop Head Red Ale**: ABV: 6%. Dry hops: Amarillo. IBU: 45. Source: Web.

**West Coast IPA**: ABV: 7-7.3%. Malt: 84% Pale malt, 8% CaraPils malt, 8% Carastan 30-37L malt. Hops: Simcoe, Columbus, Centennial. Late hops: Cascade. Dry hops: Simcoe, Cascade, Centennial, Amarillo. IBU: 95. Source: CYBI/Web.

**Double Stout**: ABV: 8.8%. Malt: Golden naked oats. Hops: Target. IBU: 45. Source: Web.

**Imperial India Pale Ale**: ABV: 9.4%. Hops: Nugget, Summit. IBU: 101. Source: Web.

**Trippel**: ABV: 9.7%. Malt: Pale malt. Hops: Styrian Goldings, Saaz. IBU: 24. Source: Web.

**Extra Pale Ale**: Malt: Pale malt. Hops: Cascade, Chinook. Source: Web.

**Ruby Red Ale**: Malt: Munich malt. Source: Web.

### . Gritty McDuff's Brewing Company, Portland, ME

**Black Fly Stout**: OG: 1048. Malt: Pale malt, Crystal malt, Black malt, Roast barley. Hops: Chinook. Late hops: Goldings, Cascade. Source: NACB.

**Best Brown Ale**: OG: 1055-57. Malt: Pale malt, CaraMunich malt, Chocolate malt, Crystal malt. Hops: Northern Brewer. Late hops: Willamette, Goldings. Source: BC.

### . *Haines Brewing Company, Haines, AK*

**Lookout Stout**: OG: 1059. Malt: Maris Otter pale malt, Crystal malt, Flaked barley, Roast barley. Hops: Northern Brewer. Late hops: Northern Brewer. Source: 150.

### . *Hair of the Dog Brewing Company, Portland, OR*

**Golden Rose**: OG: 1074. Malt: Pale malt, Aromatic malt, Honey malt, Candi sugar. Hops: Hallertau. Source: GAM.

**Adambier**: OG: 1094. Malt: Pale malt, Crystal malt, Patent black malt, Chocolate malt, Munich malt, Peat-smoked malt. Hops: Northern Brewer, Tettnang. Source: GAM.

**Fred**: OG: 1098. Malt: Pale malt, Aromatic malt, Rye malt, Crystal malt. Hops: Bramling Cross, Fuggles, Hallertau, Willamette, Eroica. Late hops: Target, Northern Brewer, Goldings, Saaz, Cascade. Source: NACB.

### . *Hammer & Nail Brewers, Watertown, CT*

**Brown Ale**: OG: 1045. Malt: Mild ale malt, Crystal malt, Chocolate malt. Hops: Willamette. Late hops: Willamette. Source: NACB.

**Vienna-Style Lager**: OG: 1045. Malt: Pilsner malt, Vienna malt, CaraPils malt, Munich malt, Crystal malt. Hops: Hallertau. Late hops: Saaz. Source: NACB.

**Scotch Classic-Style Ale**: OG: 1071-73. Malt: Pale malt, Munich malt, Crystal malt, CaraMunich malt, Roast barley, Peat-smoked malt. Hops: Willamette. Source: BC.

### . *Harpoon Brewery, Boston, MA. Www.harpoonbrewery.com*

**Harpoon UFO Hefeweizen**: OG: 1050. Malt: Lager malt, Wheat malt, CaraPils malt. Hops: Hallertau. Late hops: Hallertau. IBU: 19. EBC: 10. Source: NACB/Web.

**Winter Warmer**: OG: 1056. Malt: Pale malt, CaraPils malt, Crystal malt. Hops: Cluster. Others: Cinnamon, Nutmeg. Source: 150.

**Harpoon Spring Maibock**: OG: 1060. Malt: Lager malt, Crystal malt, Munich malt. Hops: Spalt. Late hops: Tettnang. Source: NACB.

**Belgian Pale Ale**: °P: 15.4. Malt: Pale malt, Caramel malt, Munich malt. Hops: Amarillo, Apollo. IBU: 33. EBC: 20. Source: Web.

**IPA**: °P: 15.5. Malt: Pale malt and 2 other malts. Hops: Cascade. IBU: 42. EBC: 15. Source: Web.

**Single Hop ESB**: Hops: Delta. Late hops: Delta. Source: BA.

Notes Formerly Mass. Bay Brewing Company.

## . *Hart, Seattle, WA*

**Pyramid Wheaten Ale**: OG: 1042. Malt: Caramel malt, Wheat malt. Hops: Nugget, Perle. Source: GAM.

**Pyramid Hefeweizen Ale**: OG: 1045. Malt: Caramel malt, Wheat malt. Hops: Nugget, Perle. Source: GAM.

**Pyramid Apricot Ale**: OG: 1045. Malt: Caramel malt, Wheat malt. Hops: Nugget, Perle. Others: Apricots. Source: GAM.

**Pyramid Pale Ale**: OG: 1048. Malt: Caramel malt. Hops: Cascade. Source: GAM.

**Pyramid Best Brown Ale**: OG: 1052. Malt: Caramel malt, Roast barley, Munich malt, Dark Carastan malt. Hops: Nugget, Liberty. Source: GAM.

**Espresso Stout**: OG: 1062. Malt: Caramel malt, Roast barley, Patent black malt, Munich malt. Hops: Nugget, Liberty. Source: GAM.

## . *Hartmann, Bridgeport, CT*

**1905 Holiday Ale**: OG: 1055. Malt: Pale malt, Caramel 120L malt, Corn sugar. Hops: Cluster. Yeast: Wyeast #1098/Wyeast #1056. Others: Salt. IBU: 46. SRM: 17. Source: BYO.

## . *John Harvard's Brewhouse, Westport, CT*

**Imperial Stout**: OG: 1097. Malt: Pale malt, Vienna malt, Flaked barley, Crystal malt, Roast barley, Patent black malt. Hops: Chinook. Source: BC.

## . *The Hatuey Brewery, Winston-Salem, NC*

**Hatuey**: OG: 1053-54. Malt: Lager malt, Flaked maize, Crystal malt. Hops: Saaz. Late hops: Tettnang. Source: CB.

## . *Heartland Brewery, New York, NY. Www.heartlandbrewery.com*

**Indian River Ale**: ABV: 4%. Malt: Pale malt, Victory malt, Crystal 60L malt, Corn sugar. Hops: Galena. Late hops: Cascade. Others: Orange peel, Coriander, Kosher salt. Yeast: Wyeast #1056. Source: SMB.

**Harvest Wheat Ale**: ABV: 4.5%. Malt: Pale malt, Red wheat malt. Source: Web.

**Cornhusker lager**: ABV: 4.75%. Malt: Flaked maize. Source: Web.

**Smiling Pumpkin Ale**: ABV: 5.5%. Malt: Pale malt, Crystal 60L malt, Honey, Corn sugar. Hops: Cluster. Late hops: Cascade, Mount Hood. Others: Pumpkin, Cinnamon, Nutmeg, Cloves, Kosher or Sea salt. Source: SMB. Others: Honey-roast pumpkins, Ginger, Cloves, Cinnamon, Nutmeg. Source: Web.

**Stumbling Buffalo Ale**: ABV: 5.5%. Malt: "plenty of" Chocolate malt. Source: Web.

**Red Rooster Ale**: ABV: 5.5%. Malt: Caramel malt, Munich malt. Source: Web.

**Farmer Jon's Oatmeal Stout**: ABV: 6%. Malt: Pale malt, Roast barley, Flaked oats, Flaked barley, Crystal 20L malt, Flaked wheat. Hops: Cluster, Mount Hood. Late hops: Hallertau. Others: Kosher salt. Source: SMB.

**Bavarian Black Lager**: ABV: 6.5%. Malt: Caramel malt, Chocolate malt. Source: Web.

### . Heckler, Tahoe City, CA

**Heckler Brau Hell Lager**: OG: 1050. Malt: CaraPils malt, Caramel malt, Crystal malt. Hops: Saaz, Tettnang. Source: GAM.

**Heckler Brau Oktoberfest**: OG: 1054. Hops: Saaz. Source: GAM.

**Heckler Brau Doppel Bock**: OG: 1072. Malt: Pilsner malt, Caramel malt, Munich malt, Chocolate malt. Hops: Tettnang, Northern Brewer. Source: GAM.

### . High Falls Brewing Company, Rochester, NY

**Genesee Light**: ABV: 3.6%. Malt: 2-row malt, 6-row malt. Source: geneseebeer.com.

**Genesee Beer**: ABV: 4.5%. Malt: 6-row malt, Corn grits. Hops: Yakima. Source: geneseebeer.com.

**Michael Shea's Black & Tan**: OG: 1050. Note: This is a blend of two beers; a porter and a lager. Porter Malt: Pale malt, Black malt, Chocolate malt. Porter hops: Fuggles. Porter late hops: Goldings. Lager Malt: Lager malt, CaraPils malt. Lager hops: Saaz. Lager late hops: Hallertau. Source: NACB.

**Dundee Pale Ale**: ABV: 5.3%. Hops: Cascade, Columbus, Amarillo. IBU: 35. Source: dundeebeer.com.

**Dundee Pale Bock Lager**: ABV: 6.25%. Hops: Magnum, Saaz. IBU: 25. Source: dundeebeer.com.

**Dundee India Pale Ale**: ABV: 6.3%. Malt: Crystal malt. Hops: Amarillo, Simcoe. IBU: 60. Source: dundeebeer.com.

### . High Point Brewing, Denver, CO

**ESB Ale**: OG: 1062. Malt: Pale malt, Caramel malt. Hops: Columbus, Centennial, Cascade, Willamette, Hallertau. Source: GAM.

### . Highland Brewing Company, Asheville, NC. Www.highlandbrewing.com

**Highland Heather Ale**: OG: 1048. Malt: Maris Otter pale malt, Roast barley. Hops: Goldings, Hersbrücker. Others: Heather tips. Source: 150.

**Gaelic Ale**: OG: 1056. Malt: Pale malt, Crystal malt, Munich malt, Extra Special malt. Hops: Chinook. Late hops: Willamette, Cascade. Source: 150/Web.

### . Hill Country Brewing Company, Austin, TX

**Balcones Fault Pale Malt**: OG: 1045. Malt: Pale malt, CaraVienne malt, Wheat malt, CaraPils malt. Hops: Goldings, Fuggles. Source: GAM.

**Balcones Fault Red Granite**: OG: 1045. Malt: Pale malt, CaraVienne malt, Wheat malt, Chocolate malt, Crystal malt. Hops: Fuggles. Source: GAM.

### . Historical recipes

**Washington's Small Beer**: Malt: Bran, Molasses. Source: DAW.

**Corn Beer**: Malt: Corn syrup. Source: DAW.

**Ginger Beer**: Malt: Molasses. Others: Ground ginger. Source: DAW.

**Spruce Beer**: Malt: Molasses. Others: Spruce tips. Source: DAW.

**Birch Beer**: Malt: Corn syrup. Others: Essence of Wintergreen, Oak essence. Source: DAW.

**Two Penny**: Malt: Pale malt, Crystal malt. Hops: Goldings. Source: DAW.

**Small Ale for the Stone**: Malt: Brown malt, Crystal malt. Source: DAW.

### . Holy Cow! Casino Cafe Brewery, Las Vegas, NV

**Vegas Gold Hefe Weizen**: OG: 1050. Malt: Wheat malt, CaraPils malt. Hops: Willamette. Source: GAM. Malt: Pale malt, Wheat malt. Hops: Tettnang. Late hops: Tettnang. Source: SMB.

**Rebel Red English Brown**: OG: 1056. Malt: Pale malt, Caramel 60L malt, Caramel 90L malt / Caramel 80L malt, CaraPils malt, optional Roast barley. Hops: Fuggles. Late hops: Fuggles. Source: GAM/SMB.

**Amber Gambler Classic English Pale Ale**: OG: 1056. Malt: Pale malt, Caramel 40L malt, Munich malt, optional CaraPils malt. Hops: Fuggles. Late hops: Cascade. Source: GAM/SMB.

**Holy Cow! Stout**: OG: 1062. Malt: Pale malt, Caramel malt, Patent black malt. Source: GAM.

### . Hops Grill & Bar, Clearwater, FL

**Clearwater Light**: OG: 1041. Malt: Pale malt, CaraPils malt, Wheat malt. Hops: Hallertau. Late hops: Saaz. Source: 150.

### . Hudenpohl-Schoenling, Cincinnati, OH

**Hudy Delight**: OG: 1030. Malt: Lager malt, Corn syrup. Hops: Cluster, Cascade. Source: GAM.

**Morlein's Cincinnati Select Lager Beer**: OG: 1048. Malt: Pale malt, Caramel malt. Hops: Cluster, Saaz, Mount Hood. Source: GAM.

**Christian Moerlein Bock**: OG: 1049. Malt: Pale malt, Caramel malt, Patent black malt. Hops: Cluster, Mount Hood. Source: GAM.

**Little Kings Red**: OG: 1052. Malt: Pale malt, Caramel malt, Chocolate malt. Hops: Cascade, Mount Hood. Source: GAM.

**Little Kings Cream Ale**: OG: 1053. Malt: Lager malt, Corn grits, Corn syrup. Hops: Hallertau. Source: GAM.

**Little Kings Ice Cream Ale**: OG: 1058. Malt: Lager malt, Corn grits, Corn syrup. Hops: Hallertau. Source: GAM.

### .  *Joseph Huber Brewing Company, Monroe, WI*

**Berghoff Dark**: OG: 1045. Malt: Lager malt, Munich malt, Black malt, CaraPils malt. Hops: Tettnang. Late hops: Tettnang. Source: NACB.

**Dempsey's Extra Stout**: OG: 1050. Malt: Pale malt, Crystal malt, Munich malt, Roast barley. Hops: Cluster. Late hops: Willamette. Source: NACB.

### .  *Hyland Orchard and Brewery, Sturbridge, MA*

**Hyland's American Pale Ale**: OG: 1048. Malt: Pale malt, Crystal malt. Hops: Nugget. Late hops: Cascade. Dry hops: Willamette. Source: NACB.

### .  *Ipswich Brewing Company, Ipswich, MA and Baltimore, MD*

**Extra Special Bitter**: OG: 1046. Malt: Pale malt, Crystal malt, Wheat malt. Hops: Cascade. Late hops: Chinook. Source: NACB.

**Oatmeal Stout**: OG: 1073. Malt: Pale malt, Toasted Flaked oats, Roast barley, Chocolate malt, Crystal malt, Black malt. Hops: Galena. Late hops: Willamette, Cascade. Source: BC.

### .  *J&L Brewing Company, San Rafael, CA*

**San Rafael Red Diamond Ale**: OG: 1050. Malt: Pale malt, Crystal 60-80L malt, Crystal 90-110L malt, Crystal 135-155L malt, Munich malt, Wheat. Hops: Bullion, Cascade, Willamette, Tettnang. Source: GAM.

**San Rafael Golden Ale**: OG: 1054. Malt: Pale malt, Wheat. Hops: Cascade, Tettnang. Source: GAM.

**San Rafael Amber Ale**: OG: 1060. Malt: Pale malt, Crystal 60-80L malt, Crystal 90-110L malt, Crystal 135-155L malt, Munich malt. Hops: Tettnang, Bullion, Cascade, Willamette. Source: GAM.

Note: Contract brewed by Cold Spring Brewing Company, Cold Spring, MN.

### .  *Jasper Murdoch's Alehouse, Norwich, VT*

**Whistling Pig Red Ale**: OG: 1048. Malt: Pale malt, CaraPils malt, Crystal malt, Brown malt. Hops: Fuggles, Goldings. Late hops: Goldings. Source: NACB.

### Jester King, Austin, TX. Www.jesterkingbrewery.com

**Commercial Suicide**: OG: 1024. Malt: 72% Pilsner malt, 7% Brown malt, 7% Crystal 45L malt, 6% Chocolate malt, 6% Flaked oats, 3% Amber malt. Hops: Goldings. Yeast: Wyeast #3711 and optional souring yeast/bacteria. IBU: 20. Source: Web.

**Wytchmaker Rye IPA**: OG: 1059. Malt: 85% Pale malt, 15% Rye malt. Hops: Goldings. Late hops: Chinook, Falconer's Flight, Zythos. Dry hops: Simcoe, Falconer's Flight, Citra. Yeast: Wyeast #3711 and optional souring yeast/bacteria. IBU: 55. Source: Web.

**Black Metal**: OG: 1085. Malt: 77% Pale malt, 5% Roast barley, 4% Chocolate malt, 4% Black malt, 2% Crystal 60L malt, 2% Crystal 120L malt, 2% Brown malt, 4% Carafa® III malt. Hops: Columbus. Yeast: Wyeast #3711 and optional souring yeast/bacteria. IBU: 30. Source: Web.

### Jigger Hill Brewery, Tunbridge and South Royalton, VT

**Tunbridge Sap Brew**: OG: 1040. Malt: Pale malt, CaraPils malt, Biscuit malt, Maple syrup. Hops: Willamette. Source: NACB.

### Jones Brewing Company, Smithton, PA

**Eureka Gold Light Lager**: ABW: 3.09%. Malt: Corn grits. Hops: Cluster. Source: GAM.

**Stoney's Light Beer**: ABW: 3.2%. Malt: Corn grits. Hops: Cluster. Source: GAM.

**Eureka 1881 Red Irish Amber Lager**: ABW: 3.5%. Malt: Corn grits. Hops: Cluster. Source: GAM.

**Eureka Black & Tan Welsh Dark**: ABW: 3.5%. Malt: Caramel malt, Corn grits. Hops: Cluster. Source: GAM.

**Stoney's Beer**: OG: 1042. Malt: Corn grits. Hops: Cluster. Source: GAM.

**Eureka Gold Lager**: ABW: 3.54%. Malt: Corn grits. Hops: Cluster. Source: GAM.

**Esquire Extra Dry**: OG: 1044. Malt: Corn grits. Hops: Cluster. Source: GAM.

### Kalamazoo Brewing Company, Kalamazoo, MI

**Bell's Oberon Ale**: OG: 1042. Malt: Lager malt, Wheat malt, CaraPils malt. Hops: Saaz. Others: Coriander seeds. Source: NACB.

**Bell's Porter**: OG: 1050. Malt: Pale malt, Crystal malt, Black malt, Chocolate malt. Hops: Goldings. Late hops: Fuggles. Source: NACB.

Note: This brewery became Bell's Brewery in 2005.

### KelSo Beer Company, Brooklyn, NY. Www.kelsobeer.com

**Carrollgaarden Wit**: ABV: 5%. Malt: Pilsner malt, Wheat malt, Acid malt, Oats. Hops: Hallertau. Others: Orange peel, Coriander, Chamomile. IBU: 20. Source: Web.

**Saison**: ABV: 5%. Malt: Pilsner malt, Wheat malt, Honey malt. Hops: Goldings, Fuggles, Hallertau. IBU: 22. Source: Web.

**Pilsner**: ABV: 5.5%. Malt: Pilsner malt, Light Munich malt. Hops: Sterling. IBU: 23. Source: Web.

**Winter Lager**: ABV: 5.5%. Malt: Pale malt, Caramel malt, Chocolate malt, Caramel 60L malt. Hops: Galena, Willamette. IBU: 23. Source: Web.

**Pale Ale**: ABV: 5.75%. Malt: Golden Promise pale malt, Pale crystal malt. Hops: Citra, Cascade, Horizon. IBU: 34. Source: Web.

**Nut Brown Lager**: ABV: 5.75%. Malt: Pilsner malt, Munich malt, Chocolate malt. Hops: Fuggles, Hallertau, Northern Brewer. IBU: 19. Source: Web.

**India Pale Ale**: ABV: 6%. Malt: Golden Promise pale malt, Pale crystal malt. Hops: Columbus, Cascade, Nelson Sauvin. IBU: 64. Source: Web/BA.

**Kellerfest**: ABV: 6%. Malt: Pilsner malt, Caramel malts, Munich malt, Vienna malt. Hops: Select, Styrian Goldings. IBU: 34. Source: Web.

**Resessionator**: ABV: 8%. Malt: Pilsner malt, Caramel malt, Munich malt, Vienna malt. Hops: Hallertau, Saaz, Chinook, Horizon. IBU: 25. Source: Web.

**Imperial IPA**: ABV: 10%. Malt: Maris Otter pale malt, Pale crystal malt. Hops: "Name one...over half a dozen varieties. IBU: 100. Source: Web.

### . *Thomas Kemper Brewing Company, Seattle, WA*

**Weizen-berry**: OG: 1045. Malt: Lager malt, CaraPils malt, Wheat malt, Crystal malt. Hops: Hallertau. Late hops: Hallertau. Others: Raspberries. Source: NACB. OG: 1050. Malt: Wheat malt. Hops: Nugget, Liberty. Source: GAM.

**Pale Lager**: OG: 1048. Malt: Caramel 40L malt, Patent black malt, Munich malt. Hops: Nugget, Liberty. Source: GAM.

**Honey Weizen**: OG: 1050. Malt: Pale malt, Wheat malt. Hops: Nugget, Liberty. Source: GAM.

**Hefeweizen**: OG: 1050. Malt: Wheat malt. Hops: Nugget, Liberty. Source: GAM.

**Amber Ale**: OG: 1052. Malt: Caramel 40L malt, Caramel 80L malt, Munich malt. Hops: Saaz, Nugget, Liberty. Source: GAM.

**Dark Lager**: OG: 1058. Malt: Caramel 40L malt, Caramel 80L malt, Munich malt, Chocolate malt. Hops: Nugget, Styrian Goldings. Source: GAM.

### . *Kennebunkport Brewing Company, Kennebunkport, ME*

**Shipyard Longfellow Ale**: OG: 1065-66. Malt: Pale malt, Crystal malt, Chocolate malt, Flaked barley, Roast barley. Hops: Northern Brewer. Late hops: Tettnang, Cascade, Goldings. Dry hops: Goldings, Cascade. Source: BC.

**Prelude Ale**: OG: 1078. Malt: Pale malt, Torrefied wheat, Chocolate malt, Crystal malt. Hops: Cascade, American Goldings, Fuggles, Tettnang. Source: GAM.

### . *Kross Brewing Company, Morrisville, VT*

**Brueghel Blonde Ale**: OG: 1048. Malt: Belgian Pilsner malt, CaraVienne malt, Wheat malt, Flaked wheat, Crystal malt. Hops: Willamette. Others: Coriander seed. Source: NACB.

### . *La Conner Brewing Company, La Conner, WA*

**La Conner Pilsner**: OG: 1051-56. Malt: Pilsner malt. Hops: Northern Brewer. Late hops: Saaz, Hersbrücker. Source: 150.

### . *Lagunitas Brewing Company, Petaluma, CA*

**IPA**: OG: 1059. Malt: Pale malt, Dextrin malt, Crystal malt, Munich malt. Hops: Horizon. Late hops: Cascade, Willamette, Cascade. Source: 150. °P: 14.82. Malt: 75% Pale malt, 6% Wheat malt, 5.7% Munich 10L malt, 3.8% Crystal 60L malt, 9% Caramel 15L malt. Hops: 0.3g/l Horizon, 0.05g/l Summit, Apollo, Bravo or Columbus. Late hops (30 minutes): 1g/l Willamette, 0.5g/l Centennial. Late hops (Whirlpool): 1.5g/l Cascade. Dry hops: Cascade, Centennial. Yeast: Wyeast #1968. Notes: Mash temperature = 160°F, Final gravity = 4.5°P. Source: CYBI.

**Censored Ale**: °P: 16. Malt: 74% Pale malt, 8% Wheat malt, 6.5% Caramel 60L malt, 10% Munich 10L malt, 0.04% Roast barley. Hops: 0.2g/l Horizon or Nugget, 0.3g/l Willamette. Late hops (30 minutes): 0.7g/l Willamette, 0.1g/l Centennial, 0.2g/l Cascade. Late hops (Whirlpool): 0.4g/l Centennial, 0.4g/l Liberty. Dry hops: No. Yeast: Wyeast #1968. Notes: Mash temperature = 156°F, Final gravity = 4.5-5°P. Source: CYBI.

**Cappuccino Stout**: OG: 1070. Malt: Pale malt, Crystal malt, Chocolate malt, Wheat malt, Coffee, Sugar. Hops: Horizon. Late hops: Willamette, Cascade. Source: 150.

**Brown Shugga**: OG: 1059. Malt: 71.6% Pale malt, 17% Wheat malt, 4.7% Caramel 60L malt, 4.5% Munich 10L malt, 1.3% Caramel 120L malt, 1% Crystal 135-165L malt, 12g/l Brown sugar. Hops: 0.36g/l Willamette, Hop oil. Late hops (30 minutes): 0.3g/l Horizon or Nugget, 1.2g/l Willamette. Late hops (Whirlpool): 0.15g/l Horizon, 0.9g/l Centennial, 0.5g/l Liberty. Dry hops: No. Yeast: Wyeast #1968. IBU: 55. Notes: Mash temperature = 155°F or stepped mash, Final gravity = 5-6°P. Source: CYBI.

### . *Lake Placid Pub & Brewery, Lake Placid, NY*

**Ubu Ale**: OG: 1069. Malt: Maris Otter pale malt, Wheat malt, Crystal malt, Chocolate malt, Patent black malt. Hops: Fuggles. Late hops: Cluster, Mount Hood. Source: 150.

### . *Lakefront Brewery, Milwaukee, WI*

**Pumpkin Lager Beer**: OG: 1055. Malt: Pale malt, Crystal malt, Munich malt, CaraPils malt. Hops: Cluster. Others: Pumpkins, Salt, Cinnamon, Nutmeg. Source: GAM.

**Eastside Dark**: OG: 1060. Malt: Pale malt, Munich malt, Chocolate malt, Patent black malt. Hops: Mount Hood. Late hops: Mount Hood. Source: 150/GAM.

**Riverwest Stein Beer**: OG: 1060. Malt: Pale malt, Roast barley, Crystal malt. Hops: Mount Hood, Cascade. Source: GAM.

**Cream City Pale Ale**: OG: 1060. Malt: Pale malt, Caramel malt, Munich malt, CaraPils malt. Hops: Cluster, Cascade. Source: GAM.

**Klisch Pilsner**: OG: 1060. Malt: Pale malt. Hops: Mount Hood. Source: GAM.

### . Latrobe Brewing Company, Latrobe, PA

**Rolling Rock Beer**: OG: 1040. Malt: Lager malt, CaraPils malt, Flaked maize. Hops: Hallertau. Late hops: Hallertau. Source: NACB.

### . Left Hand Brewing Company, Longmont, CO

**Black Jack Porter**: OG: 1048. Malt: Pale malt, Black malt, Munich malt, Chocolate malt, Crystal malt. Hops: Goldings. Late hops: Cascade. Source: NACB.

### . Jacob Leinenkugel, Chippewa Falls, WI

**Honey Weiss Bier**: ABW: 3.85%. Malt: Pale malt, Wheat malt. Hops: Yakima. Source: GAM.

**Red Lager**: ABW: 3.85%. Malt: Pale malt, Lager malt, Caramel malt, CaraPils malt. Hops: Cluster, Mount Hood. Source: GAM.

### . Lone Star Brewing Company, Longview, TX

**Lone Star**: OG: 1037. Malt: Pale malt, Flaked maize, Crystal malt. Hops: Tettnang, Styrian Goldings. Late hops: Saaz, Tettnang. Source: BC.

### . Lonetree, Denver, CO

**Country Cream Ale**: OG: 1050. Malt: Lager malt, Wheat malt, Crystal malt. Hops: Mount Hood, Northern Brewer, Hallertau. Source: GAM.

**Horizon Honey Ale**: OG: 1052. Malt: Pale malt, Caramel malt, Colorado Honey. Hops: Cascade. Source: GAM.

**Sunset Red Ale**: OG: 1054. Malt: Caramel malt, Lager malt. Hops: Northern Brewer, Tettnang, Hallertau. Source: GAM.

**Iron Horse Dark Ale**: OG: 1064. Malt: Roast barley, Chocolate malt. Hops: Perle, Willamette. Source: GAM.

### . Long Trail, Bridgewater Corners, VT

**Harvest Ale**: ABW: 3.4%. Malt: Pale malt, Chocolate malt, Crystal malt. Source: GAM.

**Stout**: OG: 1045. Malt: Pale malt, Chocolate malt. Hops: Chinook. Source: GAM.

**Long Trail Ale**: OG: 1046. Malt: Pilsner malt, Wheat malt, Crystal malt, Munich malt. Hops: Tettnang. Late hops: Tettnang. Source: NACB. Malt: Pale malt, Chocolate malt, Crystal malt. Hops: Willamette, Cascade. Source: GAM.

**Kölsch**: OG: 1046. Malt: Lager malt, CaraPils malt, Wheat malt. Hops: Tettnang. Late hops: Spalt. Source: NACB. OG: 1045. Malt: Pale malt, Wheat malt. Hops: German varieties. Source: GAM.

**Hibernator**: OG: 1058. Malt: Pale malt, Chocolate malt, Crystal malt, Black malt, Honey. Hops: Willamette. Source: GAM.

**Double Bag Ale**: OG: 1065. Malt: Pale malt, Chocolate malt, Crystal malt. Source: GAM.

### . Longshore Brewing, Garden City, NY

**Longshore Lager**: OG: 1042. Malt: Lager malt, Munich malt, CaraPils malt. Hops: Spalt. Late hops: Saaz. Dry hops: Saaz. Source: NACB.

**Rough Rider Brown Ale**: OG: 1053-54. Malt: Pale malt, Dextrin malt, Munich malt, Crystal malt, CaraMunich malt, Chocolate malt. Hops: Chinook. Late hops: Willamette, Chinook. Source: BC.

**Leviathan**: OG: 1105-106. Malt: Pale malt, Munich malt, Crystal malt. Hops: Chinook. Late hops: Willamette, Goldings. Source: BC.

### . Lost Coast Brewery, Eureka, CA

**Downtown Brown Ale**: OG: 1044. Malt: Mild ale malt, Brown malt, Black malt, Chocolate malt, Crystal malt. Hops: Willamette. Late hops: Cascade. Source: NACB. OG: 1050. Malt: Roast barley, Chocolate malt. Hops: Chinook, Cascade, Mount Hood. Source: GAM.

**Alleycat Amber Ale**: OG: 1050. Malt: Crystal malt, CaraPils malt. Hops: Mount Hood, Cascade, Liberty. Source: GAM.

### . Mac & Jack's Brewery, Redmond, WA

**African Amber**: OG: 1060. Malt: Pale malt, CaraPils malt, Crystal malt, Munich malt. Hops: Centennial. Late hops: Cascade. Dry hops: Cascade. Source: 150.

### . McNeill's Brewery, Brattleboro, VT

**Alle Tage Altbier**: OG: 1046. Hops: German noble. Source: GAM.

**Big Nose Blond**: OG: 1046. Malt: Pale malt, Wheat malt, Crystal malt, Munich malt. Hops: Cascade, Northern Brewer, Hallertau. Source: GAM.

**Duck's Breath Ale**: OG: 1048. Malt: Maris Otter pale malt, Crystal malt. Hops: Goldings. Source: GAM.

**Firehouse Amber Ale**: OG: 1048-56. Malt: Pale malt, Crystal malt. Hops: Northern Brewer or Goldings. Late hops: Northern Brewer, Cascade or Goldings. Dry hops: Cascade. Source: NACB/BC/GAM.

**Champ Ale**: OG: 1050. Malt: Pale malt, Crystal malt. Hops: Cascade. Source: GAM.

**ESB**: OG: 1054. Malt: Pale malt, Crystal malt. Hops: Cascade. Source: GAM.

**Pullman's Porter**: OG: 1054. Malt: Pale malt, Roast barley, Chocolate malt, Crystal malt, Patent black malt. Hops: Northern Brewer, Cascade. Source: GAM.

**Dead Horse IPA**: OG: 1056. Malt: Pale malt, Crystal malt, Dextrin malt. Hops: Goldings. Source: GAM.

**Oatmeal Stout**: OG: 1058. Malt: Pale malt, Roast barley, Chocolate malt, Munich malt, Patent black malt, Crystal malt, Flaked oats, Dextrin malt. Hops: Fuggles. Source: GAM.

### . McSorley's Brewing, Detroit, MI

**McSorley's Black & Tan**: OG: 1044. Malt: Pale malt, Lager malt, CaraPils malt, Munich malt, Crystal malt, Roast barley. Hops: Northern Brewer. Late hops: Hallertau, Northern Brewer. Source: NACB.

### . Mad River Brewing Company, Blue Lake, CA

**Steelhead Extra Pale Ale**: OG: 1054. Malt: Pale malt. Hops: Tettnang, Cluster, Cascade, Willamette, Chinook. Source: GAM.

**Jamaica Brand Red Ale**: OG: 1065. Malt: Pale malt, Dark crystal malt, Crystal malt. Hops: Cluster, Cascade, Willamette, Chinook. Source: GAM.

**Steelhead Extra Stout**: OG: 1071. Malt: Pale malt, Crystal malt, Dark crystal malt, Chocolate malt, Patent black malt. Hops: Cluster, Cascade, Willamette. Source: GAM.

### . Mad Tree Brewing Company, Cincinnati, OH.
### Www.madtreebrewing.com

**Sol Drifter**: OG: 1040. Malt: 71% Pale malt, 10.5% Red wheat malt, 12% Vienna malt, 3.6% CaraPils malt, 3% Caramel 60L malt. Hops: 3.9% Galena, 13.5% Fuggles. Late hops: Wakatu, 16.6% Zythos, 8.3% Motueka, 8.3% Pilgrim. Dry hops: 20.8% Motueka, 16.6% Wakatu, 0.5% Pilgrim. IBU: 18. Source: Web.

**Flölsch**: OG: 1042. Malt: 80% Pale malt, 10% Red wheat malt, 3.3% Caramel 60L malt, 3.3% Vienna malt, 3.3% Flaked barley. Hops: 15.2% Galena. Late hops: 24.2% Cascade, 60.6% Pacifica. Others: Lime juice, Fresh ginger, Ancho chillies. IBU: 12. Source: Web.

**Misnomer**: OG: 1043. Malt: 56.3% Pale malt, 28.2% Red wheat malt, 12.1% Munich 10L malt, 3.4% CaraPils malt. Hops: 6.7% Galena, 18.1% Fuggles. Late hops: 22.5% Falconer's Flight. Dry hops: 20.7% Falconer's Flight, 32.2% Zythos. IBU: 25. Source: Web.

**Sprye**: OG: 1044. Malt: 71.4% Pale malt, 5.7% Rye malt, 2.4% Flaked barley, 16.3% Munich 10L malt, 4.1% Melanoidin malt. Hops: 10.3% Galena, 9.6% Centennial. Late hops: 17.1% Chinook, 8% Centennial. Dry hops: 54.8% Simcoe. IBU: 38. Source: Web.

**The Pilgrim**: OG: 1044. Malt: 70.2% Pale malt, 16.7% Munich 10L malt, 6.7% Rye malt, 3.7% Melanoidin malt, 2.7% Flaked barley. Hops: 30% Galena. Late hops: 70% Pilgrim. Others: Frozen cranberries, Chopped walnuts, Vanilla. IBU: 15. Source: Web.

**Lift**: OG: 1045. Malt: 82.8% Pale malt, 10.3% Red wheat malt, 3.4% Vienna malt, 3.4% Flaked barley. Hops: 11.5% Galena. Late hops: 59.9% Pacifica, 7.2% Cascade, 21.4% Hallertau Mittelfrüh. IBU: 11. Source: Web.

**Madmann Blackberry Gose**: OG: 1052. Malt: 50% Wheat malt, 37.5% Pilsner malt, 12.5% Acid malt. Hops: 13.5% Perle. Dry hops: 86.5% Sorachi Ace. Others: Sea salt, Blackberry puree, Lactic acid. IBU: 10. Source: Web.

**Wheat Eater**: OG: 1052. Malt: 80% Pilsner malt, 20% Red wheat malt. Hops: 16.4% Galena. Late hops: 63.3% Pacifica, 20.3% Falconer's Flight. IBU: 15-30. Source: Web.

**Happy Amber**: OG: 1054. Malt: 67.7% Pale malt, 5.2% Caramel 80L malt, 10.4% Munich 10L malt, 11.5% Melanoidin malt, 5.2% Victory malt. Hops: 13.1% Galena, 10.6% Chinook, 6.8% Cascade. Late hops: 17.7% Cascade, 12% Chinook. Dry hops: 39% Cascade. IBU: 30. Source: Web.

**Black Forest**: OG: 1055. Malt: 68.4% Pale malt, 8.9% Chocolate malt, 7.9% Caramel 90L malt, 5.3% Victory malt, 2.6% Black malt, 6.9% Lactose. Hops: 28.1% Galena, 33% Styrian Goldings. Late hops: 38.9% Cascade. IBU: 17. Source: Web.

**Flight of Simcoe**: OG: 1056. Malt: 79.3% Pale malt, 16.6% Vienna malt, 2.1% Caramel 40L malt, 2% CaraPils malt. Hops: 22.3% Chinook, 20.8% Centennial. Late hops: 31.4% Centennial, 20.3% Cascade. Dry hops: 2.6% Simcoe, 2.6% Falconer's Flight. IBU: 70. Source: Web.

**Batch One**: OG: 1061. Malt: 70.2% Pale malt, 4.6% Caramel 80L malt, 10.3% Munich 10L malt, 9.5% Melanoidin malt, 5.4% Victory malt. Hops: 25.7% Cascade, 15.2% Chinook. Late hops: 17% Chinook, 22.6% Cascade. Dry hops: 19.4% Cascade. IBU: 25-40. Source: Web.

**PsycHOPathy**: OG: 1061. Malt: 78.6% Pale malt, 2.4% Caramel 40L malt, 16.7% Vienna malt, 2.4% CaraPils malt. Hops: 7.2% Galena, 6% Chinook, 12.9% Centennial. Late hops: 18.8% Centennial, 9.6% Cascade. Dry hops: 25.2% Centennial, 20.4% Chinook. IBU: 71. Source: Web.

**Identity Crisis**: OG: 1062. Malt: 85.1% Pale malt, 1.8% Roast barley, 1.8% Chocolate malt, 2.4% Caramel 60L malt, 2.6% Extra Special malt, 3.7% Carafa® III malt, 2.6% Black malt. Hops: 7.6% Galena, 13.1% Chinook. Late hops: 12.3% Amarillo, 14.3% Simcoe. Dry hops: 26.3% Amarillo, 26.3% Simcoe. IBU: 58. Source: Web.

**Gnarly Brown**: OG: 1065. Malt: 69.8% Pale malt, 2.3% Roast barley, 2.3% Pale chocolate malt, 15.8% Victory malt, 6.8% Extra Special malt, 3.2% Brown malt. Hops: 15.6% Galena, 14.9% Chinook, 34.8% Cascade. Late hops: 34.7% Cascade. IBU: 30. Source: Web.

**Gnarly Brown Coffee**: **Gnarly Brown** with Others: Crushed coffee beans. Source: Web.

**Rubus Cacao**: OG: 1066. Malt: 62.5% Pale malt, 12.9% Vienna malt, 8.6% Chocolate malt, 6.5% Caramel 60L malt, 1.3% Roast barley, 1.7% Black malt, 2.2% CaraPils malt, 4.3% Flaked oats. Hops: 52.9% Galena. Late hops: 47.1% Experimental hop 05256. Others: Cacao nibs, Raspberry puree. IBU: 15. Source: Web.

**Rounding Third**: OG: 1066. Malt: 82.9% Pale malt, 9.2% Munich malt, 4.6% Caramel 60L malt, 2.3% CaraPils malt, 0.9% Chocolate malt. Hops: 3.4% Nugget, 8.1% Simcoe, 9.4% Cascade. Late hops: 18.8% Simcoe, 21.6% Cascade. Dry hops: 38.8% Falconer's Flight. IBU: 51. Source: Web.

**The Great Pumpcan**: OG: 1070. Malt: 73% Pale malt, 9.4% Crystal 60L malt, 7.5% Victory malt, 4.6% Extra Special malt, 2.4% Melanoidin malt, 1.3% CaraPils malt, 1.8% Molasses. Others: Fresh ginger, Crushed nutmeg, Cinnamon stick. Hops: 26.3% Galena. Late hops: 73.7% Fuggles. IBU: 15. Source: Web.

**Everything Went Black**: ABV: 7%. Malt: Pale malt, Carafa® III malt, Caramel 40L malt, Rye malt. Hops: Millennium, Centennial, Nugget. Source: Web.

**Blacktart**: OG: 1074. Malt: 59.9% Pale malt, 12% Victory malt, 8% Extra Special malt, 8% Caramel 120L malt, 4% Wheat malt, 2% Chocolate malt, 2.2% Carafa® III malt, 8% Acid malt, 4% Sucrose, 0.7% Lactose. Hops: 50% Apollo. Late hops: 50% Experimental hop 05256. Others: Blackberry puree, Cinnamon stick, Lactic acid. IBU: 25. Source: Web.

**Thundersnow**: OG: 1074. Malt: 75.7% Pale malt, 7.2% Crystal 90L malt, 5.4% Extra Special malt, 5.4% Victory malt, 2.5% Melanoidin malt, 2% Chocolate rye malt, 1.8% Dark chocolate malt. Hops: 8.8% Chinook, 7.4% Northern Brewer, 23.6% Perle. Late hops: 35.4% Perle, 24.8% Northern Brewer. Others: Vanilla bean, Fresh ginger, Crushed nutmeg, Cinnamon stick. Yeast: White Labs WLP028. IBU: 18. Source: Web.

**Un-Happy Amber**: OG: 1080. Malt: 76.5% Pale malt, 7.3% Crystal 60L malt, 7.3% Victory malt, 3.6% Extra Special malt, 4% Melanoidin malt, 1.3% CaraPils malt. Hops: 20.3% Galena, 21.4% Chinook, 17.1% Cascade. Late hops: 18.4% Chinook, 22.7% Cascade. Dry hops: 7% Cascade, 13% Nugget. IBU: 71. Source: Web.

**Citra High**: OG: 1084. Malt: 72.4% Pale malt, 15.5% Vienna malt, 3.4% Caramel 40L malt, 1.7% CaraPils malt, 6.9% Corn sugar. Hops: 14.1% Simcoe, 5.8% Apollo. Late hops: 12.9% Simcoe, 16.1% Citra. Dry hops: 17% Simcoe, 34% Citra. IBU: 124. Source: Web.

**Dead Flowers**: OG: 1089. Malt: 78.4% Pale malt, 9.8% Victory malt, 1.3% Extra Special malt, 7.2% Melanoidin malt, 3.3% Caramel 40L malt. Others: Chamomile, Elderflowers. Hops: 40% Galena. Late hops: 27.5% Chinook, 17.5% Perle, Dry hops: 15% Perle. IBU: 29. Source: Web.

**Ye Olde Battering Ram**: OG: 1092. Malt: 83% Pale malt, 7.5% Wheat malt, 5.7% Caramel 120L malt, 3.8% CaraPils malt. Hops: Experimental hop 05256. Late hops: Experimental hop 05256. IBU: 117. Source: Web.

**Galaxy High**: OG: 1096. Malt: 71.9% Pale malt, 15.4% Vienna malt, 3.4% Caramel 40L malt, 2.4% CaraPils malt, 6.8% Corn sugar. Hops: 5.7% Galena, 13.1% Topaz. Late hops: 13.2% Topaz, 21.4% Galaxy. Dry hops: 35.2% Galaxy, 17.6% Topaz. IBU: 118. Source: Web.

**Bourbon Barrel Aged Axis Mundi**: ABV: 10.5%. Malt: "A metric shit ton". Hops: Cascade, Perle. IBU: 72. Source: Web.

. *Magic Hat Brewing Company, South Burlington, VT. Www.magichat.net*

**Hocus Pocus**: OG: 1045. Malt: Pale malt, Wheat malt. Hops: Centennial. IBU: 13. SRM: 4.5. Source: Web.

**Participation Ale**: OG: 1045. Malt: Pale malt, Dark Crystal malt, Chocolate malt. Hops: Fuggles. IBU: 28. SRM: 54.0. Source: Web.

**Mother Lager**: OG: 1046. Malt: Pilsner malt. Hops: Northern Brewer, Saaz. IBU: 17. SRM: 3.2. Source: Web.

**#9**: OG: 1047. Malt: Pale malt, Crystal malt. Hops: Cascade, Warrior. IBU: 18. SRM: 9.0. Source: Web. OG: 1051-53. Malt: Pale malt, Wheat malt, Crystal malt. Hops: Tettnang. Late hops: Willamette, Cascade. Others: Apricot flavouring. Source: CB.

**Single Chair Ale**: OG: 1048. Malt: Pilsner malt. Hops: Hallertau, Columbus. IBU: 17. SRM: 3.3. Source: Web.

**Lemon Ginger Hocus Pocus**: OG: 1050. Malt: Pale malt, Wheat malt. Hops: Warrior, Chinook. IBU: 13. SRM: 4.5. Source: Web.

**Heart of Darkness Stout**: OG: 1050. Malt: Pale malt, Crystal malt, Roast barley. Hops: Northern Brewer. Late hops: Northern Brewer. Source: NACB.

**Humble Patience**: OG: 1051. Malt: Pale malt, Crystal malt, Chocolate malt, Caramalt, Roast barley. Hops: Warrior, Cascade. IBU: 29. SRM: 37.4. Source: Web.

**Fat Angel**: OG: 1052. Malt: Pale malt, Crystal malt, Munich malt. Hops: Fuggles, Warrior. IBU: 26. SRM: 9.2. Source: Web.

**Circus Boy**: OG: 1055. Malt: Pale malt, Wheat malt. Hops: Amarillo, Magnum. IBU: 18. SRM: 5.0. Source: Web.

**Blind Faith IPA**: OG: 1055. Malt: Pale malt, Crystal malt, Chocolate malt. Hops: Warrior, Cascade. IBU: 38. SRM: 12.5. Source: Web. OG: 1061-62. Malt: Pale malt, Wheat malt, Crystal malt, Chocolate malt. Hops: Cascade. Late hops: Willamette, Progress, Cascade. Dry hops: Willamette, Cascade. Source: BC.

**Ravell**: OG: 1056. Malt: Pale malt, Crystal malt, Chocolate malt. Hops: Warrior, Fuggles. IBU: 22. SRM: 63.6. Source: Web.

**Feast of Fools**: OG: 1060. Malt: Pale malt, Crystal malt, CaraPils malt, Chocolate malt, Roast barley, Molasses. Hops: Warrior. Others: Raspberries. Source: 150.

**Batch 373**: OG: 1060. Malt: Pale malt, Biscuit malt, Black malt, Munich malt, Chocolate malt, Special B malt. Hops: Styrian Goldings, Amarillo. IBU: 30. SRM: 30.0. Source: Web.

**Roxy Rolles**: OG: 1062. Malt: Pale malt, Crystal malt, Dark Crystal malt. Hops: Brewers Gold, Simcoe. IBU: 40. SRM: 25.0. Source: Web.

**Batch 314**: OG: 1064. Malt: Pale malt, Crystal malt, Caramalt, Munich malt, Roast barley. Hops: Columbus. IBU: 20. SRM: 30.0. Source: Web.

**hI.P.A.**: OG: 1066. Malt: Pale malt. Hops: Warrior. IBU: 45. SRM: 6.8. Source: Web.

**Batch 621**: OG: 1066. Malt: Pale malt, Crystal malt, Victory malt, Munich malt, Vienna malt, Chocolate malt. Hops: Warrior, Centennial, Tettnang. SRM: 24.0. Source: Web.

**Jinx**: OG: 1066. Malt: Pale malt, Crystal malt, Peat-smoked malt, Chocolate malt, Munich malt. Hops: Warrior, Centennial. IBU: 20. SRM: 22.0. Source: Web.

**Batch 375**: OG: 1080. Malt: Pale malt. Hops: Columbus, Brewers Gold. IBU: 75. SRM: 15.0. Source: Web.

### . Main Street Brewing Company, Corona, CA

**Bishop's Tippel Trippel**: OG: 1090. Malt: Pale malt, CaraPils malt, Candi sugar. Hops: Perle, Saaz. Yeast: White Labs WLP500. IBU: 48. Source: BLAM.

### . Maine Beer Company, Freeport, ME. Www.mainebeercompany.com

**Peeper**: OG: 1047. Malt: Pale malt, Red wheat malt, CaraPils malt, Vienna malt. Hops: Cascade, Centennial, Amarillo, Magnum. Source: Web.

**A Tiny Beautiful Something Pale Ale**: OG: 1049. Malt: Pale malt, Caramel 40L malt, CaraPils malt, Flaked oats. Hops: El Dorado, Warrior. Source: Web.

**Mo**: OG: 1051. Malt: Pale malt, CaraPils malt, Red wheat malt, Caramel 40L malt. Hops: Simcoe, Falconer's Flight. Source: Web.

**Another One**: OG: 1059. Malt: Pale malt, Red wheat malt, CaraPils malt. Hops: Simcoe, Warrior, Citra, Cascade. Source: Web.

**Lunch**: OG: 1059. Malt: Pale malt, Red wheat malt, Munich 10L malt, CaraPils malt, Caramel 40L malt. Hops: Simcoe, Centennial, Warrior, Amarillo. Source: Web.

**Zoe**: OG: 1064. Malt: Maris Otter pale malt, Pale malt, Chocolate malt, Munich 10L malt, Caramel 40L malt, Caramel 80L malt, Victory malt. Hops: Simcoe, Centennial, Columbus. Source: Web.

**Mean Old Tom**: OG: 1068. Malt: Pale malt, Wheat malt, Roast barley, Chocolate malt, Caramel 40L malt, Flaked oats. Hops: Magnum, Centennial. Source: Web.

**Dinner**: OG: 1069. Malt: Pale malt, Caramel 40L malt, CaraPils malt, Dextrose. Hops: Citra, Falconer's Flight, Mosaic, Simcoe. Source: Web.

**Red Wheelbarrow**: OG: 1070. Malt: Pale malt, Munich malt, Victory malt, Special B malt, Abbey malt, VC-80. Hops: Columbus, Amarillo, Falconer's Flight. Source: Web.

**Weez**: OG: 1070. Malt: Maris Otter pale malt, Pale malt, Caramel 80L malt, Wheat malt, Roast barley, Chocolate malt, Caramel 80L malt, Munich malt, Flaked wheat. Hops: Simcoe, Warrior, Citra, Cascade. Source: Web.

**King Titus**: OG: 1075. Malt: Pale malt, Chocolate malt, Munich malt, Munich 10L malt, Flaked oats, Caramel 40L malt, Caramel 80L malt, Roast wheat. Hops: Centennial, Columbus. Source: Web.

### . *Market Street Brewing Company & Restaurant, Corning, NY*

**Vanilla Crème Ale**: OG: 1040. Malt: Pale malt, Crystal malt, Wheat malt. Hops: Nugget. Late hops: Mount Hood. Others: Vanilla beans. Source: 150.

### . *Massachusetts Bay Brewing Company, Boston, MA*

**Harpoon Ale**: OG: 1044. Malt: Pale malt, Caramel 40L malt. Hops: Cascade, Cluster. Source: GAM.

**Harpoon IPA**: OG: 1060. Malt: Pale malt, Munich malt, Victory malt. Hops: Centennial. Late hops: Goldings. Dry hops: Liberty. Source: 150. OG: 1061-63. Malt: Pale malt, Crystal malt, Toasted pale malt, Roast barley. Hops: Cluster. Late hops: Fuggles, Cascade. Source: CB. Malt: Pale malt, Caramel 40L malt, Roast barley. Hops: Cluster, Cascade, Fuggles. Source: GAM.

**Harpoon Golden Lager**: Malt: Pale malt. Hops: Cluster. Source: GAM.

**Harpoon Light**: Malt: Pale malt. Hops: Cluster, Cascade. Source: GAM.

**Harpoon Octoberfest**: Malt: Pale malt, Crystal 80L malt. Hops: Cluster. Source: GAM.

**Harpoon Stout**: Malt: Pale malt, Caramel 80L malt, Wheat malt, Patent black malt, Chocolate malt. Hops: Cluster, Fuggles, Goldings. Source: GAM.

**Harpoon Winter Warmer**: Malt: Pale malt, Caramel 80L malt. Hops: Cluster. Source: GAM.

Note: Now Harpoon Brewery.

### . *F.X.Matt Brewing Company, Utica, NY*

**Saranac Black & Tan**: ABW: 3.85%. Malt: Caramel malt, Roast barley, Chocolate malt, Patent black malt, Crystal malt. Hops: Cascade, Goldings, Hallertau. Source: GAM.

**Saranac Golden Pilsner**: ABW: 3.9%. Malt: Wheat malt. Hops: Cascade, Cluster, Tettnang. Source: GAM.

**Saranac Adirondack Amber / Saranac Adirondack Lager / Saranac 1888**: ABW: 4%. Malt: Pale malt, Caramel malt. Hops: Mount Hood, Cluster, Cascade, Hallertau. Source: GAM.

**Saranac Wild Berry Wheat**: ABW: 4.1%. Malt: Caramel malt, Wheat malt. Hops: Saaz, Perle. Source: GAM.

**Saranac Chocolate Amber**: ABW: 4.4%. Malt: Pale malt, Caramel malt, Wheat malt, Chocolate malt, Munich malt. Hops: Northern Brewer, Hersbrücker. Source: GAM.

**Saranac Black Forest Lager**: OG: 1050. Malt: Lager malt, CaraPils malt, Black malt, Munich malt, Roast barley. Hops: Tettnang. Late hops: Perle. Source: NACB.

**Saranac Pale Ale**: OG: 1055. Malt: Pale malt. Hops: Cascade, Goldings. Source: GAM.

**Saranac Mountain Berry Ale**: Malt: Caramel malt, Wheat malt, Chocolate malt. Hops: Cluster, Cascade. Source: GAM.

**Saranac Season's Best**: Malt: Chocolate malt. Hops: Cluster, Cascade. Source: GAM.

Note: See Saranac Brewing.

### . *Mayflower Brewing Company, Plymouth, MA.*
*www.mayflowerbrewing.com*

**Golden Ale**: °P: 10.8. Malt: Pilsner malt, CaraPils® malt. Hops: Galena, Liberty. IBU: 15. Source: Web.

**Pale Ale**: °P: 11.9. Malt: Pale malt, Munich 40L malt, Victory malt. Hops: Nugget, Goldings. IBU: 26. Source: Web.

**Porter**: °P: 14.3. Malt: Pale malt, CaraMunich malt, Chocolate malt, Peat-smoked malt, Brown malt. Hops: Pilgrim, Glacier. IBU: 34. Source: Web.

**IPA**: °P: 16.8. Malt: Pale malt, Munich malt, Munich 40L malt. Hops: Simcoe, Glacier, Nugget, Amarillo. IBU: 77. Source: Web.

**Summer Rye Ale**: Malt: Pilsner malt, Wheat malt, Rye malt. Hops: American. Source: Web.

### . *Mendocino Brewing Company, Ukiah, CA*

**Red Tail Ale**: OG: 1052. Malt: Pale malt, Victory malt, Crystal malt. Hops: Cluster. Late hops: Cascade. Source: 150. Malt: Pale malt, Caramel malt. Hops: Cluster, Cascade. Source: GAM.

**Black Hawk Stout**: ABW: 4.5%. Malt: Pale malt, Caramel malt, Patent black malt. Hops: Cascade, Cluster. Source: GAM.

**Blue Heron Ale**: ABW: 5.25%. Malt: Pale malt. Hops: Cluster, Cascade. Source: GAM.

**Frolic Shipwreck Scottish Ale**: Malt: Caramel malt, Carastan malt. Hops: Goldings, Fuggles. Source: GAM.

**The Eye of the Hawk Strong Ale**: Malt: Pale malt, Caramel malt. Source: GAM.

**Yuletide Porter**: Malt: Pale malt, Caramel malt, Patent black malt. Hops: Cluster, Cascade. Source: GAM.

### . Middlesex Brewing Company, Wilmington, MA

**Raspberry Wheat**: OG: 1042. Malt: Pale malt, Wheat malt. Hops: Cascade. Source: GAM.

**Brown Ale**: OG: 1044. Malt: Pale malt, Chocolate malt, Crystal malt, Munich malt. Hops: Willamette, Chinook, Cascade. Source: GAM.

**Oatmeal Stout**: OG: 1050. Malt: Pale malt, Roast barley, Chocolate malt, Crystal malt, Oats. Hops: Willamette, Chinook, Cascade. Source: GAM.

### . Mill City Brewing Company, Lowell, MA

**Harvest Wheat**: OG: 1043. Malt: Pale malt, Wheat malt. Hops: Perle, Cascade, Mount Hood, Tettnang. Source: GAM.

**Chocolate Raspberry Wheat**: OG: 1046. Malt: Chocolate malt, Patent black malt. Hops: Northern Brewer, Cascade, Willamette. Source: GAM.

**Octoberfest**: ABW: 4.9%. Malt: Pale malt, Munich malt, Vienna malt. Hops: Saaz. Source: GAM.

**Boarding House Ale**: OG: 1050. Malt: Pale malt, Caramel malt. Hops: Willamette, Cascade. Source: GAM.

**Spindle Porter**: OG: 1051. Malt: Pale malt, Caramel malt, Chocolate malt, Patent black malt. Hops: Willamette, Northern Brewer, Cascade, Chinook. Source: GAM.

**IPA**: OG: 1055. Malt: Pale malt, Caramel malt, Victory malt. Hops: Cascade, Willamette. Source: GAM.

**Old Nutcracker**: OG: 1057. Malt: Pale malt, Caramel malt, Victory malt, Patent black malt. Hops: Cascade, Willamette. Source: GAM.

**Oatmeal Stout**: OG: 1064. Malt: Pale malt, Lager malt, Wheat malt, Roast barley, Chocolate malt, Caramel malt, Patent black malt, Oatmeal, Flaked barley, CaraPils malt. Hops: Northern Brewer, Goldings. Source: GAM.

### . Millstream Brewing Company, Amana, IA

**Schild Brau Amber**: OG: 1057. Malt: Lager malt, CaraPils malt, Crystal malt, Roast barley. Hops: Cluster. Late hops: Hallertau. Source: NACB.

### . Minneapolis Town Hall Brewery, Minneapolis, MN

**Hope and King Scotch Ale**: OG: 1063. Malt: Golden Promise pale malt, Flaked barley, Crystal malt, Munich malt, Chocolate malt, Roast barley. Hops: Centennial. Late hops: Goldings. Source: 150.

### Minnesota Brewing Company, St. Paul, MN

**Grain Belt Premium Beer**: OG: 1044. Malt: Lager malt, CaraPils malt, Flaked rice. Hops: Tettnang. Late hops: Perle. Source: NACB.

### Mishawaka Brewing Company, Mishawaka, IN

**Founder's Stout**: OG: 1050. Malt: Pale malt, Patent black malt, Roast barley, Crystal malt, Black malt. Hops: Perle, Willamette, Mount Hood. Source: GAM.

**Four Horsemen Ale**: OG: 1050. Malt: Pale malt, Victory malt, Chocolate malt, Munich malt, Crystal malt. Hops: Perle, Willamette, Mount Hood. Source: GAM.

**Ankenbrock Weizen**: OG: 1050. Malt: Lager malt, Wheat malt. Hops: Saaz, Perle. Source: GAM.

**Lake Effect Pale Ale**: OG: 1052. Malt: Pale malt, CaraPils malt. Hops: Cascade, Willamette, Perle. Source: GAM.

**Indiana Ale**: OG: 1063. Malt: Victory malt, CaraPils malt, Caramel malt, Vienna malt. Hops: Mount Hood, Chinook, Willamette. Source: GAM.

**India Pale Ale**: Malt: Pale malt, Victory malt, CaraPils malt. Hops: Centennial, Cascade, Chinook. Source: GAM.

### Modern Times Beer, San Diego, CA. Www.moderntimesbeer.com

**Fortunate Islands**: ABV: 5%. Malt: 49.4% Pale malt, 44.8% Wheat malt, 3.9% CaraVienne malt, 1.9% Acid malt. Hops: Hop extract. Late hops: Citra, Amarillo. Dry hops: Citra, Amarillo. Yeast: Wyeast #1056. IBU: 30. SRM: 3. Source: Web/BSC.

**Oneida**: ABV: 5.2%. Malt: 91.4% Pale malt, 6.8% CaraPils malt, 1.9% Acid malt. Hops: Hop extract. Late hops: Nelson Sauvin, Cascade. Dry hops: Cascade, Nelson Sauvin. Yeast: White Labs WLP001. IBU: 45. SRM: 4. Source: Web/BSC.

**Lomaland**: ABV: 5-5.5%. Malt: 61.2% Pilsner malt, 19.9% Wheat malt, 7.6% Flaked maize, 16.8% Pale malt, 2.1% Acid malt. Hops: Hop extract. Late hops: Saaz. Yeast: 95% Dupont, Westmalle. IBU: 28-30. SRM: 3. Source: Web/BSC.

**Sleepless City Coffee Brown**: OG: 1054. Malt: 77.8% Pale malt, 7.7% Caramel 15L malt, 7% Caramel 75L malt, 4.7% Flaked oats, 2.7% Chocolate malt. Hops: Palisade. Late hops: Palisade. Others: Kenya Nyera Othaya Peaberry Coffee. Yeast: Wyeast #1056. IBU: 32. SRM: 18. Source: Web/BSC.

**Mount Remarkable**: ABV: 5.5%. Hops: Helga, Ella. IBU: 55. Source: Web.

**Black House**: ABV: 5.8%. Malt: 52.2% Pale malt, 1.7% Roast barley, 8.4% Pale chocolate malt, 11% Crystal 60L malt, 13.9% Flaked oats, 6.4% Biscuit malt, optional Black malt, 3.2% Carafa® Special III malt. Hops: $CO_2$ Extract. Others: 2.4% Ethiopian coffee, 0.8% Sumatran coffee. Yeast: Wyeast #1056. IBU: 30-40. SRM: 35. Source: Web/BSC.

**Roraima**: ABV: 6.5%. Malt: 68% Pale malt, 27.2% Wheat malt, Roast barley, 3.7% CaraWheat® malt, 1.1% Carafa® III malt. Hops: Hop extract. Late hops: Triskel, Motueka, Cascade. Dry hops: Triskel, Motueka, Cascade. Yeast: Brett Brux Trois. IBU: 34. SRM: 12. Source: Web/BSC.

**Aurora**: ABV: 6.7%. Malt: Pale malt, Rye malt, Chocolate rye malt, CaraRed® malt, Crystal rye malt, Melanoidin malt. Hops: Equinox, Centennial, Motueka, Experimental hop 07270. IBU: 75. Source: Web.

**Blazing World**: ABV: 6.8%. Malt: 87.3% Pale malt, 1.5% Wheat malt, 11.2% Munich malt. Hops: Hop extract, Columbus. Mash hops: Simcoe. Late hops: Nelson Sauvin, Mosaic, Simcoe. Dry hops: Nelson Sauvin, Mosaic, Simcoe. Yeast: Wyeast #1056. IBU: 65. SRM: 9. Source: Web/BSC.

**Booming Rollers**: ABV: 6.8%. Malt: 89.8% Pale malt, 6.1% Wheat malt, 4.1% Crystal 10L malt, optional CaraPils malt. Hops: Hop extract. Late hops: Motueka, Centennial, Citra. Dry hops: Centennial, Motueka, Citra. IBU: 79. SRM: 5. Source: Web/BSC.

**Southern Lands**: ABV: 6.8%. Malt: 77.4% Pale malt, 15.5% Wheat malt, 3,1% Acid malt, 3.1% CaraPils malt. Hops: Hop extract. Late hops: Centennial, Calypso. Dry hops: Centennial, Calypso. Yeast: Brett Brux Trois. IBU: 59. SRM: 5. Source: Web/BSC.

**Orderville**: ABV: 6.8%. Hops: Fresh Simcoe, fresh Chinook, fresh Mosaic. IBU: 85. Source: Web.

**Protocosmos**: ABV: 7%. Hops: Ahtanum, Centennial, Galaxy. IBU: 90. Source: Web.

**Neverwhere**: ABV: 7%. Malt: 74.6% Pale malt, 19.6% Wheat malt, 2.9% Acid malt, 2.9% CaraPils malt. Hops: Hop extract. Dry hops: Citra, Centennial, Chinook. Yeast: Brett Brux Trois. IBU: 39. SRM: 4. Source: Web/BSC.

**New Harmony**: ABV: 7.2%. Hops: Huell Melon. Yeast: Trappist. IBU: 30. Source: Web.

**City of the Sun**: ABV: 7.5%. Malt: 13.2% Maris Otter pale malt, 62.4% Pale malt, 20.8% Wheat malt, 2.5% CaraVienne malt, 1% Acid malt. Hops: Hop extract, Bravo. Late hops: Motueka, Simcoe, Mosaic. Dry hops: Motueka, Simcoe, Mosaic. Yeast: White Labs WLP001. IBU: 70. SRM: 5. Source: Web/BSC.

**Lost Horizon**: ABV: 8.5%. Malt: 84.8% Pale malt, 6.1% ESB pale malt, 4.5% Crystal 10L malt, 4.5% Dextrose. Hops: Hop extract. Late hops: Simcoe, Centennial, Chinook, Calypso. Dry hops: Centennial, Simcoe. Yeast: White Labs WLP001. IBU: 78. SRM: 5. Source: Web/BSC.

**Mega Black House**: OG: 1099. Malt: 75.4% Pale malt, 5% Biscuit malt, 3.8% Patent black malt, 3.8% Chocolate malt, 3.8% Oat malt, 2.5% Black malt, 2.5% Roast barley. Hops: Magnum. Others: 3.2% Coffee. Yeast: White Labs WLP001. IBU: 66. SRM: 57. Source: Web/BSC.

### National Brewing Company, Baltimore, MD

**Colt 45 Strong Export Lager**: OG: 1047. Malt: Lager malt, Crystal malt, Flaked maize. Hops: Hallertau. Source: DL.

### New Amsterdam Brewing, Utica, NY

**Amber**: OG: 1031. Malt: Roast barley. Hops: Cascade, Hallertau. Source: GAM.

**Blonde Lager**: OG: 1046. Malt: Pale malt, CaraVienne malt, Wheat malt, Roast barley. Hops: Saaz, Cascade, Tettnang. Source: GAM.

**New York Ale**: OG: 1048. Malt: Pale malt, Caramel malt, Roast barley. Hops: Cascade, Hallertau. Dry hops: Yes. Source: GAM.

**India Dark Ale**: OG: 1049. Malt: Pale malt, Caramel malt, Victory malt, Roast barley, Chocolate malt, Patent black malt. Hops: Northern Brewer, Cluster. Source: GAM.

**Black & Tan**: OG: 1050. Malt: Pale malt, Caramel malt, Wheat malt, Roast barley, Chocolate malt, Patent black malt, Flaked oats. Hops: Cluster, Cascade, Goldings, Fuggles, Hallertau. Source: GAM.

**IPA**: OG: 1060. Malt: Pale malt, Crystal malt, Amber malt, Roast barley. Hops: Centennial. Late hops: Centennial, Cascade. Dry hops: Cascade. Source: NACB.

**Harpoon Spring Maibock**: OG: 1060. Malt: Lager malt, Crystal malt, Munich malt. Hops: Spalt. Late hops: Tettnang. Source: NACB.

### New Belgium Brewing Company, Fort Collins, CO

**Sunshine Wheat Beer**: OG: 1048. Malt: Pale malt, 50% Wheat malt. Others: Coriander, Orange peel. Source: GAM.

**Fat Tire Amber Ale**: OG: 1050. Malt: Pale malt, CaraPils malt, Crystal malt, Biscuit malt, Munich malt, Chocolate malt. Hops: Willamette. Late hops: Fuggles. Source: 150. OG: 1048-50. Malt: Pilsner malt, Crystal malt, Munich malt, Biscuit malt, Victory malt. Hops: Yakima Magnum. Late hops: Hersbrücker, Willamette. Source: BC. Malt: Pale malt, Chocolate malt, Victory malt, Caramel 40L malt. Source: GAM.

**Fat Tire Ale**: OG: 1058. Malt: Belgian pale malt, Special B malt, Munich malt, Crystal malt. Hops: Brewers Gold. Late hops: Saaz. Source: NACB.

**Old Cherry Ale**: OG: 1058. Malt: Pale malt, Caramel 40L malt, Victory malt, Chocolate malt, Colorado Montmorency Cherries. Source: GAM.

**Saison Belgian Style Farmhouse Ale**: OG: 1058. Malt: Pale malt, CaraPils malt, Crystal malt. Hops: Hallertau. Late hops: Strisselspalt. Others: Cardamom, Coriander, Orange peel. Source: 150.

**La Folie**: OG: 1062. Malt: Pale malt, Munich malt, Crystal malt, Wheat. Hops: Cantillion Iris. Source: 150.

**Abbey**: OG: 1063. Malt: Pale malt, CaraPils malt, Munich malt, Caramel 80L malt, Chocolate malt. Hops: Target, Willamette, Liberty. IBU: 24. Source: BLAM. OG: 1064. Malt: Pale malt, Caramel 80L malt, Victory malt, Chocolate malt, Demerara sugar. Source: GAM.

**Trippel**: OG: 1073. Malt: Pale malt, Caramel 40L malt, Victory malt. Hops: Saaz. Source: GAM.

### . *New England Brewing Company, Norwalk, CT*

**Light Lager**: OG: 1034. Malt: Pale malt. Hops: Saaz, Perle, Hersbrücker. Source: GAM.

**Gold Stock Ale**: OG: 1044. Malt: Pale malt, Caramel malt. Hops: Saaz, Perle, Northern Brewer, Cascade, Tettnang, Hersbrücker. Source: GAM.

**Atlantic Amber**: OG: 1048-51. Malt: Pale malt, Crystal malt. Hops: Northern Brewer. Late hops: Cascade, Saaz. Source: CB/GAM.

**American Wheat**: OG: 1050. Malt: Pale malt, Wheat malt. Hops: Northern Brewer, Cascade, Tettnang. Source: GAM.

**Oatmeal Stout**: OG: 1052. Malt: Pale malt, Roast barley. Hops: Northern Brewer, Tettnang. Source: GAM.

**Holiday Ale**: OG: 1054. Malt: Pale malt, Wheat malt, Chocolate malt, Crystal malt, Munich malt. Hops: Perle. Source: GAM.

**New England IPA**: OG: 1063-64. Malt: Pale malt, Crystal malt, Munich malt, Victory malt, Roast barley. Hops: Northern Brewer. Late hops: Willamette, Cascade. Dry hops: Willamette, Cascade. Other: Oak chips. Source: BC.

**Tom Mik's Imperial Stout**: OG: 1108-109. Malt: Maris Otter pale malt, Wheat malt, Crystal malt, Patent black malt, Chocolate malt, Victory malt, Roast barley. Hops: Challenger, Goldings. Late hops: Fuggles. Source: BC.

### . *New Glarus Brewing Company, New Glarus, WI*

**Hearty Hop Ale**: OG: 1060. Malt: Pale malt, Crystal malt. Hops: Cascade, Goldings. Late hops: Cascade. Dry hops: Cascade, Goldings. Source: NACB.

**Wisconsin Belgian Red**: OG: 1065. Malt: Pale malt, Crystal malt, Wheat malt. Hops: Any aged variety. Others: Cherries. Source: NACB.

### . *New Haven Brewing Company, New Haven, CT*

**Mr. Mike's Light Ale**: Malt: Pale malt, Wheat malt. Hops: Hallertau. Source: GAM.

**Elm City**: OG: 1047. Malt: Pale malt, Roast barley, Crystal malt. Hops: Northern Brewer, Willamette, Hallertau. Source: GAM.

**Elm City Connecticut Ale**: OG: 1048-51. Malt: Pale malt, Munich malt, Crystal malt, Roast barley. Hops: Northern Brewer. Late hops: Willamette, Goldings. Source: CB.

**Blackwell Stout**: OG: 1051. Malt: Wheat malt, Flaked barley, Munich malt, Crystal malt, CaraPils malt. Hops: Northern Brewer, Cascade. Source: GAM.

## . North Coast Brewing Company, Fort Bragg, CA

**Schimshaw Pilsner Style Beer**: OG: 1045. Malt: Munich malt. Hops: Hallertau, Tettnang. Source: GAM.

**Blue Star Wheat Beer**: OG: 1046. Malt: Wheat malt, Pale malt, CaraPils malt. Hops: Cascade. Late hops: Cascade. Source: 150/GAM.

**Acme IPA**: OG: 1062. Malt: Pale malt, CaraPils malt, Vienna malt, Munich malt. Hops: Cluster. Late hops: Cluster, Northern Brewer. Source: 150.

**Old No. 38 Stout**: OG: 1056. Malt: Roast barley. Hops: Yakima. Source: GAM.

**Ruedrich's Red Seal Ale**: OG: 1057. Malt: Pale malt. Hops: Yakima. Source: GAM.

**PranQster**: OG: 1070. Malt: American 2-row malt, Wheat malt, Wheat, Munich malt, Invert sugar. Hops: Tettnang, Liberty. IBU: 19. Source: BLAM. OG: 1075. Malt: Belgian pale malt, Crystal malt, CaraVienne malt, Candi sugar. Hops: Willamette. Source: NACB.

**Old Rasputin Imperial Stout**: OG: 1091-2. Malt: Pale malt, Carastan malt, Brown malt, Chocolate malt, Crystal malt, Roast barley. Hops: Cluster. Late hops: Northern Brewer, Centennial. Source: 150. Malt: Pale malt, Chocolate malt, Roast barley, Patent black malt, Crystal malt, Victory malt. Hops: Cluster. Late hops: Centennial, Northern Brewer, Liberty. Dry hops: Liberty. Source: BC.

## . Nor'wester Brewing Company, Portland, OR

**Honey Weizen**: OG: 1042. Malt: Pale malt, Crystal malt, Honey malt, Toasted pale malt, Wheat malt, Clover honey. Hops: Mount Hood. Late hops: Mount Hood. Source: NACB.

**Hefe Weizen**: OG: 1048. Malt: Pale malt, Wheat malt. Hops: Oregon Mount Hood, Tettnang, Hallertau. Source: GAM.

**Peach Creme Ale**: OG: 1048. Malt: Pale malt, Wheat malt, Light roast barley, Red Peach concentrate. Hops: Mount Hood. Source: GAM.

**Raspberry Weizen**: OG: 1048. Malt: Pale malt, Wheat malt, Light roast barley. Hops: Mount Hood. Source: GAM.

**Dunkel Weizen**: OG: 1050. Malt: Wheat malt, Roast barley, Barley. Hops: Mount Hood, Tettnang, Hallertau. Source: GAM.

**Blacksmith Porter**: OG: 1051. Malt: Pale malt, Roast barley. Hops: Oregon Willamette. Source: GAM.

**Best Bitter Ale**: OG: 1054. Malt: Pale malt, Roast barley. Hops: Oregon Willamette, Cascade, British Columbian Goldings. Source: GAM.

**Winter Weizen**: OG: 1064. Malt: Pale malt, Torrefied wheat, Light roast barley. Hops: Goldings, Willamette. Source: GAM.

. *Norwich Inn, Norwich, VT*

**Jasper Murdock's Whistling Pig Red Ale**: OG: 1058-59. Malt: Pale malt, Wheat malt, Crystal malt, Roast barley. Hops: Chinook. Late hops: Fuggles, Goldings. Source: BC.

. *Oasis, Boulder, CO*

**Pale Ale**: OG: 1051. Malt: Pale malt, Caramel malt. Hops: Goldings. Source: GAM.

**Scarab Red**: OG: 1053. Malt: Pale malt, Caramel malt, Toasted pale malt. Hops: Mount Hood. Source: GAM.

**Tut Brown Ale**: OG: 1055. Malt: Pale malt, Caramel malt, Patent black malt. Hops: Cascade. Source: GAM.

**Capstone Extra Special Bitter Ale**: OG: 1056. Malt: Pale malt, Caramel malt, Roast barley. Hops: Nugget, Willamette. Source: GAM.

**Zoser Oatmeal Stout**: OG: 1060. Malt: Pale malt, Caramel malt, Patent black malt, Roast barley, Chocolate malt, Oats. Hops: Centennial. Source: GAM.

. *Odell Brewing Company, Fort Collins, CO*

**East Street Wheat**: OG: 1045. Malt: Pale malt, Wheat malt, Crystal malt, Munich malt. Hops: Cascade. Late hops: Saaz, Tettnang. Source: 150.

**Cutthroat Porter**: OG: 1052. Malt: Pale malt, Caramalt, Crystal malt, Amber / Brown malt, Munich malt, Chocolate malt, Roast barley. Hops: Fuggles. Late hops: Goldings, Northern Brewer. Source: 150.

. *O'Fallon Brewery, O'Fallon, MO*

**Cherry Chocolate Beer**: OG: 1051. Malt: Pale malt, Wheat malt, Crystal malt, Dextrin malt, Chocolate malt. Hops: Northern Brewer. Late hops: Northern Brewer. Others: Chocolate extract, Cherry essence. Source: 150.

. *Old Dominion Brewing Company, Ashburn, VA*

**Dominion Lager**: OG: 1052. Malt: Lager malt, CaraPils malt, Munich malt, Crystal malt. Hops: Perle, Hallertau. Late hops: Tettnang, Hallertau, Saaz. Source: NACB.

**Oak Barrel Stout**: OG: 1056. Malt: Pale malt, Munich malt, Crystal malt, CaraPils malt, Wheat malt, Rauchmalz, Chocolate malt, Roast barley. Hops: Perle. Late hops: Willamette. Source: 150.

. *Old Harbor Brewing Company, Hudson, MA*

**Pilgrim Nut Brown Ale**: OG: 1048. Malt: Pale malt, Crystal malt, Chocolate malt. Hops: Northern Brewer, Cascade. Source: GAM.

**Pilgrim ESB**: OG: 1052. Malt: Pale malt, Crystal malt, Chocolate malt. Hops: Northern Brewer, Nugget, Willamette. Source: GAM.

**Pilgrim Harvest IPA**: OG: 1054. Malt: Pale malt, Special roast malt, Crystal malt. Hops: Northern Brewer, Nugget, Cascade, Willamette. Source: GAM.

**Dog's Breath Bitter**: OG: 1055. Malt: Pale malt, Crystal malt, Chocolate malt. Hops: Cascade, Nugget, Northern Brewer, Tettnang. Source: GAM.

**Pilgrim Stout**: OG: 1060. Malt: Pale malt, Black malt, Flaked barley. Hops: Northern Brewer. Source: GAM.

## . Old Nutfield Brewing Company, Derry, NH

**Black 47 Stout**: OG: 1047. Malt: Pale malt, Roast barley, Crystal malt, Black malt. Hops: Northern Brewer. Late hops: Fuggles. Source: NACB.

## . Olde Heurich Brewing Company, Washington, D.C.

**Heurich's Foggy Bottom Ale**: Malt: Pale malt, Caramel malt. Hops: Cascade, Tettnang, Hallertau. Source: GAM.

**Olde Heurich Marzen Beer**: Malt: Pale malt, Caramel malt. Hops: Saaz, Cascade, Tettnang. Source: GAM.

## . Old World Brewing Company, Staten Island, NY

**New York Style Harbor Amber Ale**: OG: 1052. Malt: Pale malt, Caramel malt, Munich malt. Hops: Chinook, Cascade, Hallertau. Source: GAM.

**New York Style Harbor Dark Ale**: OG: 1056. Malt: Pale malt, Caramel malt, Chocolate malt, Patent black malt. Hops: Willamette, Cascade. Source: GAM.

## . Olde Wyndham Brewery, Willamantic, CT

**Frog 'n' Hound Pub Ale**: OG: 1044. Malt: Pale malt, Crystal malt. Hops: Cascade. Late hops: Willamette. Source: NACB.

## . Oldenberg, Fort Mitchell, KY

**Premium Verum Amber**: OG: 1046. Malt: Pale malt, Dextrin malt, Black malt, Munich malt. Hops: Saaz, Cascade. Source: GAM.

**Holy Grail Nut Brown Ale**: OG: 1050. Malt: Pale malt, Dextrin malt, Victory malt, Chocolate malt, Munich malt, Vienna malt. Hops: Northern Brewer, Willamette, Fuggles. Source: GAM.

## . Brewery Ommegang, Cooperstown, NY

**Hennepin**: OG: 1070. Malt: Pilsner malt, Pale malt, Candi sugar. Hops: Styrian Goldings. Late hops: Saaz. Others: Dried Ginger, Bitter orange peel. Source: 150. OG: 1073-76. Malt: Pilsner malt, Flaked maize, Aromatic malt, Biscuit malt, Candi sugar. Hops: Styrian Goldings. Late hops: Styrian Goldings, Saaz. Source: BC.

**Ommegang Abbey Ale**: OG: 1074. Malt: Pilsner malt, Aromatic malt, Crystal malt, Special roast malt, Corn sugar. Hops: Styrian Goldings. Late hops: Styrian Goldings. Others: Curaçao Orange peel, Liquorice root. Source: 150.

**Ommegang**: OG: 1076. Malt: Pilsner malt, Amber malt, Aromatic malt, Glucose. Hops: Styrian Goldings, Saaz. Others: 5 various Spices. IBU: 20. Source: BLAM. OG: 1082. Malt: Belgian pale malt, Munich malt, Special B malt, Candi sugar. Hops: Hallertau. Late hops: Hallertau. Source: NACB. OG: 1085-87. Malt: Pilsner malt, Aromatic malt, Crystal malt, Chocolate malt, Honey malt, Candi sugar. Hops: Styrian Goldings. Late hops: Saaz. Source: BC.

## . *Oregon Ale & Beer Company, Cincinnati, OH and Portland, OR*

**Oregon Hefeweizen**: OG: 1048. Malt: Caramel 60L malt, Wheat malt. Hops: Northern Brewer, Willamette. Source: GAM.

**Nut Brown Ale**: OG: 1050. Malt: Caramel 60L malt, Roast barley, Victory malt, Special roast malt. Hops: Northern Brewer, Willamette. Source: GAM.

**Raspberry Wheat**: OG: 1051. Malt: Caramel 60L malt, Wheat malt. Hops: Northern Brewer, Willamette. Source: GAM.

**Honey Red Ale**: OG: 1053. Malt: Caramel 60L malt, Munich malt. Hops: Ultra, Mount Hood. Source: GAM.

**Oregon Original India Pale Ale**: OG: 1060. Malt: Pale malt, Crystal malt, Biscuit malt. Hops: Chinook. Late hops: Cascade. Dry hops: Cascade. Source: NACB. OG: 1055. Malt: Caramel 60L malt, Wheat malt. Hops: Saaz, Northern Brewer, Cascade. Source: GAM.

## . *Oregon Trail Brewery, Corvallis, OR*

**White Ale**: OG: 1043. Malt: Pale malt, Wheat malt, Crystal malt. Hops: Perle, Mount Hood. Source: GAM.

## . *Otter Creek, Middlebury, VT*

**Summer Wheat Ale**: OG: 1038. Malt: Pale malt, Wheat malt. Hops: Cascade, Willamette. Source: GAM.

**Helles Alt Beer**: OG: 1043. Malt: Pale malt, Munich malt, CaraPils malt. Hops: Chinook, Tettnang, Hallertau. Source: GAM.

**Pale Ale**: OG: 1048. Malt: Pale malt, Caramel malt, Red wheat malt. Hops: Cascade. Dry hops: Cascade. IBU: 23. Source: 150.

**Hickory Switch Smoked Amber Ale**: OG: 1050. Malt: Pale malt, Caramel 60L malt, Chocolate malt, Munich malt, CaraPils malt. Hops: Chinook, Cascade, Willamette, Tettnang, Hallertau. Source: GAM.

**Stovepipe Porter**: OG: 1055. Malt: Pale malt, Chocolate malt, Black malt, Munich malt, Crystal malt. Hops: Nugget. Late hops: Galena, Willamette. IBU: 30. Source: NACB. OG:

1058-59. Malt: Pale malt, CaraMunich malt, Crystal malt, Chocolate malt, Roast barley. Hops: Chinook. Late hops: Cascade, Willamette. Source: BC. OG: 1054. Malt: Pale malt, Caramel 60L malt, Roast barley, Chocolate malt, CaraPils malt. Hops: Chinook, Cascade, Willamette. Source: GAM.

**Copper Ale**: OG: 1055-58. Malt: Pale malt, Dextrin malt, Crystal malt, Munich malt, Chocolate malt, Roast barley. Hops: Chinook. Late hops: Hersbrücker, Tettnang. Dry hops: Tettnang. Source: CB. OG: 1050. Malt: Pale malt, Caramel 20L malt, Caramel 40L malt, Munich malt, Roast barley, CaraPils malt. Hops: Chinook, Tettnang, Hallertau. Source: GAM.

**Mud Bock Spring Ale**: OG: 1058. Malt: Pale malt, Crystal malt, Dextrin malt, Munich malt, Chocolate malt, Wheat malt. Hops: Cascade. Source: 150. OG: 1059. Malt: Pale malt, Caramel 20L malt, Wheat malt, Chocolate malt, Caramel 40L malt, Munich malt, CaraPils malt. Hops: Cascade. Source: GAM.

### . *Otto Brothers Brewing Company, Jackson Hole, WY and Victor, ID*

**Teton Ale**: OG: 1048. Malt: Caramel malt, Roast barley, Munich malt. Source: GAM.

**Moose Juice Stout**: OG: 1055. Malt: Pale malt, Crystal malt, Black malt, Roast barley. Hops: Chinook. Late hops: Chinook, Cascade. Source: NACB. Malt: Caramel malt, Roast barley, Chocolate malt, Munich malt. Hops: Chinook, Cascade. Source: GAM.

**Old Faithful Ale**: Hops: Cascade, Willamette. Source: GAM.

Note: Became Grand Teton Brewing Company in 2000.

### . *Ould Newbury Brewing Company, Newburyport, MA*

**Plum Island Extra Pale**: OG: 1038. Malt: Pale malt, Carastan malt, Wheat malt. Hops: Nugget, Tettnang. Source: GAM.

**Yankee Ale**: OG: 1042. Malt: Pale malt, Carastan malt, Chocolate malt, Munich malt, Crystal 60L malt. Hops: Cascade, Willamette, Nugget, Tettnang. Source: GAM.

**Great Glen Scottish Ale**: OG: 1044. Malt: Pale malt, Wheat malt, Roast barley, Crystal 120L malt. Hops: Willamette, Nugget. Source: GAM.

**Porter**: OG: 1047. Malt: Pale malt, Roast barley, Chocolate malt, Patent black malt, Crystal 60L malt. Hops: Perle, Cascade, Nugget. Source: GAM.

**Rye Ale**: OG: 1050. Malt: Pale malt, Flaked rye, Chocolate malt, Crystal 60L malt. Hops: Perle, Nugget. Source: GAM.

**Haystack India Pale**: OG: 1055. Malt: Pale malt, Crystal 60L malt. Hops: Cascade, Nugget. Source: GAM.

**Spiced Ale**: OG: 1060. Malt: Pale malt, Crystal 60L malt, Glucose. Hops: Cascade, Mount Hood, Nugget. Others: Cinnamon, Nutmeg, Ginger, Cloves, Coriander. Source: GAM.

## Pacific Coast Brewing Company, Oakland, CA.
Www.pacificcoastbrewing.com

**Orca Porter**: OG: 1048. Malt: Chocolate malt. IBU: 50. Source: Web.

**Killer Whale Stout**: OG: 1050. Malt: Light malt extract, Crystal 120L malt, Black malt, Chocolate malt, Roast barley. Hops: Nugget, Chinook. Late hops: Willamette. IBU: 50. Source: SMB/Web.

**Gray Whale Ale**: OG: 1054. Malt: Light malt extract, Crystal 20L malt. Hops: Nugget, Chinook. Late hops: Willamette, Perle. IBU: 30. Source: SMB/Web.

**Columbus I.P.A.**: OG: 1060. Malt: Light malt extract, Crystal 120L malt. Hops: Columbus. IBU: 80. Source: SMB/Web.

**Emerald Ale**: OG: 1060. Hops: Centennial. IBU: 30. Source: Web.

**Blue Whale Ale**: OG: 1070. Malt: Pale malt, Crystal malt. Hops: Nugget, Chinook. Late hops: Willamette, Centennial, Perle, Chinook. Dry hops: Centennial. Other: Oak chips. Source: 150. Malt: Light malt extract, Crystal 40L malt, Crystal 120L malt. Hops: Nugget, Chinook. Late hops: Willamette, Perle, Centennial. Dry hops: Yes. Others: Oak chips. IBU: 70. Source: SMB/Web.

**Cade Blue Barleywine**: ABV: 10%. Notes: Similar to **Blue Whale Ale** but stronger and Dry hops: No. Source: Web.

**Leviathan Imperial Stout**: OG: 1100. Malt: Light malt extract, Crystal 120L malt, Black malt, Chocolate malt, Roast barley, Honey. Hops: Nugget, Chinook. Late hops: Chinook. IBU: 50. Source: SMB/Web.

## Paper City Brewing, Holyoke, MA

**Winter Palace Wee Heavy**: OG: 1075. Malt: Pale malt, Roast barley. Hops: Cascade. Source: 150.

**Winter Solstice Ale**: OG: 1078. Malt: Maris Otter pale malt, Crystal malt, Candi sugar. Hops: Magnum. Late hops: Saaz. Source: NACB.

## Pavichevich, Elmhurst, IL

**Baderbräu Pilsener Beer**: ABW: 3.7%. Malt: Pale malt, Lager malt, Caramel malt. Hops: 95% Saaz. Source: GAM.

**Baderbräu Bock Beer**: ABW: 4.6%. Malt: Pale malt, Lager malt, Chocolate malt, Caramel malt. Hops: 95% Saaz. Source: GAM.

## Penn Brewing, Pittsburgh, PA

**Helles Gold**: OG: 1046. Malt: Pale malt, Special roast barley. Hops: Hallertau. Source: GAM.

**Penn Pilsner**: OG: 1050. Malt: Pale malt, Special roast barley. Hops: Hallertau. Source: GAM.

**Penn Dark**: OG: 1051. Malt: Pale malt, Special roast barley. Hops: Hallertau. Source: GAM.

**Oktoberfest**: ABV: 5.6%. Malt: Pale malt, Caramalt. Hops: Hallertau. Source: HB.

**St. Nikolaus Bock**: ABV: 8.4%. Malt: Pale malt, Munich malt, Caramalt, Dark malt. Hops: Hallertau. Source: HB.

## . *Pete's Brewing Company, Palo Alto, CA*

**Pete's Signature Pilsner**: OG: 1048. Malt: Lager malt, CaraPils malt, Munich malt. Hops: Saaz. Late hops: Saaz, Hallertau. Source: NACB.

**Pete's Wicked Bohemian Pilsner**: OG: 1048. Malt: Pale malt, Caramel malt. Hops: Tettnang, Saaz, Cluster. Source: GAM.

**Pete's Wicked Summer Brew**: OG: 1048. Malt: Pale malt, Wheat malt. Hops: Tettnang. Source: GAM.

**Pete's Wicked Strawberry Blonde**: OG: 1050. Malt: Pale malt, Wheat malt. Hops: Tettnang, Cluster. Others: Strawberry flavouring. Source: GAM.

**Pete's Wicked Amber Ale**: OG: 1050. Malt: Pale malt, Caramel malt, Munich malt. Hops: Tettnang, Cluster, Cascade. Source: GAM.

**Pete's Wicked Honey Wheat**: OG: 1051. Malt: Pale malt, Caramel malt, Wheat malt, Clover honey. Hops: Cascade, Tettnang. Source: GAM.

**Pete's Wicked Ale**: OG: 1052-54. Malt: Pale malt, Crystal malt, Chocolate malt. Hops: Brewers Gold. Late hops: Goldings. Dry hops: Cascade. Source: CB. OG: 1055. Malt: Pale malt, Caramel malt, Roast chocolate malt. Hops: Cascade, Brewers Gold. Source: GAM.

**Pete's Wicked Winter Brew**: OG: 1052. Malt: Pale malt, Caramel malt. Hops: Cascade, Liberty, Tettnang. Others: Raspberries, Nutmeg. Source: GAM.

**Pete's Wicked Maple Porter**: OG: 1055. Malt: Pale malt, Caramel malt, Chocolate malt. Hops: Tettnang, Mount Hood, Cluster. Source: GAM.

**Pete's Wicked Multi Grain**: OG: 1055. Malt: Caramel malt, Wheat malt, Rye malt, Oats. Source: GAM.

**Pete's Wicked Pale Ale**: OG: 1055. Malt: Pale malt, Wheat malt. Hops: Cascade, Cluster, Saaz. Source: GAM.

## . *Pike Brewery, Seattle, WA. Www.pikebrewing.com*

**Porter**: OG: 1045. Malt: Pale malt, CaraPils malt, Crystal malt, Chocolate malt, Biscuit malt, Munich malt, Special B malt, Patent black malt. Hops: Cluster, Goldings. Source: GAM.

**Weisse**: OG: 1046. Malt: Pale malt, Wheat malt, Munich malt. Hops: Perle, Saaz. IBU: 24. Source: Web.

**Naughty Nellie**: OG: 1048. Malt: Organic pale malt, Carastan malt, Aromatic malt, Munich malt. Hops: Centennial, Cascade, Select. IBU: 24. Source: Web.

**Auld Acquaintance**: OG: 1052. Malt: Pale malt, Crystal malt. Hops: Cluster, Goldings. Source: GAM. Malt: Pale malt, Wheat malt, Crystal malt, Munich malt. Hops: Magnum, Willamette, Goldings. IBU: 32. Source: Web.

**Bride Ale**: OG: 1052. Malt: Pale malt, Wheat malt, Munich malt, Crystal malt. Hops: Magnum, Goldings, Willamette. IBU: 32. Source: Web.

**Pale Ale**: OG: 1053-54. Malt: Pale malt, Munich malt, Crystal malt, CaraMunich malt. Hops: Magnum. Late hops: Goldings, Willamette. Source: BC. OG: 1052. Malt: Pale malt, Crystal malt. Hops: Goldings. Source: GAM. Malt: Pale malt, Wheat malt, Munich malt, Crystal malt. Hops: Magnum, Goldings, Willamette. IBU: 32. Source: Web.

**FSB**: OG: 1058. Malt: Maris Otter pale malt, Vienna malt, Flaked oats, Crystal malt. Hops: Magnum, Northern Brewer, Nugget, Willamette. IBU: 58. Source: Web.

**India Pale Ale**: OG: 1062. Malt: Pale malt, Amber malt, CaraPils malt, Munich malt, Crystal malt. Hops: Magnum. Late hops: Chinook, Goldings. Dry hops: Goldings. Source: NACB. Malt: Pale malt, Crystal malt, Munich malt. Hops: Columbus, Willamette, Goldings, Chinook. IBU: 60. Source: Web. OG: 1064. Malt: Pale malt, Munich malt, Crystal malt, CaraPils malt. Hops: Chinook, Goldings. Source: GAM.

**Kilt-Lifter Scotch-Style Ale**: OG: 1067-68. Malt: Pale malt, Wheat malt, Munich malt, Crystal malt, CaraMunich malt, Peat-smoked malt. Hops: Yakima Magnum. Late hops: Willamette, Goldings. Source: BC. OG: 1064. Malt: Pale malt, Munich malt, Peat-smoked malt, Crystal malt. Hops: Magnum, Goldings. IBU: 27. Source: Web.

**Tandem**: OG: 1070. Malt: Pale malt, Crystal wheat malt, Roast malt. Hops: Northern Brewer, Mount Hood. IBU: 25. Source: Web.

**Pike Street Stout**: OG: 1072. Malt: Maris Otter pale malt, Roast barley, Crystal malt. Hops: Chinook, Goldings. Source: GAM.

**XXXXX Stout**: OG: 1073. Malt: Pale malt, Roast malt, Crystal malt. Hops: Chinook, Willamette, Goldings. IBU: 65. Source: Web.

**Monk's Uncle**: OG: 1075. Malt: Pale malt, Pilsner malt, Wheat malt, Aromatic malt. Hops: Saaz, Nugget. IBU: 38. Source: Web.

**Old Bawdy 1998**: OG: 1095. Malt: Maris Otter pale malt, Crystal malt, Peat-smoked malt. Hops: Magnum. Late hops: Chinook, Cascade. Source: NACB. OG: 1101-105. Malt: Pale malt, Munich malt, Crystal malt, Chocolate malt, Peat-smoked malt. Hops: Yakima Magnum. Late hops: Hersbrücker, Mount Hood, Saaz. Source: BC. OG: 1096. Malt: Pale malt, Peat-smoked malt, Roast barley, Crystal malt. Source: GAM. Malt: Pale malt, Crystal malt, Peat-smoked malt, Munich malt, Black malt. Hops: Chinook. Late hops: Centennial, Goldings. Source: SMB. Malt: Pale malt, Crystal malt, Peat-smoked malt, Wheat malt. Hops: Chinook, Centennial, Magnum, Columbus. IBU: 90. Source: Web.

## Pinehurst Village Brewing, Aberdeen, NC

**Double Eagle Scotch Ale**: OG: 1072. Malt: Pale malt, Amber malt, CaraPils malt, Black malt, Flaked oats, Torrefied wheat, Roast barley. Hops: Nugget. Late hops: Willamette, Styrian Goldings. Source: NACB.

## Pizza Port Brewing Company, Solana Beach, CA

**Mo' Betta Bretta**: OG: 1060. Malt: Pale malt, CaraPils malt, Munich malt, Flaked oats. Hops: Magnum. Source: 150.

## Portland Brewing Company, Portland, OR

**Haystack Black Ale**: OG: 1050. Malt: Pale malt, Crystal malt, Black malt, Chocolate malt. Hops: Galena. Late hops: Fuggles, Cascade. Dry hops: Cascade. Source: NACB.

**MacTarnahan's Amber Ale**: OG: 1055-55. Malt: Pale malt, Peat-smoked malt, Crystal malt, Roast barley. Hops: Cascade, Northern Brewer. Late hops: Northern Brewer, Cascade. Source: BC.

**Haystack Black Porter**: OG: 1055-56. Malt: Pale malt, Crystal malt, Chocolate malt, Patent black malt. Hops: Nugget. Late hops: Willamette, Goldings. Source: BC.

**Woodstock IPA**: OG: 1066-67. Malt: Pale malt, Crystal malt. Hops: Challenger. Late hops: Goldings, Challenger. Dry hops: Challenger, Goldings. Others: Oak chips. Source: BC.

## Portsmouth Brewery, Portsmouth, NH

**Navish's Oatmeal Stout**: OG: 1065. Malt: Pale malt, Caramel malt, Black malt, Chocolate malt, Roast barley, Oats. Hops: Chinook. Source: 150.

## Potomac River Brewing Company, Chantilly, VA

**Rapahannock Red Ale**: OG: 1048. Malt: Pale malt, Crystal malt, Black malt, Wheat malt. Hops: Chinook. Late hops: Cascade. Source: NACB.

## Pyramid Breweries, Berkeley, CA, Seattle and Kalama, WA.
*Www.pyramidbrew.com*

**Curve Ball Kölsch**: ABV: 4.9%. Malt: 2-row malt, 60% Wheat malt. Hops: Vanguard, Perle. Source: Web.

**Apricot Weizen**: ABV: 5.1%. Malt: 2-row malt, 60% Wheat malt, Caramel malt. Hops: Nugget. Others: Apricots. Source: Web.

**Apricot Ale**: ABV: 5.1%. Malt: 50% Pale malt, 50% Wheat malt. Hops: Nugget/Summit. Others: Apricots. Source: Web.

**Amber Weizen**: ABV: 5.1%. Malt: 2-row malt, 60% Wheat malt, Caramel malt. Hops: Nugget. Source: Web.

**Hefe Weizen**: ABV: 5.2%. Malt: 39% 2-row malt, 60% Wheat malt, 1% Caramel malt. Hops: Nugget, Liberty, Willamette/Mount Hood. Source: Web.

**Crystal Wheat Ale**: ABV: 5.3%. Malt: 61% Pale malt, 29% Wheat malt. Hops: Spalt, Mount Hood, Tettnang. Source: Web.

**Pyramid Traditional ESB**: OG: 1055. Malt: Pale malt, Toasted pale malt, Crystal malt, Torrefied wheat. Hops: Goldings. Late hops: Goldings. Dry hops: Goldings. Source: NACB.

**Broken Rake**: ABV: 6.1%. Malt: Pale malt, Caramel 40L malt, Caramel 80L malt, CaraPils malt. Hops: Cascade. Source: Web.

**ThunderHead/India Pale Ale**: ABV: 6.7%. Malt: 2-row malt, Munich 10L malt, Caramel malt, CaraPils malt. Hops: Nugget/Summit/ Columbus. IBU: 67. Source: Web.

**Snow Cap Ale**: ABV: 7%. Malt: Pale malt, Chocolate malt, Caramel 80L malt. Hops: Willamette, optional Nugget. Late hops: Willamette, Goldings. Source: 150/Web.

## . *Ram Big Horn Brewing Company, Lake Oswego, OR*

**Total Disorder Porter**: OG: 1055. Malt: Pale malt, Crystal malt, Chocolate malt, Wheat malt. Hops: Cascade. Late hops: Willamette, Cascade. Source: 150.

## . *Ranger Creek, San Antonio, TX. Www.drinkrangercreek.com*

**Mission Trail Ale**: OG: 1048-52. Malt: 88% Pilsner malt, 12% Munich malt. Hops: Hallertau. Lare hops: Hallertau. Yeast: European ale. IBU: 20. SRM: 4. Source: Web.

**OPA**: OG: 1054-7. Malt: 77% Pale malt, 7% Crystal 60L malt, 16% Oat malt. Hops: Centennial. Late hops: Centennial, Citra. Dry hops: Centennial, Citra. Yeast: English ale. IBU: 35. SRM: 9. Source: Web.

**UNO**: OG: 1054-7. Malt: 65.5% Pale malt, 6.5% Crystal 60L malt, 10% Oat malt, 18% Rye malt. Hops: Centennial. Late hops: Centennial, Citra. Dry hops: Centennial, Citra. Yeast: English ale. Notes: Oak aged. IBU: 35. SRM: 11. Source: Web.

**Saison Oscura**: OG: 1955-60. Malt: 85.5% Pilsner malt, 6.5% Wheat malt, 4% Chocolate malt, 4% Light sugar. Hops: Goldings. Late hops: Fuggles, Goldings. Yeast: Saison/Farmhouse. IBU: 25. SRM: 20. Source: Web.

**Mesquite Smoked Porter**: OG: 1060-4. Malt: 54% Maris Otter pale malt, 3.5% Chocolate malt, 29% Mesquite-smoked Maris Otter pale malt, 11% Crystal 60L malt, 2.5% Black malt. Hops: Fuggles. Late hops: Fuggles, Tettnang. Yeast: English ale. IBU: 60. SRM: 40+. Source: Web.

**La Bestia Aimable**: OG: 1078-80. Malt: 79% Pilsner malt, 8% CaraMunich, 8% Dark sugar, 3.5% Light sugar, 1.5% Local honey. Hops: Tettnang. Late hops: Tettnang. Yeast: Belgian ale. IBU: 21. SRM: 15-20. Source: Web.

## Red Hook Brewery, Woodinville, WA and Portsmouth, NH.
*Www.redhook.com*

**Sunrye**: OG: 1039. Malt: Pale malt, Speciality malts. Hops: Mount Hood, Hersbrücker. IBU: 16. SRM: 4.6. Source: Web.

**Wheat Hook Ale**: OG: 1046. Malt: Pale malt, Wheat malt, Munich malt. Hops: Mount Hood, Willamette, Yakima Hersbrücker. Source: GAM.

**Blonde Ale**: OG: 1050. Malt: Pale malt, Wheat malt, Caramel malts. Hops: Saaz. IBU: 18.3. SRM: 8.1. Source: Web.

**Blackhook Porter**: OG: 1050. Malt: Pale malt, Caramel malt, Black malt, Roast barley. Hops: Willamette, Northern Brewer, Cascade. IBU: 40. SRM: 51.0. Source: Web. OG: 1056. Malt: Pale malt, Crystal malt, Patent black malt. Hops: Eroica. Late hops: Tettnang. Source: NACB. OG: 1049. Malt: Pale malt, Caramel 40L malt, Patent black malt, Roast barley. Hops: Willamette, Eroica, Cascade. Source: GAM. OG: 1052: Malt: Pale malt, Roast barley, Chocolate malt, Munich malt, Flaked barley, Crystal malt, Patent black malt. Hops: Goldings, Hersbrücker. Late hops: Cascade. Source: Jeff Benjamin, HF.

**Red Hook Rye**: OG: 1052. Malt: Pale malt, Munich malt, Flaked rye. Hops: Mount Hood, Yakima Hersbrücker. Source: GAM.

**CopperHook**: OG: 1053. Malt: Caramel malt, CaraPils malt. Hops: Willamette, Saaz. IBU: 20. SRM: 11. Source: Web.

**ESB**: OG: 1054. Malt: Pale malt, CaraMunich malt, CaraPils malt. Hops: Willamette. Late hops: Tettnang, Willamette. Source: 150. Malt: Pale malt, Caramel malt. Hops: Tettnang, Willamette. IBU: 28. SRM: 13.2. Source: GAM/Web. OG: 1054-57. Malt: Pale malt, Crystal malt. Hops: Tettnang. Late hops: Willamette, Tettnang. Source: CB. OG: 1050. Malt: Crystal malt, Maltodextrin. Hops: Willamette. Late hops: Tettnang. Yeast: Wyeast #1098. Source: Michael G. Lloyd, MHF.

**WinterHook**: OG: 1056. Malt: Pale malt, Carastan malt, CaraVienne malt, CaraPils malt. Hops: Willamette. Late hops: Tettnang, Willamette. Source: 150. OG: 1057. Malt: Munich malt, Caramel malt. Hops: Northern Brewer, Cascade. IBU: 29. SRM: 21.7. Source: Web.

**Long Hammer IPA**: OG: 1058. Malt: Pale malt, Munich malt, Crystal malt. Hops: Willamette, Northern Brewer, Cascade. IBU: 38.5. SRM: 8.4. Source: Web.

**Ya Sure Ya Betcha Ballard Bitter**: OG: 1059. Malt: Pale malt, Caramel 40L malt, Munich malt. Hops: Northern Brewer, Willamette, Cascade. Source: GAM.

**Late Harvest Autumn Ale**: OG: 1060. Malt: Smoked Munich malt, Crystal malt, Caramel malt, Roast malt. Hops: Northern Brewer, Saaz. IBU: 32. SRM: 21.0. Source: Web.

**Double Black Stout**: OG: 1069. Malt: Pale malt, Crystal malt, Wheat malt, Patent black malt, Chocolate malt, Roast barley, Espresso Coffee. Hops: Northern Brewer. Late hops: Cascade. Source: 150. OG: 1073. Malt: Pale malt, Wheat malt, Roast barley, Munich malt, Patent black malt, Starbucks Coffee. Hops: Chinook, Northern Brewer. Source: GAM.

. *Rochester Mills Beer Company, Rochester, MI. Www.beercos.com*

**Milkshake Stout**: ABV: 5%. Others: Lactose. Source: Web.

**Paint Creek Porter**: ABV: 5.6%. Malt: Chocolate malt. Source: Web.

**Wits Organic**: ABV: 6.1%. Others: Coriander, Sweet orange peel. Source: Web.

**Pleszures Pale Ale**: ABV: 6.1%. Hops: Amarillo. Source: Web.

**Belgian Dubbel**: ABV: 9.5%. Malt: Candi sugar. Source: Web.

. *Rock Creek Brewing Company, Richmond, VA*

**River City IPA**: OG: 1050. Malt: Pale malt, Crystal malt, Toasted pale malt, Black malt, Wheat malt. Hops: Fuggles. Late hops: Fuggles, Goldings. Source: NACB.

**Devil's Elbow IPA**: OG: 1070. Malt: Pale malt, Crystal malt, Biscuit malt, Wheat malt. Hops: Fuggles. Late hops: Goldings. Dry hops: Goldings. Source: NACB.

. *Rockies Brewing Company, Boulder, CO*

**Boulder Stout**: OG: 1050. Malt: Pale malt, Crystal malt, Munich malt, Roast barley. Hops: Northern Brewer. Source: NACB. OG: 1066. Malt: Pale malt, Crystal malt, Patent black malt, Chocolate malt. Hops: Nugget, Willamette, Hallertau. Source: GAM.

**Buffalo Gold Premium Ale**: OG: 1051. Malt: Pale malt, Crystal malt. Hops: Nugget, Willamette, Cascade. Source: GAM.

**Boulder Amber Ale**: OG: 1054. Malt: Pale malt, Caramel 40L malt. Hops: Chinook, Willamette, Cascade. Source: GAM.

**Boulder Extra Pale Ale**: OG: 1054. Malt: Pale malt, Caramel 40L malt. Hops: Chinook, Cascade, Hallertau. Source: GAM.

**Boulder Fall Fest Ale**: OG: 1054. Malt: Pale malt, Crystal 50-60L malt, Patent black malt, Roast barley. Hops: Mount Hood, Willamette. Source: GAM.

**Boulder Porter**: OG: 1056. Malt: Pale malt, Crystal malt, Patent black malt. Hops: Chinook, Hallertau. Source: GAM.

**Wrigley Red**: OG: 1056. Malt: Pale malt, Crystal 20-80L malt, Roast barley. Hops: Nugget, Willamette, Cascade. Source: GAM.

. *Rocky River Brewing Company, Rocky River, OH*

**Chocolate Jitters**: OG: 1071. Malt: Pale malt, Munich malt, Aromatic malt, Carafa® III malt, Chocolate malt, Lactose, Belgian Chocolate, Jamaican Blue Mountain Coffee. Hops: Tettnang. Late hops: Liberty. Others: Vanilla. Source: 150.

## Rockyard Brewing Company, Castle Rock, CO. Www.rockyard.com

**Redhawk Ale**: ABV: 5%. Malt: Pale malt, Caramel malt. Hops: Goldings. Source: Web.

**Double Eagle Ale**: OG: 1052. Malt: Pale malt, Munich malt, Wheat malt. Hops: Perle. Late hops: Hallertau. Source: 150. Malt: Pale malt, Wheat malt. Hops: Hallertau. Source: Web.

**Hopyard IPA**: ABV: 5.3%. Malt: Pale malt, Vienna malt, Munich malt, CaraAmber® malt. Hops: Amarillo. Source: Web.

## Rogue Ales, Newport, OR. Www.rogue.com

**Chipotle Ale**: °P: 12. Malt: Pale malt, Munich malt. Hops: Cascade, Willamette. Others: Chipotle chillies. IBU: 35. °L: 23. Source: Web.

**Honey Cream Ale**: °P: 12. Malt: Pale malt, Munich malt, Honey. Hops: Crystal. IBU: 30. °L: 10. Source: Web.

**Kells Irish Lager**: °P: 11.5-12. Malt: Pale malt, CaraPils malt or Pale malt, Crystal malt, Wheat malt, Acid malt. Hops: Sterling. IBU: 25-28. °L: 9.8. Source: Web.

**Morimoto Black Obi Soba**: °P: 12. Malt: Pale malt, Roast buckwheat/soba, Munich malt, Crystal malts or Pale malt, Roast buckwheat/soba, Munich malt, Caramel 15L malt, Caramel 60L malt, Carafa® Special II malt. Hops: Horizon, Sterling, Cascade. IBU: 30. °L: 36. Source: Web.

**Morimoto Soba**: °P: 12. Malt: Roast buckwheat/soba, Pale malt, Munich malt, Caramel 15L malt or Roast buckwheat/soba, Pale malt, Munich malt, Crystal malt, Carastan malt. Hops: Crystal. IBU: 30. °L: 14. Source: Web.

**Younger's Special Bitter / YSB**: °P: 12. Malt: Pale malt, Crystal 50-60L malt. Hops: Willamette, Goldings. IBU: 35. °L: 17. Source: GAM/Web.

**Hazelnut Brown Nectar**: °P: 12. Malt: Pale malt, Munich malt, Crystal malts, Brown malt, Carastan malt, Chocolate malt. Hops: Perle, Sterling. Others: Hazelnut extract. IBU: 28. °L: 9.8. Source: Web. °P: 14. Malt: Pale malt, Munich malt, Crystal malt, Brown malt, Carastan malt, Pale chocolate malt. Others: Hazelnut extract. Hops: Saaz, Perle. IBU: 33. °L: 36. Source: 150/Web.

**Rogue-N-Berry**: OG: 1048. Malt: Carastan malt, Chocolate malt. Hops: Saaz. Others: Marionberries. Source: GAM.

**Mocha Porter**: OG: 1050. Malt: Pale malt, Crystal malt, Munich malt, Chocolate malt. Hops: Perle. Late hops: Centennial. Source: NACB/GAM. °P: 13. Malt: Pale malt, Crystal malt, Chocolate malt, Black malt, Munich malt, Carastan malt. Hops: Perle, Centennial. IBU: 54. °L: 77. Source: Web.

**Bullfrog Ale**: °P: 12.5. Malt: Pale malt, Wheat malt. Hops: Mount Hood, Saaz, Horizon. IBU: 16. °L: 5. Source: Web.

**Honey Orange Wheat**: °P: 13. Malt: Pale malt, Wheat malt, #48 Oregon Wildflower honey, Orange juice. Hops: Willamette. IBU: 10. °L: 3.5. Source: Web.

**American Amber Ale**: °P: 13. Malt: Pale malt, Crystal 95-115L malt, Crystal 135-165L malt. Hops: Goldings, Cascade. IBU: 53. °L: 33. Source: Web.

**Chamomellow**: °P: 13. Malt: Pale malt, 18% Munich malt. Hops: Cascade, Goldings. Others: Chamomile. IBU: 34. °L: 3.2. Source: Web.

**Half-E-Weizen/Mom Hefeweizen**: °P: 13. Malt: Pale malt, Wheat malt. Hops: Saaz. Others: Coriander, Ginger. IBU: 34. °L: 3. Source: Web.

**Oregon Golden Ale**: °P: 13. Malt: Pale malt, 18% Munich malt. Hops: Cascade, Goldings/Willamette. IBU: 35. °L: 10. Source: Web. OG: 1052. Malt: Munich malt. Hops: Willamette. Source: GAM.

**Saint Rogue Red**: °P: 13. Malt: Pale malt, Munich malt, Crystal malt, Carastan malt. Hops: Chinook, Centennial. Dry hops: Centennial. IBU: 44. °L: 27. Source: 150/GAM/Web.

**Juniper Pale Ale**: °P: 13. Malt: Pale malt, Triumph pale malt, Munich malt, Crystal malt, Caramel 15L malt. Hops: Styrian Goldings, Amarillo. Others: Juniper berries. IBU: 34. °L: 3. Source: Web.

**Santa's Private Reserve**: °P: 13. Malt: Pale malt, Munich malt, Crystal 60-70L malt, Carastan 30-37L malt, Carastan 13-17L malt. Hops: Chinook, Centennial, "Rudolph" mystery hop. IBU: 44. °L: 26. Source: Web.

**Oktoberfest**: °P: 14. Malt: Pilsner malt, Munich malt, Acid malt. Hops: Perle. IBU: 29. °L: 4.2. Source: Web.

**Mexicali Rouge**: OG: 1052. Malt: Munich malt. Hops: Willamette, Cascade. Others: Chipotle chillies. Source: GAM.

**Saint Rogue Dry Hopped**: OG: 1052. Malt: Pale malt, Carastan malt, Crystal malt, Munich malt. Hops: Fresh Centennial. Source: GAM.

**XS Smoke Ale / Smoke / Welkommen**: OG: 1058. °P: 14.5. Malt: Pale malt, Alder- and/or Beech-smoked malt, Crystal malt, Munich malt or Pale malt, Alder-smoked Munich malt, Rauchmalz, Crystal malt, Carastan 30-37L malt, Carastan 13-17L malt. Hops: Perle, Saaz. Late hops: Saaz, Perle. IBU: 48. °L: 20.6. Source: NACB/Web. Malt: Carastan malt, Crystal malt, Hand-smoked Munich malt. Hops: Saaz, Perle. Source: GAM.

**Captain Sig's Deadliest Ale**: °P: 14.5. Malt: Pale malt, Chocolate malt, Munich malt, Carastan malt. Hops: Amarillo, Cascade. IBU: 80. °L: 20. Source: Web.

**Brutal Bitter**: °P: 15. Malt: Pipkin / Maris Otter pale malt, CaraVienne malt, CaraWheat® malt. Hops: Crystal. Dry hops: No. IBU: 59. °L: 14.2. Source: Web.

**Chocolate Stout**: °P: 15. Malt: Pale malt, Crystal 135-165L malt, Chocolate malt, Flaked oats, Roast barley, Natural/Dutch bittersweet Chocolate. Hops: Cascade. IBU: 69. °L: 135. Source: Web.

**Shakespeare Stout**: °P: 15. Malt: Pale malt, Crystal 135-165L malt, Chocolate malt, Roast barley, Flaked oats. Hops: Cascade. Late hops: Cascade. Yeast: Wyeast #2220. IBU: 69. °L: 135. SRM: 68. Source: GAM/Web/BYO.

**Independence Hop Ale**: °P: 15. Malt: Pale malt, Munich malt, CaraWheat® malt, CaraFoam® malt. Hops: Fresh Centennial, Fresh Cascade. IBU: 80. °L: 14.1. Source: Web.

**Yellow Snow IPA**: °P: 15. Malt: Pale malt, Melanoidin malt, CaraFoam® malt. Hops: Amarillo. IBU: 70. °L: 14. Source: Web.

**Paul's Black Lager**: °P: 15. Malt: Pale malt, Melanoidin malt, Black malt, Carafa® Special II malt, Chocolate malt. Hops: Hallertau, Perle. IBU: 28. Source: Web.

**Golden Frog**: ABV: 6%. °P: 15. Malt: Pilsner malt. Hops: Saaz. IBU: 39. Source: Web.

**Dead Guy Ale**: °P: 16. Malt: Pale malt, Munich malt, Carastan malt. Hops: Perle, Saaz. IBU: 40. °L: 16. Source: GAM/Web. OG: 1063-64. Malt: Pale malt, Dextrin malt, CaraMunich malt, Munich malt, Crystal malt. Hops: Perle. Late hops: Saaz, Perle. Source: BC.

**Hoppy Frog IPA**: ABV: 6.5%. °P: 13. Malt: Maris Otter pale malt. Hops: Amarillo. IBU: 75. Source: Web.

**Two Frog**: ABV: 6.5%. °P: 16. Malt: Pilsner malt, CaraVienne malt, Candi sugar. Hops: Saaz. IBU: 25. Source: Web.

**Mogul Ale**: OG: 1066. Malt: Chocolate malt, Munich malt, Crystal malt. Hops: Saaz, Perle, Cascade, Centennial, Willamette, Chinook. Source: GAM.

**Imperial Younger's Special Bitter**: °P: 16.7. Malt: Maris Otter pale malt, Crystal malt. Hops: Willamette, Goldings. Late hops: Amarillo. IBU: 50. Source: Web.

**Dad's Little Helper**: °P: 17. Malt: Pale malt, Flaked maize. Hops: Crystal. IBU: 25. °L: 10. Source: Web.

**Trackdown IPA**: ABV: 7%. °P: 17. Malt: 100% Maris Otter pale malt. Hops: 100% Amarillo. IBU: 85. °L: 10. Source: Web.

**Monk Madness**: °P: 18. Malt: Pale malt, Munich malt, Special B malt, Melanoidin malt, Amber malt. Hops: Chinook, Amarillo, Centennial, Summit, Belgian noble hops. IBU: 108. °L: 66. Source: Web.

**Morimoto Imperial Pilsner**: ABV: 8.8%. °P: 18. Malt: 100% Pilsner malt. Hops: 100% Sterling. IBU: 74. °L: 16. Source: Web.

**Menage Frog**: ABV: 9%. °P: 20. Malt: Pilsner malt, "Huge amount of" Candi sugar. Hops: Saaz. IBU: 30. Source: Web.

**Imperial India Pale Ale / I2PA**: ABV: 9.5%. °P: 20. Malt: Pipkin pale malt. Hops: Cascade, Goldings, Saaz. IBU: 74. °L: 13. Source: Web. OG: 1080. Hops: Newport. Late hops: Cascade, Sterling. Dry hops: Amarillo. Source: 150.

**Double Dead Guy Ale**: °P: 20. Malt: Pale malt, Munich malt, Caramel 15L malt. Hops: Cascade. IBU: 60. °L: 25. Source: Web.

**Brew 10,000**: ABV: 10%. °P: 21. Malt: Maris Otter pale malt, Vienna malt, French Special aromatic malt. Hops: Yakima Summit, Saphir. IBU: 83. °L: 18. Source: Web.

**Old Crustacean**: ABV: 11.5%. °P: 25. Malt: Pale malt, Carastan malt, Munich malt. Hops: Chinook, Centennial. IBU: 110. °L: 57. Source: Web. OG: 1090-94. Malt: Pale malt, Munich malt, Crystal malt, Chocolate malt. Hops: Chinook. Late hops: Centennial. Source: CB/GAM.

**Imperial Stout**: ABV: 11%. °P: 26. Malt: Pale malt, Black malt, Chocolate malt, Munich malt, Flaked oats, 2 secret ingredients, optional XLT-80 malt. Hops: Cascade, Chinook, Willamette. IBU: 88. °L: 256. Source: Web.

. *Russian River Brewing Company, Santa Rosa, CA.*
*Www.russianriverbrewing.com*

**Aud Blonde**: OG: 1046. Malt: Pilsner malt. Hops: Crystal. IBU: 20. Source: Web.

**Little White Lie**: OG: 1047. Malt: 40% Wheat. Hops: Crystal. IBU: 20. Source: Web.

**Dr. Zeus**: OG: 1056. Hops: Zeus. IBU: 45. Source: Web.

**Sanctification**: OG: 1056. Malt: Pale or Pilsner malt, Vienna malt, Acid malt. Hops: Sterling. Late hops: Sterling. Source: 150.

**Rejection**: OG: 1058. Malt: De-bittered black malt. IBU: 27. Source: Web.

**Temptation**: OG: 1062. Malt: Pilsner malt, Wheat. Hops: Styrian Goldings, Sterling. IBU: 27. Yeast: White Labs WLP510. Source: BLAM.

**Damnation**: OG: 1066. Malt: American 2-row pale malt, Pilsner malt, Dextrose. Hops: Styrian Goldings, Sterling. IBU: 25. Yeast: White Labs WLP500. Source: BLAM.

**Pliney the Elder**: OG: 1074. Malt: Pale malt, CaraPils malt, Crystal malt, Dextrose. Mash hops: Chinook. Hops: Warrior, Chinook. Late hops: Simcoe, Columbus, Centennial. Dry hops: Columbus, Centennial, Simcoe. Source: 150.

. *Saint Arnold Brewing Company, Houston, TX. Www.saintarnold.com*

**Fancy Lawnmower**: OG: 1045. Malt: Pilsner malt, Wheat malt. Hops: Hallertau. Late hops: Hallertau. IBU: 20. Source: Web.

**Texas Wheat**: OG: 1049. Malt: 50% Pale malt, 50% Wheat malt. Hops: Perle. Late hops: Liberty. IBU: 18. Source: Web.

**Summer Pils**: OG: 1050. Malt: Pilsner malt. Hops: Saaz, Hallertau. IBU: 41. Source: Web. OG: 1048. Malt: Pilsner malt, Munich malt. Hops: Hallertau. Late hops: Saaz, Hallertau. Source: 150.

**Amber Ale**: OG: 1054. Malt: Pale malt, CaraVienne malt. Hops: Cascade. Late hops: Cascade, Liberty. IBU: 31. Source: Web.

**Elissa IPA**: OG: 1061. Malt: Maris Otter pale malt, Crystal malt. Hops: Cascade. Late hops: Cascade. Dry hops: Cascade. IBU: Approximately 60. Source: 150/Web.

**Saint Arnold Christmas Ale**: OG: 1066. Malt: Pale malt, Munich malt, CaraMunich malt, Special B malt, CaraVienne malt. Hops: Perle. Late hops: Liberty. Source: 150.

**Double IPA**: OG: 1082. Malt: Maris Otter pale malt, Wheat malt, CaraVienne malt, CaraPils malt, Crystal malt, Honey, Molasses. Hops: Chinook, Centennial, Ahtanum. Dry hops: Cascade. Source: Web.

**Abbey American Quadruppel**: OG: 1093. Malt: Maris Otter pale malt, Munich malt, Victory malt, Special B malt, Brown sugar. Hops: Perle, Liberty, Saaz. Source: Web.

**Barleywine**: OG: 1099. Malt: Maris Otter pale malt, Munich malt, Chocolate malt. Hops: Cascade, Northern Brewer. Dry hops: Saaz. Source: Web.

### . *St. Stan's Brewing Company, Modesto, CA*

**Red Sky Ale**: OG: 1045. Malt: Pale malt, Crystal malt, Wheat malt. Hops: Chinook. Late hops: Cascade, Willamette. Source: NACB.

### . *Salmon Creek Brewery, Vancouver, WA*

**Brother Larry's Belgian**: OG: 1082. Malt: Pilsner malt, Munich malt, Aromatic malt, Special B malt, Biscuit malt, CaraPils malt, Candi sugar. Hops: Northern Brewer, Hallertau. Late hops: Hallertau, Goldings. Source: BYO[27].

### . *San Andreas Brewing Company, Hollister, CA*

**Earthquake Porter**: Malt: Pale malt, Crystal malt, Chocolate malt, Roast barley. Hops: Chinook, Goldings, Cluster. Source: GAM.

**Seismic Ale**: Malt: Crystal malt, Munich malt. Hops: Cascade, Chinook, Cluster, Goldings. Source: GAM.

**Earthquake Pale Ale**: Malt: Crystal malt. Hops: Tettnang, Cascade, Chinook. Source: GAM.

**Kit Fox Amber**: Malt: Crystal malt, Munich malt. Hops: Chinook, Cluster, Cascade, Goldings. Source: GAM.

**Survivor Stout**: Malt: Roast barley, Chocolate malt. Hops: Chinook, Goldings, Cluster. Source: GAM.

---

[27] http://byo.com/recipe/1580.html

## San Francisco Brewing Company, San Francisco, CA

**Andromeda Wheat**: OG: 1040. Malt: Wheat malt. Hops: Saaz, Hallertau. Source: GAM.

**Pony Express Amber Ale**: OG: 1043. Malt: Caramel malt, CaraPils malt. Hops: Cascade. Source: GAM.

**Albatross Lager**: OG: 1046. Malt: Caramel malt. Hops: Hallertau, Saaz. Source: GAM.

**Emperor Norton Lager**: OG: 1056. Malt: Caramel malt, CaraPils malt, Munich malt. Hops: Saaz. Source: GAM.

**Shanghai IPA**: OG: 1061. Malt: Caramel malt. Hops: Cascade, Goldings, Chinook. Source: GAM.

**Gripman's Porter**: OG: 1062. Malt: Caramel malt. Hops: Cascade. Source: GAM.

## Sand Creek Brewing Company, Black River Falls, WI

**Oscar's Chocolate Oatmeal Stout**: OG: 1056. Malt: Pale malt, Munich malt, Chocolate malt, Wheat malt, Roast barley, Flaked oats. Hops: Goldings. Late hops: Goldings. Source: 150.

## Santa Cruz Brewing Company, Santa Cruz, CA

**Lighthouse Amber**: ABW: 3.8%. Malt: Pale malt, Caramel malt. Hops: Northern Brewer, Chinook, Tettnang, Hallertau. Source: GAM.

**Lighthouse Lager**: ABW: 3.8%. Malt: Pale malt. Hops: Hallertau, Cluster. Source: GAM.

## Saranac Brewing / F.X. Matt Brewing Company, Utica, NY

**Adirondack Amber**: OG: 1055. Malt: Pilsner malt, Crystal malt, Munich malt. Hops: Cascade. Late hops: Hallertau. Source: NACB.

## Saxer Brewing Company, Lake Oswego, OR

**Three Finger Amber**: ABW: 4%. Malt: Pale malt, Dark CaraPils malt, Munich malt. Hops: Saaz, Hersbrücker. Source: GAM.

**Lemon Lager**: OG: 1040. Malt: Pale malt. Hops: Yakima Perle, Saaz. Others: Lemon juice extract. Source: GAM.

**Three Finger Jack-Stout**: OG: 1048. Malt: Pale malt, Roast barley, Munich malt. Source: GAM.

**Three Finger Jack Hefedunkel**: OG: 1050. Malt: Caramel malt, Munich malt, Patent black malt. Hops: Hersbrücker. Source: GAM.

## August Schell Brewing Company, New Ulm, MN.
Www.schellsbrewery.com

**Light**: ABV: 4%. Malt: 80% Malt, 20% Maize. Hops: Cascade, Cluster. Source: Web.

**Hefeweizen**: ABV: 4.4%. Malt: 40% Pale malt, 60% Wheat malt. Hops: Cascade, Mount Hood. Source: Web.

**Original**: ABV: 4.8%. Malt: 70% Malt, 30% Maize. Hops: Cascade, Cluster. Source: Web.

**Dark**: ABV: 4.8%. Malt: Pale malt, Black malt, Corn extract. Hops: Cluster. Source: Web.

**Firebrick**: ABV: 5%. Malt: Pale malt, Caramel malt, CaraPils malt, Munich malt. Hops: Vanguard, Chinook, Hallertau. Source: Web.

**Zommerfest**: ABV: 5%. Malt: Pale malt, Wheat malt. Hops: Vanguard, Tettnang. Source: Web.

**Schmalz's Alt**: ABV: 5.1%. Malt: Pale malt, CaraPils malt, Munich malt, Black malt, Chocolate malt. Hops: Chinook, Hallertau. Source: Web.

**Maifest**: OG: 1055. Malt: Lager malt, CaraPils malt, Wheat malt, Vienna malt. Hops: Tettnang. Late hops: Hallertau. Source: NACB. ABV: 6.9%. Malt: Pale malt, CaraPils malt, Munich malt. Hops: Mount Hood, Cascade, Hallertau. Source: Web.

**Octoberfest**: ABV: 5.5%. Malt: Pale malt, Caramel malt, CaraPils malt, Black malt. Hops: Nugget, Cascade. Source: Web.

**Pilsner**: ABV: 5.6%. Malt: 100% Pale malt. Hops: Cascade, Hallertau. Source: Web.

**Pale Ale**: ABV: 5.75%. Malt: Pale malt, Carastan malt, CaraPils malt, Munich malt. Hops: Cascade, Chinook, Goldings. Source: Web.

**Caramel Bock**: ABV: 5.8%. Malt: Pale malt, Caramel malt, CaraPils malt, Black malt. Hops: Cluster, Mount Hood. Source: Web.

**Doppel Bock**: ABV: 6.9%. Malt: Pale malt, Caramel malt, CaraPils malt, Munich malt, Black malt. Hops: Mount Hood, Cascade, Centennial. Source: Web.

**Snowstorm**: Note: Recipe and ABV changes annually. Source: Web.

## *Schirf, Salt Lake City, UT*

**Wasatch Premium Ale**: OG: 1040. Malt: Crystal malt, Wheat malt, Chocolate malt, CaraPils malt, Vienna malt. Hops: Chinook, Cascade. Source: GAM.

**Wasatch Raspberry Wheat Beer**: OG: 1040. Malt: Wheat malt, Crystal malt, CaraPils malt. Hops: Perle, Chinook, Willamette, Tettnang. Source: GAM.

**Wasatch Slickrock Lager**: OG: 1040. Malt: Wheat malt, CaraPils malt, Vienna malt. Hops: Saaz, Cascade. Source: GAM.

**Wasatch Irish Stout**: OG: 1040. Malt: Wheat malt, Patent black malt, Chocolate malt, Munich malt, Crystal malt. Hops: Chinook, Cascade. Source: GAM.

**Wasatch Weizenbier**: OG: 1040. Malt: Wheat malt, Crystal malt, CaraPils malt. Hops: Chinook, Willamette, Perle, Tettnang. Source: GAM.

### Joseph Schlitz Brewing Company

**Schlitz**: OG: 1048. Malt: Lager malt, Flaked maize. Hops: Hallertau. Source: DL.

### Scorched Earth, Algonquin, IL. Www.ScorchedEarthBrewing.com

**Pit Master**: ABV: 4%. Others: Peaches, Candied ginger. IBU: 4. Source: Web.

**Sweetie Pie**: ABV: 4.2%. Others: Strawberries, Rhubarb. IBU: 4. Source: Web.

**Twisted Hickster**: ABV: 4.8%. Hops: Summit. IBU: 14. Source: Web.

**Fielders Wit**: ABV: 5.2%. Others: Blueberries. IBU: 15. Source: Web.

**Berry Fool**: ABV: 5.4%. Malt: 87% Pilsner malt, 10% Flaked rye, 3% Aromatic malt. Hops: Aramis. Others: Raspberries, Grains of Paradise. IBU: 25. Source: Web.

**Wet Willie**: ABV: 5.4%. Hops: Fresh Cascade. IBU: 50. Source: Web.

**Public Servant**: ABV: 6%. Malt: Rye malt. IBU: 60. Source: Web.

**Base Jumper**: ABV: 7.2%. Others: Orange juice. Pink grapefruit juice. IBU: 80. Source: Web.

**Saint Monty**: ABV: 8.1. Others: Montmorency cherry juice. IBU: 20. Source: Web.

**Crypt Keeper**: ABV: 8.3%. Others: Chocolate, Coffee, Pumpkins, Spices. IBU: 25. Source: Web.

**The Bitter Chocolatier**: ABV: 9.1%. Malt: Chocolate malt, Flaked oats. Others: Cocoa nibs, Chocolate. IBU: 25. Source: Web.

### Sea Dog Brewing Company, Bangor, ME

**Riverdriver Hazelnut Porter**: OG: 1045. Malt: Pale malt, Toasted pale malt, Crystal malt, Black malt, Chocolate malt. Hops: Goldings. Others: Noirot Hazelnut liqueur concentrate. Source: NACB.

**Old Gollywobbler Brown Ale**: OG: 1045. Malt: Pale malt, Patent black malt, Roast barley, Crystal malt. Hops: Cascade, Willamette, Tettnang. Source: GAM.

**Windjammer Blonde Ale**: OG: 1050. Malt: Pale malt, Crystal malt. Hops: Cascade. Source: GAM.

**Old East India Pale Ale**: OG: 1068. Malt: Pale malt, Chocolate malt, Crystal malt. Hops: Cascade, Willamette, Tettnang. Source: GAM.

### Shenandoah Brewing Company, Alexandria, VA

**Stony Man Stout**: OG: 1050. Malt: Pale malt, Crystal malt, Roast barley, Black malt, Chocolate malt. Hops: Northern Brewer. Late hops: Willamette. Source: NACB.

## Shipyard Brewing Company, Portland, ME

**Goat Island Light Ale**: OG: 1034. Malt: Pale malt, Flaked maize. Hops: Willamette, Tettnang. Source: GAM.

**Wheat Ale**: ABV: 4.5%. Hops: Delta. Source: BA.

**Shipyard Export Ale**: OG: 1048-54. Malt: Pale malt, Crystal malt, Wheat malt. Hops: Cascade. Late hops: Willamette, Tettnang. Source: 150/GAM.

**Chamberlain Pale Ale**: OG: 1050. Malt: Pale malt, Crystal malt, Chocolate malt. Hops: Cascade, Fuggles, Tettnang. Source: GAM.

**Mystic Seaport Pale Ale**: OG: 1050. Malt: Pale malt, Crystal malt, Chocolate malt. Hops: Cascade, Fuggles, Tettnang. Source: GAM.

**Blue Fin Stout**: OG: 1052. Malt: Pale malt, Roast barley, Chocolate malt, Crystal malt, Patent black malt. Hops: Northern Brewer, Cascade, Goldings, Tettnang. Source: GAM.

**Fuggles IPA**: OG: 1055. Malt: Pale malt, Crystal malt. Hops: Fuggles. Late hops: Fuggles. Dry hops: Fuggles. Source: NACB.

**Old Thumper Extra Special Ale**: OG: 1058. Malt: Pale malt, Crystal malt, Chocolate malt. Hops: Challenger, Progress, Goldings. Source: GAM.

**Longfellow Winter Ale**: OG: 1062. Malt: Roast barley, Chocolate malt, Crystal malt. Hops: Northern Brewer, Cascade, Goldings, Tettnang. Source: GAM.

## Sierra Nevada Brewing Company, Chico, CA

**Summerfest**: OG: 1046. Malt: Pale malt, Dextrin malt. Hops: Hallertau. Source: GAM.

**Pale Ale**: OG: 1052. Malt: Pale malt, Crystal malt. Hops: Magnum, Perle. Late hops: Cascade. Dry hops: Cascade. Source: 150. OG: 1057-59. Malt: Pale malt, Dextrin malt, Crystal malt. Hops: Nugget. Late hops: Perle, Cascade. Dry hops: Cascade. Source: CB. Malt: Crystal malt. Hops: Cascade. Late hops: Cascade. Yeast: Wyeast #1056. Source: Mark Garetz, MHF.

**Sierra Nevada Porter**: OG: 1054. Malt: Pale malt, Crystal malt, Black malt, Chocolate malt. Hops: Fuggles. Late hops: Goldings. Source: NACB. OG: 1061-62. Hops: Nugget, Centennial. Late hops: Cascade. Source: BC. OG: 1058. Malt: Pale malt, Caramel malt, Dextrin malt, Patent black malt, Chocolate malt. Hops: Willamette, Nugget. Source: GAM.

**Pale Bock**: OG: 1064. Malt: Pale malt, Dextrin malt. Hops: Perle, Mount Hood. Source: GAM.

**Stout**: OG: 1064. Malt: Pale malt, Caramel malt, Patent black malt, Dextrin malt. Hops: Chinook, Cascade. Source: GAM.

**Celebration Ale**: OG: 1064-67. Malt: Pale malt, Crystal malt, optional CaraPils malt. Hops: Chinook. Late hops: Cascade. Dry hops: Cascade, Centennial. Source: 150/BC.

Malt: Pale malt, Caramel malt, Dextrin malt. Hops: Chinook, Cascade, Centennial. Source: GAM.

**Torpedo Extra IPA**: ABV: 7.2%. Hops: Citra. Source: BA.

**Bigfoot**: OG: 1095-1105. Malt: Pale malt, Crystal malt/Caramel malt. Hops: Nugget. Late hops: Cascade. Dry hops: Cascade, Centennial. Source: NACB/BC/GAM.

### . Sin City Brewing Company, Las Vegas, NV

**Sin City Amber**: OG: 1053. Malt: Pilsner malt, Munich malt. Hops: Hersbrücker. Late hops: Hersbrücker. Source: 150.

### . Sleeping Giant Brewing Company, MT

**Black Country Scottish Ale**: OG: 1051-52. Malt: Pale malt, Crystal malt, Roast barley, Peat-smoked malt. Hops: Goldings. Late hops: Willamette, Goldings. Source: BC.

### . SLO Brewing Company, San Luis Obispo, CA

**Brickhouse Extra Pale Ale**: OG: 1048. Malt: Pale malt, Crystal malt, Toasted pale malt. Hops: Goldings, Cluster. Dry hops: Cascade. Source: NACB. OG: 1045. Malt: Pale malt, Crystal 10L malt, Munich malt. Hops: Nugget, Northern Brewer, Willamette. Source: GAM.

**Holidaze Ale**: OG: 1050. Malt: Pale malt, Crystal 50-60L malt, Munich malt, Crystal 95-115L malt, Roast barley. Hops: Nugget, Centennial. Others: Herbs. Source: GAM.

**Garden Alley Amber Ale**: OG: 1056. Malt: Pale malt, Crystal 10L malt, Crystal 50-60L malt, Crystal 95-115L malt. Hops: Centennial, Nugget. Source: GAM.

**Cole Porter**: OG: 1064. Malt: Pale malt, Munich malt, Crystal 50-60L malt, Crystal 95-115L malt, Chocolate malt, Patent black malt, Roast barley. Hops: Nugget, Willamette. Source: GAM.

### . Snake River, Jackson, WY

**Pale Ale**: OG: 1050. Malt: Pale malt, Munich 7L malt, Carastan 34L malt. Hops: Washington Chinook, Washington Cascade. Source: GAM.

**Lager**: ABW: 5.6%. Malt: Pale malt, Caramel 75L malt, Caramel 150L malt, Munich 7L malt, Carastan 34L malt. Hops: Perle, Tettnang. Source: GAM.

**Zonker Stout**: OG: 1060. Malt: Pale malt, Caramel 75L malt, Chocolate malt, Patent black malt, Caramel 150L malt, Carastan 34L malt. Hops: Washington Willamette, Chinook, Goldings. Source: GAM.

### . Smuttynose Brewing Company, Portsmouth, NH

**Old Brown Dog Ale**: OG: 1050. Malt: Mild ale malt, Crystal malt, Toasted pale malt, Brown malt, Chocolate malt. Hops: Willamette. Source: NACB.

**Smuttynose Scotch-Style Ale**: OG: 1068. Malt: Pale malt, Crystal malt, Amber malt, Roast barley. Hops: Fuggles. Source: NACB.

**Smuttynose Imperial Stout**: OG: 1070. Malt: Pale malt, Roast barley, Crystal malt. Hops: Challenger. Late hops: Fuggles. Dry hops: Fuggles. Source: NACB.

### . *Southampton Publick House, Southampton, NY*

**Southampton Abbot 12**: OG: 1096. Malt: 2-row pale malt, Pilsner malt, Special B malt, Sucrose, Dark candi sugar. Hops: Styrian Goldings, Perle. IBU: 22. Source: BLAM.

### . *Spanish Peaks Brewing, Bozeman, MT*

**Black Dog Ale**: OG: 1045. Malt: Pale malt, Crystal malt, Wheat malt. Hops: Willamette. Late hops: Mount Hood. Source: NACB. OG: 1050. Malt: Pale malt, Carastan malt, Crystal malt, Chocolate malt, Munich malt. Source: GAM.

**Honey Raspberry Ale**: OG: 1046. Malt: Wildflower honey. Others: Raspberries. Source: GAM.

**Sweetwater Wheat Ale**: OG: 1046. Malt: Pale malt, Wheat malt. Source: GAM.

**Yellowstone Pale Ale**: OG: 1056. Malt: Pale malt, Carastan malt, Crystal malt, Munich malt. Source: GAM.

### . *Spencer Brewing, Saint Joseph's Abbey, Spencer, MA*

**Spencer Trappist Ale**: OG: 1058: Malt: Pale malt, Pilsner malt, CaraMunich malt. Hops: Nugget. Late hops: Willamette. Yeast: Wyeast #3787 or White Labs WLP530. IBU: 25. SRM: 8. Source: BYO.

### . *Spoetzl Brewery, Shiner, TX*

**Shiner Bock**: OG: 1060. Malt: Lager malt, CaraPils malt, Munich malt, Black malt. Hops: Northern Brewer. Late hops: Hallertau. Source: NACB. OG: 1043. Malt: Pale malt, Vienna malt, Corn grits, Crystal malt, Roast barley. Hops: Brewers Gold. Source: 150.

### . *Sprecher Brewing, Milwaukee, WI*

**Hefe Weiss**: OG: 1044. Malt: Pale malt, Wheat malt, CaraPils malt. Hops: Cascade, Mount Hood, Tettnang. Source: GAM.

**Special Amber Lager**: OG: 1052. Malt: Pilsner malt, Munich malt, CaraVienne malt, Crystal malt. Hops: Cascade. Late hops: Mount Hood. Source: 150. Malt: Pale malt, Caramel malt, CaraPils malt. Hops: Cascade, Mount Hood, Tettnang. Source: GAM.

**Black Bavarian-Style Lager**: OG: 1055. Malt: Lager malt, Black malt, Crystal malt, Chocolate malt, Munich malt. Hops: Hallertau. Late hops: Tettnang. Source: NACB. OG: 1060. Malt: Pale malt, Caramel malt, Patent black malt. Hops: Cascade, Mount Hood, Chinook, Tettnang. Source: GAM.

**Belgian Style Ale**: OG: 1075. Malt: Pale malt, Dextrin malt, Munich malt, Vienna malt. Hops: Mount Hood, Willamette, Tettnang. Source: GAM.

. *Spring Street Brewing Company, St. Paul, MN*

**Wit Original 1444 Recipe**: OG: 1046. Malt: Wheat malt. Hops: Cluster, Tettnang. Source: GAM.

**Wit Amber Harvest 1444 Recipe**: OG: 1050. Malt: Wheat malt, Roast wheat, Roast barley. Hops: Cluster, Tettnang. Source: GAM.

**Wit Black**: OG: 1053-54. Malt: Pale malt, Wheat malt, Roast wheat malt, Roast barley. Hops: Tettnang. Others: Anise. Source: CB.

. *Springfield Brewing Company, Springfield, MO.*
*Www.springfieldbrewingco.com*

**Mueller Wheat**: OG: 1045. Malt: Wheat malt, Wheat, Pale malt. Hops: Perle. Late hops: Liberty. IBU: 15. Source: 150/Web.

**Pale Ale**: °P: 12.5. Malt: Caramel malt, Pale malt. Hops: Cascade: IBU: 25. Source: Web.

. *Squatters Pub Brewery, Salt Lake City, UT. Www.squatters.com*

**Full Suspension Pale Ale**: OG: 1048. Malt: Pale malt, CaraMunich malt. Hops: Nugget. Late hops: Columbus. Source: 150.

**Captain Bastard's Oatmeal Stout**: Malt: Pale malt, Caramel malt, Chocolate malt, Roast barley, Oatmeal. Hops: Chinook. Source: Web.

. *Star, Portland, OR*

**Bright Star Pineapple Ale**: OG: 1048. Malt: Carastan 30-37L malt, Munich malt. Hops: Mount Hood, Liberty. Source: GAM.

**Raspberry Wheat Ale**: OG: 1050. Malt: Carastan 30-37L malt, Munich malt, Wheat malt. Hops: Liberty. Source: GAM.

**Dark Star Nut Brown Ale**: OG: 1052. Malt: Pale malt, Wheat malt, Chocolate malt, Munich malt, Crystal 50-60L malt. Hops: Perle, Northern Brewer, Tettnang. Source: GAM.

**Black Cherry Stout**: OG: 1060. Malt: Wheat malt, Roast barley, Crystal 80L malt, Munich malt. Hops: Northern Brewer, Tettnang. Others: Black Cherries. Source: GAM.

. *Steelhead Brewing Company, Burlingame, CA*

**Wee Heavy Scotch Ale**: OG: 1105. Malt: Pale malt, Special B malt, Biscuit malt, Chocolate malt. Hops: Nugget. Late hops: Mount Hood. Source: 150.

. *Stevens Point Brewery, Stevens Point, WI*

**Point Amber**: OG: 1048. Malt: Lager malt, Vienna malt, Crystal malt. Hops: Perle. Late hops: Mount Hood, Hallertau. Source: NACB.

**Pale Ale**: OG: 1056. Malt: Pale malt, Crystal 60L malt, Crystal 75L malt. Hops: Magnum. Late hops: Ahtanum. Yeast: White Labs WLP002. IBU: 45. SRM: 18. Source: BYO.

**Pale Ale 2.0**: ABV: 6%. Hops: Magnum, Herkules, Mandarina Bavaria. IBU: 55. Source: Web.

**Smoked Porter**: OG: 1064. Malt: Pale malt, Chocolate malt, Peat-smoked malt, Crystal 75L malt. Hops: Perle. Late hops: Mount Hood. Yeast: White Labs WLP002. IBU: 53. SRM: 46. Source: BYO. Notes: Stone have also brewed **Smoked Porter with Chipotle Peppers**, **Smoked Porter with Vanilla Beans**. Source: Web.

**IPA**: OG: 1065. Malt: Pale malt, Crystal 15L malt. Hops: optional Perle, Magnum. Late hops: Centennial. Dry hops: Centennial, Chinook. Yeast: White Labs WLP002. IBU: 77. SRM: 8. Source: BYO/Web.

**Cali-Belgique IPA**: ABV: 6.0%. IPA brewed with Belgian yeast. IBU: 77. Source: Web.

**Saison**: ABV: 6%. Others: Lemon zest, Grains of Paradise, Lemon thyme, Lavender. IBU: 35. Source: Web.

**10.10.10 Vertical Epic Ale**: OG: 1069. Malt: 80% Pale malt, 11% Flaked triticale, 9% Amber candi sugar. Hops: Perle. Others: Dried chamomile flowers, Grape juice. Yeast: Wyeast #3522. IBU: 45. Source: Web.

**Enjoy After 07.04.16 Brett IPA** (b-c): ABV: 7%. Yeast: Brettanomyces. IBU: 70. Source: Web.

**Ruination IPA**: OG: 1075. Malt: Pale malt, Crystal malt. Hops: Magnum. Late hops: Centennial. IBU: 100+. Source: 150/Web. Malt: Pale malt, Crystal 15L malt. Hops: Magnum. Late hops: Centennial. Dry hops: Centennial. Yeast: White Labs WLP002. IBU: 100+. SRM: 6. Source: BYO.

**02.02.02 Vertical Epic Ale**: OG: 1075. Malt: 48.5% Pale malt, 40.25% Flaked red wheat, 6.25% Oats, 5% Rice hulls. Hops: 63.7% Centennial. Others: 9% Orange peel, 14% Curaçao Orange peel, 12.8% crushed coriander seeds, 0.6% ground black pepper. Yeast: White Labs WLP400. IBU: 45. Source: Web.

**04.04.04 Vertical Epic Ale**: OG: 1076. Malt: 95% Pale malt, 5% Flaked wheat. Hops: Sterling. Others: Kaffir lime leaves. Yeast: White Labs WLP510. IBU: 35. Source: Web.

**08.08.08 Vertical Epic Ale**: OG: 1076. Malt: 87% Pale malt, 6.5% Flaked oats, 5.5% Light candi sugar syrup, 1% Blonde Candi sugar powder. Hops: Simcoe, Amarillo. Late hops: Ahtanum. Dry hops: Simcoe, Amarillo. Yeast: White Labs WLP570. IBU: 65. Source: Web.

**Delicious IPA**: ABV: 7.7%. Hops: Lemondrop, El Dorado. IBU: 80. Source: Web.

**Ruination IPA**: ABV: 7.8%. Malt: Pale malt, Crystal malt. Hops: Columbus. Late hops: Columbus. Notes: Aged in Kentucky Bourbon barrels. IBU: 59. Source: Web.

**03.03.03 Vertical Epic Ale**: OG: 1078. Malt: 89.45% Pale malt, 6.8% Flaked red wheat, 1.25% Chocolate wheat malt, 2.5% Special B malt. Hops: Warrior. Dry hops: Centennial. Others: Coriander, Grains of Paradise. Yeast: White Labs WLP500. IBU: 48. Source: Web.

**07.07.07 Vertical Epic Ale**: OG: 1078. Malt: 71.6% Pale malt, 14.5% Wheat malt, 5% Light Munich malt, 5% Vienna malt, 3.9% Blonde Candi sugar. Hops: Glacier, Crystal. Others: Ground ginger, Cardamom, Dried Grapefruit peel, Dried Orange peel, Dried Lemon peel. Yeast: White Labs WLP566, WLP565 and WLP550. IBU: 20-25. Source: Web.

**09.09.09 Vertical Epic Ale**: OG: 1080. Malt: 73.1% Pale malt, 5.4% Chocolate malt, 10.4% Crystal 75-80L malt, 4.3% Aromatic malt, 1.7% Black malt, 1.7% Carafa® malt, 3.4% Dark candi sugar. Hops: Perle, Magnum. Others: Dried tangerine peel, Vanilla bean, French oak chips. Yeast: Wyeast #3522. Source: Web.

**111.11.11 Vertical Epic Ale**: OG: 1082. Malt: 80.25% Pale malt, 9.1% Light Munich malt, 1.05% Crystal 75-80L malt, 4% CaraBohemian® malt, 5.6% Special B malt. Hops: Perle, Warrior. Late hops: Pacific Jade, Target. Others: Anaheim chillies, Cinnamon. Yeast: Wyeast #3220. IBU: 65. Source: Web.

**05.05.05 Vertical Epic Ale**: OG: 1083. Malt: 89.75% Pale malt, 9% Caramel 150L malt, 1.25% Chocolate wheat malt. Hops: Amarillo. Yeast: White Labs WLP550. IBU: 45. Source: Web.

**06.06.06 Vertical Epic Ale**: OG: 1083. Malt: 87.5% Pale malt, 7% Dark wheat malt, 5% Carafa® Special II malt, 0.5% White wheat. Hops: Magnum. Late hops: Mount Hood. Yeast: White Labs WLP500. IBU: 25-30. Source: Web.

**Ruination IPA 2.0**: ABV: 8.5%. Hops: Magnum, Nugget, Centennial, Simcoe, Citra, Azacca. IBU: 100+. Source: Web.

**Thunderstruck IPA**: ABV: 8.7%. Hops: Topaz, Galaxy, Ella, Vic Secret. IBU: 95. Source: Web.

**Do These Hops Make My Beer Look Big? IPA**: ABV: 8.8%. Hops: HBC #291. IBU: 65. Source: Web.

**Xocoveza Charred**: ABV: 8.9%. Malt: Maris Otter pale malt, Pale malt, Chocolate malt, Crystal malt, Patent black malt, Coffee malt, Lactose, Flaked oats. Hops: Challenger, Goldings. Others: Nutmeg, Coffee, Vanilla, Pasilla peppers, Cinnamon, Cocoa. Notes: Aged in Kentucky Bourbon barrels. IBU: 31. Source: Web.

**Imperial Mutt Brown Ale**: ABV: 9%. Malt: Chocolate wheat malt, Honey malt, Victory malt, Vienna malt, Turbinado sugar. IBU: 45. Source: Web.

**Enjoy by 09.02.15 IPA**: ABV: 9.4. Hops: "More than a dozen hops". Source: Web.

**Bitter Chocolate Oatmeal Stout**: OG: 1094. Malt: Pale malt, Roast barley, Chocolate malt, Crystal 15L malt, CaraPils malt, Flaked oats, Black malt, Cocoa. Hops: Galena,

Ahtanum, Summit, Willamette. Yeast: White Labs WLP002. IBU: 45. SRM: 64. Source: BYO.

**Imperial Russian Stout** (b-c): OG: 1096. Malt: Pale malt, Amber malt, Roast barley, Black malt. Hops: Warrior. Yeast: White Labs WLP002. IBU: 90+. SRM: 93. Source: BYO.

**Old Guardian**: ABV: 10.5%. Malt: Pale malt, Maris Otter Crystal malt. Hops: Warrior, Columbus. Late hops: Columbus, Ahtanum. Notes: Aged in Temecula red wine barrels. IBU: 53. Source: Web.

**Chai-spiced Imperial Russian Stout**: ABV: 10.6%. Others: Cinnamon, Cardamom, Cloves, Ginger, Black pepper, Black tea. IBU: 65. Source: Web.

**Old Guardian**: ABV: 11%. Malt: Low colour Maris Otter pale malt, Maris Otter Crystal malt. Hops: Warrior, Columbus. Late hops: Columbus, Ahtanum. Notes: Aged in Kentucky Bourbon barrels. IBU: 50. Source: Web.

**Winter Harvest**: ABV: 11.3%. Malt: Pilsner malt, Candi sugar. Hops: Magnum. Late hops: Hallertau. Others: Merlot grapes. Notes: Aged in red wine barrels. IBU: 36. Source: Web.

**Xocoveza Extra Añejo**: ABV: 11.3%. Malt: Maris Otter pale malt, Pale malt, Chocolate malt, Crystal malt, Patent black malt, Coffee malt, Lactose, Flaked oats. Hops: Challenger, Goldings. Others: Nutmeg, Coffee, Vanilla, Pasilla peppers, Cinnamon, Cocoa. Notes: Aged in Extra Añejo Tequila barrels that previously held Bordeaux red wine. IBU: 31. Source: Web.

**Stygian Descent**: ABV: 11.6%. Malt: Pale malt, Caramel malt, Carafa® III malt. Hops: Chinook. Late hops: Amarillo, Simcoe. Notes: Aged in Kentucky rye whiskey barrels. IBU: 77. Source: Web.

**Highway 78 Scotch Ale**: ABV: 12.2 or 12.5%. Malt: Maris Otter pale malt, Golden Promise pale malt, Chocolate malt, Crystal malt, Sucanat cane sugar. Hops: Goldings, Target. Notes: Aged in Scotch whisky barrels. IBU: 17. Source: Web.

**Old Guardian**: ABV: 13%. Malt: Pale malt, Maris Otter Crystal malt. Hops: Warrior, Columbus. Late hops: Columbus, Ahtanum. Notes: Aged in Kentucky Rye whiskey barrels. IBU: 46. Source: Web.

**Fyodor's Classic**: ABV: 13-13.9%. Malt: Pale malt, Roast barley, Amber malt, Black malt. Hops: Warrior. Notes: Aged in Kentucky bourbon barrels. IBU: 38-43. Source: Web.

**Guardian's Slumber**: ABV: 14.9%. Malt: Pale malt, Maris Otter Crystal malt. Hops: Warrior. Late hops: Delta, Chinook, Columbus. Notes: Aged in Kentucky bourbon barrels. IBU: 68. Source: Web.

### . *Stone City Brewing Company, Solon, IA*

**John's Generations Ale**: OG: 1048. Malt: Belgian Pilsner malt, Wheat malt, Flaked wheat, CaraPils malt. Hops: Saaz. Others: Coriander seeds, Dried curaçao Orange peel. Source: NACB.

**Stein Bock**: OG: 1055. Malt: Lager malt, Vienna malt, CaraPils malt. Hops: Hallertau. Late hops: Perle, Tettnang. Source: NACB.

### . *Stone Coast Brewing Company, Portland and Bethel, ME*

**Sunsplash Golden Ale**: OG: 1048. Malt: Pale malt, Crystal malt, Wheat malt, CaraPils malt. Hops: Mount Hood. Late hops: Willamette, Mount Hood. Source: NACB.

### . *Stoudt's, Adamstown, PA. Www.stoudtsbeer.com*

**Pilsner**: OG: 1050. Malt: Pale malt, Wheat malt. Hops: Perle, Cluster, Saaz. Source: GAM.

**American Pale Ale**: ABV: 5%. Malt: Pale malt, Caramel malt, Munich malt. Hops: Cascade, Warrior. Late hops: Cascade. IBU: 41. Source: Web.

**Gold**: OG: 1052. Malt: Pale malt, Crystal malt, Munich malt. Hops: Cluster, Hallertau. Source: GAM. ABV: 4.7%. Malt: Pale malt, Munich malt, Vienna malt. Hops: Perle, Hallertau. Late hops: Saaz, Hallertau. IBU: 25. Source: Web.

**Scarlet Lady Ale**: ABV: 5%. Malt: Maris Otter pale malt, Caramel malt, Carafa® III malt. Hops: Perle. Late hops: Willamette. IBU: 32. Source: Web.

**Weizen**: ABV: 5%. Malt: Pale malt, Wheat malt. Hops: Hallertau. IBU: 12. Source: Web.

**Stoudt's Ale**: OG: 1052. Malt: Pale malt, Crystal malt. Hops: Willamette. Source: GAM.

**Oktober Fest**: ABV: 5%. Malt: Pale malt, Munich malt. Hops: Perle, Hallertau. Late hops: Hallertau, Saaz. IBU: 26. Source: Web.

**Fest**: OG: 1052. Malt: Pale malt, Crystal malt, Munich malt. Hops: Cluster, Tettnang, Hallertau. Source: GAM.

**Amber**: OG: 1056. Malt: Pale malt, Crystal malt, Munich malt. Hops: Cascade. Source: GAM.

**Festbier**: OG: 1060. Malt: Lager malt, Crystal malt, Munich malt, Vienna malt, Black malt. Hops: Saaz. Late hops: Saaz, Tettnang. Source: NACB.

**Fat Dog Stout**: OG: 1064. Malt: Pale malt, Victory malt, Patent black malt, Chocolate malt, Munich malt, Crystal malt. Hops: Goldings, Fuggles. Source: GAM.

**Bock**: OG: 1064. Malt: Pale malt, Crystal malt, Munich malt. Hops: Perle, Cluster, Tettnang, Hallertau. Source: GAM.

**Blonde Double Mai Bock**: OG: 1068. Malt: Pale malt, Crystal malt, Munich malt. Hops: Perle, Cluster, Hallertau, Saaz. Source: GAM. ABV: 7%. Malt: Pale malt, Munich malt,

Clover honey. Hops: Perle, Warrior, Hallertau. Late hops: Hallertau, Saaz. IBU: 35. Source: Web.

**Abbey Double**: ABV: 7%. Malt: Pale malt, Crystal malt, Munich malt and 2 other malts. Hops: Hallertau. Source: HB. OG: 1072. Malt: Pale malt, Crystal malt, Munich malt. Hops: Perle, Cluster, Tettnang, Hallertau. Source: GAM.

**Anniversary Double Bock**: ABV: 7%. Malt: Pale malt, Munich malt, Caramalt. Hops: Hallertau. Source: HB.

**Smooth Hoperator**: ABV: 7.2%. Malt: Pale malt, Vienna malt, Others. Hops: Summit. Late hops: Amarillo. IBU: 50. Source: Web.

**Honey Double Bock**: OG: 1072. Malt: Pale malt, Crystal malt, Munich malt. Hops: Perle, Cluster, Tettnang, Hallertau. Source: GAM.

**Triple**: OG: 1080. Malt: Pale malt, Crystal malt, Munich malt. Hops: Perle, Cluster, Tettnang, Hallertau. Source: GAM. ABV: 9%. Malt: Pale malt, Wheat malt. Hops: Perle, Warrior. Late hops: Hallertau, Saaz. IBU: 37. Source: Web.

**Old Abominable Barley Wine**: ABV: 8.5%. Malt: 80% Maris Otter pale malt, Caramel malt. Hops: Warrior. Late hops: Ahtanum. IBU: 55. Source: Web.

**Fat Dog Stout**: ABV: 9%. Malt: "Too many malts to mention". Hops: Goldings, Warrior. Late hops: Goldings, Willamette. IBU: 55. Source: Web.

**Double India Pale Ale**: ABV: 10%. Malt: Pale malt, Munich malt. Hops: Warrior. Late hops: Cascade, Willamette. IBU: 90. Source: Web.

**Winter Ale**: Note: Recipe changes every other year. Source: Web.

## . *Karl Strauss' Old Columbia Brewery, San Diego, CA*

**Amber Lager**: OG: 1050. Malt: Caramel malt. Source: GAM.

**Big Barrel IPA**: ABV: 9%. Hops: Nelson Sauvin. IBU: 40. Source: BA.

## . *Sudwerk Privatbrauerei Hübsch, Davis, CA*

**Hübsch Lager**: OG: 1047. Malt: Pale malt, Crystal malt, Munich malt, CaraPils malt. Hops: Perle, Tettnang, Hallertau. Source: GAM.

**Hübsch Pilsner**: OG: 1050. Malt: Pale malt. Hops: Tettnang, Hallertau, Perle. Source: GAM.

**Hübsch Märzen**: OG: 1053. Malt: Pale malt, Crystal 20-30L malt, Crystal 40-70L malt, Munich malt, CaraPils malt. Hops: Tettnang, Hallertau, Perle. Source: GAM. OG: 1060. Malt: Pilsner malt, CaraPils malt, Munich malt, CaraMunich malt, Wheat malt. Hops: Tettnang. Late hops: Saaz. Source: NACB. OG: 1054. Malt: Pilsner malt, Munich malt, CaraPils malt, CaraMunich II malt. Hops: Tettnang. Late hops: Hallertau. Source: 150/HB.

**Maibock**: ABV: 6.5%. Malt: Pale malt, Caramalt, Munich malt, Roast malt. Hops: Tettnang. Source: HB/GAM.

**Doppelbock**: ABV: 7.1%. Malt: Pale malt, Chocolate malt. Hops: Hallertau, Tettnang. Source: HB/GAM.

. *Summit Brewing Company, St. Paul, MN. Www.summitbrewing.com*

**Scandia Ale**: ABV: 4.8%. Malt: Pale malt, Wheat malt, Oat malt. Hops: Saaz. IBU: 17. °L: 5.3. Source: Web.

**Pilsener**: ABV: 5.0%. Malt: Pale malt, Caramel malt. Hops: Horizon, Vanguard, Saaz. IBU: 25. °L: 5. Source: Web.

**Dusseldorfer Style Alt Bier**: OG: 1050. Malt: Pale malt, Caramel malt, Wheat malt, Munich malt. Hops: Saaz, Northern Brewer, Tettnang. Source: GAM.

**Extra Special Bitter**: ABV: 5.1%. Malt: Golden Promise pale malt, Maris Otter pale malt. Hops: Fuggles, Target, Northdown. IBU: 50. °L: 26. Source: Web.

**Extra Pale Ale**: ABV: 5.3%. Malt: Pale malt, Caramel malt. Hops: Fuggles, Horizon, Cascade. IBU: 40-45. °L: 14. Source: Web. OG: 1048. Malt: Pale malt, Caramel malt. Hops: Eroica, Cascade, Fuggles. Source: GAM.

**Great Northern Porter**: ABV: 5.6%. Malt: Pale malt, Caramel malt, Black malt. Hops: Fuggles, Horizon, Cascade. IBU: 50. °L: 60. Source: Web. OG: 1048. Malt: Pale malt, Crystal malt, Black malt, Chocolate malt. Hops: Styrian Goldings. Late hops: Styrian Goldings. Source: NACB. OG: 1053. Malt: Pale malt, Caramel malt, Patent black malt. Hops: Eroica, Cascade, Fuggles. Source: GAM.

**Winter Ale**: OG: 1058. Malt: Pale malt, Crystal malt, Patent black malt. Hops: Willamette. Late hops: Fuggles, Tettnang. IBU: 36. °L: 42. Source: GAM/150/Web.

**India Pale Ale**: ABV: 6.4%. Malt: Pale malt, Caramel malt, Special B malt. Hops: Northern Brewer, Goldings. Dry hops: Goldings. IBU: 60-65. °L: 24. Source: Web. ABW: 4.7%. Malt: Pale malt, Caramel malt. Hops: Goldings. Source: GAM.

**Maibock / Heimertingen Maibock**: ABV: 6.7%. Malt: Pale malt, Munich malt. Hops: Saaz, Mount Hood. IBU: 40. °L: 10. Source: GAM/Web.

**Oktoberfest**: ABV: 7.4%. Malt: Pale malt, Munich malt, Caramel malt. Hops: Northern Brewer, Saaz, Tettnang. IBU: 25. °L: 15. Source: Web.

. *Tabernash Brewing Company, Longmont, CO*

**Tabernnash Weiss**: OG: 1045. Malt: Pale malt, Wheat malt, CaraPils malt. Hops: Hallertau. Late hops: Spalt. Source: NACB.

### . TableRock Brewpub and Grill, Boise, ID

**TableRock Nut Brown Ale**: OG: 1054. Malt: Pale malt, Dextrin malt, Carastan malt, Brown malt, Crystal malt, Patent black malt, Chocolate malt. Hops: Willamette. Source: 150.

### . Ten Springs Brewing Company, Saratoga, NY

**Fat Bear Stout**: OG: 1048. Malt: Pale malt, Roast barley, Crystal malt, Chocolate malt. Hops: Target. Late hops: Fuggles. Source: NACB.

### . Terrapin Beer Company, Athens, GA. Www.terrapinbeer.com

**Golden Ale**: ABV: 5%. Malt: Pale malt, Vienna malt, Wheat malt, Munich malt, Flaked maize. Hops: Mount Hood, Santiam, Cascade. IBU: 21. Source: Web.

**Rye Pale Ale**: OG: 1054. Malt: Pale malt, Rye malt, Victory / Biscuit malt, Munich malt, Honey malt. Hops: Magnum. Late hops: Fuggles, Goldings, Cascade. Late hops: Amarillo. IBU: 45. Source: 150/Web.

**All-American Imperial Pilsner**: ABV: 7.5%. Malt: Pale malt, CaraPils malt. Hops: Warrior, Mount Hood, Santiam, Liberty. Dry hops: Saaz. IBU: 75. Source: Web.

**Wake-n-Bake Coffee Oatmeal Stout**: ABV: 7.5%. Malt: Pale malt, Chocolate malt, Black malt, Flaked oats, Roast barley, Flaked barley. Hops: Columbus, Northern Brewer. IBU: 75. Source: Web.

**Big Hoppy Monster**: ABV: 8%. Malt: Pale malt, Crystal malts, Munich malt. Hops: Ahtanum, Centennial, Simcoe, Warrior, Cascade. IBU: 75. Source: Web.

**Rye Squared**: ABV: 8.5%. Malt: Pale malt, Rye malt, Biscuit malt, Munich malt, Honey malt. Hops: Amarillo, Goldings, Fuggles, Magnum, Cascade. IBU: 80. Source: Web.

Note: I'd like to thank Jim Smith of Atlanta who provided myself, my wife and some fellow members of Scottish Craft Brewers with some Terrapin beers and US hops during a pleasant evening in Edinburgh in 2006.

### . Thirsty Dog Brewing Company, Independence, OH. Www.thirstydog.com

**Golding's Retriever**: °P: 15. Malt: Caramel malt, Munich malt. Hops: Goldings, Cascade: IBU: 26. Source: Web.

**Old Leghumper Porter**: OG: 1061. Malt: Pale malt, Munich malt, Crystal malt, Chocolate malt, Flaked barley. Hops: Northern Brewer. Late hops: Liberty. Source: 150.

### . Three Floyds Brewing Company, Munster, IA. Www.threefloydspub.com

**Xtra Pale Ale**: OG: 1045. Malt: Pale malt, Crystal malt, Wheat malt. Hops: Goldings, Cascade. Late hops: Cascade. Source: NACB.

**Alpha King Pale Ale**: OG: 1062. Malt: Pale malt, CaraPils malt, Melanoidin malt, CaraMunich malt, Caramel malt, Special B malt, Red wheat. Hops: Warrior, Centennial.

Late hops: Cascade. Dry hops: Cascade, Columbus, Centennial. IBU: 66. Source: 150/Web.

**Dreadnought**: OG: 1084. Malt: Pale malt, Melanoidin malt. Hops: Warrior. Late hops: Centennial, Cascade. Dry hops: Cascade. Source: 150.

. Tin Whiskers Brewing Co., Saint Paul, MN. Www.twbrewing.com

**Parity Pilsner**: OG: 1050. Malt: 6-row pale malt, Pilsner malt, Flaked maize. Hops: Liberty. Late hops: Liberty, Crystal. Yeast: Wyeast #2035. IBU: 42.5. Source: Web.

**Schottky Pumpkin Ale**: OG: 1052. Malt: Maris Otter pale malt, Victory malt, Crystal 80L malt, Crystal 60L malt, Munich malt. Hops: Nugget. Others: Pumpkins, Pumpkin pie spices. Yeast: Wyeast #1272. IBU: 28.5. Source: Web.

**Wheatstone Bridge**: OG: 1054. Malt: Pale malt, White wheat malt, Honey. Hops: Glacier. Others: Chamomile flowers. Yeast: Wyeast #1010. IBU: 12.7. Source: Web.

**Ampere Amber**: OG: 1054. Malt: Pale malt, Roast barley, Chocolate malt, Crystal 35L malt, Melanoidin malt. Hops: Northern Brewer. Late hops: Perle, Willamette. Yeast: Wyeast #2112. IBU: 48.5. Source: Web.

**Flip Switch IPA**: OG: 1054. Malt: Maris Otter pale malt, Crystal 15L malt, Crystal 35L malt, CaraPils malt. Hops: Chinook. Late hops: Warrior, Centennial, Citra. Dry hops: Warrior, Citra. Yeast: Wyeast #1272. IBU: 63.9. Source: Web.

**Lecky Scottish Ale**: OG: 1063. Malt: Maris Otter pale malt, Organic Amber malt, Brown malt, Chocolate malt, Peat-smoked malt. Hops: Nugget. Late hops: Goldings. Yeast: Wyeast #1084. IBU: 36. Source: Web.

**Short Circuit Stout**: OG: 1065. Malt: Maris Otter pale malt, Oat malt, Roast barley, Chocolate malt, Black malt, Crystal 120L malt, Flaked barley, Lactose. Hops: Nugget. Late hops: Goldings. Yeast: Wyeast #1084. IBU: 55. Source: Web.

**Watts Wheat Wine**: OG: 1075. Malt: White wheat malt, Pilsner malt, Flaked wheat. Hops: Vanguard. Others: Orange peel, Chamomile, Peppercorns, Coriander. Yeast: Wyeast #1010 and Wyeast #3844. IBU: 15. Source: Web.

**Barrel Shifter Porter**: OG: 1076. Malt: Maris Otter pale malt, White wheat malt, Chocolate malt, Caramel 120L malt. Hops: Chinook. Late hops: Goldings. Others: White American oak, Medium toast cherrywood. Yeast: Wyeast #1084. Source: Web.

. *Tommyknocker Brewery, Idaho Springs, CO. Www.tommyknocker.com*

**Maple Nut Brown**: OG: 1055-56. Malt: Pale malt, CaraMunich malt, Crystal malt, Chocolate malt, Munich malt, Maple syrup. Hops: Perle. Late hops: Liberty, Cascade. Source: BC.

**Imperial Nut Brown**: OG: 1080. Malt: Pale malt, Munich malt, Crystal malt, Chocolate malt, Maple syrup. Hops: Willamette. Source: 150/Web.

**Butt Head Bock**: ABV: 8.2%. Malt: Munich malt, Caramel malt, Chocolate malt. Hops: Hallertau. Source: Web.

### . Traverse Brewing Company, Williamsburg, MI

**Old Mission Lighthouse Ale**: OG: 1048. Malt: Pale malt, Crystal malt, Wheat malt. Hops: Cluster. Late hops: Cascade. Source: NACB.

### . Tröegs Brewing Company, Harrisburg, PA

**HopBack Amber Ale**: OG: 1063. Malt: Pilsner malt, Crystal malt, Chocolate malt. Hops: Nugget. Late hops: Nugget, Liberty, Simcoe. Source: 150.

**Nugget Nectar**: ABV: 7.5%. Notes: Based on HopBack Amber Ale but "cranked to 11". Source: BA.

### . Trout River Brewing Company, Lyndonville, VT

**Rainbow Red Ale**: OG: 1047. Malt: Pale malt, Crystal malts, Roast barley. Hops: Northern Brewer. Late hops: Cascade. Source: 150/BYO[28].

### . Tun Tavern Brewing Company, Abington, PA

**Tun Tavern Lager**: ABW: 3.56%. Malt: Caramel malt, Munich malt. Hops: Saaz, Mount Hood. Source: GAM.

### . Tupper's Hop Pocket Brewing Company

**Tupper's Hop Pocket Ale**: OG: 1055. Malt: Pale malt, Crystal malt, Wheat malt. Hops: Mount Hood. Late hops: Mount Hood, Cascade. Dry hops: Cascade. Source: NACB. Note: Brewed by Old Dominion.

### . Turtle Mountain Brewing Company, Rio Rancho, NM.
Www.turtlemountainbrewing.com

**Red Rye**: OG: 1048. Malt: Flaked rye. IBU: 20. Source: Web.

**Fat Squirrel Pale Ale**: OG: 1052. Hops: Goldings. IBU: 45. Source: Web.

**Steam Ale**: OG: 1052. Hops: Northern Brewer, Cascade. IBU: 35. Source: Web.

### . Uinta Brewing, Salt Lake City, UT

**Sum'r Organic Summer Ale**: ABV: 4%. Hops: Sorachi Ace. Source: BA.

**King's Peak Porter**: OG: 1052. Malt: Pale malt, Crystal malt, Munich malt, Chocolate malt, Black malt, Roast barley. Hops: Chinook. Late hops: Willamette, Tettnang. Source: NACB.

---

[28] http://byo.com/recipe/1490.html

**Burly Irish Red**: OG: 1045. Malt: Maris Otter pale malt, Roast barley, Light crystal malt, Dark crystal malt, Barley. Hops: Perle. IBU: 16. SRM: 12.5. Source: Web.

**New World Silk Ale**: OG: 1046. Malt: Maris Otter pale malt, Crystal malt, Red wheat malt, Chocolate malt. Hops: Hallertau. IBU: 20. SRM: 10.3. Source: Web.

**Grand Slam Baseball Beer**: OG: 1048. Malt: Maris Otter pale malt, Red wheat malt, Chocolate malt. Hops: Perle. IBU: 18. SRM: 6. Source: Web.

**Curacao White Beer / Wit**: OG: 1048. Malt: Pilsner malt, Red wheat malt. Hops: Horizon, Tettnang, Saaz. Others: Sweet and bitter curacao orange peel, Coriander. Note: Sour mashed. IBU: 15. SRM: 2.5. Source: Web.

**Betelguise / Beetlejuice**: OG: 1048. Malt: Pilsner malt, Red wheat malt. Hops: Perle, Hallertau. IBU: 12. SRM: 2.8. Note: Sour mashed. Source: Web.

**Helles Alt**: OG: 1048. Malt: Munich malt. Hops: Tettnang. IBU: 15. SRM: 6. Source: Web.

**Handsome Mick's Stout**: OG: 1050. Malt: Maris Otter pale malt, Roast barley, Crystal malt, Oat malt, Chocolate malt, Barley. Hops: Perle, Fuggles. IBU: 18. SRM: 28. Note: Malt is smoked over Apple, Maple and Hickory smudge. Source: Web.

**Ethan Alien Vermont Lager**: OG: 1052. Malt: Pilsner malt, Caramalt, Light crystal malt, Barley. Hops: Saaz, Perle. IBU: 25. SRM: 3.5. Source: Web.

**Dogbite Bitter ESB**: OG: 1052. Malt: Maris Otter pale malt, Crystal malt, Red wheat malt, Chocolate malt. Hops: Goldings, Fuggles. IBU: 40. SRM: 8.5. Source: Web.

**Bombay Grab India Ale**: OG: 1052. Malt: Maris Otter pale malt, Crystal malt, Red wheat malt. Hops: Magnum, Cascade, Chinook. IBU: 90. SRM: 6. Source: Web. Malt: Pale malt, Wheat malt, Crystal 50L malt, CaraPils malt. Hops: Cascade. Late hops: Perle. Dry hops: Cascade. IBU: 75. SRM: 8. Source: SMB.

**Spuyten Duyvil / Spittin' Devil**: OG: 1052. Malt: Maris Otter pale malt, Rye malt, Crystal malt. Hops: Simcoe, Hallertau. IBU: 26. SRM: 11. Note: Sour mashed. Brettanomyces. Source: Web.

**Vermont Smoked Porter**: OG: 1055. Malt: Pale malt, Smoked malt, Patent black malt, Chocolate malt. Hops: Chinook. Late hops: Goldings. Source: 150.

**Rocktoberfest**: OG: 1056. Malt: Pilsner malt, Crystal malt, Pale crystal malt, Barley. Hops: Hallertau. IBU: 18. SRM: 3.5. Source: Web.

**Blackwatch IPA**: OG: 1058. Malt: Maris Otter pale malt,Crystal malt, Red wheat malt, Chocolate malt. Hops: Simcoe, Fuggles. IBU: 60. SRM: 18. Source: Web.

**Forbidden Fruit**: OG: 1070. Malt: Pilsner malt, Caramalt, Red wheat malt. Hops: Perle. Others: Raspberries. IBU: 10. SRM: 5. Notes: Sour mashed. Oak aged. Source: Web.

**The Wee Heavy**: OG: 1101. Malt: Maris Otter pale malt, Roast barley, Barley. Hops: Perle, Goldings. IBU: 26. SRM: 12.5. Source: Web. OG: 1097. Malt: Pale malt, Roast barley. Hops: Goldings / Fuggles. Late hops: Fuggles / Goldings. IBU: 75. SRM: 15. Source: SMB.

### . Victory Brewing Company, Downingtown, PA

**Prima Pils**: OG: 1050. Malt: Lager malt, CaraPils malt, Vienna malt. Hops: Hallertau. Late hops: Spalt. Source: NACB.

**Hop Devil India Pale Ale**: OG: 1067-69. Malt: Pilsner malt, Crystal malt, Munich malt, CaraMunich malt. Hops: Centennial. Late hops: Goldings, Cascade. Dry hops: Cascade. Source: BC.

**Golden Monkey**: OG: 1085. Malt: Pilsner malt, Sucrose. Hops: Tettnang, Saaz. Others: Coriander. IBU: 28-30. Source: BLAM.

### . Wachusett Brewing Company, Winchester, MA

**Quinn's Irish-Style Ale**: OG: 1048. Malt: Pale malt, Crystal malt, Black malt, Brown malt, Roast barley. Hops: Target. Late hops: Northern Brewer, Goldings. Source: NACB.

### . Weidman's Brew Pub, Fort Smith, AR

**Rope Swing Red Ale**: OG: 1036. Malt: Pale malt, Caramel malt. Source: GAM.

**Naked Nut Brown Ale**: OG: 1042. Malt: Pale malt, Caramel malt, Roast barley, Chocolate malt. Source: GAM.

**Danny Boy Stout**: OG: 1050. Malt: Pale malt, Caramel malt, Roast barley, Chocolate malt, Black malt. Source: GAM.

### . Whale Tale Brewing Company, Old Orchard Beach, ME

**Whale Tail Brown Ale**: OG: 1043. Malt: Pale malt, Crystal malt, Black malt, Chocolate malt, Brown malt, Sugar. Hops: Fuggles. Late hops: Cascade. Source: NACB.

### . Widmer Bros. Brewing Company, Portland, OR. Www.widmer.com

**Citra Blonde Summer Ale**: ABV: 4.3%. Dry hops: Citra. Source: BA.

**Widmer Summerbräu**: OG: 1045. Malt: Lager malt, CaraPils malt, Vienna malt, Wheat malt. Hops: Spalt. Late hops: Tettnang. Source: NACB.

**Widmer Hefeweizen**: ABV: 4.9%. Malt: Pale malt, Wheat malt, Caramel malt, Munich malt. Hops: Alchemy. Late hops: Willamette, Cascade. IBU: 30. Source: Web. OG: 1047. Malt: Caramel malt, Munich malt. Hops: Cascade, Tettnang. Source: GAM.

**Blackbier**: ABW: 5%. Malt: Caramel malt, Patent black malt, Roast barley, Chocolate malt. Hops: Perle, Tettnang. Source: GAM.

**Drop Top Amber**: ABV: 5%. Malt: Pale malt, Honey malt, Caramel malt, Extra Special malt. Hops: Alchemy, Simcoe. IBU: 20. Source: Web.

**W'07 Pale Ale**: ABV: 5.4%. Malt: Pale malt, CaraVienne malt, CaraPils malt, Caramel malt. Hops: Alchemy. Late hops: Alchemy, Summit. Dry hops: Summit, Chinook. IBU: 34. Source: Web.

**Okto**: ABV: 5.5%. Malt: Pale malt, CaraPils malt, CaraMunich malt, Extra Special malt. Hops: Alchemy. Late hops: Mount Hood, Tettnang. IBU: 25. Source: Web.

**Snowplow**: ABV: 5.5%. Malt: Pale malt, Wheat malt, Caramel malt, CaraPils malt, Oat malt, Roast barley. Hops: Alchemy. Late hops: Willamette. IBU: 28. Source: Web.

**Hop Jack Pale Ale**: OG: 1056. Malt: Pale malt, Vienna malt, Crystal malt, Munich malt, Dextrin malt. Hops: Willamette, Cascade. Late hops: Cascade, Centennial. Source: 150.

**Broken Halo IPA**: ABV: 6%. Malt: Pale malt, Caramel malt, CaraPils malt. Hops: Alchemy, Zeus, Cascade. IBU: 45. Source: Web.

**Snowplough Milk Stout**: OG: 1068. Malt: Pale malt, CaraPils malt, Patent black malt, Crystal malt, Wheat malt, Flaked oats, Roast barley, Lactose. Hops: Magnum. Late hops: Willamette. Source: 150.

**TEAser XPA**: Hops: Teamaker. Source: BA.

### . Wild Boar, Atlanta, GA

**Classic Pilsner**: OG: 1049. Malt: Pale malt, CaraPils malt. Hops: Saaz. Source: GAM.

**Black Forest Wheat**: Malt: Wheat malt, Chocolate malt. Others: Cherry puree. Source: GAM.

**Special Amber**: OG: 1052. Malt: Pale malt, Caramel malt. Hops: Cascade, Tettnang. Source: GAM.

**Wild Wheat**: OG: 1052. Malt: Pale malt, Wheat malt. Hops: Tettnang. Source: GAM.

**Wild Winter**: OG: 1052. Malt: Caramel malt, Chocolate malt. Hops: Cascade. Source: GAM.

### . Wild Goose Brewery, Frederick, MD

**Golden Ale**: OG: 1044. Malt: Pale malt, Wheat malt. Hops: Cascade, Hallertau, Goldings, Tettnang. Source: GAM.

**India Pale Ale**: OG: 1050. Malt: Pale malt, Crystal malt, Wheat malt. Hops: Target. Late hops: Fuggles, Cascade. Source: NACB. OG: 1056. Malt: Pale malt, Wheat malt, Crystal malt. Hops: Cascade, Willamette, Goldings, Tettnang. Source: GAM.

**Amber**: OG: 1051. Malt: Pale malt, Wheat malt, Crystal malt, Chocolate malt. Hops: Willamette, Cascade, Tettnang, Hallertau. Source: GAM.

**Porter**: OG: 1054. Malt: Pale malt, Patent black malt, Crystal malt, Chocolate malt. Hops: Cascade, Willamette, Goldings, Tettnang, Hallertau. Source: GAM.

**Spring Wheat Ale**: OG: 1058. Malt: Pale malt, Crystal malt. Hops: Saaz, Willamette, Cascade. Source: GAM.

**Winter Ale**: ABW: 6.4%. Malt: Pale malt, Roast barley, Crystal malt. Hops: Cascade, Willamette, Goldings, Fuggles. Source: GAM.

**Wild Goose Oatmeal Stout**: OG: 1065. Malt: Pale malt, Flaked oats, Roast barley, Munich malt, Crystal malt, Black malt, Chocolate malt. Hops: Cascade, Willamette, Tettnang. Late hops: Cascade, Willamette. Source: NACB.

## . William & Scott, Huntington Beach, CA

**Rhino Chasers Peach Honey Wheat**: OG: 1049. Malt: Pale malt, Roast wheat malt, Munich malt. Hops: Cluster, Mount Hood, Tettnang. Source: GAM.

**Rhino Chasers American Amber Ale**: OG: 1050. Malt: Pale malt, Caramel malt. Hops: Mount Hood, Cascade, Fuggles, Willamette. Source: GAM.

**Rhino Chasers Dark Roasted Lager**: OG: 1051. Malt: Pale malt, Caramel malt, Patent black malt, CaraPils malt. Hops: Saaz, Mount Hood, Cluster, Perle. Source: GAM.

**Rhino Chasers Winterful**: OG: 1052. Malt: Pale malt, Caramel malt, Patent black malt, CaraPils malt. Hops: Cascade, Liberty, Yakima. Source: GAM.

## . Woodstock Brewing Company, Kingston, NY

**St. James Ale**: OG: 1042. Malt: Pale malt, Caramel malt, Vienna malt. Hops: Cluster, Cascade. Source: GAM.

**Hudson Lager**: OG: 1051. Malt: Pale malt, Munich malt. Hops: Tettnang, Hallertau. Source: GAM.

**Big Indian Porter**: OG: 1070. Malt: Pale malt, Chocolate malt, Patent black malt, Crystal malt. Hops: Cluster, Tettnang, Hallertau. Source: GAM.

**Ichabod Crane Holiday Lager**: OG: 1098. Malt: Pale malt, Caramel malt, Munich malt. Hops: Cluster, Hallertau. Others: Nutmeg, Cinnamon, Cloves, Pumpkins. Source: GAM.

## . Wynkoop Brewing Company, Denver, CO

**Railyard Ale**: OG: 1045. Malt: Pale malt, Wheat malt, Crystal malt. Hops: Goldings. Late hops: Cascade. Dry hops: Cascade. Source: NACB. ABV: 4.2%. Malt: Pale malt, Crystal malt, Caramel malt, Munich malt. Hops: Tettnang, Hallertau. Source: GAM.

**Silverback Pale Ale**: ABV: 5.5%. Hops: Centennial. Others: Grains of Paradise. Source: BA.

## . Yakima Brewing and Maltng Company, Yakima, WA

**Grant's Celtic Ale**: OG: 1034. Malt: Pale malt, Caramel malt, Patent black malt. Hops: Cascade. Source: GAM.

**Grant's Apple Honey Ale**: OG: 1044. Malt: Pale malt, Honey. Hops: Cascade. Others: Apple concentrate. Source: GAM.

**Bert Grant's Hefeweizen**: OG: 1045. Malt: Light Pilsner malt, CaraPils malt, Crystal malt, Wheat malt. Hops: Hallertau. Late hops: Hallertau. Source: NACB.

**Grant's India Pale Ale**: OG: 1046. Malt: Pale malt. Hops: Galena, Cascade. Source: GAM.

**Grant's Weis Beer**: OG: 1046. Malt: Pale malt, Wheat malt. Hops: Cascade. Source: GAM.

**Grant's Scottish Ale**: ABW: 4.7%. Malt: Pale malt, Caramel malt. Hops: Cascade. Source: GAM.

**Grant's Perfect Porter**: OG: 1048. Malt: Pale malt, Caramel malt, Patent black malt, Chocolate malt, Peat-smoked malt. Hops: Willamette. Source: GAM.

**Bert Grant's Fresh Hop Ale**: OG: 1053-54. Malt: Pale malt, Crystal malt. Hops: Galena. Late hops: Willamette, Cascade. Dry hops: Cascade. Source: BC.

**Grant's Imperial Stout**: OG: 1070. Malt: Pale malt, Patent black malt, Caramel malt, Honey. Hops: Galena, Cascade. Source: GAM.

. *Ybor City Brewing Company, Tampa, FL*

**Calusa Wheat Beer**: OG: 1040. Malt: Wheat malt, Lager malt, CaraPils malt. Hops: Hallertau. Late hops: Hallertau. Source: NACB.

. *Yellow Rose Brewing Company, San Antonio, TX*

**Honcho Grande Brown Ale**: OG: 1048. Malt: Pale malt, Crystal malt, Black malt, Chocolate malt. Hops: Willamette. Source: NACB.

. *D. G. Yuengling & Son, Pottsville, PA*

**Yuengling Porter**: OG: 1048-49. Malt: Pale malt, Corn grits / Flaked maize, Crystal malt, Black malt. Hops: Cluster, Cascade. Late hops: Cascade. Source: CB.

# Vietnam

. *B.G.I. Tien Giang, Da Nang*

**33 Export**: OG: 1052. Malt: Rice, Lager malt, Crystal malt, Rice syrup. Hops: Tettnang. Late hops: Saaz, Tettnang. Source: CB.

# Wales

. *Craft Brewing Association: www.craftbrewing.org.uk*

. *Aberystwyth Ales, Llanrhystyd*

**Dinas Dark Mild**: OG: 1036. Malt: Maris Otter pale malt, Crystal malt. Hops: Goldings. Source: RP4/5.

**Dinas Draught**: OG: 1038. Malt: Maris Otter pale malt, Crystal malt. Hops: Goldings, Target. Source: RP4/5.

**Aberystwyth Premium**: OG: 1046. Malt: Maris Otter pale malt. Hops: Goldings, Target' Source: RP4/5.

. *Bragdy Ceredigion, Pentregat*

**Gwrach Ddu** (b-c): ABV: 4%. Malt: Maris Otter pale malt, Crystal malt, Amber malt. Hops: Northern Brewer or First Gold. Source: JE2/3/4/5.

**Barcud Coch** (b-c): ABV: 4.3%. Malt: Maris Otter pale malt, Crystal malt, Amber malt. Hops: Challenger, Bramling Cross, optional Target. Source: JE1/2. Hops: Challenger, First Gold/Goldings. Source: JE3/4/5.

**Ddraig Aur** (b-c): ABV: 5%. Malt: Maris Otter pale malt, Crystal malt, Amber malt. Hops: Challenger. Source: JE2. ABV: 4.3%. Source: JE3. ABV: 4.2%. Hops: Challenger, Fuggles. Source: JE4/5.

**Blodeuwedd** (b-c): ABV: 4.5%. Malt: Pale malt. Hops: Hallertau. Source: JE3/4/5.

**Cwrw 2000** (b-c): ABV: 5%. Malt: Maris Otter pale malt, Crystal malt, Pale chocolate malt, Amber malt. Hops: Challenger, Fuggles. Source: JE4/5.

**Nadolig** (b-c): ABV: 6.2%. Malt: Maris Otter pale malt, Crystal malt, Pale chocolate malt, Amber malt. Hops: Challenger, Fuggles, Goldings. Others: Cinnamon, Nutmeg, Other Spices. Source: JE4/5.

**Yr Hen Darw Du** (b-c): ABV: 6.2%. Malt: Maris Otter pale malt, Crystal malt, Amber malt, Chocolate malt, Black malt. Hops: Challenger, optional Target. Source: JE1/2/3/4/5.

. *Bragdy Ynys Môn, Llangefni*

**Medra** (b-c): ABV: 4%. Malt: Maris Otter pale malt, Crystal malt. Hops: Cascade, Fuggles. Source: JE4/5.

**Wennol** (b-c): ABV: 4.1%. Malt: Maris Otter pale malt, Crystal malt. Hops: Cascade. Source: JE3/4/5.

**Sospan Fach** (b-c): ABV: 4.3%. Malt: Pale malt, Crystal malt. Hops: First Gold. Source: JE4/5.

**Tarw Du** (b-c): ABV: 4.5%. Malt: Maris Otter pale malt, Crystal malt, Chocolate malt, Black malt, Roast barley. Hops: Fuggles, Cascade. Source: JE3/4/5.

**Amnesia** (b-c): ABV: 4.9%. Malt: Maris Otter pale malt, Crystal malt. Hops: Fuggles, Cascade. Source: JE3/4/5.

### . S. A. Brain & Company, Cardiff

**Red Dragon Dark / Dark**: OG: 1035. Malt: Pale malt, Chocolate malt, Invert sugar, Glucose. Hops: Fuggles, Goldings. Source: RP1/2/3/4/5.

**MA**: OG: 1035. Malt: Pale malt, Chocolate malt, Crystal malt, Invert sugar, Glucose. Hops: Goldings. Source: RP4/5.

**Bitter / Light**: OG: 1035. Malt: Pale malt, Crystal malt, Invert sugar, Glucose. Hops: Fuggles, Goldings. Source: RP1/2/3/4/5.

**Bread of Heaven**: ABV: 4%. Hops: Styrian Goldings, Cascade, Target. Source: W.

**Brains Traditional Welsh Ale**: OG: 1041-43. Malt: Pale malt, Crystal malt, Sugar. Hops: Fuggles. Late hops: Fuggles, Goldings. Source: CB.

**SA Best Bitter**: OG: 1042. Malt: Pale malt, Crystal malt, Invert sugar, Glucose. Hops: Fuggles, Goldings. Source: RP1/2/3/4/5.

**SA Gold**: ABV: 4.7%. Late hops: Cascade, Styrian Goldings. Source: WB.

### . The Breconshire Brewery, Brecon

**Golden Valley** (b-c): ABV: 4.2%. Malt: Optic pale malt, Crystal malt. Hops: Progress. Source: JE5/6.

**Brecknock Best** (b-c): ABV: 4.5%. Malt: Optic pale malt, Dark crystal malt, Black malt. Hops: Bramling Cross, Pilot. Source: JE6.

**Red Dragon** (b-c): ABV: 4.7%. Malt: Optic pale malt, Crystal malt, Torrefied wheat. Hops: First Gold, Goldings, Pioneer, Susan. Source: JE5. Malt: Optic pale malt, Dark crystal malt, Wheat malt. Hops: Goldings, Pioneer, First Gold. Source: JE6.

**Ramblers Ruin** (b-c): ABV: 5%. Malt: Optic pale malt, Crystal malt, Black malt. Hops: First Gold, Goldings, Progress. Source: JE5/6.

**Winter Beacon** (b-c): ABV: 5.3%. Malt: Optic pale malt, Crystal malt, Wheat malt, Black malt, Low colour malt. Hops: Goldings, Fuggles, First Gold. Source: JE6.

### . Bullmastiff Brewery, Cardiff

**Brewery Bitter / Bitter**: OG: 1036. Malt: 85% Maris Otter pale malt, 15% Crystal malt, 5% Sugar. Hops: Goldings. Source: RP3/4/5.

**Best Bitter**: OG: 1040. Malt: 85% Maris Otter pale malt, 15% Crystal malt, 5% Sugar. Hops: Goldings. Source: RP3/4/5.

**Ebony Dark**: OG: 1040. Malt: 85% Pipkin pale malt, 6% Crystal malt, 9% Chocolate malt, 5% Dark sugar. Hops: Fuggles. Source: RP3/4/5.

**Son of a Bitch**: OG: 1062. Malt: 90% Maris Otter pale malt, 10% Crystal malt, 5% Sugar. Hops: Goldings. Source: RP3/4/5.

### . *Bragdy Ceredigion, Ceredigion*

**Gwrach Ddu** (b-c): ABV: 4%. Malt: Maris Otter pale malt, Crystal malt, Amber malt. Hops: First Gold. Source: JE6.

**Draig Aur** (b-c): ABV: 4.2%. Malt: Maris Otter pale malt, Crystal malt, Amber malt. Hops: Fuggles, Challenger. Source: JE6.

**Barcud Coch** (b-c): ABV: 4.3%. Malt: Maris Otter pale malt, Crystal malt, Amber malt. Hops: Fuggles, Challenger. Source: JE6.

**Blodeuwedd** (b-c): ABV: 4.5%. Malt: Pale malt. Hops: Hallertau. Source: JE6.

**Cwrw 2000** (b-c): ABV: 5%. Malt: Maris Otter pale malt, Crystal malt, Amber malt, Pale chocolate malt. Hops: Challenger, Fuggles. Source: JE6.

**Nadolig** (b-c): ABV: 6.2%. Malt: Maris Otter pale malt, Crystal malt, Amber malt, Pale chocolate malt. Hops: Challenger, Fuggles, Goldings. Others: Spices, Cinnamon, Nutmeg. Source: JE6.

**Yr Hen Darw Du** (b-c): ABV: 6.2%. Malt: Maris Otter pale malt, Crystal malt, Amber malt, Chocolate malt, Black malt. Hops: Challenger. Source: JE6.

### . *Conwy Brewery, Conwy*

**Castle Bitter / Cwrw Castell** (b-c): ABV: 3.8%. Malt: Maris Otter pale malt, Crystal malt, Chocolate malt, Wheat malt. Hops: Pioneer, Cascade. Source: JE6.

**Sun Dance / Dawns Haul** (b-c): ABV: 4%. Malt: Low colour Maris Otter pale malt, Wheat malt. Hops: Styrian Goldings. Source: JE6.

**Celebration Ale / Cwrw Gwledd** (b-c): ABV: 4.2%. Malt: Maris Otter pale malt, Crystal malt, Chocolate malt. Hops: Cascade. Source: JE5.

**Welsh Pride / Balchder Cymru** (b-c): ABV: 4.4%. Malt: Maris Otter pale malt, Crystal malt. Hops: Challenger, Goldings. Source: JE6.

**Honey Fayre / Cwrw Mêl** (b-c): ABV: 4.5%. Malt: Maris Otter pale malt, Crystal malt, Wheat malt, Welsh honey. Hops: Pioneer, Challenger. Source: JE6.

**Special / Arbennig** (b-c): ABV: 4.5%. Malt: Maris Otter pale malt, Crystal malt, Wheat malt, Roast barley. Hops: Pioneer, Challenger. Source: JE6.

**Telford Porter** (b-c): ABV: 5.6%. Malt: Maris Otter pale malt, Crystal malt, Roast barley. Hops: Pioneer, Challenger, Goldings. Source: JE6.

## Crown Buckley, Llanelli

**Buckley's Mild / Dark / 4X**: OG: 1032. Malt: Maris Otter pale malt, 8% Black malt, Wheat malt, Flaked maize. Hops: Challenger, Fuggles, Goldings, Hallertau Brewers Gold. Source: RP1.

**Buckley's Dark Mild**: OG: 1034. Malt: Maris Otter pale malt, 11% Black malt, Wheat malt/Torrefied wheat, optional Invert sugar. Hops: Challenger, Fuggles, Bramling Cross, Goldings, WGV. Source: RP.

**Crown Pale Ale**: OG: 1033. Malt: 80% Maris Otter pale malt and Pipkin pale malt, 8% Torrefied wheat, 12% Invert sugar. Hops: Challenger, Fuggles, Goldings. IBU: 20. EBC: 25. Source: RP4/5.

**Buckley's Best Bitter**: OG: 1036. Malt: Maris Otter pale malt, 8% Wheat malt, Flaked maize. Hops: Challenger, Fuggles, Goldings, Hallertau Brewers Gold, optional WGV. Source: RP1/2.

**Best Bitter**: OG: 1036. Malt: Maris Otter pale malt, Torrefied wheat, Invert sugar. Hops: Challenger, Fuggles, Goldings. Source: RP3/4/5.

**Crown SBB / Special Best Bitter**: OG: 1037. Malt: Maris Otter pale malt, 9-11% Torrefied wheat, Flaked barley, Invert sugar. Hops: Bramling Cross, Fuggles, Goldings, small % Saaz. Source: RP.

**James Buckley Ale**: OG: 1038. Malt: 98% Maris Otter pale malt and Pipkin pale malt, 2% Crystal malt. Hops: Challenger, Fuggles, Goldings. IBU: 21. EBC: 26. Source: RP4.

**Crown 1041**: OG: 1041. Malt: Maris Otter pale malt, 14% Crystal malt, Flaked maize. Hops: Bramling Cross, Fuggles, Goldings, Saaz. Source: RP1.

**Reverend James Original Bitter**: OG: 1045. Malt: Maris Otter pale malt, Wheat malt / Torrefied wheat, Flaked maize, Invert sugar. Hops: Challenger, Bramling Cross, Fuggles, Goldings, WGV. Source: RP.

## Dyffryn Clwyd, Denbigh

**Cysur Bitter / Comfort Bitter**: OG: 1036. Malt: Halcyon pale malt, Crystal malt, Chocolate malt. Hops: Challenger. Source: RP4.

**Cwrw Castell / Castle Bitter**: OG: 1042. Malt: Halcyon pale malt, Crystal malt, Chocolate malt. Hops: Challenger. Source: RP4/5.

**Jolly Jack Tar Porter**: OG: 1045. Malt: Halcyon pale malt, Pale malt Chocolate malt, Roast barley. Hops: Challenger. Source: RP4/5.

**Pedwar Bawd / Four Thumbs**: OG: 1045. Malt: Halcyon pale malt, Crystal malt, Wheat malt. Hops: Challenger, Styrian Goldings. Source: RP4/5.

**De Laceys**: OG: 1062. Malt: Halcyon pale malt, Crystal malt, Pale chocolate malt. Hops: Challenger. Source: RP4.

### Evan Evans, Llandeilo

**FBA**: ABV: 4.5%. Hops: Perle, Goldings, Fuggles. Source: W.

### Felinfoel Brewery Company, Llanelli

**Dark**: OG: 1032. Malt: 75% Pipkin pale malt, 3% Crystal malt, 8-12% Torrefied wheat, 10-12% No.1 invert sugar, 0-2% Caramel. Hops: 20% Bramling Cross, 60% Challenger, 20% WGV. IBU: 28. EBC: 75. Source: RP.

**Bitter Ale**: OG: 1032. Malt: 85% Triumph pale malt, 15% Torrefied wheat, Invert sugar. Hops: Bramling Cross, Challenger, Fuggles. Source: RP1. Malt: 75% Pipkin pale malt, 3% Crystal malt, 8-12% Torrefied wheat, 10-14% No.1 invert sugar. Hops: 20% Bramling Cross, 60% Challenger, 20% WGV. IBU: 28. EBC: 20. Source: RP4/5.

**Cambrian Bitter**: OG: 1036. Malt: 85% Pipkin pale malt, 3% Crystal malt, 12% Torrefied wheat, Invert sugar. Hops: Bramling Cross, Challenger, WGV. IBU: 22. Source: RP2.

**Double Dragon**: OG: 1048. Malt: 85% Triumph pale malt, 15% Torrefied wheat, Invert sugar. Hops: Bramling Cross, Challenger, Fuggles. Source: RP1. Malt: 85% Pipkin pale malt, 3% Crystal malt, 12% Torrefied wheat, Invert sugar. Hops: Bramling Cross, Challenger, WGV. IBU: 25. Source: RP2. Malt: 75% Pipkin pale malt, 3% Crystal malt, 8-12% Torrefied wheat, 10-14% No.1 invert sugar. Hops: 20% Bramling Cross, 60% Challenger, 20% WGV. IBU: 25. EBC: 30. Source: RP4/5.

### Jolly Brewer, Wrexham

**Benno's** (b-c): ABV: 4%. Malt: Lager malt. Hops: Hallertau. Source: JE6.

**Suzanne's Stout** (b-c): ABV: 4%. Malt: Maris Otter pale malt, Roast barley, Flaked barley. Hops: Challenger, Target. Source: JE6.

**Taid's Garden** (b-c): ABV: 4.2%. Malt: Pilsner malt, Maris Otter pale malt, Wheat malt. Hops: Goldings, Fuggles, Hallertau. Source: JE6.

**Diod y Gymraef** (b-c): ABV: 4.5%. Malt: Maris Otter pale malt. Hops: Goldings, Fuggles. Source: JE6.

**Lucinda's Lager** (b-c): ABV: 4.5%. Malt: Pilsner malt, Wheat malt. Hops: Goldings, Fuggles, Hallertau. Source: JE6.

**Taffy's Tipple** (b-c): ABV: 4.5%. Malt: Maris Otter pale malt, Amber malt, Chocolate malt. Hops: Goldings, Challenger, Target, Northern Brewer. Source: JE6.

**Y Ddraig Goch** (b-c): ABV: 4.5%. Malt: Maris Otter pale malt, Chocolate malt, Flaked barley. Hops: Challenger, Goldings, Northern Brewer. Source: JE6.

**Tommy's** (b-c): ABV: 5.5%. Malt: Maris Otter pale malt, Chocolate malt. Hops: Hallertau. Source: JE6.

. *Kingstone, Tintern. Www.kingstonebrewery.co.uk*

**Tewdric's Tipple Ale**: ABV: 3.8%. Malt: Pale malt, Crystal malt. Hops: Fuggles, Northern Brewer. Source: Web.

**Challenger Ale**: ABV: 4%. Malt: Pale malt, Wheat malt. Hops: Challenger. Late hops: Challenger. Source: Web.

**Kingstone Gold Fine Ale**: ABV: 4%. Malt: Pale malt, Wheat malt. Hops: Fuggles, First Gold. Source: Web.

**No. 1 Premium Stout**: ABV: 4.4%. Malt: Pale malt, Roast barley, Flaked barley. Hops: Target, Challenger. Source: Web.

**Classic Bitter** (b-c): ABV: 4.5%. Malt: Maris Otter pale malt, Crystal malt. Hops: Cascade, Northern Brewer, Bramling Cross, optional Willamette. Source: JE6/Web.

**Millers Ale** (b-c): ABV: 4.9%. Malt: Maris Otter pale malt, Crystal malt, Wheat malt. Hops: Fuggles, First Gold. Source: JE6.

**Gatehouse Ale** (b-c): ABV: 5.1%. Malt: Maris Otter pale malt, Crystal malt. Hops: Challenger, Northern Brewer. Source: JE6.

**Abbey Ale**: ABV: 5.1%. Hops: Northern Brewer, Challenger. Source: Web.

. *Newmans Brewery, Caerphilly*

**Red Stag**: ABV: 3.6%. Hops: Cascade, First Gold. Source: W.

. *Otley, Pontypridd*

**O4 Colomb-O**: ABV: 4%. Hops: Columbus. Source: WB.

**O Rosie**: ABV: 4.3%. Others: Rosemary. Source: WB.

**Thai Bo**: ABV: 4.6%. Others: Lemon grass, Kaffir lime leaves, Galangal. Source: WB.

. *North Wales Brewery / Bragdy Gogledd Cymru, Abergele*
  *www.northwalesbrewery.net*

**Moelfre IPA**: ABV: 4%. Malt: Lager malt. Source: Web.

**Dandelion and Burdock**: ABV: 4%. Malt: Lager malt. Source: Web.

. *Pembroke Brewery Company, Pembroke*

**The Darklin**: OG: 1035. Malt: 85% Halcyon pale malt, 3% Chocolate malt, 12% Roast barley. Hops: Target, USA Fuggles. Source: RP4/5.

**Main Street Bitter**: OG: 1040. Malt: 95% Halcyon pale malt, 5% Crystal malt. Hops: Target, USA Fuggles. Source: RP4/5.

**Golden Hill Ale**: OG: 1045. Malt: 95% Halcyon pale malt, 5% Wheat malt. Hops: Target, USA Fuggles. Source: RP4/5.

### Pembrokeshire's own Ales, Narberth

**Benfro Bitter**: OG: 1036. Malt: Maris Otter pale malt, Crystal malt, 10% Torrefied wheat. Hops: Goldings, Hallertau. Source: RP1.

**Benfro Extra**: OG: 1041. Malt: Maris Otter pale malt, Crystal malt, 10% Torrefied wheat. Hops: Goldings, Hallertau. Source: RP1.

### Pen-Ion Cottage Brewery, Llanarth

**Lambs Gold** (b-c): ABV: 3.2%. Malt: Maris Otter pale malt, Light crystal malt. Hops: Target, Tettnang, Willamette. Source: JE6.

**Tipsy Tup** (b-c): ABV: 3.8%. Malt: Maris Otter pale malt, Light crystal malt. Hops: Target, Tettnang, Willamette. Source: JE6.

**Stock Ram** (b-c): ABV: 4.5%. Malt: Optic lager malt, Roast barley, Flaked barley. Hops: Target, Tettnang, Nugget. Source: JE6.

**Twin Ram** (b-c): ABV: 4.8%. Malt: Maris Otter pale malt, Light crystal malt. Hops: Target, Tettnang, Willamette. Source: JE6.

**Ewes Frolic** (b-c): ABV: 5.2%. Malt: Optic lager malt, Light crystal malt. Hops: Target, Tettnang, Sterling. Source: JE6.

**Ramnesia** (b-c): ABV: 5.6%. Malt: Maris Otter pale malt, Light crystal malt. Hops: Target, Tettnang, Willamette. Source: JE6.

### Plassey Brewery, Wrexham

**Farmhouse Bitter**: OG: 1039. Malt: 100% Pale malt, Coloured sugar. Hops: Fuggles. Source: RP1.

**Bitter**: OG: 1040. Malt: 95% Pale malt, 5% Crystal malt. Hops: Fuggles, Hallertau, Tettnang. Late hops: Tettnang. IBU: 32. Source: RP2/3/4/5.

**Fusilier** (b-c): ABV: 4.5%. Malt: Maris Otter pale malt, Crystal malt, Chocolate malt, CaraPils malt. Hops: Cascade, Styrian Goldings, Saaz, Pacific Gem. Source: JE3/4/5.

**Cwrw Tudno**: OG: 1047. Malt: 97% Pale malt, 2% Crystal malt, 1% Chocolate malt. Hops: Northern Brewer, Hallertau, Tettnang. Late hops: Tettnang. IBU: 35. Source: RP2/3/4/5/JHF.

**Dragon's Breath**: OG: 1060. Malt: Maris Otter pale malt, Crystal malt, Chocolate malt, Wheat malt, Roast barley. Hops: Styrian Goldings, Hallertau, Tettnang. EBC: 80. Source: RP4/5.

### Sam Powell Brewery, Newtown

**Best Bitter**: OG: 1034. Malt: 86% Pale malt, 5.5% Crystal malt, 1% Chocolate malt, 7.5% Wheat flour. Hops: Fuggles, Goldings. Source: RP1.

**Original Bitter**: OG: 1038. Malt: 86% Pale malt, 5.5% Crystal malt, 1% Chocolate malt, 7.5% Wheat flour. Hops: Fuggles, Goldings. Source: RP1.

**Samson Ale**: OG: 1048. Malt: 86.5% Pale malt, 5.5% Crystal malt, 1% Chocolate malt, 7% Wheat flour. Hops: Fuggles, Goldings. Source: RP1.

### . *Purple Moose, Porthmadog*

**Cwrw Eryri / Snowdonia Ale** (b-c): ABV: 3.6%. Malt: Maris Otter pale malt, Crystal malt, Torrefied wheat. Hops: Pioneer, Goldings, Hallertau. Source: JE6.

**Cwrw Madog / Madog's Ale** (b-c): ABV: 3.7%. Malt: Maris Otter pale malt, Dark crystal malt, Crystal malt, Torrefied wheat. Hops: Pioneer, Goldings. Source: JE6.

**Cwrw Glaslyn / Glaslyn Ale** (b-c): ABV: 4.2%. Malt: Maris Otter pale malt, Crystal malt, Torrefied wheat. Hops: Pioneer, Goldings, Hallertau. Source: JE6.

**Ochr Tywylly y Mws / Dark Side of the Moose** (b-c): ABV: 4.6%. Malt: Maris Otter pale malt, Roast barley, Dark crystal malt, Crystal malt. Hops: Pioneer, Bramling Cross. Source: JE6.

### . *Reckless Eric's Brewing & Supply Company, Cilfynydd*

**Retribution**: OG: 1034. Malt: 87% Maris Otter pale malt, 12% Crystal malt. Hops: Challenger. Late hops: USA Fuggles. Source: RP4.

**Renown**: OG: 1040. Malt: 85% Maris Otter pale malt, 10% Wheat malt, 5% Crystal malt. Hops: Challenger. Late hops: USA Fuggles. Source: RP4.

**Restoration**: OG: 1043. Malt: 81% Maris Otter pale malt, 6% Wheat malt, 6.5% Amber malt, 6.5% Crystal malt. Hops: Challenger. Late hops: USA Fuggles. Source: RP4.

**Recked 'Em**: OG: 1052. Malt: 80% Maris Otter pale malt, 6% Wheat malt, 6% Amber malt, 2% Roast malt, 6% Crystal malt. Hops: Challenger. Late hops: Fuggles. Source: RP4.

**Rejoice**: OG: 1060. Malt: 66% Maris Otter pale malt, 29% Crystal malt, 3% Roast barley, 1% Black malt. Hops: Challenger. Late hops: USA Fuggles. Source: RP4.

### . *Snowdonia Brewery Company, Gellilydan*

**Mel Y Moelwyn**: OG: 1037. Malt: Maris Otter pale malt, Crystal malt, Black malt. Hops: Fuggles, Goldings. Source: RP3.

**Choir Porter**: OG: 1045. Malt: Maris Otter pale malt, Crystal malt, Black malt. Hops: Fuggles. Source: RP3.

**Snowdon**: OG: 1050. Malt: Maris Otter pale malt, Crystal malt. Hops: Goldings. Late hops: Goldings. Source: RP3.

### . *Warcop, St. Brides Wentloog*

**Drillers** (b-c): ABV: 4%. Malt: Maris Otter and Halcyon pale malt, Crystal malt. Hops: Goldings. Source: JE3/4/5.

**Steelers** (b-c): ABV: 4.2%. Malt: Maris Otter and Halcyon pale malt, Crystal malt, Chocolate malt. Hops: Goldings. Source: JE4/5.

**YA No. 3** (b-c): ABV: 4.3%. Malt: Maris Otter pale malt. Hops: Fuggles. Source: JE4/5.

**Zen** (b-c): ABV: 4.4%. Malt: Halcyon and/or Maris Otter pale malt, Crystal malt. Hops: Goldings. Source: JE3/4/5.

**Riggers** (b-c): ABV: 4.5%. Malt: Halcyon and/or Maris Otter pale malt, Crystal malt. Hops: Goldings. Source: JE3/4/5.

**Rockers** (b-c): ABV: 4.8%. Malt: Maris Otter and Halcyon pale malt, Lager malt. Hops: Fuggles. Source: JE4/5.

**Deep Pit** (b-c): ABV: 5%. Malt: Halcyon and/or Maris Otter pale malt, Crystal malt, Chocolate malt. Hops: Goldings. Source: JE2/3/4/5.

**Dockers** (b-c): ABV: 5%. Malt: Halcyon and/or Maris Otter pale malt, Crystal malt. Hops: Goldings. Source: JE2/3/4/5.

**Black and Amber Extra** (b-c): ABV: 6%. Malt: Halcyon pale malt, Crystal malt, Chocolate malt. Hops: Goldings. Source: JE2/4/5.

**QE2** (b-c): ABV: 6%. Malt: Maris Otter and Halcyon pale malt, Lager malt. Hops: Fuggles. Source: JE4/5.

**Red Hot Furnace** (b-c): ABV: 9%. Malt: Maris Otter and/or Halcyon pale malt, Crystal malt, Chocolate malt. Hops: Goldings. Source: JE2/3/4/5.

### . *Welsh Brewers, Cardiff*

**Worthington Dark**: OG: 1032.5. Malt: 83% Pale malt, Sugar. Hops: Challenger, Northdown. IBU: 20. EBC: 70. Source: RP3/4/5.

**Hancock's HB**: OG: 1036.5. Malt: 84% Pipkin and Halcyon pale malt, High Maltose syrup. Hops: Challenger, Northdown. IBU: 22. EBC: 22. Source: RP3/4/5.

**Worthington Best Bitter**: OG: 1036.5. Malt: 84% Pale malt, Sugar. Hops: Challenger, Northdown. IBU: 22. EBC: 22. Source: RP3/4/5.

# *Zimbabwe*

### . *National Breweries, Harare*

**Zambezi Premium Export Lager**: OG: 1045. Malt: Crystal malt, Lager malt, Flaked maize, Sugar. Hops: Spalt. Late hops: Hersbrücker, Saaz. Source: CB.

# Further Ingredients

Throughout history brewers have used a wide range of ingredients beyond the usual grains and hops. During researching this book I discovered a range ingredients that are no longer routinely used. As well as the ingredients listed in the Recipe Information, here is a list of other ingredients you may wish to experiment with but please take care not to poison anyone! I cannot take any responsibility for any adverse affects.

. *Agrimony*

Alternative names: Common agrimony, Church steeples, Sticklewort. Latin name: *Agrimonia eupatoria*. Notes: Astringent bitter. Source: A,G&B/SHB.

. *Alder*

Alders are a group of trees and shrubs of the birch family *Betulaceae*. The catkins are very astringent and the bark has traditionally been used in several medicinal applications. Source: SHB/Web.

. *Allspice*

The dried fruit of *Pimenta dioica*. Has a flavour similar to a combination of cinnamon, cloves and other spices. Alternative names: Jamaica pepper, Myrtle pepper. Source: HF/botanical.com

. *Ascorbic acid*

This can be used as an anti-oxidant in brewing. I've used it myself on several occasions and not noticed any adverse effects. Alternative name: Vitamin C. Source: HF.

. *Avens*

Avens has a pleasant clove-like flavour, has been used in herbal medicine and is used in Augsburg ales. Alternative names: Wood avens, Herb Bennet, Colewort, St. Benedict's herb. Latin name: *Geum urbanum*. Source: SHB/botanical.com.

. *Bayberry*

Considered as poor substitute for bog myrtle. Alternative names: Sweet-oak, Candleberry, Wild myrtle. Latin name: *Myrica cerifera*. Source: A,G&B.

. *Betony*

A bitter grassland plant. Popular medicinal herb. Alternative name: Bishopswort. Latin name: *Betonica officinalis / Stachys officinalis*. Source: A,G&B/SHB.

. *Birch*

Both the sap and branches may be used. Birch is rich in methyl salicylate which is similar to aspirin and is analgesic and anti-inflammatory. Has wintergreen flavour. Source: SHB/DAW.

. *Blessed thistle*

Bitter. Antiseptic. Used in bitter liqueurs. Can be irritant. Alternative names: Carduus, Culpepper, Holy thistle. Latin name: *Cnicus benedictus*. Source: A,G&B/DAW/botanical.com.

. *Bog Myrtle*

Commonly used. Gingery, bitter, balsamic, spicy, astringent. Antiseptic. Has expectorant and sedative properties. The branches are used as a hop substitute in Yorkshire in Gale Beer. Alternative names: Sweet gale, Gawle, Porst, Pors, Gagellan. Latin name: *Myrica gale*. Source: A,G&B/SHB/DAW/botanical.com.

. *Bogbean*

Bitter. Used in herbal teas. Alternative names: Buckbean, Marsh trefoil, Water trefoil, Marsh clover. Latin name: *Menyanthes trifoliata*. Source: A,G&B/SHB/DAW/botanical.com.

. *Borage*

Very refreshing cucumber-like flavour. Latin name: *Borago officinalis*. Source: SHB/botanical.com.

## . Bracken fern

In Siberia and in Norway, the fronds have been used with malt for brewing a type of beer. Latin name: *Pterdium aquilinum*. Source: SHB/botanical.com.

## . Broom

Probably a popular flavouring in the 17th and 18th centuries in Great Britain. Broom is bitter, tannic and a preservative. It contains a hallucinogen and has been used to treat various conditions, including dropsy. An excessive amount can result in unpleasant effects. Alternative name: Scotch broom. Latin name: *Cytisus scoparius* / *Sarothamnus scoparius*. Source: A,G&B/SHB.

## . Burdock

Antibiotic, antifungal, antiseptic and has several medicinal applications. Latin name: *Arctium lappa*. Source: SHB.

## . Burnet

Astringent, used in Herb beer. Latin name: *Sanguisorba officinalis* / *Poterium sanguisorba*. Source: SHB/botanical.com.

## . Caraway seeds

Commonly used in cooking. Alternative name: Karawya. Latin name: *Carum carvi*. Source: SHB.

## . Cardamom

Aromatic spice. Latin name: *Elettaria cardamomum*. Source: SHB/HF.

## . Centaury

Bitter. Used in herbal wines and liqueurs. Alternative names: Feverwort, Christ's Ladder. Latin name: *Centaurium erythraea*. Source: A,G&B/botanical.com.

## . Chamomile

Frequently used in herbal teas. Latin name: *Matricaria chamomilla*. Source: SHB.

## . China root

Has been used as a remedy for several conditions and as a tonic. Alternative names: Sarsparilla. Latin name: *Smilax spp.* Source: SHB.

## . Clary

Relative of sage. Has a strong, warm aromatic flavour. It was used as an adulterant by German wine merchants who infused it with elderflowers and added the liquid to wine to convert it into Muscatel. It was also used as a hop substitute in beer providing bitterness and an intoxicating effect followed by a severe headache. Alternative name: Eyebright. Latin name: *Salvia sclarea.* Source: A,G&B/botanical.com.

## . Clivers

Traditionally used in nettle beer. Alternative name: Goosegrass, Barweed, Robin-run-in-the-grass, Catchweed. Latin name: *Galium aparine.* Source: A,G&B/botanical.com.

## . Coltsfoot

Used as a cough remedy. Used for making Cleats Beer. Alternative names: Coughwort, Cleats, Foalfoot. Latin name: *Tussilago farfara.* Source: A,G&B/SHB.

## . Comfrey root

In cookery, young leaves are used as a spinach substitute and to flavour cakes etc. Older plants have a coarse, unpleasant taste. Alternative name: Blackwort, Ass ear. Latin name: *Symphytum officinale.* Source: A,G&B/DAW./botanical.com

## . Coriander

The volatile oils in the seeds are better extracted by alcohol so they may be added to the fermentation. Latin name: *Coriandrum sativum.* Source: SHB/HF/DAW.

## . Corn mint

"Apples and gingerbread" aroma. Antioxidant. Antimicrobial. Latin name: *Mentha arvensis.* Source: A,G&B.

### . Costmary

Balsamic flavour. Has been used to add a spicy flavour to beer. Alternative name: Alecost. Latin name: *Tanacetum balsamita*. Source: A,G&B/SHB/DAW/botanical.com.

### . Cow parsnip

Latin name: *Heracleum lanatum*. Source: SHB.

### . Cowslip

Popular. The flowers have a distinctive fragrance, have narcotic properties and are used in Cowslip wine. Alternative names: Plumrocks, Mayflower, Password, Paralysio. Latin name: *Primula veris*. Source: SHB/botanical.com.

### . Dandelion

Used in soft drinks. Possible slight narcotic. Different parts of the plant have different properties. Has been shown to be effective in the treatment of gallstones, pneumonia, bronchitis and gout. Latin name: *Taraxacum officinale*. Source: A,G&B/SHB.

### . Darnel

Grassy plant that malts well and may be accidentally included due to growing among grain crops. Strongly intoxicating. Alternative name: Roseger. Latin name: *Lolium temulentum*. Source: A,G&B/SHB.

### . Dock

Latin name: *Rumex acetus*. Source: SHB.

### . Elder

**Elderflowers**: These have a lovely delicate scent, but some trees can produce flowers having an unpleasant scent. **Elderberries**: The red berries of *Sambucus racemosa* are toxic. The edible black berries of other varieties are used in wine, a beer called Ebulon and preserves. Elder has laxative properties and many other medical uses. Latin name: *Sambucus spp*. Source: SHB.

. *Elecampane*

Bitter. Antiseptic. Latin name: *Inula helenium*. Source: A,G&B/SHB/DAW.

. *Eyebright*

Bitter and tannic. Used to treat eye problems. Common drink ingredient in Middle ages. Latin name: *Euphrasia officinalis*. Source: A,G&B/SHB/DAW.

. *Fennel*

May contain a hallucinogen. Used to treat stomach cramps. Latin name: *Foeniculum vulgare*. Source: A,G&B/SHB.

. *Fir*

Several traditional medicinal uses. Source: SHB.

. *Garlic*

Source: A,G&B/HF.

. *Gentian*

Extremely bitter. Latin name: *Gentiana lutea*. Source: SHB.

. *Ginger*

Has beneficial effects on blood circulation, digestion, reducing cholesterol, nausea, fever and many other effects. Latin name: *Zingiber officinale*. Source: SHB/HF.

. *Grains of Paradise*

Hot, pepper-like. Latin name: *Amomum Melegueta / Aframomum melegueta*. Source: SHB.

. *Ground-ivy*

Popular. Bitter. Tannic. Fining aid. Alternative names: Alehoof, Alehove, Tunhoof, Gill-go-over-the-Ground, Robin-run-i'-t'-hedge, Creeping Jenny. Latin name: *Glechoma hederacea*. Source: A,G&B/SHB, DAW.

. *Ground pine*

Turpentine-like smell. Latin name: *Ajuga chamaepitys*. Source: SHB.

. *Hay*

Cut and dried grass. Source: A,G&B.

. *Hazel*

Source: SHB.

. *Heather*

Alternative name: Bell heather. Latin name: *Erica cinerea*. Source: A,G&B.

. *Henbane*

Powerful narcotic poison, in large amounts can cause a number of unpleasant effects. Can be fatal. Latin name: *Hyoscyamus niger*. Source: SHB

. *Herb Bennet root*

Clove-scented. Antiseptic. Alternative names: Common avens, Wood avens, Colewort, Wild rye, Clove root. Latin name: *Geum urbanum*. Source: A,G&B.

. *Horehound*

Extremely bitter. Used as a cough remedy. Horehound juice was used to adulterate old hops to make them seem new. Alternative name: White horehound, Mountain hops. Latin name: *Marrubium vulgare*. Source: A,G&B/SHB/DAW.

. *Horseradish*

Latin name: *Cochlearia armoracia*. Source: A,G&B.

. *Hyssop*

Popular. Aromatic, astringent, bitter. Fining aid. Latin name: *Hyssopus officilanis*. Source: A,G&B/SHB.

. *Juniper*

Traditionally used for brewing in the Scandinavian countries. Berries and/or branches may be used. **Juniper berries**: Source: A,G&B/SHB. **Juniper wood**: Source: SHB

. *Lemon balm*

Popular. Used to treat depression, stress and anxiety. Smells of lemons. An ingredient in Benedictine. Widely used in ales of Middle ages. Alternative name: Balm. Latin name: *Melissa officinalis*. Source: A,G&B/SHB.

. *Lesser burnet*

Latin name: *Pimpinella saxifraga*. Source: SHB.

. *Lignum Vitae*

Latin name: *Guaiacum officinale* or *Guaiacum sanctum*. Source: SHB.

. *Liquorice*

Has several herbal medicine applications but can produce significant side-effects. Alternative names: Licorice. Latin name: *Glycyrrhiza glabra*. Source: SHB/HF.

. *Ling*

Alternative name: Viking heather. Latin name: *Calluna vulgaris / Fraoch Lochlannach*. Source: A,G&B.

. *Long pepper*

Hot flavour. Latin name: *Piper officinarum / Piper retrofractum*. Source: A,G&B.

. *Mandrake*

Has similar effects to henbane. Aphrodisiac. Latin name: *Atropa mandragora / Mandragora offininarum*. Source: SHB.

. *Maple*

Maple syrup or sap may be used. Very nutricious and has medicinal uses. Source: SHB/DAW.

. *Marigold*

Alternative names: Calendula. Latin name: *Calendula officinalis*. Source: SHB.

. *Marjoram*

Latin name: *Origanum vulgare*. Source: SHB/DAW.

. *Marsh rosemary*

Probably considered to be an inferior alternative to bog myrtle. Possibly causes headache, delirium, vertigo etc. Alternative names: Wild rosemary, Schweineporst (pigs gale), Falscher Porst (false gale), Finnmark pors. Latin name: *Ledum palustre*. Source: A,G&B/SHB.

. *Meadowsweet*

May have been used for flavouring meads and wines rather than ale. Preservative. Alternative name: Meadwort. Latin name: *Filipendula ulmara*. Source: A,G&B/SHB.

. *Molasses*

Source: SHB.

. *Mountain Ash*

Source: SHB.

. *Mugwort*

Used dried rather than fresh. A member of the same family as wormwood but milder in its effdcts. Latin name: *Artemisia vulgaris*. Source: A,G&B/SHB/DAW.

. *Mustard*

Latin name: *Brassica nigra / B. alba*. Source: SHB.

. *Nettles*

Has several medicinal applications, including treatment of Alzheimer's disease, Parkinson's disease, multiple sclerosis, arthritis, rheumatism, hay fever, asthma and bronchitis. Nettles are a rich source of minerals and vitamins. Nettle beer apparently has a very pleasant flavour and typically uses a large quantity of nettles which allegedly provides many health benefits. Latin name: *Urtica dioica*. Source: A,G&B/SHB.

## . Nutmeg

Source: HF/SHB.

## . Oak

Astringent. Oak chips are sometimes used in brewing to impart an oak character that may mimic the effect of using oak casks. Source: SHB/HF.

## . Orris root

Violet scent. Slightly bitter. May cause nausea or vomiting. Latin name: *Iris germanica*. Source: A,G&B/SHB.

## . Pennyroyal

Popular but now considered to be poisonous. Can induce abortion. Now an endangered species. Bitter, pungent. Latin name: *Mentha pulegium / Hedeoma pulegioides*. Source: A,G&B/SHB/DAW.

## . Peony seeds

Used as a cure for nightmares. Source: A,G&B.

## . Peppermint

Latin name: *Mentha piperita*. Source: SHB.

## . Pine

The needles have a pleasant taste and have antiseptic, expectorant and diuretic properties. The resin is a strong expectorant. The bark is high in tannins. Pine has several traditional medicinal uses. Source: SHB.

## . Roman wormwood

Less bitter than wormwood. Source: A,G&B.

## Rosemary

Popular. Sprigs of rosemary may have been added directly to ale before drinking in the 14ᵗʰ century. Antioxidant, antiseptic. Latin name: *Rosmarinus officinalis*. Source: A,G&B/SHB.

## Rowan

Latin name: Sorbu aucuparia. **Rowanberries**: Alternative name: Mountain ash berries. Source: A,G&B. **Rowan wood**: Source: SHB.

## Rue

Very bitter. Used as a culinary herb in Italian cuisine. Can cause abortion in large doses. Alternative names: Herb of grace. Latin name: *Ruta graveolens*. Source: SHB.

## Saffron

Expensive. Has been shown to be effective at lowering blood pressure. May have some narcotic effect. Latin name: *Crocus sativa*. Source: SHB

## Sage

Popular. Highly Antibacterial. Possible hallucinogen. Has several medical uses and may inhibit Alzheimer's disease. Latin name: *Salvia officinalis*. Source: A,G&B/SHB/DAW.

## St.-John's-wort

Antideppressant, anti-viral, anti-bacterial and other medicinal properties. Latin name: *Hypericum perforatum*. Source: SHB.

## Sassafras

Herbal medicine banned in the USA. Used in Creole cooking. Alternative name: Winauk. Latin name: *Sassafras officinale / S. albidum*. Source: SHB.

## Scurvy-grass

Popular. Sharp, pungent aroma. Bitter, salty taste. High in vitamin C. Used as treatment for scurvy and as a tonic. Alternative name: Gittings. Latin name: *Cochlearia officinalis*. Source: A,G&B/SHB.

. *Serviceberry*

Latin name: *Amelanchier alnifolia*. Source: SHB.

. *Spanish Juice*

Source: SHB.

. *Spearmint*

Antioxidant. Antimicrobial. Latin name: *Mentha spicata*. Source: A,G&B.

. *Spruce*

Preservative. Strong flavour. Has had several medicinal uses. Alternative name: Black spruce. Latin name: *Picea mariana*. Source: A,G&B/SHB/HF/DAW.

. *Squinancywort*

Alternative name: Squinanth. Latin name: *Asperula cynanchica*. Source: A,G&B.

. *Sumac*

Alternative names: Staghorn sumac. Latin name: *Rhus typhina*. Source: DAW.

. *Sweet flag*

Pleasant odour. Spicy flavour. Alternative name: Calamus. Latin name: *Acorus calamus*. Source: SHB.

. *Sycamore*

Source: SHB.

. *Tansy*

Very bitter. Tannic. Pungent, camphor aroma. Antibacterial. Can be poisonous. Alternative name: Olkall. Latin name: *Chrysanthemum vulgare / Tanacetum vulgare*. Source: A,G&B/SHB.

. *Tormentil roots*

Bitter. Can cause vomiting. Smell of roses. Alternative name: Bloodroot. Latin name: *Potentilla tortmentilla*. Source: A,G&B.

### . Valerian

Latin name: *Valeriana officinalis*. Source: HF.

### . Water mint

Smokey aroma. Antioxidant. Antimicrobial. Latin name: *Mentha aquatica.* Source: A,G&B.

### . Wild carrot seed

This is the same as the garden carrot plant. Has been shown to have a significant preventative role in cancer and cardiovascular disease. Alternative names: Queen Anne's lace. Latin name: *Daucus carota*. Source: SHB.

### . Wild celery

Latin name: *Apium graveolens*. Source: A,G&B.

### . Wild ginger

Although not related to ginger, it has been used in the same way and has similar properties. Latin name: *Asarum canadense*. Source: SHB.

### . Wild lettuce

Bitter. Alternative names: Prickly lettuce. Latin name: *Lactuca svirosa / L. serriola*. Source: SHB.

### . Wild sarsparilla

Balsamic, aromatic odour. Used as tonic and medicine. Latin name: *Aralia nudacaulis*. Source: SHB.

### . Wild Service Tree berries

Relative of rowan tree. Alternative name: Chequer tree berries. Latin name: *Sorbus torminalis*. Source: A,G&B.

### . Willow

Source: SHB.

. *Wintergreen*

Contains methyl salicylate, an analgesic related to aspirin. Toxic in too large a dose. Latin name: *Gaultheria procumbens*. Source: SHB.

. *Wood Sage*

Source: DAW.

. *Woodruff*

Source: DAW.

. *Wormwood*

Probably a popular flavouring in the 17th and 18th centuries in Great Britain. Bitter. Contains an addictive hallucinogen. An ingredient in Absinthe. Latin name: *Artemisia absinthium*. Source: A,G&B/SHB.

. *Yarrow*

Widely used. Bitter. Preservative. May contain a hallucinogen, cause dizzyness, ringing in the ears and/or madness. Has had several medical uses. Latin name: *Achillea millefolium*. Source: A,G&B/SHB/DAW.

# About the Author

Les Howarth attempted his first full mash home brew in 1979 in spite of not having the appropriate equipment. The result was a comedy of errors with grain, water, hops and wort ending up being distributed over his mother's kitchen in Liverpool. Nevertheless, the resulting brew turned out to be the best beer he had brewed up until that date. But these brewing difficulties meant that he did not attempt to perform another full mash until two years later, when his continuing dissatisfaction with the tinned beer kits of the time resulted in his investing in a "Bruheat" masher/boiler. This was the start of a highly enjoyable and satisfying pastime with progressive improvements in equipment, ingredients and technique, leading to even better beers. Les is a life member of CAMRA (Campaign for Real Ale) and a honorary life member of Scottish Craft Brewers.

Les is happily married to Mariana and works as an industrial R&D scientist.

**The author (centre) being presented with Honorary Life Membership of Scottish Craft Brewers by Norrie Pederson (left) and Ian McManus (right).**

# Index

I have not included unspecified pale malt in this index since it is fairly ubiquitous in usage. I have also indexed fruit extracts, purees, juices etc. under the parent fruit.

441